Victor Hirtzler

The

Hotel St. Francis Cook Book

By Victor Hirtzler

Former Chef of Hotel St. Francis
San Francisco

Creative Cookbooks
Monterrey, California

The Hotel St. Francis Cook Book

by
Victor Hirtzler

ISBN: 1-58963-302-4

Creative Cookbooks
An Imprint of Fredonia Books
Monterey, California
http://www.creativecookbooks.com

PREFACE

IN THIS, my book, I have endeavored to give expression to the art of cookery as developed in recent years in keeping with the importance of the catering business, in particular the hotel business, which, in America, now leads the world.

I have been fortunate in studying under the great masters of the art in Europe and America; and since my graduation as Chef I have made several journeys of observation to New York, and to England, France and Switzerland to learn the new in cooking and catering.

I have named my book The Hotel St. Francis Cook Book in compliment to the house which has given me in so generous measure the opportunity to produce and reproduce, always with the object of reflecting a cuisine that is the best possible.

VICTOR HIRTZLER.

JANUARY 1

BREAKFAST
Sliced oranges
Farina with cream
Calf's liver and bacon
Lyonnaise potatoes
Rolls
Coffee

LUNCHEON
Eggs Oriental
Tripe and potatoes, family style
Cold ham and tongue
Celery root, field and beet salad
Port de Salut cheese
Crackers
Coffee

DINNER
Consommé d'Orleans
Boiled whitefish, Netherland sauce
Squab pot pie, à l'Anglaise
Lettuce and tomatoes, mayonnaise
Savarin Montmorency
Demi tasse

Eggs Oriental. Put on a plate one slice of tomato fried in butter, on top of the tomato place six slices of cucumber simmered in butter and well seasoned, on top of that one poached egg, and cover with sauce Hollandaise.

Tripe and potatoes, family style. Slice the white ends of six leeks very fine, put in sauce pan with four ounces of butter and simmer for five minutes. Then add a scant spoonful of flour and simmer again. Then add one pound of tripe cut in pieces one inch square, one pint of bouillon, two raw potatoes sliced fine, some chopped parsley, salt and pepper, and one-half glass of white wine. Cover and cook for an hour, or until all is soft.

Boiled whitefish, Netherland style. Boil, and serve on napkin with small boiled potatoes, lemon and parsley. Serve melted butter separate.

Squab pot pie, à l'Anglaise. Roast the squabs and cut in two. Fry a thin slice of fillet of beef on both sides, over a quick fire, in melted butter. Put both in a pie dish with a chopped shallot that was merely heated with the fillet, six heads of canned or fresh mushrooms, one-half of a hard-boiled egg, a little chopped parsley, and some flour gravy made from the roasted squab juice, and well seasoned with a little Worcestershire sauce. Cover with pie dough and bake for twenty minutes. This is for an individual pie; make in the same proportions for a large pie.

Lemon water ice. One quart of water, one pound of sugar, and four lemons. Dissolve the sugar in the water, add the rinds of two lemons and the juice of four lemons. Strain and freeze.

Orange water ice. One quart of water, one pound of sugar, three oranges and one lemon. Melt the sugar in the water, add the juice of the oranges and the lemon, and one drop of coloring. Strain and freeze.

Strawberry water ice. One-half pound of sugar, one pint of water, one pint of strawberry pulp, the juice of one lemon, and coloring. Strain and freeze.

Raspberry water ice. Same directions as for strawberry water ice. Use raspberry pulp instead.

Cantaloupe water ice. Add to one quart of cantaloupe pulp the juice of three lemons and a half pound of sugar. Pass through a fine sieve and freeze.

JANUARY 2

BREAKFAST
Grape nuts with cream
Kippered herring
Rolls
Coffee

LUNCHEON
Omelet with oysters
Perch sauté, meunière
Browned hashed potatoes
Lobster salad with anchovies
Floating island
Napoleon cake
Coffee

DINNER
Little Neck clams
Codfish chowder
Planked shad and roe
Artichokes au gratin
Hearts of romaine, Roquefort
  dressing
Peach Melba
Caroline cakes
Coffee

Omelet with oysters. Parboil six oysters, add one spoonful of cream sauce and season well. Make the omelet, and before turning over on platter place the oysters in the center. Serve with light cream around the omelet.

Perch sauté, meunière. Season the fish well with salt and pepper, roll in flour, put in frying pan and cook with butter. When done, put fish on platter, and put a fresh piece of butter in pan, over fire, and allow to become hazelnut color. Pour the butter and the juice of a lemon over the fish, sprinkle with chopped parsley, and garnish with quartered lemons and parsley in branches.

Browned hashed potatoes. Hash three cold boiled potatoes. Melt three ounces of butter in a frying pan, add the potatoes, season with salt and pepper, and fry evenly. When nearly done form in the pan in the shape of a rolled omelet and fry again until well browned on the top. Turn over on platter in the same manner as an omelet, and sprinkle with chopped parsley.

Lobster salad. Take the tails of two boiled lobsters, season with salt and pepper and a teaspoonful of vinegar, and let stand for a half hour, then add one cup of mayonnaise sauce. Put some sliced lettuce in the bottom of a salad bowl, the lobster salad on top, a few nice lettuce leaves around the sides, cover the salad again with mayonnaise, and decorate with hard-boiled eggs, beets and olives.

Lobster salad with anchovies. Same as above. Decorate with fillets of anchovies.

Floating island. Beat the whites of six eggs very stiff, add six ounces of powdered sugar and the inside of a vanilla bean. Mix well. Boil one quart of milk, one-quarter pound of sugar, and the remainder of the vanilla bean, in a wide vessel. Dip a tablespoon in hot water and form the beaten eggs, or meringue, into the shape and size of an egg, and drop into the boiling milk. Dip the spoon in hot water each time so the meringue will not stick. Take off the fire and let stand for a few minutes, turning the floating eggs several times. Then take out of the milk and dress on napkin to cool. Boil the milk again and bind with the yolks of two eggs, strain and cool. Put the sauce in a bowl, or deep dish, and float the "islands" on top. Serve very cold.

JANUARY 3

BREAKFAST
  Orange Juice
  Waffles and honey
  Chocolate and whipped cream

LUNCHEON
  Chicken salad, Victor
  Rolls
  Coffee

DINNER
  Potage Normande
  Fillet of turbot, Daumont
  Sirloin of beef, Clermont
  Endives salad
  Rolled oats pudding
  Coffee

Chicken salad, Victor. Cut the breast of a boiled soup hen or boiled chicken in half-inch squares, add one-half cup of string beans cut in pieces one inch long, a cup of boiled rice, one peeled tomato cut in small squares and one sliced truffle. Season with salt, fresh-ground black pepper, a little chives, chervil, parsley, one spoonful of tarragon vinegar and two spoonsful of best olive oil. Mix well and serve on lettuce leaves.

Potage Normande. Velouté with Julienne of carrots and turnips.

Fillet of turbot, Daumont. Put the fillet in a buttered pan, season with salt and pepper, and add one glass of white wine. Boil six fresh mushrooms in a little water and strain the juice over the fish, or use the juice of canned mushrooms. Cook the fish, remove to platter, and reduce the sauce to glace, then add one pint of sauce au vin blanc (white wine sauce), strain, and before pouring over the fish add two ounces of sweet butter and the juice of one lemon.

Sirloin of beef, Clermont. Roast sirloin of beef, sauce Madère, garnished with tomatoes stuffed with whole chestnuts, and Bermuda onions stuffed with cabbage.

Boiled chestnuts. Cut the chestnut shells with a sharp knife and put on pan in oven for ten minutes. Then peel, put in vessel with a small piece of celery, salt, and cover with water. Boil slowly so they will remain whole when done. Use for garnishing, stuffing, etc.

Tomatoes stuffed with chestnuts. Peel four nice fresh tomatoes, cut off the tops, scoop out the insides, and fill with boiled chestnuts. Put a small piece of butter on top, and put in oven for five minutes. Serve as a garnish, or as an entrée with Madeira sauce.

Boiled cabbage. Cut a head of cabbage in four, trim and wash well. Have a kettle with salt water boiling. Put the cabbage in the kettle and cook until nearly soft, then drain off nine-tenths of the water, add a small piece of ham, or ham bone, and simmer till soft. Remove the ham or bone and prepare the cabbage with cream, or any other style. For stuffing onions, cut the cabbage up, add a little butter, and season with salt and pepper.

Stuffed onions with cabbage. Peel four large Bermuda or Spanish onions. Boil them in salt water until nearly done, then remove from the fire and allow to cool. Take out the inside and fill with cabbage prepared as above. Put the stuffed onions on a buttered dish with a piece of butter on top, and bake in oven.

JANUARY 4

BREAKFAST
    Hothouse raspberries with cream
    Baked beans, Boston style
    Brown bread
    Coffee

LUNCHEON
    Canapé of fresh caviar
    Consommé Julienne
    Boiled Salmon, sauce Princess
    Corned beef hash with poached eggs
    Escarole salad
    French pastry   Coffee

DINNER
    Lynn Haven oysters
    Strained chicken okra, in cups
    Cheese straws
    Salted English walnuts
    Fillet of sole, Gasser
    Stuffed capon, St. Antoine
    Asparagus Hollandaise
    Gauffrette potatoes
    Season salad   Coupe St. Jacques
    Assorted cakes   Coffee

Consommé Julienne. The word "Julienne" is a common kitchen term, signifying cut in slender strips, or match shape. For consommé garnish cut "Julienne" style one carrot, one turnip, one leek, a small piece of celery, four leaves of cabbage, and one-half of an onion. Season with a spoonful of salt, and one-half teaspoonful of sugar. Mix well. Put in a well-buttered casserole, cover with buttered paper and the casserole cover, put in oven moderately hot, and allow to simmer slowly. Turn occasionally, using a fork to avoid breaking the vegetables. They should simmer without adding liquid, but should they be too dry, a half cup of consommé may be added. Cook until soft, and drain on a sieve so all the juice will run off. Combine with two quarts of consommé, and before serving add a few peas and some chervil.

Fillet of sole, Gasser. Put four fillets of sole in cold milk seasoned with salt and pepper, and leave for four hours. Then wrap around raw potatoes, cut like a cork, and about three inches long. Let one side extend over the potato, and fasten with a toothpick. Fry slowly in swimming lard until golden brown, then take out, remove the toothpick, push out the potato, and fill the center of the sole with a very thick filling composed of two-thirds Bearnaise sauce and one-third of reduced tomato sauce. Serve on napkin with fried parsley, and tomato sauce, separate.

Boiled salmon, sauce Princess. Boil the salmon, serve the sauce separate. Make the sauce as follows: One pint of Hollandaise sauce, one spoonful of meat extract, and twelve parboiled oysters, thoroughly mixed.

Stuffed capon, St. Antoine. Season the capon well, both inside and out, and put in ice box. Prepare a stuffing as follows: The bread crumbs made from a five-cent loaf of bread, twelve whole boiled chestnuts, three boiled fresh, or canned, apricots, six stewed prunes, three boiled, or canned, pears, and two peaches. Put in a bowl, add an egg and one gill of brandy, and mix well. Fill the capon, wrap a piece of fat pork around it, and put in roasting pan with a carrot, onion, bouquet garni, and three ounces of butter. Put in oven and roast slowly, basting continually until done. Remove the capon to a platter and take off the fat pork. Return the pan to fire and bring to a boil. When the fat is clear drain it off and add to the pan one-half cup of bouillon and one cup of brown gravy. Season, boil, strain and pour over the capon. Garnish with watercress.

JANUARY 5

BREAKFAST
  Baked apples with cream
  Fried hominy
  Maple syrup
  Coffee

LUNCHEON
  Shirred eggs, Mornay
  Fried smelts, Tartar
  Broiled spareribs and sauerkraut
  Plain boiled potatoes
  American cheese and crackers
  Coffee

DINNER
  Potage Marquis
  Celery
  Stuffed lobster
  Boiled beef, sauce piquante
  Maitre d'hotel potatoes
  Brussels sprouts and chestnuts
  Spinach, English style
  Savarin Mirabelle
  Coffee

Shirred eggs, Mornay. Put on a buttered shirred egg dish one spoonful of cream sauce, break two fresh eggs on top, season with salt and pepper, cover the eggs with sauce Mornay, sprinkle with grated cheese and bake in oven.

Potage Marquis. Cream of rice with breast of boiled chicken cut in small squares.

Stuffed lobster. Prepare the lobster as for croquettes. Clean the shells and fill with the prepared lobster. Sprinkle the top with cheese and bread crumbs mixed with a small piece of butter, and bake in oven. Serve on napkin with quartered lemon and parsley.

Maitre d'hotel potatoes. Peel and slice two boiled potatoes and put in pan. Season with salt and pepper, cover with thick cream, and boil for a few minutes. Then add two ounces of sweet butter and mix well, being careful not to break the potatoes. Just before serving add the juice of one-half lemon and some chopped parsley.

Boiled Brussels sprouts. Clean and wash the sprouts, boil in salt water till soft. Drain and cool. Be careful that the sprouts remain whole.

Brussels sprouts with chestnuts. Melt three ounces of butter in pan, add two cups of fresh-boiled sprouts, season with salt and pepper, and fry for a few minutes. Then add a cup of fresh-boiled chestnuts, mix well, and serve with a sprinkle of parsley on top.

Boiled spinach. Clean the spinach and wash in four or five waters, as it is difficult to remove the sand. It is sometimes necessary to wash as many as ten times to remove it all. Put a gallon of water and a handful of salt in a pot and bring to the boiling point. Add the spinach, and boil over a very hot fire, so it will remain green. It will require from five to ten minutes, depending upon the tenderness of the spinach. Drain off water and serve plain. Or, cool with cold water, press dry with the hand, and prepare as desired.

Spinach, English style. Add a small piece of butter to plain spinach.

JANUARY 6

BREAKFAST
  Sliced pineapple
  Waffles
  Honey in comb
  Rolls
  Coffee

LUNCHEON
  Croquettes Liviannienne
  Eggs Beaujolais
  Camembert cheese and crackers
  Coffee

DINNER
  Potage Victoria
  Bass, Provençale
  Stuffed lamb chops, Maréchal
  Curried Lima beans
  Château potatoes
  Lettuce salad
  Nectarine ice cream
  Assorted cakes
  Coffee

Croquettes Liviannienne. Mix four leaves of melted gelatine with one pint of mayonnaise and use to bind some crab meat. Cool and form in small croquettes, roll in chopped yolks of hard-boiled eggs mixed with chopped parsley.

Eggs Beaujolais. Poached eggs on toast covered with sauce Colbert.

Potage Victoria. Half velouté of chicken and half purée of tomatoes. Garnish with turnip cut in small squares, string beans cut in half-inch lengths, and a few peas.

Bass, Provençale. Split a bass, remove the bones and skin, put in buttered pan, season with salt and pepper, put some sliced tomatoes and a few small pieces of butter on top, and bake in oven. When done cover with white wine sauce with a few pieces of tomato in it.

Stuffed lamb chops, Maréchal. Broil the lamb chops on one side. Cover that side with force meat of veal quenelles decorated with chopped tongue and truffles, put in buttered pan, cover with buttered paper, and bake in oven for ten minutes. Serve with fresh mushroom sauce. (See veal force meat recipe Jan. 11.)

Macedoine water ice. Two pounds of sugar, three quarts of water, and six lemons. Dissolve the sugar in the water, add the rind of four lemons and the juice of six, strain and freeze. When frozen add one quart of assorted fruit, such as small seedless grapes, stoned cherries, and apricots, strawberries, and pineapple cut in small dices, or any other kind in season, or canned. Before adding the fruit to the water ice put it in a bowl with a little powdered sugar and kirschwasser, and leave for an hour. This will prevent the fruit from freezing too hard.

Normandie water ice. Two pounds of sugar, two quarts of water, and the juice of six lemons. Mix together, add one quart of crabapple pulp and one gill of cognac. Freeze.

Curried Lima beans. Put some boiled Lima beans in a sauce pan and cover with well seasoned curry sauce. Before serving add a small piece of fresh butter and some chopped parsley.

JANUARY 7

BREAKFAST
  Stewed rhubarb
  Boiled eggs
  Dry toast
  Coffee

LUNCHEON
  Consommé favorite
  Broiled shad roe, maitre d'hotel
  Mirabeau salad
  Lemon pie
  Coffee

DINNER
  Potage à l'Anglaise
  Fillet of flounder, Meissonier
  Chicken, Valencienne
  Jets de houblons
  Sybil potatoes
  Hearts of romaine
  Macédoine water ice
  Lady fingers
  Coffee

Consommé favorite. Garnish the consommé with asparagus tips cut in small pieces, and chicken dumplings stuffed with goose liver, the size of a large olive. Teaspoons may be used to form the dumplings.

Broiled shad roe, maitre d'hotel. Season the roe well with salt and pepper, roll in olive oil, and broil. Serve with maitre d'hotel sauce, and garnish with quartered lemon and parsley.

Mirabeau salad. Cut in one-inch squares one cucumber, two tomatoes, and one potato. Put in salad bowl separately, cover with vinaigrette sauce. Add one teaspoonful of French mustard in the vinaigrette. Lay anchovies over the top, and a green olive cut in strips, in the middle.

Potage à l'Anglaise. Put in vessel two pounds of lean mutton, and one pound of barley. Cover with water, season with salt, add a bouquet garni, and boil for two hours. Then remove the bouquet and the meat, strain through a fine sieve, add one pint of boiling thick cream, three ounces of sweet butter, and a little Cayenne pepper.

Fillet of flounder, Meissonier. Cook the fillets in white wine. Make a white wine sauce and add a Julienne of vegetables, and pour over the fish before serving.

Chicken, Valencienne. Salt and pepper a jointed chicken and sauté in pan with butter. Put on platter and serve with suprême with truffles and fresh mushrooms, cut in small squares, and quenelles (chicken dumplings), teaspoon size. Garnish with heart-shaped fried crusts of bread.

Coupe St. Jacques. Slice some fresh fruits, such as oranges, pineapple, pears and bananas, and add all fresh berries in season. Put in a bowl with one-quarter pound of sugar, and a small glass of kirschwasser and of maraschino. Let stand for about two hours. Then fill coupe glasses about half full with the fruit, and fill the remainder with two kinds of water ice, raspberry and lemon. Smooth the top with a knife, and decorate with some of the fruit used for filling.

JANUARY 8

BREAKFAST
  Baked apples
  Scrambled eggs with parsley
  Rolls
  Coffee

LUNCHEON
  Hors d'oeuvres variés
  Pilaff à la Turc
  Pont l'Evêque cheese
  Crackers
  Fruit
  Coffee

DINNER
  Potage Quirinal
  Fillet of sole, Normande
  Squab en compote
  Artichoke Hollandaise
  Peach ice cream
  Pound cake
  Coffee

Risotto. In a vessel put one chopped onion, two ounces of butter, and the marrow of a beef bone chopped fine; and simmer until the onions are done. Then stir in one pound of rice, and put in oven for five minutes. Then add one and one-half pints of bouillon and a pinch of salt, cover, and place in oven for twenty minutes. Add a half cup of grated cheese before serving.

Pilaff à la Turc. Make a ring of risotto on a round platter, and in center put some well-seasoned chickens' livers, sauté au Madère.

Potage Quirinal. Make in the same manner as purée of game, but use pheasants only. Garnish with Julienne of breast of pheasants, truffles, and some dry sherry. Season with Cayenne pepper.

Fillet of sole, Normande. Cook the fillets "au vin blanc." Garnish individually with mussels, oysters, mushrooms, small Parisian potatoes, and very small fried fish. If small fish are not obtainable cut a fillet of sole in strips one-quarter-inch thick and two inches long, breaded and fry. Before serving place a slice of truffle on top of each piece of sole.

Peach ice cream. One pint of cream, one quart of milk, the yolks of eight eggs, one-half pound of sugar, one pint of peach pulp, and a few drops of peach kernel extract. Put the milk and one-half of the sugar on the fire to boil. Mix the other half of the sugar with the eggs, stir into the boiling milk, and cook until it becomes creamy, but do not let it come to the boiling point after adding the eggs. Remove from the fire, add the cream, pulp and extract, and freeze.

Banana ice cream. Same as the above, except substitute the pulp of six bananas and extract, in place of the peach pulp.

Pineapple ice cream. Add one pint of finely cut pineapple instead of the peach pulp.

Hazelnut ice cream. Roast one-half pound of hazelnuts, pound to a fine paste, mix with a little milk and two ounces of sugar. Use instead of the peach pulp.

Raspberry ice cream. Use one pint of raspberry pulp in place of the peach pulp.

JANUARY 9

BREAKFAST
　Preserved figs with cream
　Waffles
　Coffee

LUNCHEON
　Omelet with soft clams
　Ripe olives
　Broiled Spanish mackerel, fine herbs
　Hollandaise potatoes
　Cucumber salad
　German huckleberry pie
　Coffee

DINNER
　Bisque of California oysters
　Salted pecans
　Frogs' legs, Michels
　Roast pheasant, bread sauce and
　　bread crumbs
　Compote of spiced peaches
　Sweet potatoes, southern style
　Asparagus, Polonaise
　Banana ice cream
　Lady fingers
　Coffee

Omelet with soft clams. Take the bellies of six soft clams and put in pan, season with salt and pepper, add a small piece of butter, and heat through. Mix with two spoonsful of cream sauce. Make an omelet, and garnish with the clams in cream.

Broiled Spanish Mackerel, aux fines herbes. Season the mackerel with salt and pepper, roll in oil, and broil. Prepare a maitre d'hotel sauce with chopped chervil and chives, and pour over the fish. Garnish with quartered lemon and parsley in branches.

Cucumber salad. Slice some iced cucumbers and serve with French dressing. Or: Slice a cucumber and put in salad bowl, salt well and let stand for an hour, then squeeze the salt water out gently, and use dressing desired, as French dressing, Thousand Island dressing, etc. Or: Slice the cucumbers, cover with very thick cream, season with salt and paprika, and just before serving add the juice of one lemon.

Bisque of California oysters. Put one pint of California oysters, with their juice, in a pot and bring to the boiling point. Then skim, and add one pint of cream sauce, one-half pint of milk, a bouquet garni, and boil for ten minutes. Remove the bouquet garni, strain the broth through a fine sieve and return to the pot. Heat a pint of cream and strain into the soup, add three ounces of sweet butter, and season to taste.

Roast pheasant. Pheasant should be kept one week to season, before cooking. Clean, wrap in a slice of fresh lard, and roast in the same manner as chicken. Serve bread sauce and fried bread crumbs separate.

Bread sauce. Boil one cup of milk, add half of an onion, a little salt, one-third of a cup of fresh bread crumbs, and boil for five minutes. Remove the onion, add a piece of butter the size of a walnut, and season with Cayenne pepper.

Bread crumbs. Put in frying pan three ounces of butter and three-quarters of a cup of fresh bread crumbs, and fry until brown. Then drain off the butter and serve the dry crumbs in a sauce boat.

JANUARY 10

BREAKFAST
  Oatmeal with cream
  Rolls
  Coffee

LUNCHEON
  Oysters Yaquino
  Cold assorted meats
  Potato salad
  Brie cheese and crackers
  Oolong tea

DINNER
  Potage Grande Mère
  Cold goosebreast with jelly
  Fillet of sole, royale
  Plain potted squab chicken
  Potatoes à la Reine
  Stuffed fresh mushrooms
  Hearts of romaine salad
  Pineapple ice cream
  Assorted cakes
  Coffee

Oysters Yaquino. Season one dozen oysters on the deep shell, with salt and paprika, put on each a piece of butter and some chopped chives. Place in oven, bake, and serve very hot.

Potage Grande Mére. Take equal parts of leeks, cabbage, onions and celery and cut in very small dices. Put in pot, cover with water, season with salt and pepper, and boil. When soft, add hot milk, and serve.

Fillet of sole, royale. Same as fillet of sole, Joinville.

Potted squab chicken. Prepare the chicken as for roasting. Season well, and put a small piece of fresh butter in each. Place in a sauté pan with butter and a piece of onion, brown well, basting from time to time. When almost done drain off the butter, add a cup of stock and a little brown gravy, and finish roasting. Strain the gravy over the chicken when serving. Serve in a casserole.

Potatoes à la Reine. Mix well, one cup of boiling water, one ounce of butter, and a half cup of flour; cool a little, and add the yolks of two eggs. Mix this dough with equal parts of fresh-boiled potatoes passed through a fine sieve, season with salt and a little grated nutmeg. Take up, with a spoon, in pieces the size of an egg, and drop one by one in warm swimming lard, heating gradually, so the potato will have time to swell (soufflé), before becoming a golden brown color. When done, salt, and serve on napkin.

D'Uxelles. Put in flat sauce pan three ounces of butter, one chopped onion, and a slice of ham cut in small dices. Simmer for five minutes. Add the stems of fresh or canned mushrooms chopped very fine, and simmer again for five minutes; then add one-half glass of white wine and reduce. Then add one-half pint of brown gravy and boil for ten minutes. Finally stir in one-half cup of fresh bread crumbs, the yolks of two eggs, and season with salt and Cayenne pepper, and chopped parsley. D'Uxelles is used for garnishing in many ways.

Stuffed fresh mushrooms. Cut the stems from six fresh mushrooms, wash the heads well, season with salt and pepper, and fill with D'Uxelles. Place on a buttered dish, sprinkle with grated cheese, put a piece of butter on the top of each, and bake in a moderate oven.

JANUARY 11

BREAKFAST
Grapefruit juice
Pettijohn's with cream
Crescents
Cocoa

LUNCHEON
Pancake Molosol
Scotch consommé
Sweetbread patties with cream
Meringue glacé with raspberries
Coffee

DINNER
Blue Points on shell
Potage Bagration
Celery. Ripe olives
Paupiette of flounder, Bignon
Roast ribs of beef
Anna potatoes
New peas
Escarole salad
Bavarois au chocolat
Assorted cakes
Coffee

Pancake Molosol. Spread some very thin French pancakes with fresh Russian caviar, roll up, and cut in diamond shapes. Serve on napkin, garnished with leaves of lettuce filled with chopped onions, quartered lemons, and parsley in branches. The pancakes must be fresh.

Scotch consommé. Boil a piece of mutton very slowly in consommé. When done strain the broth, add the mutton, cut in small dices, some brunoise, and some boiled barley.

Sweetbread patties with cream. Cut some parboiled sweetbreads in small dices and simmer a few minutes with a piece of butter. Add a little cream and cream sauce, season with salt and Cayenne pepper, boil for ten minutes. Have some hot patty shells, and fill.

Potage Bagration. Add to cream of chicken some boiled macaroni cut in pieces one-quarter inch in length.

Paupiette of flounder, Bignon. Stuff some fillets with fish force meat. Bread, and fry. Serve tomato sauce separate.

Fish force meat. Quarter pound trimmings of fish chopped fine, passed through sieve, and add one yolk of egg and a tablespoonful of cream. Salt and pepper.

Veal force meat. Quarter pound raw veal chopped fine, passed through sieve; add one raw yolk of egg, salt and pepper, and tablespoonful of cream.

Chicken force meat. Quarter pound raw chicken meat, chopped fine, and passed through sieve. Add one yolk of egg and a tablespoonful of cream. Salt and white pepper.

Anna potatoes. Peel some potatoes to a round shape, about the size of a dollar, and slice very thin, like Saratoga chips. Season with salt and pepper. Melt some butter in a round mould or hot frying pan, and lay the potatoes around the bottom; add layer upon layer until they are about two inches in height. Put some melted butter over them, and bake in a moderate oven for about a half hour. Drain off the butter and turn out upon a napkin on a platter.

Meringue glacée, with raspberries. Fill meringue shells with raspberry ice cream and garnish with fresh raspberries.

JANUARY 12

BREAKFAST
Stewed prunes
Boiled eggs
Dry toast
Coffee

LUNCHEON
Eggs Mirabeau
Hasenpfeffer (hare stew)
Noodles
Coffee éclairs
Rolls
Tea

DINNER
Consommé d'Artagnan
Pickles
New England boiled dinner
Apple pie
Coffee

Eggs Mirabeau. Place some stuffed eggs in a buttered shirred egg dish, cover with cream sauce, and bake in oven.

Hasenpfeffer (hare stew). Cut up a hare in three-inch pieces. Save the blood and liver in separate dish. Put the cut up meat in an earthen pot and cover with one-half claret, or white wine, and one-half water. Add one sliced carrot, one sliced onion, a bouquet garni with plenty of thyme in it, salt, and a spoonful of whole black peppers. Let stand for forty-eight hours, then drain, strain the juice, and put the meat on a platter. Put in a pan on the stove one-half pound of butter; when hot add two heaping spoonsful of flour, and allow to become nice and yellow, stirring all the while to prevent its burning. Then add the pieces of hare and simmer for a few minutes; then add the juice and a glass of water or bouillon, bring to the boiling point, cover and let simmer slowly. Parboil and fry in butter one dozen small onions; also cut up one-half pound of salt pork in half-inch squares, and parboil and fry them. When stew is about three-quarters cooked, add the onions, pork, and a can of French mushrooms, and cook until done. Now chop the liver fine, mix with the blood, and stir into the stew just before removing from the fire. Do not let it boil after adding the liver. Season to taste, and serve with a sprinkle of chopped parsley.

Consommé d'Artagnan. In the bottom of a buttered pan place one sliced carrot, one onion, a stalk of celery, a piece of raw ham, a sprig of thyme, one bay leaf, and some pepper berries. On top place three calf's feet, and simmer for a few minutes. Then add one-half glass of white wine and one-half glass of sherry, and three quarts of bouillon or stock. Clarify with the whites of six eggs, bringing to a boil slowly. Cook until the feet are soft. Strain the broth through cheese cloth, cut the calf's feet in small pieces and add to the consommé.

New England boiled dinner. Put a shoulder of salt pork in a pot, cover with water, bring to a boil, and then allow to become cool. Then put the pork in a pot with five pounds of brisket of beef, cover with water, add a little salt, a bouquet garni, three whole turnips, three beets, three carrots and a small head of cabbage. Cook until the vegetables are soft, then remove, and continue cooking the meat until well done. Place the meat on a platter, slice, and place the vegetables around the meat; add some plain boiled potatoes, pour a little of the broth over all, and serve hot.

JANUARY 13

BREAKFAST
Stewed rhubarb
Broiled finnan haddie
Baked potatoes
Rolls
Coffee

LUNCHEON
Oyster stew
Eggs Gambetta
Mutton chops
French fried potatoes
String beans
Camembert cheese and crackers
Coffee

DINNER
Potage Venitienne
Aiguillettes of bass, à la Russe
Beef steak, Provençale
Georgette potatoes
Lettuce and tomato salad
Fancy ice cream
Assorted cakes
Coffee

Oyster stew. Put in a pot six oysters with their own juice, bring to the boiling point, and skim. Then add one cup of boiling milk, one ounce of sweet butter, and salt. Serve crackers separate.

Eggs Gambetta. Dip four cold poached eggs in some beaten eggs, then in bread crumbs, and fry in swimming fat. Place on toast, garnish with boiled calf's brains and sliced truffles, and serve with Madeira sauce.

Potage Venitienne. Beat two spoonfuls of farina, two whole eggs and a half cup of milk together, stir into one quart of boiling consommé, and cook for twelve minutes.

Aiguillettes of bass, à la Russe. Remove the skin from the fillets of bass, and cut in slices (aiguillettes) about one and one-half inches wide and five inches long. Place in a buttered pan, season with salt and pepper, place on each piece three or four round slices of cooked carrots, add half a glass of white wine, cover with buttered paper, and cook slowly. Add some finely cut chervil to some white wine sauce, and pour over the fish.

Beef steak, Provençale. Cook a small sirloin steak sauté in butter, and season well. Cover one-half of the steak with Béarnaise sauce, and the other half with Béarnaise sauce mixed with a little purée of tomatoes. On top of each half place a round potato croquette the size of a walnut, and some Julienne potatoes around the steak.

Béarnaise sauce. Put in a sauce pan six very finely-chopped shallots, a spoonful of crushed white peppers, and a glass of tarragon vinegar, and reduce until nearly dry. Then put the pan in another vessel containing hot water, add the yolks of five eggs and stir in well. Then add one pound of sweet butter cut in small pieces. Stir the butter in piece by piece, and as it melts the sauce will become thick, like mayonnaise. Be careful that the sauce does not become too hot. Salt, strain through cheese cloth, add one teaspoonful of melted meat extract, some chopped fresh tarragon, and a little Cayenne pepper.

Béarnaise tomatée. One cup of thick purée of tomatoes mixed with two cups of Béarnaise sauce.

Choron sauce. Same as Bearnaise tomatée.

JANUARY 14

BREAKFAST
Grapefruit juice
Grape-nuts with cream
Rolls
Coffee

LUNCHEON
Barquette à l'aurore.
Salmon steak with anchovies
Baked potatoes
Cheese cake
Coffee

DINNER
Consommé crème de volaille
Salted English walnuts
Frogs' legs, sauté à sec
Lamb chops, sauce Soubise
Stewed tomatoes
Brussels sprouts
Hearts of romaine
Meringue Chantilly
Coffee

Barquette à l'aurore. Small tartelettes filled with Italian salad and covered with pink mayonnaise sauce.

Italian salad. Use equal parts of carrots, turnips, string beans, and roast beef cut in small squares, and of boiled peas. Season with salt, pepper, tarragon vinegar and olive oil, and garnish with beets and flageolet beans.

Pink mayonnaise. Add to two cups of mayonnaise, one-half cup of cold purée of tomatoes.

Consommé crème de volaille. Put some very light chicken force meat (quenelle) in small round buttered timbale moulds, and cook in bain-marie (double boiler). When done, slice thin and serve in hot consommé. (See chicken force meat recipe Jan. 11.)

Cheese cake. One and one-half pounds of cottage cheese, one-half pound of sugar, one-half pound of butter, the yolks of five eggs, one-half pint of milk, the whites of three eggs well beaten, and some vanilla extract. Mix the butter with the sugar, then the cheese, and the yolks of the eggs, one by one. Then add the milk, flour, and vanilla, and finally the beaten whites of eggs should be stirred in very slowly. Pour on pie dish or pan lined with a thin tartelette dough, and bake in a moderate oven.

Sauce Soubise. Parboil six sliced onions, and then pour off the water. Put in vessel with cold water and salt, and boil till done. Drain off the water, pass the onions through a fine sieve, add one pint of cream sauce, mix well, and season with salt and Cayenne pepper.

Soubise (for stuffing crabs, etc.). Slice a dozen onions, put in vessel with cold water and salt, bring to the boiling point, and allow to cool. Then put the onions in a well buttered casserole, add a half-pound of parboiled rice, a little salt, and two ounces of butter. Cover with a buttered paper and the casserole cover, put in oven and cook until soft. Then strain through a fine sieve; put in a vessel and add two spoonsful of thick cream sauce, heat well, and bind with the yolks of four eggs, season with salt and Cayenne pepper, and allow to cool. When cold mix with a spoon, and use as needed.

JANUARY 15

BREAKFAST
Broiled Yarmouth bloaters
Lyonnaise potatoes
Corn muffins
Coffee

LUNCHEON
Grapefruit with cherries
Scrambled eggs, Turbico
Curried lamb with rice
Chocolate éclairs
Coffee

DINNER
Blue Point oysters
Potage Marie Louise
Salted hazelnuts
Fillet of sole, Castelanne
Squab en compote
Spinach
Endive salad, French dressing
Coupe St. Jacques
Assorted cakes
Coffee

Scrambled eggs, Turbico. Mix with six scrambled eggs one-half cup of Créole sauce.

Curried lamb with rice. Cut three pounds of shoulder and breast of lean lamb in pieces two and one-half inches square. Parboil and put on fire in cold water with one carrot, one onion, a bouquet garni, and salt. Boil until the lamb is done; remove the vegetables, and strain the broth. Put in another vessel three ounces of butter, melt, add two spoonsful of curry powder and two of flour, heat, then add a sliced apple and banana fried in butter, and one-half cup of chutney sauce. Boil for twenty minutes. Strain over the lamb, and serve with boiled rice.

Potage Marie Louise. Mix one quart of purée of white beans with one pint of thick consommé tapioca.

Fillet of sole, Castelanne. Put six fillets in a buttered pan, season with salt and pepper, add one-half glass of white wine, cover, and bake in oven for ten minutes. Make on a round platter a border of boiled rice. Place the fillets in the center. Strain the fish broth, mix with Créole sauce, and pour over the fish, completely covering same.

Squab en compote. Prepare four squab as for roasting, except the stuffing. Season well, and put in earthen pot with an onion, carrot, and two ounces of butter. Put in oven and roast well, basting continually so they will retain their juice. To a brown gravy, or sauce Madère, add the following: Eight small onions boiled and fried, eight heads of fresh mushrooms sauté in butter, eight small boiled French carrots, and two small pickles cut in two. Serve with the squabs.

JANUARY 16

BREAKFAST
  Oatmeal with cream
  Boiled eggs
  Dry toast
  Chocolate

LUNCHEON
  Clam broth in cups
  Broiled striped bass
  Vogeleier omelet
  Field salad
  Tartelette au Bar le Duc
  Coffee

DINNER
  Consommé, de la mariée
  Boiled codfish, oyster sauce
  Roast ribs of beef
  Lima beans
  Potato croquettes
  Escarole and chicory salad
  Savarin Montmorency
  Coffee

Vogeleier omelet. Cut a roll in very thin slices, put in omelet pan with two ounces of butter, and fry until crisp. Add eight beaten eggs, with salt, pepper, and plenty of chives, and make into an omelet.

Tartelette au Bar le Duc. Line the moulds with tartelette dough, fill with raw white beans, and bake. When the dough is done remove the beans, and fill the tartelettes with imported Bar le Duc jelly. Decorate with whipped cream.

Consommé de la Mariée. Boil one quart of consommé. Put the yolks of four eggs in a soup tureen and stir well, adding the consommé slowly. Season with a little Cayenne pepper.

Oyster sauce. Parboil a dozen oysters in their own juice for two minutes. Then strain the broth through a napkin into one pint of cream or Allemande sauce, add the oysters, and season.

Lima beans. Boil the beans in salt water until soft, drain off, add sweet butter and a little pepper, and simmer for a few minutes. Serve with a sprinkle of chopped parsley.

Peas in cream. Boil the peas in salt water until nearly done. Drain off the water and add just enough thick cream to wet them, and simmer for five minutes. Then add a cup of cream sauce and cook until the peas are very soft. Add a little salt and a pinch of sugar.

Coupe oriental. Slice some fresh fruit, such as oranges, pineapple, bananas, etc., add all kinds of berries in season, and put in a bowl with some sugar and a small glass of kirsch or maraschino. Allow to macerate for a couple of hours. Then fill coupe glasses half way to the top with the fruit, and fill the remainder with vanilla ice cream. Place a strawberry or cherry on top. Cook about one-quarter of a pound of sugar so that it will crack when cold. It will require about 310 degrees. Dip a tablespoon into it and shake it over a stick, to form filé sugar (commonly called spun sugar). Cut this sugar in pieces and form in the shape of a ball, and put on top of the cup before serving.

JANUARY 17

BREAKFAST
Baked apples with cream
Poached eggs on toast
Puff paste crescents
English breakfast tea

LUNCHEON
Pain mane
Cold roast beef
Fresh vegetable salad
Roquefort cheese and crackers
Coffee

DINNER
Potage Andalouse
Ripe olives
Fillet of Spanish mackerel,
   Montebello
Olivette potatoes
Leg of lamb, au jus
Mixed string beans
Tomato salad
Vanilla custard pie
Coffee

Pain mane. Small dinner rolls, split, toasted, and filled with a purée of sweet-and-sour bananas, and garnished with pimentos.

Fresh vegetable salad. For this salad use any kind of fresh vegetables in season, such as string beans, Lima beans, carrots, cauliflower, asparagus, Brussels sprouts, tomatoes, peas, boiled celery, boiled celery roots, spring turnips, Jerusalem artichokes, fresh buttons of artichokes, etc. Place them in separate bouquets in a salad bowl, and use French dressing, or any other dressing desired.

Potage Andalouse. To velouté of beef add some cooked tapioca.

Fillet of Spanish mackerel, Montebello. Put the fillets in a buttered dish, season with salt and a little Cayenne pepper, cover with buttered paper, and bake in oven. Dress on a platter, and cover with sauce Béarnaise tomatée.

Olivette potatoes. Cut potatoes with a Parisian potato spoon to the shape of an olive. Put in a vessel with cold water, bring to the boiling point, and drain. Melt some butter in a sauté pan, add the potatoes, and bake in oven until a nice golden brown. Drain off the butter, and season with salt.

Sweet potatoes, rissolées. Boil some small sweet potatoes. When done peel and put in a pan with butter, and roast until brown. Season with salt.

JANUARY 18

BREAKFAST
Baked beans, Boston style
Brown bread
Omelet with jelly
Coffee

LUNCHEON
Hors d'oeuvres variés
Consommé Impératrice
Beef steak, Foch
Gendarme potatoes
Lettuce salad
Meringue glacée au chocolat
Coffee

DINNER
Oysters on half shell
Crème Maintenon
Queen olives
Fillet of sole, Lord Curzon
Stuffed goose, with chestnuts
Apple sauce
Sweet potatoes, rissolées
Peas in cream
Cold asparagus, mustard sauce
Coupe Oriental
Assorted cakes
Coffee

Consommé Impératrice. Consommé garnished with small lobster dumplings and asparagus tips in equal parts, and a sprinkle of chopped chervil.

Beaf steak, Foch. Use sirloin, tenderloin, or rump steak. Season well, and sauté in butter. Place on a platter and put a thick piece of parboiled beef marrow, with one fried egg, on top. Serve with the pan gravy.

Meringue glacée au chocolat. Fill two meringue shells with chocolate ice cream, place together, and decorate with whipped cream.

Crème Maintenon (soup). Three parts crème à la Reine soup, and one part thick consommé Brunoise.

Fillet of sole, Lord Curzon. Put six fillets in a buttered pan, season with salt and a teaspoonful of curry powder, add one-half glass of white wine, cover with buttered paper, and bake in oven. When done put the fish on a platter, strain the broth into a pint of white wine sauce, add one chopped shallot, one tomato cut in squares, one red pepper, and two fresh mushrooms cut in squares and simmered in butter. Mix, season well, and pour over the fish.

Stuffed goose with chestnuts. Clean a goose, and keep the liver and gizzard. Fill with a chestnut stuffing, put in a roasting pan, salt, add a spoonful of water and place in the oven. The water will soon evaporate and the fat begin to melt. Baste well until the goose is done. Then remove the goose to a platter; save the grease for other purposes; and add to the pan one-half glass of bouillon or stock, and one spoonful of meat extract. Boil for five minutes. Serve the gravy separately. Also serve giblet sauce and apple sauce separately. The goose should be served very hot.

JANUARY 19

BREAKFAST
Hothouse raspberries in cream
Scrambled eggs with bacon
Dry toast
Coffee

LUNCHEON
Consommé in cups
Ripe California olives
Broiled fillet of sole, maitre d'hotel
Cucumber salad
Deviled turkeys' legs, with chow chow
Mashed potatoes au gratin
Brie cheese and crackers
Coffee

DINNER
Potage gentilhomme
Fish dumplings, cream sauce
Small tenderloin steak, Florentine
Romaine salad, Roquefort dressing
English breakfast tea ice cream
Assorted cakes
Coffee

Deviled turkey's legs, with chow chow. Use the legs from a boiled or roasted turkey. Season with salt and pepper, spread some French mustard all over the surface, roll in bread crumbs, and broil; or fry in pan with a piece of butter. When nice and brown dish up on platter, and garnish with large leaves of lettuce filled with chow chow.

Mashed potatoes au gratin. Put some mashed potatoes in a buttered shirred egg dish or pie plate. Sprinkle with grated Parmesan or Swiss cheese, put small bits of butter on top, and bake until brown.

Potage gentilhomme. Potato soup with Julienne of carrots.

Julienne. Julienne is the term used in cooking for vegetables, or any kind of meat, etc., cut in long strips, like matches. Vegetable Julienne should be prepared and cooked as follows: Cut the vegetables in strips, add salt and a very little sugar, put in a well-buttered casserole, cover with buttered paper and the casserole cover. Put in oven and smother until soft. Turn gently once or twice, with a fork, so as not to break the vegetables.

Small tenderloin steak, Florentine. Broiled tenderloin steak, with sauce Madere, or brown sauce. Garnish with risotto, and just before serving garnish the risotto with truffles, ham and tongue cut in small squares.

Roquefort dressing, for salads. For four persons take four ounces of Roquefort cheese, put in salad bowl and mash well with a fork. Add one-half teaspoonful of salt, two pinches of ground black pepper, two tablespoonsful of vinegar, and three tablespoonsful of olive oil. Mix well and pour over the salad. If desired, one teaspoonful of Worcestershire sauce and a pinch of paprika may be added.

English breakfast tea ice cream. Prepare in the same manner as vanilla ice cream. Before freezing add some strong tea made of one ounce of English breakfast tea and one cup of boiling water.

JANUARY 20

BREAKFAST
Stewed rhubarb
Boiled eggs
Buttered toast
Coffee

LUNCHEON
Eggs Oudinot
Fricassee of veal, with noodle-
Chocolate profiteroles
Coffee

DINNER
Potage McDonald
Lyon sausage
Fried chicken, Maryland
Cheese cake
Coffee

Eggs Oudinot. Put some stuffed eggs in a shirred egg dish, cover with cream sauce, sprinkle with the chopped yolks of hard-boiled eggs, put a small piece of butter on the top of each, and bake in oven until brown.

Fricassee of veal. Cut five pounds of shoulder and breast of veal in pieces two and one-half inches square, put on fire in cold water, bring to the boiling point, and then cool. Put back in vessel, cover with water, add one carrot, one onion, a bouquet garni, a little salt, and boil until soft. Remove the vegetables and bouquet, and use the broth to make the fricassee sauce. Put in casserole on stove, six ounces of butter, when hot add three-quarters cup of flour, heat through, then add three pints of the veal broth, stir well and boil for ten minutes, then bind with the yolks of three eggs and a cup of cream. Season and strain the sauce over the pieces of veal. Allow to stand five minutes before serving. Noodles, spaghetti, or other paste, should be served, either separate or on the side of plate with the stew.

Noodle dough. Mix one pound of flour with five whole eggs, with a very little or no salt, and a pony of kirschwasser, if desired. Mix well, roll out very thin, and then let the dough become nearly dry. Then cut in strips. Have a vessel on the fire, with about a gallon and a half of boiling water. Add the noodles, and boil for seven minutes over a quick fire, so they will not stick together. Drain off the water and pour two ounces of hot melted butter over the noodles. A little grated nutmeg may be added, if desired. Noodles, like macaroni, may be prepared in many ways.

Chocolate profiteroles. Make some small cream puffs and fill with whipped cream. Place on a deep dish and cover with a sauce made of one pint of water, one-half pound of sugar, and three ounces of cocoa. Boil the water with the sugar, then add the cocoa and stir well. Boil for five minutes.

Potage McDonald. Boil one calf's brains in chicken broth. Make one quart of cream of barley soup, and strain both together through a fine sieve. Put in vessel and add one ounce of sweet butter, and, when melted, serve. Do not let the soup boil after the two have been joined.

Fried chicken, Maryland. Cut up a spring chicken, put in flour, then in eggs, and then in bread crumbs. Season with salt and pepper. Melt three ounces of butter in a frying pan, and when hot add the breaded chicken and fry until golden brown, but be careful not to burn it. It will require about twelve minutes for a young chicken. When done, put on platter with cream sauce over the bottom, and garnish with four corn fritters, four small potato croquettes the size of an ordinary cork, and four strips of fried bacon on top.

JANUARY 21

BREAKFAST
  Preserved figs
  Oatmeal with cream
  Rolls
  Cocoa

LUNCHEON
  Eggs Mery
  Roast fresh leg of pork, au jus
  Apple sauce
  Spinach
  Swiss cheese
  Crackers
  Coffee

DINNER
  Petite marmite
  Radishes
  Boiled beef, horseradish sauce
  Boiled potatoes
  Pickled beets
  Apple Charlotte
  Coffee

Eggs Mery. Scramble eight eggs, well seasoned. Just before they are done add one sliced truffle and two sliced pimentos. Serve in croustades.

Roast leg of fresh pork. Put on bottom of roasting pan one sliced carrot, one onion, three bay leaves, six cloves, one spoonful of pepper berries, and a piece of celery. Season the leg of pork with salt and pepper, and a little sage, if desired. Put on top of the vegetables, and place in oven to roast. Baste well. When done take out the pork, remove the fat in the pan, and add to the gravy a cup of stock or bouillon, and one tablespoonful of meat extract. Boil, strain, and season to taste.

Apple Charlotte. Chop six peeled apples and fry in butter with one-quarter pound of sugar, and one-half teaspoonful of ground cinnamon. Line a charlotte mould with slices of white bread cut as thin as possible, and buttered with fresh butter. Fill the mould with the fried apple and bake in even for twenty-five minutes. Serve with brandy sauce.

JANUARY 22

BREAKFAST
Stewed prunes
Pettijohn's with cream
Rolls
Coffee

LUNCHEON
Canape of fresh caviar
Scrambled eggs with morilles
Planked sirloin steak
Romaine salad
Camembert cheese
Crackers
Coffee

DINNER
Consommé Bretonne
Lyon sausage
Lobster Thermidor
Noisettes of lamb, Cendrillon
Peas au beurre
Celery mayonnaise
Apple water ice
Cakes
Coffee

Scrambled eggs with morilles. Morilles are a species of mushroom rarely found in the United States. They come principally from Europe in cans, or dried. When fresh ones are used, sauté in butter and mix with the scrambled eggs. When in can, drain off the water, put in sauce pan with a piece of butter, season with salt and pepper, simmer for ten minutes, and add to the eggs. When dried, soak them in cold water over night, wash, and then proceed in the same manner as with the canned ones.

Planked sirloin steak. Broil the steak in the usual manner. When nearly done put on a meat plank, put four slices of broiled tomatoes on top, place four strips of broiled bacon across the tomatoes, and roast in oven for five minutes. Cover with maitre d'hotel sauce, and garnish with Parisian potatoes, parsley in branches, and quartered lemon.

Consommé Bretonne. Make a Julienne of equal parts of celery, onions and leeks, and serve in consommé.

Lobster Thermidor. Cut a live lobster in two lengthwise, sprinkle with olive oil, season with salt and pepper, and put in oven and bake. When done remove the meat from the shell and cut in small squares. Then make a sauce as follows: Chop two shallots, a little parsley and tarragon, add one spoonful of meat extract, or some good meat gravy, and reduce by boiling until nearly dry. Then add one spoonful of dry mustard, one cup of cream sauce, and two ounces of fresh butter. Put some of the sauce in the bottom of the shells, put the lobster in the sauce, and pour the remainder over the top. Sprinkle with grated cheese, and bake in oven until brown.

JANUARY 23

BREAKFAST
  Poached eggs on toast
  Broiled ham
  Rolls
  Ceylon tea

LUNCHEON
  Mariniert herring
  Potato salad
  Lemon pie
  Coffee

DINNER
  California oyster cocktails
  Bisque of crabs
  Ripe olives
  Frogs' legs, marinière
  Roast chicken, au jus
  Watercress salad
  Asparagus Hollandaise
  Peach Melba
  Carolines (cakes)
  Coffee

Bisque of crabs. Take two large raw Pacific crabs and put in vessel with cold water, season with salt and a bouquet garni, and boil for one-half hour. Then crack the shells and remove the meat. Use the meat for salad, an entrée dish, or to garnish the soup. Put the shell in a mortar and smash fine. In a vessel put one-quarter pound of butter and the broken shell, and simmer. Then add one pint of the water used to boil the crab, and one pint of milk, and boil for ten minutes. Then add one quart of cream sauce, boil again, and strain through a fine sieve. Put back in pot, add one pint of boiling thick cream, salt and Cayenne pepper, and just before serving add three ounces of sweet butter and one cup of crab meat cut in small pieces.

Cocktail sauce, for oysters (1). One cup of tomato ketchup, one pinch of salt, a little Cayenne pepper, paprika, and celery salt, one teaspoonful of Worcestershire sauce, and one tablespoonful of tarragon vinegar.

(2). One cup of tomato ketchup, one-half teaspoonful of paprika, one spoonful of grated horseradish sauce, salt, one spoonful of Worcestershire sauce, and the juice of one lemon.

Oyster cocktail. Use California oysters, Toke Points, Blue Points, Lynn-havens, Seapuits, or any other kind. Put in an oyster cocktail glass and mix with plenty of cocktail sauce. Set the glass in ice, and serve with lemons cut in half.

Frogs' legs, marinière. Cut the hind legs of two dozen small frogs in two. Put in sauté pan with three ounces of butter, season with salt and pepper, and simmer for five minutes. Then add six chopped shallots and simmer for three minutes. Then one-half glass of white wine and boil until nearly dry. Then add one pint of Allemande sauce, fricassee sauce, or sauce au vin blanc, and boil for five minutes. Serve with a sprinkle of chopped chives and parsley over the top.

JANUARY 24

BREAKFAST
    Preserved strawberries
    Finnan haddie in cream
    Baked potatoes
    Corn muffins
    Coffee

LUNCHEON
    Eggs Chipolata
    Tripe à la mode de Caen
    Chocolate éclairs
    Coffee

DINNER
    Consommé parfait
    Pimentos à l'huile
    Sand dabs, meunière
    Leg of lamb, Boulangère
    Chiffonade salad
    Rolled oats pudding
    Coffee

Eggs Chipolata. Make some shirred eggs and garnish with sauce Madère, to which has been added two small roasted onions, two heads of mushrooms, two small French carrots, three boiled chestnuts, and two very small fried sausages.

Consommé parfait. To one pint of lukewarm consommé tapioca add four raw beaten eggs, put in buttered mould, set in pan in boiling water, and put in moderate oven for ten minutes. Allow to cool, cut in slices, and serve in consommé.

Pimentos à l'huile. This is a plain hors d'oeuvres. Take a can of pimentos, drain off the juice, cut the pepper in four, place on a platter, season with salt and pepper, add one part vinegar and two parts olive oil, and sprinkle with chopped parsley.

Leg of lamb, Boulangère. Season a leg of lamb with salt and pepper, and rub with garlic and butter. Put in roasting pan with a cup of water and a bouquet garni. Slice two large onions very fine, also six raw potatoes the size of a silver dollar, mix, season with salt and pepper, and place around the leg of lamb. Put small pieces of butter on top, put in oven, and baste the meat only. It will require about one and one-quarter hours to cook. Do not disturb the potatoes while cooking. When done remove the bouquet garni, and serve the meat and potatoes very hot, with chopped parsley on top.

Rolled oats pudding. Boil one pint of milk with half of a split vanilla bean; add two ounces of rolled oats and two ounces of sugar, and cook for about ten minutes. Remove from the fire. Separate the yolks and whites of four eggs, add the yolks to the rolled oats and mix well. Beat the whites very hard with a whip, and add to the batter lightly. Put in buttered pudding mould and bake in bain-marie (hot water bath) for about thirty minutes. Take out of mould and serve with vanilla cream sauce.

Vanilla cream sauce. Boil one pint of milk with one-quarter of a split vanilla bean. Mix one-quarter of a pound of sugar with two eggs and one spoonful of sifted flour. Pour the boiling milk over this mixture, and put back on the fire, stir well, and allow to become thick. Then add one cup of cream, strain and serve.

Cream sauce (sweet—quick). One pint of cream, two ounces of sugar, and some flavoring. Mix well, and serve hot or cold.

JANUARY 25

BREAKFAST
　Oatmeal with cream
　Boiled eggs
　Dry toast
　Coffee

LUNCHEON
　Hors d'oeuvres variés
　Clam broth in cups
　Cheese straws
　Broiled lamb chops
　French fried potatoes
　Cold artichokes, mustard sauce
　Apple pie
　Coffee

DINNER
　Chicken okra
　Queen olives
　Fillet of sole, Rose Caron
　Vol au vent, Toulouse
　Roast saddle of venison
　Purée of chestnuts
　Peas au cerfeuil
　Sweet potatoes, Southern style
　Lettuce salad
　Omelette soufflé à la vanille
　Coffee

Fillet of sole, Rose Caron. Skin the four fillets of one large sole and place on a buttered pan. Put on top of each, three slices of cooked lobster, season with salt and paprika, add one-half glass of white wine, cover with buttered paper, put in oven and cook for twelve minutes. Remove the fillets to a platter, taking care that the lobster does not fall off. To the gravy in the pan add one pint of white wine sauce and boil for ten minutes, then add two tablespoonsful of écrevisse butter, and strain the sauce over the fish. Heat in sherry wine sixteen slices of truffles, and put four on top of each fillet, after the sauce has been added. Garnish with fleurons.

Sweet potatoes, Southern style. Peel and slice some boiled sweet potatoes and put in buttered shirred egg dishes, or pie plates. Add a little salt, molasses and maple syrup, sprinkle with powdered sugar, put some small bits of butter on top, and bake in oven until brown.

Vol au vent, or patty shells. Take some puff paste, with six turns, and roll out to about one-quarter inch in thickness. With a round pastry cutter about three inches in diameter, cut the paste. Then moisten with egg, and with the tip of a small knife trace a ring on each patty about one-half inch from the edge. Bake in a hot oven for about twenty minutes. Take out of the oven and with the knife point lift off the center cover within the traced circle, and empty of the uncooked paste inside.

Garniture Toulouse. Cut the garnishing to agree with the size of the patty. For the size described above cut in pieces about one-half inch square. For larger patties cut from an inch to an inch and a half square. Use the boiled breast of chicken, sweetbreads boiled in chicken broth, and French mushrooms in equal parts, one-half of a sliced truffle to each person, three chicken dumplings, teaspoon size cut in two, rooster kidneys and rooster combs. Mix well, and stew in a sauce Allemande made of chicken broth and well seasoned. Fill the hot patty shells and serve on platter, garnished with parsley in branches.

JANUARY 26

BREAKFAST
Waffles
Honey in comb
Coffee

LUNCHEON
Grapefruit with sherry
Mixed grill
Cup custard
Lady fingers
Coffee

DINNER
Purée Crécy
Radishes
Bouillabaisse Marseillaise
Roast leg of mutton, currant jelly
String beans
Hashed in cream potatoes
Escarole salad
Napoleon cake
Coffee

Mixed grill. Broil one lamb chop, one breakfast sausage, one slice of tomato, one whole fresh mushroom head, and one whole lamb kidney. Put all on a plate, cover with maitre d'hotel sauce, and serve hot. Garnish with watercress.

Cup custard. Mix four eggs, one-quarter pound of sugar, one pint of milk, and flavor with vanilla. Strain, pour into cups, and bake in bain-marie until firm. It will require about one-half hour in a moderate oven.

Bain-marie. This is a term used in cookery for a vessel holding hot water in which another vessel may be heated at a temperature not above that of boiling water. Different dishes are variously allowed to stand, cook or bake in bain-marie. For example, Hollandaise sauce should be kept in bain-marie in hot water. Hollandaise or Béarnaise sauce, if kept in boiling water, would turn. A cream soup should be kept in boiling water, as extra cooking will not harm it. Timbale of chicken, custard for soup, or cup custard, should be cooked in bain-marie.

Purée Crécy (soup). Slice six carrots very thin, put in casserole with three ounces of butter, and simmer for thirty minutes. Then add three pints of well-seasoned chicken broth, and boil for one hour. Strain through a fine sieve. Serve in a separate dish small squares of bread fried in butter.

Roast leg of mutton. The leg of mutton should hang in the ice box at least four days before using. If too fresh it will be tough. Rub the mutton with salt and pepper and, if desired, a little garlic. Put in a roasting pan, one sliced onion, one sliced carrot, one bay leaf and two cloves. Now put in the mutton, with a piece of butter on top, and place in oven to roast. Baste continually. It will require from forty-five to sixty minutes to cook. If desired well done cook for another thirty minutes. When done take out the leg, drain off the fat, and make a gravy by adding one cup of stock and one spoonful of meat extract; boil, season, and strain.

JANUARY 27

BREAKFAST
Stewed rhubarb
Ham and eggs
Rolls
Coffee

LUNCHEON
Salade thon mariné
Stuffed breast of veal, au jus
Asparagus tips, au gratin
Potato salad
Savarin au rhum
Coffee

DINNER
Potato and leek soup
Corned beef and cabbage
Plain boiled potatoes
Broiled chicken on toast
Lettuce with egg dressing
Coupe St. Jacques
Assorted cakes
Coffee

Thon mariné salad. Tunny fish can be obtained in cans, the best quality being the French brands. Break up the fish with the fingers, and place on a platter with leaves of lettuce. The fish should be in pieces about one inch and a half thick. Sprinkle with salt, pepper, chopped parsley, chervil, and a little finely sliced chives, and a sauce of one-third vinegar and two-thirds olive oil.

Stuffed breast of veal, au jus. Have your butcher prepare a breast of veal ready for stuffing. Use the same dressing as for chicken, and sew up the end so the dressing will not fall out while roasting. Put in the roasting pan one sliced onion and one carrot. Put in the veal and sprinkle with salt and pepper. Put bits of butter all over the top and roast in oven, basting often. It will take about an hour to cook in a moderate oven. Remove the veal to platter when done, and make a sauce by adding to the gravy in pan one cup of bouillon and one spoonful of meat extract, boil for five minutes, and strain.

Asparagus tips, au gratin. Put the tips in a buttered pan or silver dish, cover with well-seasoned cream sauce, sprinkle with grated cheese and small bits of butter and bake in oven until brown.

Corned beef and cabbage. The best corned beef is that made from the brisket. Put on fire in cold water and skim when it comes to the boiling point. Cover and let it boil slowly until about three-quarters done. Then add two heads of well-washed cabbage cut in four, and cook with the beef for at least one hour.

JANUARY 28

BREAKFAST
Farina with cream
Omelet with fine herbs
Rolls
Coffee

LUNCHEON
Grapefruit and orange en suprême
Ripe olives
Eggs Marigny
Russian salad
Caramel custard
Coffee

DINNER
Tomate Parisienne (cold)
Consommé parfait
Boiled salmon, Hollandaise
Potatoes nature
Fricandeau of veal, au jus
Sorrel with eggs
Carrots with cream
Baba au rhum
Coffee

Russian salad. Equal parts of boiled carrots, turnips, beets and potatoes, cut in small dice, boiled peas, boiled string beans cut in small pieces, and one slice of cold roast beef cut in small squares. Put all in salad bowl, season with salt, pepper, a little Cayenne pepper, and just enough tarragon vinegar to wet the mixture. Let stand for one hour, drain off the liquid, if any, and form the salad in pyramid shape in the bowl. Spread some thick mayonnaise over all, and garnish with boiled potatoes and truffles, cut like a five-cent piece, linking one to the other around the base of the salad like a chain. On top put a small flower of a boiled and seasoned cauliflower, and serve very cold.

Caramel custard. Put two ounces of sugar in a copper pan and cook until it is brown in color, then pour into a custard mould and allow to become cold. Mix four eggs with one-quarter of a pound of sugar, flavor with vanilla, add one pint of milk, and strain. Pour over the burned sugar, and fill the mould. Put in bain-marie and cook until firm. When cool, reverse the custard on a dish, and serve. The caramel at the bottom of the mould will serve as a sauce.

Tomate Parisienne (Hors d'oeuvres). Peel and slice four tomatoes and lay on platter with lettuce leaves. Cut the inside of a stalk of celery in very small dice, and six anchovies in small squares. Put in a bowl, add a pinch of salt, some fresh-ground black pepper, some chives, parsley and chervil chopped fine, and one spoonful of vinegar and two of olive oil. Mix well and pour over the tomatoes.

Sorrel. Sorrel is a fine vegetable for the promotion of health. Remove the stems from a peck of sorrel and wash the leaves in four different waters, to remove all the sand. Have a kettle with salted water on the fire. Put the sorrel into the boiling water and cook for ten minutes, stirring often. Pour off the water and let stand in the colander fifteen minutes so it will drain dry, then strain through a fine sieve. Then put the sorrel in a sauce pan with three ounces of butter and bring to the boiling point. Season with salt and pepper, and bind with two whole eggs, beaten. Do not let it boil after adding the eggs, but let it get just hot enough to give the sorrel a firm body. Garnish with the half of a hard boiled egg, if desired.

JANUARY 29

BREAKFAST
Orange juice
Boiled eggs
Rolls
Coffee

LUNCHEON
Hors d'oeuvres variés
Eggs à la Russe
Boiled beef tongue with spinach
Mashed potatoes
French pastry
Coffee

DINNER
Cream of canned peas
Sardines on toast
Roast beef au jus
Lima beans
Rissolées potatoes
Romaine salad
Raspberry Bavarois
Assorted cakes
Coffee

Eggs à la Russe. Spread a piece of toast with fresh caviar, put an egg fried in oil on top, and put anchovy sauce around the edge on the platter.

Eggs fried in oil. Fry the eggs one at a time. Have a very small frying pan with plenty of very hot olive oil in it. Drop a fresh egg in it, and turn with a wooden spoon. If any other kind of spoon is used the egg will stick to it. When of a good yellow color, take out and place on a towel, so the oil can drain off, and season with salt. The eggs should be soft inside, like a poached egg.

Anchovy sauce. To a cup of cream add one spoonful of essence of anchovies, or one teaspoonful of anchovy paste. Anchovy sauce is also made with sauce Allemande, white wine sauce, or even a brown sauce, if desired. The cream sauce with the essence is more commonly used with eggs.

Boiled beef tongue. Put a fresh beef tongue in cold water and bring to the boiling point, skim, add salt, one carrot, one onion, a bouquet garni, one stalk of celery, and one of leek. Boil until tongue is soft. The bouillon may be used for stock or soup, or to make caper sauce. For beef tongue with spinach, put plain boiled spinach on platter, sliced tongue on top, and pour a little of the broth over all.

Raspberry Bavarois. (For four or five persons.) One pint of milk, one pint of whipped cream, the yolks of four eggs, one-quarter pound of sugar, six sheets of French gelatine, and one-half pint of raspberry juice. Boil the milk with the sugar, then pour over the yolks, and set on the fire again until it thickens, but do not let it boil. Wash the gelatine in cold water, add to the mixture, and stir until melted. Then set aside until cold. Mix the raspberry pulp with the whipped cream, and stir into the mixture. Put in mould and place in ice box until set. Turn out on platter, and serve with whipped cream or raspberry syrup, separate or around the bavarois.

Sardines on toast. Take sardines from can and put on a fine thin wire broiler and heat quickly. Serve on toast with maitre d'hotel butter on top, and garnish with quartered lemons and parsley.

JANUARY 30

BREAKFAST
Baked apples with cream
Scrambled eggs with smoked beef
Rolls
English breakfast tea

LUNCHEON
Grapefruit with chestnuts
Consommé in cups
Deviled crab
Lemon pie
Coffee

DINNER
Toke Point oysters
Potage tapioca, Crécy
Terrapin, Maryland
Squab chicken, Michels
Stewed tomatoes
Cèpes Tyrolienne (cold)
Fancy ice cream
Cakes
Coffee

Grapefruit with chestnuts. Cut a grapefruit in two and cut free the sections with a pointed knife. Pour a little maraschino in the center, and place a marron glacé (candied chestnut) on top.

Deviled crabs. Simmer the flakes of two crabs and one-half of a chopped onion in butter. Season with salt and Cayenne pepper, add two cups of thick cream sauce, one dash of Worcestershire sauce, one spoonful of English mustard, and a little chopped chives. Bring to a boil, and bind with the yolks of two eggs. Then fill the crab shells, spread a little French mustard over the top, sprinkle with bread crumbs, place a small piece of butter on each, and bake in the oven. When brown serve on napkin with lemon and parsley.

Potage tapioca, Crécy. Half consommé tapioca and half potage Crécy, mixed. No croûtons.

Stewed tomatoes. Peel six tomatoes, and cut in four. Squeeze out half of the juice, and put the tomatoes in a vessel with three ounces of butter, season with salt, pepper and a pinch of powdered sugar, cover, and simmer until done.

Cèpes Tyrolienne (cold). Cut in small dices one carrot and one celery root, and put in casserole with one chopped onion and two ounces of butter. Simmer. Then add one glass of white wine and reduce. Then add one-half cup of tomato sauce, some chopped chervil, and one can of sliced cèpes. Serve cold.

Squab chicken à la Michels. Season four squab chickens well with salt and pepper, both inside and out. Put in iron pot with a quarter of a pound of sweet butter and one onion cut in two. Put the pot on the fire and simmer slowly, until the chicken and onion are of a good yellow color, turning them often while cooking. Then add one tablespoonful of white wine and one of chicken broth, cover, and put in oven for ten minutes, basting frequently. Put the chickens on a platter, take out the onion, and boil the sauce remaining in pot with the addition of one teaspoonful of meat extract. Strain over the chicken.

JANUARY 31

BREAKFAST
  Oatmeal with cream
  Calf's liver and bacon
  Rolls
  Coffee

LUNCHEON
  Oysters Kirkpatrick
  Country sausages with baked apples
  Potato salad
  Cabinet pudding
  Coffee

DINNER
  Potage Windsor
  Green olives
  Fillet of sole, Admiral
  Saddle of lamb, mint sauce
  String beans
  Potato croquettes
  Hearts of lettuce
  Pineapple biscuit glacé
  Assorted cakes
  Coffee

Oysters Kirkpatrick. Season some oysters on half shell with salt, pepper and a little Worcestershire sauce, cover with tomato ketchup, sprinkle with grated cheese, put a small piece of butter on top of each, and bake in their own shells for five minutes. Serve quartered lemon separate.

Cabinet pudding. Fill a well-buttered pudding mould with left-over pieces of sponge, layer or other kinds of cake, cut in small squares, and mix with one-quarter pound of seedless raisins. Then make a custard of three eggs, one-quarter pound of sugar, one pint of milk and a little vanilla flavoring. Mix well, strain, and pour over the cake in the moulds, and bake in bain-marie for about forty minutes. Remove from the mould and serve hot, with vanilla cream sauce.

Fillet of sole, Admiral. Put fillets of sole in a buttered sauté pan, decorate the top with fish force meat in the shape of an anchor, and cook in white wine. When done serve with a white wine sauce, with shrimps, oysters and clams cut in small pieces, in it. Garnish with fleurons.

Potage Windsor. Put in roasting pan five pounds of veal bones, one carrot and one onion sliced, a piece of leek, a piece of celery, a bouquet garni, and three ounces of butter. Roast in oven until well browned, then transfer to a pot and add one gallon of water, six calf's feet and a little salt, and boil until the feet are cooked. Strain the broth. Allow the feet to cool, remove the meat from the bones, and slice in very thin strips. Now put four ounces of butter in a vessel, heat, and add four ounces of flour and cook until golden brown. Then add two quarts of the broth, and boil for thirty minutes. Strain, add the calf's feet, one carrot boiled and cut in very thin round slices, some small chicken dumplings, a few French peas, and one-half cup of sherry wine. Season with salt and Cayenne pepper.

FEBRUARY 1

BREAKFAST
Fried hominy
Currant jelly
Crescents
Coffee

LUNCHEON
Poached eggs with clams, Créole
Chicken croquettes with peas
Camembert cheese and crackers
Coffee

DINNER
Oxtail soup, English style
Boiled brook trout, Hollandaise
Potatoes nature
Roast staffed duckling, apple sauce
Broiled sweet potatoes
Brussels sprouts in bouillon
Romaine salad
French pancake
Coffee

Clams, Créole. Heat two dozen clams in their own juice, but do not allow them to boil. Then add one pint of Créole sauce.

Poached eggs with clams, Créole. Serve poached eggs on toast, covered with clams Créole.

Ox tail, English style. Cut two ox tails in small pieces, put on the fire in cold water, salt, and bring to the boiling point. Take off the stove and allow to cool. Put in sauce pan four ounces of butter, melt, add the oxtail, and roast until colored. Then sprinkle the pieces with two large spoonsful of flour, and cook again until of a good brown color. Then add one gallon of bouillon, stock or hot water; bring to a boil, and skim. Then boil for one hour. Now add three carrots and two turnips cut in very small squares, and one pound of whole barley, and boil for two hours. Then add one pint of purée of tomatoes, one spoonful of Worcestershire sauce, salt, pepper, a little Cayenne, some chopped parsley, and one-half cup of tomato ketchup. Boil again for ten minutes, and before serving add one glass of sherry wine.

Broiled sweet potatoes. Peel four boiled sweet potatoes, and slice length-wise, one-quarter inch in thickness. Sprinkle with salt, wet with olive oil, and broil on both sides on an iron broiler. Serve on a platter with melted butter poured over them.

Brussels sprouts in bouillon. Clean and wash thoroughly one quart of Brussels sprouts. Put a vessel on the fire, with one gallon of water and a tablespoonful of salt. When boiling add the sprouts and cook for five minutes; then cool off with cold water. Put the cold sprouts in a casserole, add two ounces of butter, salt, pepper, one cup of bouillon and a little chopped parsley. Cover, and simmer until well done. Sprouts should be served whole, so do not touch with spoon while cooking.

FEBRUARY 2

BREAKFAST
Stewed rhubarb
Boiled eggs
Dry toast
Coffee

LUNCHEON
Smoked goosebreast
Tomcods, meunière
Broiled fresh spareribs, with lentils
Vanilla bavarois, with Bar le Duc
Cookies
Demi tasse

DINNER
Consommé Doria
Scallops, Jerusalem
Spring lamb tenderloin, Thomas
Fried egg plant
Chicory and escarole salad
Homemade apple pudding
Coffee

Tomcods, meunière. Season six tomcods with salt and pepper, and roll in flour. Melt four ounces of butter in a frying pan, put in the tomcods and fry. When done put on platter and sprinkle with chopped parsley and the juice of two lemons. Put four ounces of butter in the pan and cook to the color of a hazelnut. Pour the butter over the fish, garnish with quartered lemon and parsley in branches.

Broiled spareribs with lentils. Broil some spareribs and place on platter. Garnish with lentils, and serve with a border of Madeira sauce.

Lentils. Soak two pounds of lentils in cold water for six hours, then put on fire with one quart of water, a pinch of salt, one ham bone, one carrot, one onion and a bouquet garni. Boil for about two hours, when the lentils should be soft; remove the vegetables and the bouquet, and drain off the water. Then chop two large onions very fine, put in casserole with three ounces of butter, cover, and simmer until done. Add the lentils and a cup of brown meat gravy, some chopped parsley and ground pepper, simmer for twenty minutes, and serve hot.

Lentil salad. Take some of the boiled lentils, before the onions and brown gravy have been added, and serve with French dressing.

Vanilla Bavarois with Bar le Duc. Bar le Duc is a currant jelly made in the village of Bar le Duc, France. There are two kinds, red and white. Make a vanilla bavarois, place on platter, and pour some red Bar le Duc around the base.

Homemade cookies. Work one-quarter pound of butter and one-quarter pound of sugar together until creamy, then add three eggs, one by one, and whip well. Then add one-quarter pound of sifted flour and some flavoring, preferably the rind of a lemon. Dress the batter in fancy, or plain round, shapes, on a buttered pan, and bake in a quick oven.

FEBRUARY 3

BREAKFAST
  Grapefruit
  Ham and eggs
  Rolls
  Coffee

LUNCHEON
  Canapé of sardines
  Eggs Benedict
  Sweetbread cutlets, cream sauce
  Broiled fresh mushrooms
  Fruit salad, Chantilly
  Coffee

DINNER
  Potage Lamballe
  Frogs' legs, sauté à sec
  Wiener schnitzel
  Spaghetti Milanaise
  Terrine de foie gras, cold
  Lettuce salad
  Nesselrode pudding
  Cakes
  Coffee

Eggs Benedict. Cut an English muffin in two, toast, and put on platter. Put a slice of broiled ham on top of each half, a poached egg on top of the ham, cover all with Hollandaise, and lay a slice of truffle on top of the sauce.

Wiener Schnitzel. Cut from a leg of veal some cutlets; or have your butcher cut them for you. Season with salt and pepper, roll in flour, then in beaten eggs, and then in bread crumbs. Put some melted butter in a frying pan and fry the cutlets, or schnitzel, on both sides, until yellow and well done. Dish up on a platter with tomato sauce. Put on each schnitzel a thin slice of lemon. Roll a fillet of anchovy around your finger to form a ring, place on a slice of lemon and fill the ring with capers.

Fruit salad, Chantilly. Slice some fresh fruit, such as oranges, pears, pineapple, apples, strawberries, cherries, etc. Put in a bowl, add one spoonful of granulated sugar, one pony of kirschwasser or maraschino, and allow to macerate for about an hour. Put in glasses or saucers, and serve with whipped cream on top.

Fruit salad au kirsch. Same as above, but use kirschwasser only, to macerate, and omit the whipped cream.

Fruit salad au marasquin. Same as au kirsch, only use maraschino instead of kirschwasser.

FEBRUARY 4

BREAKFAST
  Guava jelly
  Rolled oats with cream
  Plain omelet
  Rolls
  Coffee

LUNCHEON
  Hors d'oeuvres variés
  Fillet of halibut, au vin blanc
  Broiled pig's feet, special
  Celery root, field and beet salad
  Assorted fruit
  Coffee

Bisque of clams
Broiled Alaska black cod
Breast of squab under glass,
  St. Francis
Asparagus Polonaise
Coupe Viviane
Assorted cakes
Coffee

Broiled Alaska black cod. This Alaskan fish is brought from the north frozen, and is very fine, being rich and fat. Broiling is the best way of preparing it, as it needs a quick fire to cook the oil in the fish. Season well, and serve with maitre d'hotel sauce made with plenty of lemon juice.

Asparagus Polonaise. Put four pounds of boiled fresh, or two cans, of asparagus on a platter. Have the asparagus very hot. Sprinkle the tips with salt and pepper, one chopped boiled egg, and some chopped parsley. Melt in a pan, three ounces of sweet butter, add two tablespoonsful of bread crumbs, fry until brown, and pour over the tips of the asparagus.

Breast of squab under glass, St. Francis. Season the breast of a raw squab with salt and pepper, and roll in flour. Fry in butter for two minutes, or until nice and brown. Fry in the same butter, very lightly, one slice of Virginia ham. Then fry in same pan the heads of four fresh mushrooms, well seasoned. Put a slice of toast in a buttered shirred egg dish, put the ham on the toast, the breast of squab on the ham, and the mushrooms on top. Pour well-seasoned cream sauce over all, cover with a glass bell that fits just inside of the edge of the shirred egg dish, put in the oven and cook for ten minutes.

Boiled lettuce. Boil six heads of lettuce in salted water. When done strain off the water and pound the lettuce through a fine colander. Add two ounces of butter and one cup of cream, heat well, and serve.

FEBRUARY 5

BREAKFAST
Baked apples with cream
Buttered toast
Cocoa

LUNCHEON
Omelet with soft clams, Newburg
Breaded lamb chops, tomato sauce
New string beans
Potatoes au gratin
Mince pie
Coffee

DINNER
Seapuit oysters
Potage Talleyrand
Planked smelts
Tournedos Rossini
Jets de houblons
Gauffrette potatoes
Romaine salad, Roquefort dressing
Curaçao sorbet
Alsatian wafers
Demi tasse

Sauce Newburg. Put in a vessel one cup of well-seasoned cream sauce, one cup of thick cream and one gill of sherry wine. Bring to the boiling point and bind with the yolk of one egg and a little cream. Then stir slowly into the sauce two tablespoonsful of lobster or crayfish butter. This sauce is used a great deal in hotel and restaurant cookery.

Soft clams, Newburg. Take the bellies of two dozen soft clams and put in a buttered sauté pan, add one spoonful of Madeira wine, cover the pan, and warm them through. Do not stir, as the clams will break easily. Then add one and one-half cups of sauce Newburg, well seasoned with salt, pepper and a litle Cayenne pepper. Mix and serve in a chafing dish.

Omelet with soft clams. Make a plain well-seasoned omelet. Put at each end a bouquet of clams Newburg, and pour on each side of the omelet a litle sauce Newburg.

Potage Talleyrand. Put in soup tureen one quart of consommé tapioca, one grated fresh, or two grated canned truffles, one glass of dry sherry wine, a pinch of Cayenne pepper.

Tournedos. Tournedos are small tenderloin beef steaks, trimmed free of fat. They may be either broiled or sautéed, and served with maitre d'hotel sauce. Mostly used as an entrée with fancy garniture.

Tournedos Rossini. Salt and pepper the tournedos, sauté in butter, and put on a platter. Take one slice of fresh goose liver (or Strassbourg goose liver au natural), season, roll in flour, sauté in butter, and put on top of the tournedo. Simmer a large head of fresh mushroom in butter, and place on top of the goose liver, lay two slices of truffle on top of the mushroom, and pour well-seasoned Madeira sauce over all.

FEBRUARY 6

BREAKFAST
  Preserved figs
  Scrambled eggs with bacon
  Rolls
  Coffee

LUNCHEON
  Antipasto
  Essence of chicken in cups
  Cheese straws
  Bear steak, port wine sauce
  Chestnuts and prunes
  Fried egg plant
  Mexican salad
  Corn meal pudding
  Coffee

DINNER
  Clam chowder
  Ripe olives
  Striped bass sauté, miller style
  O'Brien potatoes
  Asparagus Hollandaise
  Cold Westphalia ham
  Omelette soufflée à la vanille
  Coffee

Scrambled eggs with bacon (1). Put some plain scrambled eggs in a deep platter with strips of broiled bacon over the eggs.

(2) Cut six slices of bacon in small squares, put in casserole with one-half ounce of butter and fry slowly until crisp. Add ten beaten eggs mixed with one-half cup of cream, season with salt and pepper, and cook in the usual manner.

Antipasto. This is an Italian relish (hors d'oeuvre), and can be obtained in cans. It consists of tunny fish, sardines, pickles, capers, etc., preserved in oil. Serve on a napkin, in the can, with quartered lemons and parsley around the sides.

Essence of chicken. Put in a casserole one chopped raw fowl, or plenty of carcasses, necks, etc., of raw chickens. Add the whites of three eggs, stir well, and add slowly two quarts of strong chicken broth. Bring to a boil, strain through a napkin, and serve in cups.

O'Brien potatoes. Peel two large boiled potatoes, cut in one-half inch squares, and put in hot fat to gain color. Cut two red peppers (pimentos) in small squares and put in a sauté pan with one ounce of butter. When the peppers are hot add the potatoes, season with salt and pepper, and mix carefully so the potatoes will not break.

Omelette Soufflée. Mix one-half pound of sugar with the yolks of two eggs, add one-half of a split vanilla bean, and beat until light and fluffly. Remove the pieces of vanilla bean. Beat the whites of eight eggs until absolutely stiff, and then add to the batter lightly. Arrange on a silver platter in fancy shape, and decorate with a pastry bag with a fine tube. Dust with powdered sugar, and bake in a rather hot oven for a few minutes.

FEBRUARY 7

BREAKFAST
  Cactus fruit with lemon
  Broiled pigs' feet, Chili sauce
  Shirred eggs with parsley
  Dry toast
  Cocoa

LUNCHEON
  Eggs Lackmée
  Lamb steak, Bércy
  String beans
  Mashed potatoes
  Fruit salad au Marasquin
  Coffee

DINNER
  Consommé Julienne
  Fillet of flounder, Cansale
  Tenderloin of beef, Malvina
  Escarole and chicory salad
  Almond cake
  Coffee

Cactus fruit with lemon. Slice some cactus fruit and serve on ice, with powdered sugar and lemon separate. No cream.

Broiled pigs' feet, Chili sauce. Split some cooked pigs' feet, season, roll in bread crumbs, sprinkle with oil and broil. Put on platter and garnish with lemon and parsley. Serve hot or cold Chili sauce, separate.

Shirred eggs with parsley. Crack two eggs on a buttered shirred egg dish, season with salt and pepper, sprinkle with fresh-chopped parsley, and bake in oven for three minutes.

Eggs Lackmée. Put four poached eggs on toast. Chop some boiled chicken very fine, add one cup of cream sauce, one-half cup of cream, put on the stove and bring to the boiling point, season with salt and a little Cayenne pepper, and pour over the eggs.

Lamb steak. Cut the steak crosswise from a leg of young lamb, and about one inch in thickness. Season with salt and pepper, roll in oil and broil; or sauté in pan with butter. Use as an entrée dish, or in place of the roast.

Garniture Bércy. Bércy is used with steaks, chops, fish, etc. Prepare as follows: Mix one-quarter pound of fresh butter with salt, pepper, three fine chopped shallots, one small piece of garlic mashed fine, some chopped parsley, chervil and chives. Spread over the meats or fish, and put in hot oven for two minutes. (Called also sauce Bércy.)

Fillet of flounder, Cansale. Put four fillets of flounder in a buttered pan, season with salt and pepper, add the juice of one dozen oysters, one-half wineglass full of white wine, cover with buttered paper, and bake in oven. When done remove the fillets and add to the pan one-half pint of white wine sauce, and boil for ten minutes. Bind with the yolk of one egg, and strain. Poach the dozen oysters, and, with a small can of French mushrooms, add to the sauce, and pour over the fish.

Tenderloin of beef, Malvina. A roast tenderloin with sauce Madère, garnished with small onions sauté, potatoes rissolées, and whole chestnuts glacé au Madère.

Chestnuts glacé. Put one-half pound of boiled chestnuts in a sauté pan with two spoonsful of meat extract, and cook for ten minutes.

Chestnuts glacé au Madère. Add to chestnuts glacé a little sauce Madère, just before serving.

FEBRUARY 8

BREAKFAST
    Baked apples with cream
    Boiled eggs
    Dry toast
    Chocolate with whipped cream

LUNCHEON
    Omelette Louis XIV
    Chickens' livers sauté, au Madère
    Purée of Lima beans
    Sago pudding
    Coffee

DINNER
    Seapuit oysters
    Cream of celery, Kalamazoo
    Ripe California olives
    Fillet of pompano, en papillote
    Roast chicken
    Watercress salad
    Château potatoes
    Fresh asparagus, Hollandaise
    Peach Mona Lisa
    Assorted cakes
    Coffee

Omelette Louis XIV. Chop the white meat of a boiled fowl very fine, mix with one truffle cut in small dices and one-half cup of well-seasoned cream sauce. Place in the center of a plain omelet, turn on a platter, and pour some cream sauce around the edge.

Chickens' livers sauté, Forestière. Clean a dozen chicken livers, cut in two, and season with salt and pepper. Melt a piece of butter in frying pan, add the livers, and sauté over a quick fire for a few minutes. Slice one pound of fresh mushrooms and fry them in butter. Then put the mushrooms and livers together in a sauce pot on the stove, and cover with two cupsful of brown gravy or Madeira sauce. Get as hot as possible without boiling, serve in deep dish, or chafing dish, with chopped parsley on top.

Purée of Lima beans. Take one can, or a pound of fresh boiled Lima beans, and pass through a fine sieve. Put in pot, add two ounces of butter, season with salt and pepper, and serve hot. If too thick add a soupspoonful of cream or consommé.

Cream of celery, Kalamazoo. Make a cream of celery soup. Take the inside of two stalks of celery and cut in very small dices boiled, and use for garnishing.

Fillet of pompano en papillote. Take four small Pacific pompano, or the fillets of a large Florida pompano, season, roll in flour, and put in pan in two ounces of hot butter. Fry on both sides until nearly done. Simmer two chopped shallots in one ounce of butter for a minute, then add six chopped fresh mushrooms, and simmer for ten minutes. Now add one spoonful of Madeira sauce, season with salt and pepper, and cook for five minutes to a purée. Add the juice of a lemon, some chopped parsley, and one ounce of sweet butter. Now cut four pieces of manilla paper in the shape of a heart about ten inches high and fourteen inches wide. Fold in center, then open out flat on the table and oil well on one side. Put a teaspoonful of the mushroom purée on one half of the paper, place the pompano on top, and another spoonful of the purée on top of the fish. Now fold the free side of the paper over the top, and turn in the edges to close tight the opening. Put on a flat pan and place in an oven for a few minutes. Be careful not to burn, and serve in the papers on a silver platter. Other fish may be substituted for pompano if desired.

Papillote, club style (for fish). Fry the fish as above. Omit the purée of mushrooms and use, instead, a piece of butter, a slice of fresh-boiled hot potato, and one slice of lime. Finish as above.

Veal chops en papillote. Season four veal chops with salt and pepper, fry in butter, and finish in paper, with the purée of mushrooms and the addition of a slice of cooked ham on top, before folding the paper.

FEBRUARY 9

BREAKFAST
Stewed prunes
Broiled salt mackerel, melted
  butter
Baked potatoes
Rolls
Coffee

LUNCHEON
Eggs Henri IV
Pork tenderloin, sauce Madère
Fried sweet potatoes
Stewed apples
Sherry wine jelly
Coffee

DINNER
Consommé national
Radishes
Fried fillet of sole, Maréchal
Roast rack of lamb, mint sauce
String beans
Mashed potatoes
Nesselrode pudding
Cakes
Coffee

Wine jelly. Dissolve four ounces of French gelatine in two quarts of water, add one pound of sugar, the rind and juice of six lemons, the juice of three oranges, a piece of cinnamon stick, and six cloves. Stir well and put on fire to boil. Then stir quickly into the jelly the whites of six eggs, partly beaten, and boil again. Then take off the fire and strain through a flannel jelly bag, and add the flavoring desired. Pour into jelly moulds and put on ice until firm. To remove the jelly, dip the moulds in hot water, and turn out on a cold dish. For the following jellies use a wine glassful of the respective wines or liqueurs for flavoring: Sherry wine, maraschino, Rhein wine, claret, port wine, anisette, kirschwasser, champagne, Burgundy, Moselle wine, Chartreuse, brandy, Bénédictine, Cognac, fine champagne, etc.

Fruit jelly. Cut or slice all kinds of fresh fruit in season, put in jelly mould and cover with wine jelly. Put in ice box until firm.

Jelly à la Russe. Put some empty jelly moulds on ice until cold, then pour a little wine jelly in the bottom and allow to set. Do not let the balance of the jelly set, but add a pony of Russian kümmel, put in bowl and beat with a whip until it looks like white frost. Then fill the moulds to the top with the beaten jelly, and set in the ice box until needed.

Fillet of sole, Maréchal. Salt and pepper the fillets, dip in milk, then in flour, then in beaten eggs, and finally in bread crumbs. Fry in swimming lard, and serve on napkin with lemon and fried parsley. Serve the following sauce separate: Two cups of cream sauce, one dozen parboiled oysters, one-quarter pound of picked shrimps, and six sliced canned mushrooms.

FEBRUARY 10

BREAKFAST
Grapefruit
Omelet with chives
Corn muffins
Coffee

LUNCHEON
Pickled oysters
Toasted rye bread
Consommé vermicelli
Calf's head à la poulette
Potato croquettes
Hot mince pie
American cheese
Coffee

DINNER
Purée of pheasant, St. Hubert
Planked smelts
Bacon and cabbage
Boiled potatoes
Roast ribs of beef, au jus
Chiffonnade salad
Tutti frutti ice cream
Assorted cakes
Coffee

Consommé vermicelli. Boil one-half pound of vermicelli in two quarts of salt water for five minutes. Drain, and add to three pints of consommé. Serve grated cheese separate.

Calf's head, poulette. Take one boiled calf's head and cut in pieces two inches square. Mix with one quart of poulette sauce, and serve in chafing dish.

Purée of pheasant, St. Hubert. Remove the breast of a roasted pheasant and cut in small squares. Put the rest of the pheasant in a pot and cover with two quarts of bouillon, add a bouquet garni, and boil for one hour. In a sauce pot put three ounces of butter; when hot add three spoonsful of flour, and allow to become nice and brown. Then strain the broth into the sauce pot and boil for thirty minutes. Chop the pheasant very fine and add to the soup, boil again, and strain through a fine sieve. Season with salt and pepper, add the cut-up pheasant breast, and a glass of fine dry sherry wine.

Bacon and cabbage. Cut a large head of cabbage in four, wash well, and put in two quarts of water, with a little salt, and boil. Then drain off the water, add fresh water and two pounds of bacon, and boil until the bacon is well done. Put the cabbage on a platter, slice the bacon and put on top of the cabbage.

Tutti frutti ice cream. Macerate one-quarter of a pound of chopped candied mixed fruit in a pony of maraschino. Mix thoroughly with one quart of vanilla ice cream. Put in the bottom of a mould a little raspberry water ice, and fill to the top with the ice cream and fruit. Pack in ice and rock salt, and leave for about an hour and a half. Turn out on platter and decorate with candied cherries and angelica.

FEBRUARY 11

BREAKFAST
Oatmeal with cream
Rolls
Chocolate
Whipped cream

LUNCHEON
Eggs Brésilienne
Sirloin steak, marchand de vin
Fried egg plant
Farina pudding
Coffee

DINNER
Potage Waldaise
Fish dumplings, white wine sauce
Mutton chops, provençale
Mashed potatoes
String beans
Hearts of romaine
Fancy ice cream
Cakes   Coffee

Eggs Brésilienne. Put some boiled rice on a platter, place a poached egg on top, and cover with tomato sauce mixed with a little chopped ham.

Sirloin steak, marchand de vin. Cut four slices of sirloin steak about one-half inch thick, season with salt and pepper, and roll in flour. Have three ounces of hot butter in a pan and fry the steaks for two minutes. Remove the steaks to platter. Chop two shallots very fine and put in pan, allow to become hot, add one-half glass of claret, and reduce one-half. Then add one spoonful of meat extract, the juice of one lemon, and some chopped parsley and pour over the steaks. Garnish with Parisian potatoes.

Parisian potatoes. Take some large potatoes and cut out a quart of small potatoes with a round Parisian spoon. Put on fire in cold water, with one spoonful of salt, and boil for three minutes. Drain off the water and put the potatoes in a flat sauté pan with three ounces of butter. Put in oven and roast for about twelve minutes, or until golden yellow. Try with fingers to see if done. Serve in a deep dish.

Potage Waldaise. Mix one quart of consommé tapioca with one quart of purée of tomato soup, add four slices of boiled ham cut in small squares.

Fish dumplings, white wine sauce. Remove the skin and bones from one pound of halibut, sole, salmon or other fish, put in mortar, mash well, and mix with the following dough: One cup of boiling water, one ounce of butter, and one-half cup of flour, well mixed. Let cool, stir in the yolks of two eggs, and mix with the mashed fish. Season with salt and a little Cayenne pepper, strain through a fine sieve, place in a pan on ice, and stir in slowly one-quarter pint of thick cream, adding it little by little. To make dumplings, drop teaspoonful of this forcemeat, or stuffing, into boiling fish broth, bouillon, or water with salt, and cook very slowly for five minutes. Serve in chafing dish covered with white wine sauce. These dumplings are also called quenelles of fish, and are used for fish patties, vol au vent, or garniture for fish. If made very small, can be served with clam broth. The forcemeat can be used for fish timbales and stuffing for fish.

Timbale of bass. Make a force meat as above, with any kind of bass, fill small well-buttered timbale moulds, and boil in bain-marie. Then cover with buttered paper and put in oven for ten minutes. Turn out on platter, and serve with any kind of fish sauce. For a fancy decoration slices of truffles or pimentos may be cut in the shape of stars, crescents, initials, etc., and placed in the bottom of the timbale moulds, then fill with the forcemeat and cook.

FEBRUARY 12

BREAKFAST
  Sliced pineapple
  Broiled lamb kidneys with bacon
  Lyonnaise potatoes
  Rolls
  Coffee

LUNCHEON
  Eggs à la tripe
  Kingfish sauté meunière
  Cucumber salad
  Chicken sauté, Parisienne
  French peas
  Corn meal pudding
  Coffee

DINNER
  Potage Minestra
  Queen olives
  Fillet of barbel, regence
  Tournedos Beresford
  Potatoes château
  Asparagus Hollandaise
  Baked Alaska
  Coffee

Eggs à la tripe. Slice an onion very fine, put in casserole with two ounces of butter, cover, and simmer. Cook until the onions are soft, but not colored. Then add two spoonsful of flour, allow to get hot, pour in one pint of boiling milk, season with salt and pepper, and boil for five minutes. Slice eight hard-boiled eggs about one-quarter inch in thickness, put in the sauce and cook until hot. Serve in chafing dish, or deep dish, with chopped parsley on top.

Chicken sauté, Parisienne (1). Joint a young chicken and sauté in pan with two ounces of butter. Season with salt and pepper, and when done add two cups of tomato sauce and one dozen sliced canned French mushrooms. Cook for two minutes in the sauce, dress the chicken on platter, pour the sauce over it, and garnish with macaroni in cream.

(2) Joint the chicken and put in sauté pan with two ounces of butter, and season with salt and pepper. When nearly done, add two chopped shallots and heat them through, only. Add one cup of sauce Madère, the juice of one lemon, and some chopped parsley. Serve with Parisian potatoes.

Sago pudding. One quart of milk, one-half of a split vanilla bean, one-quarter pound of sago, six ounces of sugar, the yolks of six eggs and the whites of six eggs. Boil the milk and the vanilla bean together, add the sago, and cook until well done and like a stiff batter. Take off the fire, add the sugar and the yolks, and mix well. Beat the whites until very stiff and dry, and then add to the batter and mix lightly. Put in buttered moulds and bake in moderate oven for nearly an hour. Turn out of moulds and serve with vanilla sauce.
  Corn meal, rice, tapioca and farina puddings are made in the same manner as sago pudding.

Sago pudding, family style. One quart of milk, one-half of a split vanilla bean, three ounces of sago, six ounces of sugar, two eggs and one cup of cream. Boil the milk with the vanilla bean (or one-half teaspoonful of vanilla extract), add the sago, and cook well. Mix the sugar, eggs and cream, and add to the milk and sago. Pour in pudding dishes or bowl, put in hot oven to color the top, and serve either hot or cold, with cream separate.

Rice, corn meal, tapioca, farina or vermicelli puddings, family style, are made in the same manner as sago pudding, family style.

FEBRUARY 13

BREAKFAST
  Stewed prunes
  Boiled eggs
  Buttered toast
  Cocoa with whipped cream

LUNCHEON
  Eggs Troubadour
  Haricot of mutton
  French pastry
  Coffee

DINNER
  Potage Voisin
  Smoked goosebreast
  Fillet of sole, Choisy
  Sweetbreads Eugénie
  Roast leg of lamb, au jus
  Julienne potatoes
  Celery mayonnaise
  Curaçao jelly
  Coffee

Eggs Troubadour. Spread four pieces of toast with purée de foie gras (goose liver pâté), put a poached egg on top of each, and cover with sauce Périgord.

Haricot of mutton (stew). Cut five pounds of lean shoulder of mutton in pieces two inches square. Put in roasting pan with a little butter or fat, season with salt and pepper, and roast in oven until nice and brown. Add four spoonsful of flour and roast again until the flour is brown. Then put in a casserole and cover with boiling water, add a bouquet garni, six French carrots, six turnips cut in small pieces, season with salt and pepper, and boil for one hour. Remove the bouquet garni, and add one pint of purée of tomatoes, or a can of tomatoes strained through a fine sieve, and boil again, with the pot covered, until done. Before serving add some boiled string beans and chopped parsley. A little Worcestershire sauce may be added if desired.

French pastry. This is a term used in hotels and restaurants for a platter of mixed individual fancy cakes, such as éclairs, fruit tartelettes, moka cake, Napoleons, apple turnovers, Pont Neuf cakes, jalousie, cream puffs, etc.

Potage Voisin. Half purée of peas and half purée Crécy. Before serving add a handful of boiled rice.

Smoked goosebreast (Hors d'oeuvre). The most common goosebreast is imported from Germany; that made in the United States is seldom to be found in the markets. Do not cook; slice very thin, and serve on an ice-cold china platter, decorated with chopped meat jelly, and garnished with parsley in branches.

Fillet of sole, Choisy. Put the four fillets of a sole in a buttered pan, season with salt and a little Cayenne pepper, add one-half glass of white wine, cover with a buttered paper, and bake in oven. When done dress on a platter, and cover with green Hollandaise sauce, with a slice of truffle on top.

Green coloring (Vert d'épinards). Mash in mortar a peck of well-washed spinach. When very fine strain through a piece of cheesecloth, put in a bowl, set in hot water (bain-marie), and boil until set. When cold it will be a firm green mass, and may be used for coloring sauces, soups, etc.

Green Hollandaise sauce. Mix one pint of Hollandaise sauce with one spoonful of green coloring (Vert d'épinards).

FEBRUARY 14

BREAKFAST
Stewed rhubarb
Plain omelet
Rolls
Coffee

LUNCHEON
Smoked eels
Pumpernickel with sweet butter
Roast loin of pork with sauerkraut
Plain boiled potatoes
German huckleberry pie
Coffee

DINNER
Lynn Haven oysters
Cream of cauliflower
Pickles
Broiled Spanish mackerel, sauce
fleurette
Chicken sauté, Portugaise
Artichokes Hollandaise
Hearts of lettuce, French dressing
Diplomate pudding
Assorted cakes
Coffee

Smoked eels. Imported German canned eels. Serve on napkin with quartered lemons and parsley in branches.

Sauerkraut, Alsatian style. Spread one-quarter of a pound of goose grease (lard will do) in the bottom of a casserole, then put in one pound of sauerkraut, then two pounds of bacon, then another pound of sauerkraut, and another quarter pound of goose grease on top. Then add a pint of white wine and a pint of bouillon, cover with a buttered paper and the casserole cover, put on the stove and bring to a boil. Then put in oven and cook for an hour and a half. Serve the sauerkraut on a platter, with the bacon sliced, as a garnish.

Sauerkraut, German style. Put one-quarter pound of lard in a casserole, add one pound of sauerkraut, two pounds of salt pork, one bouquet garni, one whole onion, one carrot, and on top another pound of sauerkraut. Then add one glass of vinegar, two spoonsful of sugar, and one pint of bouillon. Cover, and cook in oven for two hours. Then remove the bouquet garni, onion and carrot, and serve the sauerkraut with the salt pork.

Sauerkraut, Hungarian style. Put in a casserole one-quarter pound of lard and one pound of sauerkraut. Sprinkle on top one spoonful of paprika and three peeled and chopped tomatoes. Then add two pounds of bacon and another pound of sauerkraut, and sprinkle again with another spoonful of paprika and three chopped tomatoes. Add a pint of sweet white wine and a pint of bouillon, and one bouquet garni. Cover and bake in oven for one hour and a half. Remove the bouquet garni, and serve with the bacon sliced.

Special notice for sauerkraut. Avoid salt, as the sauerkraut is seasoned, and the bacon and salt pork are salty also. If the raw sauerkraut is too salty, lay it in a dish pan, cover with water, and squeeze out with the hands immediately. Do not let it remain in the water but a second.

Other meats may be cooked in the sauerkraut, as beef and pork together lamb and pork, beef and lamb, or pheasant or other game.

FEBRUARY 15

BREAKFAST
  Baked apples with cream
  Baked beans, Boston style
  Boston brown bread
  Coffee

LUNCHEON
  Eggs Bagration
  Chicken hash on toast
  Chocolate éclairs
  Coffee

DINNER
  Hors d'oeuvres varies
  Mock turtle soup
  Ripe California olives
  Aiguillettes of sole, hotelière
  Sweetbreads braisé, Clamart
  Roast partridge, bread sauce
  Jets de houblons
  Soufflée potatoes
  Endives salad
  Fancy ice cream
  Assorted cakes
  Coffee

Eggs Bagration. Put on a platter some boiled rice, lay a fresh hard-boiled egg, cut in two, on top, and cover with the following sauce. Take any kind of cold meats that may be left over, such as lamb, beef, ham or tongue, and cut in small dices. Also a few mushrooms and truffles cut in the same way. Put in a casserole with a cup of cream sauce, season with salt and pepper, and bring to a boil.

Chicken hash on toast. Cut the breast of a boiled fowl in small squares. Put in a casserole one cup of cream sauce, one gill of thick cream and the chicken, season with salt and pepper, and cook together. Serve on a platter on dry toast.

Aiguillettes of sole, hotelière. Put aiguillettes of sole (long fillets) in a buttered pan, season with salt and pepper, cover with a glass of white wine, and cook for ten minutes. Then put the sole on a platter, and reduce the wine until nearly dry. Then add a pint of Béarnaise sauce and pour over the fish.

Mock turtle soup. Put in pan six pounds of cut veal bones, two sliced onions and one carrot, and four ounces of butter, and roast until brown. Then add one-quarter pound of flour and brown again. Change to a vessel, add two gallons of water, one can of tomatoes, a bouquet garni, some salt, a spoonful of black pepper berries, and two cloves, and boil for two hours. Add one pint of cooking sherry and boil again for thirty minutes. Skim, and remove the grease from the top, and strain through a cheesecloth. Then take one-quarter of a boiled calf's head and cut in small squares and put in a casserole with one glass of dry sherry wine, a little salt and Cayenne pepper, and boil for five minutes. Now add the strained soup to the calf's head. Before serving add three thin slices of smoked beef tongue cut in small diamond shapes, three chopped hard-boiled eggs, and a truffle cut in small squares.

Roast partridge. Tie a piece of fresh fat pork over the breast of the dressed partridge, season inside and out with salt and pepper, put in roasting pan with a piece of butter, and put in oven. Baste often so the meat will not become dry. It will require about thirty minutes to cook. Serve with lemon and watercress, and bread sauce separate.

Bread sauce, for game. To a pint of boiling milk add one whole onion, a bay leaf with two cloves stuck through it, and one and one-half cups of fresh bread crumbs, and boil for a few minutes. Then remove the onion and bay leaf and cloves, and season with salt and Cayenne pepper. Before serving add two ounces of sweet butter.

Bread crumbs, for game. Put in frying pan four ounces of sweet butter. When just warm add a cupful of fresh bread crumbs, and fry until golden yellow. Drain off the butter (which may be kept for roasting, etc.), and serve the crumbs in a small bowl. This is usually served in addition to bread sauce, with quail, pheasant, partridge, etc.

FEBRUARY 16

BREAKFAST
- Hominy with cream
- Plain scrambled eggs
- Rolls
- English breakfast tea

LUNCHEON
- Crab salad
- Mutton chops, Robinson
- String beans
- Napoleon cake
- Coffee

DINNER
- Pea soup
- Radishes
- Broiled shad, maître d'hôtel
- Roast chicken, au jus
- Hot asparagus, Hollandaise
- Potato croquettes
- Watercress salad
- Peach Mona Lisa
- Assorted cakes
- Coffee

Crab salad. Season the flakes of a crab with salt and pepper, add a spoonful of mayonnaise, and mix. Put a few leaves of lettuce around the inside of a salad bowl, put the crab in the center, cover with mayonnaise, and garnish with a hard-boiled egg cut in four, two fillets of anchovies, and one green olive.

Mutton chops, Robinson. Broil four mutton chops and season well. Cut in four a half dozen chicken livers, season with salt and pepper and fry in butter. Cut up a small can of mushrooms, put in a casserole with the livers, and cover with a cup of sauce Madère. Cook together and pour over the chops.

Watercress salad (1). Clean and wash the watercress well, and season with salt and vinegar.

(2) Use French dressing with a very little oil. Watercress does not require much oil.

Peach Mona Lisa. Make a fancy form in the shape of a peach of vanilla ice cream with a brandied peach in the center. Put a spoonful of raspberry sauce (see raspberry sauce), in the center of a small plate. Put a round piece of sponge cake, about three inches in diameter and one-half inch thick, on the plate. Dust the ice cream peach with some sugar, colored pink, and place on the sponge cake. Stick two sugar peach leaves under the edge of the peach, and serve.

Napoleon cake. When making vol au vent, patty shells, or anything else with puff paste, save the trimmings, roll together and give two turns, in the same manner as when making fresh puff paste. Leave in ice box for one-half hour and then roll out to one-eighth inch in thickness. Put on a pastry pan, prick all over with a fork, and bake in oven until very dry. When done, divide and cut into three strips, and allow to become cold. Put the three strips one on top of the other, with pastry cream between. Glace the top with vanilla icing, and sprinkle a band one-half inch wide along the edge with chopped pistache nuts. Then cut into individual portions about two by four inches in size.

FEBRUARY 17

BREAKFAST
Grapefruit marmalade
Boiled eggs
Buttered toast
Ceylon tea

LUNCHEON
Eggs Benedict
Tripe sauté, Lyonnaise
Potatoes hashed in cream
Romaine salad
Camembert cheese and crackers
Coffee

DINNER
Consommé Rachel
Sardines. Olives
Boiled sheepshead, cream sauce
Potatoes Hollandaise
Roast leg of mutton, currant jelly
Baked Hubbard squash
German fried potatoes
Celery Mayonnaise
Plum pudding, hard and brandy
    sauces
Coffee

Tripe sauté, Lyonnaise. Cut two pounds of tripe in narrow strips. Put in large frying pan four ounces of butter and four sliced onions, and cook until half fried, then add the tripe, which must be dry; season with salt and pepper, and fry until both are of a nice yellow color. Drain off the butter and serve the tripe dry, garnished with quartered lemons and chopped parsley. Vinegar may be served instead of the lemons if desired.

Consommé Rachel (1). Plain consommé garnished with asparagus tips. (2) Plain consommé garnished with chicken dumplings and small peas.

Boiled sheepshead, cream sauce. Put a whole sheepshead in cold water with one glass of milk, season with salt, and bring to the boiling point. Then put on side of range where it will keep very hot without boiling, and let stand for twenty minutes. Serve on napkin with small boiled potatoes, quartered lemons and parsley. Cream sauce separate.

Plum pudding. One pound of well-chopped beef suet, one pound of sifted flour, one-half pound of bread crumbs; two lemons, both juice and rinds; one pound of brown sugar, four eggs, one-half teaspoonful each of powdered nutmeg, ginger, cloves and cinnamon; one pound of currant raisins; one-half pound each of malaga raisins, orange peel, citron peel and lemon peel, all chopped fine; one cup of molasses, and one-half pint of good brandy. Mix all together in a bowl, putting the liquids in last, making a thick, heavy mixture. Put in a buttered mould or in a cloth, and boil in water, or steam cook, for about three hours. This pudding, if kept in a cool place, will keep indefinitely. Warm the pudding until very hot before serving, sprinkle some powdered sugar over the top, pour on some brandy, and burn.

Brandy sauce. Put in a vessel one-half pint of apricot pulp, made from fresh or preserved fruit; one pint of water, and a half pound of sugar, and boil. Moisten a teaspoonful of arrowroot with a little water and add it to the boiling sauce, stirring so it will not get lumpy. Then strain and add a small glassful of brandy.

Hard sauce. Put in a bowl three-quarters of a pound of sweet butter, one pound of sugar, the white of an egg, and flavor with lemon, vanilla or a little brandy, and work into a cream. Put into a pastry bag with a tube, and dress on a pan in small round shapes. Place in the ice box to get hard.

FEBRUARY 18

BREAKFAST
  Waffles
  Honey in comb
  Boiled eggs
  Dry toast
  Coffee

LUNCHEON
  Grapefruit and oranges en suprême
  Chicken broth in cups
  Olives
  Small sirloin steak, Bordelaise
  Potato croquettes
  Lettuce and tomato salad
  French pastry
  Coffee

DINNER
  Potage Westmoreland
  Oysters à l'ancienne
  Chicken pot pie, home style
  Combination salad
  Moka cake
  Demi tasse

Grapefruit and oranges en suprême. Sliced oranges and grapefruit in equal parts, add a little sugar and maraschino, and serve in suprême glasses. Tie a ribbon around the glass, with a nice bow.

Potage Westmoreland. Equal parts of mock turtle soup, thick consommé tapioca, and thick consommé brunoise. Before serving add a glass of dry sherry wine.

Oysters à l'ancienne. Take a dozen oysters on the deep half shell, season with salt and pepper, put a small piece of butter, some chopped parsley, a little lemon juice, and a thin slice of salt pork on each, and bake in a hot oven for about four minutes.

Chicken pot pie, home style. Take a young fat hen and cut up as for fricassee. Wash well and put in a vessel with one quart of water, season with salt, bring to a boil, skim, and add a bouquet garni. After boiling for about thirty minutes remove the bouquet and add twelve small round potatoes, twelve very small onions, and one-quarter pound of parboiled salt pork cut in small squares. Boil all together until well done. Mix in a cup three spoonsful of flour and one-half cup of water, and stir into the stewing chicken. Boil again for about ten minutes, then put in a deep dish, sprinkle with chopped parsley, and when nearly cold cover with thin pie, or puff paste, brush over with the yolk of an egg, and bake in oven until well browned. Serve on a napkin. Dumplings and a few small French carrots may be added before covering with the paste, if desired.

Moka cake. Take three layers of cake and fill between with moka filling. For the filling beat a half pound of sweet butter with a half pound of powdered sugar until it is white and light. Then add the yolks of three eggs, one by one, and a half cup of rich cream, beating until very smooth. Flavor with some strong coffee or coffee extract. Finish the cake by glacing the top with coffee frosting, and decorate with some of the moka filling.

FEBRUARY 19

BREAKFAST
Stewed prunes
Scrambled eggs with chives
Toasted muffins
Coffee

LUNCHEON
Canapé of raw meat
Radishes
Broiled shad, maître d'hôtel
Potatoes au gratin
Cauliflower mayonnaise
Pont l'Évêque cheese
Crackers
Coffee

DINNER
Cream of Lima beans
Celery
Frogs' legs, Jerusalem
Roast squab chicken
Individual artichokes, au gratin
Julienne potatoes
Endives salad
Vanilla ice cream
Assorted cakes
Coffee

Canapé of raw meat. Take a quarter pound of lean fresh beef tenderloin or sirloin and chop very fine and season with a little salt and pepper. Toast some thin slices of rye or white bread lightly, spread with a little sweet butter, and then spread the chopped meat on top. Serve on a napkin, garnished with quartered lemon and parsley.

Broiled shad, maître d'hôtel. Split a shad, season with salt and pepper, sprinkle with oil, and broil on both sides. Dish up on a platter, cover with maître d'hôtel sauce, and garnish with quartered lemons and parsley.

Cream of Lima beans. Put in a vessel two ounces of butter and one leek cut in small pieces. Simmer for a few minutes, then add one-half cup of flour and simmer again. When hot add one quart of milk and a can of Lima beans, or one pound of fresh beans. When soft strain through a fine sieve, put back in vessel, bring to a boil, and add one-half pint of thick cream and two ounces of best butter. Stir well, and season with salt and pepper and a little Cayenne pepper. In place of the cream, use half chicken broth, light bouillon, veal broth, or half stock and half milk, if desired.

Frogs' legs, Jerusalem. Put in a sauté pan one soupspoonful of chopped celery, three chopped shallots, and three ounces of butter, and simmer for about five minutes. Then add one dozen cut up frogs' legs, season with salt and pepper, and simmer for five minutes. Then add one cup of cream, or one cup of cream sauce, and boil for ten minutes. Serve in chafing dish.

Artichokes au gratin. Remove the leaves from four boiled artichokes and cut the bottoms in slices. Butter four individual shirred egg dishes, put one spoonful of cream sauce in the bottom, then put in the sliced artichokes, season with salt and pepper, cover with cream sauce, sprinkle with grated cheese, put a small piece of butter on top of each, and bake in oven until brown.

FEBRUARY 20

BREAKFAST
  Oatmeal
  Boiled salt mackerel
  Baked potatoes
  Rolls   Coffee

LUNCHEON
  Poached eggs, Rothschild
  Fried chicken, Maryland
  Field salad
  Roquefort cheese, crackers   Coffee

DINNER
  Potage de santé
  Salmon, Chambord
  Leg of mutton, à la Busse
  Spinach with cream   Parisian potatoes
  Sliced tomatoes, mayonnaise
  Anise seed cake

Poached eggs, Rothschild. Put a spoonful of purée of game on a plate, a poached egg on top, and cover with sauce Périgueux.

Purée of game. After serving roast venison, duck, quail, bear, reindeer, hare, or other game, take the remainder, remove the meat from the bones and mash very fine in a mortar, add just enough thick brown gravy to make a paste, and pass through a fine sieve. Season with salt and pepper, heat well, and use as a garnish.

Salmon, Chambord. Put in a buttered shallow sauce pan two slices of salmon, season with salt and pepper, add half a glass of red wine, and half a glass of stock, bouillon, fish stock or water, cover with buttered paper, and put in the oven and cook until done. With its broth make a sauce Génoise, and add to it one dozen small French mushrooms, one dozen parboiled clams, and one sliced truffle. Pour the sauce over the fish, and garnish with plain-boiled small écrevisses (crayfish).

Leg of mutton, à la Busse. Roast a leg of mutton, serve with its own gravy, and garnish with fresh mushrooms sauté in butter, and onions glacés.

Fresh mushrooms sauté in butter. Clean and wash one pound of fresh mushrooms and dry in a towel. Put in a sauté pan on the range, two ounces of butter; when hot add the mushrooms, season with salt and pepper, and sauté slowly for about ten minutes. Serve on toast with their own gravy, or use as a garnish for entrées, stews, etc.

Onions glacés. Peel one dozen small white onions and put in one quart of cold water with a spoonful of salt. Put on fire, boil for about five minutes, drain off water, and put the onions in a shallow sauté pan with one ounce of butter. Put in oven and roast until brown. Then add one spoonful of meat extract, let them glacé in this for a few minutes, and then serve. If preferred the onions may be glacéd by sprinkling with powdered sugar, and omitting the meat extract. Or take one pint of strong beef consommé and reduce one-half, then add at the same time as the onions, and they will glacé while reducing.

Anise seed cake. One-half pound of sugar, four eggs, one-half pound of flour, and one-half ounce of anise seed. Beat the sugar and eggs together over a slow fire until blood warm, then remove and continue beating until cold and firm. Then add the sifted flour and anise seed. Mix, and lay out on a greased and floured pan in drops about one and one-half inches in diameter. Put in a dry warm place until a crust forms on top (a few hours will be required), and then bake in a slow oven.

Spinach in cream. Boil a peck of well-washed spinach in salted water. Drain off and pound through a fine colander, add two ounces of butter, one cup of thick cream, heat well and serve. Salt and pepper if necessary.

FEBRUARY 21

BREAKFAST
    Baked apples with cream
    Plain omelet
    Rolls
    English breakfast tea

LUNCHEON
    Fillet of herring, mariné
    Potato salad
    Minced tenderloin, à l'estragon
    Mashed potatoes au gratin
    American cheese, crackers   Coffee

DINNER
    Consommé Florentine   Ripe olives
    Fillet of sole, Bercy
    Sweetbreads braisé, with peas
    Roast squab, au jus.   Gauffrette potatoes
    Cold asparagus, mustard sauce
    Coupe Lyonnaise. Assorted cakes. Coffee

Fillet of herring, mariné. Take two marinated herrings, remove the skins and bones, and cut in long strips. Put on platter, strain a little of its own sauce over them, and decorate with sliced lemons.

Minced tenderloin of beef, à l'estragon. Slice one pound of tenderloin of beef in strips one-eighth inch thick and two inches wide, using trimmings or the end piece. Put two ounces of melted butter in frying pan, and when red-hot add the slices of meat, season with salt and pepper, and fry very quickly over a hot fire; about one minute is required. Then remove the meat and sprinkle the pan with one spoonful of flour, and allow to become brown, then add one cup of bouillon or stock, boil for five minutes, add one teaspoonful of chopped fresh tarragon, and test as to seasoning. Then add one ounce of fresh butter and the juice of one lemon. Pour over the fillets, which have been kept warm in a deep dish.

Consommé Florentine. In consommé put some plain boiled spinach cut in small pieces, also thin pancake cut same way. Serve grated cheese separate.

Fillet of sole, Bercy. Put in a buttered flat sauté pan three finely-chopped shallots, the four fillets of a sole on top of the shallots, and a little chopped parsley and chervil on top of the fillets. Season with salt and pepper, add one-half glass of white wine, cover with buttered paper, put on top of the stove and bring to the boiling point. Then put in oven and finish cooking. Remove the fillets to a platter, and put in the sauté pan one pint of white wine sauce, cook for a few minutes, and pour over the fish. Do not strain the sauce. Other fish besides sole may be used if desired.

Roast squab, au jus. Season four squabs, put a piece of fresh fat pork over the breast, and place in roasting pan with one sliced carrot, one onion, one bay leaf, a clove, a few pepper berries, and three ounces of butter. Roast in a hot oven for about thirty-five minutes, basting often. Then put the squabs on a platter, and place the pan on the fire and cook until the butter is clarified. Drain off, add one cup of bouillon and one spoonful of meat extract, reduce one-half, strain, and pour over the squabs. Garnish with watercress.

Waffle potatoes. Cut the potatoes with a special cutter called a potato waffle machine. Put them in warm swimming lard and let it become hot gradually so the potatoes will not become brown too quick. When cooked soft take them out and put them for a second into very hot fat so they will become crisp and golden yellow. Serve on a napkin, sprinkled with salt.

Sybil and Gauffrette potatoes. Same as waffle potatoes.

Coupe Lyonnaise. Fill a glass with vanilla ice cream, and put on top one large marron glacé.

FEBRUARY 22

BREAKFAST
Orange marmalade
Buckwheat cakes
Rolls
Coffee

LUNCHEON
Canapé Julia
Consommé in cups
Cheese straws
Sand dabs, meunière
Broiled chicken on toast
Sybil potatoes
Baked Hubbard squash
Hearts of lettuce
Meringue glacé à la vanille
Coffee

DINNER
Seapuit oysters
Clear green turtle, au Pemartin
Crisp celery.   Queen olives
Salted almonds
Fillet of bass, 1905
Noisettes of lamb, Ducale
Breast of chicken with Virginia ham
Peas au beurre
Soufflée potatoes
Alligator pear salad
Apple Moscovite
Assorted cakes   Coffee

Canapé Julia. Chop the tail of a lobster very fine and put in a vessel on the range. When hot add one cup of thick cream sauce, bring to a boil, and season with salt and Cayenne pepper. Add the yolks of two eggs, but do not boil, heat just enough to bind the lobster. Make four pieces of toast, put the lobster on top, cover with grated cheese, put a bit of butter on the top of each, and bake in the oven. Serve on napkins, with lemons and parsley.

Noisettes of lamb. Noisettes are cut from the saddle of lamb, free from fat and skin, and in the shape of a small tenderloin steak. Broil or sauté in butter, and serve with Colbert, Béarnaise, or any other meat sauce.

Ducale. Artichoke bottoms filled with French peas, sauce Madère. Use as a garnish for lamb, beef, sweetbreads, etc.

Breast of chicken. Cut the breast from two raw roasting chickens, remove the skin, season with salt and pepper, roll in flour. Put two ounces of butter in a shallow sauté pan, and fry the breasts for about fifteen minutes, or until golden brown. Serve with Virginia ham or bacon, figs, or with sauce Colbert, Madère, cream, etc. If Virginia ham is served take four slices and just heat through on the broiler, or in pan with a little butter. Do not allow to become hard or crisp.

Alligator pear salad. (1). Select ripe, soft pears, but not mushy. Cut in half, remove the stone, fill with French dressing, and serve on cracked ice.

(2). Put in the bottom of a salad bowl some lettuce leaves, scoop out the inside of the pears with a soup spoon, put on the lettuce leaves, and cover with French dressing.

Apple Moscovite. Take four large apples and remove the insides with a sharp spoon, leaving only a firm shell. Put a spoonful of apple sauce on the bottom of the apples. Whip the whites of six eggs very hard, and mix with a half pint of sweet apple sauce. Fill the apples with this, dust over with powdered sugar, and bake in a moderate oven.

FEBRUARY 23

BREAKFAST
    Stewed prunes
    Boiled eggs
    Dry toast
    Coffee

LUNCHEON
    Hors d'oeuvres variés
    Mutton chops, Daumont
    Julienne potatoes
    Swiss cheese and crackers
    Coffee

DINNER
    Potage Kroumir
    Aiguillettes of sole, marinière
    Chicken, Montmorency
    Artichokes with melted butter
    Chiffonnade salad
    Kirschwasser jelly
    Lady fingers
    Coffee

Mutton chops, Daumont. Bread four mutton chops and fry in a flat sauté pan. Dish up on a long platter, and garnish with artichoke bottoms filled with cauliflower. Pour sauce Périgueux around the chops.

Artichokes filled with cauliflower. Remove the leaves and trim the bottoms of four cold artichokes. Cut in four a boiled and well-seasoned cauliflower, squeeze out the water, and use to fill the artichoke bottoms. Cover with a little thick cream sauce, sprinkle with grated cheese, place small bits of butter on top of each, put on a buttered pan with a spoonful of bouillon, and bake in the oven.

Potage Kroumir. One quart of purée of tomato soup mixed with one pint of consommé tapioca.

Aiguillettes of sole, marinière. Take the four fillets from one sole and lay them flat in a buttered pan, sprinkle with three chopped shallots, season with salt and pepper, add one-half glass of white wine, one-half cup of stock or water, cover with buttered paper, and bring to a boil on top of the stove. Then put in oven and cook for about seven minutes. Put the fillets on a platter, and reduce the broth until nearly dry. Then add two cups of white wine sauce and boil for a minute. Bind the sauce with the yolk of an egg mixed with a spoonful of cream, add a little chopped chives, and pour over the fish.

Chicken sauté, Montmorency. Joint a chicken, season with salt and pepper, put three ounces of butter in a sauté pan and sauté the chicken. When done remove the chicken to a platter, and put in the pan one cup of brown gravy or sauce Madère, and one can of French mushrooms. Boil for a few minutes. Then pour over the chicken. Garnish with croustades filled with small French peas.

Croustades. One cup of flour, one cup of milk, the whites of three eggs, a teaspoonful of olive oil, a teaspoonful of corn starch, and a little salt. Mix well and strain. Keep the croustade iron very hot in swimming lard. Dip the iron in the dough for a few seconds, then dip in the swimming lard, coated with the dough, and fry until a nice golden color. Take out, and when cold the croustades will be very crisp. Croustade irons can be obtained in any first-class store.

FEBRUARY 24

BREAKFAST
  Grapefruit with cherries
  Omelet with ham
  Rolls
  Coffee

LUNCHEON
  Eggs Talleyrand
  Oysters à la Hyde
  French pastry
  Coffee

DINNER
  Cream of frogs' legs
  Olives
  Scallops, Newburg
  Roast Easter kid, mint sauce
  Sweetbreads sauté, with green peas
  Endives salad
  Fancy ice cream
  Assorted cakes
  Coffee

Eggs Talleyrand. Trim the bottoms of four fresh artichokes and put a little terrine de foie gras in each, and keep hot. Put a poached egg on top of each and cover with sauce Périgueux.

Cream of frogs' legs. Take the backs and front legs of two dozen frogs, reserving the hind legs for an entrée. Put in vessel with two quarts of bouillon or chicken broth, and boil for thirty minutes. Then take one-half pound of rice flour and mix with one pint of cream. Let it run into the boiling soup, and cook for ten minutes. Strain through a fine colander, put back in the vessel, season with salt and a little Cayenne pepper, and add three ounces of sweet butter. Stir the soup so the butter will melt slowly. Serve croûtons soufflés separate.

Scallops, Newburg. Put one pint of scallops in a sauté pan with one ounce of butter, season with salt and pepper, and sauté for about three minutes over a hot fire; then drain off and add one pint of sauce Newburg. Do not cook further, and serve in chafing dish.

Roast Easter kid. Kid when young is a delicious morsel. Prepare in the same manner as lamb for roasting.

Sweet potatoes sauté. Peel and slice two large boiled sweet potatoes. Put three ounces of butter in a sauté pan, when hot add the potatoes and sauté until nice and brown. Season with salt and pepper.

FEBRUARY 25

BREAKFAST
Waffles
Honey
Coffee

LUNCHEON
Poached eggs, Martha
Hungarian beef goulash
Noodles, Polonaise
Savarin Chantilly
Coffee

DINNER
Consommé Colbert
Broiled Alaska candlefish
Sweetbreads, Théodora
Roast ribs of beef, au jus
Saratoga potatoes
Celery Victor
Fruit cake
Coffee

Poached eggs, Martha. On top of four pieces of toast put some lobster croquette preparation in a layer about one-quarter of an inch thick, put a piece of butter on top of each, and bake in oven. Put a poached egg on top and cover with cream sauce.

Noodles, Polonaise. On a large platter put one pound of plain boiled noodles. In a frying pan put one-quarter pound of butter, and one-half cup of fresh bread crumbs. Fry until golden brown, and pour over the noodles.

Consommé Colbert. Equal parts of carrots, turnips, peas, string beans, cauliflower, and flageolet beans. Cut the carrots and turnips in small squares. Boil the cauliflower and cut off the small flowers. Then put all in hot consommé, with one poached egg to each person. Add a little chopped chervil before serving.

Broiled Alaska candlefish. As this fish is very oily it is better broiled. Season with salt and pepper, and serve on platter, with plenty of lemon and parsley in branches.

Sweetbreads, Théodora. Split four large sweetbreads, fill with chicken forcemeat, and braise them. Serve with sauce Madère, and garnish with stuffed fresh mushrooms.

Fruit cake (white). One pound each of butter, sugar and flour, one-half teaspoonful of baking powder, ten eggs, one-quarter pound of currant sultana raisins, one pony of rum, and one-quarter pound of chopped glacé fruits. Work the butter and the sugar together until creamy, then add the eggs two by two, and work well, then add the rum, and finally the flour, baking powder and fruit. Mix lightly, and bake in a buttered pan lined with paper.

FEBRUARY 26

BREAKFAST
Stewed prunes
Boiled eggs
Buttered toast
Coffee

LUNCHEON
Eggs à la Colonel
English lamb chops, Tavern
Lettuce salad
Pont l'évêque cheese
Crackers
Coffee

DINNER
Cream of rice
Ripe olives
Rock cod, en court bouillon
Potatoes nature
Squab chicken sauté, Sutro
Olivette potatoes
Endives salad
Orange soufflé, St. Francis
Assorted cakes
Coffee

Eggs à la Colonel. Cut two tomatoes in half, squeeze out the juice, bread them, and fry. Put a poached egg on top of each piece, and cover with sauce Madère with fresh mushrooms.

English lamb chops, Tavern. Broil an English lamb chop until nearly done, then put in an earthern casserole, with some sauté potatoes on one side and some stewed lamb kidneys on the other. Put in the oven for a minute or two, and serve with chopped parsley on top.

English mutton chop, Tavern. Same as English lamb chop, Tavern.

Rock cod, en court bouillon. Put in a flat pan three spoonsful of olive oil, one onion sliced very fine, three sliced green and one red pepper, one bouquet garni, and about five pounds of codfish cut in slices two inches thick. Season with salt and pepper, add two glasses of white wine and one pint of water, and a little chopped parsley. Simmer slowly for about forty minutes. Remove the bouquet garni, and serve on a deep platter with broth and all. Any fish may be prepared in the same manner.

Squab chicken sauté, Sutro. Cut two squab chickens in six pieces each. Two legs, two wings, and the breast and carcass split. Season with salt and pepper, and sauté in pan with two ounces of butter. Prepare as follows: Two fresh artichoke bottoms boiled and cut in four; one-half pound of fresh mushrooms sauté in butter; one can of cèpes sauté in butter; the livers of the chickens whole, and one parboiled sweetbread sliced and sauté in butter. Mix all together with the chicken, season well, and add some chopped parsley and chives.

Orange Soufflé, St. Francis. Cut "lids" from the tops of four large oranges and remove the insides. Have the openings about an inch and one-half in diameter. Fill about one-third full with some sliced fresh fruit, such as oranges, apples, bananas, pineapple, etc. Then add a few drops of maraschino, fill another third with vanilla ice cream. Beat the whites of six eggs until stiff, mixed with one-half pound of sugar and the grated rind of an orange, and fill the final third of the orange. Dust with powdered sugar, and brown on top in a very hot oven. It will take but a second to brown, and they should be served at once.

FEBRUARY 27

BREAKFAST
Orange marmalade
Ham and eggs
Corn muffins
Coffee

LUNCHEON
Omelet with Virginia ham and
  peppers
Calf's head, vinaigrette
Baked potatoes
Apricot layer cake
Coffee

DINNER
Strained gumbo soup, in cups
Radishes
Barracouda, maitre d'hotel
Stuffed capon, Bruxelloise
Asparagus, Hollandaise
Champs Elysées potatoes
Hearts of romaine, Roquefort
  dressing
Chocolate parfait
Lady fingers
Coffee

Omelet with Virginia ham and peppers. Cut two slices of Virginia ham and one green pepper in small squares, put in frying pan with one ounce of butter, and simmer for about two minutes. Add eight beaten eggs and two red peppers cut in small squares, season with salt and pepper, and proceed in the same manner as for a plain omelet.

Calf's head, vinaigrette. Dish up on a napkin some boiled calf's head with the brains and the tongue sliced. Garnish the platter with pickles, pickled beets, quartered lemons, parsley in branches, and two hard-boiled eggs cut in two. Serve vinaigrette sauce separate.

Strained gumbo soup, in cups. Make a chicken okra soup, strain through cheese cloth, and serve in cups.

Stuffed capon, Bruxelloise. Soak half of a loaf of white bread in milk, then squeeze out the milk, mince fine, add salt and pepper, a little chopped parsley, one pound of finely chopped salted almonds, and one egg. Mix well together and fill the capon. Tie a slice of fresh fat pork over the breast, and roast in the same manner as chicken or other fowl.

Layer cake. Eight eggs, one-half pound of flour, one-quarter pound of melted butter, and a few drops of vanilla extract. Beat the eggs with the sugar over a slow fire until thoroughly warm, then take off the range and continue beating until cold. Put in the flour, mixing lightly, and add the melted butter and vanilla extract. Bake in buttered flat tin cake moulds, for about ten minutes.

French layer cake. The same as above with the exception that it is baked in one thick cake and then cut into layers.

Chocolate layer cake. Use three or four layers, filling between with chocolate cream. Glacé with chocolate frosting, and decorate the top with glacé fruits. See pastry cream for directions for filling.

Apricot layer cake. Same as chocolate layer cake, but fill with apricot marmalade, glacé the top with vanilla frosting, and decorate with glacé fruit.

FEBRUARY 28

BREAKFAST
Shredded wheat with cream
Crescents
Cocoa

LUNCHEON
Eggs à la Reine
Tripe à la mode de Caën
Camembert cheese and crackers
Coffee

DINNER
Consommé d'Orleans
Celery
Fillet of sole, Victoria
Leg of mutton, Réforme
Carrots, Vichy
Potato salad
Peach Melba
Assorted cakes
Coffee

Poached eggs, à la Reine. Spread some purée de foie gras on a piece of toast. Put a poached egg on top, cover with cream sauce, and sprinkle with finely chopped truffles. After the truffles have been chopped put in a napkin and squeeze out the juice, and then chop again. They will then be dry, and easy to sprinkle.

Fillet of sole, Victoria. Put four fillets in a buttered sauté pan, season with salt and pepper, add one-half glass of white wine. When done put on platter and pour a lobster sauce over the fish, with lobster and truffles cut in small squares, in it.

Leg of mutton, Réforme. Roast a leg of mutton, and serve the following sauce separate: Ham, tongue, pickles, mushrooms, and chicken in equal parts, cut Julienne style, and mixed with sauce poivrade.

Sauce poivrade. Crush one-half cup of black pepper berries and put in vessel with one dozen chopped shallots, a little parsley, and one pint of white wine vinegar. Boil and reduce until nearly dry, then add one quart of brown sauce, or sauce Madère, and boil for five minutes, then strain, and stir in three ounces of sweet butter slowly.

Tripe à la mode de Caën. Parboil eight pounds of raw tripe and four ox feet. Cut both the tripe and the feet in pieces two inches square. Chop one pound of raw beef suet and four large onions very fine. Put in an earthen pot half of the suet and onions, then half of the tripe and feet, then the remainder of the suet and onions, followed by the rest of the tripe and feet. Season with salt and pepper, add one bouquet garni, one-half pint of brandy, one pint of white wine, and fill the remainder of the space in the pot with water. Put a cover on the pot and seal with any kind of paste or dough, so that no air or steam can escape. Then put the pot in a moderate oven and leave for about eight hours; then take out of oven, take off the cover, and remove the bouquet garni. If there should be too much fat on top a little may be taken off. Ordinarily there will not be too much. Season to taste with salt and pepper, add one-half pint of dry apple cider and one glass of brandy, and boil for two minutes. Serve hot. The proper way to serve tripe à la mode de Caën is in small individual earthen pots, on a large plate, with red-hot ashes under the pot

MARCH 1

BREAKFAST
  Strawberries with cream
  Boiled eggs
  Dry toast
  Coffee

LUNCHEON
  Grapefruit en suprême
  Consommé in cups
  Cheese straws
  Sweet-and-sour beef tongue
  String beans
  Mashed potatoes
  Chocolate éclairs   Coffee

DINNER
  Oysters on half shell
  Onion soup au gratin
  Kingfish sauté, meunière
  Roast chicken
  Succotash
  Potato cakes
  Escarole salad
  Corn meal pudding   Coffee

Sweet-and-sour sauce. Procure one-half pound of unsweetened spiced fish cake from your grocer, break it in small pieces, put in a bowl, cover with one pint of vinegar and one pound of brown sugar. Soak for about an hour, then stir well, and add one cup of fish broth or meat stock, depending upon whether it is to be used for fish or meat. Season with salt and a little Cayenne pepper, then add one pound of seedless raisins, and boil again for five minutes.

Sweet-and-sour beef tongue. Boil a fresh beef tongue in the same manner as boiled beef. When done cut in thin slices, put in a flat pan, cover with sweet-and-sour sauce, and simmer for five minutes. Serve on a platter covered with the sauce.

Omelette Suzanne. Cut six macaroons in four and mix with a little whipped cream. Cut six lady fingers in two and sprinkle with powdered cocoa and powdered sugar. Melt some Bar le Duc jelly. Make an omelet in the usual manner, powder with plenty of sugar, and burn bands across the top with a hot iron. At one end of the omelet place the lady fingers, at the other end the macaroons, and pour some of the Bar le Duc jelly on each side. Pour a pony of Chartreuse over the omelet, then a pony of fine champagne, and light it.

Cheese straws. Roll out some puff paste (a good way to utilize any trimmings you may have) very thin, about one-eighth inch. Wash the top with eggs and spread with grated Parmesan cheese mixed with a little Cayenne pepper. Cut in narrow strips, one-half inch by six, lay on a baking pan and bake in a moderate oven until brown and crisp.

Onion soup, au gratin. Slice three onions very fine, put in a casserole with three ounces of butter, put on the cover, and simmer until of a golden color. Then add one quart of consommé, stock or any good broth (consommé preferred), season well, and boil for five minutes. Slice three rolls very thin and put in oven and allow to remain until brown and dry, like toast. Put the soup in an earthen casserole, float the slices of rolls on top, spread a cup of grated cheese over the bread, put in a hot oven and cook until brown on top. Serve very hot.

Potato cakes. Whenever there is mashed potatoes left over, make into little cakes about one inch thick and two inches in diameter, roll in flour, and fry in pan with a little butter, until brown on both sides. If the potato should be too thin add the raw yolk of an egg.

MARCH 2

BREAKFAST
Oatmeal with cream
Broiled finnan haddie
Lyonnaise potatoes
Rolls
Coffee

LUNCHEON
Eggs Bordelaise
Lamb chops, Victor **Hugo**
Julienne potatoes
Stewed tomatoes
Brie cheese, crackers   Coffee

DINNER
Cream of lettuce   Radishes
Scallops, Mornay
Croustades financière
Roast leg of mutton, currant jelly
Potato croquettes
Cold asparagus, mustard sauce
Fruit salad, au marasquin
Lady fingers   Coffee

Eggs Bordelaise. Fry the eggs in oil, put on toast, cover with Bordelaise sauce, and lay two slices of truffle on each egg.

Lamb chops, Victor Hugo. Broil or sauté six lamb chops on one side only, and allow to become cold. Grate two horseradish roots and put in a sauce pot with two ounces of butter, and simmer. Then add one cup of thick cream sauce, and bring to a boil; season well and bind with the yolks of two eggs. When this stuffing is cold put on top of the chops, make smooth with a knife, sprinkle with a little grated Parmesan cheese mixed with bread crumbs, put small bits of butter on each chop, place on a buttered pan, and put in a hot oven, so they will cook from the bottom. Cook until the tops are nice and brown, and serve on a platter with brown gravy, and two slices of truffle on each.

Cream of lettuce. Take the trimmings of six heads of lettuce, in volume about the same as two heads of lettuce, wash well and cut in small bits. Take two quarts of chicken broth, or any kind of clear broth or stock, add the lettuce to it and boil for thirty minutes. Put in a separate vessel four ounces of butter, and heat; add three spoonfuls of flour and heat again; add the broth containing the lettuce and boil for ten minutes. Boil a pint of cream, mix with the soup, and strain through a fine sieve. Put back in vessel, add two or three ounces of sweet butter, and stir until the butter is melted. Season with salt and a little Cayenne pepper.

Scallops, Mornay. Put one pint of scallops in a sauté pan with an ounce of butter, season with salt and pepper, and heat through. Then remove the juice and add one cup of thick cream sauce, mix well, put in a deep dish, sprinkle with grated Parmesan or Swiss cheese, put small bits of butter on top, and bake in hot oven until brown.

Croustades financière. Make a financière, but cut a little smaller than for garniture. Fill the croustades, and serve on napkin with parsley in branches.

Financière (garniture). Cut two parboiled sweetbreads in slices, and sauté in butter; add one-half can of French mushrooms, or one-quarter pound of fresh mushrooms cut in two and sautéed, rooster combs and kidneys, sliced truffles, small chicken dumplings, and a few green olives with the stones removed. Put all in a casserole, season well, add a pint of good Madeira sauce, and serve hot. This garnish may be used for filling croustades, vol au vents, small patties, or as an entrée.

MARCH 3

BREAKFAST
  Griddle cakes with maple syrup
  Buttered toast
  Oolong tea

DINNER
  Toke Point oysters
  Pannade soup
  Boiled sea bass, Hollandaise
  Potatoes nature
  Chicken sauté, Salonika
  Peas au cerfeuil
  Chiffonnade salad
  Biscuit glacé
  Assorted cakes
  Coffee

LUNCHEON
  Poached eggs, Monnet Sully
  Imported Frankfort sausages
  Sauerkraut
  Boiled potatoes
  Limberger cheese and crackers
  Coffee

SUPPER
  Golden buck

Poached eggs, Monnet Sully. Place a poached egg on a canapé of chicken and pour Béarnaise sauce over it.

Canapé of chicken. Take the breast of a boiled fowl and chop very fine, season with salt and pepper, mix well with two ounces of sweet butter, and spread on fresh toast.

Pannade soup. Take a half loaf of stale white bread, or some rolls, and put in a pot with three pints of water, season with salt and pepper, add one-quarter of a pound of butter, cover, and boil slowly for one hour. It will then be of the consistency of gruel. Mix the yolks of two eggs with a cup of cream and a half cup of milk, and stir slowly into the boiling soup. This is an excellent plain soup, and fine for the digestion.

Peas au cerfeuil. Put three ounces of butter in a casserole, add one quart of parboiled peas, some chopped chervil (cerfeuil), season with salt and a pinch of sugar, and simmer for five minutes.

Boiled sea bass, Hollandaise. Put a whole sea bass, including the head and tail, in a fish kettle, in cold water. Season with salt, some whole black pepper berries, and a bouquet garni. Add one sliced onion, and one carrot, bring to a boil and then set on the side for fifteen minutes. Serve on a napkin with small boiled potatoes, quartered lemons and parsley. Hollandaise sauce separate.

Fried artichokes. Trim the bottoms of six boiled artichokes, cut in four, put in flour, then in milk, then in beaten egg, then in fresh bread crumbs, and fry in swimming fat. Serve on napkin with lemon and parsley.

Chicken sauté, Salonika. Joint a chicken and season with salt and pepper. Put two spoonfuls of olive oil in a sauté pan, and when very hot add the chicken. Sauté until nice and brown, then add one chopped shallot. When the shallot is hot pour off the oil, add one cup of brown gravy, and simmer for five minutes. Dish up on a flat platter, pour the sauce over it, sprinkle with chopped parsley, and garnish both ends of the platter with fried artichokes.

Golden buck. A Welsh rabbit with a poached egg on top.

MARCH 4

BREAKFAST
  Sliced pineapple
  Bacon and eggs
  Rolls
  Coffee

DINNER
  California oyster cocktail
  Ox tail soup, English style
  Frogs' legs, Jerusalem
  Filet mignon, Bayard
  Flageolet beans
  Sybil potatoes
  Hearts of lettuce
  Raspberry water ice
  Assorted cakes
  Coffee

LUNCHEON
  Mussels marinière
  Reindeer chop, port wine sauce
  Sweet potatoes, sauté
  Lettuce braisé
  Waldorf salad
  French pastry
  Coffee

SUPPER
  Hangtown fry

Sauce marinière. Cut fine six shallots, put in casserole with one ounce of butter, and simmer just enough to have the shallots hot, then add one glass of white wine and boil until reduced nearly dry. Then add one pint of sauce Allemande and boil for five minutes. Season with salt and pepper, and sprinkle with a little chopped parsley and chives.

Sauce Allemande. Put four ounces of butter and three spoonfuls of flour in a casserole and place on the stove. When hot add one quart of chicken or veal broth, and boil for twenty minutes, then bind with the yolks of three eggs mixed with one-half cup of thick cream. Strain and season well with salt and a little Cayenne pepper.

Mussels, marinière. Wash the mussels well to free them from all sand. Put in casserole with one-half glass of white wine and one cup of water, bring to the boiling point, then add six chopped shallots, and boil until the mussels are open. Remove the mussels to another vessel, strain the broth, and reduce. Then add one pint of sauce marinière, and pour over the mussels. The mussels may be served with the entire shells attached; on the half shell, or removed from the shells altogether, after they have been boiled.

Reindeer chop. Reindeer should be hung up for at least two weeks before being cooked, otherwise it will be very tough. The meat is very good, and easily prepared. Salt and pepper the chops, roll in olive oil, and broil; or fry in frying pan, in the same manner as any other kind of chop or steak. Serve with maître d'hôtel, or some fancy meat sauce.

Port wine sauce. Take the brown gravy from a roast, or use any kind of brown sauce, or sauce Madère; add one glass of port wine and boil for two minutes. This sauce is excellent with game. If a sweeter sauce is desired one-half cup of hot currant jelly may be added.

Filet mignon, Bayard. Sauté in butter, or broil, small tenderloin steaks, place on toast, spread with purée de foie gras, cover with sauce Madère with sliced truffles, and garnish with small round chicken croquettes.

Hangtown fry. Mix plain scrambled eggs with one dozen small fried California oysters.

MARCH 5

BREAKFAST
Pearl grits with cream
Broiled smoked salmon
Toast Melba
Coffee

LUNCHEON
Eggs, Meyerbeer
Paprika schnitzel with spätzel
Gorgonzola cheese with crackers
Coffee

DINNER
Cream of bananas
Ripe California olives
Fillet of bass, Nanon
Chicken sauté, Créole
Boiled rice
Escarole and chicory salad
Nesselrode pudding
Assorted cakes
Coffee

Pearl grits. To one quart of boiling water add eight ounces of pearl grits, season with salt, and boil for twenty minutes. Serve cream separate.

Eggs, Meyerbeer. For each person cook two eggs on a shirred egg dish. Have the eggs very soft. Place a broiled split lamb's kidney in the center of each dish and cover with a little sauce Madère. Place two slices of truffle on top. Season well.

Broiled smoked salmon. Slice the salmon about one-half inch thick, roll in olive oil, and broil. When done put on platter, cover with maître d'hôtel sauce, and garnish with quartered lemons and parsley.

Toast Melba. Cut some white bread in very thin slices, trim, put on a pan and bake in the oven until brown.

Paprika schnitzel. Cut four slices from a leg of veal. The slices should be about one-half inch thick, two and one-half inches wide and six inches long. Season them with salt and paprika. Melt three ounces of butter in a sauté pan, when hot put the slices of meat in the pan and sauté for about five minutes. Then add one cup of very thick cream, a little more salt, one teaspoonful of paprika, and simmer for five minutes. If the sauce should be too thin add one spoonful of cream sauce and simmer for a few minutes.

Nesselrode pudding. Beat over the fire the yolks of eight eggs, one-half pound of sugar, and one pony of good rum, until light and creamy. Then remove from the fire and continue beating until cold. Then add one quart of whipped cream and one-half pound of broken marrons glacés. Mix well, and put in one large, or in individual moulds, pack in ice and salt, and leave until hard. It will require about two hours to freeze. To serve, remove from mould, decorate the top with a marron glacé, and pour maraschino sauce around the bottom of the pudding.

Spätzel. These are small flour dumplings, but made harder than the usual dumpling. Mix well one cup of flour, one whole egg and the yolk of an egg, one-third of a cup of milk, a little salt and pepper, and a very little grated nutmeg. Form in small bits and drop into boiling salted water and boil for about five minutes, then pour off the water. In a frying pan put two ounces of butter and cook until brown, then pour over the spätzel and mix.

Cream of bananas. Make a cream of chicken soup, heat six bananas in it, and strain through a fine sieve.

MARCH 6

BREAKFAST
  Bar le Duc jelly
  Spanish omelet
  Dry toast
  Chocolate with whipped cream

LUNCHEON
  Grapefruit with cherries
  Fried tomcods, Tartar sauce
  Turkeys' livers en brochette
  Flageolet beans
  French pastry
  Coffee

DINNER
  Consommé royal
  Soft clams, bâtelière
  Roast turkey, cranberry sauce
  Sweet potato croquettes
  Asparagus Hollandaise
  Chiffonnade salad
  Mince pie
  American cheese
  Coffee

Spanish omelet. Make a plain omelet and pour one cup of Créole sauce around it.

Fried tomcods. Clean eight tomcods, wash well, and dry with a towel. Roll in milk, then in flour, and fry in swimming fat for about five minutes, or until nice and brown. The fat must be very hot. Serve on a napkin with fried parsley, quartered lemons, and Tartar sauce separate.

Turkeys' livers en brochette. Take three turkey livers and cut each in four slices. Broil three slices of bacon, and cut in four pieces also. Now stick a piece of liver on a skewer, then a piece of bacon, then another piece of liver, then another piece of bacon, and so continue until the skewer is full. Season with salt and pepper, roll in fresh bread crumbs, sprinkle with olive oil, and broil. When done on all sides place on a piece of toast, put some maître d'hôtel sauce over it, and garnish with quarters of lemon and water-cress.

Clams bâtelière. Separate the bellies from one dozen soft clams and put them back in their half shells. Season with salt and pepper, cover with maître d'hôtel sauce, put a thin slice of salt pork over the top, and place in oven and bake. Garnish with quartered lemon and parsley.

Roast turkey. Season the turkey well, fill with any kind of stuffing, and roast in the same manner as roast turkey stuffed with chestnuts.

MARCH 7

BREAKFAST
Fresh strawberries with cream
Boiled eggs
Rolls
Coffee

LUNCHEON
Eggs Sarah Bernhardt
Reindeer stew
Mashed potatoes
Camembert cheese and crackers
Coffee

DINNER
Cherrystone oysters on half shell
Cream of farina
Fillet of turbot, Bonnefoy
Lamb chops, charcutière
Succotash
French fried potatoes
Romaine salad
Fancy ice cream
Assorted cakes   Coffee

Eggs Sarah Bernhardt. Cut six hard-boiled eggs in two, remove the yolks, mash them up and mix with a little salt, pepper, celery salt, one spoonful of fresh bread crumbs, one spoonful of chopped chicken meat, and the yolk of one raw egg. Stuff the halved whites of eggs with this, put on a buttered dish and place in the oven for four minutes. Dress on a silver platter, and cover with sauce Perigueux.

Sauce Perigueux. Chop a small can of truffles and put in a casserole with one glass of Madeira, and reduce until nearly dry. Then add one pint of brown gravy and season with salt and Cayenne pepper.

Sauce Perigord. Slice one small can of truffles, put in casserole with one glass of Madeira or sherry wine, reduce, add one pint of brown gravy and boil again for twelve minutes. Season with salt and Cayenne pepper.

Reindeer stew. Cut about five pounds of shoulder and breast of reindeer in pieces two inches square. Put in sauté pan with one-quarter pound of butter, season with salt and pepper, and sauté until nice and brown. Then add two spoonfuls of flour and simmer until the flour is slightly brown; add one pint of claret and one quart of boiling water, a bouquet garni, and bring to a boil; skim, cover and let slowly cook until nearly done. Sauté in butter twelve heads of fresh mushrooms, and parboil twelve very small potatoes and fry in butter, add them to the stew and cook until soft. Season well with salt and pepper.

Cream of farina. Boil one pound of farina in one quart of milk. When done add one pint of well-seasoned chicken broth, and strain through a fine sieve. Put back in pot, add two ounces of sweet butter and one pint of boiling cream. Season with salt and a little Cayenne pepper.

Fillet of turbot, Bonnefoy. Cut the turbot in fillets about one and one-half inches wide and three inches long. Put in sauté pan, season with salt and pepper, add six very finely chopped shallots, one small can of mushrooms, or a half pound of fresh mushrooms, and one glass of claret. Cover with buttered manilla paper, put in oven and simmer for ten minutes, then remove the fish to a platter. Put the pan with the gravy on the fire, add one pint of tomato sauce and boil for five minutes. Then stir in well one ounce of good butter, and pour over the fish.

Lamb chops, charcutière. Broil some lamb chops and cover with brown sauce with which has been mixed some sliced pickle and sliced green olives in equal parts. Season the sauce well.

MARCH 8

BREAKFAST
Stewed prunes
Scrambled eggs with bacon
Buttered toast
English breakfast tea

LUNCHEON
Canapé of fresh caviar
Consommé in cups
Cheese straws
Spring lamb Irish stew
Cream puffs
Coffee

DINNER
Purée d'Artois (soup)
Salted pecans
Broiled shad, Albert
Chicken à l'Estragon
Potatoes au gratin
Artichokes, sauce Hollandaise
Omelette soufflée
Coffee

Purée d'Artois. Same as purée of peas.

Broiled shad, Albert. Broiled shad with horseradish sauce.

Chicken à l'Estragon. Boil a whole chicken in a quart of water with salt and a bouquet garni. When done pull the skin off but leave the chicken whole. Make the sauce in the following manner: Put three ounces of butter in a casserole, when hot add two and one-half spoonfuls of flour and one and one-half pints of the chicken broth, boil for ten minutes, add a little chopped tarragon and boil for another ten minutes. Bind with the yolks of two eggs and a half cup of cream, strain, and season with salt and Cayenne pepper. Pour the sauce over the chicken, and lay a few leaves of tarragon on top.

Omelette soufflée. Mix a cup of powdered sugar with the yolks of two eggs and the inside of a vanilla bean, and beat until it is light and fluffy. Beat the whites of eight eggs until they are very stiff, then add to the batter, mixing lightly. Place this on a buttered silver platter that has been dusted with powdered sugar, form into a fancy shape, decorate through a pastry bag with some of the same preparation, dust with powdered sugar, and bake in a rather hot oven for about ten minutes.

Omelette soufflée en surprise. Cut a piece of sponge cake into an oval shape about one-half inch thick, three inches wide and six inches long. Put on top of the cake one pint of vanilla ice cream that has been frozen very hard, cover with omelette soufflée preparation, decorate in the same manner as above, dust with powdered sugar, and bake in a very hot oven for two minutes.

MARCH 9

BREAKFAST
Orange marmalade
Boiled eggs
Dry toast
Ceylon tea

LUNCHEON
Eggs Maltaise
Calf's head, à la Française
Plain boiled potatoes
Brie cheese and crackers   Coffee

DINNER
Cream of green corn
Matelote of fish
Leg of mutton, Bretonne
Field salad
Sand tart   Coffee

Eggs Maltaise. Fill a croustade with purée of fresh mushrooms, put a poached egg on top, and cover with cream sauce.

Calf's head, à la Française. Boil a calf's head, with the tongue and brains, and dish up on a china platter. Make a macédoine of vegetables as follows: Boil in salt water a carrot and a turnip, and when cold cut up in small dices. Add one-half pound of cold cooked string beans cut in pieces about one-half inch long, one-quarter pound of boiled peas, and one-half can of flageolet beans. Put this macédoine in a salad bowl, add one teaspoonful of salt, one-half teaspoonful of fresh-ground black pepper, a little parsley and chervil, one-half cup of white wine vinegar, and one and one-half cups of olive oil. Mix well and pour over the calf's head.

Cream of green corn. Soak five pounds of green corn in cold water over night. Then put on fire in pot with one-half gallon of bouillon, and cook until soft. Then strain through a fine sieve, put back in pot, add one quart of boiling cream, and season with salt and a little Cayenne pepper. Before serving add four ounces of sweet butter, and stir well until melted.

White beans, Bretonne. Soak 3 pounds of white beans in cold water over night. Put in a vessel with three quarts of water, a ham bone, a bouquet garni, and a small handful of salt. Boil until soft, then remove the ham bone and bouquet, and drain off the water. Chop three large onions very fine, put in casserole with three ounces of butter, and simmer until cooked, then add a teaspoonful of chopped garlic and heat through, pour in a cupful of purée of tomatoes and some chopped parsley, add the beans, season well with fresh-ground black pepper, and cook for ten minutes.

Leg of mutton, Bretonne. Roast leg of mutton garnished with beans Bretonne.

Matelote of fish. Take the solid meat of any kind of fresh fish such as bass, carp, perch, etc., and cut about four pounds in slices two inches thick. Put in buttered pan, season with salt and pepper, add one pint of claret, one cup of stock, fish broth, or water, and a bouquet garni. Cover, put over a slow fire and boil for about twenty minutes, or until soft. Put the fish in a deep dish, cover with matelote sauce, and garnish with boiled écrevisses. To make the matelote sauce put three ounces of butter in a casserole and allow to become hot. then add two spoonfuls of flour, heat well, and then pour in the strained broth from the fish, boil for ten minutes, add one spoonful of meat extract and one teaspoonful of essence of anchovies, and strain. Peel one dozen very small white onions, parboil then and fry in butter until soft. Add the onions and one can of French mushrooms to the sauce, season well, and boil.

Sand tart (Sablé). One pound of sugar, one pound of flour, the yolks of five eggs, six ounces of butter, and three tablespoonfuls of thick sour milk in which has been dissolved one pinch of soda. Mix to a hard dough and roll **very** thin. Beat the whites of two eggs and use to moisten the top of the rolled dough. Cut in the desired shape, sprinkle with sugar mixed with a little powdered cinnamon and chopped almonds, put on buttered pan and bake quick.

MARCH 10

BREAKFAST
   Sliced bananas with cream
   Broiled finnan haddie
   Baked potatoes
   Rolls
   Coffee

LUNCHEON
   Eggs Renaissance
   Mutton chops, Signora
   Fried egg plant
   Romaine salad
   Meringued peaches   Coffee

DINNER
   Mock turtle soup
   Oysters, Victor
   Croustades Laguipierre
   Roast capon, au jus
   Fresh asparagus, Hollandaise
   Champs Élysées potatoes
   Escarole salad
   Fancy ice cream
   Assorted cakes   Coffee

Eggs Renaissance. Put a little cream sauce in the bottom of a buttered cocotte dish, add a raw egg, season with salt and pepper, then add a few sliced canned mushrooms and sliced truffles, cover with cream sauce, sprinkle with grated cheese, put bits of butter on top, and bake in oven.

Mutton chops, Signora. Split open four mutton chops, season with salt and pepper, put three slices of truffle in each chop and fold together, roll in flour, then in beaten egg, and finally in bread crumbs. Fry the chops for ten minutes in hot melted butter. Serve cream sauce to which has been added some chopped truffles.

Meringued peaches. (Pêche meringuée). Cook one quarter pound of rice in one quart of milk for about one-half hour. The rice should be stiff when done. Add one pony of cream, one ounce of butter, two ounces of sugar, and mix well. Spread on a dish about one inch deep, and place on top some halved preserved peaches, or some fresh peaches cooked in syrup. Make a meringue paste with the whites of four eggs beaten stiff and a half pound of sugar. Cover the peaches with the meringue, using a pastry bag with a fancy tube. Dust over with powdered sugar, and bake in a rather cool oven until it becomes a little dry and brown.

Oysters Victor. Wash the heads of three fresh mushrooms, dry them in a towel, and chop very fine, also chop very fine six walnuts and put in salad bowl with the mushrooms, season with salt and pepper, add three ounces of butter and a little chopped parsley, and mix well together. Spread this paste on top of a dozen oysters on the half shell, and bake in oven for about five minutes. Serve with halves of lemon.

Croustades Laguipierre. Use equal parts of chickens' livers, sauté in butter, sliced sweetbreads sauté, boiled rooster combs, sliced green olives, sliced truffles, and French mushrooms cut in two. Stir into hot Madeira sauce, season well, and fill the croustades.

MARCH 11

BREAKFAST
Fresh strawberries with cream
Scrambled eggs with truffles
Crescents
Coffee

LUNCHEON
Hors d'oeuvres variés
Potato omelet
Roquefort cheese and crackers
Hungarian beef goulash
Coffee

DINNER
Consommé Du Barry
Queen olives
Fillet of sole, Turbigo
Veal kidney roast
Carrots in butter
Mashed potatoes
Chicory salad
Fried cream
Coffee

Scrambled eggs with truffles. Cut a truffle in small dices and put in sauce pan, on the range, with one ounce of butter. When hot add six beaten eggs, a little salt and pepper, one spoonful of cream, and then scramble in the usual manner. Dish up and lay six slices of heated truffles on top.

Potato omelet. Cut a boiled potato in small dices. Put one ounce of butter in a frying pan with the potato, and fry until brown, then add six beaten eggs, season with salt and pepper, and cook into an omelet in the usual manner.

Consommé Du Barry. Boil a cauliflower in salt water. When done cut the tips of the flowers from the stems and add to boiling consommé.

Fillet of sole, Turbigo. Cut the fillets from a sole, and remove the skin. Spread with fish force meat, (see fish dumplings), fold in half, place in buttered sauté pan, season with salt and pepper, add one-half glass of white wine, and boil. When done remove the fish to a platter; add to the gravy in the pan one cup of white wine sauce, boil for ten minutes, and strain. Cut the tail of a lobster in slices, heat them and lay on top of fillets and cover with the sauce.

Carrots in butter. Wash and peel three dozen small French carrots, and boil in two quarts of salted water. When done drain off the water, add two ounces of sweet butter, and simmer for two minutes. Sprinkle with a little chopped parsley.

Fried cream. One quart of milk, one-half pound of sugar, the yolks of eight eggs, four ounces of flour, and one-half of a vanilla bean. Boil the milk with the vanilla bean. Mix the sugar, flour and the yolks of the eggs, and then pour into the boiling milk. Continue cooking, stirring all the time until stiff. Then pour into a flat pan in a layer about three-quarters of an inch thick, allow to become cold, and then cut into two inch squares. Roll in flour, then in beaten egg, and finally in cake, macaroon, or bread crumbs, and fry in swimming lard until brown. Serve dusted with powdered sugar, or with a lump of sugar covered with brandy, and burning.

Beef tongue, Parisian style. Wash a fresh beef tongue, put in a pot, cover with hot water, add a cup of white wine vinegar, two carrots, two onions, a bay leaf, a few cloves, a crushed garlic clove, some thyme, the green tops of a bunch of celery, and some salt. Simmer slowly for three hours, or until when pricked with a fork it has the consistency of jelly. Then peel and trim. Reduce the broth, and make a brown gravy, adding a glass of Madeira wine. In another pan boil a dozen or so small onions. Glacé and simmer them in plenty of butter, but do not brown, add a can of mushroom heads and quarter of a pound of salt pork that has been boiled and diced, and simmer again. Add two tablespoonfuls of minced parsley and a wine glass of sherry, then mix with the brown Madeira sauce. Put the whole tongue on a platter, and pour the sauce over it.

MARCH 12

BREAKFAST
  Stewed rhubarb
  Boiled eggs
  Rolls
  Coffee

LUNCHEON
  Grapefruit with maraschino
  Fried tomcods, Tartar
  Broiled honeycomb tripe
  Celery root, field and beet salad
  Lyonnaise potatoes
  Cherry tart   Coffee

DINNER
  Potage Lamballe   Radishes
  Bass, Dijonaise
  Roast chicken
  Fonds d'artichauts, Feypell
  Julienne potatoes
  Sliced tomatoes, French dressing
  Vanilla ice cream
  Cakes   Coffee

Bass, Dijonaise. Put four fillets of bass in a buttered pan, season with salt and pepper, sprinkle with two finely-chopped shallots, add one-half cup of water, cover, and put in hot oven for fifteen minutes. Then place the fillets on a platter, and reduce the broth until nearly dry, add one spoonful of French mustard and two cups of cream sauce, and boil for two minutes. Add some chopped chives, and pour over the fish.

Fonds d'artichauts, Feypell. (Artichoke bottoms, Feypell). Remove the leaves, and trim the bottoms of twelve boiled artichokes. Cut six of them into one-half inch squares. Prepare one cup of purée of fresh mushrooms and one-half cup of grated cheese. Put in a sauté pan one ounce of fresh butter, and when hot add the cut-up artichoke bottoms, and season with salt and pepper. Fry until of a light golden yellow color, then add the grated cheese, mix well, add the mushrooms purée, and boil for a minute or two. Finally stir in the yolk of an egg, mixing quickly, and a little chopped parsley. Cover thickly the six whole artichoke bottoms with this filling, place on a buttered dish or pan, lay a thin slice of raw bacon about an inch and a half long on top of each, and put in the oven and bake. Serve as a vegetable course with Madeira or tomato sauce, or as a garnish, plain.

Canapé St. Francis. Trim small pieces of toast, and cut in fancy shapes, or circular. Spread with caviar. Place a slice of tomato on top and over this strips of caviar. Place on lettuce leaves that have been dressed with French dressing mixed with finely-chopped herbs.

Potatoes Ritz. Allow one large potato for each individual. Peel, and cut into half-inch dices. Boil in salt water for ten minutes, drain, and brown with butter. When done the potatoes should be in small free pieces, and browned on all sides.

Asparagus Polonaise. Put four pounds of boiled fresh asparagus, (for four persons), on a platter. In a frying pan put three ounces of fresh butter, and one-half cup of fresh bread crumbs, and fry until the crumbs are golden yellow. Then pour over the tips of the asparagus, sprinkle with a little pepper and chopped parsley. A hard-boiled egg chopped fine, may be added if desired.

MARCH 13

BREAKFAST
  Grapefruit marmalade
  Buckwheat cakes
  Breakfast sausages
  Maple syrup
  Rolls   Coffee
DINNER
  Toke Point Oysters, mignonette
  Potage Mongol
  Ripe California olives
  Fillet of sole, Villeroi
  Roast loin of lamb, mint sauce
  Asparagus Polonaise   Potato salad
  Savarin aux fruits   Coffee

LUNCHEON
  Eggs gastronome
  Calf's brains au beurre noir
  Persillade potatoes
  Hearts of lettuce, French dressing
  French pastry   Coffee
SUPPER
  Yorkshire buck
  Coffee

Eggs gastronome. Boil six eggs until hard, remove the shells, and cut in two lengthwise. Chop up the yolks and put in a bowl. Chop very fine one can of French mushrooms, and add to the yolks, season with salt and pepper, add the raw yolk of one egg, one-half cup of fresh bread crumbs and a little chopped parsley, and mix well. Fill the hard-boiled whites with this filling, put on a platter, cover with brown gravy and bake in oven.

Calf's brains au beurre noir. Put two calf's brains in cold water and leave for one hour; then remove the reddish-black outside skin with the fingers, and put again in fresh cold water so the blood will run out, and the brains remain white after being cooked. Now put in a casserole two quarts of water, a heaping spoonful of salt, one-half glass of vinegar, two onions, one-half of a carrot, and a bouquet garni. Boil for five minutes, and then add the brains and boil for two minutes, then let it stand in the hot broth for about one-half hour. Then remove the brains, cut in two lengthwise and lay on a platter, sprinkle with salt and fresh-ground black pepper, one spoonful of French capers, and a little chopped parsley, chives and chervil. Put in a frying pan three ounces of sweet butter and cook until very dark brown, nearly black; and pour over the brains. Then put in the same pan one-third of a cup of vinegar, let it become hot, and pour over the brains also.

Potatoes persillade. Cut two dozen potatoes to the shape of a small egg. Put in a pot, cover with cold water, add a spoonful of salt, and boil slowly so they will not break. When they are nearly soft drain off the water, add one ounce of butter, cover, and simmer until the butter is melted. Then sprinkle with chopped parsley.

Fillet of sole, Villeroi. Put the fillets of a large sole in a buttered pan, add some salt and a glass of milk, bring to a boil, and then set on the side of the stove for ten minutes; then remove the fish to a platter. Mix in a cup one spoonful of flour and one spoonful of butter; add this to the broth in the pan from which the fish has been removed, and boil for five minutes; then add one cup of cream, and two ounces of sweet butter and whip well until melted, season with salt and pepper, and strain over the fish.

Boiled fresh asparagus. Fresh asparagus should be peeled very thin with a sharp knife, and well washed. If to be served hot, put in boiling salt water over a hot fire about twenty minutes before serving. They should not be cooked in advance. If to be served cold, as soon as the asparagus is done pour a glass of cold water over them so they will not continue cooking and become too soft. Allow to cool in the broth, and before serving lay on a towel or napkin to allow the water to drip off.

MARCH 14

BREAKFAST
Baked beans, Boston style
Brown bread
Buttermilk
Coffee

LUNCHEON
Omelet with oysters
Veal chops, sauté in butter
Purée of salad
Camembert cheese, crackers Coffee

DINNER
Little Neck clams
Chicken okra soup
Salted almonds
Aiguillettes of bass, Massena
Vol au vent Toulouse
Roast capon, giblet sauce
Stewed asparagus Château potatoes
Endives salad
Parfait Napolitain
Assorted cakes   Coffee

Purée of salad. (Vegetable). Boil in salted water, lettuce or any other kind of green salad. When done drain off the water and press through a fine colander. Add butter and a little cream.

Aiguillettes of bass, Massena. Put four fillets of bass in a buttered pan, season with salt and pepper; add one-half glass of white wine and one-half glass of stock, bouillon, fish broth or water, cover with buttered paper, and put in oven to bake. When done place the aiguillettes on a platter and cover with the following sauce: Heat one and one-half ounces of butter in a sauce pan, add one spoonful of flour and allow to become brown, add the fish broth left from cooking the bass, one spoonful of meat extract, and one-half spoonful of Worcestershire sauce. Boil for ten minutes, then add one-half teaspoonful of essence of anchovies, and strain through cheese cloth. Boil one dozen clams and cut in two; cut half of the tail of a lobster in small squares, and six heads of mushrooms cut in two. Put all of this in the strained sauce, and season well.

Giblet sauce. Clean the giblets of chickens, turkeys, or other fowl, boil in salt water, and chop. Put in casserole two chopped onions, and two ounces of butter, and simmer for ten minutes, or until soft and yellow. Then add one tablespoonful of flour, and simmer again until brown. Add the gravy from a roast, the chopped giblets and a little of the water the giblets were boiled in. Cook for half an hour, season with salt and pepper and chopped parsley. A little sherry wine may be added before serving, if desired.

Stewed asparagus. Cut up some asparagus tips and cook in a casserole in salt water until soft. Mix a spoonful of flour and one ounce of butter and add to the asparagus, with some of the water used for boiling. Use only enough water to cover the asparagus. Sprinkle with chopped parsley and pepper, and serve in a deep dish.

White bean soup. Soak a quart of beans over night. Put in a vessel with four quarts of water, or a mild soup stock. Add a half pound of lean bacon, and a shinbone, if desired. Start to boil rapidly, then remove to back of stove and cook for several hours until the beans drop to pieces. Skim from time to time. Meanwhile chop very fine an onion, a carrot and a stalk of celery, and simmer in butter until they take on a slightly brown color. Add a spoonful of flour, a potato cut in small dices, and the water from the beans. Strain the beans, and to the purée add the cooked vegetables; cut the bacon in small pieces, and cook all together for twenty minutes. Season with salt, pepper and chopped parsley.

MARCH 15

BREAKFAST
Bananas with cream
Scrambled eggs with asparagus tips
Toast
Coffee

LUNCHEON
Crab salad
Consommé in cups   Cheese straws
Fried whitebait, rémoulade
Lamb chops   Sauté potatoes
Escarole and chicory salad
Roquefort cheese, crackers   Coffee

DINNER
Pot au feu
Loin of pork, baker's oven style
Mashed turnips
Celery root and field salad
Fancy ice cream
Assorted cakes   Coffee

Fried whitebait. Wash the whitebait well and dry on a towel or napkin. Roll in milk, then in flour, and fry in very hot swimming lard, just enough to make them crisp. Lay them on a napkin, sprinkle with salt, and garnish with fried parsley and quartered lemons. Serve brown bread and butter sandwiches and sauce Tartar or rémoulade.

Pot au feu. Put in a pot one brisket of beef; or five pounds of short ribs of beef; two gallons of cold water, and a handful of salt. Bring slowly to a boil and skim well, so the broth will remain clear. When the boiling point is reached add two whole carrots, two turnips, three stalks of leeks, one stalk of celery, a bouquet garni, one small head of Savoy cabbage, and two large onions, all well washed. Bring to the boiling point again, cover, and put on the side of the stove where it will simmer slowly. The vegetables will be done before the meat, so when they are cooked remove them and throw out the bouguet garni. Let the beef cook until very soft. Cut the vegetables, with the exception of the onions, in thin slices; and when the beef is done strain the broth over the vegetables. Give it another boil, season well, add some chopped chervil, and serve with toasted bread crusts, separate.

The boiled beef may be served as an extra course, usually after the soup, if no fish is served.

Loin of pork, baker's oven style. For a large family, take eight pounds of pork ribs, season with salt and pepper, rub with a piece of garlic thoroughly, and put into a stoneware pot. Cut six large potatoes in strips lengthwise and one inch square, slice three onions and add, with three pints of water, a bay leaf and two cloves, to the meat. Your baker will bake it for you in a brick oven, and it will be a dish quite different from the usual roasted pork. If necessary, put it in your own oven, baking for not less than four hours with a slow, even fire. However, it is preferable to have it baked in a brick oven.

Fried chicken, Vienna style. Cut a chicken in six pieces; two legs, two wings, and two pieces of breast. Season with salt and pepper, roll in flour, then in beaten eggs, and finally in fresh bread crumbs. Put in a sauté pan in two spoonfuls of hot butter, and fry. When done dish up on a platter, garnish with corn fritters, and serve sauce suprême separate.

Peas, farmer style. Shell enough peas to make two cupsful. Take twelve firm large asparagus tips, an onion, a firm head of lettuce cut fine, six small French carrots cut in two, three ounces of butter, a pinch of salt and one of sugar. Add enough water to cover, and simmer slowly until all the vegetables are thoroughly done.

MARCH 16

BREAKFAST
  Grapefruit
  Fried eggs
  Dry toast
  English breakfast tea

LUNCHEON
  Sardines, vinaigrette
  Paprika schnitzel with spätzel
  German apple cake
  Coffee

DINNER
  Blue Point oysters on half shell
  Purée paysanne
  Pompano sauté, meunière
  Tame duckling, apple sauce
  Young beets in butter
  Sweet potatoes sauté
  Waldorf salad
  Lemon pie
  Coffee

Sardines, vinaigrette. Remove the skins from a can of sardines, and arrange on a platter, on a lettuce leaf. Sprinkle with salt and fresh-ground black pepper, pour a spoonful of vinaigre and one of olive oil over them, and sprinkle with chopped parsley. Garnish with a lemon cut in half, two hard-boiled eggs cut in two, some chopped onion on a small leaf of lettuce, and another small leaf filled with small French capers.

Purée paysanne. (Soup). Slice a carrot, an onion, a turnip, one-half of a stalk of celery, two stalks of leeks, three leaves of cabbage, one-half pound of squash or other fresh vegetable such as asparagus or tomatoes. Put them in a vessel with one-half pound of fresh peas, and one-quarter pound of fresh Lima beans. Cover with two quarts of bouillon and cook until soft. Strain through a fine colander, put back in the vessel, bring to a boil, season with salt and pepper, add two ounces of butter and mix well.

Young beets in butter. Cut some young boiled beets in thin slices, put in sauté pan with butter, season with salt and pepper, and simmer for a few minutes.

Fillet of sole, Villeroi. Put the fillets of a large sole in a buttered pan, add some salt and a glass of milk, and bring to a boil, then set on side of stove for ten minutes. Then remove the fillets to a platter. Mix in a cup one spoonful of flour and one spoonful of butter, and add this to the milk broth in the pan, which has been kept boiling, and cook for five minutes. Then add one cup of cream and two ounces of sweet butter, whip well until melted, season with salt and pepper, and strain over the fish.

Sponge cake. One-half pound of sugar, six yolks of egg and six whole eggs, one-half pound of flour, and flavoring. Beat the eggs and yolks and sugar over a slow fire until blood warm. Then remove and continue beating until cold and very light and spongy. Then add the flour and vanilla, or other flavoring, and mix lightly. Put into paper-lined moulds or pan, and bake in medium hot oven. Serve with powdered sugar dusted on top, or frosted.

Caroline cake. (Chocolate or coffee). Make a dough as for cream puffs, and dress on a pan in drops about quarter the size as for regular cream puffs. Bake in a moderate oven; when done make a hole in the bottom of each with a pointed stick, and fill with pastry cream, or sweetened whipped cream. Place on a wire grill about one-quarter inch apart, and glacé with chocolate or coffee icing. Let the icing dry, and serve in paper cases.

MARCH 17

BREAKFAST
Fresh strawberries with cream
Boiled eggs
Dry toast
Chocolate with whipped cream

LUNCHEON
Eggs Princesse
Chicken sauté, Hongroise
Mashed potatoes
Lettuce salad
Brie cheese and crackers
Coffee

DINNER
Little Neck clams
Consommé Camino
Fillet of bass, Menton
Roast leg of lamb
String beans
Château potatoes
Chiffonnade salad
Fancy ice cream
Assorted cakes
Coffee

Eggs Princesse. Put some purée of fresh mushrooms in the bottom of small croustades, lay a poached egg on top, and cover with sauce Perigueux.

Chicken sauté, Hongroise. Joint a chicken and put in a sauté pan with two ounces of butter, season with salt and a little paprika, simmer for five minutes; then add a sliced onion and simmer slowly for ten minutes with the cover over the pan. Then add a cup of cream and cook for four minutes, and add one-half cup of cream sauce. Remove the chicken to a platter, pour the sauce over it, and garnish both ends of the platter with macédoine of vegetables.

Macédoine of vegetables. Macédoine is a mixture of vegetables, and may be obtained in cans, but is easily made at home. If the canned sort is used drain off the juice, put in casserole in cold water, bring to a boil, and then drain off the water, season with salt and pepper, and simmer for a minute or so. To make macédoine, use equal parts of carrots, turnips, string beans, cut in squares about one-quarter inch in diameter, and peas and flageolet beans. Boil each separately in salt water, and mix afterwards, season with salt and pepper and one ounce of butter, and simmer as above. Flageolet beans come in cans, or dry like dry peas. They may be omitted if desired.

Consommé Camino. Boil one-quarter of a pound of macaroni in salt water; when soft, drain, and cool in cold water. Then cut in small pieces about one-half inch in length, and serve in a quart of consommé. Serve grated cheese separate.

Fillet of bass, Menton. Cut four fillets of bass; and prepare some fish dumpling mixture. Spread some of the mixture over the fillets, and fold in half, place in buttered sauté pan, add a little salt and one-half glass of white wine, cover with buttered paper, and place in oven for fifteen minutes. Dish up on a platter and cover with white wine sauce.

Beans, Normandy. Soak two pounds beans over night, then put to boil with three pints of water, sliced carrot, a yellow turnip, an onion, and a bouquet garni, season with salt, and cook for an hour. Put two big spoonfuls of butter and a spoonful of flour in a pan, and make a creamy sauce by adding the water from the beans. Now fill a baking dish; first a layer of sliced potatoes mixed with minced onions, then the semi-cooked beans, then potatoes, and so on until filled. Then add half a glass of white vinegar and bake until the potatoes are done, by which time the beans will be done also.

MARCH 18

BREAKFAST
Baked apple with cream
Fried hominy
Bar le Duc jelly
Rolls
Coffee

LUNCHEON
Oranges en suprême
Clam broth in cup
Fillet of sole, Orly
Tripe and oysters in cream
Baked potatoes
Diplomate pudding
Coffee

DINNER
Cream of celery
Pompano, Café Anglaise
Chicken sauté, Portugaise
Fresh asparagus, Hollandaise
Julienne potatoes
Romaine salad
Sponge cake
Compote of mixed fruits
Coffee

Orange en suprême. Slice six oranges, put in bowl with three spoonfuls of powdered sugar and two ponys of Curaçao, let stand for thirty minutes, and serve in suprême glasses.

Fillet of sole, Orly. Roll four fillets of sole in the form of cigars, put in flour, then in beaten eggs, and finally in bread crumbs, and fry in hot swimming lard. When done lay on napkin, garnish with quartered lemon and fried parsley, and serve tomato sauce separate.

Diplomate pudding. Take sponge, or any kind of left over cake and cut in small pieces, using enough to fill a pudding mould. Add about a teaspoonful of chopped candied fruit to each person. Make a custard with one quart of milk, six eggs and a half pound of sugar; pour over the cake in the mould, and bake. Serve with brandy sauce with some chopped candied fruit in it.

Pompano, Café Anglaise. Put four small whole pompano and four fillets of pompano in a buttered sauté pan, and season with salt and pepper. Put in another vessel one dozen clams and one dozen oysters, with their own juice, and bring to a boil. Then strain the broth over the pompano and boil until done. Remove the fish to platter, reduce the broth, then add one cup of cream sauce and one cup of white wine sauce, and strain. Put the oysters and clams and one dozen écrevisse tails in the sauce and pour over the fish. The sauce should be well seasoned. Garnish with small fried fillets of sole.

Small fried fillets of sole. Cut fillets of sole into small strips about one-quarter inch thick and two inches long, roll in milk and then in flour, and fry in hot swimming lard. When crisp take out of the fat and sprinkle with salt. Serve with Tartar sauce as fried fillet of sole, or use as a garnish for fish.

Chicken sauté, Portugaise. Joint a chicken and season with salt and pepper. Put in sauté pan one spoonful of olive oil and one of butter, heat, add the chicken, and sauté until golden yellow; then add three finely chopped shallots and simmer for a minute; add one can of French, or one-half pound of fresh mushrooms sauté in butter; two peeled and quartered tomatoes, or the same amount of canned ones, using the pulp only, and simmer for five minutes. Add one cup of tomato sauce, and simmer again for five minutes. Put the chicken on a platter, pour the sauce with its garnishing on top, and sprinkle with chopped parsley. A little chopped garlic may be added at the same time as the chopped shallots, if desired.

MARCH 19

BREAKFAST
Preserved figs with cream
Scrambled eggs with parsley
Puff paste crescents
Oolong tea

LUNCHEON
Eggs Du Barry
Boiled ham, Leonard
Stewed tomatoes, Brazilian
Mashed potatoes
Roquefort cheese, crackers   Coffee

DINNER
Velvet soup
Ripe California olives
Skatefish au beurre noir
Baked chicken with rice
Chiffonnade salad
Bavarois à la vanille
Assorted cakes   Coffee

Baked chicken with rice. Put in a saucepan a fat hen with all of its fat, cover with hot water, season with salt, and when it comes to a boil, skim off the foam but leave the fat. Add a soup bouquet with the addition of some spices and a bay leaf. When the hen is half done, which will be in about an hour, remove the bouquet, and add a cup of washed rice. Boil until the rice is nearly done, by which time it has absorbed most of the broth; then put into a porcelain baking dish and bake until brown.

Eggs Du Barry. Line an egg cocotte with a forcemeat made of truffles and beef tongue, drop an egg into this, set the dish in hot water and cook in the oven for from five to ten minutes. When done cover with hot purée of cauliflower.

Purée of cauliflower. Boil a head of cauliflower in salted water. When soft drain off the water and press the cauliflower through a fine colander. Season with salt and pepper, and add a spoonful of cream sauce.

Forcemeat of truffles and tongue. Put through a fine sieve two slices of beef tongue, then add a truffle chopped fine, the yolk of one egg, and a little pepper.

Boiled ham, à la Leonard. Soak a smoked ham in cold water for twelve hours, after having cut off the handle bone and shortening the hip bone. Set on the fire and bring to the boiling point very gradually, then drain off the water, and replace with water of tepid warmth. Add four or five carrots, two bay leaves, a small bunch of thyme, sage and basil and a bunch of celery tops, all tied in a bunch. Season with mace, cloves and pepper berries, let it come to bubbling heat, and then set on back of stove, where it may simmer at an even temperature. When done; allowing about a quarter of an hour for each pound of meat; peel, and serve with a sauce made of some clear soup stock, Madeira sauce, three spoonfuls of molasses and a spoonful of French mustard. The ham should be basted frequently while cooking.

Velvet soup. Mince fine the red part of a few carrots, stew them with butter, salt, sugar and a little broth. When done strain through a sieve. Put a quart of clear broth on to boil, mix in four tablespoonfuls of tapioca, let it stand for twenty-five minutes on the side of the fire, skimming well. At the last minute before serving add the carrot purée, season, boil up once or twice more, and serve in a tureen.

Tomato stew, Brazilian. Dice a piece of white bread and simmer with two ounces of butter, slightly browning it. Add four peeled tomatoes and a can of Lima beans with the water drained off, and season. Then add a half cup of chicken broth or well-flavored stock, and simmer for twenty minutes.

MARCH 20

BREAKFAST
    Strawberries with cream
    Boiled eggs
    Dry toast
    Coffee

LUNCHEON
    Raisin cocktail
    Consommé in cups
    Broiled shad roe with bacon
    Cold roast beef
    Cole slaw
    French pastry
    Coffee

DINNER
    Purée Célestine
    Radishes
    Paupiettes of bass
    Mutton chops, Milanaise
    Peas, farmer style
    Homemade apple pudding
    Coffee

Broiled shad roe with bacon. Season four shad roes with salt and pepper, lay in oil, and broil. When done place on platter and cover with maître d'hôtel sauce. Lay eight crisp-broiled slices of bacon on top of the roe, and garnish with quartered lemon and parsley.

Purée Célestine. Same as purée of potatoes.

Purée of potatoes. Peel four well-washed white potatoes, and cut in pieces. Put in a vessel with one quart of stock and two cut-up stalks of leeks, and boil until done. Then strain through a fine sieve, put back in vessel, season with salt and pepper, add two ounces of butter, and stir well until the butter is melted.

Paupiettes of bass. Cut four fillets of bass about one-quarter of an inch thick, two inches wide and six inches long. Lay them flat on the table and spread with a thin layer of fish dumpling preparation. Roll them up and place standing in a buttered sauté pan, season with salt and white pepper, add one-half glass of white wine and one-half cup of stock or hot water, cover with buttered paper, and put in oven for fifteen minutes. Then remove the fish to a platter, reduce the broth until nearly dry, add one pint of white wine sauce, strain, and pour over the fish. Decorate the tops with chopped hard-boiled eggs, chopped parsley, and lobster corals chopped very fine.

Lobster corals. In lobsters may be found a solid red substance which is known as lobster corals. Remove the corals from a boiled lobster, put on a covered plate and dry on the stove until very hard. Chop fine, and use for decorating fish, salads, etc. It will keep a long time in a dry place.

Raisin cocktail. Soak seedless raisins in sherry wine for fifteen minutes, then put a heaping spoonful in each cocktail glass. Make a sauce of tomato ketchup, tobasco sauce, celery seed, and the juice of two lemons; allowing the latter to a half pint of ketchup. Add a few chopped almonds, fill the glasses and chill, or serve with ice around the glasses.

Homemade apple pudding. Fry four sliced apples in a little butter and a pinch of powdered cinnamon. Cut half of a five cent loaf of milk bread into small squares, mix with the apple and put in a pudding mould. Mix half a pound of sugar with four eggs and one quart of milk, strain, and pour into the mould. Allow to soak for a half hour, and bake in a moderate oven.

Maraschino sauce for iced pudding. One-half pint of cream, one pony of maraschino, one-quarter of a pound of sugar. Beat all together until a little thick, and serve very cold.

MARCH 21

BREAKFAST
  Oatmeal and cream
  Broiled kippered herring
  Baked potatoes
  Rolls
  Coffee

LUNCHEON
  Canapé St. Francis
  Eggs, Carême
  Hot buckwurst with potato salad
  Limburger cheese and crackers
  Coffee

DINNER
  Potage Eliza
  Terrapin, Maryland
  Beef tongue, Parisian style
  Potatoes Ritz
  Beans, Normandy
  Hearts of lettuce
  Savarin au kirsch
  Coffee

Broiled kippered herring. Kippered herring may be obtained in cans. Dip in oil and broil very lightly, cover with maître d'hôtel sauce, and garnish with lemon and parsley.

Eggs, Carême. Butter a shirred egg dish, crack two eggs into it, and season with salt and pepper. Slice a truffle and a few canned mushrooms, mix with a little cream sauce, and pour over the eggs. Bake in oven.

Hot buckwurst. Secure the buckwurst from your butcher, lay them in boiling water for ten minutes, but do not let the water boil after they have been put in it.

Potage Eliza. Same as potage santé.

How to boil terrapin. Put two live terrapin into boiling water and leave for two minutes. Then remove the outer skin from the feet, neck and head, with a towel. Put the terrapin in a kettle with two quarts of cold water, an onion, a carrot, a bay leaf, and one clove, and boil until the feet are soft. The time required depends upon the age of the terrapin, some being cooked in fifteen minutes, and others requiring two or three hours. When done open the shell, take out all the meat, and the liver, removing the gall from the latter with scissors. Remove the tail and claws and head. Cut up the legs in inch-long pieces, or at the joints, as preferred. Reduce the broth by boiling down to about a cupful, and put in a jar with the meat, and add a whiskey glass of sherry wine. The terrapin is then ready to prepare in any style desired.

Terrapin, Maryland. Put one cup of terrapin, prepared as above, in a flat pan, add a little grated nutmeg, salt and pepper, and half a glass of dry sherry. Boil until half reduced, then add a cup of thick cream, boil, and thicken with the yolks of two eggs, a quarter of a cup of thick cream and an ounce of butter beaten together. Heat, but do not boil. Serve in chafing dish, with dry sherry, and toast on the side.

Terrapin, Jockey club. Same as Terrapin, Maryland. Before serving add two ponies of Cognac and six slices of truffles.

Terrapin, Baltimore. One cup of the prepared terrapin without the liver. Put in saucepan with salt, pepper, nutmeg, celery salt, and a glass of dry sherry. Boil for five minutes. Mash the liver in a salad bowl, add the yolks of two raw eggs, one ounce of sweet butter, and strain through a fine sieve. Add a cup of brown sauce to the simmering terrapin, then add the liver prepared as above, pouring in gradually. Heat barely enough to thicken. Before serving add half a glass of dry sherry.

MARCH 22

BREAKFAST
Fresh raspberries with cream
Scrambled eggs with smoked beef
Rolls
Coffee

LUNCHEON
Grapefruit en suprême
Crab meat, Monza
Loin of pork, baker's oven style
Field salad
Prune soufflé   Coffee

DINNER
Little Neck clams
White bean soup
Salt codfish, Nova Scotia
Fried chicken, Vienna style
Corn fritters   Mashed potatoes
Romaine salad
Diplomate pudding, glacé   Coffee

Crab in chafing dish. Mince a shallot onion and brown slightly with two spoonfuls of butter. Add a spoonful of flour, mixing well, then add a half pint of sweet milk, and stir to a smooth cream. Add the meat of a California crab (or six eastern crabs) and a tablespoonful of sherry. Place toast, cut in fancy shapes, on a deep platter, and cover with the crab. This is a favorite way of preparing crab.

Crab meat au gratin. Shred the meat of one crab, mix with a cup of cream sauce and a little paprika, or Cayenne; or if this is too strong use white pepper. Fill individual baking dishes, and sprinkle the top liberally with grated Parmesan cheese. Bake in an oven until the top is an even brown.

Crab meat, Gourmet. Put a quarter of a pound of picked shrimps in a saucepan, add one ounce of butter and one-half whiskey-glassful of dry sherry wine. Simmer for five minutes, then add the meat of one crab, prepared Monza.

Crab meat, Suzette. Bake four good-sized potatoes, and cut off one side like the cover of a box. Scoop the insides out with a spoon, and fill with the meat of one crab prepared in cream. Sprinkle some grated Parmesan or Swiss cheese on top, and bake in oven until nice and brown. Serve on napkins, garnished with parsley in branches and quartered lemons.

Oysters or crab, à la Poulette. If for oysters, boil them in their own liquid for about five minutes. If the small California oysters are used boil for half that time. Into this liquid of, say, a pint of oysters, stir a heaping teaspoonful of corn starch mixed with a half pint of white wine. Then beat the yolks of two eggs with half a cup of cream, and stir slowly into the above, add two large spoonfuls of butter, and keep on the stove but do not let it boil. Finally squeeze in the juice of half a small lemon. If crab is used, cut the meat in small pieces, and make the sauce in the same manner, but instead of beginning with the juice of oysters for the foundation of the sauce, begin with a cup and a half of cream and water in equal proportions, thicken with corn starch, then add the yolks of eggs, etc., as above. The oysters or the crab meat should be added last.

Crab meat, à la Louise. Have the crab meat thoroughly chilled, and allow one crab to three or four people, according to the size of the fish. Use small fancy fish plates, or salad plates. Lay on each plate some slices of the white hearts of firm heads of lettuce. Lay on top some canned Spanish pimentos, using the brilliant red variety, which is sweet. On top of this place the crab meat, taking care not to break it too small. Over all pour French dressing made with tarragon vinegar, well-seasoned with freshly-ground black pepper.

MARCH 23

BREAKFAST
  Hominy and cream
  Ham and eggs
  Rolls
  Coffee

LUNCHEON
  Sardines with lemon
  Clam broth in cups
  Sand dabs, meunière
  Plain boiled potatoes
  Asparagus, vinaigrette
  Edam cheese and crackers
  Coffee

DINNER
  Potage Coquelin
  Radishes and olives
  Broiled pompano, Havanaise
  Leg of mutton, Clamart
  Rissolées potatoes
  Lettuce and tomato salad
  Fancy ice cream
  Assorted cakes
  Coffee

SUPPER
  Eggs Pocahontas

Eggs Pocahontas. Fry six strips of bacon, and two dozen California, or one dozen Blue Point, oysters. Scramble ten eggs and mix with the above. Season well.

Potage Coquelin. Garnish purée of pea soup with chicken and leeks cut Julienne style, and boiled in broth.

Broiled pompano, Havanaise. Serve broiled pompano with a Colbert sauce, to which has been added two red peppers (pimentos), cut Julienne style. Pour the sauce over the fish, or serve separate, as desired.

Leg of mutton, Clamart. Roast leg of mutton garnished with purée of peas. Serve brown gravy.

Lettuce and tomato salad. Put the leaves of a head of lettuce in a salad bowl. In the center place four peeled and sliced, or quartered, tomatoes. Pour one-half cup of French dressing or mayonnaise over the tomatoes.

Crab meat, Belle Helene. Put six whole tomatoes in hot water for fifteen seconds, then cool immediately, and remove the skins. Cut a hole in the tops the size of a quarter of a dollar, scoop out the insides, season the inside of the shells with salt and pepper, fill with crab meat Monza, and bake in oven for ten minutes. Serve on platters, garnished with parsley and quartered lemons.

Prune soufflé. Wash a cupful of prunes thoroughly, and soak them over night. Boil them in the water in which they were soaked, flavoring with half of a vanilla bean, and sweetened with a cupful of sugar. When done pour off and save the juice. Strain the pulp through a colander or wire sieve, making a good firm purée, and about a cupful in quantity. Whip the whites of six eggs until dry, then whip in the prune pulp, and bake in the same manner as an omelette soufflé. Bake on a platter, formed into a symmetrical mound; or in a buttered pudding mould. Serve hot or cold, with a sauce made of the flavored juice in which the prunes were cooked, or it may be served with whipped cream. Other fruit may be prepared in the same manner, if desired.

Salt codfish, Nova Scotia. Soak two pounds of salt codfish in cold water for six hours. Then put in casserole in one pint of water, boil for ten minutes, drain, add one pint of Créole sauce, boil slowly for five minutes, and serve hot with fresh-boiled rice.

MARCH 24

BREAKFAST
    Stewed prunes
    Boiled eggs
    Buttered toast
    English breakfast tea

LUNCHEON
    Crab cocktail, Victor
    Broiled shad roe, ravigote
    Tripe sauté, Lyonnaise
    Château potatoes
    Escarole salad
    Caroline cake
    Coffee

DINNER
    Clam chowder, Boston style
    Fillet of sole, under glass
    Roast chicken
    Julienne potatoes
    Asparagus, Hollandaise
    Baked Alaska
    Coffee

Broiled shad roe, ravigote. Broil the roe, place on a platter, and cover with a sauce made by mixing one-half cup of maître d'hôtel sauce with two chopped vinegar pickles and one teaspoonful of French mustard.

Fillet of sole under glass. Cut the fillets into pieces two inches square. Into a buttered shirred egg dish put a piece of toast; on top of this place the fish, season with salt and pepper, put three fresh mushroom heads on each portion of fish, add a piece of butter about the size of an egg, and over all squeeze the juice of half a lemon, and sprinkle with finely-chopped parsley. Cover with a glass cover, such as used for mushrooms, put in a moderate oven and cook for twenty minutes; being careful that the oven is not hot enough to burn the toast. Then take from the oven, pour velouté sauce and a spoonful of white wine over each portion, and return, to cook for another five minutes. Any other fish may be substituted for sole, if desired.

Clam chowder, Boston style. Put fifty clams, with their liquid, into a saucepan and boil for three minutes. Then set the clams aside, strain the broth and return to the fire. Chop fine, a medium-sized onion, and cut into dice four slices of salt pork. Put a piece of butter into a pan, and fry the pork and onion until light brown in color; stir in two tablespoonfuls of flour and cook thoroughly, add the clam juice, a half pint of rich soup stock, and the same amount of cream, a couple of diced potatoes, and a bit of thyme if the flavor is liked. Cook for about ten minutes. Chop the clams, and add last of all, as they do not require much cooking. Just before serving add a few hard crackers broken into bits.

Crab cocktail, Victor. Place a boiled crab on ice and chill thoroughly, then remove the meat, taking care not to break the pieces more than necessary. Make a sauce with three-quarters of a cup of tomato ketchup, a teaspoonful of Worcestershire sauce, two tablespoonfuls of tarragon vinegar, and a good pinch of freshly-ground pepper. Mix with the crab meat, fill the cocktail glasses, place them in cracked ice, and serve.

Baked Alaska. (Individual). Slice some sponge cake about one-half inch thick, and cut with a round cutter two inches in diameter. Place the discs of cake on a silver platter, put a ball of vanilla cream in the center of each, and cover with meringue paste. Make the meringue with the whites of four eggs, beaten well and mixed with one-half pound of powdered sugar. Use a pastry bag with a fancy tube, and cover carefully; dust with powdered sugar, and bake in a very hot oven for a couple of minutes. Put a French cherry on top of each before serving.

MARCH 25

BREAKFAST
Fresh strawberries with cream
Bacon with eggs
Rolls
Coffee

LUNCHEON
Grapefruit with cherries
Chicken broth with rice
Crab meat, Gourmet
Rolled veal, Huguenin
Onions, Hongroise
Camembert cheese, crackers Coffee

DINNER
Toke Points on half shell
Potage Esau
Shrimps with mushrooms
Rack of lamb, mint sauce
String beans   Potato croquettes
Chiffonnade salad
Peach Melba
Assorted cakes   Coffee

Rolled veal, Huguenin. Cut four thin slices of veal and flatten out smoothly. Chop fine two young green onions and two slices of bacon; and crush and chop fine, half of a clove of garlic, add a little pepper, and spread over the veal, roll up tight and tie with a string. In a saucepan put a piece of butter the size of an egg, and the veal, and simmer for three-quarters of an hour, basting frequently. Before serving season with salt and sprinkle with parsley.

Shrimps with mushrooms. Fry two cups of shrimps and half a cup of fresh mushrooms in plenty of butter. Season with nutmeg, salt and pepper, and the juice of half a lemon. Add two spoonfuls of tomato sauce, half a cup of stock, and a few bread crumbs. Sprinkle with chopped parsley.

Onions, Hongroise. Chop fine a large Bermuda onion, cover with water, and cook until tender. Drain, add half a pound of fresh cream cheese, a pint of sweet cream, a large can of pimentos, and a teaspoonful of paprika. Serve in a chafing dish. Do not salt.

Peach Melba. Peel some large fresh peaches, and cook them whole in a light syrup; or use whole preserved peaches. From vanilla ice cream, that is frozen very hard, cut some round pieces about three inches in diameter and an inch thick. Place the ice cream on plates, place a peach on the center of each, and pour Melba sauce over them.

Raspberry Melba sauce. Mix well a half pint of strained raspberry pulp, the juice of one lemon, and half a pound of powdered sugar; place in an earthen pot and let it set over night. Then pack in ice, stir well, add a cup of powdered sugar, and stir every half hour until smooth and thick. Keep in ice until used.

Potage Esau. Same as purée of lentils.

Diplomate pudding glacé. Mix in a bowl one pint of preserved fruit; or fresh fruit that has been cooked in syrup; cut in small dices, add a pony of kirsch and one of maraschino, and allow to macerate for one hour. Beat the yolks of four eggs with a quarter of a pound of sugar and half of a split vanilla bean, over the fire, until light and creamy; then remove from the fire and continue beating until cold. Then add one pint of whipped cream and the prepared fruit, and mix well together. Put in a pudding mould, pack in ice and rock salt, and freeze for about two hours. Serve with cold brandy sauce with chopped fruit in it.

MARCH 26

BREAKFAST
Preserved figs
Omelet with tomatoes
Rolls
Coffee

LUNCHEON
Hors d'oeuvres variés
Sand dabs, meunière
Broiled rump steak
French fried potatoes
Smothered onions
Romaine salad
Eclairs   Coffee

DINNER
Viennese bean soup
Crab meat en Bellevue
Chicken, Tyrolienne
Boiled rice
Asparagus, Hollandaise
Strawberry pie   Coffee

Viennese bean soup. Wash a pint of beans, then put them in water and let them soak over night. Then put in a vessel with three quarts of water and a quarter of a pound of lean salt pork, and cook slowly for three hours, by which time the beans should be done. Meanwhile mince an onion, a large carrot, and a stalk of celery; fry them in butter, but do not brown. Add a spoonful of flour and two cups of the beans, making a thick sauce; add this to the beans in the pot, and cook slowly for another hour. Season to taste, and sprinkle with chopped parsley before serving. Cut the pork in very thin slices, and serve one slice to each plate.

Chicken, Tyrolienne. Joint a tender fowl, and dust lightly with flour. Put into a pan with plenty of butter, and simmer slowly for about fifteen minutes, turning frequently so it will become brown on all sides. Then sprinkle liberally with salt and pepper, add a spoonful of sherry and half a cup of brown gravy, a slice of boiled ham diced fine, and one large tomato cut in small pieces. Simmer slowly again for ten minutes. Dish up on a platter, sprinkle with chopped parsley, and garnish with apples fried in butter.

Peach pie. Slice about five peaches for each pie, add sugar and cinnamon to taste, cover, and finish in the same manner as apple pie. For preserved peaches very little sugar is required.

Apricot, pear and pineapple pies. Make in the same manner as peach pie.

Strawberry pie. Clean and wash the berries, and add three ounces of sugar for each pie. Line the pie plate with dough, and put a handful of biscuit crumbs on the bottom, before putting in the berries. The crumbs will prevent the juice from running.

Raspberry, blackberry, huckleberry, gooseberry, currant, grape and cherry pies, prepare in the same manner as strawberry pie.

English gooseberry pie. Fill a deep china vegetable dish with gooseberries, add one-quarter pound of sugar and two cloves to each individual dish, wet the edges of the dish, cover with pie dough, wash the top with eggs, and bake. When done dust the top with powdered sugar, allow to cool, and serve cream separate.

English huckleberry or currant pie, same as English gooseberry pie.

English rhubarb pie. Remove the outer skin from rhubarb, cut in small pieces, and prepare the same as English gooseberry pie.

English grape pie. Same as gooseberry, but use a little less sugar.

MARCH 27

BREAKFAST
Sliced oranges
Omelet with kidneys
Rolls
Coffee

LUNCHEON
Indian canapé
Rack of lamb, jardinière
Lettuce salad
Floating island
Lady fingers   Coffee

DINNER
Cream of chicken, à la Reine   Queen olives
Fillet of rock cod, Nantaise
Sweetbreads braisé, Henri IV
Julienne potatoes
Fresh artichokes, sauce mousseline
Paté de foie gras   Lettuce salad
Pudding à la Rossini   Coffee

Omelet with kidneys. Make a plain omelet, and before turning over on platter put a small spoonful of kidney stew (see kidney stew), in the center. Put some stewed kidneys at each end of the omelet.

Rack of lamb. Have the butcher cut a rack of lamb consisting of about ten chops. Season with salt and pepper, and put in a small roasting pan with a sliced onion and carrot, and two ounces of butter. Put in a hot oven to roast, basting every few seconds so it will not become dry. If necessary, add a spoonful of water to prevent the vegetables from burning. After twenty minutes remove the lamb to a platter, and add a spoonful of flour to the pan, and simmer for five minutes; then add one cup of stock or hot water, and one spoonful of meat extract. Season, strain, and pour over the rack of lamb. Garnish with fresh watercress.

Rack of lamb, jardinière. Garnish the lack of lamb with a bouquet of peas, and a bouquet of string beans, cauliflower, spring carrots in butter, or any kind of fresh vegetables. Some kind of potatoes, such as Parisian, Julienne, etc., may be added, if desired.

Sweetbreads braisé, Henry IV. Braised sweetbreads with sauce Béarnaise, garnished with Julienne potatoes, and sliced truffles cut in triangles, placed on top of the sweetbreads.

Pudding à la Rossini. Cut six large thin pancakes in strips one inch wide, and line a buttered pudding mould with them, one overlapping the other. Boil a pint of milk, add one-quarter of a pound of flour to it, and stir well to a thick batter; then remove from the fire, whip in one-quarter pound of sugar and two ounces of butter, two ounces of grated cocoanut, the rind of a lemon, and the yolks of six eggs. Beat the whites of six eggs very stiff and add, mixing lightly. Fill the lined pudding mould, and bake in a slow oven for about forty minutes. Serve hot, with orange sauce.

Orange sauce. Boil together one pint of water, one-half pound of sugar, and the grated rind of an orange. While boiling, stir in one teaspoonful of corn starch dissolved in a little cold water, boil for a few minutes, remove from the fire and add the juice of one or two oranges. Strain.

Lemon sauce. Same as orange sauce, using lemons instead of oranges, and in the same proportions.

Fillet of rock cod, Nantaise. Season four fillets of rock cod with salt and pepper, dip in oil and broil. When done place on platter and cover with the following butter: Press six sardines through a fine sieve, mix with two ounces of butter, the juice of two lemons, and some chopped parsley.

MARCH 28

BREAKFAST
    Fresh strawberries with cream
    Boiled eggs
    Dry toast
    Coffee

LUNCHEON
    Matjes herring, potato salad
    Chicken croquettes, cream sauce
    Asparagus tips
    Tapioca pudding
    Coffee

DINNER
    Giblet soup, à l'Anglaise
    Radishes
    Terrapin, Jockey Club
    Baby lamb steak, horticulture
    Escarole salad
    Bavarois noisettes
    Alsatian wafers
    Coffee

Matjes herring. This is an imported salted herring. Lay six herrings in cold water for an hour, and then clean. Put them in a stone pot, add a sliced onion, one-quarter cup of whole black pepper berries, two bay leaves, four cloves, one-half cup of vinegar, two cups of cream, and a little salt if necessary. Allow to stand for a couple of days, and then serve on lettuce leaves, with its own sauce, and with sliced lemon on top.

Baby lamb steak, horticulture. Cut a steak from the leg of a spring lamb, season with salt and pepper, roll in oil, and broil. When done dish up on a platter, cover with Madeira sauce, and garnish with different vegetables, such as peas, carrots, stuffed tomatoes, stuffed peppers, string beans, cauliflower, asparagus tips, artichokes, etc. Arrange the vegetables in bouquets, and use as many kinds as you desire.

Bavarois noisette. The yolks of eight eggs, one quart of milk, one-half of a split vanilla bean, one-half pound of sugar, one-quarter pound of ground hazelnuts, one pint of whipped cream, and five sheets of French gelatine. Boil the milk with the vanilla. Roast the hazelnuts, grind, or chop them very fine, and mix with the yolks of eggs and sugar. Add the boiling milk, and stir over the fire until it thickens, but do not let it boil. Remove from the fire and add the gelatine (which has been washed) in cold water, and stir with a spoon until melted. Allow to become cold, remove the vanilla bean, add the whipped cream, mix well, put in a fancy mould, and set in the ice box for two hours. Serve with whipped cream with chopped hazelnuts in it.

Indian Canapé. Use one hard-boiled egg for each person to be served, and force through a sieve. For six eggs add a quarter of a pound of sweet butter, a half teaspoonful of curry, and beat into a smooth paste. Toward the last add a tablespoonful of cream. Spread over toast, and place a little chopped chutney on top of each.

Pommes d'arbre, 1915 (apple, 1915). Peel and core six apples and cook them in syrup, with the addition of half of a vanilla bean. Drain, and allow to become cold. Make a cream sauce with half a pint of cream, two ounces of sugar, and two sheets of gelatine, and pour over the apples, coating them nice and smooth. Sprinkle the top with nonpareil candies, and place in ice box. Serve in suprême glasses, with vanilla cream in the bottom of the glass.

MARCH 29

BREAKFAST
    Oatmeal and cream
    Broiled kippered herrings
    Lyonnaise potatoes
    Rolls
    English breakfast tea

LUNCHEON
    Omelet with soft clams
    Blood pudding
    Mashed turnips
    Mashed potatoes
    Roquefort cheese and crackers
    Coffee

DINNER
    German lentil soup
    Salted almonds
    Crab meat, au gratin
    Tournedos, Rossini
    Château potatoes
    Chiffonade salad
    Pommes d'arbre, 1915
    Assorted cakes
    Coffee

German lentil soup. To a purée of lentils, add before serving, some sliced Frankfurter sausages, and a little bacon cut in small strips and fried.

Quince jelly. To each pound of cut-up quinces add a cup of water, put in a kettle and stew until soft. Then put in a jelly bag to drain, but do not crush. Add a pound of sugar to each pint of liquor, boil gently until the sugar is dissolved, then boil more quickly. Pour into glasses, and when cold cover with paraffine.

Preserved pears. Peel, halve, and remove the cores from Bartlett or Seckle pears. Allow one pound of sugar to each pound of fruit. Put the sugar on to melt, with a few spoonfuls of water. Stick a clove in each piece of fruit, and boil in the sugar until thoroughly done. Put the fruit in glass jars, cover with the syrup, and seal. The rind of one lemon to every five pounds of fruit may be used instead of the cloves, if desired, or both may be used.

Pineapple preserves. Pare and slice the pineapples, then weigh out one pound of cane sugar to each pound of fruit. Put a layer of the slices in a stone jar, sprinkle with the sugar, continue until fruit and sugar are used up, and allow to stand over night. Then remove the pineapple and cook the syrup until it thickens, add the fruit, and boil for fifteen minutes, remove the fruit and let it cool, then put in jars and pour the syrup over it. A very little ginger root boiled in the syrup will improve it.

Citron preserves. Pare some sound fruit, divide into quarters, remove the seeds, and cut in small pieces. To every pound of fruit allow one-half pound of granulated cane sugar. Cook the citron in water until quite clear, then drain through a colander. Melt the sugar with a few spoonfuls of water, and boil until very clear, then put in the drained citron, add two sliced large lemons, a small piece of ginger root, and cook for about fifteen minutes. Fill the jars with the citron, and cover with the syrup.

MARCH 30

BREAKFAST
Honey in comb
Scrambled eggs with chives
Rolls
Coffee

LUNCHEON
Canapé of fresh Astrachan caviar
Saddle of hare, sour cream sauce
Palestine potatoes
Spatzle
Green peas au beurre
French pastry   Coffee

DINNER
Lobster chowder
Ripe California olives
Broiled barracouda
Roast leg of lamb, mint sauce
String beans
Alsatian potatoes
Escarole salad
Biscuit Tortoni
Assorted cakes
Coffee

Scrambled eggs with chives. Make some plain scrambled eggs, and just before serving add some finely-cut chives, mix, and season well.

Sweet potato croquettes. Boil four large potatoes in salt water, when soft, peel, and pass through a sieve. Then put in a casserole, add two ounces of butter, the yolks of three eggs, season with salt and pepper, and mix well. When cold, roll in flour, shape in the form of a large cork, then roll in beaten eggs and bread crumbs, and fry in very hot swimming lard. When nice and brown serve on a napkin.

Palestine potatoes. Sweet potato croquettes formed in the shape of a small pear. When fried, dress on a napkin with the pointed end up, and stick a sprig of parsley in the top.

Alsatian potatoes. Put in a casserole two ounces of butter and one chopped onion, and simmer until golden yellow. Add four potatoes cut in small dices, one bay leaf, one clove, one cup of water, and season with salt and pepper. Cover, and simmer slowly for thirty minutes. Add fresh chopped parsley before serving.

Biscuit Tortoni. Same as biscuit glacé, with the addition of a pony of good maraschino and two ounces of macaroon crumbs. To make the crumbs, crush some dry macaroons and pass through a sieve or colander. Put in round paper cases, filling above the edge, and allow to set in ice box for several hours until frozen. Dip the top of the biscuit in macaroon crumbs before serving.

Saddle of hare, sour cream sauce. Remove the skins from the saddles of two hares, and lard them with thin strips of larding pork. Put them in an agate pan, add a little salt, and one-half cup of whole black peppers wrapped in cheese cloth. Cover with from two to three quarts of sour cream, and stand in a cool place for forty-eight hours. Then put the saddles in a roasting pan with a sliced onion and carrot, and a little butter on top, and roast in a hot oven for about ten minutes, or until brown. Then strain the sour cream, and add little by little to the saddles, while roasting. Baste continually, and after forty minutes you should have a nice brown sauce. Remove the saddles to a platter, reduce the sauce one-half, season with salt if necessary, and a little paprika, strain part over the saddles, and serve the remainder in a bowl.

MARCH 31

BREAKFAST
  Hothouse raspberries with cream
  Browned corned beef hash
  Poached eggs on toast
  Rolls
  Coffee

LUNCHEON
  Grapefruit with cherries
  Frogs' legs, sauté à sec
  Lamb chops
  Watercress salad
  French fried potatoes
  Camembert cheese with crackers
  Coffee

DINNER
  Petite marmite
  Radishes
  Crab à la Louis
  Boiled beef, horseradish sauce
  Boiled potatoes
  Stuffed cabbage
  Hearts of lettuce salad
  Apple water ice
  Cakes
  Coffee

Corned beef hash. Chop an onion very fine and put in a casserole with two ounces of butter. Simmer until the onion is cooked, then add two pounds of boiled corned beef cut in small dices, and one pound of boiled potatoes cut very small, or chopped. Mix well, season with a little pepper, and salt if necessary, add one cup of bouillon, and simmer for ten minutes. Before serving add a little chopped parsley.

Browned corned beef hash. Same as above, but use only one-half cup of bouillon. Before serving put the hash in a frying pan with two ounces of butter, and allow it to brown. Serve in the shape of an omelet.

Corned beef hash au gratin. Make a corned beef hash and put in a buttered, deep, silver vegetable dish, sprinkle with bread crumbs, put a small piece of butter on top, and bake in oven until brown.

Lamb cutlets in papers. Fry the cutlets in a sauté pan, in melted fat pork, turning frequently. Brown only slightly, allowing them to remain rare. Then remove the cutlets, and in the fat simmer some minced onions, mushrooms and parsley for a few minutes. When nearly done add some shredded lean ham. Now prepare some oiled paper, tearing it heart-shaped, lay the cutlet on one half, surrounding it with the minced herbs, with a little on top also; then fold over the paper, creasing the edges together like a hem. Lay on a buttered dish, and set in oven until nicely colored.

Purée of onions (Soubise). Peel and slice one dozen large white onions, put in a casserole with one-quarter pound of butter, cover, and put in oven for about forty-five minutes, or until soft; but do not allow them to become brown. Then drain off the butter and add one pint of thick cream sauce, season well with salt and white pepper, and strain through a fine sieve.

Apple water ice. See Normandy water ice.

APRIL 1

BREAKFAST
Fresh strawberries with cream
Boiled eggs
Dry toast
Coffee

LUNCHEON
Canapé Romanoff
Eggs, Voltaire
Tripe à la mode de Caen
Baked potatoes
Coffee éclairs   Demi tasse

DINNER
Cream of chicken, Reine Hortense
Ripe olives
Terrapin Baltimore
Roast saddle of mutton   Château potatoes
Braised sweetbreads, Marie Louise
Lettuce salad
Pears in syrup
Lady fingers   Coffee

SUPPER
Venetian egg in chafing dish

Venetian egg in chafing dish. Mince an onion and cook in sauté pan in two ounces of butter, then add half a can of firm tomatoes and cook for twenty minutes. Add a pound of eastern cheese, broken into small bits; season with salt, paprika, a little Worcestershire sauce, and half a teaspoonful of mustard. Stir continuously. Last, add three lightly beaten eggs, and stir until thick. It should be of the same consistency as a Welsh rabbit. Serve either with, or on, toast or toasted crackers.

Eggs, Voltaire. In the bottom of a buttered cocotte or egg dish place a spoonful of chicken hash, on top break a raw egg, and season. Cover with cream sauce and grated cheese. Bake until the tops are brown.

Cream of chicken, Reine Hortense. Make a cream of chicken soup in the usual way. Take a cup of peeled almonds to each quart of the soup, pound into a pulp in a mortar, pulverizing thoroughly; mix with milk, strain, and add to the soup.

Canapé Romanoff. Mix a boxful of smoked Norwegian sardines with three ounces of hot butter, mash fine, and force through a sieve. Stir in four spoonfuls of cream, and spread over toast cut in fancy shapes. Garnish with ripe and green olives. Serve as a fancy sandwich at tea or bridge parties, or as an appetiser for dinner.

Braised sweetbreads, Marie Louise. Soak the sweetbreads in cold water for no less than three hours, changing the water two or three times. This draws all the blood from the sweetbreads. Then put into a large pot, with plenty of cold water, and bring to the boiling point; then drench with cold water to cool. In a saucepan put a sliced carrot, a sliced onion, a bay leaf, a clove, parsley in branches, a piece of salt pork rind, butter the size of half an egg, and one cup of stock or broth of any kind. Place the sweetbreads on top, and place in oven and cook for half an hour, basting frequently. The sweetbreads should turn an even yellow. Trim some artichoke bottoms, cut in half, and place the sweetbreads on top. Mix the juice from the baked sweetbreads with a cup of cream sauce and a sherry glassful of dry sherry. Pour this over the top, sprinkle with chopped parsley, and return to oven for two minutes.

Pears in syrup. Make a syrup with a cup of sugar, and water enough to cover. Add the juice or rind of a lemon, a few cloves, and a stick of cinnamon. Quarter the pears, remove the cores, and cook in the syrup for eight or ten minutes, or until tender. Old hard pears may require a half an hour or more before they are sufficiently cooked. A little claret or white wine may be added, if desired.

APRIL 2

BREAKFAST
Preserved figs with cream
Ham and eggs
Rolls
Coffee

LUNCHEON
Terrine de foie gras à la gelée
Eggs, Texas clover
Broiled squab with fresh mushrooms
French fried potatoes
Romaine salad
Brie cheese and crackers
Coffee

DINNER
Blue Point oysters on half shell
Clear green turtle soup, au Madère
Queen olives
Crab poulette
Roast chicken
Fresh asparagus, Hollandaise
Rissolée potatoes
Sliced tomatoes, French dressing
Omelette Robespierre
Coffee

Eggs, Texas clover. Chop a green pepper, put in casserole with one ounce of butter, and simmer until the peppers are soft; then add ten beaten eggs, season with salt and pepper, and scramble. Before serving add a dozen par-boiled oysters, a little cream, and a piece of fresh butter.

Terrine de foie gras à la gelée. Serve as an appetiser, cold, with meat jelly. The foie gras comes from Europe, being a particular specialty of Stras-bourg, Alsace. It is a goose liver pie, baked in terrines.

Broiled squab. Split the squab, season well, roll in oil and broil. Serve on a piece of freshly-made toast, cover with maître d'hôtel sauce, and garnish with half a lemon and watercress.

Broiled squab with fresh mushrooms. Prepare as above, with the addi-tion of four broiled heads of fresh mushrooms on top of the squab.

Clear green turtle soup. May be made from live turtle, or the Florida canned turtle, which is the most common for home use. Put a can of green turtle meat in a pot and bring to a boil, then drain off the broth, and save. Cut the meat in one-half inch squares. In a casserole put one sprig of thyme, one sprig of sweet basilic herb, one glass of sherry, and reduce until nearly dry. Then add two quarts of strong consommé, bring to a boil, and thicken with a soupspoonful of arrowroot diluted with a little cold water. Add the arrow-root while the consommé is boiling. After boiling for five minutes strain through a fine cloth, put back in the casserole, add the turtle meat, and season with salt and Cayenne pepper. Before serving add a glass of very old Madeira and the turtle juice.

Omelette Robespierre. Take six canned apricots, or six fresh apricots boiled in syrup, and cut in one-quarter inch squares. Make an omelette with ten eggs, and with very little salt. Make the omelet soft. Put on a platter, sprinkle with plenty of powdered sugar, and burn with a red-hot poker. Warm the apricots, and put at both ends of the omelet; pour two ponies of absinthe over the top, and light before bringing to the table. Anisette liqueur may be used in place of the absinthe if more convenient.

APRIL 3

BREAKFAST
Fresh raspberries with cream
Broiled Yarmouth bloaters
Potatoes hashed in cream
Rolls
Coffee

LUNCHEON
Eggs, St. Laurent
Clam broth in cups
Planked shad and roe
Chicory and beet salad
Cream puffs   Demi tasse

DINNER
Oyster soup, family style
Radishes
Fillet of turbot, Nesles   Fondante potatoes
Salmon steak, Chambord sauce
Peas au cerfeuil
Hot baked apples
Macaroons   Coffee

Poached eggs, St. Laurent. Put four slices of smoked salmon on four pieces of toast, and set in oven for a minute, to warm the salmon. Then lay a poached egg on each piece, and cover with cream sauce.

Planked shad and roe. Split a shad and lay on a buttered plank, with the roe on the side. Season with salt and pepper and bits of butter, and put in a moderate oven. After fifteen minutes turn over the roe, and leave in the oven for another two minutes. Then take out and make a border around the fish with potato croquette preparation, and bake again until the border is brown. Serve with maître d'hôtel butter, and garnish with quartered lemons and parsley in branches.

Fillet of turbot, Nesles. Put four fillets of turbot in a buttered pan, season with salt and a little Cayenne pepper, add a cup of cream, and boil for twelve minutes. Then remove the fillets to a platter, add to the cream in the pan a cup of cream sauce, bring to the boiling point, then add two spoonfuls of grated cheese, and pour over the fish. Have the sauce well seasoned.

Fondante potatoes. Cut a quart of small potatoes to the size of pigeons' eggs, put in a casserole and cover with cold water, add a pinch of salt, and bring to a boil. Then drain off the water and put the potatoes in a flat sauté pan with two ounces of butter, and simmer very slowly until they are golden yellow. Then add a spoonful of chicken broth and simmer again until nearly dry. Sprinkle with fresh-chopped parsley, season with salt and pepper.

Chicken sauté, chasseur. Joint a chicken, and season with salt and pepper. In a sauté pan put one ounce of butter and a spoonful of olive oil, heat, and then add the chicken. When the chicken is golden yellow add three chopped shallots, and simmer, but not enough to color the shallots. Then add one gill of white wine and boil for two minutes; add one peeled and chopped tomato and half of a can of French mushrooms, and boil for ten minutes more. Finally add half a dozen small onions glacé, and then dress the chicken on a platter. Season the sauce well, reduce one-half, add a little chopped parsley, and pour over the chicken.

Roast saddle of mutton. Secure the saddle from the butcher ready prepared for roasting. Put a sliced onion and carrot in a roasting pan, place the saddle on top, season well with salt and pepper, put a piece of butter on top, and place in hot oven. Bast frequently. It will require from thirty-five to forty-five minutes to roast, depending upon the thickness. When done, place the saddle on a platter, drain off the fat in the pan, add a half cup of stock and a spoonful of meat extract, and bring to a boil. Strain and pour over the saddle. Serve hot.

APRIL 4

BREAKFAST
  Guava jelly
  Oatmeal with cream
  Rolls
  Cocoa with whipped cream

LUNCHEON
  Grapefruit and orange en surprise
  Eggs, Crossy
  Chicken sauté, chasseur
  Parisian potatoes
  Endives salad
  Soufflé au fromage
  Coffee

DINNER
  Potage Solferino
  Ripe olives
  Brook trout, sauté meunière
  Roast leg of lamb, mint sauce
  Stewed asparagus
  Rissolées potatoes
  Neapolitan ice cream
  Assorted cakes
  Coffee

Eggs, Crossy. Make a cupful of purée of spinach and spread on four round pieces of toast, lay a poached egg on top of each, and pour a little brown gravy around them.

Soufflé au fromage. Heat a pint of milk in a double boiler. Mix a quarter of a pound of butter with a quarter of a pound of flour, working them well together, then add to the boiling milk and cook until it thickens. Remove from the fire and add the yolks of six eggs, whipping slightly. Then add a quarter of a pound of grated Parmesan cheese, season with salt and pepper, and stir in the whites of the six eggs, which have been whipped dry. Put into large, or individual, buttered moulds, sprinkle with cheese, and bake for twenty minutes.

Potage Solferino. Cut six fresh tomatoes in pieces and cook in half a cup of consommé until well done. Strain through a fine sieve, and add to two quarts of consommé. Garnish with small squares of carrots and potatoes that have been cooked separately, and peas and chervil.

Brook trout, sauté meunière. Clean and wash well six small brook trout, season with salt and pepper, and roll in flour. Put three ounces of butter in a frying pan, melt, add the fish and sauté till nice and brown. When done put the fish on a platter, sprinkle with chopped parsley and the juice of two lemons. Melt two ounces of fresh butter in the frying pan and pour over the fish. Garnish with quartered lemons and parsley in branches.

Stewed asparagus. Cut off two pounds of tips about one inch in length, from fresh asparagus. Put in casserole and cover with a cup of bouillon, season with salt and pepper, cover, and boil slowly for about eighteen minutes. Then mix half a cupful of water and a spoonful of flour, and pour slowly into the boiling asparagus. Add a little chopped parsley before serving.

Neapolitan ice cream. Fill a brick-shaped mould with three layers of different ices, such as pistache, vanilla and strawberry ice cream, or lemon water ice, strawberry and pistache, or chocolate, ice cream. Cover mould well, and pack in ice and salt, and let stand for an hour. To serve, dip the mould in warm water and remove the ice cream, cut in slices about one inch thick, and crossways of the brick, to show the different colors.

APRIL 5

BREAKFAST
Fresh strawberries with cream
Waffles with maple syrup
Coffee

LUNCHEON
Poached eggs, Jeanne d'Arc
Breaded pork chops, cream sauce
Spaghetti Caruso
Field salad
Roquefort cheese and crackers
Coffee

DINNER
Potato soup à la Faubonne
Radishes and salted almonds
Clams with port wine
Sweetbreads braisé, Clamart
Roast chicken
Sybil potatoes
Cold asparagus, mustard sauce
Almond cake
Coffee

SUPPER
Sandwich Carême

Sandwiches, Carême. Mince fine one-half dozen sweet mixed pickles. Shred the meat of one lobster, and mix with the pickles, season with salt and pepper, and add a whiskey glass of tarragon. Let stand for a few minutes, then squeeze out the vinegar and add half a cup of mayonnaise. Spread over toast or salted crackers. The above may be mixed with three hard-boiled eggs, and served on lettuce leaves as a salad.

Clams with wine sauce. Take as many large clams as you desire to use. Remove from the shells, cut away the neck, retaining only the bellies. Cook in Madeira wine for two or three minutes, then put in half as much sweet cream as you have wine, and heat to boiling. If for six persons, thicken with the yolks of three eggs, add another half cup of rich cream, and season with Cayenne pepper and salt. Serve in a chafing dish, with small thin bits of toast on the side.

Potato soup, Faubonne. Put one quart of purée of potato soup and one quart of consommé Julienne in a casserole and bring to a boil. Bind with the yolks of three eggs mixed with a cup of cream. Serve with a little chopped parsley and chervil.

Sweetbreads braisé, Clamart. Place four sweetbreads braisé on a platter, garnish with a purée of fresh or canned peas, and pour brown gravy around the bottom.

Almond cake. Mix three-quarters of a pound of almond paste, one-half pound of sugar, and four whole eggs, and work until creamy and smooth. Add the yolks of sixteen eggs, one by one, stirring all the while, and flavor with the rind of a lemon. Beat the whites of eight eggs very stiff, and add to the mixture lightly, stirring in at the same time one-half pound of sifted flour. Bake in a cake pan or mould, in a moderate oven. When cold finish with white frosting, and decorate with split almonds.

Almond cream cake. Cut an almond cake in three or four layers and spread between with whipped cream sweetened with vanilla sugar, and mixed with fine-chopped roasted almonds. Cover with white frosting, and decorate with whipped cream and split almonds.

Eggs, Jeanne d'Arc. Place four very soft poached eggs on a buttered dish, cover with a thick tomato sauce, sprinkle with grated cheese, put small bits of butter on top, and bake in a hot oven for two minutes.

APRIL 6

BREAKFAST
  Orange juice
  Buckwheat cakes with maple syrup
  Chocolate with whipped cream

LUNCHEON
  Tartine Russe
  Consommé parfait
  Crab en brochette
  Chow chow
  Chocolate macaroons
  Coffee

DINNER
  Potage Reine Mogador
  Queen olives
  Catfish sauté, meunière
  Roast loin of lamb, au jus
  Timbale of croquette potatoes
  Chiffonnade salad
  Saxony pudding
  Coffee

Tartine Russe. Toasted rye bread, buttered, spread with caviar, and garnished around the edges with chopped boiled eggs, and some chopped beets in the center.

Consommé parfait. To a pint of cold consommé tapioca add three raw eggs and two additional yolks, put in a buttered mould and cook in a bain marie. When done allow to cool, slice, and serve in hot consommé. (This is tapioca royal).

Crab en brochette. Alternate on a skewer a crab leg, then a piece of broiled bacon, and so on, until the skewer is full. Season with salt and pepper, roll in oil and fresh bread crumbs, and broil. When done place on toast, cover with maitre d'hôtel sauce, and garnish with lemon and parsley.

Chocolate macaroons. One pound of almond paste, one pound of granulated sugar, two ounces of melted cocoa, one spoonful of flour, and the whites of five eggs. Mix the almond paste with the sugar, add the whites of eggs, and work well. Then add the cocoa and flour, mix well, and dress on paper, in the same manner as ordinary macaroons. Moisten the tops with a brush, and bake in a moderate oven.

Saxony pudding. Sift one-half pound of flour into a sauce pan, and add a pint of boiling milk and four ounces of butter. Stir with a wooden spoon until the flour is free from the bottom of the pan. Then remove from the fire and add four ounces of sugar and the yolks of eight eggs, four ounces of candied fruit chopped fine, and the whites of six eggs beaten very hard. Put in a mould and cook in bain marie in a moderate oven. When done remove from mould and serve with apricot sauce flavored with kirschwasser. Make the sauce in the same manner as brandy sauce, but use kirschwasser in place of brandy.

Potage Reine Mogador. Half cream of chicken and half purée of potatoes. Bind with the yolks of two eggs and half a cup of cream.

Catfish sauté, meunière. Clean six catfish, season with salt and pepper, roll in milk and then in flour. Melt three ounces of butter in a frying pan, add the fish, and sauté until nice and brown. Then put on a platter, sprinkle with chopped parsley and the juice of two lemons. Add to the sauce in the pan two ounces of fresh butter, and cook until hazelnut brown, then pour over the fish. Garnish with parsley and quartered lemons.

APRIL 7

BREAKFAST
  Fresh raspberries with cream
  Boiled eggs
  Dry toast·
  Coffee

LUNCHEON
  Yarmouth bloaters in oil
  Poached eggs, Talleyrand
  Fricandeau of veal, au jus
  Sorrel   Mashed potatoes
  Pont l'êveque cheese and crackers
  Coffee

DINNER
  Potage Saxe
  Lyon sausages and radishes
  Curried crab
  Sirloin steak, Dickinson   Soufflé potatoes
  Cauliflower au gratin
  Hearts of romaine, roquefort dressing
  Vanilla and chocolate ice cream
  Assorted cakes   Coffee

Yarmouth bloaters in oil. Skin and split four Yarmouth bloaters, and remove the bones. Lay them in an earthen pot, add the juice of one lemon, one-half cup of olive oil, four bay leaves, two cloves and one spoonful of whole black peppers. Allow to stand for twenty-four hours. Serve on lettuce leaves with a little of its juice.

Poached eggs, Talleyrand. On four round pieces of toast spread some foie gras, lay a poached egg on top of each piece, and cover with sauce Perigueux.

Fricandeau of veal, au jus. Obtain from the butcher the nut of a leg of veal and lard it with thin strips of larding pork. Put in a sauté pan a sliced onion and carrot, some parsley in branches, one bay leaf, one clove, and six pepper berries. Place the veal on top, season with salt and pepper, put three ounces of butter on top of all, and roast in a hot oven, basting frequently. Add a little water when necessary, so the vegetables will not burn. It will require from fifty minutes to one hour to cook. When done place the fricandeau on a platter, and boil the gravy; if necessary add a little stock or bouillon, season well, and strain over the veal.

Potage Saxe. To two quarts of boiling consommé add the bread crumbs made from a small loaf of bread, two beaten eggs, and some chopped chervil. Stir well, boil and serve.

Sirloin steak, Dickinson. Broil a steak and place on a platter. Parboil six slices of beef marrow in salt water, and lay on top of the steak. Heat a pimento, cut in triangles, and place on top of the marrow. Cover all with sauce Colbert with sliced truffle in it.

Curried crab. Cut the crab meat into small pieces. Put in a frying pan a piece of butter the size of an egg, and a teaspoonful of chopped onion or shallot, and fry until golden brown. Add a heaping teaspoonful of flour and a small teaspoonful of curry powder, and stir into the butter and onion until thoroughly mixed. Add a cup of hot soup stock and a cup of cream, and boil for three minutes. Then add the crab meat and simmer slowly for about five minutes. Serve with boiled rice.

Spaghetti Caruso. Boil a pound of whole spaghetti in salt water. Soak one pound of dried mushrooms over night. Heat in a casserole two ounces of butter, add a chopped shallot and a little garlic. When hot add the mushrooms and three peeled and cut up tomatoes, and simmer for five minutes. Then add the cooked spaghetti and two cups of grated parmesan cheese, season with salt and white pepper, and serve very hot.

APRIL 8

BREAKFAST
Hominy with cream
Ham and eggs
Rolls
Coffee

LUNCHEON
Grapefruit à l'anisette
Oyster broth in cups
Crackers
Broiled brook trout with bacon
Cucumber salad
Lamb chops, grilled
Julienne potatoes
Chicory salad
French pastry
Coffee

DINNER
Potage Viennoise
Curried oysters with boiled rice
Saddle of mutton with currant jelly
String beans à l'Alsacienne
Laurette potatoes
Dandelion salad
Gastaner pudding
Coffee

Grapefruit à l'anisette. Cut the grapefruit in half and loosen the inside from the skin with a pointed knife. Put a teaspoonful of powdered sugar and a half pony of anisette on each half. Serve on cracked ice.

Oyster broth. In a casserole put two dozen oysters with their own juice, and one quart of water. Add a bouquet garni and put on the fire. When boiling remove the bouquet garni, and strain the broth through a napkin, season with salt and a little Cayenne pepper, and serve in cups. The oysters may be saved for other purposes.

Curried oysters. In a casserole melt three ounces of butter, then add two spoonfuls of flour, one spoonful of curry powder, and one pint of oyster broth. Boil for a minute, then add one apple fried in butter, one tablespoonful of chutney sauce, one teaspoonful of Worcestershire sauce, and a little salt and Cayenne pepper. Boil for five minutes, and bind with the yolk of an egg and a spoonful of cream. Strain the sauce, and add two dozen well-seasoned parboiled oysters.

Pudding à la Gastaner. Decorate the bottoms of buttered moulds with chopped pastry cherries and angelique, arranging in alternating lines of green and red. Cut some lady fingers to fit the depth of the mould, and moisten them well with Curaçao. Stand them up around the inside of the mould one-half inch apart. Cook four ounces of farina in one quart of milk, and mix with the rind and juice of a lemon, five eggs, four ounces of sugar, and one cup of apricot pulp, and fill the moulds with same. Serve with strawberry sauce flavored with a pony of brandy.

Broiled brook trout with bacon. Clean and wash well, one-half dozen brook trout, and dry them on a towel or napkin. Season with salt and pepper, roll in oil, and broil. When done put on a platter with maître d'hôtel sauce. Lay six slices of broiled bacon on top. Garnish with quartered lemons and parsley in branches.

Potage Viennoise. Cream of barley with royal cut in small squares as garnishing.

Potage Venitienne. Half velouté of chicken soup and half consommé tapioca. Add a little chopped chives.

APRIL 9

BREAKFAST
  Grapefruit marmalade
  Shirred eggs
  Dry toast
  Coffee

LUNCHEON
  Eggs St. George
  Lamb cutlets in papers
  Cold asparagus, mayonnaise
  Brown Betty pudding
  Coffee

DINNER
  Potage Venitienne
  Crab in chafing dish
  Roast duckling, apple sauce
  Sweet potato croquettes
  Artichokes, mustard sauce
  Lemon water ice
  Cocoa cake   Coffee

AFTERNOON TEA
  Oysters poulette, or sweetbreads
    Monza   Salted almonds
  Windsor sandwiches
  Cream of almond sandwiches
  Olive sandwiches
  Shrimp salad
  Vanilla ice cream
  Pound cake   Fruit cake
  Apple tarts
  Salted pecans
  Créole sandwiches
  Dubney sandwiches
  Bread and butter sandwiches
  Chicken salad
  Pineapple water ice
  Strawberry pie
  Chocolate, coffee or tea
  Rolls   Toast Melba
  Assorted cakes

Cocoa cake. Half a cup of butter, a cup of sugar, three eggs, a teaspoonful of vanilla, three-fourths of a cup of milk, six level tablespoonfuls of cocoa, two teaspoonfuls of baking powder, and one and three-fourth cups of sifted flour. Cream the butter, adding the sugar gradually, then add the eggs one by one, whipping vigorously. Sift together half of the flour, the cocoa and the baking powder, then add the milk and the rest of the flour, making a mixture that will drop from the spoon. When all is mixed together put in a pan or mould, and bake for thirty-five minutes. Cover the cake with a plain icing. A cake is baked when it shrinks from the pan, or if, when you press it it springs back.

Dubney sandwiches. To a cupful of chopped chicken or turkey meat add a spoonful of mayonnaise, a teaspoonful of minced onion, two minced shallots, a pinch of chopped chives, and season with salt and pepper. Spread on well-buttered warm toast.

Cream of almond sandwiches. Mix a soft cream cheese with a cup of crushed salted almonds, and a liqueur glassful of kirsch. Spread on thin slices of brown bread.

Olive sandwiches. Chop equal parts of olives and onions together, add a few drops of olive oil and a little pepper, but no salt, as the olives have enough. Spread on thin slices of buttered bread.

Windsor sandwiches. Chop enough chicken or turkey to make a cup of meat, add half as much chopped ham, and half a dozen chopped olives. Bind together with mayonnaise. Spread on white and on brown buttered bread.

Creole sandwiches. Chop some fresh or canned sweet peppers, bind together with mayonnaise, and add a bit of minced parsley. Spread on both white and brown bread. Always make the sandwiches dainty and thin.

Brown Betty. Pull half a loaf of white bread to bits, or use bread crumbs. The pulled bread makes the lighter pudding. Butter the inside of a pudding dish liberally, put in a layer of crumbs, then twice as much sliced apple or other fruit, sprinkle with sugar, nutmeg and bits of butter, add another layer of crumbs, and so on, for about three layers, having the crumbs last. Bake until brown, and the fruit well done, or about twenty minutes. Serve with cream.

APRIL 10

BREAKFAST
    Oatmeal with cream
    Boiled eggs
    Toast
    English breakfast tea

LUNCHEON
    Kieler sprotten
    Omelette Schofield
    Mixed vegetable salad
    Camembert cheese with crackers
    Coffee

DINNER
    Fish chowder
    Ripe olives
    Fillet of sole, Bretonne
    Planked shad and roe
    Lettuce salad
    Hot asparagus with melted butter
    Coffee custard
    Demi tasse

Kieler sprotten. This is a canned fish. Serve cold on lettuce leaves, garnished with quartered lemons.

Omelette Schofield. Boil a shad roe in salt water for ten minutes. Allow to cool, and cut in dices one-quarter inch square. Heat a cup of cream sauce, add the roe, and season with salt and Cayenne pepper. When making the omelet place a little of the roe in the center; dress on a platter, and pour the roe and cream sauce around the edge.

Fish chowder. Cut a pound of some white fish, such as bass, codfish, or sole, in dices about one-quarter inch square, and free from skin and bones. Put the bones of the fish in a casserole and add three quarts of water, one bouquet garni, and two tablespoonfuls of salt. Boil for thirty minutes, and strain. Cut two pounds of potatoes in quarter inch squares, and boil in the fish stock until soft, then add the fish and boil for five minutes, then add one pint of boiling-hot cream, and season well with salt and white pepper. Before serving add a little chopped parsley. Serve broken crackers separate.

Fillet of sole, Bretonne. Boil four fillets of sole in a little salt water. Dish up on a platter and cover with equal parts of Hollandaise and tomato sauce mixed. Garnish with rings of fried onions.

Coffee custard. Grind fine (but not pulverized), a half pound of Java or other mildly flavored coffee. Put it into a quart of boiling milk and let it infuse on the back of the stove for a half hour, then strain through cheese cloth. Beat the yolks of six eggs with six ounces of sugar, add a spoonful of cream, and stir into the hot milk, which has been heated again after straining off the coffee. Let it cream, but do not boil; and then add the beaten whites of three eggs. Use any flavoring desired, a dash of brandy or cognac being very good. Fill the moulds, stand them in hot water, and place in a moderate oven. When done, cool, serve with English cream, apricot juice or just plain cream.

Grapefruit marmalade. Shave two clean whole grapefruit very thin, rejecting nothing but the seeds and cores. Measure the fruit, and add three times the quantity of water, and let it stand in an earthenware dish over night. Then boil for ten minutes, and let it stand another night. Then add an equal quantity of sugar, and boil briskly until the mixture jells.

Eggs St. George. Butter four cocotte dishes, put purée of onions on bottom, a poached egg on top, cover with cream sauce, and sprinkle with grated cheese. Bake in hot oven to color only.

APRIL 11

BREAKFAST
  Fresh strawberries with cream
  Omelet with fine herbs
  Crescents
  Chocolate

LUNCHEON
  Scrambled eggs with truffles
  Lamb chops, sauce Soubise
  Julienne potatoes
  Lettuce salad
  Raspberry shortcake
  Coffee

DINNER
  Potage Châtelaine
  Radishes
  Crab meat au gratin
  Roast chicken
  Mashed potatoes
  Cold asparagus, mayonnaise
  Vanilla ice cream
  Assorted cakes
  Coffee

Omelet with fine herbs. Mix equal parts of chopped parsley, chervil, and chives with the beaten eggs, season well with salt and white pepper, and make the omelet in the usual manner.

Lamb chops, sauce Soubise. Season the chops well, roll in oil, then in bread crumbs, and broil. Put a cupful of sauce Soubise on a platter, and lay the broiled chops on top.

Strawberry shortcake. Bake two layers of sponge cake (see layer cake). Place on top of one some well-sweetened strawberries, put the other cake on top, and press well together. Cut in individual portions, put some selected berries on top, and decorate with sweetened whipped cream. Serve cream separate.

Old fashioned strawberry shortcake. Make some biscuit dough as follows: Mix three-quarters of a pound of flour, one ounce of baking powder, two ounces of sugar, two ounces of butter, and a pinch of salt. Mix to a dough with half a pint of milk. Roll out about one-half inch thick, and bake. When cold split in two, place on one layer some crushed strawberries, and spread some sugar over them. Put the other layer on top and cut in squares. Serve with well-sweetened crushed strawberries on top, and plain cream separate.

Raspberry shortcake. Prepare in the same manner as either of the above, using raspberries in place of strawberries.

Potage Châtelaine. Simmer in two ounces of butter one onion, one-half stalk of celery, and one leek, all chopped very fine. Then add one-half pound of lean beef cut in small squares, sprinkle with three ounces of flour, and simmer until well browned. Then add two quarts of stock or bouillon and boil for an hour. Season with salt and fresh-ground black pepper, and add a glass of good sherry wine before serving.

String beans, Alsacienne. Simmer in a casserole in three ounces of butter one chopped onion. When just colored golden yellow, add one spoonful of flour, one quart of bouillon, stock, or chicken broth, and three pounds of cleaned and well-washed string beans. Season with salt and pepper, cover, and simmer for forty minutes. Then add one-half glass of white wine and cook for fifteen minutes. Do not add the wine to the beans until they are soft. Sprinkle with chopped parsley before serving.

APRIL 12

BREAKFAST
　Baked apples with **cream**
　Waffles
　Honey in comb
　Coffee

LUNCHEON
　Poached eggs, Virginia
　Minced tenderloin of beef,
　　à l'Estragon
　Lyonnaise potatoes
　Escarole salad
　Port de Salut cheese with crackers
　Coffee

DINNER
　Potage Portugaise
　Salted pecans
　Fillet of turbot, Sarcey
　Boiled ham with spinach
　Hollandaise potatoes
　Lallah Rookh
　Lady fingers
　Coffee

Boiled ham with spinach. Soak an eight-pound ham in water over night. Then put on fire, in a pot, covered with cold water, and bring to a boil. Then set to side of stove where it will simmer, but not boil, for about three and one-half hours, when the ham should be done. Try to pull off the skin. If it comes off easily the ham is cooked. Serve with plain spinach, and with either champagne or Madeira sauce, or plain bouillon.

Dandelion salad. Clean and wash the dandelion well, and dry in a towel Put in a salad bowl, lay two hard-boiled eggs cut in four, on top, sprinkle with salt and pepper, and one-third vinegar to two-thirds of olive oil. Mix just before serving.

Dandelion salad, German style. Put the salad in a bowl. Cut six slices of bacon in small dices, and fry until crisp. Pour the hot fat and bacon over the salad, add a spoonful of vinegar, salt if necessary, and a little fresh-ground black pepper. Mix well.

Poached eggs, Virginia. Put four corn fritters on a platter, lay a poached egg on each, and cover with tomato sauce.

Potage Portugaise. Mix one quart of tomato sauce with one quart of consommé and bring to a boil. Season with salt and pepper, and add a cup of boiled rice before serving.

Fillet of turbot, Sarcey. This is fillet of sole au vin blanc. Before serving lay three slices of truffle on each fillet.

Lallah Rookh. To a quart of vanilla ice cream add a pony of Jamaica rum, and mix well. Serve flat in glasses with a little rum on top.

Apple sauce. Peel and core six apples and cut in small pieces. Put into a vessel, add a pony of white wine, two ounces of water, one ounce of sweet butter, two ounces of sugar, and a small stick of cinnamon. Cover, boil for thirty minutes, and strain through a fine sieve.

Rump of beef, Windsor. Larded rump of beef, braisé, with its own gravy, garnished with Parisian potatoes, fresh green peas, and beets Frouard.

Virginia ham and eggs. Broil or fry two slices of Virginia ham and place on platter. Lay two fried eggs on top.

APRIL 13

BREAKFAST
Fresh raspberries with cream
Bacon and eggs
Rolls
Coffee

LUNCHEON
Crab, Portola (cold)
Eggs, Coquelin
Calf's head, sauce piquante
Fondante potatoes
Apple strudel   Coffee

DINNER
Blue Points on half shell
Crème Parisienne (soup)
Sand dabs, meunière
Roast tenderloin of beef
Summer squash
Potatoes rissolées
Chartreuse jelly
Assorted cakes   Coffee

Eggs, Coquelin. Cut in two, six hard-boiled eggs. Mix the yolks with a cupful of well-seasoned purée of mushrooms, and fill the half eggs. Set them on a buttered china platter, cover with cream, and put in the oven to bake. When very hot remove, lay twelve fillets of anchovies over the eggs, and serve.

Calf's head, sauce piquante. Boiled calf's head served on a napkin, with the brain and tongue. Garnish with parsley in branches, sliced pickles, sliced pickled beets, and lemon in halves. Serve sauce piquante separate.

Apple strudel. Roll out some puff paste about one-eighth inch thick and eight inches wide. On it spread some sliced apples mixed with sugar and powdered cinnamon. Wet the edges and fold up both sides, forming a roll. Place on a baking pan, wash the top with egg, and bake in a hot oven. When done cut in slices about two inches wide, and serve hot, with hard and brandy sauces.

Crab, Portola. Remove the boiled crab meat from the shell, taking care to keep as entire as possible. On a salad plate arrange hearts of lettuce, cut into eighths. On the lettuce lay a whole sweet red pimento, using the canned ones which come ready for use. On top of the pepper place three spoonfuls of crab meat. Cover all with French dressing made with tarragon vinegar, using one spoonful to three of olive oil; seasoned with salt and some fresh-ground pepper.

Crème Parisienne. Cream of chicken and cream of chicory soups mixed. Serve bread cut in small squares and fried in butter.

Stuffed tomatoes with anchovies. Chop the contents of one bottle of anchovies in oil, in small pieces, add two hard-boiled eggs chopped fine, a little fresh-ground pepper, and two spoonfuls of mayonnaise. Peel six tomatoes, cut off the tops and scoop out the insides with a spoon. Then fill with the prepared anchovies, cover with the piece cut from the top, and serve on leaves of lettuce garnished with quartered lemons and parsley in branches.

Brook trout sauté, Miller style. Clean four brook trout and dry in a napkin. Season with salt and pepper, roll in flour, put in a frying pan with two spoonfuls of butter and the grease from two slices of salt pork that have been fried in their own fat. Fry the trout on both sides, place on platter, and lay the fried pork on top. Then put in the same frying pan two ounces of butter, and cook until the color of chestnuts. Pour over the fish, and sprinkle with some chopped parsley and the juice of two lemons. Garnish with parsley in branches.

APRIL 14

BREAKFAST
Grapefruit juice
Wheatcakes
Breakfast sausages
Rolls
Coffee

LUNCHEON
Sardines with lemon
Scrambled eggs, Raspail
Fillet mignon, Trianon
Peas
Pineapple, Créole
Coffee

DINNER
Consommé aux quenelles
Fillet of sole, Voisin
Sweetbreads braisé, ancienne
Roast rack of mutton
Fresh string beans
Potato croquettes
Alligator pear salad
Punch Palermitaine
Assorted cakes
Coffee

Scrambled eggs, Raspail. Cut a stalk of celery in small dices, wash well, and boil in salt water. When soft drain off the water. In a pot put two ounces of butter and two peeled tomatoes cut in small dices. Simmer for five minutes, add ten beaten eggs and the celery, season with salt and pepper, and add one-half cup of thick cream. Cook and serve.

Fillet mignon. A very small tenderloin steak. Broil or sauté in pan with butter. Serve maître d'hôtel sauce, and garnish with watercress and half of lemon.

Fillet mignon, Trianon. Dress the fillet on a platter and cover with Béarnaise sauce. Lay three triangular shaped pieces of truffle on top and garnish with Julienne potatoes.

Pineapple, Créole. Cook a quarter pound of rice in a quart of milk. Add a quarter pound of sugar and one cup chopped fresh or canned pineapple, and mix well. Dress on a platter and decorate the top with sliced pineapple and candied cherries. Serve hot with apricot sauce poured over all.

Consommé aux quenelles. Make small chicken dumplings from chicken force meat, boil them in, and serve with, consommé. These small dumplings are called in French, quenelles.

Fillet of sole, Voisin. In a buttered sauce pan put four fillets of sole, sprinkle with one-half teaspoonful of very finely chopped onions, a little chopped parsley, chives, chervil, and one peeled and finely chopped tomato. Season with salt and pepper, add one-half glass of white wine, cover, and put in oven for fifteen minutes. Then remove the fish to a platter, and put in the same sauté pan one pint of white wine; cook and mix well, and pour over the fish.

Sweetbreads braisé, ancienne. Dish up on a platter four sweetbreads braisé, and garnish with four croustades financière. Pour sauce Madère around the sweetbreads on platter.

Roast rack of mutton. Secure from the butcher a rack of mutton of ten chops, season well with salt and pepper, place in a roasting pan with sliced carrots, onions, a spoonful of pepper berries, and a small piece of butter on top; and roast, basting well, for ten minutes. Then put the rack on a platter; drain off the grease and add to the pan one-half cup of stock and a spoonful of meat extract, season well, bring to a boil, and strain over the roast.

APRIL 15

BREAKFAST
Stewed rhubarb
Boiled eggs
Buttered toast
Coffee

LUNCHEON
Grapefruit en suprême, with kirsch
Eggs, Lorraine
Corned beef hash
French pastry
Demi tasse

DINNER
Purée St. Germain
Salmon Mirabeau
Fillet of beef, Charcutière
Stewed canned corn
Baked potatoes
Endives salad
Floating island
Macaroons
Coffee

Grapefruit en suprême with kirsch. Add to sliced grapefruit, for each person, a spoonful of powdered sugar and one pony of kirschwasser. Mix well and serve in suprême glasses.

Eggs, Lorraine. Same as eggs Chipolata with the addition of a strip of bacon across the top.

Purée St. Germain. Add to a purée of peas some fresh-cooked green or canned peas.

Salmon Mirabeau. Put in a buttered flat pan two thick slices of salmon, season with salt and pepper, add one-half glass of claret or white wine, cover, and cook until done. Put on a platter, cover with tarragon sauce (sauce à l'estragon), garnish with stuffed olives, and lay six fillets of anchovies on top of each slice of fish.

Tarragon sauce (Sauce à l'estragon). Chop some tarragon very fine, add one-half glass of claret or white wine, and reduce by boiling until nearly dry. Then add one pint of brown gravy and boil for five minutes. Season with salt and pepper, add two ounces of fresh butter and whip well into the hot sauce. Serve with fish or meats.

Fillet of beef, Charcutière. Roast tenderloin of beef. Serve with brown gravy (sauce Madère), to which has been added twelve small glaced onions, six sliced sour pickles, and twelve heads of French mushrooms or fresh mushrooms sauté in butter. Before serving add a cup of tomato sauce, and season well with salt and pepper.

Stewed canned corn. Empty a can of corn into a sauce pan, add one ounce of fresh butter, season with salt and pepper, and boil. If too thick add a spoonful of thick cream.

Punch Palermitaine. Serve orange water ice in glasses with a little Curaçao on top.

Scalloped halibut with cheese. Prepare one quart of cream sauce. Take four pounds of halibut, clear of bones and skin, and cut in thin slices about one-quarter inch thick, and two inches square. Butter a shallow earthen dish, put some cream sauce in the bottom, sprinkle with grated cheese, then put in a layer of halibut, season with salt and pepper; then sauce, cheese and fish in turn; and continue for about five layers, with cream and sauce on top. Put bits of butter on top and bake in a moderate oven for from forty-five minutes to one hour, or until fish is done and top is nicely browned.

APRIL 16

BREAKFAST
Fresh raspberries with cream
Codfish cakes
Broiled bacon
Rolls
Coffee

LUNCHEON
Hors d'oeuvres assorted
Poached eggs, Paulus
Filet mignon, maître d'hôtel
Potatoes hashed in cream
Cold asparagus, vinaigrette
Fruit salad, Chantilly
Lady fingers
Coffee

DINNER
Consommé Daumont
Baked shad, with raisins
Chicken sauté, Austin
Jeanette potatoes
Carrots, Vichy
Lettuce salad
Charlotte Russe
Coffee

Codfish cakes. Prepare the fish as for codfish balls. Form into flat cakes about one inch thick and two and one-half inches in diameter. Roll in flour and fry in melted butter. Serve on napkin with lemon and parsley in branches.

Poached eggs, Paulus. Put four very soft poached eggs on four slices of toast, cover with cream sauce with sliced truffles, sprinkle with grated cheese, and bake in hot oven just long enough to become slightly brown.

Consommé Daumont. To some chicken force meat add some truffles chopped fine, mix well and form into small dumplings. Cook the dumplings in consommé. Cut two turnips in small squares and boil in salt water. When done add to the consommé, with one-half cup of boiled rice, and croutons soufflés prepared with grated cheese.

Chicken sauté, Austin. Joint a chicken, season well with salt and pepper, put in sauté pan with two ounces of hot melted butter, and fry until brown on both sides. Then add one cup of brown gravy, two sliced truffles, and one spoonful of chopped tarragon. Boil for five minutes.

Jeanette potatoes. Prepare the potatoes as for croquettes, put into a pastry bag with a large star tube, and press through onto a buttered pan, in the form and size of a large rose. Brush the top with yolks of eggs, and bake in oven until brown. Serve on a napkin.

Charlotte Russe. (I). Line a pudding mould with lady fingers, fill with sweetened whipped cream, unmould on a plate and decorate with whipped cream.

(II). Whip to a frost one pint of cream, add one-quarter pound of sugar and a glass of sherry wine. Dissolve two sheets of gelatine in a little hot water, strain, and pour into the cream, heating well. Line a pudding mould with lady fingers and fill with the prepared cream. Allow to stand in the ice box for an hour and a half before serving. Decorate with whipped cream.

Baked shad with raisins. Split the fish and lay at full length on a long buttered dish. Cover the top of the fish with slices of tomato. Put bits of butter on top of the tomato; for a medium sized shad using a lump of butter the size of an egg. Sprinkle chopped parsley over all, and strew seedless raisins around the fish. Then add a half glass of wine, and put in a moderate oven to bake. The fish will be very tender when thoroughly done, but the time required will depend upon the thickness of the fish. From thirty to forty-five minutes is usually sufficient.

APRIL 17

BREAKFAST
  Orange juice
  Hominy with cream
  Crescents
  Chocolate with whipped cream

LUNCHEON
  Oysters mignonette
  Eggs à la tripe
  Small tenderloin steak, Demidoff
  Sauté potatoes
  Escarole salad
  Camembert cheese with crackers
  Coffee

DINNER
  Potage Mongol
  Perch sauté, meunière
  Roast leg of mutton
  String beans with butter
  Potatoes au gratin
  Field salad
  Roman punch
  Pound cake
  Coffee

Oysters mignonette. Put six oysters on half shell on cracked or shaved ice, with a small glass or hollow green pepper filled with mignonette sauce, in the center.

Small tenderloin steak, Demidoff. Put four small broiled tenderloin steaks on a platter, and cover with brown gravy containing olives and sliced canned mushrooms. Garnish both ends of the platter with asparagus tips.

Roman punch. Dress lemon water ice in glasses in pointed shapes, and pour a little rum on top.

Beets, Frouard. Cut some boiled beets with a Parisian spoon into the shape of olives, put in a sauté pan with melted butter, season with salt and pepper, and heat through. Serve in a vegetable dish, or use for garnishing.

Deviled crab in shells. Secure some empty shells from a first-class grocer. Allow one shell to each person and fill with the following: Take the meat of one crab, which is sufficient for four persons, shred it, add a cup of velouté sauce, a teaspoonful of English mustard, a soupspoonful of Worcestershire sauce, a half-teaspoonful of finely chopped parsley, salt, pepper and a bit of Cayenne. Mix well. Fill the shells, covering evenly. Make a paste of a teaspoonful each of English and French mustard and two spoonfuls of melted butter. Spread this over the top, and cover with bread crumbs. Bake for about ten minutes, or until the top is browned.

Roast leg of reindeer. Put in a roasting pan a sliced onion, a sliced carrot, a piece of skin of salt pork, a stalk of celery, some parsley in branches, two bay leaves, two cloves, and one sprig of thyme. Season the leg of reindeer well and lay on top. Put three ounces of butter on the leg, and place in the oven to roast. Baste continually, adding a little water or stock from time to time, to prevent the vegetables from burning. When the roast is done remove to a platter, and make a brown gravy with the contents of the pan by adding a spoonful of flour, simmer, add one cup of stock, season well, and strain over the meat. Some may be reserved to serve in a bowl, separate. Also serve currant jelly and port wine sauce.

Asparagus tips au gratin. Cut the tips from fresh-cooked asparagus, place in a buttered dish, season with salt and pepper, cover with cream sauce, sprinkle with grated Swiss cheese, put small bits of butter on top, and bake in oven until brown.

APRIL 18

BREAKFAST
Rice cakes
Apricot marmalade
Rolls
Coffee

LUNCHEON
Eggs Epicurienne
Tripe and oysters in cream
Baked potatoes
Strawberries Romanoff
Lady fingers
Demi tasse

DINNER
Little Neck clams
Consommé Sévigné. II.
Ripe California olives
Fillet of sole, St. Cloud
Roast chicken
Sybil potatoes
Cold asparagus, mustard sauce
Fruit salad glacé
Assorted cakes
Coffee

Eggs Epicurienne. Shir the eggs. When nearly done add a brown gravy to which has been added some small pieces of terrine de foie gras, four slices of truffle, and one sliced canned mushroom.

Strawberries Romanoff. Put some nice ripe strawberries into a bowl, pour some Curaçao over them, and serve with well-sweetened whipped cream, flavored with vanilla, on top. Serve very cold.

Consommé Sévigné, II. Consommé Brunoise with small quenelles (chicken dumplings). Add some chopped chirvil and a little Cayenne pepper. Serve very hot.

Flannel cakes. One pound of flour, one ounce of baking powder, two ounces of sugar, two ounces of butter, two eggs, and a pinch of mace. Mix all together with sufficient milk to make a medium dough, or batter. Beat until smooth, and bake on a hot griddle.

Rice cakes. Boil one-quarter pound of well-washed rice in water for five minutes. Drain off the water and add one pint of milk, cook until rice is soft, drain off the milk and add the rice to a flannel cake batter. Bake in the usual manner.

Fillet of sole, St. Cloud. In a buttered sauté pan put four fillets of sole, season with salt and white pepper, add one-half glass of white wine and a little stock, and boil for ten minutes. Make a white wine sauce and add the following to it: Two dozen boiled mussels and one dozen boiled oysters removed from the shells, six heads of canned mushrooms and twelve slices of truffle. Put the fish on a platter and cover with the sauce.

Fruit salad glacé. One sliced orange and one sliced grapefruit, six slices of pineapple, one banana, one dozen strawberries and a handful of raspberries. Put all in bowl, add two spoonfuls of sugar, a glassful of maraschino and a pony of kirchwasser. Allow to stand in the ice box for an hour. Serve in small individual dishes with a spoonful of vanilla ice cream on top.

Grapefruit cocktail. Slice one grapefruit and one-half orange and put in bowl with a spoonful of sugar and a pony of kirschwasser. Allow to stand for an hour. Serve in grapefruit suprême glasses, decorated on top with brandied cherries.

APRIL 19

BREAKFAST
  Raspberries with cream
  Plain omelet
  Rolls
  English breakfast tea

LUNCHEON
  Fillet of mariniert herring
  Potato salad
  Consommé in cups
  Sweetbread patties in cream
  Cold artichokes, vinaigrette
  Roquefort cheese and crackers
  Coffee

DINNER
  Purée of spinach
  Crab meat, Suzette
  Roast tenderloin of beef, Cubaine
  Gendarme potatoes
  Peas and carrots in cream
  Lettuce and alligator pear salad
  Frozen egg nogg
  Macaroons
  Coffee

Sweetbread patties in cream. Soak two pounds of sweetbreads in cold water for two hours, to cause the blood to flow out. Then put them on the fire in one quart of water and two ounces of salt, bring to a boil, and then allow to become cold. Pull off the skin and cut the sweetbreads in pieces one-half inch square. Put in vessel with one cup of bouillon, and boil till soft. Then add a cup of cream, season with salt and a little Cayenne pepper, and boil for five minutes. Knead one ounce of butter with one ounce of flour, and use for thickening. Boil again for five minutes. Serve in hot patty shells, on napkin, garnished with parsley in branches. (Patty shells, Jan. 25).

Purée of spinach (Soup). Bring to a boil two quarts of chicken broth, add one peck of well-washed spinach and two ounces of butter, and boil for an hour. Strain through a fine sieve, and put back in the casserole. It should now be of the thickness of a purée of pea soup. Season well with salt and pepper, and stir in, while boiling, one-quarter pound of sweet butter. Serve with small squares of bread fried in butter.

Roast tenderloin of beef, Cubaine. Roast the beef in the usual manner. Serve with sauce Madère, and garnish with stuffed green or red peppers.

Candied sweet potatoes. Boil four sweet potatoes, remove the skins, and cut in egg shapes. Put in sauté pan with two ounces of butter, and roast slowly. When nearly brown add a spoonful of powdered sugar and continue roasting till sugar and potatoes are brown.

Cole slaw, ravigote. Slice a white cabbage very thin and put in a salad bowl. Cover with highly seasoned sauce Tartar, and mix thoroughly.

Frozen egg nogg. One quart of milk, six eggs, one-half pound of sugar, one pony of brandy, one pony of rum, and one-half teaspoonful of grated nutmeg. Mix well, strain, and freeze. Serve in glasses.

APRIL 20

BREAKFAST
  Stewed prunes
  Plain shirred eggs
  Rolls
  Coffee

LUNCHEON
  Grapefruit cocktail
  Eggs en cocotte, Valentine
  Roast loin of pork, apple sauce
  Candied sweet potatoes
  Cole slaw, ravigote
  Vanilla custard pie
  Demi tasse

DINNER
  Consommé Théodora
  Scalloped halibut with cheese
  Rump of beef
  Peas
  Parisian potatoes
  Beets Frouard
  Chocolate ice cream
  Assorted cakes
  Coffee

Eggs en cocotte, Valentine. Mix some crab meat with a little well-seasoned cream sauce. Put a spoonful in the bottom of a buttered cocotte dish, break an egg on top, salt and pepper the egg, put a little more crab meat and cream on top, sprinkle with grated Parmesan cheese, put some bits of butter on top, and bake in oven for five minutes.

Consommé Théodora. Put in the consommé, equal parts of small chicken dumplings, royal, and boiled asparagus tips. Before serving add some chopped chervil.

Vanilla custard pie. Six eggs, one quart of milk, one-quarter pound of sugar, one-half of a vanilla bean. Boil the milk with the vanilla bean. Mix the eggs with the sugar and add to the milk. Strain, and fill a large pie dish lined with a thin pie dough, and bake in a moderate oven until set.

Lemon custard pie. Same as vanilla custard pie, except use the grated rind and the juice of two lemons instead of the vanilla bean.

Orange custard pie. Same as lemon custard pie, but use two oranges instead of the lemons.

Cocoanut custard pie. Same as vanilla custard pie, but put a handful of shredded cocoanut in the bottom of the pie before filling.

Vanilla meringue pie. Same as vanilla custard pie, but when baked, cover, and ornament the top with meringue paste, dust with powdered sugar, and put back in oven to color.

Meringue paste for pie. The whites of four eggs beaten firm and stiff; then add one-half pound of powdered sugar and mix well. Flavor to taste.

Lemon meringue pie. Same as lemon custard pie, but cover and ornament with meringue paste, and bake until colored.

Orange meringue pie. Same directions as for lemon meringue pie.

Lemon pie, special. The yolks of eight eggs, six ounces of sugar, three lemons, the whites of four eggs. Mix the yolks, sugar, and the grated rinds and the juice of the lemons, and beat over a fire until thick. Then add the whites of eggs well beaten, and pour into a large pie dish lined with thin pie dough. Bake slowly. Serve with powdered sugar on top.

Cocoanut meringue pie. Same as cocoanut custard pie, but cover with meringue paste, and bake until colored.

APRIL 21

BREAKFAST
Strawberries with cream
Virginia ham and eggs
Rolls
Cocoa with whipped cream

LUNCHEON
Antipasto
Fried smelts, sauce rémoulade
Spring lamb Irish stew
Chiffonnade salad
Old fashioned raspberry shortcake
Coffee

DINNER
Toke Points on half shell
Potage santé
Boiled salmon, Villers
Roast capon, au jus
Parsnips with cream
Duchess potatoes
Endive salad, Victor dressing
Frankfort pudding, sauce Sabayon
Coffee

Boiled salmon, Villers. Cut two slices of salmon about one and one-half inch thick. Put in vessel with one quart of water, a bouquet garni, one spoonful of salt, a teaspoonful of whole black peppers, and one spoonful of white wine vinegar. Boil slowly for twenty minutes. In a casserole put two ounces of butter, heat, and then add two ounces of flour. When the flour is hot add a pint and a half of the fish broth from the salmon, and boil for five minutes. Then add the yolk of one egg and one cup of cream, mix well, season with salt and pepper, and strain. Add to the sauce one can of sliced mushrooms and half a pound of picked shrimps. Place the salmon on a platter and pour the sauce over it.

Frankfort pudding. One-quarter pound of butter, one-quarter pound of sugar, the yolks of seven eggs, six ounces of cake crumbs, the whites of six eggs, and some vanilla flavoring. Mix the butter with the sugar, and work well with a wooden spoon until creamy, then add the yolks, one by one, and mix thoroughly. Add the cake crumbs; which are made by passing left-over cake through a colander with large holes; flavor with the vanilla extract, and mix well. Beat the whites to snow, and add to the batter, mixing very lightly. Put in a buttered pudding mould and bake. Serve hot Sabayon sauce separate, or pour over the pudding.

Sabayon sauce. In a copper kettle put six yolks of eggs and six ounces of powdered sugar. Set on a slow fire, or bain-marie, and beat until warm. Add a glass of Marsala or sherry wine and whip until it thickens. Serve either hot or cold.

Boiled parsnips. Peel a half dozen parsnips, wash, and boil whole in salt water. When done cut in slices, or some fancy shape, and put in sauce pan with two ounces of butter. Heat through. Season with salt and pepper.

Parsnips in cream. Cut boiled parsnips in pieces two inches long, put in sauce pan with one cup of cream sauce, season with salt and white pepper. Serve in deep vegetable dish, and very hot.

Victor dressing. Two pinches of salt, one pinch of fresh-ground black pepper, one spoonful of tarragon vinegar, two spoonfuls of olive oil, and one teaspoonful of chopped chervil.

APRIL 22

BREAKFAST
Fresh cherries
Flannel cakes with maple syrup
Rolls
Coffee

LUNCHEON
Grapefruit with chestnuts
Austrian chicken fritters
Cold asparagus, mustard sauce
Lemon pie, special
Demi tasse

DINNER
Consommé Soubise
Ripe olives with garlic and oil
Deviled crabs in shells
Tenderloin of beef, Cumberland
Stuffed cucumbers
Sweet potatoes, Southern style, II.
California sherbet
Assorted cakes
Coffee

Consommé Soubise. Mix one cup of purée of onions, one pint of cold chicken broth, three whole eggs and the yolks of three eggs; season with salt, pepper, and a little grated nutmeg. Strain through a fine sieve, put in buttered moulds, and cook in bain-marie. Allow to set, slice, and serve in hot consommé.

Ripe olives with garlic and oil. Rub an olive dish or salad bowl with garlic. Put the olives in the dish, add a spoonful of olive oil, and roll the olives in the dish for a few minutes.

Austrian chicken fritters. Chop the meat of a boiled or baked fowl, season with salt, pepper, nutmeg and herbs; place in a saucepan, and add enough cream or white sauce to moisten. To each cup of the meat and cream add the yolk of one egg. Cut some sandwich bread into thick slices. Mix a pint of milk with two well-beaten eggs. Spread the sandwich bread with a thick layer of the creamed chicken, press two pieces of the bread together, as if making a sandwich, dip this in the egg and milk mixture, then roll in sifted bread crumbs, and fry in hot lard to an even brown color; and in the same manner as for pancakes.

Sweet potatoes, Southern, II. Peel some sweet potatoes and cut lengthwise into strips about an eighth of an inch thick. Put some butter into a sauté pan, and the potatoes, and sprinkle them with brown sugar. Then place on top another layer of potatoes, sprinkle them with sugar, and so on, filling the pan. Add hot water, cover the dish, and set in the oven and bake until soft.

California sherbet. Fill glasses with orange water ice, and on top place five strawberries that have been soaked in California brandy.

Tenderloin of beef, Cumberland. Roast tenderloin of beef, sauce poivrade, garnished with stuffed cucumbers.

Stuffed cucumbers. Peel two cucumbers and cut in pieces one and one-half inches thick. Put in casserole and cover with a quart of water, season with a pinch of salt, bring to a boil, and cool off. With a round cutter remove the inside from the cucumbers, leaving firm rings. Place these on a buttered sauté pan and fill with the following stuffing: Mix a cup of bread crumbs with a cup of purée of fresh mushrooms; season with salt and pepper, add the yolks of two raw eggs, and some fresh-chopped parsley. Mix well, and fill the cucumbers. Cover with buttered manilla paper, put a cup of bouillon in the bottom of the pan, and bake in oven for twenty minutes. Serve as a garnishing for entrées, or fish; or as a vegetable course, on a platter, with tomato sauce or meat gravy.

APRIL 23

BREAKFAST
  Baked apples with cream
  Boiled eggs
  Dry toast
  Coffee

LUNCHEON
  Oysters mariné
  Clam broth in cups   Cheese straws
  English chuck steak, maître d'hôtel
  White beans with tomatoes
  French fried potatoes
  Cocoanut meringue pie   Coffee

DINNER
  Potato soup, Dieppoise
  Broiled herring, cream sauce
  Hollandaise potatoes
  Roast leg of reindeer, port wine sauce
  Sweet potatoes flambé with rum
  Asparagus tips au gratin
  Vanilla charlotte glacé   Demi tasse

English chuck steak, maître d'hôtel. This steak is cut from the end of the saddle, near the legs. It should be cut all the way across the saddle, and about an inch and a half thick. Season with salt and pepper, dip in oil, and broil. When done put on a platter, cover with maître d'hôtel sauce, and garnish with lemon and watercress.

White beans and tomatoes. Soak two pounds of white beans in cold water, over night. Then put the beans in a vessel with three quarts of water, a ham bone, a bouquet garni, and a handful of salt. Bring to the boiling point, skim, cover, and boil until well done. Remove the ham bone and the bouquet, and drain off the water. In a casserole put two ounces of butter and a chopped onion, and simmer until nice and yellow. Then add four peeled and chopped fresh tomatoes, or a quart of canned tomatoes, and simmer for thirty minutes. Then add the beans, season with salt and pepper, and simmer all together for fifteen minutes.

Oysters, mariné. Same as pickled oysters.

Potato soup, Dieppoise. In a sauce pan put three ounces of butter, one sliced celery root, two leeks, a half dozen sliced parsley roots, and simmer for five minutes. Then add two pounds of potatoes sliced very thin, and two quarts of bouillon. Season with salt and pepper, and boil for forty-five minutes. Just before serving add two rolls that have been sliced thin and toasted in the oven, and a little fresh-chopped parsley.

Sweet potatoes flambé with rum. Boil and peel four sweet potatoes, and cut in egg shapes. Put in pan with two ounces of butter and roast until nice and yellow. Then add a little salt and a teaspoonful of sugar, heat, and then put in chafing dish. Pour two ponies of rum on top, light, and bring to the table flaming.

Vanilla chocolate glacée. Line a pudding mould with lady fingers, fill with vanilla ice cream, unmould, and decorate with whipped cream and glacé cherries.

Dartois Chantilly. Roll some puff paste with six turns, and about one-quarter inch thick. Cut in strips two inches wide and four inches long. Place them in a wet pan about one-half inch apart, and let them set for a few minutes, then brush over with egg, and with the point of a small knife mark a line about one-eighth inch deep all around the cakes, and about one-quarter inch from the edges. Bake in rather hot oven for about twenty-five minutes. Remove the top while hot, and empty the cake, leaving only the dry crust. Fill with sweetened whipped cream, vanilla flavor, after cooling.

APRIL 24

BREAKFAST
  Orange marmalade
  Finnan haddie in cream
  Baked potatoes
  Rolls
  Oolong tea

LUNCHEON
  Eggs en cocotte, plain
  Ripe California olives
  Sand dabs, meunière
  Cold asparagus, vinaigrette
  Strawberry short cake
  Coffee

DINNER
  Little neck clams
  Burned farina soup
  Radishes
  Fillet of sole, sauce cardinal
  Olivette potatoes
  Roast shad and roe, à l'Américaine
  Artichokes, Hollandaise
  Lettuce salad
  English rice pudding
  Coffee

Eggs en cocotte, plain. Break one or two eggs in a buttered cocotte dish, season with salt and pepper, put a little butter on top, and bake in oven for a few minutes. Serve on napkin or paper doily.

Burned farina soup. Melt in a casserole one-half pound of butter; when hot add three-quarters of a pound of farina, and roast on top of the range, stirring with a wooden spoon so it will not stick to the bottom. Cook until the color of a chestnut, then add two quarts of boiling water, season with salt and pepper, and boil for one hour. This is a good soup for Friday.

Fillet of sole, cardinal. In a buttered sauté pan put four fillets of sole, season with salt and white pepper, add one-half gass of white wine, cover with buttered paper, and bake in oven for ten minutes. Remove the fillets to a platter, and to the sauté pan add one pint of white wine sauce. Bring to a boil and then stir in two tablespoonfuls of lobster butter. When the butter is melted strain the sauce over the fish.

Roast shad and roe, à l'Américaine. Secure from the fish dealer a fresh shad with the roe inside, and without the belly cut open. In a roasting pan put four ounces of butter, one chopped onion, a carrot cut in very small dices, a spoonful of chopped parsley, and a bay leaf, clove, and a garlic clove, all chopped fine. Place the fish on top, season well with salt and pepper, put a few bits of butter on top of the fish, and place in the oven. Baste continually, and if the pan becomes too dry, add one-half glass of white wine, baste, and then add one-half glass of water. Bake for about an hour in a moderate oven. When done place on a platter and pour the sauce in the pan over the fish. A spoonful of Worcestershire sauce, and the juice of a lemon or two, may be added to the sauce if desired.

English rice pudding. Three pints of milk, one-quarter of a pound of rice, one-quarter of a pound of sugar, and one-half of a vanilla bean split in two. Boil the milk with the vanilla bean, then add the washed rice, and cook for about forty minutes. Add the sugar and boil again for a few minutes, turning carefully with a wooden spoon, so it will not stick to the bottom. Then remove from the fire, add one cup of thick cream, and pour into deep china vegetable dishes, and bake in a hot oven until brown on top. Use one large dish for baking, or individual ones, as desired.

APRIL 25

BREAKFAST
    Grapefruit à la Rose
    Boiled eggs
    Dry toast
    Coffee

LUNCHEON
    Consommé in cup
    Fillets of sand dabs, sauce verte
    Leberkloese (liver dumplings)
    Sauerkraut
    Boiled potatoes
    Escarole and chicory salad
    Port de Salut cheese and crackers
    Coffee

DINNER
    Cream of potatoes
    Pickles
    Tenderloin steak, à la Polonaise
    Spinach with eggs
    Mashed potatoes
    Lettuce and alligator pear salad
    Orange custard pie
    Coffee

Grapefruit à la Rose. Peel and slice two grapefruit and put in salad bowl. Mix one-half cup of fresh strawberries and one-half cup of fresh raspberries and two spoonfuls of powdered sugar, and strain through a fine colander. Have all very cold. Put the grapefruit in glasses and pour the fresh fruit sauce over it.

Fillet of sand dabs, fried. Cut the fillets from four sand dabs, season with salt and pepper, roll in flour, then in beaten eggs, then in bread crumbs, and fry in hot swimming lard. When done serve on napkins with fried parsley and quartered lemons. Serve sauce Tartar or sauce verte separate.

Sauce verte. In a mortar mash equal parts of chives, chervil and parsley. When very fine add some mayonnaise sauce, mix well, and strain through a cheese cloth. Season well before serving.

Leberkloese (liver dumplings). Remove the skin from a calf's liver of good size, and scrape well with a fork to remove all the nerves. Then put in a bowl and add four cups of fresh bread crumbs, three eggs, a little salt, pepper, grated nutmeg, chopped parsley, chopped garlic, one chopped onion and four chopped shallots fried in butter, a teaspoonful of chopped thyme leaves, and one bay leaf chopped almost to a powder. Mix all well together, and drop with a soupspoon into boiling bouillon or salt water, and cook slowly for about twelve minutes. Place on a platter with a little brown gravy; or, in a pan put three ounces of butter with one cup of bread cut in small squares and fry until nice and yellow, then pour over the dumplings, and sprinkle chopped parsley on top.

Tenderloin steak, Polonaise. Broil the steak, put on a platter, cover with maître d'hôtel sauce, and garnish with cauliflower Polonaise.

APRIL 26

BREAKFAST
Sliced oranges
Ham and eggs
Rolls
Coffee

LUNCHEON
Eggs gourmet
Honeycomb tripe with cream and peppers
Baked potatoes
Fresh vegetable salad
Imperial pancake
Demi tasse

DINNER
Consommé à la Russe
Salted Brazil nuts
Frogs' legs, sauté à sec
Breast of tame duck, Virginia style
Fried apples
Wax beans in butter
Romaine salad
Neapolitan ice cream
Assorted cakes
Coffee

SUPPER
Angels on horseback
Chicken à la King
Coffee

Eggs gourmet. Spread some terrine de foie gras on four pieces of toast, lay a poached egg on top of each piece, and cover with sauce Perigord.

Honeycomb tripe with cream and peppers. Cut three pounds of tripe in strips about two inches long and one-half inch wide, and put in casserole with cold water and a spoonful of salt. Bring to a boil and cook for ten minutes. Then drain off the water, add one pint of milk, season with salt, and boil for thirty minutes. Cut six green peppers in small squares, and put in casserole with three ounces of butter, simmer until done, then add one pint of cream sauce, boil for a minute, and add to the tripe. Boil together for five minutes.

Imperial pancakes. Make some thin pancakes, and cut in circular shapes with a three-inch round cutter. With the same cutter cut some sponge cake, and about one-half inch thick. Put some apple sauce on top of the cake, then one of the round pieces of pancake, and repeat until you have four layers with the pancake on top. Decorate with meringue paste, with a pastry bag and a fancy tube, and form in the shape of a crown on top. Put in oven to give a light color.

Consommé à la Russe. To consommé brunoise add a spoonful of boiled barley and a few squares of boiled smoked beef tongue for each person.

Breast of tame duck. Cut the breasts from a tame duck, season with salt and pepper. Put a piece of butter in a sauté pan, add the breasts and sauté for about fifteen minutes if the duck is a young one. Serve on a platter covered with sauce Colbert.

Breast of duck, Virginia style. Broil two slices of Virginia ham and lay on top of the breasts prepared as above.

Boiled wax beans. Cut the strings from both sides of the beans, and cut the beans in two. Boil in salted water until done, then drain off the water, and to each pound of beans add two ounces of butter and a little salt and pepper. Simmer for a few minutes, and sprinkle with chopped parsley before serving.

Angels on horseback. Select large eastern oysters, wrap a slice of thin raw bacon around each oyster, and fasten with a wooden toothpick. Dip them in beaten eggs mixed with a little Worcestershire and English mustard, then roll in fresh bread crumbs, and place in a buttered sauté pan with bits of butter on top of each oyster. Bake in hot oven for about eight minutes, and serve on toast. Pour maître d'hôtel sauce on top, and garnish with parsley in branches and halves of lemon.

APRIL 27

BREAKFAST
Grapefruit juice
Oatmeal and cream
Rolls
Cocoa

LUNCHEON
Poached eggs, d'Artois
Turkey hash in cream
Alligator pear salad
Vanilla meringue pie
Demi tasse

DINNER
Purée of green asparagus
Lyon sausage. Radishes
Fillet of turbot, Windsor
Leg of mutton, Choiseul
O'Brien potatoes
Escarole and chicory salad
Jam roll pudding
Coffee

Poached eggs, d'Artois. Place the poached eggs on toast and pour thick tomato sauce over them.

Purée of green asparagus. Heat in a casserole three ounces of butter, then add three ounces of flour and four pounds of green asparagus cut in small pieces, one quart of milk, one quart of chicken broth or bouillon, a bouquet garni, a little salt, and one teaspoonful of sugar. Boil for an hour, and strain through a very fine sieve. Then put back in casserole and add the yolks of two eggs mixed with one cup of cream. Cut some bread in small squares, fry in butter, and add just before serving.

Fillet of turbot, Windsor. Cut six fillets of fish, put in a buttered sauté pan, season with salt and white pepper, add one-half glass of white wine and one-half glass of stock, cover with buttered manilla paper, and boil until done. Make a white wine sauce and add to it one dozen parboiled oysters and the tail of a lobster cut in slices. Place the fillets on a platter, pour the sauce over them, and garnish with six fried shrimps.

Leg of mutton, Choiseul. Roast leg of mutton, sauce Madère, garnished with small croustades of purée of peas and purée of spinach, and fresh mushrooms sauté in butter.

Jam roll pudding. Mince fine one pound of suet, add a pound of flour, a pinch of salt and a cup of milk, making a rather hard dough. Roll out to the thickness of a quarter of an inch or less. Cover evenly with a layer of any kind of fruit jam, then roll up like a sausage, wrap in a wet cloth, tie with a string so it will not become loose, and steam for an hour. Cut into individual pieces, and serve warm, with hard and soft sauces.

Peach Norelli. Fill two meringue shells with a small tablespoonful of vanilla ice cream. On a fancy plate place an ice cold whole preserved peach, or a fresh peach that has been cooked in syrup. On two sides of the peach press the filled meringue shells, decorate the center with whipped cream, and on the top place a whole marron glacé.

APRIL 28

BREAKFAST
Honey in comb
Plain scrambled eggs
Buttered toast
Coffee

LUNCHEON
Stuffed tomatoes with anchovies
Clam broth in cups
Cheese straws
Planked shad and roe
Cucumber salad
Roquefort cheese with crackers
Coffee

DINNER
Consommé Célestine
Brook trout sauté, miller style
Larded tenderloin of beef, Montpasson
Onion glacés
Quartered artichokes
Parisian potatoes
Field salad
Meringue glacé au chocolat
Coffee

Consommé Célestine. Make some thin pancakes, cut in strips like matches, and serve in consommé.

Larded tenderloin of beef. Lard a tenderloin of beef, after removing the fat and skin. Put in a roasting pan with a sliced onion, carrot, celery, a little leek, parsley, one bay leaf, six cloves, and one spoonful of whole black peppers. Put some small bits of butter on top of the tenderloin, season with salt and pepper, and place in a hot oven. Baste frequently. After the fillet is done remove to a platter, place the pan on top of the stove and take off the fat except about one spoonful. Then add one spoonful of flour, stir well, and add two cups of stock and a spoonful of meat extract, season with salt and pepper, boil for five minutes, and strain. Add one-half glass of good Madeira wine, pour half of the sauce over the tenderloin, and serve the rest in a sauceboat.

Larded tenderloin of beef, Montbasson. Cook the tenderloin as above, but serve with sauce Madère, and garnish with a bouquet of quartered artichokes, glacéd onions, and Parisian potatoes.

Quartered artichokes. Cut four large artichokes in quarters, remove the fuzzy parts on the inside, and immediately rub the quarters with lemon so they will not become black. Boil in salt water until soft.

Pears Bourdaloue. Peel and cook some nice pears in a light syrup, which can be made of one pint of water and one pound of sugar. Mix a half pound of sugar with the yolks of eight eggs and two ounces of flour. Boil one quart of milk with half of a vanilla bean, and pour into the yolks and sugar, and cook until it thickens. Add two ounces of sweet butter and mix well, making a nice smooth cream. Put some of this cream on a plate and put the cooked pears on top. The pears may be cut in half and cored, if desired. Cover the pears with the rest of the cream, sprinkle some macaroon crumbs on top, and put in a hot oven to brown. Serve very hot.

APRIL 29

BREAKFAST
  Strawberries with cream
  Fried hominy
  Country sausages
  Rolls
  Coffee

LUNCHEON
  Pickled salmon, St. Francis
  Eggs, Commodore
  Hashed fillet of beef, Sam Ward
  Cocoanut custard pie
  Demi tasse

DINNER
  Cream of parsnips
  Ripe olives
  Tomcods, Montmorency
  Chicken sauté, Madeleine
  Alligator pear salad
  Omelette au cognac   Coffee

Pickled salmon, St. Francis. Cut in small pieces two pounds of raw salmon and put in sauté pan, add a can of sliced cèpes, a cupful of sliced sour pickles, one-half cup of sliced green olives, a glass of white wine, a pint of tomato ketchup, one spoonful of salt, one tablespoonful of paprika, and four peeled tomaotes, squeezed and cut in small pieces. Put on fire, bring to the boiling point, set on back of the stove and let stand for a half hour. Then put in earthen jar and place in ice box. Serve cold.

Eggs, Commodore. Cook the eggs en cocotte, just before serving pour a little Béarnaise sauce on top.

Hashed fillet of beef, Sam Ward. Take the unused portions of roasted or larded tenderloin of beef and cut in small squares. Also an equal amount of boiled potatoes cut in the same way. In a sauté pan put one chopped onion and two green peppers cut in small dices, with two ounces of butter. Simmer until soft, then add the potato and meat, one cup of bouillon, or two cups, if necessary, season with salt, cover, put in oven and cook for thirty minutes. Serve on platter with chopped parsley on top, and garnished with small pieces of toast.

Cream of parsnips. Peel and slice six parsnips and put in vessel with one pint of chicken broth, boil, and when soft add one pint of cream sauce. Boil for ten minutes and then pass through a fine sieve. Put back in vessel, add one pint of thick cream, season with salt and pepper, and add two ounces of sweet butter before serving.

Tomcods, Montmorency. Put four tomcods on a buttered flat sauté pan, season with salt and pepper, put four canned heads of mushrooms on top of each fish, cover with Italian sauce, sprinkle with a little grated cheese, put small bits of butter on top, and bake in a moderate oven for twenty minutes. Before serving pour the juice of two lemons over the fish, sprinkle with chopped parsley, and serve in same pan.

Chicken sauté, Madeleine. Joint two spring chickens and put in sauté pan with three ounces of butter, season with salt and pepper, and then simmer for five minutes. Then sprinkle two spoonfuls of sifted flour over the chicken and simmer for two minutes. Add one pint of boiling milk and boil for ten minutes. Then remove the chicken to a platter, bring the sauce to a boil, add one cup of cream, and strain over the chicken. See that the sauce is well seasoned. Sprinkle about one and one-half cupfuls of macédoine vegetables over all.

Omelet au cognac. Sprinkle a plain omelet with plenty of powdered sugar, burn with a red-hot poker, pour two ponies of cognac around the omelet, and set afire before bringing to the table.

APRIL 30

BREAKFAST
  Raspberries with cream
  Waffles
  Chocolate with whipped cream
  Crescents

LUNCHEON
  Grapefruit en suprême
  Eggs à la Turque
  Chickens' legs, deviled
  Asparagus Hollandaise
  Gauffrette potatoes
  Apple pie
  American cheese
  Coffee

DINNER
  Consommé printanier royal
  Salted almonds
  Halibut, Richmond
  Roast tame duck with olive sauce
  Sweet potatoes, country style
  Stewed tomatoes, family fashion.
  Cold asparagus, mayonnaise
  Biscuit Tortoni
  Assorted cakes
  Coffee

Eggs à la Turque. To shirred eggs add a few chickens' livers sauté, in brown gravy. Place a slice of truffle on top of each egg.

Deviled chickens' legs. Left over boiled or broiled chickens' legs may be utilized. Season with salt and pepper, spread with a little French mustard mixed with a little powdered mustard and Worcestershire sauce. Roll in fresh bread crumbs, and broil over a slow fire. When done serve on a platter with devil sauce, or sauce poivrade.

Devil sauce. In a casserole put one chopped shallot and one ounce of butter, and merely warm, then add the juice of a lemon, one spoonful of French mustard, one spoonful of Worcestershire sauce, and one pint of brown gravy. Season with salt and pepper, boil for five minutes, and strain.

Consommé printanier. Cut all kinds of spring vegetables in fancy or dice shapes, boil in salt water, and serve in hot consommé. Just before serving add some small leaves of chervil. The vegetables commonly used are carrots, turnips, peas, string beans, small green asparagus tips, small flowers of cauliflower, etc.

Halibut, Richmond. Make a border with a potato croquette preparation, around a silver platter. Remove the skin and bones from two pounds of halibut and boil in salt water for ten minutes. Then put in vessel, add one-half pint of cream and one pint of cream sauce, season with salt and Cayenne pepper, and boil together for five minutes. Then place inside the border on the silver platter, sprinkle with grated cheese, put small bits of butter on top, and bake in oven until nicely colored.

Olive sauce. Remove the stones from twenty-four green olives, cut the olives in two, and put in a casserole with a glass of sherry or Madeira wine, and boil until nearly dry. Then add one pint of brown gravy, season with salt and a little Cayenne pepper, and boil for five minutes. Serve with any meat.

Stewed tomatoes, family fashion. Peel six tomatoes and cut each in eight pieces. Put in a casserole with three ounces of butter, season with salt and pepper, add a pinch of sugar and two slices of bread cut in small squares, cover, and simmer on a slow fire for about forty minutes.

MAY 1

BREAKFAST
Stewed prunes
Melba toast
Ceylon tea

LUNCHEON
Little Neck clam cocktail
Broiled striped bass, maître d'hôtel
Potatoes natural
Lettuce and tomato salad
French pancakes
Coffee

DINNER
Bisque of crabs
Radishes
Fillet of sole, Marguery
Vol au vent of salmon, Génoise
Planked shad and roe
Cucumber salad
Fancy ice cream
Alsatian wafers
Demi tasse

SUPPER
Canapé of sardines
Yorkshire buck
Coffee

Fillet of sole, Marguery. Put four fillets of sole in a buttered sauté pan. Season each fillet with salt and a little Cayenne pepper, add one-half glass of white wine, and cover with buttered manilla paper. Put in oven and cook for six minutes. Remove the fillets to a buttered silver platter, place six boiled mussels and one head of canned mushrooms on top of each fillet. Now add to what wine is left, in the sauce pan one spoonful of white wine sauce, and bring to a boil, and bind with the yolks of two eggs and two ounces of butter. Stir well so the butter will be thoroughly melted. Strain and pour over the fish, sprinkle with grated bread crusts, and bake in a very hot oven just long enough to acquire a light golden color.

Vol au vent of salmon, Génoise. Make one large, or four individual, vol au vents shells. Boil one pound of salmon in salted water; when done cut in pieces one inch square, put in casserole, cover with one-half pint of Génoise sauce, add eight heads of canned mushrooms, season well, and fill the shells.

Chicken sauté, Montpensier. Joint a spring chicken and season with salt and pepper. Melt in a sauté pan one ounce of butter; when hot add the chicken and sauté until nice and brown. Then sprinkle with one-half spoonful of flour and let that get brown; add one-half cup of bouillon and a spoonful of meat extract, and simmer without being covered for five minutes. Then remove the chicken to a platter, season the sauce well and pour over it. Garnish with quartered tomatoes sauté in butter, and chopped parsley and chives, and also with small pieces of bread cut in heart shapes and fried in butter.

Yorkshire buck. Welsh rabbit on anchovy toast with a poached egg and two strips of broiled bacon on top.

MAY 2

BREAKFAST
Cherries
Omelet with bacon
Rolls
Coffee

LUNCHEON
Stuffed eggs, mayonnaise sauce
Broiled spareribs with lentils
Breast of squab, sauce Périgord
Potato croquettes
Port de Salut cheese with crackers
Coffee

DINNER
Farina soup, Francis Joseph
Fillet of flounder, Pompadour
Larded sirloin of beef, D'Orsay
Artichokes jardinière
Rissolées potatoes
Romaine salad
Burgundy wine jelly
Assorted cakes
Coffee

Breast of squab, Périgord. Cut the breasts from four squabs, season with salt and pepper, roll in flour, and fry in sauté pan in three ounces of butter. When done place on toast and cover with sauce Périgord.

Fillet of flounder, Pompadour. Cut the fillets from a flounder and place them on a china platter, season with salt, pepper, the juice of a lemon, and a spoonful of olive oil. Set in the ice box for twelve hours; then take out and roll in flour, then in beaten eggs, and finally in bread crumbs, and fry in swimming lard. When done place on a platter on a napkin, and garnish with fried parsley and quartered lemons. Make a sauce of six fillets of anchovies cut in small slices, mixed with sauce Tartare, well seasoned, and serve separate.

Artichokes jardinière. Boiled artichoke bottoms filled with macédoine of vegetables.

Farina soup, Francis Joseph. Roast a pheasant in the oven for five minutes to obtain a slight color, then put in fresh-prepared consommé and boil until soft. Then strain the consommé, bring to a boil, add three pints of farina and boil for fifteen minutes. Then bind with the yolks of two eggs and one-half cup of cream, add a glass of sherry wine, one spoonful of grated cheese; season with salt, a little cayenne pepper and the juice of a lemon. Cut the breast of the pheasant in thin slices and put in the soup tureen and pour the soup over it; give it a sprinkle of chopped parsley, and serve hot.

MAY 3

BREAKFAST
  Baked apples with cream
  Buckwheat cakes, maple syrup
  Rolls
  English breakfast tea

LUNCHEON
  Suprême of oysters, St. Francis
  Eggs Malakoff
  Broiled chicken
  Soufflé potatoes
  Lettuce salad
  Old fashioned strawberry shortcake
  Coffee

DINNER
  Consommé chiffonnade
  Ripe California olives
  Fillet of smelts, Stanley
  Chicken sauté, Demidoff
  Turnips glacés
  Potato croquettes
  Endives salad
  Biscuit glacé, au peppermint
  Macaroons
  Coffee

Suprême of oysters, St. Francis. For about eight people. Use twenty California oysters or seven Eastern oysters for each person. Serve like an oyster cocktail in grapefruit suprême glasses in the following sauce: Mix one cup of tomato ketchup, a short cup of cream, one teaspoonful of Worcestershire sauce, one teaspoonful of lemon juice, season with salt, a dash of tobasco, and paprika. The cream should be added last. Keep the sauce on ice until needed.

Eggs, Malakoff. Spread some fresh caviar on four pieces of toast, lay a poached egg on each, and cover the eggs with horseradish sauce and cream.

Consommé chiffonnade. Cut equal parts of lettuce and sorrel in Julienne style, put in casserole, cover with water, bring to a boil, then drain off water and allow to become cool. Then put back in casserole, add two quarts of consommé, and boil very slowly for about thirty minutes. Before serving add a little chopped parsley and chervil.

Fillet of smelts, Stanley. Split six smelts, remove the bones, season with salt and pepper, place in a buttered sauté pan, add one-half glass of white wine, and cover with buttered paper. Bake in oven for five minutes, and then place the fillets on a platter. Make a cardinal sauce but add to it the tail of a lobster cut in small squares, twelve slices of truffles, and six heads of canned mushrooms, sliced. Pour over the fish.

Cardinal sauce. One pint of sauce au vin blanc; bring to a boil and stir in two spoonfuls of lobster butter.

Chicken sauté, Demidoff. Joint a spring chicken, season with salt and pepper and put in sauté pan with two ounces of butter. Heat, add the chicken, and sauté on both sides for fifteen minutes. Then add a cup of Madeira sauce, and dress on a platter with sauce over it. Garnish the platter with turnips glacé; onions glacé; queen olives with the stones removed, and warmed in sherry wine; and French carrots.

MAY 4

BREAKFAST
Raspberries with cream
Boiled eggs
Buttered toast
Coffee

LUNCHEON
Canapé Riga
Sand dabs, meunière
Ox tail braisé
Noodles Polonaise
Cole slaw, 1,000 Island dressing
Lemon custard pie
Coffee

DINNER
Purée of red kidney beans
Radishes
Fillet of halibut, Bristol
Sweetbreads braisé, Zurich
New peas, au cerfeuil
Julienne potatoes
Roast chicken, au jus
Lettuce and grapefruit salad
Savarin Mirabelle
Coffee

Ox tail braisé. Cut two ox tails in pieces three inches long, wash well and dry with a towel or cloth. Season with salt and pepper. In a casserole put three ounces of butter, put on the stove, and when hot add the ox tail. Sauté until nice and brown, then add three spoonfuls of flour, and let that become brown also. Then add one quart of boiling water, a bouquet garni, a little salt, one-half can of tomatoes, or four chopped fresh tomatoes, one piece of garlic, an onion and a carrot. Cover the casserole and put in the oven until the ox tail is soft. It will require two or three hours. When done remove the ox tail to a platter, reduce the sauce, season well, and strain over the ox tail on the platter.

Purée of kidney beans. Soak three pounds of dry red kidney beans in cold water over night. Then put on fire with two quarts of cold water, a handful of salt, a ham bone, an onion, a carrot and a bouquet garni. Skim well, and when it boils, cover and cook until soft. Remove the ham bone, carrot, onion, and bouquet garni, and strain the beans through a fine sieve. Put back in casserole, boil again, then season with salt and pepper, and add three ounces of butter, little by little, and stir well until thoroughly melted. Serve with bread cut in small squares and fried in butter.

Fillet of halibut, Bristol. Put four fillets of halibut in a buttered sauté pan, season with salt and pepper, cover with buttered paper, add one-half glass of milk and water mixed, and cook. When done place the fish on a buttered platter, garnish with two dozen parboiled oysters, and cover all with cream sauce. Sprinkle with grated cheese, put small bits of butter on top, put in oven and bake until colored.

Sweetbreads braisé, Zurich. Put some braised sweetbreads on a platter and garnish with croustades financière and sauce Madère.

MAY 5

BREAKFAST
  Gooseberries in cream
  Waffles
  Honey in comb
  Coffee

LUNCHEON
  Oranges en suprême au Curaçao
  Clam broth in cups
  Cheese straws
  Broiled squab on toast
  Olivette potatoes
  Cold asparagus, mustard sauce
  Chocolate éclairs
  Coffee

DINNER
  Consommé croûte au pot
  Crab legs, Josephine
  Fillet of beef, Cendrillon
  Paté de foie gras
  Hearts of lettuce
  Omelet with fresh strawberries
  Demi tasse

Oranges en suprême au Curaçao. Slice two oranges, sprinkle with a spoonful of powdered sugar, and add one pony of Curaçao. Have well iced, and serve in large suprême glasses.

Consommé croûte au pot. Cut carrots, turnips, cabbage and leeks in small thin squares, parboil, and finish cooking in consommé. Serve with sliced French bread browned in oven.

Crab legs, Josephine. Bread the crab legs with fresh bread crumbs, and fry in a pan, with butter. Dish up on a round platter, with sliced fresh mushrooms sauté in butter in center. Serve sauce Colbert separate.

Fillet of beef, Cendrillon. Roast tenderloin of beef, sauce Madère, garnished with the following: Shape some potato croquettes in the form of small patties, about one and one-half inch in diameter and one inch high. Roll in flour, beaten eggs, and bread crumbs. Mark about an eighth inch deep on top with a small round cutter, and fry in swimming lard. Then lay out on a towel, lift out the cover formed by the cutter, and save. Scoop out the center, fill with a soubise (purée of onions), and replace the cover.

MAY 6

BREAKFAST
Strawberries and raspberries, with
   cream
  Scrambled eggs
  Rolls
  Oolong tea

LUNCHEON
  Hors d'oeuvres variés
  Eggs Châteaubriand
  Breaded lamb chops, reformé
  Endives salad
  Roquefort cheese and crackers
  Coffee

DINNER
  Lamb broth à la Grecque
  Ripe California olives
  Lake Tahoe trout, maître d'hôtel
  Calf's head, Providence
  Roast chicken
  Peas
  Potatoes au gratin
  Watercress salad
  French pastry
  Coffee

Eggs Châteaubriand. Spread some foie gras on a piece of toast, lay a poached egg on top, and cover with tomato sauce.

Breaded lamb chops, reformé. Mix the crumbs made from one loaf of bread with two slices of chopped ham and one spoonful of chopped parsley. Season eight chops with salt and pepper, roll in flour, then in beaten eggs, and finally in the crumbs mixed as above. Fry in hot butter, and when done place on a platter and pour around them the following sauce: Cut in small strips, and in equal parts, some gherkins, beets, fresh mushrooms sauté in butter, or canned mushrooms, smoked beef tongue, and the whites of hard-boiled eggs. Add one pint of good meat gravy and a spoonful of melted currant jelly. Season with salt and Cayenne pepper. Serve some of the sauce separate.

Lamb broth, à la Grecque. Cut a pound of raw lamb, from the shoulder or leg, in dices about one-half inch square. In a casserole put three ounces of butter and set on the stove. When hot add the lamb and one chopped onion and simmer together for ten or fifteen minutes. Then add two spoonfuls of flour and one spoonful of curry powder, and simmer for five minutes, then add two quarts of stock, bouillon or hot water. If water is used add a bouquet garni. Bring to a boil and cook for fifteen minutes, then add a cup of washed rice and boil until soft. Season with salt and pepper, remove the bouquet garni if used, add one tablespoonful of Worcestershire sauce and a teaspoonful of sugar. Serve with a little chopped parsley.

Calf's head, Providence. Boil a calf's head with the brain and tongue. Place one piece of each, for each person, on a platter, cover with sauce Madère with mushrooms and olives.

MAY 7

BREAKFAST
Sliced bananas with cream
Ham and eggs
Rolls
Coffee

LUNCHEON
Crab salad, Louis
Braised mutton chops with string
beans
Gendarme potatoes
Orange meringue pie
Demi tasse

DINNER
Little Neck clams
Consommé Vivieurs
Fillet of sole, Suchet
Sweetbreads braisé, Godard
Roast leg of reindeer, au jus
Sweet potatoes, Southern style
Purée of salad (vegetable)
Vanilla ice cream
Assorted cakes
Coffee

Crab salad, Louis. Arrange lettuce leaves around the inside of a salad bowl, with a few sliced leaves on the bottom. Put crab meat on top of the sliced leaves, and a few sliced hard-boiled eggs and sliced chives on top of the crab meat. In another bowl mix one-half cup of French dressing with one-half cup of Chili sauce, two spoonfuls of mayonnaise, salt, pepper, and one teaspoonful of Worcestershire sauce. Pour over the salad, and serve very cold.

Braised mutton chops. Have six chops cut one and one-half inches thick, season with salt and pepper. In a sauté pan on the stove put one spoonful of fat or lard, and when hot add the chops and fry on both sides until brown. Then drain off the fat, add two ounces of butter, sprinkle with a spoonful of flour, add one pint of stock, one crushed tomato, one bay leaf, one clove; and then simmer slowly for an hour and a half. When done place the chops on a platter, season the sauce well, and strain over the chops.

Consommé Vivieurs. Make a Julienne of beets, leeks and celery, in equal parts, parboil in salt water, and finish cooking in consommé. Then add the breast of a boiled chicken also cut Julienne. Chop a raw beet, press out the juice and add to the consommé. This will give it a nice reddish color. Serve croûtons diablé separate.

Croûtons diablé (for soup). Use either white or rye bread, and cut in round pieces the size of a quarter of a dollar. Mix some grated Parmesan cheese with Cayenne pepper, and put on the round pieces of bread. Place on a flat pan and bake in oven until brown. Serve on a napkin.

Fillet of sole, Suchet. Make a Julienne of vegetables in the same manner as for consommé. Prepare a fillet of sole, au vin blanc. When the sole is done add the Julienne of vegetables to the white wine sauce, together with a little chopped tarragon, and pour over the fish. Have the sauce well seasoned.

Sweetbreads braisé, Godard. Braise the sweetbreads and dish up on a platter. Garnish with whole truffles heated in sherry wine, and whole heads of mushrooms fried in butter, rooster combs, rooster fries, and sauce Madère around the platter.

MAY 8

BREAKFAST
  Guava jelly
  Rice cakes
  Breakfast sausages
  Chocolate with whipped cream
  Rolls

LUNCHEON
  Grapefruit en suprême au marasquin
  Consommé in cups
  Finnan haddie in cream
  Baked potatoes
  Italian salad
  Camembert cheese
  Coffee

DINNER
  Consommé with royal and carrots
  Ripe California olives
  Crab meat, Belle Hélène
  Tournedos Bordelaise
  Julienne potatoes
  Cauliflower au gratin
  Fresh strawberry coupe
  Assorted cakes
  Coffee

Consommé with royal and carrots. Boil one quart of French carrots in salted water. When done, drain off the water and pass the carrots through a fine sieve. Take a cup of this carrot purée and mix with two whole eggs and one yolk, season with salt and pepper, and strain again. Put in a small buttered pudding mould and cook in a bain-marie. When set, allow to become cool, remove from mould, and cut in any fancy shape desired. Serve in hot consommé.

Tournedos Bordelaise. Either fry in butter or broil a small tenderloin steak. Dish up on a platter, put some sliced parboiled beef marrow on top, and cover with Bordelaise sauce.

Fresh strawberry coupe. Select some nice strawberries and put them in a bowl with powdered sugar and a little maraschino, and mix well. Fill some coupe glasses about half full, pour some of the juice over each, and fill the remainder of the glass with vanilla ice cream. Decorate the top with selected strawberries.

Fresh raspberry coupe. Use raspberries, and prepare as above.

Banana coupe. Use sliced bananas, and prepare in the same manner as for strawberries.

Orange coupe. Use sliced oranges, and prepare as above.

Grapefruit coupe. Same as orange coupe, but use a little more sugar.

MAY 9

BREAKFAST	LUNCHEON
Orange juice	Crab ravigote
Omelet with cèpes	Consommé in cups
Rolls	Chicken à la King
Coffee	Knickerbocker salad
	Baba au rhum
	Coffee

DINNER
Purée of white beans, Soubise
Fillet of bass, Duglère
Rack of lamb, Montjo
Sybil potatoes
Artichokes, Hollandaise
Chiffonnade salad
Peach Norelli
Assorted cakes
Coffee

Knickerbocker salad. On a long leaf of romaine salad put one slice of grapefruit, then one slice of orange, and so on until the leaf is full. Then put four fresh strawberries on top, cover with French dressing and garnish with whipped cream. Serve on individual plates.

Purée of white beans, Soubise. Soak two pounds of white beans in cold water over night. Then put on fire with two quarts of water, six whole white onions, one bouquet garni, one ham bone, and two pounds of veal bones. Season with salt; and skim when it comes to a boil. When the beans are soft remove the bouquet garni, ham and veal bones, strain the rest through a fine sieve, and put back on the fire. Bring to a boil, and stir in three ounces of butter, adding it little by little. Season with salt and pepper, and if too thick add a little bouillon. Serve separate, some small squares of bread fried in butter.

Crab ravigote. Mix the meat of one boiled crab with a cup of Tartar sauce and a little Cayenne pepper. With this fill four Eastern crab shells. These shells are smaller and daintier than the Pacific Coast variety, and can be obtained from first-class grocers. Sprinkle the tops with finely chopped parsley, then lay a band of pimento across the center, parallel this with chopped yolk of egg on one side, and with chopped whites on the other, and fringe the whole with chopped parsley. Serve with quartered lemon and parsley.

Fillet of bass, Duglère. On a buttered platter put four fillets of bass, and season with salt and pepper. Sprinkle with a half of an onion, chopped fine, and a little chopped parsley, tarragon and chervil. Peel and chop two tomatoes and spread over the top of the fish. Put around the platter a little brown gravy and one-half glass of white wine. A spoonful of meat extract diluted with warm water may be used in place of the gravy if desired. Put a small piece of butter on top of each fillet, then place the platter in a moderate oven and bake for about thirty-five minutes. Serve on the same platter.

Rack of lamb, Montjo. Roast a rack of lamb, and serve with sauce Madère, to which has been added a can of French mushrooms and some stuffed olives.

Omelet with cèpes. Melt two ounces of butter in an omelet pan, then add a can of sliced cèpes, season with salt and pepper, and fry them. Then add twelve beaten eggs, and make the omelet. Pour some brown gravy around the omelet. Cream or tomato sauce may be used, if desired.

MAY 10

BREAKFAST
Cherries
Poached eggs on toast
Broiled bacon
Rolls
Coffee

LUNCHEON
Crab meat in cream
Radishes
Loin of lamb chops, jardinière
Soufflé potatoes
Cold artichokes, mustard sauce
Assorted cheese with crackers
Coffee

DINNER
Consommé Valentienne
Salted almonds
Lake Tahoe trout, meunière
Chicken sauté, Montpensier
Duchesse potatoes
Jets de houblons
Dandelion salad
Dartois Chantilly
Coffee

Loin of lamb chops, jardinière. Season four lamb chops with salt and pepper, roll in oil, and broil. Then place on a platter, cover with Madeira sauce, and garnish with bouquets of fresh vegetables; such as peas in butter, cauliflower Hollandaise; or asparagus tips, string beans, young carrots, etc. Also add some kind of potatoes.

Consommé Valentienne. Make some small dumplings of cream puff paste and boil in salt water for two minutes. Cook some lettuce, cut Julienne style, in consommé. Boil some Italian paste. Serve equal parts of each in boiling consommé.

Suggestions and recipes for preserves, jellies and pickles. For jelly select your fruit before it is too ripe, as the flavor will then be much better. Put it on the stove and bring to a heat, to facilitate the easy extraction of the juice. Have a funnel-shaped bag made of flannel, to strain the juice through. The first time it is strained use a wire sieve with a revolving wire to crush the fruit. The juice should always be strained twice, and the second time if the flannel bag is used, and it is allowed to hang over night and drip, it will be much clearer. Put on the juice over a good fire and allow it to come to a heat, then add the sugar, which should be first heated in the oven. Boil rapidly in a pan with a very large bottom, so that as much surface can be on the stove as possible. If it is desired that the color be light add a little gelatine. From fifteen to twenty minutes is long enough to boil it, but it should not stop boiling during this time. Better success will probably be had if the jelly is cooked in small quantities. After pouring the jelly in glasses set in the hot sun until set, and then cover with melted paraffine.

If corn starch be put in the juice before adding the sugar it will make it clearer. Use two teaspoonfuls in two tablespoonfuls of water, to three pints of juice. A teaspoonful of sugar on top of jelly, in the glass, prevents moulding. (To one pint of juice 1½lbs. sugar).

Preserves. Small stone jars are best for preserves. If glass jars are used they should be wrapped in paper to exclude the light. To prevent preserves from sugaring add a little tartaric acid after they are cooked.

Pickles. Cider vinegar is best for pickles. If vinegar is too strong dilute it with water. The pickles should be tightly sealed to prevent the air reaching the vinegar, as this kills it. The vinegar should always be poured on hot, just as it comes to the first scald—never allowing it to boil.

Never put up pickles in anything that has held grease; and never let them freeze. If pickles are put into brine it should be strong enough to bear an egg. To make the brine, use a heaping pint of salt to each gallon of water. Put the pickles in bottles, and seal while the brine is hot. A half bushel of grape leaves added to the barrel of salt pickles will keep them sound and firm. A slice of horseradish added to each jar or bottle of vinegar pickles will keep the vinegar clear.

MAY 11

BREAKFAST
Fresh raspberries with cream
Boiled eggs
Buttered toast
English breakfast tea

LUNCHEON
Sardines in oil
Chicken broth in cups
Fried tomcods, Tartar sauce
Broiled honeycomb tripe, Chili sauce
Browned mashed potatoes
Field and beet salad
Lemon meringue pie
Coffee

DINNER
Potage santé
Crab meat, Suzette
Roast ribs of beef, Yorkshire pudding
Stewed corn
French peas
Chiffonnade salad
Grapefruit coupe
Assorted cakes
Coffee

Broiled honeycomb tripe, Chili sauce. Roll four pieces of well seasoned boiled tripe in oil, then in fresh bread crumbs, and then broil. Heat one-half bottle of Chili sauce, pour on a platter and lay the tripe on top.

Preserves. Amount of fruit required. Seven and one-half pounds of cherries and seven and one-half pounds of sugar will make one gallon of preserves.

Fourteen pounds of berries and fourteen pounds of sugar will make five quarts of jam.

Two quarts of stemmed currants will make two pints of juice. Added to two pounds of sugar it will make three tumblers of jelly.

Always wash strawberries before removing the hulls, and then put in a colander to drain. Always select strawberries for their flavor rather than for their size.

Strawberry preserves. Prepare a small quantity at a time to secure the best results. Make a syrup in a kettle with two pounds of cane sugar and half a cup of water. Drop the berries into it and cook rapidly for twenty minutes. Do not stir, but remove any scum which may arise. After twenty minutes remove the berries and put in tumblers. Cook the syrup to a jelly and fill up the tumblers with it. Allow to become cold before covering.

Blackberry jam. Four quarts of blackberries, two quarts of nice cooked apples, four quarts of cane sugar. Boil for twenty-five or thirty minutes.

Raspberry or loganberry jam. In making raspberry jam, if two-thirds red raspberries and one-third currants are used the jam will be better, as the berries alone do not contain enough acid. Loganberries are sufficiently acid. Mash the fruit well, and boil it for twenty minutes. Weigh, and to every pound of fruit use three-quarters of a pound of sugar. Boil until when some is placed on a saucer no juice will gather around it. Put in small jars or glasses, in the same manner as jelly.

Canned strawberries. Wash well before hulling. Weigh, and to each pound of berries add one-quarter pound of cane sugar. Boil for fifteen minutes. Put in pint jars and seal while hot.

Apple jelly. Take ripe Belleflower, or other fine-flavored cooking apples. Cut in quarters and remove the cores. Drop in water as fast as cut, to prevent them from turning black. Add a little lemon juice to the water. When all are ready drain off the water, and put the apples in a copper preserving kettle. Pour a little water over them and cook until soft, then strain through a flannel bag. Boil the juice with an equal weight of sugar, until it jells, and pour while hot into jelly glasses.

Blackberry jelly. Heat the berries to the boiling point, mash, and strain through a flannel bag. Add an equal weight of sugar to the juice, and boil briskly for twenty-five minutes. Pour into glasses while hot.

MAY 12

BREAKFAST
Nutmeg melon
Shirred eggs
Rolls
Coffee

LUNCHEON
Ecrevisses en buisson
Chicken patties, Toulouse
Broiled Virginia ham
French fried potatoes
Panachée salad
Savarin with strawberries
Coffee

DINNER
Consommé Ravioli
Queen olives
Shad roe, Bordelaise
Fillet of beef, Lombarde
Cold asparagus, vinaigrette
Soufflé pudding, Dame Blanche
Coffee

Chicken patties, Toulouse. Fill some patty shells with Toulouse filling, prepared in the same manner as for Vol au vent Toulouse.

Broiled Virginia ham. Use either boiled or raw Virginia ham. Cut in thin slices, broil, and serve on platter, garnished with parsley in branches.

Panachée salad. This is a mixed salad of two kinds of vegetables such as beans and flageolets, peas and carrots, potatoes and lettuce, beets and field, etc.

Consommé Ravioli. Make some small raviolis and boil them for five or ten minutes in consommé.

Shad roe, Bordelaise. Season four roes with salt and pepper, roll in oil, and broil; when done put on a platter. Parboil one-half pound of beef marrow, slice very thin, and lay on top of the broiled roe. Cover with Bordelaise sauce.

Fillet of beef, Lombarde. Roast tenderloin of beef, sauce Madère, garnished with stuffed tomatoes and potato croquettes.

Soufflé pudding, Dame Blanche. One-quarter pound of butter, one-quarter pound of sugar, three ounces of flour, one pint of milk, the yolks of eight eggs, the whites of eight eggs, and three ounces of ground blanched almonds. Put the almonds in boiling water for one second, then immediately put them into cold water, then remove the skins, and chop them very fine. Mix the butter, flour and sugar into a hard batter. Put the milk and the almonds on the stove to boil, then add the batter, and stir until it becomes a creamy mixture. Then remove from the fire, and add the yolks one by one, mixing well. Beat the whites of eggs to snow, and mix with the rest. Put in a buttered mould and bake in a moderate oven for about forty minutes. Serve hot, with cream sauce to which chopped almonds have been added.

MAY 13

BREAKFAST	LUNCHEON
Baked apple with cream	Cantaloupe
Griddle cakes	Strained onion soup
Maple syrup	Croûtons Parmesanne
Coffee	Pickelsteiner stew
	Roquefort cheese with crackers
	Coffee

DINNER
Potage Turinoise Salted Brazil nuts
Sand dabs, David
Chicken sauté, au Madère
String beans in butter
Persillade potatoes
Romaine salad
Peaches Bordaloue
Assorted cakes   Coffee

Croûtons Parmesanne. Four yolks of eggs, two ounces of grated Parmesan cheese, one-half ounce of salt, a pinch of Cayenne pepper, and the whites of three eggs. Beat well together the yolks of eggs, grated cheese, salt and Cayenne pepper. Then add the whites of eggs, beaten very hard. Put in a buttered pan and bake in a moderate oven. Cut in diamond shapes while warm.

Pickelsteiner stew. Two pounds of veal, two pounds of shoulder of lamb, and two pounds of pork cut in pieces one and one-half inches square. Put in a sauté pan with two ounces of butter, season with salt and pepper, and cook until brown; then put in casserole with an onion chopped fine, and let it become brown, then add one-half cup of flower; one pint of purée of tomatoes; one quart of bouillon, stock, or hot water, and a bouquet garni. Cover, and cook for half an hour; then add two pounds of potates cut in one inch squares, and cook until soft. Serve in casserole, or individual cocotte dishes.

Potage Turinoise. One quart of purée of tomatoes and two quarts of consommé, mixed. Garnish with cooked spaghetti cut one inch long. Serve about two cupfuls of grated cheese separate.

Salted Brazil nuts. Roast in oven one pound of shelled Brazil nuts until they are brown. Then rub them together to loosen the second skin, which should be removed. Wet them with a little melted gum Arabic, and sprinkle with about an ounce of fine table salt. Stir until dry.

Sand dabs, David. Salt and pepper four sand dabs, roll in flour, and fry in butter. Then place on platter and sprinkle with chopped parsley and the juice of one lemon Put two ounces of fresh butter in the frying pan, add one-half cup of fresh bread crumbs, and fry until golden yellow. Pour over the fish.

Chicken sauté, au Madère. Joint a spring chicken, season with salt and pepper. Put a small piece of butter in a frying pan, heat, and add the chicken. When nice and brown sprinkle with a spoonful of flour and brown again. Then add a half glass of Madeira wine, simmer a few minutes, add a cupful of stock or bouillon, and a spoonful of meat extract, and boil for five minutes. Dress the chicken on a platter, reduce the sauce one half, season well, and train through a fine cloth or sieve. Before pouring over the chicken add a spoonful of dry sherry wine.

Peaches Bourdaloue. Prepare in the same manner as Pears Bourdaloue.

MAY 14

BREAKFAST
  Fresh strawberry preserves
  Scrambled eggs, asparagus tips
  Rolls
  Coffee

LUNCHEON
  Alligator pear cocktail
  Broiled Alaska black codfish
  Maître d'hôtel potatoes
  Fricadellen
  Spinach with eggs
  Banana coupe
  Macaroons
  Demi tasse

DINNER
  Consommé Diablé
  Ripe California olives
  Boiled salmon, Fidgi
  Saddle of lamb, Carnot
  Watercress salad
  Omelette soufflée à la vanille
  Coffee

Alligator pear cocktail. Scoop out the inside of one large, or two small, ripe alligator pears and cut in small pieces. Add one-half cup of tomato ketchup, one-half teaspoonful of Worcestershire sauce, one-half teaspoonful of lemon juice, a little salt and paprika, a dash of Tabasco sauce, and last of all, one-half cup of cream. Mix lightly, and serve in glasses set in ice. The cocktails should be very cold.

Fricadellen (Balls of cooked meat). Use any kind of meat that may be left over, such as boiled beef, roast lamb, etc. Chop very fine. To each two pounds of meat add one chopped onion fried in butter, one cup of bread crumbs, two whole eggs, and some chopped parsley. Season with salt and pepper and a little grated nutmeg. Mix well, and make into small balls, like Hamburger. Roll them in bread crumbs, and fry in pan, with melted butter. When well browned serve on a platter with any kind of brown gravy, or tomato sauce, or brown butter.

Consommé Diablé. Cut three thin slices of bread, as for sandwiches, and spread with two cups of grated Parmesan or Swiss cheese, that has been mixed with the yolks of two eggs and plenty of Cayenne pepper. Bake in a hot oven until brown. Cut in small squares or circles, and serve on a napkin on a platter. Serve the consommé very hot.

Boiled salmon, Fidgi. Boil the salmon and serve on a napkin, garnished with small round boiled potatoes, quartered lemons, and parsley in branches. Serve sauce Fidgi separate.

Sauce Fidgi. One cup of sauce Hollandaise and one cup of sauce Riche, mixed with one spoonful of melted meat extract. Season well.

Saddle of lamb, Carnot. Roast saddle of lamb, with sauce Madère. Garnish the saddle with six stuffed fresh mushrooms and Parisian potatoes.

MAY 15

BREAKFAST
  Cantaloupe
  Ham and eggs
  Rolls
  Coffee

LUNCHEON
  Eggs ministerielle
  Koenigsberger klobs
  Mashed potatoes
  Stewed tomatoes
  Ginger snaps
  Coffee

DINNER
  Potage Fontange
  Radishes
  Fillet of sole, Doria
  Tenderloin of beef, Brillat Savarin
  Spinach in cream
  Lettuce salad
  Strawberry ice cream
  Assorted cakes
  Coffee

Koenigsberger klobs. With a medium-fine meat chopper cut six ounces of shoulder of lamb, six ounces of shoulder of veal, and ten ounces of fat and lean pork. Simmer one chopped onion and six shallots in butter, and add to the meat. Season with salt, pepper, a little grated nutmeg and Cayenne pepper, and chopped parsley. Add a glassful of water, one dozen chopped anchovies, a little chopped garlic, two raw eggs, and some chives, chopped fine. Roll into small round balls about one inch in diameter. Bring two quarts of thin caper sauce to a boil, and boil the meat balls in it for about a half hour. Serve in a deep dish with the sauce.

Ginger snaps. Work one-half pound of sugar and one-quarter pound of butter together until creamy. Then add one egg, and work well again. Add one gill of molasses, one teaspoonful of powdered ginger, one-half ounce of soda dissolved in a gill of water; and mix in lightly one pound of flour. Roll out about one-eighth inch thick, and cut with a round cutter the size desired. Put them in a buttered pan, brush with egg, and bake in a moderate oven.

Potage Fontange. Make a purée of white beans. Simmer some sliced sorrel in butter, and add to the soup before serving.

Fillet of sole, Doria. Put four fillets of sole in a buttered sauté pan, season with salt and pepper, add a half glass of claret, and cover with buttered paper. Bake in oven, and when done remove the fish to a platter. Put in a casserole one ounce of butter, and heat same. Add to the hot butter one ounce of flour, one cup of stock or bouillon, the remainder of the claret used in cooking the fish, and one spoonful of meat extract. Season with salt, pepper, and a teaspoonful of Worcestershire sauce, boil for five minutes, and strain. Cut some cucumbers in round balls and simmer in butter. Add to the sauce, and pour over the fish.

Tenderloin of beef, Brillat Savarin. Roast tenderloin of beef, sauce Madère, garnished with stuffed fresh mushrooms and stuffed tomatoes.

MAY 16

BREAKFAST
 Blackberry jam
 Buckwheat cakes
 Rolls
 Coffee

LUNCHEON
 Canapé St. Francis
 Eggs Mirabel
 Sour schmorrbraten
 Noodles
 Roquefort cheese and crackers
 Coffee

DINNER
 Consommé Tosca
 Lyon sausage and pimentos
 Crab meat in chafing dish
 Chicken sauté, Amphitian
 Timbale of rice, Créole
 Parisian potatoes
 Romaine salad
 Savarin au kirsch
 Demi tasse

Eggs Mirabel. Spread some foie gras on four pieces of toast, lay a poached egg on top of each piece, and cover with sauce Perigueux.

Sour schmorrbraten. Rub a six pound piece of rump of beef with salt and pepper, and a piece of garlic. Place in an earthern pot, add one sliced onion, one carrot, a little celery, leeks, parsley, two bay leaves, one sprig of thyme, and two cloves. Boil one quart of white wine vinegar, pour over all in the earthen jar, and allow to stand in the ice box from thirty-six to forty-eight hours. Then put two ounces of butter in a casserole and heat. When hot put in the piece of meat and fry on all sides until nice and brown, and then remove. Then put two spoonfuls of flour in the casserole and allow to brown, add one glass of the vinegar used to pickle the beef, and one and one-half quarts of bouillon or stock. Then put in the beef again, bring to a boil, and add three chopped tomatoes. When the beef is soft, slice fine. Reduce the sauce, season well, and strain over the beef.

Consommé Tosca. Peel and cut a cucumber in small squares, boil in salt water until soft, and then allow to become cool. Cut one-half stalk of celery Julienne style, and cook in salt water until soft. Cook one-half pound of large barley in salt water for two hours, and cool. Boil two quarts of consommé, add two peeled tomatoes cut in small squares, and boil for two minutes. Add the cucumber. celery and barley, and serve.

Chicken sauté Amphitian. Joint a chicken, season with salt and pepper, and sauté in butter. When done place on a platter. Slice four heads of fresh mushrooms, put in a casserole with one ounce of butter, season with salt and pepper, and simmer till soft. Then add two sliced truffles, and one-half glass of sherry wine, and boil for five minutes. Then add one cup of brown gravy (meat or chicken gravy); and pour over the chicken. Garnish the platter with four timbales of rice, à la Créole.

Timbales of rice, Créole. Prepare some rice Créole, as described December 23. Butter four timbale moulds, fill with the rice, and then turn them out. Serve as a garnish, or as a vegetable with tomato sauce.

MAY 17

BREAKFAST
  Apple jelly
  Omelet with onions
  Rolls
  Coffee

LUNCHEON
  Poached eggs, St. Pierre
  Sand dabs, miller style
  Lamb hash with peppers
  Chow chow
  Neapolitan sandwich (ice cream)
  Assorted cakes   Coffee

DINNER
  Crème Bagration   Salted Jordan almonds
  Fillet of flounder, Circassienne
  Tournedos Niçoise   Duchesse potatoes
  Asparagus, Hollandaise
  Escarole and chicory salad
  Cherry pie   Coffee

Omelet with onions. Chop an onion very fine. Simmer slowly until soft, in an omelet pan in one ounce of butter. Then add eight beaten eggs, season with salt and pepper; and make the omelet in the usual manner.

Poached eggs, St. Pierre. Lay four poached eggs on four pieces of anchovy toast, and cover with anchovy sauce.

Anchovy toast. 1. Mix one spoonful of anchovy paste with one spoonful of butter, and spread on toast.

2. Soak two dozen salt anchovies in cold water for fifteen minutes. Then dry them and force them through a fine sieve. Mix with two ounces of butter, and spread on toast.

Lamb hash with peppers. Chop an onion and two green peppers, and put in a casserole with two ounces of butter. Simmer till soft, then add two pounds of roast or boiled lamb, cut in small squares, and one pound of chopped boiled potatoes, one cup of bouillon or stock, a little salt and pepper, and six red peppers (pimentos) cut in small squares. Mix well, cover, and simmer in oven for forty minutes. Serve on a platter, garnished with toast cut in triangles, and with chopped parsley on top. If desired, a spoonful of Worcestershire sauce may be added when mixing the hash.

Neapolitan sandwich. In a brick-shaped mould put three layers of ice cream of different colors, such as pistache, vanilla and strawberry. Freeze very hard. Make a layer of sponge cake about one-half inch thick. Put the brick of ice cream on top of a slice of the cake, and lay another slice of cake on top of the ice cream. Serve in slices about one inch thick. The cake should be trimmed to the size of the brick, and should be cut through crosswise to serve.

Crème Bagration. Cream of chicken with small pieces of boiled macaroni served in it.

Fillet of flounder, Circassienne. Put four fillets of flounders in a flat buttered pan, season with salt and pepper. Lay a slice of cucumber on top of each fillet, then one slice of peeled tomatoes, then a few slices of pickles and a teaspoonful of capers. Season with salt and pepper again, add a glass of white wine, and one-half ounce of butter on top of each piece of fish, and bake in the oven. Serve hot, direct from the oven.

Tournedos Niçoise. Broil, or sauté in butter, a small tenderloin steak. Dish up on a platter, with Madeira sauce with stuffed olives.

Stuffed olives. Cut the stones out of a dozen large green olives, and fill with chicken force meat (chicken dumplings). Boil in bouillon, stock, water, white sauce, or any other kind of sauce. Stuffed olives are used principally in sauces, or as a garnish for meats and fish.

MAY 18

BREAKFAST
California marmalade
Boiled eggs
Butter toast
Chocolate with whipped cream

LUNCHEON
Assorted hors d'oeuvres
Clam broth, Bellevue
Crab meat, au gratin
Broiled mutton chops
French fried potatoes
Sliced tomatoes, French dressing
Lillian Russell
Lady fingers
Demi tasse

DINNER
Consommé aux éclairs
Fillet of sole, Lord Curzon
Roast chicken
Potato croquettes
Cold artichokes, mustard sauce
Broiled fresh mushrooms on toast
Orange coupe
Macaroons
Coffee

California marmalade. One grapefruit, one orange, and two lemons. Shave the fruit very thin, discarding the seeds only. Pack lightly into an earthern vessel, add just water enough to cover, and allow to stand from twelve to twenty-four hours. Then bring to a boil, and simmer for fifteen minutes. Return to the earthern vessel and allow to stand for another twenty-four hours. Then measure, and add an equal quantity of sugar, return to stove and boil until it jells. Put up in jelly glasses.

Lillian Russell. Cut a nice cantaloupe in half, remove the seeds, and set each half in cracked ice. Fill with ice cream, with a sprinkle of maraschino on top.

Consommé aux éclairs. Make some small éclairs about one inch long. Chop a little white meat of chicken very fine, add some salt and a little whipped cream, and mix well. Split the éclairs and fill with the prepared chicken meat. Serve on a napkin. Have the consommé very hot, with a little Cayenne pepper in it.

Fillet of sole, Lord Curzon. Cut one green pepper, three heads of fresh mushrooms, and one peeled tomato in small squares. Put in a sauté pan with one ounce of butter, and simmer. Lay four fillets of flounder in a frying pan, season with salt and pepper and a chopped shallot, spread the simmered vegetables on top, add one glass of white wine, sprinkle with a spoonful of curry powder, cover, and bake ten minutes. Then remove the fish to a platter. To the pan add one cupful of Hollandaise sauce and one and one-half cupfuls of tomato sauce. Mix well and pour over the fish. Now place the platter with the fish and sauce in a very hot oven and brown slightly.

MAY 19

BREAKFAST
    Fresh raspberries with cream
    Waffles
    Honey in the comb
    Coffee

LUNCHEON
    Cantaloupe
    Eggs, Waterloo
    Breaded pork chops, tomato sauce
    Lorraine potatoes
    Cole slaw
    French pastry
    Coffee

DINNER
    Veloutine aurore
    Lake Tahoe trout, meunière
    Cucumber salad
    Leg of lamb, Rénaissance
    Château potatoes
    Millionaire punch
    Assorted cakes
    Coffee

Eggs, Waterloo. Spread some foie gras on four pieces of toast, place a poached egg on each, and cover with Béarnaise sauce.

Veloutine aurore. Mix two pints of velouté of chicken soup with one pint of purée of tomatoes.

Leg of lamb, Renaissance. Garnish a roast leg of lamb with small croûstades filled with chickens' livers sauté au Madère, and artichokes bottoms filled with macédoine of vegetables. Serve sauce Périgueux separate.

Millionaire punch. Sliced mixed fruits and a few berries soaked in Chartreuse. Serve in punch glasses with lemon water ice on top.

Raspberry juice. Mash some clean ripe raspberries to a pulp, and allow to stand over night. Then strain through a jelly bag, and to each pint of juice add one cupful of granulated sugar. Boil for three minutes, and seal hermetically in bottles, while hot. Other berries or fruit may be prepared in the same manner. This is a good substitute for brandy or wine, for puddings or sauces. It also makes a nice drink when added to a glass of ice water.

Boiled cider. Put five quarts of sweet newly-made cider, before fermentation has set in, in a granite kettle, put on the fire and boil slowly until reduced to one quart. Seal in a bottle while hot. For mince pies, fruit cake, etc., use about a gill to a quart of mince meat, or cake dough.

Peach with brandy sauce. Bring one pint of water and one pound of sugar to the boiling point, add four peeled peaches, and cook slowly until they are soft. Remove the peaches to a bowl. Reduce the syrup one-half, add a large pony of brandy, and pour over the peaches.

MAY 20

BREAKFAST
  Quince jelly
  Oatmeal with cream
  Crescents
  Chocolate with whipped cream

LUNCHEON
  Grapefruit with cherries
  Eggs en cocotte, Porto Rico
  Filet mignon, Maréchale
  New peas
  Lettuce salad
  Camembert cheese with crackers
  Coffee

DINNER
  Little Neck clams
  Consommé Sarah Bernhardt
  Ripe California olives
  Boiled Tahoe trout, Vatchett
  Broiled Porterhouse steak, Bércy
  French fried potatoes
  String beans
  Sliced tomatoes, mayonnaise
  Peaches, brandy sauce
  Assorted cakes
  Coffee

Eggs en cocotte, Porto Rico. Butter four cocotte dishes. Cut a peeled tomato in small squares and distribute in the four dishes, season with salt and pepper, and simmer for two minutes. Then add a slice of boiled ham cut in small dices, and a few fresh-cooked asparagus tips. Break an egg in each dish, season with salt and pepper, put a small piece of butter on top, and bake in oven for about five minutes.

Filet mignon, Maréchale. Broil or sauté four small tenderloin of beef steaks, and season well. Slice four heads of fresh mushrooms and chop four shallots. Put them in a casserole and simmer until done, then add two truffles sliced fine, and a small glass of sherry wine, and reduce until nearly dry. Then add two cupfuls of brown gravy, and cook again for five minutes, season with salt and Cayenne pepper, and pour over the fillets, on a platter.

Consommé Sarah Bernhardt. Consommé tapioca with small lobster dumplings. Cook a few leaves of fresh tarragon in clear consommé, and strain into the consommé tapioca before serving.

Boiled Tahoe trout, Vatchett. Put two nice Lake Tahoe trout in cold water, with a little salt, one sliced onion, one carrot, a bay leaf and a clove, some parsley and chervil. Bring to the boiling point, then set on side of the range for fifteen minutes. Serve on a napkin, with small round boiled potatoes, parsley in branches, and quartered lemons. Serve separate a sauce formed by mixing one cup of Hollandaise sauce, one and one-half cupfuls of tomato sauce, and a few chopped truffles.

Broiled Porterhouse steak, Bércy. Season a four pound Porterhouse steak with salt and pepper, roll it in oil, and broil. When nearly done place on a china platter and put on top a mixture of three ounces of butter, four shallots chopped very fine, a spoonful of chopped parsley, a little chives sliced very fine, a spoonful of meat extract, and the juice of two lemons. Put in oven and cook for five minutes. Garnish with plenty of well-washed watercress, and three lemons cut in half.

MAY 21

BREAKFAST
Pineapple preserves
Boiled eggs
Dry toast
Coffee

LUNCHEON
Antipasto
Consommé in cups
Beef à la mode
Baked potatoes
Hearts of romaine salad
Strawberry cream pie
Coffee

DINNER
Purée Camelia
Radishes. Salted almonds
Boiled salmon, Hollandaise
Potatoes natural
Roast tame duckling
Apple sauce
Potatoes au gratin
Cold asparagus, mustard sauce
Chocolate ice cream
Lady fingers   Coffee

Purée Camelia. Boil two pounds of green peas in one quart of chicken broth; with the addition of a bouquet garni. When the peas are soft remove the bouquet, and strain the soup through a fine sieve. Put back in casserole, bring to a boil, season with salt and white pepper; and add three ounces of sweet butter, stirring well to ensure its being melted.

Beef à la mode. Take about five pounds of rump of beef and lard it with a special larding needle with fresh larding pork. Season with salt and pepper, and lay in earthen pot. Cover with half claret and half water, add one sliced onion, one sliced carrot, one bouquet garni; and allow to stand for twenty-four hours. In a casserole put one spoonful of melted butter, and when the casserole is hot put the piece of beef in it and fry brown on both sides. Put the beef on a platter, and add to the casserole one ounce of fresh butter and two spoonfuls of flour, let it become brown, then add the wine, water and vegetables used in the earthen pot, bring to the boiling point, put the beef in it and simmer until the beef is soft. Place the beef on a platter, and strain the sauce through a fine sieve. Garnish the beef with carrots, onions glacés, peas and potatoes.

MAY 22

BREAKFAST
Fresh blackberries with cream
Scrambled eggs with bacon
Southern corn pone
Coffee

LUNCHEON
Canapé of raw beef
Clam broth en Bellevue
Sand dabs, meunière
Potatoes au gratin
Chiffonnade salad
Strawberries Parisienne
Coffee

DINNER
Consommé, quenelles Doria
Broiled halibut, Alcide
Smoked beef tongue with spinach
Baked potatoes
Sorbet Eau de Vie de Dantzig
Assorted cakes
Coffee

Canapé of raw beef. Chop one-half pound of lean fresh beef very fine, and season with salt and pepper. Spread four slices of rye bread, first with sweet butter, and then with the chopped beef. Place on a napkin and garnish with lettuce leaves filled with chopped onions, sliced pickles, ripe olives, and two lemons cut in half.

Strawberries, Parisienne. Put some nice ripe strawberries in a bowl and put in the ice box until very cold. Make a sauce by mixing one-half pint of strawberry pulp, made by passing some strawberries through a fine strainer or sieve; one-quarter pound of powdered sugar, the juice of one lemon, and a half pint of whipped cream. Do not whip the cream too hard. When well mixed pour over the strawberries, and serve on cracked ice.

Consommé, quenelles Doria. Make a cream puff paste. When cold, form into small balls the size of a pea, and fry in swimming lard. Serve on a napkin with hot consommé.

Broiled halibut, Alcide. Cut the halibut in slices one and one-half inches thick, season with salt and pepper, roll them in oil, and broil. To a Colbert sauce add two chopped hard-boiled eggs, and pour over the fish; which has been placed on a platter. Garnish with six small fried smelts.

Southern corn pone. Mix one quart of yellow corn meal with cold water, into a soft dough. Add one teaspoonful of salt, a little melted lard, and a little sugar. Shape with the hands into oval cakes, so that the impression of the fingers will show. Bake in a well-greased pan in a very hot oven.

Smoked beef tongue with spinach. Put a smoked tongue in a casserole and cover with cold water, bring to a boil, and then set at the side of the stove and simmer slowly until soft. Cook some spinach English style, and place on platter. Slice the beef tongue and place on top of the spinach. Serve with it either sauce Madère, Champagne sauce, or plain bouillon.

Sorbet Eau de Vie de Dantzig. One pound of sugar, three pints of water, the juice of two lemons and one orange, and the whites of two eggs beaten with one gill of maraschino. Freeze, and serve in sorbet glasses, with Eau de Vie de Dantzig on top. Pour the Eau de Vie on immediately before serving, so the silver leaves will show.

MAY 23

BREAKFAST
    Sliced apricots with cream
    Plain shirred eggs
    Dry toast
    Coffee

LUNCHEON
    Eggs Hongroise
    Calf's liver sauté, sauce Robert
    Lyonnaise potatoes
    String bean salad
    Raspberry cream pie
    Demi tasse

DINNER
    Little Neck clams
    Cooper soup
    Queen olives
    Crab meat, Suzette
    Roast capon, au jus
    Potato croquettes
    Cold artichokes, mayonnaise
    Caramel ice cream
    Macaroons
    Coffee

Eggs, Hongroise. Boil a cup of rice, and spread on a platter, lay four poached eggs on top. Place some chickens' livers, that have been cooked sauté in butter, around the rice; and cover all with sauce Périgueux.

Calf's liver sauté, sauce Robert. Slice some calf's liver three-quarters of an inch thick. Season with salt and pepper, roll in flour, and fry in melted butter. Place on a platter and cover with sauce Robert.

Sauce Robert. Slice two onions very fine and put in casserole with two ounces of butter. Simmer slowly until soft; then add a spoonful of flour and simmer again. Then add one pint of bouillon, one spoonful of vinegar, two spoonfuls of French mustard, one spoonful of meat extract, and some salt and pepper. Cook for thirty minutes. Before serving add some chopped parsley. Serve with boiled beef, tongue, etc.

String bean salad. Boil two quarts of cleaned string beans in salt water. Allow to become cool, place in salad bowl, season with salt and pepper, add two spoonfuls of white wine vinegar, five of olive oil, and a little chopped parsley. Mix well.

Strawberry cream pie. Line a plate with pie dough and bake it. (Put some white beans in the pie so it will not lose its shape while baking. When done remove the beans.) Place a handful of biscuit crumbs in the bottom, and fill with strawberries. Dust with powdered sugar, and garnish with whipped cream on top.

Raspberry cream pie. Make in the same manner as strawberry cream pie.

Banana cream pie. Use sliced bananas, and make in the same manner as strawberry cream pie.

Cooper soup. Slice three large onions and put in casserole with two ounces of butter. Cover, and simmer until the onions are done. Then add one and one-half quarts of bouillon, consommé or chicken broth; season with salt and pepper, and boil for thirty minutes. Strain. Serve toasted French bread and grated Parmesan cheese separate.

Caramel ice cream. Boil one and one-half pounds of sugar with one pint of water until slightly brown. Add two quarts of milk and stir until the sugar is dissolved. Mix one pint of milk with the yolks of eight eggs and stir gradually into the boiling milk until well mixed. Remove from the fire, add one quart of cream, and freeze.

MAY 24

BREAKFAST
Pineapple preserves
Breakfast sausages
Flannel cakes
Rolls
Coffee

LUNCHEON
Cantaloupe
Fried smelts, **Tartar sauce**
English mutton chops, **XX Century Club**
Celery root, beet and field salad
Cottage cheese and crackers
Coffee

DINNER
Consommé aux perles de **Nizam**
Fillet of perch, St. Charles
Shoulder of lamb, baker's oven style
Romaine salad
Baba au rhum
Coffee

English mutton chop, XX Century Club. Secure from the butcher four English mutton chops with the kidneys. Season with salt and pepper, roll in oil, and broil. Place on a platter and cover with sauce Madère. Garnish with four red peppers (pimentos) stuffed with purée of sweet potatoes.

Cottage cheese. Let two quarts of milk become sour. Put in a cheese cloth and allow to hang for twenty-four hours, so all the water can drain out. Then put the curd in a salad bowl, season with salt and pepper, mix well until smooth; or strain it through a fine sieve; then add a cup of sweet cream, and some chives cut very fine.

Consommé aux perles de Nizam. Perles de Nizam is large pearl tapioca. Boil two quarts of consommé, then add slowly one-half pound of pearl tapioca, and cook slowly until soft.

Fillet of perch, St. Charles. Cut four fillets of perch and place in sauté pan with butter, salt, white pepper, and one-half glass of white wine. Cover with buttered paper and simmer for ten minutes, then remove the fish to a platter. Put in the same sauté pan one pint of white wine sauce, and boil for five minutes. Strain, and add a few slices of truffle, and the tail of a lobster cut in thin slices. Pour over the fish, and sprinkle some chopped lobster corals over all.

Shoulder of lamb, baker's oven style. Season a shoulder of lamb with salt and pepper, and rub with a piece of garlic. Then place in a deep earthen flat pan, or a roasting pan about two inches deep. Slice eight potatoes to the size of a silver dollar, and slice six onions very fine. Mix together and put on top and around the piece of lamb. Add a bay leaf and two cloves to the pan, sprinkle with salt, fresh-ground pepper, and some chopped parsley, add two quarts of water, and put in a baker's oven; or in the stove oven; and simmer slowly for about two and one-half hours. Do not cover while cooking, and if the stove oven is used do not have it too hot. Serve from the pan in which it was cooked.

MAY 25

BREAKFAST
Strawberries with cream
Boiled eggs
Buttered toast
Chocolate with whipped cream

LUNCHEON
Scrambled eggs, Marseillaise
Crab meat, Louise
Corned beef hash, au gratin
Lettuce salad with French dressing
Banana cream pie
Demi tasse

DINNER
Cream soup, à l'Algerienne
Salted pecans
Sole, Colbert
Filet mignon, Chéron
Olivette potatoes
Chicory salad
Victoria punch
Assorted cakes
Coffee

Scrambled eggs, Marseillaise. Peel and slice two fresh tomatoes and put in casserole with two ounces of butter. Simmer for five minutes. Rub the inside of a bowl with garlic, break twelve eggs in the bowl and beat them. Add salt and pepper and half a cup of cream, pour into the casserole and scramble in the usual manner.

Cream soup, à l'Algerienne. Boil two sweet potatoes, and force through a fine sieve. Add two quarts of cream of chicken soup. If too thick add a little plain chicken broth, or boiling milk, season well, and strain. Before serving add two cups of boiled rice.

Sole, Colbert. Cut off the head of a large sole, and pull off the black skin. Lift off the four fillets complete, spreading the two sides apart with two toothpicks, so they will not touch. Dip in milk, then in flour, and then in beaten eggs and fresh bread crumbs, the lower side only. Dip the top side in milk and flour. Season well with salt and pepper, and place in a pan with butter, and two ounces of butter on top of the fish. Bake in the oven, basting continually until done. Then put the sole on a platter, remove the toothpicks and fill the space with two ounces of butter that has been mixed with salt, pepper, a little chopped parsley, one spoonful of meat extract, and the juice of one lemon. Place the platter in the oven just long enough to melt the butter. Garnish with parsley in branches and lemons cut in half. The whole sole may be fried in swimming lard instead of baking, if desired. This way is easier, but is not the correct one.

Filet mignon, Chéron. Sprinkle four small tenderloin steaks with salt and pepper, roll in oil, and broil; or sauté in pan with butter. Place on a platter, cover with Béarnaise sauce, lay a slice of truffle on top of each, and have for each fillet one artichoke bottom filled with macedoine of vegetables.

Victoria punch. Two pounds of sugar, two quarts of water, and the juice of six oranges, mixed. Then add a small glass of rhum, a small glass of kirsch, and a glass of sauternes. Freeze. Serve in glasses, covered with a meringue made with the white of three eggs and one-half pound of sugar.

MAY 26

BREAKFAST
- Preserved pears
- Broiled salt mackerel with melted butter
- Baked potatoes
- Rolls
- Coffee

LUNCHEON
- Cantaloupe
- Poached eggs, Vanderbilt
- Breaded veal cutlets, tomato sauce
- Spaghetti in cream
- Allumettes (cake)
- Coffee

DINNER
- Consommé aux pluches
- Ripe California olives
- Fillet of halibut, sauce **Venitienne**
- Roast tame duck, apple **sauce**
- Asparagus Hollandaise
- Potatoes au gratin
- Lettuce and grapefruit **salad**
- Soufflé glacé
- Assorted cakes
- Coffee

Poached eggs, Vanderbilt. Make a purée of fresh mushrooms and spread over toast. Lay a poached egg on top, and cover with sauce Madère.

Breaded veal cutlets, tomato sauce. Have your butcher cut four veal cutlets from the leg, and about one-third of an inch thick. Season with salt and pepper, roll in flour, then in beaten eggs, and finally in fresh bread crumbs. Heat a half cup of melted butter in a frying pan, and fry the cutlets. Serve on a platter with tomato sauce.

Spaghetti in cream. Boil half a pound of spaghetti in two quarts of water seasoned with a little salt, and when soft drain off the water. Melt an ounce of butter in a casserole, add one-half spoonful of flour, one-half cup of boiling milk, and one-half cup of cream, season with salt and pepper, and boil for five minutes. Pour over the spaghetti, adding a half cup of grated Parmesan or Swiss cheese.

Consommé aux pluches. Slice a head of lettuce and two leaves of tarragon very fine. Boil in two quarts of consommé for thirty minutes. Add some chervil before serving.

Fillet of halibut, sauce Venitienne. Put four fillets of halibut in a buttered sauté pan, season with salt and pepper, add one-half glass of white wine, cover with buttered manilla paper, and bake in the oven for fifteen minutes. Then place the fish on a platter, put in the sauté pan one pint of white wine sauce, and simmer for a few minutes. Then add two spoonfuls of green coloring, and strain over fish.

Sauce Venitienne. Use any kind of white meat or fish sauce, depending upon what it is to be used with, and color with green vegetable coloring. Use enough color to make the sauce bright green.

Soufflé glacé (plain). Whip a pint of rich cream. Beat the yolks of four eggs with one-quarter pound of sugar, until very light, then add the cream to it. Beat the whites of five eggs very stiff, and add to the cream. Put into fancy paper cases, specially made for this purpose, and freeze in the ice cream box. If you have no ice cream box, put them in a thin vessel, cover tightly, and pack in cracked ice with rock salt mixed with it.

MAY 27

BREAKFAST
    Fresh raspberries with cream
    Shirred eggs with bananas
    Dry toast
    Coffee

LUNCHEON
    Eggs, presidential
    Frogs' legs, Greenway
    Broiled squab chicken on **toast**
    Soufflé potatoes
    Hearts of romaine, Roquefort dress-
      ing
    Strawberries à la mode
    Lady fingers   Coffee

DINNER
    Crème cardinal
    Radishes
    Crab meat, gourmet
    Small tenderloin steak, Fedora
    Artichokes, sauce mousseline
    Watercress, salad
    Wine jelly, au Chartreuse
    Assorted cakes   Coffee

Shirred eggs with bananas. Peel a banana and slice it very fine. Put half and half in two buttered shirred egg dishes, and allow to become hot. Then put two eggs in each dish, season with salt and pepper, put in oven and cook.

Eggs, presidential. Boil until quite soft some left-over roasted or boiled chicken, mix with a little cream sauce, season well, and pass through a fine sieve. Place on artichoke bottoms, put on a buttered dish, and set in oven to get hot. Then lay a poached egg on top, cover with well-seasoned cream sauce, and put two slices of truffle on top.

Frogs' legs, Greenway. Cut a dozen frogs' legs in two, and sprinkle with salt and pepper. Melt two ounces of butter in a sauté pan, add the frogs' legs and simmer for five minutes, then add a spoonful of flour and simmer again for a few minutes. Then add one-half glass of white wine, one cup of chicken broth, or any kind of clear white broth, some chopped chives, parsley and chervil, and cook for five minutes. Before serving season well, and bind with the yolk of one egg and one-half cup of cream.

Strawberries, à la mode. Selected strawberries with vanilla ice cream on top.

Raspberries, à la mode. Prepare in the same manner as strawberries à la mode.

Crème cardinal. Pound the shells of two lobsters very fine, in a mortar. Then put in a casserole with three ounces of butter, a sliced onion and carrot, one leek and a little celery, and simmer for twenty minutes. Take care that it does not burn, and simmer slowly. Then add three ounces of flour, mix well, add two quarts of milk, season well with salt and a little Cayenne pepper, boil for half an hour, and then strain through a fine sieve or cheese cloth. Return to the casserole, bring to a boil, and bind with the yolks of two eggs and one-half cup of cream. Put in a soup tureen. Cut the tail of a lobster and two truffles in small dices, put them in a casserole, season with salt and a little Cayenne pepper, add a pony of good brandy and a pony of dry sherry, bring to a boil, and pour into the soup.

Small tenderloin steak, Fedora. Season four small tenderloin steaks with salt and pepper, roll in oil, and broil; or sauté in butter. When done place on top of a thin slice of heated, or fresh-boiled, ham, and cover with Bordelaise sauce.

MAY 28

BREAKFAST
   Strawberry jam
   Calf's liver and bacon
   Baked potatoes
   Rolls
   Coffee

LUNCHEON
   Grapefruit with chestnuts
   Eggs, Columbus
   Broiled pig's feet, tomato sauce
   Mashed turnips
   Cannelons à la crème
   Demi tasse

DINNER
   Consommé, profiteroles
   Lyons sausage
   Sand dabs, Grenobloise
   Broiled chicken, Tyrolienne
   Potatoes château
   String beans in butter
   Chiffonnade salad
   Fresh raspberry cup
   Macaroons
   Coffee

Eggs, Columbus. Put some green peppers in hot, swimming lard for a minute. Then peel and cut in orange shape. Cut some pimentos in orange shape. Heat both in warm butter, lay two of each on each poached egg on toast.

Cannelons à la crème. Roll out half a pound of puff paste, that was made with six turns, to about one-eighth inch thick. Cut in strips eight inches long and one inch wide. Wash with egg, and roll on buttered sticks about one inch in diameter. Place on pan and bake in moderate oven. Remove the sticks while hot. When cold fill with sweetened whipped cream.

Cornets à la crème. Same as for cannelons, but roll the strips around cornecopia shaped sticks, or tins.

Consommé, profiteroles. Make a cupful of cream puff paste, add two spoonfuls of grated cheese, put in pastry bag with round tube, and dress on pan. Make very small, about the size of a pea. Put in oven and bake. Serve separate with hot consommé.

Sand dabs, Grenobloise. Remove the skins from four sand dabs, dry with a towel, season with salt and pepper, roll in flour, and fry in pan with butter. Remove to a platter. Put two ounces of butter in the pan, cook until the color of hazelnuts, and pour over the fish. Sprinkle with chopped parsley, and lay two slices of lemon on top of each fish.

Broiled chicken, Tyrolienne. Cut a spring chicken in four, lay in a deep porcelain dish, sprinkle with salt and pepper, add one shallot or small onion, chopped fine, a little chopped parsley and tarragon, two cloves, and half a cup of olive oil. Let it stand for one hour. Then take out the chicken and roll in freshly made bread crumbs, and broil slowly for fifteen minutes. Place on a platter and garnish with two lemons cut in half, and parsley in branches. Serve rémoulade sauce separate.

MAY 29

BREAKFAST
    Gooseberries with cream
    Boiled eggs
    Toast Melba
    English breakfast tea

LUNCHEON
    Assorted hors d'oeuvres
    Clam broth in cups
    Fried smelts, sauce Tartar
    Asparagus Polonaise
    Cornet à la crème
    Coffee

DINNER
    Potage Albert
    Sardines on toast
    Boiled Lake Tahoe trout, pepper
        sauce
    Hollandaise potatoes
    Shad roe, Bordelaise
    Peas and carrots in cream
    Lettuce and grapefruit salad
    Jelly roll
    Demi tasse

Potage, Albert. Two-thirds purée of potato soup and one-third very thick Consommé Julienne.

Boiled lake trout, pepper sauce. Put two trout in a fish kettle filled with water. Season with salt, add a sliced onion, one carrot, a bouquet garni, and a spoonful of whole black peppers tied in a cheese cloth. Boil until done. Put the fish on a napkin, and garnish with small round boiled potatoes, parsley in branches, and quartered lemons. Serve pepper sauce separate.

Pepper sauce. Crush with a bottle on a hardwood table or marble one spoonful of whole black peppers. Put the crushed peppers in a casserole with a glass of white wine. Boil until nearly dry, add a pint of cream sauce, boil a minute, and strain through a cheese cloth. Season with salt.

Shad roe, Bordelaise. Place four shad roe in a buttered pan, season with salt and pepper, put a few pieces of butter on top, put in oven and cook for five minutes, basting all the time. Then sprinkle with three very finely chopped shallots, a little chopped parsley, chervil and chives, and the juice of one lemon. Bake in oven, and serve on platter with its own sauce.

Jelly roll. One-half pound of flour, six eggs, one-half ounce of baking powder, and some vanilla flavoring. Sift the flour and baking powder together. Beat the sugar and eggs together until light, then add the flour and flavoring, and mix. Spread very thin on paper, place in pan and bake. When done turn over on a paper that has been dusted with sugar. Peel the paper from the bottom of the cake at once. Spread with some jelly or marmalade, and roll up tightly. When cold cut in slices.

MAY 30

BREAKFAST
  Sliced peaches with cream
  Fried eggs with chives
  Dry toast
  Coffee

LUNCHEON
  Cantaloupe
  Frogs' legs sauté à sec
  Blood pudding, sauce Robert
  Mashed potatoes
  Escarole and chicory salad
  Apple turnover
  Demi tasse

DINNER
  Consommé Venitienne
  Fillet of halibut, Lilloise
  Tournedos, Bayard
  Jets de houblons
  Potatoes à la Reine
  Green corn
  Hearts of romaine, egg dressing
  Mousse au chocolat
  Small cakes   Coffee

Fried eggs with chives. Put an ounce of butter in a frying pan, break four eggs into the pan, season with salt and pepper, sprinkle some chives, chopped very fine, on top of the eggs, and fry.

Blood pudding, sauce Robert. Get two pounds of blood pudding from the butcher, put in frying pan with one ounce of melted butter, and fry for about fifteen minutes. Serve on a platter covered with sauce Robert.

Apple turnovers. Roll out some puff paste about one-eighth inch thick. Cut with a round cutter about four inches in diameter. Wet the edges with water, place a spoonful of chopped apples mixed with sugar and a little cinnamon on the center, and fold over, bringing the edges together, press a little, wash the top with beaten eggs and bake. When nearly done dust some powdered sugar on top, and return to oven until glaced.

Consommé Venitienne. In a bowl mix one and one-half spoonfuls of flour with three whole eggs and a little salt. Let this run through a colander into a quart of boiling consommé. Continue boiling for two minutes.

Fillet of halibut, Lilloise. Place four fillets of halibut in a buttered pan, season with salt and pepper, add a half glass of white wine, cover with buttered paper, and set in oven for ten minutes. Then put the fillets on a platter, and put in the fish pan one-half pint of white wine sauce and one-half pint of tomato sauce. Bring to a boil, and strain. Cut two slices of bacon in strips like matches (Julienne style), fry, and put in the sauce. Also add six leaves of tarragon chopped fine, season well, and pour over the fish.

Tournedos, Bayard. Season four small tenderloin steaks with salt and pepper. Heat two ounces of butter in a sauté pan, and sauté the fillets. Dress on toast spread with foie gras. Pour over them sauce Madère, to which has been added some sliced fresh mushrooms sauté in butter. Garnish with small round chicken croquettes, about one inch in diameter.

Mousse au café. Mix the yolks of six eggs with one-quarter pound of syrup at about twenty-eight degrees. Put in a basin in bain-marie and cook until it thickens. Remove from the fire and beat until cold. Add one-half cup of strong coffee and one pint of whipped cream. Mix well, put in mould and freeze. Serve decorated with sweetened whipped cream.

Mousse au chocolat. Same as above, but flavor with two ounces of melted cocoa or chocolate. instead of coffee.

MAY 31

BREAKFAST
  Fresh strawberries with cream
  Breakfast sausages with apple sauce
  Rolls
  Coffee

LUNCHEON
  Canapé Norway
  Eggs Biarritz
  English mutton chops, tavern
  Camembert cheese with crackers
  Coffee

DINNER
  Crème Congalaise
  Bass, Niçoise
  Potatoes nature
  Chicken sauté, demi-deuil
  Timbale of rice
  Flageolets in butter
  Alligator pear salad
  Peach, Bourdaloue
  Assorted cakes
  Demi tasse

Canapé Norway. Spread four pieces of toast with butter, lay thin slices of smoked salmon on top, trim to diamond shape, and dress on napkin. Garnish with parsley and lemon.

Eggs, Biarritz. Spread four pieces of toast with anchovy butter, lay on each piece a hard-boiled egg cut in two. Put a stuffed olive on each half of egg.

Crème Congalaise. Add a spoonful of curry powder to a cream of chicken soup. Also add the breast of a boiled chicken cut in small dices.

Bass, Niçoise. Cut a three-pound bass in slices about one inch thick. Put in a buttered fish pan, season with salt and pepper, spread over the top one-half teaspoonful of chopped garlic, four peeled and chopped tomatoes, some chopped parsley, and three ounces of butter in small bits. Put in oven and bake for twenty minutes. Serve from pan, direct from the oven. Other large fish may be prepared in the same manner.

Chicken sauté, demi-deuil. Cut a spring chicken in four, season with salt and pepper, put in a sauté pan with two ounces of butter, and simmer for five minutes, without allowing to get color. Then sprinkle with a spoonful of flour, and simmer again. Then add a cup of chicken broth or white bouillon, and boil for ten minutes. Then remove the chicken to a platter. Mix one-half cup of thick cream and the yolks of two eggs, and let it run into the boiling sauce. Season well, and strain. Slice one-half can of French mushrooms and two truffles, and add to the sauce. Heat, and pour over the chicken.

Timbale of rice. Make a risotto. Butter four timbale moulds, fill with risotto, and turn over on a platter. Serve with any desired sauce, such as suprême, cream, tomato, Madeira, etc. Or serve plain, as a garnish.

JUNE 1

BREAKFAST
　　Blackberry jelly
　　Ham and eggs
　　Rolls
　　Coffee

LUNCHEON
　　Little Neck clams on half shell
　　Consommé in cups
　　Cheese straws
　　Fried calf's brains, tomato sauce
　　Potatoes au gratin
　　Cold asparagus, mustard sauce
　　Raspberries à la mode
　　Sponge cake　　　Demi tasse

DINNER
　　Roçol soup, à la Russe
　　Boiled salmon, sauce diplomate
　　Larded tenderloin of beef, St. Martin
　　Green corn
　　Fresh Lima beans
　　Potatoes Marquise
　　Chicory salad with a chapon
　　Vanilla plombière
　　Macaroons　　　Coffee

Fried calf's brains, tomato sauce. Cut two cold boiled calf's brains in two lengthwise, season with salt and pepper, roll in flour, then in beaten eggs, and then in fresh bread crumbs. Fry in very hot swimming fat, and serve on napkin with parsley and lemon. Serve tomato sauce separate.

Boiled calf's brains. Let two fresh calf's brains soak in cold water for an hour, so the blood will run out. Then remove the skin with the fingers. Put in a casserole, cover with cold water, add salt, a bouquet garni, one-half of an onion, sliced, one-half of a carrot, sliced, and one-half of a wine-glassful of vinegar. Bring to the boiling point, skim, and let slowly simmer for ten minutes. Remove from the water and serve on napkin, with parsley and lemon. Serve melted butter, or other sauce, separate.

Roçol soup à la Russe. In a casserole put one veal knuckle, one pound of shin of beef, two slices of raw bacon, two slices of raw ham, and one soup hen. Cover with four quarts of water, add a spoonful of salt, bring to a boil, and skim well. Then add two carrots, two onions, two turnips, and a bouquet garni. As the meats become soft remove and cut in small squares. Then strain the broth through a cheese cloth into another casserole. Take off the fat from the top and bring to a boil. While it is boiling let one-half pound of farina run slowly into it. Cook for fifteen minutes, add the meats, season with salt, pepper, and a little chopped parsley and fennel.

Boiled salmon, sauce diplomate. Serve boiled salmon on a napkin, with small round boiled potatoes, parsley in branches, and quartered lemons. Serve sauce diplomate separate.

Sauce diplomate. To a pint of cream sauce add a spoonful of lobster butter and a spoonful of anchovy paste. Stir well, add a little Cayenne pepper, and three ounces of butter, little by little. Strain and serve.

Larded tenderloin of beef, St. Martin. Roast a larded tenderloin, and make a brown gravy. Put the tenderloin on a platter, and cut one slice for each person, leaving the remainder whole. Garnish with chickens' livers sauté in butter on each side of the platter. Add three sliced truffles and one-half glass of Madeira to the brown gravy, and boil for ten or fifteen minutes. Season well, and pour over the beef.

Potatoes Marquise. Same as Duchess potatoes.

JUNE 2

BREAKFAST
 Stewed prunes
 Boiled eggs
 Dry toast
 Ceylon tea

LUNCHEON
 Cantaloupe
 Eggs, Fedora
 Lamb chops, Bradford
 Sybil potatoes
 String bean salad
 Strawberry cream pie
 Coffee

DINNER
 Consommé Caroline
 Ripe California olives in oil and
  garlic
 Fillet of trout, Rachel
 Roast duckling, apple sauce
 Artichoke bottoms, au gratin
 Fresh asparagus, Hollandaise
 Escarole salad
 Mousse au café
 Demi tasse

Eggs, Fedora. Cut four hard-boiled eggs in two, lengthwise, remove the yolks and mash with a fork, in a bowl. Then add one-half cup of fresh bread crumbs, salt, pepper, the raw yolk of an egg, a little chopped chives and parsley, and one ounce of butter. Mix well, and fill the boiled whites with the mixture. Then roll in the beaten whites of eggs, and then in bread crumbs, and fry in hot swimming fat. Serve on a napkin, with fried parsley. Serve cream of tomato sauce separate.

Lamb chops, Bradford. Broil eight nice lamb chops, place on a platter, and garnish with stuffed hot olives. Pour sauce Madère, to which has been added whole fresh mushrooms sauté in butter, over the chops.

Consommé, Caroline. Make a royal with eight eggs to a quart of milk, or four eggs to a pint; add a little salt, pepper, and some grated nutmeg. Strain into a buttered mould, set in a bain-marie and boil. When set, and cold, remove from the mould and cut in small squares. Serve in very hot consommé with one spoonful of boiled rice to each person.

Fillet of trout, Rachel. Cut the fillets from two Tahoe trout. Use the bones and head to make a sauce Génoise. Put the fillets in a buttered fish pan, season with salt and pepper, add one-half glass of claret, and one-half glass of fish stock, bouillon or water, cover, and simmer for ten minutes. Remove the fish to a platter. Add to the sauce half of the tail of a lobster, one truffle, six heads of canned mushrooms cut in small squares, and one dozen small fish dumplings. Pour over the fish.

Chicory salad with chapon. Serve the salad with French dressing. Chapon is a crust of French bread rubbed with garlic, and added to the salad to flavor same.

JUNE 3

BREAKFAST
  Preserved pears
  Omelet with parsley
  Rolls
  Coffee

LUNCHEON
  Crab legs, à la Stock
  Eggs en cocotte, D'Uxelles
  English rump steak, maître d'hôtel
  French fried potatoes
  Wax beans in butter
  Sliced peaches with whipped cream
  Lady fingers
  Demi tasse

DINNER
  Cream of green corn
  Salted almonds
  Écrevisses, Lafayette
  Roast leg of mutton, au jus
  Mashed summer squash
  Potatoes, St. Francis
  Field salad
  Burgundy punch
  Assorted cakes
  Coffee

Crab legs, Stock. For four persons, put two leaves of lettuce on each dinner plate. Slice fine a head of lettuce and put on top of the lettuce leaves. Add to each plate one slice of peeled tomatoes, and on top place four legs of crab, or some crab meat, and two fillets of anchovies on top of the crab. Put in a salad bowl one spoonful of vinegar, one of tomato ketchup, one of Chili sauce, two of olive oil, one-half teaspoonful of Worcestershire sauce, one teaspoonful of salt, a little paprika, and some chopped chives. Mix well, and pour over the salad on the plates. Serve very cold.

Eggs, D'Uxelles. For individual portions, put in a buttered cocotte dish one spoonful of D'Uxelles (Jan. 11), break an egg on top, season with salt and pepper, put a little more D'Uxelles on top of the egg, then a little grated cheese and small bits of butter, and bake in oven until egg is **set.** Serve on a napkin.

Omelet with parsley. Beat eight eggs, season with salt, pepper and chopped parsley, add a spoonful of thick cream, and cook in the usual manner.

Burgundy punch. Two pounds of sugar, two quarts of water, the juice of six lemons and the rind of one, and one piece of cinnamon stick. Let the mixture infuse for about two hours. Freeze, and then add one pint of claret, a small glass of cognac, and a drop of red coloring.

Whipped cream. Put one-half pint of double cream into a bowl and whip until quite stiff, then add two ounces of powdered sugar and a few drops of vanilla extract. Mix well, and keep in a cool place until needed.

Sliced peaches with whipped cream. Peel and slice some ripe peaches, and sprinkle with a little sugar. Serve in individual dishes with a spoonful of whipped cream on the side.

Sliced bananas with whipped cream. Prepare in the same manner as peaches.

Sliced fruits with whipped cream. Prepare oranges, pears, figs, etc., in the same manner as peaches.

Berries of all kinds with whipped cream. Hull and wash the berries, dry in cheesecloth, and prepare in the same manner as peaches.

Cream of green corn. Put two pounds of veal bones in a casserole, cover with cold water, bring to a boil, and cool off in cold water. Put the bones back in the vessel in from three to four quarts of fresh water, add a little salt and a bouquet garni, bring to the boiling point, and skim. Cook for about one hour, then add eight ears of green corn and one pint of milk, and boil for ten minutes. Then take out the ears, cut off the grains and chop very fine, or mash in a mortar. Heat three ounces of butter in a casserole, then add three spoonfuls of flour, and when heated add two quarts of the strained veal and corn stock. Bring to a boil, stirring well with a whip. Let it boil slowly, add the corn, and cook for about thirty minutes. Strain through a fine sieve or cheesecloth, put back in the casserole, season to taste with salt and a little Cayenne pepper, stir in two ounces of sweet butter, and serve hot.

Écrevisses, Lafayette. Écrevisses, crawfish and crayfish are the same. Take the tails of twenty-four of the fish and put in sauté pan with two ounces of butter, season with salt and pepper, and simmer for five minutes. Then add a half glass of sherry wine and simmer until nearly dry; then add one and one-half cups of thick cream, and boil for five minutes. Thicken with the yolks of three eggs mixed with one-half cup of cream. Do not let it quite reach the boiling point after the yolks of eggs are added. Add a pony of very dry sherry wine, and serve in chafing dish.

Mashed summer squash. Peel three pounds of summer squash, cut in half, and put in casserole with two ounces of butter, season with salt and pepper, cover, and cook in oven for thirty minutes. Then strain through a fine sieve, put back in casserole, add two additional ounces of butter, and if too thick add a spoonful of thick cream.

JUNE 4

BREAKFAST
  Sliced figs with cream
  Bacon and eggs
  Chocolate with whipped cream
  Rolls

LUNCHEON
  Cold eggs, Danoise
  Broiled sea bass, maître d'hôtel
  Breast of squab, sauté in butter
  Summer squash, Native Son
  Potatoes sauté
  Watermelon
  Coffee

DINNER
  Consommé Japonnaise
  Radishes
  Shad roe, en bordure
  Cucumber salad
  Tenderloin of beef, Voisin
  Potatoes allumette
  Lettuce and alligator pear salad
  Vanilla ice cream
  Assorted cakes
  Demi tasse

Sliced figs with cream. Peel and slice some fresh figs and serve on a compotier, with powdered sugar and cream separate.

Cold eggs, Danoise. Make four pieces of anchovy toast, and lay on each a hard-boiled egg cut in two lengthwise. Cover the eggs with mayonnaise sauce.

Breast of squab, sauté in butter. Cut out the breasts of four raw squabs, season with salt and pepper, and roll in flour. Heat two ounces of butter in a sauté pan, add the squab breast and cook for about ten minutes, or until brown on both sides. Place on a platter, pour butter sauce over them, sprinkle with a little chopped parsley, and garnish with watercress and two lemons cut in half.

Summer squash, Native Son. Cut off the corn from four ears. Peel one pound of summer squash, and cut in one inch squares. Put them, with the corn, in a bowl and add three peeled tomatoes cut in squares. In a casserole put one chopped onion with two ounces of butter, and simmer until yellow, then add the corn, tomato and squash, season with salt and pepper, cover, and simmer for thirty minutes.

Consommé Japonnaise. Consommé aux perles de Nizam colored with yellow Breton coloring.

Shad roe, en Bordure. Butter a plank, lay four shad roe on top, season with salt and pepper, put small bits of butter on top of each roe, and set in oven. After ten minutes turn the roes over, make a bordure of potato croquette mixture around the plank, and return to oven to cook until done. Pour a little maître d'hôtel sauce on top, and garnish with parsley in branches and quartered lemons.

Tenderloin of beef, Voisin. Roast tenderloin of beef, garnished with fresh artichoke bottoms filled with tomatoes cut in small squares, sautéed in butter, and well seasoned. Serve sauce Choron separate.

Potatoes, allumette. Cut four potatoes in the form of matches, dry with a napkin, and fry in hot swimming lard until yellow and crisp. Remove, salt well, and serve on a napkin.

JUNE 5

BREAKFAST
- Raspberry jam
- Salted salmon belly, melted butter
- Baked potatoes
- Rolls
- Coffee

LUNCHEON
- Shirred eggs, Monaco
- Lake Tahoe trout, meunière
- Potatoes O'Brien
- Tomatoes, Mayonnaise
- Cream fritters
- Demi tasse

DINNER
- Little Neck clams on shell
- Sorrel soup, à l'eau
- Salted hazelnuts
- Terrapin sauté, au beurre noisette
- Fillet of bass, 1905
- Asparagus, Hollandaise
- Waldorf salad
- French pastry
- Coffee

Salted salmon belly, melted butter. Soak a salted salmon belly in cold water over night. Then place in vessel and cover with fresh cold water, bring to a boil, and then set at side of the range for twenty minutes. Dish up on a napkin on a platter, garnish with parsley in branches and quartered lemons. Serve melted butter separate.

Shirred eggs, Monaco. Put six chopped shallots in a casserole with one ounce of butter. Heat slightly, then add six sliced fresh mushrooms and one peeled and sliced tomato; season with salt and pepper, and simmer for ten minutes. Butter four individual shirred egg dishes, pour in the above preparation, break two eggs in each, season with salt and pepper, and cook in oven for five minutes.

Cream fritters. Mix two ounces of corn starch, four ounces of sugar, the yolks of four eggs, and half of the peel of a lemon, and warm up in a double boiler. Bring one-half pint of milk to the boiling point and add it to the mixture. Continue boiling, and stir all the time until it becomes thick. Then spread it on a platter about a half inch thick, and allow to become cold. Cut in pieces about two inches square, roll in flour, then in beaten eggs, and finally in bread crumbs, and fry in swimming lard, or in frying pan with plenty of melted butter. Dress on a napkin, and serve vanilla cream sauce separate.

Sorrel soup, à l'eau. Clean one pound of sorrel, wash well, and slice very thin. Put in casserole with two ounces of butter, cover, and simmer for five minutes. Then add two quarts of water, season with salt and pepper, add three sliced rolls, or one-half loaf of sliced French bread, and boil slowly for one hour. Put the yolks of three eggs in a large cup and fill with cream, mix, and let it run into the boiling soup. Serve at once.

JUNE 6

BREAKFAST
Strawberries with cream
Broiled mutton chops
Lyonnaise potatoes
Rolls
Coffee

LUNCHEON
Antipasto
Eggs, Belmont
Chickens' livers, au Madère
Risotto
Camembert cheese with crackers
Coffee

DINNER
Consommé Marchand
Pim olas
Fillet of sole, Mantane
Roast chicken
Corn au gratin
Stewed tomatoes
Potato croquettes
Escarole salad
Soufflé glacé, Pavlowa
Assorted cakes
Coffee

Eggs, Belmont. Butter four timbale moulds, put in each a spoonful of D'Uxelles, break an egg on top, season with salt and pepper, put in bain-marie, and bake until the eggs are set. Then turn out on a platter and cover with tomato sauce, to which a little chopped truffle has been added.

Consommé, Marchand. Cut a truffle Julienne style; also the breast of a boiled fowl and a few slices of smoked beef tongue. Serve in one quart of boiling well-seasoned consommé.

Pim olas. Pim olas are small green olives stuffed with red peppers (pimentos). They may be obtained in bottles of any grocer.

Fillet of sole, Mantane. Cut and trim four fillets of sole, fold over, season with salt and pepper, lay in a buttered sauté pan, add one-half glass of white wine, cover with buttered manilla paper, put in oven and bake for twelve minutes. Serve on a platter covered with Béarnaise sauce.

Soufflé glacé, Pavlowa. Whip a pint of rich cream until thick. Beat the yolks of four eggs with one-quarter pound of sugar, until very light. Then add it to the cream, with a pony of maraschino. Whip the whites of five eggs very hard, and add them to the mixture, mixing lightly. Then fill fancy paper cases until about one inch higher than the edges, and set to freeze. When hard, and just before serving, dip the tops in grated chocolate.

Soufflé glacé, St. Francis. Make a soufflé glacé Pavlowa mixture, dress in fancy paper cases, using a pastry bag with a fancy tube. Sprinkle some chopped pistache nuts on top, and freeze.

JUNE 7

BREAKFAST
Blackberries **with cream**
Plain scrambled **eggs**
Dry toast
English breakfast **tea**

LUNCHEON
Cantaloupe
Baked beans, **Boston style**
Brown bread
Citron pre**serves**
Kisses
Demi tasse

DINNER
Soft clam soup, Salem
California ripe olives
Boiled Tahoe trout, **sauce mousseline**
Potatoes nature
Cucumber salad
Vol au vent Toulouse
Stuffed capon, St. **Antoine**
Peas à la Française
Cardon à la moelle
Hearts of lettuce, French **dressing**
Coupe Orientale
Allumettes
Coffee

Soft clam soup, Salem. Remove the bellies from two dozen clams and put the remainder, with their juice, in a casserole. Add a quart of water, a bouquet garni, and some salt; bring to a boil, and strain over the clam bellies, which have been placed in a vessel. Bring to a boil again and add one pint of thick cream and two ounces of sweet butter. When butter is melted, season with salt and a little Cayenne pepper, and serve in a tureen. Serve broken crackers separate.

Boiled Tahoe trout, sauce mousseline. Put two Tahoe trout in a vessel in cold water, add one-half glassful of white wine vinegar, half of an onion and half of a carrot sliced, a bouquet garni, and a small handful of salt. Bring to a boil, and set on side of the range for twenty minutes. Serve on a platter on a napkin, garnished with small round boiled potatoes, lemons cut in two, and parsley in branches. Serve sauce mousseline separate. The potatoes may be served separate if desired.

Kisses. One pound of sugar, the whites of seven eggs, and some vanilla flavoring. Mix the sugar with a little water and boil until it is thick and sticky when cooled on a saucer. Beat the whites of the eggs until very stiff and dry, then add the hot sugar and continue beating until it becomes cold. Add a few drops of vanilla extract, and dress in a fancy shape on a buttered pan. Use a pastry bag with a fancy tube for forming them. When dry bake in a nearly cool oven.

Allumettes. Roll out some puff paste that was made with six turns, until it is about one-eighth inch thick. Spread with royal icing, and cut in strips about three-quarters of an inch wide and three inches long. Place on a wet baking pan, with a little space between, and bake in a moderate oven.

Royal icing (glacé royal). Put one-half pound of icing sugar in a bowl with the whites of two eggs and a couple of drops of lemon juice. Beat with a wooden spoon until very light and firm. While beating be careful that it does not dry on the sides of the bowl, and when finished cover immediately with a damp cloth. This icing may be used for frosting cakes, or for ornamental work.

JUNE 8

BREAKFAST
  Sliced peaches with cream
  Chipped beef on toast
  Crescents and rolls
  Cocoa

LUNCHEON
  Shirred eggs, Argenteuil
  Sweetbreads braisé, St. George
  Flageolet beans, au cerfeuil
  Purée of potato salad
  French pastry
  Coffee

DINNER
  Consommé Colbert
  Salted almonds
  Boiled turbot, Jean Bart
  Potatoes, nature
  Filet mignon, Rossini
  Green corn
  Broiled egg plant
  Hearts of romaine, Roquefort dress-
    ing
  Champagne punch
  Lady fingers
  Demi tasse

Chipped beef on toast. Cut one pound of smoked beef in very thin chips, put in hot water and bring to a boil. Then drain off the water and add a cup of very thick cream, boil again, and thicken with the yolks of two eggs and half a cup of thick cream. Let it come nearly to a boil, taste to see if sufficiently salt, add a little white pepper, and serve on four pieces of dry toast.

Shirred eggs, Argenteuil. Cut the tips, about one and one-half inch long, from one pound of asparagus, put in salted water and boil until soft, then drain off the water. Butter well four shirred egg dishes, and put the asparagus tips in them in equal portions. Crack two eggs in each dish, season with salt and pepper, put small bits of butter on top, and cook in oven for five minutes.

Sweetbreads braisé, St. George. Braise some sweetbreads, place on a platter, and garnish with okra and tomatoes sauté and green peppers cut like matches and sautéed in butter. Serve sauce Choron separate.

Okra and tomatoes sauté. Cut both ends off of one pound of okra, put in cold water and bring to a boil, then drain off the water. Peel and cut in quarters two or three large tomatoes, place them in a casserole with two ounces of butter, heat through, add the okra, season with salt and pepper, cover, and allow to simmer slowly for twenty minutes. Serve as a vegetable course, or as a garnish.

Flageolet beans, au cerfeuil. Put in a casserole two cans of flageolet beans and one quart of fresh water, bring to a boil, and drain. Return the beans to the casserole, add two ounces of sweet butter, a little salt and pepper, and one spoonful of chopped chervil. Simmer for five minutes.

Purée of potato salad. Boil four white potatoes in salted water, and pass through a fine sieve. Add one spoonful of vinegar, two spoonfuls of olive oil, a little Cayenne pepper, and salt if necessary. Set in ice box until cold. Then mix well with a wooden spoon. If too thick stir in a little hot bouillon or water. Be sure it is hot, as cold will not do. Serve in a salad bowl with finely chopped parsley on top.

Fillet of turbot, Jean Bart. Place four trimmed fillets of turbot in a buttered sauté pan, and season with salt and pepper. Place on each fillet a well-washed head of fresh mushroom and two leaves of tarragon; add one-half glass of white wine and one-half cup of water. Cover with buttered paper, bring to a boil, and set in oven for fifteen minutes. Then remove the fillets to a platter, and put one pint of white wine sauce in the sauté pan, reduce to normal thickness of a fish sauce, and strain over the fillets. Have the sauce well seasoned.

Green corn. Put three gallons of water, one pint of milk, and a handful of salt on the fire and bring to a boil. Then add one dozen clean ears of green corn, bring to a boil, cover the vessel, and set to side of range for ten minutes, where it will remain at boiling heat without actually boiling. Serve on a napkin, with corn holders, and sweet butter separate.

Champagne punch (sorbet). One pint of water, one-half pint of champagne, one-half pound of sugar, the juice of three lemons and the juice of half an orange. Dissolve the sugar in the water, add the lemon and orange juice, strain and freeze. When nearly frozen add the champagne, and finish. Finally stir in an Italian meringue (see Italian meringue) made with the whites of three eggs, and serve in sherbet glasses.

Broiled egg plant. Peel an egg plant, and cut in slices three-quarters of an inch thick. Season with salt and pepper, roll in oil, and broil. Serve on a platter with a little melted butter poured over it, and garnish with parsley in branches.

JUNE 9

BREAKFAST
  Cherries
  Omelet with egg plant
  Rolls
  Coffee

LUNCHEON
  Assorted hors d'oeuvres
  Consommé in cups
  Broiled sirloin steak, Cliff House
  French fried potatoes
  Baked tomatoes
  Brie cheese with crackers
  Coffee

DINNER
  Lamb broth, Olympic Club
  Salted pecans
  Frogs' legs, Jerusalem
  Broiled chicken, maître d'hôtel
  Asparagus, Hollandaise
  Potato croquettes
  Alligator pear, French dressing
  Meringue glacé, au chocolat
  Demi tasse

Omelet with egg plant. Use any broiled egg plant that may be left over, or fresh egg plant, and cut in small squares about one-half inch in diameter. Put in sauté pan with a little butter and simmer until soft. Then put the omelet pan on the fire with a small piece of sweet butter in it, add twelve beaten eggs, season with salt and pepper, add the egg plant, and then cook the omelet in the usual manner.

Broiled sirloin steak, Cliff House. Season a two-pound steak with salt and pepper, roll in oil, broil, and when done place on a platter. Cut the steak in slices, but do not place them apart. Sprinkle with one teaspoonful of paprika, one tablespoonful of dry English mustard, one teaspoonful of Worcestershire sauce, three chopped shallots, a little chopped chives, and two ounces of butter in small bits. Set in oven until butter is melted.

Baked tomatoes. Peel four large tomatoes and place on a buttered dish. Season with salt and pepper, put small pieces of butter on top, and set in oven to bake. When done place on platter and pour tomato sauce around them, or serve with their own butter.

Lamb broth, Olympic Club. Put a shoulder of lamb in a roasting pan, season with salt and pepper, add an onion and a carrot, put small bits of butter on top, and roast in oven until done. Then remove the meat from the bones and cut in small squares about one-quarter inch thick. Put the bones and trimmings in a casserole, add an additional two pounds of lamb bones, one turnip, two leeks, two leaves of celery, one spoonful of pepper berries, one bay leaf, two cloves, a little parsley in branches, one gallon of water, and a handful of salt. Bring to a boil, skim, and let simmer for two hours. Then strain through fine cheese cloth, put back in casserole, add the cut-up lamb and one-half pound of boiled rice, give one boil, and serve.

JUNE 10

BREAKFAST
  Fresh currants
  Oatmeal with cream
  Rolls
  Coffee

LUNCHEON
  California oyster cocktails
  Eggs Agostini
  Calf's head, vinaigrette
  Boiled potatoes
  Sliced bananas with whipped cream
  Macaroons
  Demi tasse

DINNER
  Consommé Turbigo
  Black bass, sauté meunière
  Tenderloin of beef, Parisienne
  Spinach in cream
  Artichokes, sauce mousseline
  Watercress salad
  Plombière à la vanille
  Assorted cakes
  Coffee

Eggs Agostini. Put one-quarter pound of boiled rice on a platter, lay four poached eggs on top, and cover with tomato sauce.

Consommé Turbigo. Boil one-quarter pound of noodles in salt water. Boil a carrot, cut in the form of matches, in salt water until soft. Cut the breast of a soup hen or chicken in Julienne shape. Add all to two quarts of hot and well-seasoned consommé.

Plombière à la vanille (ice cream). The yolks of eight eggs, one-half pound of sugar, one quart of milk, and one vanilla bean. Mix the yolks of eggs with the sugar. Split the vanilla bean and boil it in the milk. Then pour the milk, the yolks and sugar together, set on the fire, and stir with a wooden spoon until it thickens. Do not let it come to a boil. Strain and freeze, put in moulds, and set in ice box until very hard. Serve with whipped cream.

Plombière aux marrons. Same as vanilla plombière, but add some broken marrons glacés soaked in a little rum, when ready to put in the moulds to harden. Serve with whipped cream, and a whole marron glacé on top of each portion.

Plombière aux fruits. Prepare in the same manner as for plombière aux marrons, but use chopped mixed glacé fruit instead of the marrons.

JUNE 11

BREAKFAST
Sliced fresh figs with cream
Scrambied eggs with bacon
Buttered toast
Coffee

LUNCHEON
Cantaloupe
Eggs au fondu
Broiled squab on toast
Julienne potatoes
Cold asparagus, mustard sauce
Oregon cream cheese with crackers
Demi tasse

DINNER
Cream of artichokes
Ripe olives
Fillet of flounder, Piombino
Sweetbreads braisé, Montebello
Soufflé potatoes
Roast chicken, au jus
Escarole and chicory salad
Soufflé glacé aux fraises
Assorted cakes
Coffee

Eggs au fondu. Poached eggs on toast, covered with Welsh rabbit. Serve hot.

Cream of artichokes. Make three quarts of very light stock veal or chicken broth, strain and add to it four whole artichokes. Boil until the artichokes are soft, then remove and separate the bottoms from the leaves, cut the bottoms in small squares, and place in soup tureen. Then pass the leaves through a fine sieve, and put back in the broth. Melt three ounces of butter in a casserole, add three spoonfuls of flour, heat through, add the broth and boil for ten minutes. Then add a pint of thick cream, bring to a boil, season well with salt and pepper, and strain over the cut-up artichoke bottoms in the tureen.

Fillet of flounder, Piombino. Cut four fillets from one large flounder, place in a buttered pan, season with salt and pepper, add a glassful of claret and one-half cup of water, cover with buttered paper, put in oven and bake until done. Then place the fish on a platter. Make a sauce Génoise from the head and bones of the flounder, add the tail of a lobster cut Julienne style, and four heads of fresh mushrooms cut in the same manner and sautéed in butter. Pour the sauce over the fish. If fresh mushrooms are not available canned ones may be used.

Sweetbreads braisé, Montebello. Put some braised sweetbreads on a platter with their own gravy, and garnish with artichoke bottoms filled with purée of fresh mushrooms. Serve sauce Béarnaise separate; or poured over the sweetbreads, as desired.

Soufflé glacé aux fraises. Mix one pint of whipped cream, one-half pint of fresh strawberry juice, the yolks of four eggs beaten lightly, and four ounces of powdered sugar. Whip separately the whites of five eggs, and add to the mixture. Put in paper cases, and freeze. Serve with a dot of whipped cream on top, and a nice large fresh strawberry on top of the cream.

Soufflé glacé with raspberries. Prepare in the same manner as **soufflé glacé aux fraises**, but substitute raspberries for the strawberries.

JUNE 12

BREAKFAST
Preserved pears
Griddle cakes with honey
Coffee

LUNCHEON
Carciofini
Ecrevisses en buisson
Braised beef
Noodles
French pastry
Coffee

DINNER
Consommé Ditalini
Fillet of sole, St. Nazaire
Leg of mutton, currant jelly
String beans
Green corn
Hashed potatoes in cream
Field salad
Apricot pie
Coffee

Braised beef. Have the butcher cut an eight pound piece of rump or brisket of beef. Season with salt and pepper, and rub with a small piece of garlic. Melt in a pot about two ounces of butter, and when hot add the beef and roast on top of the range until it is brown on all sides. Then remove the beef, add one ounce of fresh butter to the gravy already in the pot, and when hot add two large spoonfuls of flour, and allow it to brown. Then add three pints of water, bring to a boil, and then put in the beef again. Add two calf's feet, one onion, one carrot, a large bouquet garni, four chopped tomatoes, salt, and a spoonful of whole black peppers. When boiling season well, cover, and put in oven. It will require from three to four hours to become well done. Then remove the beef to a platter, and reduce the sauce one-half. Taste to see if more seasoning is required, and then strain. Pour some of the sauce over the beef, and serve the remainder in a sauceboat. Garnish the beef with the carrot that was cooked with it. Cut the carrot in thin slices.

Larded rump of beef. Lard a piece of rump of beef, and then prepaie in the same manner as braised beef.

Fillet of sole, St. Nazaire. Cook four fillets of Sole à la Normande, and garnish with a dozen fried oysters.

Currant jelly. Strip the currants from their stems, and wash them. Put them on to cook, and when they become hot mash them. Boil for twenty-five minutes, then pour into jelly bag and let them drip without squeezing. Measure the juice and return it to the kettle. After it has boiled about ten minutes add heated sugar, allowing a pound of sugar to a pint of juice. Cook until it jells when a little is poured on a saucer. Pour into moulds, and seal when cold.

JUNE 13

BREAKFAST
- Fresh strawberries with cream
- Broiled veal kidneys, English style
- Baked potato
- Rolls
- Coffee

LUNCHEON
- Poached eggs, Colbert
- Ombrelle d'Ostende
- Potato croquettes
- Celery Victor
- Compote of pineapple
- Sponge cake
- Demi tasse

DINNER
- Potage Arlequin
- Ripe California olives
- Pompano, Vatel
- Chicken sauté, Archiduc
- Duchess potatoes
- Jets de houblons
- Chiffonnade salad
- Peach ice cream
- Assorted cakes
- Coffee

Broiled veal kidneys, English style. Leave a little fat on two veal kidneys, split them, season with salt and pepper, and sprinkle with a tablespoonful of dry English mustard. Then sprinkle with olive oil, and broil. When done place them on four pieces of dry toast. Mix two ounces of butter with the juice of a lemon, one tablespoonful of Worcestershire sauce, a little salt, pepper, grated nutmeg, chopped parsley, and one spoonful of meat extract. Mix well, and pour over the kidneys. Garnish with watercress.

Poached eggs, Colbert. Put some poached eggs on toast, and cover with sauce Colbert.

Ombrelle d'Ostende. Put four pieces of toast on a platter and place on each a large broiled fresh mushroom, head down. Put two broiled oysters on top of the mushrooms, pour maître d'hôtel sauce over them, and lay two strips of broiled bacon across the top of each. Garnish with parsley in branches and quartered lemons.

Compote of pineapple. Pare and core a pineapple, and cut in slices. Make a syrup with one-half pound of sugar and half a pint of water, and stew the pineapple in it until tender, and the syrup is clear. Serve cold, with a few drops of kirschwasser or maraschino sprinkled over it, and a little of its syrup.

Potage Arlequin. Slice two carrots, two beets, two turnips, and add a pound of shelled new peas. Put all in a casserole, cover with two quarts of water, season with salt, add about three pounds of cut-up veal bones, bring to a boil, and skim. Then cover, and cook until soft. Remove the veal bones, and strain the remainder through a fine sieve. Then return to casserole, and if too thick add a little bouillon, chicken broth or stock. Bring to a boil, season with salt and pepper, and stir in three ounces of sweet butter. Serve with bread cut in small squares and fried in butter.

Pompano, Vatel. Use four whole California pompano; or the four fillets from one Florida fish. Put them in a buttered sauté pan, season with salt and pepper, add one-half glass of stock and the juice of a lemon, and cook in oven until done. Then place the fish on a platter. Bring one-half pint of tomato sauce to a boil, add one-half pint of cream sauce, one spoonful of chopped truffles, season well with salt and pepper, and pour over the fish.

JUNE 14

BREAKFAST
Raspberries with cream
Scrambled eggs with cheese
Rolls
Oolong tea

LUNCHEON
Half of grapefruit with cherries
Baked beans, Boston style
Brown bread
Beignets soufflés
Coffee

DINNER
Little Neck clams on half shell
Consommé Ab-del-cader
Aiguillettes of turbot, Bayard
Roast sirloin of beef, fermière
Lettuce salad
Soufflé glacé, St. Francis
Assorted cakes
Coffee

Scrambled eggs with cheese. Mix ten eggs with one-half cup of cream, and one-half cup of grated Parmesan or Swiss cheese; season with salt and pepper to taste. Melt two ounces of butter in a casserole, add the eggs, and scramble.

Beignets soufflés. One pint of water, one-quarter pound of butter, one-half pound of flour, nine eggs, and a pinch of salt. Put the butter and salt in the water and bring to a boil. Stir in the flour with a wooden spoon, and work well until it is a smooth paste. Remove from the fire and work in the eggs, one by one. Form in the size of a walnut, and drop into hot lard with a soupspoon, and fry until well browned. The fritters will turn by themselves while frying. When done roll in powdered sugar to which has been added a little cinnamon, and serve on a napkin.

Consommé Ab-del-cader. Cut some carrots and turnips in half-moon shape, and boil in salted water. Cut some royal in the same shape. Also have some profiteroles. Put equal quantities of each in hot consommé, and also one poached yolk of an egg for each person. Have the consommé well seasoned.

Aiguilletes of turbot, Bayard. Cut four fillets of turbot lengthwise, and about four inches long and two inches wide. Place in a buttered pan, season with salt and white pepper, add one-half glass of white wine and one-half cup of fish stock, or water; cover with buttered paper, and cook in oven for ten minutes. Then place the fish on a platter, reduce the broth until nearly dry, add a pint of lobster sauce to which has been added the tail of a lobster, six heads of French canned mushrooms, and two truffles, all cut Julienne style. Pour the sauce over the fish before serving.

Roast sirloin of beef, fermière. Roast sirloin of beef, sauce Madère, garnished with string beans in butter, carrots in butter, and château potatoes.

Chicken sauté, Archiduc. Joint a chicken, and season with salt and pepper. Melt two ounces of butter in a sauté pan; when hot add the chicken and sauté for five minutes. Then add two sliced green peppers, and sauté until the chicken is done. Then place the chicken on a platter, and add another ounce of butter to the sauté pan. When the butter is nice and brown pour the gravy over the chicken, sprinkle with chopped parsley, and garnish with lemons cut in half.

JUNE 15

BREAKFAST
Sliced peaches with cream
Ham and eggs
Rolls
Coffee

LUNCHEON
Poached eggs à la Reine
Cold sirloin of beef
Rachel salad
Baked apple roll
Coffee

DINNER
Cabbage soup, Normande
Radishes
Salmon steak, Hongroise
Roast chicken
Fresh asparagus, Hollandaise
Georgette potatoes
Chicory salad
Vanilla ice cream
Bouchettes
Demi tasse

Rachel salad. Cut some artichoke bottoms, boiled celery, potatoes and asparagus tips, and two truffles, in Julienne shape. Arrange the vegetables in a salad bowl in bouquets, place the truffles in the center, and pour some French dressing over all.

Baked apple roll. Roll out one pound of puff paste until it is about one-eighth inch thick. Spread with chopped apples mixed with a little powdered sugar and powdered allspice. Wet the edges of the paste with water and roll up in the form of a big stick. Put in a pan, wash the top with beaten eggs, and bake in a rather hot oven. When done cut in slices, and serve with hard and brandy sauces. Plain cream may be served separate.

Baked apricot roll, blackberry roll, huckleberry roll, or loganberry roll. Prepare in the same manner as apple roll, using the fruit desired.

Cabbage soup, Normande. Separate the outside leaves and the core of a head of cabbage. Put both the leaves and core in a casserole with five pounds of beef bones, one onion, one carrot, a bouquet garni, and a handful of salt. Bring to a boil, season, and boil for two and one-half hours. Slice the rest of the cabbage very thin, place in another casserole, add three ounces of butter, and fry until the moisture is out. Then drain off the butter, and strain the beef and cabbage broth over it. Let it boil slowly for an hour. Season with salt and pepper, and add some bread crust cut in small squares and fried in butter.

Salmon steak, Hongroise. Cut two slices of salmon one and one-half inches thick; season with salt and pepper, roll in oil, and broil on both sides until colored. Then place on a platter, put two ounces of butter on top, and put in oven to finish cooking. When done place on a platter and cover with of tomato sauce to which a tablespoonful of paprika has been added.

Bouchettes. Make a mixture as for lady fingers. Put it into a pastry bag, and press out on paper in dots the size of a "quarter." Bake in a moderate oven. Allow to become cold, spread some jam or marmalade on the bottom of one and press another one on the jam, making a ball, and so on. Coat them with a white or pink icing.

Chocolate bouchettes. Make as above, coat with chocolate icing.

Coffee bouchettes. Make as above, coat with coffee icing.

JUNE 16

BREAKFAST
Sliced figs with cream
Boiled salt mackerel
Baked potatoes
Rolls
Coffee

LUNCHEON
Grapefruit en suprême
Shirred eggs, Antoine
Hamburg steak
Lorraine potatoes
Field salad
Vanilla blanc mange
Assorted cakes
Coffee

DINNER
Consommé Andalouse
Queen olives
Frogs' legs, sauté à sec
Filet mignon, Athénienne
Potatoes au gratin
Sliced cucumbers and tomatoes
Plombière aux marrons
Lady fingers
Coffee

Shirred eggs, Antoine. Plain shirred eggs with broiled strips of bacon on top

Vanilla blanc mange. One pint of milk, one pint of cream, six ounces of sugar, one ounce of gelatine, and one-half of a vanilla bean. Soak the gelatine in cold water. Put the milk and the vanilla bean on the fire together and let them come nearly to a boil. Then remove from the fire, add the soaked gelatine, and work with a wooden spoon until melted. Strain, and allow to become nearly cold. Then add the cream, and beat, on ice, until it begins to thicken. Then put in moulds and set in ice box for one hour. Turn out of moulds to serve.

Chocolate blanc mange. Use two ounces of chocolate instead of vanilla bean.

Coffee blanc mange. Use a cup of strong coffee instead of vanilla bean.

Blanc mange aux fruits. Make a vanilla blanc mange, and just before putting in moulds mix in one-quarter pound of chopped candied fruits.

Blanc mange aux liqueurs. Add to a vanilla blanc mange a glass of liqueur, such as maraschino, kirschwasser, kummel, rum, or other liqueur. Add the liqueur just before putting into the mould.

Consommé Andalouse. To consommé vermicelli, add just before serving, one peeled raw tomato cut in very small squares.

Filet mignon, Athénienne. Season four small fillets of beef with salt and pepper, broil or sauté them, and serve on a piece of toast with a slice of broiled ham on top. Cover with sauce Hussarde, and garnish with peas in butter.

Sauce Hussarde. Bring to a boil one pint of sauce Madère, or brown gravy; add one-half cup of fresh bread crumbs and boil for two minutes. Then add one ounce of good butter, a little chopped parsley, salt and Cayenne pepper.

JUNE 17

BREAKFAST
　　Baked apples with cream
　　Oatmeal
　　Dry toast
　　Coffee

LUNCHEON
　　Poached eggs, Blanchard
　　Spring lamb tenderloin, Thomas
　　Lettuce salad
　　Sliced fruit with whipped cream
　　Cakes
　　Coffee

DINNER
　　Cream of parsnips
　　Ripe olives
　　Fillet of bass, Argentina
　　Roast duckling, apple sauce
　　Green corn
　　Cauliflower, Hollandaise
　　Romaine salad, Roquefort dressing
　　Raspberry water ice
　　Assorted cakes
　　Coffee

Poached eggs, Blanchard. Cut two English muffins in half, toast them, and lay a slice of broiled ham on each. Put a poached egg on top of the ham, and cover with cream sauce.

Cream of parsnips, II. Put three pounds of veal bones in a casserole, add three quarts of water and a handful of salt, bring to a boil, and skim. Then add six sliced parsnips and a bouquet garni, and boil for an hour; then remove the bones and the bouquet. Put three ounces of butter in another vessel, heat, then add three spoonfuls of flour, and when hot add the broth and parsnips. Boil for half an hour, then strain through a fine sieve, put back in the casserole, season with salt and pepper, and add a pint of boiling cream.

Fillet of bass, Argentina. Put two ounces of butter in a casserole, add a sliced onion and a sliced carrot, and simmer until done. Then add a can of sliced French mushrooms, one-half can of sliced pimentos, four peeled and sliced tomatoes, one cupful of tomato sauce, and a little salt and pepper. Boil for ten minutes. Place four fillets of bass in a buttered pan, season with salt and pepper, cover with the above sauce, and bake in oven until done. Serve the fish from a platter with the sauce over it.

Cranberry jelly. To three quarts of cranberries add two pounds of granulated sugar and one quart of water. Cook thoroughly, and force through a fine sieve. Cook the juice for fifteen minutes, and then pour into individual moulds.

Crab apple jelly, and marmalade. To eight quarts of crab apples add three quarts of water. Boil slowly for an hour, adding more water to make up for evaporation. Strain through a flannel bag, but do not squeeze. Measure the juice and add an equal amount of sugar. Boil for twenty minutes, pour into glasses, and seal when cold. Make a marmalade of the remainder of the apples left in the bag, by pressing through a sieve, and then adding an equal amount of cane sugar. Cook until well done. Flavor with lemon or cinnamon.

Apricot and peach marmalade. Cut some firm ripe apricots in half and remove the stones. Add a few spoonfuls of water and cook until soft. Strain through a sieve, and add three-quarters of a pound of cane sugar to every pound of fruit. Crack some of the stones and add the kernels to the fruit. Continue to stir and cook until it thickens. Then pour immediately into hot glasses. Allow to become thoroughly cold before covering. Peach marmalade may be prepared in the same manner.

Brandied cherries. Select some fine Queen Anne cherries and cut off about half of the stem with scissors. Arrange the cherries in glass jars or bottles. Melt two and one-half pounds of granulated cane sugar with a very little water, being very careful not to let it scorch. Remove from the fire and add half a vanilla bean, then add slowly one gallon of brandy. When cold pour over the cherries, seal well, and keep in a cool place.

Brandied peaches. Rub some sound white peaches with a crash towel to remove the down. Prick all over with a needle, drop in cold water, drain, put in a kettle, cover with fresh cold water, and add a small piece of alum the size of a hazelnut. Place over a fire, stir occasionally, and as they float to the surface of the liquid take them out and place in a pan of cold water. Drain, and arrange in quart glass jars. Pour over brandy enough to cover the peaches.

Seal and put away in a cool place, and let stand for two weeks. Then drain off brandy into a kettle, and allow three pounds of sugar to each gallon of brandy. Stir well to melt the sugar. Pour this over the peaches, seal hermetically, and put away in a cool place.

Preserved cherries. To each pound of stoned cherries allow one pound of granulated cane sugar. Crack some of the stones and tie the kernels in a piece of gauze, so they may be removed after the boiling. Then put all in a preserving kettle, boil, and skim, until the syrup is clear. Then put the cherries in jars; boil the syrup a little longer, and pour over the fruit.

Preserved green gage plums. Use a pound of sugar for each pound of plums. Have the fruit clean and dry, and prick all over to keep the skins from breaking. Melt the sugar with as little water as possible, and when boiling add the plums, a layer at a time. Boil for a few minutes, then lift out with a skimmer and place singly on a dish to cool. Continue in this way until the plums are removed. When the last layer is finished return the first ones cooked to the kettle, and continue in reverse order, and boil until transparent. Then take out and arrange closely in glass jars. When all are in the jars pour the hot syrup over them, and seal.

JUNE 18

BREAKFAST
Stewed prunes
Boiled eggs
Rolls
Coffee

LUNCHEON
Hors d'oeuvres variés
Pompano sauté, meunière
Cold duckling and ham
Orloff salad
Camembert cheese
Coffee

DINNER
Consommé Irma
Lyon sausage
Fillet of sole, Talleyrand
Saddle of lamb, Souvaroff
String beans in butter
Mashed potatoes
Chiffonnade salad
Angel cake
Demi tasse

Orloff salad. Cut out the flesh from two cantaloupes and cut in one-half inch squares. Arrange in a circle in a salad bowl, and in the center put four buttons of artichokes cut in the same manner. Pour one-half cup of French dressing over all.

Consommé Irma. Boil one calf's brains, cut in small squares, and add to a quart of well-seasoned consommé.

Fillet of sole, Talleyrand. Lay four fillets of sole flat on the table and spread with fish force meat (Feb. 11), and sprinkle with a little chopped truffles. On top of each lay another thin fillet, season well with salt and pepper, roll in flour, then in beaten eggs, and finally in fresh bread crumbs. Fry in swimming lard for about ten minutes. Serve on a napkin garnished with parsley in branches and quartered lemons; and with Tartar sauce separate.

Saddle of lamb, Souvaroff. Roast a saddle of lamb, place on a platter, and garnish with a canful of cèpes sauté, and raw horseradish root shaved or scraped with a knife. Cover with brown gravy made from the lamb gravy.

Angel cake, or angel food. One pint of whites of eggs (it will require about sixteen), one pound of sugar, ten ounces of flour sifted with one-half teaspoonful of cream of tartar, and the flavor desired. Beat or whip the whites of eggs very stiff, then gradually put in the sugar and vanilla, lemon or orange flavor; and finally stir in the flour. Put in mould and bake in a very slow oven. When cold glacé with white icing.

JUNE 19

BREAKFAST
Stewed rhubarb
Broiled honeycomb tripe
Saratoga chips
Rolls
Coffee

LUNCHEON
Eggs, Oudinot
Fried smelts, Tartar sauce
Paprika schnitzel
Boiled rice
Baked apricot roll
Demi tasse

DINNER
Potage paysanne
Aiguillettes of flounder, Rochefoucault
Roast squab chicken
Artichokes, sauce mousseline
Carrots, Vichy
Potato croquettes
Alligator pear salad
Blackberry pie
Coffee

Eggs, Oudinot. Cut four hard-boiled eggs in two lengthwise. Take out the yolks and put in a salad bowl, add one-half cup of fresh bread crumbs, one raw egg yolk, and season with salt, pepper, and a little chopped parsley. Mix well, and then stuff the whites of eggs. Place on a buttered dish, cover with cream sauce, sprinkle with grated cheese, put small bits of butter all over the top, and bake in oven until brown.

Potage paysanne. Cut a carrot, white turnip, parsnip, and a small head of green cabbage in round slices the size of a silver half dollar. Put in a casserole with three ounces of butter, salt and a pinch of sugar. Cover casserole and put in oven and simmer until vegetables are done. Be careful not to burn, and when turning do not break the vegetables. When the vegetables are cooked add two quarts of bouillon, stock, or chicken or beef broth, and cook for half an hour. Before serving add chopped chervil, and season with salt and pepper.

Aiguillettes of flounder, Rochefoucault. Place four flat fillets of flounder in a buttered pan, lay some sliced lobster on top, season with salt and pepper, add one-half glass of white wine and one-half glass of water, cover with buttered paper, and put in oven for ten minutes. Then remove the fillets to a platter. Reduce the broth, add one pint of white wine sauce, and strain. To the sauce add one-half can of French mushrooms sliced, and two sliced truffles. Pour the sauce over the fish.

Pompano, Bâtelière. Roll four small California pompano in flour, and season with salt and pepper. Put three ounces of butter in a frying pan, heat, add the fish, and sauté until nice and brown. Then put the fish on a platter; and in the pan put two ounces of butter, heat until the color of hazelnuts, and pour over the fish. Sprinkle with chopped parsley, and garnish with two lemons cut in half.

JUNE 20

BREAKFAST
Fresh strawberries with cream
Waffles, special, with maple syrup
Coffee

LUNCHEON
Poached eggs, Bombay
Imported Frankfort sausages
Potato salad
Brie cheese with crackers
Coffee

DINNER
Consommé Valencienne
Carciofini. Queen olives
Frogs' legs, sauté, Dilloise
Porterhouse steak, Jolly
Fresh Lima beans
Julienne potatoes
Endives salad
Chocolate and coffee bouchettes
Demi tasse

Waffles, special. One-half pound of flour, one teaspoonful of baking powder, one spoonful of sugar, one ounce of melted butter, one-half pint of milk, one pinch of salt, three yolks and three whites of eggs. Mix the baking powder with the flour, then add the sugar, salt, yolks of eggs, butter and milk, and make a batter that should not be too stiff and hard. Beat the whites of eggs very hard, add to the batter, and mix well. Bake in a well-greased hot iron. (If possible use sour milk.)

Poached eggs, Bombay. Put some boiled rice on a platter, lay four poached eggs on top, and cover with curry sauce.

Consommé Valencienne. Boil one-half pound of rice in salted water, cool; and serve in one quart of hot and well-seasoned consommé. Before serving add some small leaves of chervil, which should be specially selected. Grated Swiss cheese should be served separate.

Frogs' legs, Dilloise. Cut two dozen frogs' legs in two, season with salt and pepper, put in sauté pan with one ounce of butter, and two ounces of bacon cut in small squares. Fry for a few minutes until the bacon is nearly crisp, then add the legs, and simmer for five minutes. Then add one pint of tomato sauce and boil for ten minutes, very slowly. Add a few dashes of Tabasco sauce, and season well.

Porterhouse steak, Jolly. Get from the butcher a nice porterhouse steak, about four pounds in weight. Season with salt and pepper, roll in oil, and broil. When done place on a platter, and cover with sauce Bordelaise with beef marrow. Place a dozen heads of broiled fresh mushrooms on top, and sprinkle with chopped parsley.

JUNE 21

BREAKFAST
Cantaloupe
Boiled eggs
Buttered toast
Uncolored Japan tea

LUNCHEON
Antipasto
Shirred eggs, Amiral
Broiled pig's feet, Chili sauce
String bean salad
Italian meringue, with whipped cream
Coffee

DINNER
Little Neck clams on half shell
Purée of cucumber soup
Pompano sauté, Bâtelière
Rissolées potatoes
Roast chicken
Peas à la Française
Lettuce salad
Raspberry shortcake with plain cream
Coffee

Shirred eggs, Amiral. Put two eggs in a buttered shirred egg dish and cook. When nearly done put on top a spoonful of white wine sauce with a little chopped lobster, mushrooms and truffles in it. Finish cooking, and season well with salt and pepper.

Purée of cucumbers. Peel four cucumbers, and cut in slices. Put them in a casserole with two quarts of cold water, season with salt, and bring to a boil. Then drain off the water, cool in cold fresh water, and drain again. Put three ounces of butter in a casserole, add the cucumbers, cover, and simmer in the oven for thirty minutes. Then remove from oven, set on top of range, add three spoonfuls of flour, simmer, then add one quart of boiling milk and one quart of chicken broth, and boil for twenty minutes. Strain through a fine sieve, put back in casserole, season with salt, pepper and a pinch of sugar, add two ounces of sweet butter and a cupful of heated cream. When butter is melted add some bread that has been cut in small squares and fried in butter, and serve.

Italian meringue. Put one pound of sugar and one gill of water into a copper kettle (copper inside and out) and cook to a blow. (See below). Beat six whites of eggs very hard and dry, and then pour into the cooked sugar, stirring constantly, and beat well until cold. It will then be a very smooth meringue paste, which can be used for meringue with whipped cream, or sherbet, or to make small fancy cakes, or for use in decorating cakes, pies, tarts, etc.

How to cook sugar to a blow. Dissolve one pound of sugar in one gill of water, and put on fire to cook. After about five minutes of good boiling dip a skimmer into it and remove immediately. Let the syrup drain a little, and then blow through. If small air bubbles fly out the sugar is cooked to a blow. If no air bubbles fly continue cooking until they do. It may possibly require some time to get it right.

Peas à la Française. In a casserole put two ounces of butter and a head of lettuce sliced very fine. Simmer for five minutes, then add two pounds of shelled peas, six small raw French carrots and one dozen raw fresh asparagus tips. Season with salt and a pinch of sugar, add one pint of chicken broth, cover, and simmer for one hour. Serve with fresh-chopped chervil on top.

JUNE 22

BREAKFAST
Baked pears
Bacon and eggs
Rolls
Coffee

LUNCHEON
Canapé Riga
Sweetbreads, Lavalière
Cold roast beef
Field salad
Lemon water ice
Langues de chat
Demi tasse

DINNER
Consommé Allemande
California ripe olives
Perch au bleu
Potatoes nature
Larded tenderloin of beef, Vigo
String beans in butter
Green corn on cob
Lettuce salad, Russian dressing
Chocolate blanc mange
Assorted cakes   Coffee

Baked pears. Core one dozen pears, but leave the stems on. Put in a pan with half a pint of water and half a pound of sugar, and bake in medium hot oven until soft. Serve either hot or cold, with sauce separate.

Baked peaches. Prick one dozen peaches all over with a fork, and set them close together in a pan. Sprinkle with one-quarter pound of granulated sugar, and add just water enough to cover the bottom of the pan. Bake until soft. Serve cream separate.

Sweetbreads, Lavalière. Prepare some sweetbreads braisé, place on a platter, garnish with peas in butter, and onions glacés. In the gravy put pieces of parboiled salt pork cut in small dices, and cook for ten minutes. Pour over the sweetbreads.

Consommé Allemande. Mix in a bowl three-quarters of a cupful of sifted flour, one-quarter of a cupful of milk, two whole eggs, and a little salt. Let it run through a colander into three pints of boiling consommé, and boil for five minutes.

Consommé Xavier. Same as Consommé Allemande, with the addition of a little chopped chervil just before serving.

Perch au bleu. Put four fresh-killed perch on a platter, and pour a glassful of white wine vinegar over them. Put in a fish kettle on the fire, some water, a handful of salt; and one sliced onion, one carrot, a bay leaf, clove and parsley tied in a bouquet. Boil for five minutes, then add the fish and vinegar, bring to a boil, and then set on side of the range for fifteen minutes. Serve on a napkin garnished with small boiled potatoes, parsley in branches, and lemons cut in half. Serve Hollandaise sauce separate.

Larded tenderloin of beef, Vigo. Lard and roast the tenderloin as given elsewhere. Serve on a platter garnished with stuffed tomatoes, Créole. Cover with its own brown gravy.

Stuffed tomatoes, Créole. Make a rice Créole (Dec. 23). Peel four sliced tomatoes, scoop out the insides, season with salt and pepper both inside and out, and fill with the rice. Place on a buttered pan, put a small piece of butter on top of each, and bake in oven for ten minutes, or until the tomatoes are soft. Test with your finger. Serve with tomato sauce around them; or use as a garnish for entrées.

JUNE 23

BREAKFAST
  Fresh raspberries with cream
  Omelet with potatoes
  Rolls
  Coffee

LUNCHEON
  Eggs, Basque
  Frogs' legs, Tartar sauce
  Broiled chicken on toast
  Soufflé potatoes
  Cold artichokes, vinaigrette
  Peach compote
  Honey cake
  Coffee

DINNER
  Potage Mongol
  Radishes
  Planked shad and roe
  Roast loin of veal, au jus
  Carrots, Vichy
  Flageolets in butter
  Endives salad
  German almond strips
  Demi tasse

Omelet with potatoes. Use left-over cold baked or boiled potatoes. Chop up a cupful and put in an omelet pan with two ounces of butter and fry until golden yellow. Season with salt and pepper, and then add a dozen beaten and seasoned eggs. Cook the omelet in the usual manner.

Eggs, Basque. Put in very hot swimming fat four whole large green peppers, and fry for one minute. Then take out and remove the skin, cut the bottoms off, take out the seeds, and place each pepper in a buttered cup, with the open end up. Then crack an egg in each pepper, season with salt, and place the cups in a pan in a little water, and put in oven to bake. Put some boiled rice on a platter and turn out the peppers with eggs on top, so they will look like stuffed green peppers. Pour some brown meat gravy, or tomato sauce, or cream sauce, around them.

Roast loin of veal, au jus. See veal kidney roast, Dec. 20.

Russian dressing, for salads. Mix in a large bowl one cup of mayonnaise sauce, three soupspoonfuls of French dressing, two soupspoonfuls of Chili sauce, two soupspoonfuls of chopped pimentos, one soupspoonful of chopped green olives, one teaspoonful of Worcestershire sauce, and season with salt and pepper, if necessary.

Peach compote. Peel a dozen peaches and place them in a sauce pan, add a quart of water, one-half pound of sugar, and one-half of a vanilla bean. Boil slowly until soft. Strain off the syrup, return to the fire, and reduce one-half. Pour the syrup over the peaches, and serve when cold. The peaches may be prepared whole, or cut in half.

Fruit compotes. Apple, nectarine, apricot, prune or plum compote may be prepared in the same manner as peach compote.

Langue de chat, I. Work a quarter pound of butter with a quarter pound of sugar until creamy. Then add four eggs, one by one, and keep on working until very smooth. Add a few drops of vanilla extract and a quarter pound of flour, and mix lightly. Put into a pastry bag and dress on a buttered pan in the shape of small thin lady fingers. Bake for a few minutes in a rather hot oven.

II. One-quarter pound of sugar, one-quarter pound of butter, one-quarter pound of flour, the whites of three eggs, and a little vanilla flavor. Mix the sugar and butter until creamy; add the whites of eggs that have been well whipped to snow; add the flour and flavoring, and mix lightly. Dress on buttered pan like lady fingers, but smaller. Bake and remove from pan while hot.

German almond strips. One-half pound of sugar, one-half pound of butter, ten ounces of flour, three eggs, one-half pound of ground almonds, and the grated rind of a lemon. Work the sugar with the butter until creamy, add the lemon rind, and work in the egg. Then add the flour and almonds, and mix lightly. Set in the ice box for an hour to harden. Then roll out in thin sheets and cut in strips two inches long and one-half inch wide. Wash the tops with egg, sprinkle with chopped almonds, put on a pan and bake in a moderate oven.

Honey cake. One-half pound of honey, seven ounces of brown sugar, one pony of water, one-half teaspoonful of soda, six ounces of finely-chopped almonds, one pinch of cloves and allspice, three-quarters of a pound of flour, and two ounces of lemon and orange peel chopped fine. Boil the sugar, honey and water; then take off the fire and allow to cool to blood heat; then mix in the flour, spices, and the soda dissolved in a little water; then add the almonds and the peel. Roll out about one-half inch thick, and cut in small cakes about one inch by three; and bake in a moderate oven. When done glacé with a very thin icing.

JUNE 24

BREAKFAST
  Apricot marmalade
  Buckwheat cakes
  Breakfast sausages
  Rolls
  Coffee

LUNCHEON
  Cold poached eggs, à l'estragon
  Sand dabs, meunière
  German huckleberry cake
  American dairy cheese
  Coffee

DINNER
  Consommé Créole
  Salt codfish, Biscayenne
  Braised sweetbreads, sauce Soubise
  Roast squab
  Boiled onions
  Broiled fresh mushrooms
  Château potatoes
  Lettuce and grapefruit salad
  Baked blackberry roll
  Coffee

Cold poached eggs, à l'estragon. Select four nice lettuce leaves and place a cold poached egg on each. Cover with sauce mayonnaise, and lay four leaves of tarragon crosswise over each egg.

German huckleberry cake. Line a cake pan, that will hold enough for six persons, with thin dough. (See dough for German cake). Fill with cleaned huckleberries, sprinkle on a handful of sugar mixed with a little powdered cinnamon, and bake. Then mix one-quarter pound of sugar with one pint of milk and three eggs, and strain. Pour this over the cake when it is nearly done, and set back in oven for a few minutes until the custard is set. When cold dust with powdered sugar.

Consommé Créole. Peel and cut in small squares, two raw tomatoes, and add to a quart of boiling consommé. Also add a cupful of boiled rice, and season with a little Cayenne pepper.

Salt codfish, Biscayenne. Soak two pounds of salted codfish in cold water over night. Then drain off the water. Heat two tablespoonfuls of olive oil in a casserole, add six shallots chopped very fine, and allow them to become warmed through, but not colored. Then add six pieces of chopped garlic and half of the codfish. On top of the codfish lay two raw potatoes that have been sliced very thin, season with salt, lay two peeled and sliced tomatoes on top of the potatoes, then add the remainder of the codfish, and half a cup of water, cover, and cook in the oven for an hour. Fresh codfish may be used if desired, with the addition of a little more salt.

Braised sweetbreads, sauce Soubise. Braise the sweetbreads in the usual manner. Put some sauce Soubise on a platter, lay the sweetbreads on top, and garnish with fleurons.

JUNE 25

BREAKFAST
Sliced peaches with cream
Boiled eggs
Dry toast
English breakfast tea

LUNCHEON
Cendrillon salad
Small tenderloin steak, Marseillaise
Gnocchis à la Romaine
Camembert cheese and crackers
Coffee

DINNER
Cream Countess
Salami sausage.   Radishes
Fillet of kingfish, Ubsala
Roast tame duck, apple sauce
Carrots and peas in cream
German fried potatoes
Escarole salad
Plombière aux fruits
Assorted cakes
Demi tasse

Salad Cendrillon. Scoop out four cold baked potatoes, fill with Russian salad, and serve on a napkin, garnished with parsley in branches and canapés of anchovies.

Small tenderloin steak, Marseillaise. Chop six shallots and two pieces of garlic, and simmer in two ounces of butter. Then add a peeled tomato cut in small squares, and six chopped anchovies, and simmer for twenty minutes. Then add two cups of brown gravy (sauce Madère), boil for two minutes, add two ounces of butter, stir until melted, and season with salt and Cayenne pepper to taste.

Gnocchis à la Romaine. Put three-quarters of a pound of farina in one quart of boiling milk, and boil slowly for fifteen minutes. Then remove from the fire and bind with the yolks of six eggs and a half cup of cream. Season with salt and white pepper, and set to cool. Then cut in one and one-half inch squares, or in other desired shapes; place on a buttered pan, or deep dish, or individual shirred egg dish; sprinkle with grated Parmesan cheese, put small bits of butter on top, and bake in oven until brown.

Gnocchis au gratin. Same as above, except pour sour cream over them, sprinkle with cheese, add butter on top, and bake until brown.

Cream Countess. Make a cream of asparagus soup, and before serving bind with the yolk of one egg for each person. Color with green spinach coloring.

Kingfish, Ubsala. Put four cleaned kingfish on a buttered pan, season with salt and pepper, add one-half glass of white wine and one-half cup of fish stock, bouillon or water, and bake in an oven. Then place the fish on a platter, add one pint of white wine sauce to the juice of the fish in the pan, and reduce by boiling to the thickness of a good sauce. Strain over the fish. Garnish with fleurons.

JUNE 26

BREAKFAST
Apricot marmalade
Waffles
Buttermilk
Coffee

LUNCHEON
Eggs, Célestine
Fried chicken, Villeroi
Flageolet beans
Mashed potato salad
French pastry
Demi tasse

DINNER
Consommé Magador
Ripe olives
Salmon, Concourt
Fillet of beef sauté, Balzag
Artichokes, Hollandaise
Green corn
Potato croquettes
Romaine salad, Roquefort dressing
Blanc mange, aux liqueurs
Lady fingers
Coffee

Eggs, Célestine. Put four pieces of toast on a buttered platter, lay a slice of broiled ham on top of each, and a poached egg on top of each slice of ham. Cover with cream sauce, sprinkle with grated cheese, put a little butter on each, and bake in a hot oven until brown.

Fried chicken, Villeroi. Joint a chicken, season with salt and pepper, roll in flour, then in beaten eggs and fresh bread crumbs. Put one-half cup of melted butter in a pan, heat, and then fry the chicken. Make a pint of sauce Allemande (March 4), add one cup of fresh-boiled new peas, and season well. Put some of the sauce on a platter, lay the chicken on top, and serve the remainder of the sauce in a sauceboat.

Consommé Magador. Wash a stock of celery and cut in small dices, boil in salted water until soft. Then add to three pints of boiling consommé; season well, and serve with chopped chervil.

Salmon, Concourt. Cut the salmon in slices one inch thick, season with salt and pepper, roll in melted butter, then in fresh bread crumbs, and broil. When done place on a platter, and garnish with parsley in branches and lemons cut in half. Serve sauce Colbert separate.

Fillet of beef sauté, Balzag. Season four small tenderloin steaks with salt and pepper, and sauté in butter. Then place on a platter. Make a pint of sauce Madère, and add to it one dozen small chicken dumplings, one dozen stuffed olives and two sliced truffles. Pour over the fillets.

JUNE 27

BREAKFAST
  Strawberries with cream
  Scrambled eggs with chives
  Crescents and rolls
  Cocoa

LUNCHEON
  Cold Virginia ham
  Bretonne salad
  Lillian Russell
  Macaroons
  Coffee

DINNER
  Chicken soup, Brésilienne
  Celery
  Striped bass, Buena Vista
  Chicken fricassee, à l'ancienne
  Asparagus, sauce mousseline
  Paté de foie gras, à la gelée
  Lettuce salad
  Pancakes, Lieb
  Coffee

Salad Bretonne. Soak one pound of white beans in cold water over night. Then put on fire in two quarts of water, add a little salt, one carrot, one onion, and a bouquet garni. Cover, and boil until soft. Then remove the vegetables, drain off the water, and set the beans in a cool place. When cold put them in a salad bowl, and in the center place two tomatoes peeled and cut in small squares. Sprinkle with one teaspoonful of salt, one-half teaspoonful of fresh-ground black pepper, one-third cup of white wine vinegar, two-thirds of a cup of olive oil, and a little chopped parsley. Some chopped chives may also be added if desired. Mix on the table.

Chicken soup, Brésilienne. One pint of consommé tapioca, one pint of thick consommé brunoise, and the breast of a fowl cut in small squares. Bring to a boil, and serve.

Striped bass, Buena Vista. Put in a wide copper fish pan one cup of olive oil, two sliced onions, two sliced green peppers, and then fry. When done add four cloves of chopped garlic and let it set in the hot oil for a second; then add a pint of claret, one dozen sliced fresh mushrooms, six peeled and sliced tomatoes, and one-half canful of sliced pimentos. Bring to a boil, and then add five pounds of striped bass cut in slices two inches thick. Season with salt, pepper, and a little paprika; cover, and simmer for thirty minutes. Cut eight slices of bread the same thickness as for toasting, and fry in hot oil. Rub the fried bread with a piece of garlic, lay on a deep platter, put the fish on top of the toast, pour sauce over the fish, and sprinkle with chopped parsley.

Chicken fricassée, à l'ancienne. Cut a young roasting chicken in eight pieces, wash well, and put in a pot in one quart of cold water. Season with salt, bring to a boil, and skim. Then add one-half pint of small peeled white onions, one pint of small round raw Parisian potatoes, one pound of parboiled salt pork cut in small dices, and one bouquet garni. Boil until done; then remove the bouquet garni, and take off the fat on top of the broth. Mix in a bowl two spoonfuls of flour and one-half cup of water, and let it run into the boiling fricassee. Boil for five minutes; then bind with the yolks of two eggs and one-half cup of cream. When serving sprinkle with chopped parsley.

JUNE 28

BREAKFAST
  Crab apple marmalade
  Shirred eggs, plain
  Melba toast
  Coffee

LUNCHEON
  Cantaloupe
  Omelette Argentine
  Turkey hash, Château de Madrid
  Julienne potatoes
  Brie cheese and crackers
  Coffee

DINNER
  Consommé Bohémienne
  Queen olives and salted almonds
  Baked lobster, Lincoln
  Roast Imperial squab
  Baked potatoes
  Cold artichokes, mustard sauce
  Baked huckleberry roll
  Coffee

Omelette Argentine. Cut one-quarter pound of egg plant in one-half inch squares. Put in omelet pan with one ounce of butter and fry until cooked. Then add eight beaten eggs, season with salt and pepper, and cook in the usual manner. Serve the omelet on a platter with sauce Colbert around it.

Turkey hash, Château de Madrid. Cut the breast of a boiled turkey in small squares. Put in a sauté pan with one pint of thick cream sauce, season with salt and pepper, heat, and fill as many red peppers (pimentos) as possible. Place the filled peppers on a buttered platter, so they will have the appearance of little red caps. Put in the oven and cook for a few minutes. Serve with sauce Créole poured around them.

Consommé Bohemienne. Make three thin pancakes, and when cold cut in Julienne shape. Cut the breast of a boiled fowl also in Julienne shape. Chop a raw peeled tomato; and add all the above with a cup of fresh peas, to three pints of boiling consommé, and serve.

Baked lobster, Lincoln. Boil two lobsters. When cold, cut in two lengthwise, remove the meat, and slice it. Put in a casserole two ounces of butter, and heat; then add two chopped shallots, and two cloves of garlic chopped fine. Heat slightly and then add six sliced fresh mushrooms, and simmer for five minutes. Then add one cup of cream sauce, one teaspoonful of English mustard mixed with one tablespoonful of Worcestershire sauce, and a little chopped parsley and tarragon. Cook for ten minutes, then add the lobster, and season with salt and pepper. Fill the half lobster shells with the mixture, sprinkle with grated cheese, put small bits of butter on top, and bake in oven until well browned. Serve on a napkin, with parsley in branches, and two lemons cut in half.

JUNE 29

BREAKFAST
    Fresh sliced peaches with cream
    Griddle cakes
    Kidneys sauté, au Madère
    Rolls
    Coffee

LUNCHEON
    Cold fish à la Michels
    Lemon pie
    Buttermilk
    Coffee

DINNER
    Little Neck clams
    Sorrel soup, with rice
    Lyon sausages
    Frogs' legs, sauté à sec
    Tournedos, Vaudeville
    Sybil potatoes
    Watercress salad
    Compote of gooseberries
    Assorted cakes
    Coffee

Cold fish à la Michels. Put in a casserole one spoonful of olive oil and a small onion chopped very fine. Fry until yellow, and then add one chopped clove of garlic and a spoonful of flour. Cook this until yellow; then add two and one-half cups of water, season with salt and pepper, and boil for two minutes. Then add about two pounds of any kind of fish cut in pieces about two inches square, and some chopped parsley, and boil for thirty minutes. Put the fish in a deep porcelain dish, pour the sauce over it, and serve when cold.

Sorrel soup with rice. Wash a large handful of sorrel, remove the stems, and slice very thin. Put two ounces of butter and three ounces of rice in a casserole, and heat. Then add the sorrel and simmer for five minutes. Then add two quarts of bouillon, chicken broth or stock, season with salt and pepper, and boil slowly for thirty minutes. When rice is soft it is ready to serve.

Tournedos, Vaudeville. Season four small tenderloin steaks with salt and pepper, and broil; or sauté in pan with butter. When done place on a platter, lay on each a fresh poached egg; and garnish with four stuffed tomatoes, Créole. Cover the tournedos with sauce Madère.

Compote of gooseberries. To each pint of well-cleaned gooseberries add one-half pound of sugar and one gill of water. Cook slowly until the berries are soft.

JUNE 30

BREAKFAST
Preserved green gage plums
Boiled eggs
Doughnuts
Rolls
Coffee

LUNCHEON
Clam broth en bellevue
Chicken sauté à sec
French fried potatoes
Romaine salad
Sierra cheese and crackers
Coffee

DINNER
Consommé Xavier
Pim olas
Boiled salmon steak with peas
Roast saddle of lamb, mint sauce
Green corn
Stewed tomatoes
Lettuce and grapefruit salad
Berliner pfannenkuchen
Coffee

Doughnuts—with baking powder. One pound of flour, one-half ounce baking powder, two ounces of butter, three ounces of sugar, the yolks of four eggs, one whole egg, one-half gill of milk, and the rind of a lemon. Sift the baking powder into the flour. Mix the sugar, butter and eggs; add the milk and flour, and the lemon rind flavoring. Roll out, and cut with a doughnut cutter, and fry in hot lard or butter. Dust with powdered sugar with a little cinnamon in it, before serving.

Doughnuts—with yeast. One pound of flour, one ounce of yeast, two eggs, two ounces of butter, two ounces of sugar, one pinch of salt and the rind and juice of a lemon. Sift the flour into a bowl; add the egg, and the yeast dissolved in a little milk, and one gill of milk; making a medium stiff dough. Cover with a cloth, and allow to rise to double its original volume. It will require about an hour. Then work in the butter, salt, and flavoring, mix well, and let it rise again. Then fold the dough together, roll out to about one-quarter inch thick, cut with a doughnut cutter, allow to rise for half an hour, and fry. Dust with powdered sugar and cinnamon before serving.

Crullers. Use either the baking powder or yeast doughnut dough, cut with a cruller cutter, and fry in the same manner as doughnuts.

Coffee cake dough. One pound of flour, one ounce of yeast, two eggs, two ounces of butter, two ounces of sugar, one pinch of salt, the rind and juice of a lemon, and a little nutmeg. Put the flour into a bowl. Dissolve the yeast in a gill of luke-warm milk, and add to the flour, with the eggs. Work to a medium stiff dough. Cover with a cloth and let it rise to double its original size. Then work in the butter, sugar, salt and lemon flavoring, and mix well. Let it rise again for about an hour; when the dough will be ready to use. This dough is the foundation for all kinds of coffee cake.

Berlines pfannenkuchen. Make a coffee cake dough. Roll out some balls about the size of an egg, flatten them a little and put one-half teaspoonful of any kind of jam on top. Pinch up the dough over the jam. Lay them on a cloth, smooth side up, cover, and allow to raise to nearly double in size. Fry in swimming hot lard or clarified butter. When done dust with granulated sugar and powdered cinnamon.

JULY 1

BREAKFAST
Sliced figs with cream
Baked beans, Boston style
Rolls
Coffee

LUNCHEON
Imperial salad
Broiled lamb chops
Red kidney beans
Soufflé potatoes
St. Francis cheese, with crackers
Demi tasse

DINNER
Potage St. Marceau
Fillet of sole, Montmorency
Sweetbreads braisé, Princess
Château potatoes
Roast chicken
Chiffonnade salad
Corn starch pudding
Coffee

Imperial salad. Equal parts of sliced tomatoes, sliced artichoke bottoms, and fresh peas. Put them in a salad bowl, cover with mayonnaise sauce, and lay some sliced truffles on top.

St. Francis cheese. Scrape the skin from three Camembert cheeses, and put in a copper casserole. Add one-quarter pound of good Roquefort cheese, one-half pound of the best table butter, two tablespoonfuls of sifted flour, and one pint of the best cream. Cook until melted, and the whole becomes thick; then strain through cheese cloth. Put in an earthern pot and allow to become cool. The cheese will keep for two weeks if kept in the ice box.

Potage St. Marceau. Mix one quart of purée of split pea soup with one pint of consommé Julienne.

Fillet of sole, Montmorency. Place four fillets of sole in a buttered pan, season with salt and pepper, and lay on each fillet four heads of canned French mushrooms. Cover all with one pint of sauce Italienne, sprinkle with grated cheese, put small bits of butter on top, and bake in oven for fifteen minutes. Then remove from the oven, squeeze the juice of a lemon on top, and sprinkle with chopped parsley. Serve from the pan used in cooking, which may be placed on a platter.

Sweetbreads braisé, Princess. Braise four nice sweetbreads, and place them on fresh artichoke bottoms on a platter. Garnish with boiled cauliflower with a little Béarnaise sauce poured over it; and over the sweetbreads pour the gravy left after braising. Sauté the livers of four chickens in butter, season well with salt and pepper, and lay them around the cauliflower.

Corn starch pudding. One quart of milk, three ounces of corn starch, five ounces of sugar, four yolks and four whites of eggs, one ounce of butter, and flavoring. Dissolve the corn starch in a little cold milk. Put the rest of the milk and the sugar on the stove, and when near boiling add the dissolved corn starch and stir well. Boil for a few minutes, then take off the fire, add the butter, the yolks of eggs, and the flavoring. Beat the whites to snow, and add, mixing lightly. Put into buttered moulds and bake for about twenty minutes. Serve with fruit or cream sauce.

JULY 2

BREAKFAST
Preserved cherries
Bacon and eggs
Rolls
English breakfast tea

LUNCHEON
Crab cocktail, Crêmière
Pig's feet, St. Menehould
Cottage fried potatoes   Succotash
Coffee blanc mange
Assorted cakes   Demi tasse

DINNER
Little Neck clams
Consommé Marie Louise
Ripe olives.   Salted pecans
Halibut, Boitel
Larded sirloin of beef, Lili
Potato pancakes
Wax beans in butter
Celery Victor
Brandied peaches
Vanilla ice cream
Macaroons   Coffee

Crab cocktail, Crêmière. Same as Crab cocktail, Victor (see March 24), with the addition of a little whipped cream on top.

Cottage fried potatoes. Slice three potatoes of medium size in pieces the size and shape of a silver dollar. Heat two ounces of butter in a frying pan, add the potatoes, season with salt and pepper, and fry slowly. When done add a spoonful of grated cheese, and put in the oven for a few minutes. Then dish up, sprinkled with chopped parsley.

Pig's feet, St. Menehould. Split two boiled pigs' feet, roll in melted butter and then in fresh bread crumbs. Broil. When done dish up on a platter, and garnish with parsley in branches and two lemons cut in half. Serve tomato sauce separate, and cream sauce with chopped truffles in it.

Succotash. If canned succotash is used empty it into a casserole, add a small piece of butter, season with salt and pepper, and serve very hot.

Fresh succotash. Put two ounces of butter in a casserole, add the corn cut from six fresh ears, and simmer for ten minutes. Then add one pound of boiled fresh Lima beans, season with salt and pepper, add one spoonful of cream sauce and one spoonful of cream, and cook for five minutes.

Consommé Marie Louise. To consommé royal add a cupful of fresh boiled green peas.

Halibut, Boitel. Cut four fillets of halibut, place them in a buttered pan, season with salt and pepper, add one-half glass of white wine and one-half cup of stock or water, cover, and simmer for ten minutes. Then remove the fish to a platter, and to the pan add one can of chopped French mushrooms, and two cups of cream sauce. Season well, and boil for five minutes. Pour over the fish, and sprinkle with chopped parsley.

Larded tenderloin of beef, Lili. Roast a larded tenderloin of beef, and serve with sauce Madère, to which has been added six sliced heads of fresh mushrooms sautéed in butter, and two sliced truffles. Garnish with six peeled and quartered tomatoes sautéed in butter.

Potato pancakes. Mix one egg, one-half cup of milk, one-half cup of flour, and salt and pepper. Grate one and one-half cups of raw potato and add immediately, otherwise it will turn black. Fry in melted butter, and form the cakes by putting in a spoonful of the batter at a time. Left over boiled or baked potatoes may be used instead of the raw potatoes if desired.

JULY 3

BREAKFAST
    Sliced bananas with cream
    Flannel cakes with maple syrup
    Rolls
    Coffee

LUNCHEON
    Fresh caviar
    Dry toast
    Clams en cocotte, Californienne
    Omelet with fresh strawberries
    Coffee

DINNER
    Croute Bretonne
    Boiled Lake Tahoe trout, Hollandaise
    Potatoes nature
    Chicken sauté, Viennoise
    Green peas
    Roast leg of mutton, currant jelly
    Endive salad
    Biscuit glacé, mapleine
    Assorted cakes
    Demi tasse

Clams en cocotte, Californienne.   Remove three dozen Little Neck clams from their shells and put in an earthern casserole or cocotte dish with two ounces of butter.   Then add one-half cup of raw fine-chopped celery, two heads of fresh mushrooms chopped very fine, and a little chives sliced very fine, and some chopped parsley.   Season with salt and pepper, put two more ounces of butter on top, and place in oven to bake.   Cook for twenty minutes, and serve from the cocotte, direct from the oven.

Croute Bretonne.   Put two pounds of beef shin and five pounds of beef bones in a casserole or soup kettle.   Add one gallon of cold water, bring slowly to a boil, and skim well.   Then add one spoonful of salt, a bouquet garni, half of a small head of cabbage or kale, two turnips, two carrots, one parsnip and an onion.   Boil for three hours; then strain the broth into a soup tureen.   Chop the vegetables very fine, put in salad bowl, season with salt, pepper, and a little grated nutmeg, and add a little chopped parsley and one-half cup of grated cheese.   Cut some bread in round pieces the size of a silver half dollar, and toast on one side.   Put the purée of vegetables on the toasted side of the croutons, place on a buttered pan and bake in the oven until brown. Serve on a napkin with the broth.

Chicken sauté, Viennoise.   Joint a spring chicken, season with salt and pepper, roll in flour, then in beaten eggs, and finally in bread crumbs.   Fry in melted butter.   When done place on a platter, pour cream sauce around it, and garnish with new peas cooked in butter.

German coffee cake.   One pound of flour, one ounce of yeast, six ounces of butter, three ounces of sugar, three eggs, and the rind of a lemon.   Prepare and raise the dough in the same manner as for coffee cake.   Roll out until about one-half inch thick, or thicker, if desired.   Brush over with egg, and spread some Streusel on top (see Streusel cake).   Allow to raise, and bake in a moderate oven.

Streusel cake.   One-half pound of flower, six ounces of sugar, four ounces of melted butter, one-half ounce of cinnamon, the juice of one lemon, and the yolk of one egg.   Mix all together, and pass through a coarse sieve.   Make a coffee cake dough, roll out, and spread the above mixture over the top.   Allow to raise, and then bake.   (This cake is the same as German coffee cake.)

Cinnamon cake. Roll out some German coffee cake dough about one-half inch thick. Brush over with melted butter, and spread granulated sugar mixed with powdered cinnamon, on top. Allow to raise, and then bake.

Coffee fruit cake. Add to German coffee cake mixture three ounces of currants, three ounces of raisins, two ounces of lemon peel, and two ounces of citron chopped fine. Roll out to about one-half inch thick, allow to rise, and bake. When done ice over with very thin lemon icing.

Coffee cream cake. Roll out some German coffee cake dough very thin. Spread over with pastry cream (see pastry cream). And cover with another thin sheet of coffee cake dough. Brush over with egg, spread some Streusel over the top, allow to raise, and bake.

JULY 4

BREAKFAST
  Sliced pineapple
  Farina with cream
  Uncolored Japan tea
  Crescents

LUNCHEON
  Canapé thon marine
  Poached eggs, Créole
  Lamb chops, Robinson
  Lyonnaise potatoes
  Corn sauté in butter
  Orange compote
  Snails (cake)
  Demi tasse

DINNER
  Consommé Florentine
  Ripe olives.   Celery
  Sand dabs, meunière
  Broiled baby turkey, cranberry sauce
  Baked sweet potatoes
  Summer squash
  Lettuce salad, egg dressing
  Coupe St. Jacques
  Macaroons
  Coffee

Poached eggs, Créole. Put some boiled rice on a platter, lay four poached eggs on top, and cover with Créole sauce.

Lamb chops, Robinson. Broil eight lamb chops, and lay them on a platter. Clean a dozen chicken livers, cut in four, season with salt and pepper, put in a frying pan with two ounces of hot melted butter, and sauté for three minutes. Then sprinkle with a spoonful of flour, add a cup of bouillon or broth, boil for a minute, add a little dry sherry wine, and pour over the chops.

Corn sauté in butter. Cut the corn from eight ears, put in a sauté pan with two ounces of butter, season with salt and pepper, and cook for ten minutes.

Orange compote. Take the outside yellow skin from six oranges cut very fine in Julienne style. Cook for thirty minutes in water, changing about three times. Changing the water takes away the bitter taste. Now peel the fine skin of the six oranges very clean, and cut in two, crosswise. In a sauce pan put one pound of sugar, a gill of water, and a drop of red coloring, and boil for ten minutes. Add the cooked skins to the syrup and boil again for fifteen minutes. Put the oranges in a deep bowl and pour the syrup over them.

Consommé Florentine. Add to consommé printanier two pancakes cut Julienne style, and some chervil.

Broiled baby turkey. Split a young turkey through from the back, wash well, and dry with a towel. Season with salt and pepper, roll in oil, and broil. When done place on four pieces of buttered toast, pour a cup of maître d'hôtel sauce over it, and garnish with watercress and two lemons cut in half.

Snails (cake). Take some German coffee cake dough and roll out into a square sheet, about one-quarter inch thick. Brush over with melted butter, and spread with some currants, citron chopped fine, sugar and cinnamon. Roll the sheet of dough into a roll, and cut in slices about one-quarter inch thick. Lay them on a buttered pan and allow to raise until nearly double in size. Bake in moderate oven, and when done, and still hot, coat over with thin lemon icing.

JULY 5

BREAKFAST
  Iced grapefruit juice
  Scrambled eggs with Swiss cheese
  Rolls
  Coffee

LUNCHEON
  Cold stuffed eggs, with anchovies
  Terrine de foie gras
  Hearts of lettuce
  Assorted French pastry
  Demi tasse

DINNER
  Chicken soup, Portugaise
  Salted almonds
  Fillet of bass, Brighton
  Paprika schnitzel
  Gnocchis au gratin
  Chiffonnade salad
  Artichokes, Hollandaise
  Strawberry water ice
  Assorted cakes
  Coffee

Scrambled eggs with Swiss cheese. Cut one-quarter pound of Swiss cheese in very small squares. Put an ounce of butter in a casserole with the cheese, and heat slightly; then add ten beaten eggs, one-half cup of cream, season with salt and pepper, and scramble in the usual manner.

Chicken soup, Portugaise. Put a soup hen on the fire in three quarts of water, bring to a boil, and skim well. Then add a tablespoonful of salt, two carrots, one onion, and a bouquet garni, and boil slowly until the fowl is done. Then skim the broth, and cut the carrots and the onion in small squares, and return to the soup. Peel four tomatoes, squeeze out the juice, cut in small squares, and also add to the soup. Bring to a boil, add a cup of boiled rice, and serve.

Fillet of bass, Brighton. Place four fillets of bass in a buttered pan, season with salt and pepper, add one-half glass of white wine, cover with buttered paper, and set in oven for five minutes. Then place the fillets on a platter; and put what remains in the pan in a casserole, add one pint of well-seasoned sauce Italienne, bring to a boil, and pour over the fish. Sprinkle with grated cheese, put small bits of butter on top, and bake in oven for fifteen minutes. Sprinkle with fresh-chopped parsley and the juice of a lemon.

Fillet of fish au gratin, à l'Italienne. Use any kind of fish cut in fillets; large fish cut in slices; or whole small fish. Prepare in the same manner as Fillet of Bass, Brighton.

Cold stuffed eggs, with anchovies. Boil six eggs until hard, remove the shells, and cut in two lengthwise. Pass the yolks through a fine sieve, and mix with one dozen anchovies in oil cut in small squares, a little pepper, and a teaspoonful of mayonnaise sauce. Fill the whites of the eggs with this mixture, and serve on a napkin with parsley in branches and two lemons cut in four.

JULY 6

BREAKFAST
Boiled farina in milk
Mixed fruit compote
Dry toast
Coffee

LUNCHEON
Grapefruit with cherries
Scrambled eggs, Caroline
Veal chop sauté, in butter
Mixed flageolet and string beans
Mashed potatoes
Escarole salad
Roquefort cheese with crackers
Coffee

DINNER
Consommé, Niçoise
Queen olives
Frogs' legs sauté, aux fines herbes
Larded tenderloin of beef, jardinière
Duchesse potatoes
Alligator pear, French dressing
Sherbet au rhum
Assorted cakes
Coffee

Boiled farina in milk. Bring a quart of milk to a boil, add a small pinch of salt, and pour a half pound of farina into it slowly so dough balls will not form. Cook for fifteen minutes.

Scrambled eggs, Caroline. Cut two boiled artichoke bottoms and two slices of boiled ham in small squares. In a casserole put the ham with two ounces of butter, heat, and then add ten beaten eggs, season with salt and pepper, add one-half cup of cream, and scramble in the usual manner. Just before finishing add the artichokes.

Consommé, Niçoise. To consommé vermicelli add a peeled tomato cut in small squares. Bring to a boil, and serve with grated cheese, separate.

Watermelon preserves. Select a melon with a thick rind, and cut in any shape desired. Lay the pieces in strong salt water for two or three days; then soak in clear water for twenty-four hours, changing the water frequently. Then put in alum water for two hours to harden. To every pound of fruit use one pound of sugar. Make a syrup of the sugar and a few pieces of ginger root and one lemon sliced thin. After boiling for a few minutes, remove the lemon and ginger, add the melon, and boil until transparent. Lift carefully, and place in glass jars. Fill the jars with the syrup.

Canned pears. Peel, halve and core ten pounds of pears. Put in a vessel with five pounds of granulated sugar, one sliced lemon, one teaspoonful of ground cinnamon, a little grated nutmeg, and a small piece of ginger root. Tie the cinnamon and nutmeg loosely in a piece of gauze. Cook all together until the pears turn pink. Put in jars, and seal while still hot.

Canned peaches. Pare twelve pounds of peaches, cut in half, and lay in cold water until needed. Put on the stove three pounds of sugar with nine pints of water. Boil to a syrup. Set the jars on a cloth in hot water. Fill the jars with the cold peaches, putting a generous layer of sugar between them. When the jars are full fill up with the hot syrup, and seal immediately. Twelve pounds of fruit and three pounds of sugar will fill six quart jars.

Canned apples and quinces. Pare and cut equal quantities of apples and quinces. First cook the quinces in just sufficient water to cover. Then remove, and cook the apples in the same water. In a vessel put a layer of quinces, then a layer of apples, and so on until all are used. Pour over them a syrup made of half a pound of sugar for each pound of fruit; and allow to stand over night. Then boil for five minutes, and seal in jars.

Tomato preserves. Scald and peel carefully some small, pear-shaped, half ripe tomatoes. Prick with a needle to prevent their bursting, and put their weight in sugar over them. Let them set overnight, then pour off the liquid into a preserving kettle, and boil until it is a thick syrup. Clarify with the white of an egg, add the tomatoes, and boil until transparent. A small piece of ginger root; or a lemon sliced very thin, to each pound of fruit, and cooked in the syrup, improves it.

Apple butter. To three gallons of cooked apples add one quart of cider, five pounds of brown sugar, and several sticks of cinnamon. Boil down to about two gallons.

JULY 7

BREAKFAST
Fresh raspberries with cream
Ham and eggs
Rolls
Coffee

LUNCHEON
Cantaloupe
Cold consommé in cups
Cold larded tenderloin of beef
Cauliflower salad
Floating island
Lady fingers
Demi tasse

DINNER
Potage Honolulu
Radishes
Stuffed clams
Chicken sauté, Lafitte
Beets à la Russe
Green corn sauté
Gauffrette potatoes
Biscuit glacé, pistachio
Assorted cakes
Coffee

Cauliflower salad. Boil two heads of cauliflower in salt water for ten minutes. Allow to become cold, and serve in salad bowl with French dressing, or mayonnaise sauce.

Potage Honolulu. Put on the fire a soup hen, in three quarts of water; season with a tablespoonful of salt, and bring to a boil. Then add one bouquet garni, three onions, three green peppers, and three-quarters of a pound of rice. When the hen is boiled soft remove it, with the bouquet garni and the peppers. Strain the rice, onions and broth through a fine sieve, and put back in the casserole. Bring to a boil, and bind with the yolks of two eggs mixed with a cup of cream. Season well with salt and Cayenne pepper, and add three canned red peppers cut in small squares, before serving.

Stuffed clams. Remove the clams from twenty-four large Little Necks. Wash the shells very clean, so there will be no sand in them. Chop the clams, and mix with three fresh mushrooms chopped fine, one truffle, a little chopped parsley and three ounces of butter. Season with salt and pepper, and then fill the shells. Place on a pan, sprinkle with grated cheese, put a small piece of butter on top of each, and bake in the oven for fifteen minutes. Serve on a napkin, with parsley, and lemons cut in half.

Chicken sauté, Lafitte. Cut a spring chicken in four, and season with salt and pepper. Put two ounces of butter in a sauté pan, heat, and then add the chicken. Cook until golden yellow, then sprinkle with a tablespoonful of flour and cook until the flour is yellow. Then add half a glass of claret and a cup of stock, bouillon or chicken broth. In another frying pan put a spoonful of olive oil, heat, then add a can of cèpes, toss them while cooking slightly, and add to the chicken. Peel one tomato, cut in eight, and also add to the chicken. Simmer together for twenty minutes. Then place the chicken on a platter; boil the sauce for five minutes more, season well with salt and pepper, add some chopped parsley, and pour over the chicken. Lay six fleurons around the platter.

Beets à la Russe. Slice a dozen boiled beets, put in a sauté pan with two ounces of butter, season with salt and pepper, and simmer for about five minutes. Just before serving add six leaves of fresh mint chopped very fine.

JULY 8

BREAKFAST
  Apricots
  Shirred eggs with peppers
  Rolls
  Coffee

LUNCHEON
  Beef marrow, Princess
  Eggs, Garcia
  Bread custard pudding
  Demi tasse

DINNER
  Consommé Charles Quint
  Broiled salmon, à la Russe
  Noisettes of lamb, Montpensier
  Roast duckling, apple sauce
  Fried sweet potatoes
  Green corn
  Chicory salad
  Philadelphia vanilla ice cream
  Assorted cakes
  Coffee

Shirred eggs with peppers. Cut four whole green peppers in small squares. Take four individual shirred egg dishes and put a teaspoonful of butter in each. Divide the chopped peppers equally among the four dishes, and simmer until nearly cooked; then break two eggs in each dish, season with salt and a little pepper, and cook again until the eggs are done.

Beef marrow, Princess. Have the butcher take the marrow out of four beef shin bones. Lay them whole in cold water for an hour, so the blood will run out. Then put the marrow in a casserole, in two quarts of cold water; add a tablespoonful of salt, bring to a boil, and let the marrow stand for half an hour in the boiling water. Then place it on four pieces of dry toast, and cover with well-seasoned Bordelaise sauce. When making the Bordelaise sauce omit the marrow.

Bread custard pudding. Over half a pound of bread crumbs pour a custard made of one quart of milk, the yolks of three eggs, three whole eggs, four ounces of sugar, and the grated rind of a lemon. Put in small moulds, and bake in a bain-marie. Serve with a cream sauce.

Cocoanut pudding. One-quarter pound of grated cocoanut, one-quarter pound of bread crumbs, and custard same as for bread custard pudding. Bake in the same way, and serve with cream sauce.

Consommé Charles Quint. Serve in hot consommé equal parts of chicken dumplings and asparagus tips. Add some picked chervil leaves.

Boiled salmon à la Russe. Cut two slices of salmon about one and one-half inches thick, and season well. Roll in oil, and broil. When done place on a platter, and spread two tablespoonfuls of anchovy butter on top. Serve separate Hollandaise sauce to which has been added two tablespoonfuls of fresh caviar.

Anchovy butter. Mix two tablespoonfuls of butter with two tablespoonfuls of essence of anchovies, the juice of a lemon, and a little chopped parsley. Anchovies in salt, soaked in cold water for an hour; or anchovies in oil; forced through a fine sieve, may be used if desired. Use in the same proportion as given for the essence.

Noisettes of lamb, Montpensier. Season four noisettes of lamb with salt and pepper, roll in oil, and broil. Then place on a platter; put on one side four artichoke bottoms filled with French peas in butter, and on the other side Parisian potatoes. Put a spoonful of Béarnaise sauce on top of each noisette. and serve.

JULY 9

BREAKFAST
Sliced figs with cream
Boiled salt mackerel
Baked potatoes
Rolls
Coffee

LUNCHEON
Cantaloupe
Clam broth in cups
Scrambled eggs, Havemeyer
Roast rack of mutton
String beans
Potato salad
Roquefort cheese with crackers
Coffee

DINNER
Potage Coburg
Ripe California olives
Lobster, Becker
Roast saddle of venison, currant jelly
Red cabbage
Potatoes, nature
Knickerbocker salad
Cocoanut pudding
Demi tasse

Scrambled eggs, Havemeyer. Peel two tomatoes, cut in half, squeeze out the juice, and cut in small squares. Put in a sauce pot one ounce of butter, heat, add the tomatoes, and simmer for two minutes. Then add eight beaten eggs, and one-half cup of cream. Season with salt and pepper. Scramble in the usual manner.

Potage Coburg. Mix one quart of mock turtle soup with one pint of consommé tapioca; and just before serving add one-half cup of very small gnocchis.

Lobster, Becker. Put in a sauté pan two ounces of butter, heat, add the tails of two boiled lobsters cut in slices, season with salt and pepper, and toss in pan for five minutes. Then add one-half glass of sherry wine, and boil for five minutes. Then add a cupful of very thick table cream, and boil again for five minutes. Then bind with the yolks of two eggs mixed with two ponies of very dry sherry wine. Before serving add a dozen slices of truffle.

Roast saddle of venison. Cook the saddle larded or plain, as desired. In a roasting pan put one sliced onion, one carrot, a small piece of celery, a sprig of thyme, two bay leaves, two cloves, and a spoonful of pepper berries. Season the saddle well, and lay in the pan, with two ounces of butter on top of the venison. Put in the oven and baste continually. When the saddle is done take out of the pan, and drain off the fat. Then put in the pan one-half glass of sherry wine, and reduce by boiling until nearly dry. Then add one cup of beef or chicken stock, one spoonful of meat extract, season with salt and pepper, and boil until reduced one-half. Pour over the saddle, or serve separate, as desired.

JULY 10

BREAKFAST
Stewed prunes
Boiled eggs
Dry toast
English breakfast tea

LUNCHEON
Grapefruit, cardinal
Cold consommé in cups
Cold pheasant pie with meat jelly
Chiffonnade salad
Lemon water ice
Lady fingers
Demi tasse

DINNER
Potage Dagobert
Radishes
Fillet of sole, à la Française
Tournedos, Porte Maillot
Roast chicken
Lettuce salad
Strawberry ice cream
Assorted cakes
Coffee

Grapefruit, Cardinal. Peel four grapefruit and slice them. Drain off the juice, and put the slices in suprême glasses. Force two small baskets of fresh raspberries through a fine sieve, put in a bowl, add two spoonfuls of powdered sugar and one pony of kirschwasser, mix well, and pour over the grapefruit.

Cold pheasant pie. Cut the breasts from two pheasants, and trim carefully. Put all of the trimmings and the meat of the legs without the bones, in an earthern jar; add three chopped shallots, and a bouquet garni, cover with sherry wine, and allow to stand for two days. Simmer the bones, with an onion, carrot, and a little celery, in two ounces of butter, until slightly brown. Then cover with a quart of stock, and cook slowly until reduced one-half. Keep this to mix with the forcemeat. Pass through a fine meat chopper one pound of veal, and one pound of not-too-fat pork; and season with salt, pepper and a little allspice. Have a special game pie or paté form lined with paté dough. Put a layer of forcemeat in the bottom, then a few pieces of the breasts cut in long narrow strips, and a strip of larding pork cut the same size. Lay the strips lengthwise of the pie. Add a few peeled blanched or parboiled pistachio nuts, then another layer of forcemeat, and so continue until the form is full. Cover the top with thin layer of larding pork, and then cover all with dough. Moisten the edges where the dough comes together, and close carefully, so there will be no leak. Cut a round hole in the center and insert a little chimney made of a small piece of stiff paper; otherwise the dough will close while cooking. Put in the oven and cook for one and one-half hours. Then allow to become cold, remove the paper chimney, fill the hole with meat jelly, and put in ice box until set. Cut in thin slices.

Paté dough. One pound of flour, one-quarter pound of butter, three eggs, one-half pony of water. Mix the butter and flour between the hands, then add the eggs and water, and season with a little salt. Let the dough set in the ice box a few hours before using.

Potage Dagobert. Mix one quart of purée of peas, one pint of consommé Julienne, and one pint of consommé aux perles de Nizam.

Tournedos. Porte Maillot. Season four small tenderloin steaks with salt and pepper; roll in oil, and broil. Place on a platter, and garnish with carrots and turnips cut in small balls, boiled and tossed in butter, salt and pepper. Also four potatoes cut in the shape of wooden shoes, fried in hot swimming lard, and filled with purée of spinach. Pour sauce Madère over the meat.

Fillet of sole, à la Française. Lay four fillets of sole flat on a table, spread with fish forcemeat (see Timbale of bass), roll up and place in a buttered pan. Season with salt and white pepper, add one-half glass of white wine and one-half cup of fish stock, bouillon or water. Cover with buttered paper, and set in oven for fifteen minutes. Then take out and place the fillets on a platter. Add to the pan one pint of white wine sauce, boil for two minutes, and strain. Then add to the sauce a spoonful of well-seasoned lobster butter, one dozen French mushrooms, and two sliced truffles. Pour the sauce over the fish, and garnish with four écrevisses en buisson.

JULY 11

BREAKFAST
Fresh grapes
Omelet with bacon
Crescents
Cocoa

LUNCHEON
Canapé St. Francis
Poached eggs, gourmet
Calf's head, vinaigrette
Boiled potatoes
Apple cottage pudding
Coffee

DINNER
Consommé Cameroni
Celery
Black bass, Tournon
Roast loin of veal, Nivernaise
Maître d'hôtel potatoes
Summer squash with butter
Field salad
Biscuit glacé au chocolat
Assorted cakes
Coffee

Canapé St. Francis. Put four nice leaves of yellow lettuce on four dessert plates. Cut four round pieces of toast, two and one-half inches in diameter, spread with fresh caviar, and place on top of the lettuce. Peel two ripe tomatoes and cut in four nice slices, and lay on top of the caviar. Sprinkle each piece with one third white wine vinegar and two-thirds olive oil, and a little salt and fresh ground black pepper mixed together. Lay two fillets of anchovies crosswise over each, and finally sprinkle some fine-chopped chervil over all. Serve cold.

Poached eggs, gourmet. Spread some paté de foie gras on four pieces of toast, lay a poached egg on top of each, and cover with Béarnaise sauce.

Apple cottage pudding. One-half pound of sugar, one-half pound of butter, eight eggs, one pint of milk, one and one-half pounds of flour, one ounce of baking powder, two grated rinds of lemons, one pinch of powdered mace, and four nice apples cut in thin slices. Mix the butter and the sugar well together, then add the eggs and the milk. Sift the baking powder and the flour together, and add, mixing lightly. Then add the grated rinds, mace and apples. Bake in a buttered pan, and serve with a thin apple sauce.

Cottage pudding. Make an Apple cottage pudding batter, and add chopped candied fruits and raisins, instead of the apples. Serve with fruit sauce.

Boston brown pudding. Same as cottage pudding with the addition of a cup of molasses.

Consommé Cameroni. Add to a quart of consommé brunoise one-quarter pound of boiled spaghetti cut in pieces one-quarter inch long. Serve grated cheese separate.

Black bass, Tournon. Season two black bass with salt and pepper, roll in melted butter, and broil. Then place on a platter, garnish with parsley in branches and two lemons cut in half. Serve Colbert sauce, to which a little chopped tarragon has been added.

Roast loin of veal, Nivernaise. Same as Veal Kidney Roast. (Dec. 20). Garnish with carrots cooked in butter.

JULY 12

BREAKFAST
  Orange juice
  Oatmeal with cream
  Buttered toasted rolls
  Coffee

LUNCHEON
  Calf's foot jelly in cups
  Eggs, Moscow
  Terrine de foie gras en aspic
  Lettuce salad
  Camembert cheese with crackers
  Coffee

DINNER
  Potage Lord Mayor
  Queen olives.   Salted almonds
  Boiled Lake Tahoe trout, Hollandaise
  Potatoes, natural
  Roast ribs of beef
  Cauliflower au gratin
  Rissolée potatoes
  Sliced tomatoes
  Coffee ice cream
  Macaroons
  Demi tasse

Calf's foot jelly. Parboil four calf's feet; allow to become cool; put back in vessel with an onion and a carrot, a piece of leek, a piece of celery, one clove, a bay leaf, a sprig of thyme, a spoonful of whole black peppers, a gallon of water, a quart of white wine, and a small handful of salt. Boil until the feet are soft. Then strain the broth, let it stand for a couple of minutes, and then remove all the fat from the top. Put a spoonful of the broth on a plate and set on ice. If it sets too hard add a little water, if it is too soft boil down until it is thick enough to set. Then put six whites of eggs in a casserole, beat with a whip, add slowly to the broth, put on a slow fire and bring to the boiling point. This serves to clarify the broth. Then strain, and set to cool. If the broth is for invalids omit the spices and vegetables, use but a little salt, and do not clarify. The cooked calf's feet may be used for an entrée, or for soup or salad.

Eggs, Moscow. Poach six eggs, and set in ice box until cold. Then remove the yolks carefully by making a very small hole, and letting the soft yolks run out. Fill the eggs with fresh caviar, roll in flour, then in beaten eggs, and finally in bread crumbs; fry in very hot swimming lard or melted butter for a few seconds only; or until the crumbs are yellow. Serve immediately on a napkin, with fried parsley, and two lemons cut in half.

Terrine de foie gras en aspic. Use a jelly mould that will contain as much as six small individual moulds. Put a little melted, but not hot, meat jelly in the bottom, and set on cracked ice until it is firm. Cut some foie gras from a terrine with a spoon, and lay in the mould, then cover with a little more melted jelly, then another layer of foie gras, and so continue until the mould is full. Set in the ice box for an hour; and serve on a napkin, with parsley in branches.

JULY 13

BREAKFAST
Mixed fresh fruit
Eggs au berre noir
Rolls
Coffee

LUNCHEON
Canapé Martha
Cold roast beef
Brésilienne salad
French pastry
Demi tasse

DINNER
Consommé Palestine
Radishes.   Lyon sausages
Fillet of flounder, St. Avertin
Roast tenderloin of beef, Berthieu
Escarole salad
Cottage pudding
Coffee

Consommé Palestine. Add to hot well-seasoned consommé equal parts of peas, flageolet beans, and carrots and turnips cut in small round balls; and all boiled in salted water.

Brésilienne salad. One-third boiled fresh Lima beans, one-third sliced green peppers, and one-third celery cut Julienne style. Place in a salad bowl, separately. In the center put some French dressing. Sprinkle with chopped parsley and chervil.

Fillet of flounder, St. Avertin. Put four fillets of flounder in a pan, cover with water, add a spoonful of salt and the juice of a lemon, and boil for seven minutes. Then place on a platter, and cover with a pint of Hollandaise sauce to which has been added a spoonful of French mustard. Garnish with four or eight round potato croquettes.

Roast tenderloin of beef, Berthieu. Garnish the roasted tenderloin with stuffed cucumbers, stuffed olives, peas au beurre, and potatoes château. Serve sauce Madère separate.

Potage Lord Mayor. Put two pounds of veal bones in a roasting pan with one onion, one carrot, a little celery, leek and parsley in branches, and two ounces of butter. Roast in oven until nicely browned, then drain off the fat, put in casserole, add two fresh pig's feet, one soup hen, and three pounds of shin of beef, one bouquet garni, a handful of salt, and two gallons of water. Cook until the hen and beef are soft, when they may be removed. When the pig's feet are done take out the bone, the fat and the lean meat, so nothing is left but the skin. Cut the skin in small squares, or round pieces the size of a dime. Cut some carrots in the same shape, and boil in salted water until soft. Put one pound of chopped beef in a casserole, add the whites of six eggs, stir well, add slowly the strained broth, and bring to a boil. This will clarify it. Season with salt and Cayenne pepper to taste. Boil for fifteen minutes, strain through a cheese cloth into another pot, bring to a boil, and reduce slowly for half an hour. Mix two spoonfuls of arrow root and a cup of sherry wine well together, and let run slowly into the boiling broth. Boil again for ten minutes. Before serving add a glass of dry amontillado. The beef and the soup hen then may be used for salads, croquettes, or other purposes.

JULY 14

BREAKFAST
Sliced peaches with cream
Kidney stew
Baked potatoes
Rolls
Coffee

LUNCHEON
Eggs, Bienvenue
Kalter aufschnitt
Camembert cheese with crackers
Coffee

DINNER
Chicken mulligatawney soup
Ripe California olives
Fried smelts, Tartar sauce
Roast chicken
Artichokes, Hollandaise
Summer squash
Rissolée potatoes
Field salad
Fancy ice cream
Assorted cakes
Demi tasse

Eggs, Bienvenue. Butter four individual shirred egg dishes. Make a border of mashed (croquette) potato around each dish. Put in the bottom a spoonful of purée of fresh tomatoes. Break two eggs in each dish, season with salt and pepper, and bake in oven.

Kalter aufschnitt. Assorted cold meats, such as roast beef, ham, tongue, lamb, etc. Garnish with a lettuce leaf filled with potato salad, for each person.

Chicken mulligatawney soup. Cut the breast from an uncooked soup hen, and cut in small squares of about one-quarter inch. Make about two quarts of broth from the bones and trimmings. Heat three ounces of butter in a casserole, add the cut-up breast of chicken, and simmer for five minutes. Then add an onion chopped very fine, and simmer again until yellow. Then add two spoonfuls of flour and one spoonful of curry powder, and heat through. Now pour in the strained chicken broth and a cup of rice, and boil slowly until the rice is cooked. Cut two apples in quarter inch squares, and simmer in butter until cooked, and add to the soup. Season with salt and pepper.

To preserve limes. Remove the cores from the limes with a small tin tube made for the purpose. Then cover with salad water, using a large handful of salt to the gallon. Soak for four or five hours; then drain off the water, and throw the limes into boiling water. As soon as they are soft take them out, one by one, and drop them into cold water. Change the cold water several times. To turn the limes green again put two gallons of water in a copper pan, add two large handfuls of cooking salt, one cup of vinegar, and several handfuls of fresh spinach. Put the pan on the fire and boil for a few minutes, then put the limes in the pan, and boil up several times. Remove from the fire, and allow to stand until cold; when the limes will have resumed their natural color. Drain off the liquid and let the limes soak in fresh water for about fourteen hours, changing the water frequently. Prepare a fifteen degree syrup, testing with a syrup gauge or cooking thermometer; and when boiling throw the limes into this, boil up, and then put into a vessel and leave for twelve hours. Then pour off the syrup, and boil it to sixteen degrees, pour it over the limes again, leaving it for twelve hours. Then drain and boil again to twenty degrees, pour over the limes, stand for twelve hours, and continue every twelve hours until thirty-two degrees are reached. Then boil for two minutes, and pour into small stone jars. Seal hermetically when cool.

Jellied cherries. Stone three pounds of cherries. Crush a handful of the cherry stones, and tie in a gauze bag. Put a pound of currant juice on the fire, add the crushed cherry stones, and steep. Put the cherries in a copper pan over a slow fire, and reduce one-half. Then add three pounds of granulated cane sugar and the currant juice, after the gauze bag has been removed; and boil steadily until a little tried on a saucer will not spread. Add half a gill of kirschwasser, and pour at once into jelly glasses. Place in a cool place, and when cold pour melted paraffine over the top and cover tightly.

Candied lemon or orange peels. Put a sufficient quantity of lemon or orange peels on the fire with enough water to cover. Boil until soft to the touch, then drain, and put in cold water and soak for twenty-four hours, changing the water often. Then pour off the water, and put the peels in an earthern jar, covering with a fifteen degree boiling syrup. Use a syrup guage or cooking thermometer to determine the density. Let the peels stand for twelve hours, then pour off the syrup and boil it up to eighteen degrees. Pour again over the peels and let it set for twelve hours. Repeat this operation six or seven times, gradually increasing the density of the syrup until it reaches thirty-two degrees. The last time prepare a fresh thirty-two degree syrup. Drain the old syrup from the peels, add them to the fresh boiling syrup, and boil up once. Then put the peels in stone jars or pots, cover with the syrup, and seal when cold.

Fig jam. Select large white firm figs, remove the stems, and cut in quarters. Dissolve a half pound of sugar in a little water for each pound of figs. Bring to a boil, then add the figs and boil steadily until the marmalade coats the spoon and drops from it in beads. Then pour into hot jelly glasses.

Blackberry cordial, for medicinal purposes. Heat and strain through fine cheese cloth some ripe blackberries. To one pint of juice add one pound of granulated sugar, one-fourth ounce of powdered cinnamon, one-fourth ounce of mace, and one teaspoonful of cloves. Boil all together for twenty minutes, strain, and to each pint add a jill of French brandy. Put up in small bottles.

Vanilla brandy. Cut some vanilla beans very fine, pound in a mortar, put in bottles and cover with strong brandy. This is much better than ordinary vanilla extract.

JULY 15

BREAKFAST
Strawberries with cream
Boiled eggs
Dry toast
Russian caravan tea

LUNCHEON
Cantaloupe
Chicken jelly in cups
Cold beef à la mode
Potato salad
Boiled custard
Lady fingers
Demi tasse

DINNER
Consommé Garibaldi
Salami
Sand dabs, sauté meunière
Mutton chops, maison d'or
String beans in butter
Stewed tomatoes
Mashed potatoes
Roast squab
Lettuce salad
French pastry
Assorted fruit
Coffee

Chicken jelly. Clarify three quarts of good chicken broth with the whites of six eggs. Soak two leaves of gelatine in water, and add to the broth. Boil for twenty minutes, and strain. Set in ice box to become firm.

Cold beef à la mode. Take two pieces of rump of beef weighing about six pounds each, season with salt and pepper, place in a vessel with a spoonful of fat or butter, and roast until nice and brown all over. Then sprinkle with two spoonfuls of flour, and cook until flour is brown. Then add one quart of boiling water and a pint of claret, one bouquet garni, twenty-four small raw French carrots, twenty-four small white onions fried in butter, and four quartered tomatoes. Cover, and boil in the oven. Remove the carrots and onions when soft, and continue cooking the beef until well done. Put the beef in an earthern pot and lay the carrots and onions around it. Reduce the sauce, by boiling, to half its volume, and strain over the beef. Prepare the day before using, so it will have sufficient time to become cold.

Boiled custard. The yolks of four eggs, three whole eggs, one ounce of corn starch, one quart of milk, and flavoring. Put all of the eggs, corn starch, half of the sugar, and a few drops of the milk into a bowl and mix well together. Boil the remainder of the milk and the other half of the sugar; pour over the egg mixture, and cook until it thickens. Then take off the fire, add the flavoring, mix well, and serve either in cups or saucers.

Tipsy parsons. Cut some slices of sponge cake about one-half inch thick. Soak them in sherry wine, and place them in saucers. Cover the top with boiling custard, and serve.

Vanilla custard with meringue. Make some boiled custard flavored with vanilla. Pour in saucers, place a half meringue shell on each, and serve.

Macaronade Célestine. Soak some macaroons in maraschino. Place in a saucer and pour boiling custard over them.

Bouchettes Palmyra. Soak some bouchettes in kummel, place them on saucers, and pour boiling custard over them.

Consommé Garibaldi. Boil one-quarter pound of spaghetti and cut in pieces one inch long. Cut a dozen green queen olives Julienne style, and add, with the spaghetti, to three pints of hot consommé. Serve grated cheese separate.

Mutton chops, maison d'or. Broil four mutton chops on one side; and then set to become cold. Make a forcemeat from the breast of a chicken, and add to it some chopped truffles. Place the forcemeat on the broiled side of the chops in pyramid form, sprinkle with fresh bread crumbs, set on a buttered pan, put a small piece of butter on top of each, and cook in the oven for ten or twelve minutes. Serve on a platter, with sauce Madère.

Lamb chops, maison d'or. Prepare in the same manner as mutton chops, maison d'or.

JULY 16

BREAKFAST
Baked Bartlett pears with cream
Omelet with asparagus tips
Rolls
Coffee

LUNCHEON
Shrimp salad
Eggs, Marlborough
Cold squab and Virginia ham
Alligator pear salad
Compote of apricots
German coffee cake
Demi tasse

DINNER
Chicken soup, Piedmontaise
Pim olas.   Radishes
Black bass, Heydenreich
Sweetbreads, poulette
Roast leg of venison
Red cabbage
Boiled potatoes
Lettuce and grapefruit salad
Apple cobbler
Coffee

Eggs, Marlborough. Place four poached eggs on four pieces of anchovy toast, cover with sauce Périgueux, and lay a strip of broiled bacon across each.

Chicken soup, Piedmontaise. Mix a pint of chicken broth with a pint of purée of tomato soup, add a quarter pound of macaroni cut in one-quarter inch pieces, and the breast of a boiled chicken cut in small squares.

Black bass, Heydenreich. Place two black bass in a buttered pan, and season with salt and fresh-ground black pepper. Chop three ounces of salted almonds, and mix with one-quarter pound of chopped fresh mushrooms, three ounces of butter, and some chopped parsley. Spread over the fish, and bake in oven for twenty minutes. Pour the juice of two lemons over the fish, and serve from the pan in which it was baked.

Sweetbreads, poulette. Soak two pounds of sweetbreads in cold water for two hours, to cause the blood to run out. Then put on the fire in two quarts of water, add a spoonful of salt, bring to a boil, and then cool off in cold water. Remove the skins, and cut the sweetbreads in slices one-half inch thick. Put two ounces of butter in a sauce pan, add the sweetbreads, and simmer for two minutes. Then add a spoonful of flour, and heat through. Then add one pint of thick cream, and boil for ten minutes. Season with salt and Cayenne pepper, add a can of sliced French mushrooms and a little chopped chives, boil for two minutes, and thicken with the yolks of two eggs mixed with a little cream. Serve in a chafing dish.

Cobblers. Apple, pear, peach or apricot. Line a deep baking pan with pie dough, fill with the chopped fruit desired, sweetened with sugar, and with a little cinnamon added, cover with a sheet of pie crust paste, brush with egg, and bake. Serve with cream or wine sauce.

Wine sauce. Put in a sauce pan one pint of water, one-half pound of sugar, and the rind and juice of half a lemon. Bring to a boil, and then thicken with a teaspoonful of corn starch dissolved in a little water, and again bring to a boil. Flavor with a glassful of any kind of wine; or a pony of cognac, kirschwasser, or other cordial, as you may desire. Strain and serve with puddings, cobblers, etc.

JULY 17

BREAKFAST
  Raspberries with cream
  Broiled fillet of sole, maître d'hôtel
  Hashed browned potatoes
  Rolls
  Coffee

LUNCHEON
  Eggs, St. Catherine
  Boneless squab en aspic
  Majestic salad
  Roquefort cheese with crackers
  Coffee

DINNER
  Little Neck clams
  Consommé Talleyrand
  Ripe olives.   Lyon sausage
  Boiled salmon trout, sauce mousseline
  Potatoes, nature
  Planked sirloin steak, St. Francis
  Escarole and chicory salad
  Fancy ice cream
  Assorted cakes
  Coffee

Eggs, St. Catherine. Cut the tops from four large baked potatoes, and scoop out the insides. Lay a slice of tomato in the bottom, season with salt and pepper, break an egg in each, and cover with well-seasoned cream sauce. Sprinkle with grated cheese, put small bits of butter on top, and bake in oven for about ten minutes. Serve on napkin, with parsley in branches.

Boneless squab en aspic. Cut the squabs open at the back, and remove all the bones, being careful not to cut the skin. Spread flat on the table, season with salt and pepper, fold together and place in a buttered pan and cook until done, and of a nice color. Allow to become cold. Set an oval mould in cracked ice, garnish the bottom with sliced truffles, pour in just enough nearly cold meat jelly to cover the truffles. Place the cold squab in the mould and fill to the top with jelly. Keep in the ice box until set. When ready to serve turn over on a napkin, remove the mould, and garnish with parsley.

Majestic salad. Equal parts of celery, raw apple, and green peppers cut in Julienne style. Serve with mayonnaise dressing.

Consommé Talleyrand. Put four grated truffles in a soup tureen, add a glassful of very dry sherry wine, and a pinch of Cayenne pepper, cover, and stand for an hour. When ready to serve pour three pints of hot consommé tapioca over it.

Planked sirloin steak, St. Francis. Season a three pound sirloin steak with salt and pepper, roll in oil and broil. When done place it on a hot meat-plank sufficiently large so that it may be garnished with a bouquet of new peas cooked in butter, string beans, asparagus tips with a little Hollandaise sauce on them, and French carrots in butter. Lay a dozen fresh mushrooms on top of the steak. Around the steak and vegetables lay some Parisienne potatoes. Serve sauce Colbert separate.

JULY 18

BREAKFAST
Orange and grapefruit juice mixed
Oatmeal and cream
Corn muffins
Coffee

LUNCHEON
Chicken salad, Victor
Vogeleier omelet
Raspberry water ice
Streusel kuchen (cake)
Coffee

DINNER
Potage vert pré
Smoked eels with rye bread
Corned beef and cabbage
Boiled potatoes
Peach meringue
Demi tasse

Potage vert pré. Mix one pint of consommé tapioca with one quart of purée of pea soup. Just before serving add some chopped chervil.

Peach meringue. Dress some meringue paste (see meringue shells) on dishes or plates in round forms about three inches in diameter and three-quarters of an inch deep. Place the dishes on a pan, and set in a rather cool oven until the meringues are of a nice straw color. Put on the center of each a spoonful of pastry cream, and on top of this half of a peach cooked in syrup; or half of a preserved peach.

Apricot meringue. Prepare in the same manner as peach meringue.

Strawberry, blackberry or raspberry meringues. Prepare in the same manner as peach meringue, but use fresh uncooked berries.

Patience (cake). Beat ten whites of eggs until firm, then add one pound of powdered sugar, three quarters of a pound of flour, and some vanilla flavor Stir until firm and well mixed, and lay out like small lady fingers on a but tered pan. Set in a dry place until a crust forms on top, and then bake in a moderate oven.

JULY 19

BREAKFAST
  Grapes
  Waffles
  Honey in comb
  Toasted rolls
  Ceylon tea

LUNCHEON
  Sardines
  Scrambled eggs, Lucullus
  Galantine of capon
  Salade Cupid d'Azure
  Port de Salut cheese with crackers
  Coffee

DINNER
  Consommé Trianon
  Celery.   Olives.   Salted almonds
  Broiled barracouda, mustard sauce
  Hollandaise potatoes
  Roast leg of veal
  Carrots Vichy
  Spinach with egg
  Pickled beets
  Vanilla ice cream
  Coffee fruit cake   Demi tasse

Scrambled eggs, Lucullus. Put in a casserole one ounce of butter, and three truffles cut in dices about one-eighth inch square. Heat through, and then add eight beaten eggs, and one-half cup of cream. Season with salt and pepper, then scramble, and dish up on a china platter. Cut about a dozen slices of truffle, heat on a plate with the addition of half a spoonful of meat extract, and lay over the eggs.

Galantine of capon. Split open down the back a good-sized fowl or capon, and remove every bone, being careful not to remove any of the meat, and not to cut the skin. Lay out flat on the table skinside down, and season with salt and pepper. Prepare a forcemeat with one pound of veal, and one and one-half pounds of lean pork. Strain through a sieve, season with salt and pepper and a little grated nutmeg, and add a pint of cream. Cut in small squares the tip of a smoked boiled beef tongue, one-half pound of white fat pork, one-quarter pound of ham, one-quarter pound of peeled pistache nuts, and four truffles. Mix thoroughly with the force meat, and put on top of the fowl. Close, by drawing both sides together, forming a big sausage. Roll very tightly in a towel or napkin, and tie with a string on both ends and twice around the middle. Cook in bouillon, stock or salted water slowly for from one and one-half to two hours. When cooked, untie, remove the cloth, roll tight again and re-tie. Set in the ice box for at least eight hours. Serve sliced in the same manner as sausage, and about one-quarter inch thick. Garnish with meat jelly and parsley in branches. Galantine of chicken, squab, etc., may be prepared in the same manner.

Salade Cupid d'Azure. Cut alligator pears in slices, lay on a platter, and sprinkle with one chopped shallot, salt and pepper, one chopped green pepper, one spoonful of vinegar, and two spoonfuls of olive oil. Allow to stand for an hour. Cut two heads of well-washed romaine salad in two, and on each lay a slice of grapefruit, then a slice of alligator pear, then a slice of grapefruit, and so continue until the romaine is full. Divide the dressing over the individual salads; and if not sufficient, finish with French dressing.

Consommé Trianon. To each portion of consommé royal add six slices of truffle cut in triangle shape.

Mustard sauce. To one pint of cream sauce add two spoonfuls of French mustard, and mix well.

JULY 20

BREAKFAST
  Sliced peaches with cream
  Boiled eggs
  Popover muffins
  Coffee

LUNCHEON
  Cantaloupe
  Poached eggs, Bar le Duc
  Paprika veal   Boiled rice
  Louise salad
  Surprise fritters.   Coffee

DINNER
  Little Neck clams
  Crab grumbo   California ripe olives
  Boiled codfish, egg sauce
  Small tenderloin steak, Rachel
  Hearts of lettuce
  Apricot cobbler
  Patience   Demi tasse

Popover muffins. Five eggs, one-half ounce of salt, one quart of milk, and one pound of flour. Beat the eggs and salt well together; then beat in the milk; then add the flour and beat until smooth. This will make a very thin batter. Fill greased tall muffin moulds only half full, and bake in medium oven until very crisp.

Paprika veal. The remains of a roast leg of veal may be used. Cut in slices one-half inch thick, and as wide as the meat will allow. Put two ounces of butter and a chopped onion in a casserole and simmer until the onion is done. Then add two spoonfuls of flour and one spoonful of paprika, and simmer again for a few minutes. Then add half a pint of stock, half a cup of white wine, one spoonful of meat extract, and the veal. Season well with salt, and simmer for twenty minutes. Should the sauce be too thick add a little more stock.

Poached eggs, Bar le Duc. Place four boiled bottoms of artichokes on four pieces of toast, and lay four poached eggs on the artichokes. Cover all with well-seasoned cream sauce, to which has been added a little chopped fresh tarragon.

Louise salad. Raw celery, fresh pineapple, and pimentos in equal parts, and all cut Julienne style. Place in a salad bowl and cover with well-seasoned mayonnaise sauce with a dash of dry sherry wine in it.

Surprise fritters. One quart of milk, six ounces of butter, three-quarters of a pound of flour and eight eggs. Make a paste in the same manner as for cream puffs. Drop with a spoon in a pan of hot swimming lard and fry until crisp and brown. Fill with currant or other fruit jelly, dust with powdered sugar, and serve with cream or Sabayon sauce.

Crab Gumbo. Put two ounces of butter, one chopped onion and one chopped green pepper in a casserole and simmer until done. Then add two quarts of fish broth and one-half cup of rice, and boil very slowly for fifteen minutes. Then add three peeled tomatoes cut in small dices, one spoonful of Worcestershire sauce, the meat of two whole crabs, and a can of okra; or one pound of fresh okra cut in pieces one inch long. Cook slowly for twenty minutes, season well with salt and pepper, and sprinkle with a little chopped parsley.

Fish broth. Cover the bones of any kind of fish with water, add a bouquet garni, one onion, one carrot, and a cupful of white wine if desired. Cook for thirty minutes, and strain. The broth may be served in cups as soup; used for chowders; for bisque soups; for white wine sauce; for cooking fish, or for many other purposes.

JULY 21

BREAKFAST
Sliced fresh pineapple
Pearl grits with cream
Buttered toast
English breakfast tea

LUNCHEON
Stuffed mangoes
Scrambled eggs, Mayence
Steak Tartare
Roquefort cheese with crackers
Coffee

DINNER
Consommé Sicilienne
Chow chow.   Carciofini
Broiled salmon, St. Germain
Sweetbreads braisé, Elizabeth
Roast leg of mutton, currant jelly
Cold asparagus, mustard sauce
Cantaloupe baskets
Almond rocks
Coffee

Scrambled eggs, Mayence. Mayence, or Mainz, is a city in Germany famous for its ham. Cut four slices of Mayence or Westphalia ham in small squares, put in a casserole with two ounces of butter and simmer until heated through. Then add ten beaten eggs and one-half cup of cream, and season with pepper and a very little salt. Scramble in the usual manner.

Steak Tartare. Cut one pound of tenderloin steak very fine, season with salt and pepper, and form in two oval shaped pats. In the center on top lay the yolk of a raw egg. Garnish with two lettuce leaves filled with fine-chopped white onions and some sliced pickles; and two leaves filled with capers and chopped parsley. Serve raw.

Consommé Sicilienne. Roll out very thin a noodle paste, and cut in lozenge shapes about one inch long. Boil in salt water for about ten minutes, cool off in fresh cold water, and serve in hot consommé. Serve grated Parmesan cheese separate.

Boiled salmon, St. Germain. Cut two slices of salmon about one and one-half inches thick, roll in butter, season with salt and pepper, roll in fresh bread crumbs, and broil slowly. When done place on a platter, and garnish with Parisian potatoes. Serve sauce Béarnaise separate.

Sweetbreads braisé, Elizabeth. Braised sweetbreads served with stuffed tomatoes, stuffed mushrooms, onions glacé, and sauce Madére.

Cantaloupe baskets. Cut four cantaloupes in the form of baskets, using part of the rind for the handle. Carefully take out the pulp with a teaspoon. Fill the baskets with vanilla ice cream mixed with the pulp, and decorate with whipped cream.

Orange baskets. Cut the oranges in the form of baskets, scrape out the pulp, fill with orange water ice, and decorate with strawberries and raspberries.

Almond rocks. Beat the whites of eight eggs very stiff and dry. Add one pound of powdered sugar and three-quarters of a pound of shredded almonds, and one-half spoonful of vanilla extract. Mix lightly, and lay on a buttered and floured pan, in the shape of rocks, using a fork to form them. Bake in a slack oven. Serve cold.

Small tenderloin steak, Rachel. Broil the steaks and lay on a platter. Put a slice of terrine de foie gras on top, garnish with peas au beurre and Julienne potatoes. Serve sauce Madère.

JULY 22

BREAKFAST
    Stewed prunes
    Virginia ham **and eggs**
    Rolls
    Coffee

LUNCHEON
    Tomatoes, surprise
    Clam broth in cups
    Cold Lake Tahoe trout, vinaigrette
    Boston brown pudding
    Demi tasse

DINNER
    Cream of watercress
    Pim olas.   Celery
    Fried frog's legs, Espagnole
    Roast squab chicken, Michels
    Peach compote
    Sweet and sour string beans
    Gauffrette potatoes
    Lettuce salad, egg dressing
    Blanc mange aux fruits
    Rolled almonds wafers
    Coffee

Tomatoes, surprise. Peel four tomatoes, cut off the top, and scoop out the insides with a small sharp spoon. Cut a stalk of white celery in small dices, wash well, and set in ice box to cool. Then mix the celery with half a cup of thick mayonnaise sauce, season with salt and pepper, and fill the tomatoes. Sprinkle the tops with chopped parsley, and serve on lettuce leaves.

Cream of watercress. Heat three ounces of butter in a casserole, add three spoonfuls of flour, one pint of chicken broth, and one pint of milk; and bring to a boil. Then add one quart of well-washed watercress, and season with salt and Cayenne pepper. Boil for half an hour, strain, and put back in casserole. Again bring to a boil, and bind with the yolks of two eggs mixed with one-half pint of cream. Strain again and serve.

Fried frogs' legs, Espagnole. Season two dozen frogs' legs with salt and pepper, roll in flour, then in beaten eggs, and then in fresh bread crumbs. Fry in swimming hot lard, and serve on a napkin on a platter. Garnish with fried parsley and two lemons cut in half. Serve Créole sauce separate.

Squab chicken, Michels. Put four well-seasoned squab chickens in a casserole with three ounces of butter and one onion cut in half. Put in oven and baste very often. When both chicken and onion are nicely colored set on top of the stove, add one-half glass of white wine, cover the pot, and simmer for five minutes. Then place the chicken on a platter; and put in the pot one-half cup of chicken broth and a spoonful of meat extract, and boil for five minutes. Pour over the chicken.

Rolled almond wafers (cigarettes). Beat the whites of nine eggs, but not too hard. Stop beating when they begin to get spongy. Then stir in one-half pound of blanched chopped almonds, ten ounces of sugar, two ounces of flour, and one pinch of powdered cinnamon. Spread on a buttered pan, like wafers, and about two inches square. Bake in a hot oven. When done immediately roll them around a small wooden stick, and press the ends together. They may be served dry, or filled with whipped cream.

Sweet and sour string beans. Boil two pounds of string beans in salted water. When cooked place in a casserole, add a cupful of white wine vinegar, one cupful of brown sugar, one spoonful of meat extract, and a cupful of chicken broth, or any kind of good bouillon. Season with salt, and boil for fifteen minutes with the pot uncovered.

JULY 23

BREAKFAST
  Compote of apricots
  Buckwheat cakes with maple syrup
  Rolls
  Coffee

LUNCHEON
  Omelette Meissonier
  Pork chops, Badoise
  Schloss cheese with crackers
  Coffee

DINNER
  Consommé Chevalier
  Salted Brazil nuts.   Ripe olives
  Fillet of sole, Montmorency
  Broiled spring turkey
  Summer squash
  Lima beans
  Mashed potatoes, au gratin
  Escarole and chicory salad
  Croute aux fruits
  Demi tasse

Omelette Meissonier. Cut a carrot and a turnip in one-quarter inch squares. Boil until soft in salted water, then mix with a spoonful of cream sauce, and season with salt and pepper. Make an omelet with ten eggs, in the usual manner and before turning over on the platter place the vegetables in the center. Pour cream sauce around the omelet.

Pork chops, Badoise. Season four pork chops with salt and pepper, roll in flour, and fry in a pan. When done place on a platter, garnish one side with noodles and the other side with mashed potato. Pour tomato sauce around all.

Consommé Chevalier. Serve in hot well-seasoned consommé equal parts of small chicken dumplings, and chicken breast and smoked beef tongue cut Julienne style.

Fillet of sole, Montmorency. Place four flat fillets of sole on a buttered pan, season with salt and pepper, and lay four heads of French mushrooms and four slices of truffle on top of each. Cover with sauce Italienne, sprinkle with grated cheese, put small bits of butter on top, and bake in oven. When done sprinkle with chopped parsley and the juice of a lemon, and serve from the pan they were baked in. A silver dish is preferable for baking.

Croute aux fruits (fruit crust). Toast some slices of sponge cake, put them on a plate or saucer, and put on top different kinds of stewed fruit, (compote), flavored with a little kirschwasser or maraschino.

Crout à l'ananas (pineapple crust). Prepare in the same manner as croute aux fruits, but use pineapple. Decorate with maraschino cherries.

JULY 24

BREAKFAST
Baked pears with cream
Scrambled eggs with smoked salmon
Rolls
Coffee

LUNCHEON
Terrine de foie gras en aspic
Shirred eggs, Niçoise
Sweetbreads, Marigny
Lettuce and grapefruit salad
Blackberry meringue
Demi tasse

DINNER
Cream of flageolet beans
Antipasto.   Celery
Sea bass, Montebello
Roast tenderloin of beef, vert pré
Field and beet salad
Alexandria pudding
Coffee

Scrambled eggs with smoked salmon. Cut a half pound of raw smoked salmon in thin slices. In a casserole put the salmon with two ounces of butter, and heat through. Then add ten beaten eggs, one-half cup of cream, a little salt and pepper; and scramble in the usual manner.

Terrine de foie gras en aspic. Use small round individual moulds; or a large one for six people; as desired. Melt a little meat jelly just so it will run, but do not have it hot. Put a little in the bottom of each mould and set in the ice box to become firm. Cut the foie gras out of the terrine with a soup spoon, which should be dipped in hot water for each cut so as to give a nice smooth surface. Put a layer of foie gras in the bottom of the moulds, cover with a little more jelly, set in ice box again to become cool, and then repeat until the moulds are full. For serving dip the form in hot water for a second, and turn out on a napkin on a platter. Garnish with parsley in branches.

Shirred eggs, Niçoise. Shir some eggs, and before serving pour some tomato sauce, or purée, over the white of the eggs.

Sweetbreads, Marigny. Garnish some braised sweetbreads with an artichoke bottom filled with French peas, for each person. Serve sauce Madère.

Cream of flageolet beans. Heat three ounces of butter in a casserole, then add three spoonfuls of flour, and heat through. Then add one pint of chicken broth, one pint of milk, and two cans of French flageolet beans. Boil for thirty minutes, strain through a fine sieve, and put back in the casserole. Bring to a boil, season with salt and Cayenne pepper and a very little grated nutmeg. Then stir in a pint of boiling milk and three ounces of sweet butter. Strain again, and serve.

Sea bass, Montebello. Cut the fillets from a sea bass in the same manner as a fillet of sole. Spread a layer of fish forcemeat (see Bass Timbale) over them, season well, and fold the fillets. Put in a buttered pan, add one-half cup of fish stock or broth, one-half glass of white wine, cover with buttered paper, and cook in oven for fifteen minutes. Place on a platter, and cover with a mixture of two-thirds Béarnaise sauce and one-third tomato sauce. Garnish with fleurons.

Roast tenderloin of beef, vert pré. Roast a tenderloin of beef, and place on a platter. Garnish with French string beans in butter, and Julienne potatoes. Pour a little sauce Madère over the tenderloin; and also serve sauce separate.

JULY 25

BREAKFAST
Cantaloupe
Boiled eggs
Dry toast
Ceylon tea

LUNCHEON
Matjes herring, Krasnapolsky
Consommé in cups
Cheese straws
Broiled squab on toast
Asparagus, Hollandaise
Roquefort cheese with crackers
Mixed fruit
Coffee

DINNER
Rice soup, à l'Allemande
Salted almonds
Sand dabs, meunière
Saddle of lamb, jardinière
Romaine salad
Pear cobbler
Assorted cakes
Coffee

Matjes herring, Krasnapolsky. Get six Matjes herring from the grocer, and soak in cold water for two hours. Then remove the skins, and place the herrings on lettuce leaves on a platter. Garnish with small plain boiled potatoes and dill pickles.

Rice soup, à l'Allemande. Put three ounces of butter and two spoonfuls of raw rice in a casserole and heat through. Then add two spoonfuls of flour and heat again. Then add two quarts of strained boiling chicken broth, and boil slowly for an hour. Stir occasionally so the rice will not burn on the bottom of the pot. Season with salt and white pepper.

Saddle of lamb, jardinière. Prepare in the same manner as rack of lamb, jardinière.

Alexandria pudding. Ten ounces of bread crumbs, one quart of milk, two ounces of butter, the grated rind of a lemon, the yolks of eight eggs, the whites of six eggs, four ounces of browned and chopped almonds, and six ounces of sugar. Mix the sugar with the butter, and then add the eggs. Mix the crumbs with the almonds and lemon rind, and add to the first mixture. Beat the whites of the eggs, and mix in lightly. Bake in a buttered pan, and serve with strawberry or raspberry sauce.

JULY 26

BREAKFAST
Fresh raspberries with cream
Boiled salted salmon belly
Baked potatoes
Rolls
Coffee

LUNCHEON
Grapefruit with cherries
Broiled striped bass
Sibyl potatoes
Breast of chicken, en aspic
Louis salad
Neufchâtel cheese with crackers
Claret punch
Demi tasse

DINNER
Little Neck clams
Consommé Monte Cristo
Planked shad
Roast chicken
Château potatoes
New peas
Chiffonnade salad
Fancy ice cream
Assorted cakes
Coffee

Breast of chicken en aspic. Loosen the legs and skin of a good-sized chicken, then insert a knife between neck and wing up towards the middle of the wishbone, loosening all the meat from the breast bone. The whole side will then be in one piece with the wing attached. Do the same with the other side. Then season, and fry to a brown color in butter. Set aside to become cold. Then decorate with the hard-boiled white of eggs cut in fancy shapes; place in an oval form, cover with almost-cold meat jelly, and set in ice box to become cold. To remove, dip the form in hot water for a second, and place on a folded napkin. Garnish with parsley in branches.

Louis salad. Equal parts of raw pineapple, apple, and celery, cut Julienne style. Season with a sauce made with a cup of mayonnaise, a spoonful of cream, a spoonful of sherry wine, a dash of vinegar, and a pinch of paprika. Mix well.

Claret punch. One bottle of claret, one bottle of soda water, one-half pint of plain water, one-half pound of powdered sugar, one lemon cut in slices, and one pony of brandy. Stir all together until the sugar is dissolved. Strain, cool on ice, and serve in glasses with a very thin slice of lemon.

Consommé Monte Cristo. Consommé royal and printanier mixed.

JULY 27

BREAKFAST
Fig jam
Boiled eggs
Dry toast
English breakfast tea

LUNCHEON
Canapé of sardines
Cold clam broth
Broiled honeycomb tripe
Lyonnaise potatoes
Chiffonnade salad
Stilton cheese with crackers
Coffee

DINNER
Potage velour
California ripe olives
Fillet of turbot, Bàtelière
Sweetbreads, Metropolitan Club
Roast duckling, apple sauce
Artichokes, Hollandaise
Waldorf salad
Strawberry meringue
Demi tasse

Potage velour. Mix two pints of purée of tomato soup with one pint of consommé aux perles de Nizam.

Fillet of turbot, Bàtelière. Put four fillets of turbot in a buttered pan, season with salt and pepper, add one-half glass of claret and one-half cup of fish broth, cover, boil for ten minutes, and then place the fish on a platter. Put one ounce of butter in a small casserole and heat. Then add one ounce of flour, heat through, add the broth left from the fish and also another half cup of broth, boil for five minutes, and strain. Then add slowly two ounces of fresh butter, stir well, and when butter is melted add one cup of hot shrimps. Season well, and pour over the fish.

Sweetbreads, Metropolitan Club. Let two pounds of sweetbreads soak in cold water with a little salt in it, for two hours; to cause the blood to run out. Then put in a casserole with one-half gallon of cold water and a spoonful of salt, and bring to a boil. Cool off in cold water, and then trim them free from skin. Put three ounces of butter in a very wide earthern pot, put the sweetbreads on top, and season with salt and pepper. Add six small white onions, six heads of fresh mushrooms, and two green peppers cut in one inch squares. Simmer until nice and brown, then add one-half glass of white wine and a spoonful of meat extract. Cook in oven for fifteen minutes, basting continually. Serve from the casserole in which it was cooked.

JULY 28

BREAKFAST
  Sliced peaches with cream
  Plain shirred eggs
  Rolls

LUNCHEON
  Cantaloupe
  Poached eggs, Périgordine
  Mixed grill, special
  French fried potatoes
  Chicory salad
  Rice croquettes
  Demi tasse

DINNER
  Clam cocktail
  Consommé Inauguration
  Salted pecans
  Mousse d'écrevisses (fish)
  Roast ribs of beef, Yorkshire pudding
  Stewed corn
  Green peas
  Mashed potatoes
  Watercress salad
  Chocolate ice cream
  Assorted cakes
  Coffee

Poached eggs, Périgordine. Spread some paté de foie gras on four pieces of toast, lay a poached egg on top of each, and cover with sauce Périgordine.

Consommé Inauguration. Equal parts of Julienne, small chicken dumplings, and Italian paste, served in hot consommé.

Mousse d'écrevisses. Remove the shells from three lobsters and two dozen écrevisses (crayfish or crawfish) and smash very fine in a mortar. Put a cup of water, an ounce of butter, and a little salt and Cayenne pepper in a vessel and bring to a boil. Then stir in slowly two tablespoonfuls of flour, and continue stirring until there are no lumps. Mix this with the écrevisse and lobster meat and mashed shells. When cold strain through a very fine sieve. Place in a bowl on ice and mix with an egg and a pint of thick cream; stirring in carefully so it does not curdle. Test for seasoning, and if necessary add a little écrevisse coloring to give a rose shade. Fill small buttered moulds, and boil in bain-marie for about fifteen minutes. Turn out on a platter, and pour écrevisse sauce over all. The lobster is added for economy and strength of color. Double the amount of écrevisses may be used instead.

Écrevisse sauce. Melt two tablespoonfuls of écrevisse butter in a pint of sauce Allemande, or sauce au vin blanc. Add a few écrevisse tails.

JULY 29

BREAKFAST
Grapes
Griddle cakes, maple syrup
Coffee

LUNCHEON
Herring salad
Hot tomato broth
Eggs, Suzette
Cold tongue, meat jelly
Beet salad
Peach cobbler
Anisette cakes　　　Coffee

DINNER
Potage McDonald
Radishes
Kingfish, Argentine
Small sirloin steak, à la Russe
Summer squash
Cauliflower, Hollandaise
Potato croquettes
Sliced tomatoes
Orange basket
Assorted cakes　　　Coffee

Herring salad. Soak two salted herrings in cold water for an hour, then remove the skin and cut out the bones. Slice in thin slices, and mix with one quart of potato salad.

Hot tomato broth. Chop three pounds of shin or lean beef. Mix with the whites of six eggs and one dozen tomatoes chopped very fine. Stir well, and add slowly one gallon of bouillon or stock. Bring slowly to a boil, and simmer for an hour. Strain through cheese cloth, season with salt and pepper. Serve either hot or cold.

Eggs, Suzette. Bake four medium-sized potatoes, cut off the tops, and scoop out the insides. Mash half of the potato that has been removed, add a little butter, season with salt and pepper, and put back in the bottom of each potato shell. Break an egg in each, cover with well-seasoned cream sauce, sprinkle with grated cheese, put small bits of butter on top, and bake in medium-hot oven for ten minutes.

Anisette cake. One-half pound of sugar, five eggs, one-half pound of flour, and one teaspoonful of anise seed. Beat the sugar with the eggs until light, then add the flour and anise seeds. Put in a buttered bread pan and bake. When done allow to become cool; then cut in slices about one-half inch thick. Lay on a pan and bake until they become of a nice brown color.

Potage McDonald. Heat three ounces of butter in a casserole; then add two and one-half spoonfuls of flour, and one-half spoonful of curry powder. Heat through, and then add one pint of bouillon, stock or chicken broth, and one pint of milk; bring to a boil, and add one parboiled calf's brains. Boil for thirty minutes, and then strain through a fine sieve. Heat in another casserole one ounce of butter; then add half of a chopped onion, and fry until golden yellow. Then add the soup and boil for ten minutes. Then add the yolks of two eggs mixed with one cup of cream, stir well, and strain again. Season well with salt and pepper.

Kingfish, Argentine. Put two kingfish on a buttered platter or pan, season with salt and pepper, add a glass of white wine, put in oven and bake. Cover with Créole sauce and serve.

Small sirloin steak à la Russe. Broiled sirloin steak garnished with small patty shells filled with fresh caviar. Serve horseradish sauce separate.

JULY 30

BREAKFAST
  Apricots
  Ham and eggs
  Rolls
  Coffee

LUNCHEON
  Lobster salad
  Poached eggs, Piedmontaise
  Birds' nests
  Demi tasse
  Orangeade

DINNER
  Consommé Vanderbilt
  Salami.   Pim olas
  Striped bass, meunière
  Leg of veal, au jus
  Spinach with egg
  Laurette potatoes
  Lettuce salad
  Raspberry meringue
  Demi tasse

Poached eggs, Piedmontaise. Make a risotto, and place four poached eggs on top. Cover with cream sauce.

Birds' nests (puff paste). Bake small patties as elsewhere described. Wash with thin royal icing, and sprinkle with plenty of shredded cocoanut. Set in oven to obtain a little color. Fill the center with jelly or marmalade, and place three or four blanched almonds on top to represent the bird's eggs. Small egg-shaped candies may be used instead if desired.

Lemonade. One quart of water, the juice of five lemons, and one-half pound of powdered sugar. Dissolve the sugar in the water, and then add the lemon juice. Strain, and cool on ice.

Orangeade. One pint of water, one pint of orange juice, the juice of two lemons, and one-half pound of sugar. Dissolve the sugar in the water, add the orange and lemon juice, strain, and cool on ice.

Consommé Vanderbilt. Equal parts of boiled breast of chicken, boiled smoked beef tongue, French canned mushrooms and truffles cut in Julienne style; and one part of fresh or canned peas. Serve in hot, well-seasoned consommé.

JULY 31

BREAKFAST
Fresh strawberries with cream
Plain omelet
Rolls
Coffee

LUNCHEON
Schlemmerbroedchen
Scrambled eggs, Pluche
Westphalian ham
Red cabbage salad
Rice croquettes
Champagne punch
Demi tasse

DINNER
Little Neck clams on half shell
Potage Mexicaine
Ripe California olives
Fillet of turbot, Tempis
Roast chicken
Château potatoes
Asparagus, Hollandaise
Tomato salad
Biscuit glacé, au café
Demi tasse

Schlemmerbroedchen (sandwich). Spread four slices of rye bread with butter, cover with one-quarter pound of raw beef chopped very fine, and seasoned with salt and pepper. Spread some fresh caviar on top of the beef. Serve on a folded napkin, with two lemons cut in half.

Red cabbage salad. Slice a head of red cabbage very thin, put in a salad bowl, season with salt, pepper, one spoonful of oil, and three spoonfuls of vinegar. This salad requires more vinegar than oil.

Rice croquettes. Cook one-half pound of rice in three pints of milk, to which has been aded half of a vanilla bean. This will make a stiff batter. Add one-quarter pound of sugar and the yolks of four eggs. Allow to cool. Shape the rice in croquettes, dip in beaten eggs, then in macaroon crumbs or powder, and fry in swimming hot lard or butter. Serve with wine sauce.

Compote with rice. Prepare some rice as for croquettes. Put a large spoonful in the center of a plate and garnish with stewed fruit. Any kind of stewed fruit may be used, such as peaches, apricots, pears, etc., either singly or mixed.

Champagne punch. One quart of champagne, one quart of white wine, one bottle of soda water, one spoonful of sugar, and three apples cut in small dices. Cool, and serve in champagne cup glasses.

Potage Mexicaine. Mix one quart of purée of tomato soup with one pint of well-seasoned consommé tapioca.

Fillet of turbot, Tempis. Season four fillets of turbot with salt and pepper, and roll in flour. Put three ounces of butter in a pan and heat. Then add the fish and fry for ten minutes on both sides. Place the fish on a platter; add another ounce of butter to the pan, and cook to the color of a chestnut, and pour over the fish. Sprinkle with the juice of a large lemon, and one spoonful of chopped salted almonds.

Scrambled eggs, Pluche. Scrambled eggs with chopped herbs; such as parsley chervil and chives.

AUGUST 1

BREAKFAST
Sliced peaches with cream
Waffles with maple syrup
Ceylon tea

LUNCHEON
Eggs à la Patti
Stewed tripe, Blanchard
Puff paste roses
Coffee

DINNER
Consommé Alexandria
Lyon sausage.   Antipasto
Boiled brook trout, mousseline
Potatoes, nature
Roast saddle of mutton, currant jelly,
    mint sauce
String beans in butter
Broiled tomatoes
Escarole and chicory salad
Soufflé au fromage
Coffee

Eggs à la Patti. Make a chicken hash in cream and put on a platter. Lay four poached eggs on top, and one slice of truffle on top of each egg. Pour sauce Madère around the hash.

Puff paste roses. Roll out some puff paste about one-eighth inch thick, and out with a star cutter. Brush over with a little water, and fold the points of the stars to the center. Bake, and when nearly done dust with powdered sugar, and return to oven to finish baking. The cakes will puff up like a rose. Fill with jelly and serve.

Consommé Alexandria. Add one cupful of boiled white meat of chicken, cut in small dices, to three pints of consommé brunoise.

Orange or lemon brandy, for flavoring. Peel very thin the yellow outside from oranges or lemons. The inner white skin is not good. Crush with a little granulated sugar. Put in a bottle and cover with strong brandy. In the same manner can be prepared the kernels of cherries, plums, apricots or peaches. Pound the kernels slightly before putting them in the brandy.

Glacé fruit. Be very particular in selecting the fruit. Cherries should be large and not quite ripe, and without blemishes; and the stones must be removed. Apricots and peaches should be of medium size, and almost green. Make as small a hole as possible when removing the stones. Pears should be peeled, and the stems left on. Figs should be green. Strawberries should be very green, but full grown; wash and dry well, and leave the stems on. Nectarines should be green, and the stones removed. Any hard green plums may be used, but leave their stones in. Cut pineapple in thick slices, remove the core, and any brown outside spots. All fruit should be thoroughly washed and dried before being prepared. It is well to make new syrup for each kind of fruit. To make the syrup boil two pounds of granulated sugar and two gills of water for eight minutes. Put the fruit in the syrup piece by piece; do not let it stop boiling; and wait a few seconds between each piece, so the syrup will boil up over the fruit. Then remove piece by piece in the same order as placed in the kettle. Use a silver spoon or an aluminum skimmer to handle the fruit, and under no circumstances use a fork. Place the fruit on a thick piece of waxed paper, and set in a cool place. Repeat the process the next day, adding a pound of sugar and a gill of water to the syrup of the day before. Allow the fruit to boil hard for a minute, and remove as before. This must be continued for about eight days before the fruit will have absorbed enough sugar, and not be mushy. When the fruit is finished line a broad shallow stone jar with waxed paper, lay the fruit in singly, not allowing the pieces to touch, put waxed paper between the layers, and cover closely.

Baked pears, for canning. Wash as many ripe, firm unspecked pears as will fill a baking pan. Fill the pan almost full of boiling water. Sweeten as though for immediate use. Set the pan in the oven, baste frequently, and turn the pears around so they will brown lightly and evenly. Add a few cloves and a small stick of cinnamon. When the pears are very tender and almost candied, pack in hot glass jars, and pour the boiling syrup over them. Be sure to have enough thick syrup to cover the fruit. Seal while hot. Should the water evaporate too much while cooking, add a little more from time to time.

AUGUST 2

BREAKFAST
  Oregon cherries
  Finnan haddie in cream
  Baked potatoes
  Rolls
  Coffee

LUNCHEON
  Assorted hors d'oeuvres
  Cold consommé in cups
  Cold saddle of mutton
  White bean salad
  French pastry
  Demi tasse

DINNER
  Lamb broth à la Reine
  Queen olives
  Baked whitefish, St. Menehould
  Roast squab
  Artichokes with melted butter
  Broiled potatoes
  Celery root, field and beet salad
  Pumpkin pie
  Coffee

White bean salad. Soak a pound of navy beans over night in cold water. Then boil them in three quarts of water; to which has been added a little salt, an onion, a carrot, and a bouquet garni. When soft, remove the onion and carrot, and the bouquet garni, drain off the water, and set the beans to cool. When cold put in a salad bowl, add two shallots chopped very fine, a little chopped parsley, a little salt and some fresh-ground pepper, one spoonful of vinegar and two of olive oil. Mix well.

Lamb broth à la Reine. Put a shoulder of lamb in a roasting pan, season with salt and pepper, a little fat or a small piece of butter, and put in the oven to roast. When done remove the lean meat from the bones and cut in small squares. Put the trimmings in a casserole with five pounds of lamb bones and three quarts of water. Bring to a boil, skim well, and then add one sliced onion, one carrot, a bay leaf, six cloves, a bouquet garni, a stalk of leek and three leaves of celery, a little salt and a few whole black pepper berries. Boil slowly for one hour, without being covered, so the broth will stay clear. Strain through fine cheese cloth, add the lamb cut in small squares, and one-half pound of boiled rice. Serve hot and well seasoned.

Pumpkin pie. Make a custard with five eggs, two ounces of sugar, one pint of pumpkin pulp, one pony of molasses, three ounces of melted butter, one pinch of grated nutmeg, one pinch of cinnamon and one pinch of allspice. Mix to a custard, and finish like a custard pie.

Pumpkin pulp. Peel a pumpkin and wash out the seeds. Steam or boil until soft, and strain through a fine sieve.

Baked whitefish, St. Menehould. Take four pounds of whitefish (bass or other fish may be used), put in a vessel with two quarts of water and a spoonful of salt, and boil for five minutes. Then drain off the water, remove the skin and bones, and break the fish in two inch pieces. Make one quart of cream sauce. In a buttered baking dish put one spoonful of cream sauce, then one-third of the fish; cover with cream sauce; then another third of the fish; cover with sauce; and then the remainder of the fish, and pour the remainder of the sauce on top. The sauce should be highly seasoned. Sprinkle the top with grated Swiss or Parmesan cheese, put small bits of butter on top, and bake in oven for fifteen or twenty minutes. Sprinkle with the juice of two lemons, and serve from the baking dish.

AUGUST 3

BREAKFAST
Loganberries with cream
Bacon and eggs
Rolls
Coffee

LUNCHEON
Eggs Mollet, cream sauce
Broiled black bass, maitre d'hôtel
Sliced cucumbers, French dressing
Browned hashed potatoes
Compote with rice
Demi tasse

DINNER
Terrapin soup, Southern style
Pimentos, vinaigrette
Scalloped clams
Larded tenderloin of beef, moderne
Romaine salad
Biscuit glacé, peppermint
Assorted cakes
Coffee

Eggs Mollet, cream sauce. Eggs Mollet are soft boiled (about four minutes). Remove the shells, being careful that the eggs do not break. Put in a deep dish and cover with cream sauce.

Pimentos, vinaigrette. Drain the juice from one can of pimentos, lay them on a platter, and cover with vinaigrette sauce. Serve very cold.

Scalloped clams. Put six dozen Little Neck clams in a vessel with their juice, and bring to a boil. Heat two ounces of butter in a casserole, then add two spoonfuls of flour, and heat through. Then add the juice of the clams and half a pint of milk, and season with salt and pepper. The sauce should then be a little thick. Bind with the yolks of two eggs mixed with one-half cup of cream. Mix the clams with three-fourths of the sauce and put in a baking dish. Pour the rest of the sauce over the top, sprinkle with grated cheese, put small bits of butter on top, and bake in hot oven until brown. Serve in same dish.

Tenderloin of beef, moderne. Roast the tenderloin of beef, place on a platter, and garnish with several small patties; some of them filled with string beans, and some filled with peas in butter. Also garnish with rissolée potatoes. Serve Madeira sauce separate, besides pouring a little over the tenderloin.

Terrapin soup, Southern style. Scald two terrapin, and remove the shell, skin and intestines. Cut the terrapin in small pieces about one-quarter inch square. Heat four ounces of butter in a casserole, then add the terrapin and fry over a quick fire. Sprinkle with three tablespoonfuls of flour, add three pints of any kind of good broth and one pint of milk, season with salt and pepper, add a glass of good sherry wine, and boil until well done. Bind with the yolks of two eggs mixed with a cup of cream and a glass of dry sherry wine. Set on stove and let it come nearly to a boil, but not quite.

AUGUST 4

BREAKFAST
  Grapefruit
  Oatmeal with cream
  Rolls
  English breakfast tea

LUNCHEON
  Eggs Vilna
  Calf's liver sauté, Spanish style
  Boiled rice
  Watermelon
  Demi tasse

DINNER
  Consommé Rothschild
  California ripe olives
  Broiled striped bass, maître d'hôtel
  Sliced culemo salad
  Roast chicken
  Peas à la Française
  Mashed potatoes
  Watercress
  Apricot meringue
  Coffee

Eggs Vilna. Spread some fresh caviar on four pieces of toast, lay a poached egg on top of each, lay four fillets of anchovies crosswise over the eggs, and garnish with two lemons cut in half, and parsley in branches.

Calf's liver, Spanish style. Cut six slices of calf's liver three-quarters of an inch thick, season with salt and pepper, roll in flour, and fry in melted butter. When nearly done place on a platter and keep hot. Pour one pint of very sighly seasoned Créole sauce over the liver, and put in oven for two minutes. Sprinkle with chopped parsley, and serve.

Consommé Rothschild. Equal parts of breast of boiled fowl, beef tongue and truffles cut Julienne style, and added to very hot consommé. Add a little chervil before serving.

Sliced culemo salad. Culemo is a sort of cucumber. Peel, slice, and pour French dressing over it.

AUGUST 5

BREAKFAST
  Cantaloupe
  Boiled eggs
  Dry toast
  Crescents
  Chocolate with whipped cream

LUNCHEON
  Cold eggs with celery
  Cold chicken, with chow chow
  Asparagus, mayonnaise
  Roquefort cheese with crackers
  Coffee

DINNER
  Little Neck clams
  Potage Lamballe
  Radishes.   Lyon sausage
  Fillet of sole, Paylord
  Sweetbreads, Egyptienne
  Roast ribs of beef
  Saratoga chip potatoes
  Chiffonnade salad
  Vanilla ice cream
  Assorted cakes
  Fruit
  Coffee

Cold eggs with celery. Put four cold poached eggs on a platter and cover with a sauce made of one pinch of salt, a little fresh-ground black pepper, the heart of a stalk of celery cut in very small dices, a little chopped parsley, one spoonful of vinegar, and two tablespoonfuls of olive oil.

Fillet of sole, Paylord. Chop very fine one-half of a can of French mushrooms, put in a napkin and squeeze out the water. Then mix with half a cup of thick cream sauce. Season four fillets of sole with salt and pepper, and spread all over with mushroom purée; then roll in fresh bread crumbs, and fry in swimming hot lard. Dress on a napkin on a platter, and garnish with fried parsley and quartered lemons. Serve Tartar sauce separate.

Sweetbreads, Egyptienne. Put some braised sweetbreads on a platter and garnish with stuffed green peppers and croquettes of rice. One of each to each person. Serve Bordelaise sauce separate.

Stuffed green peppers. Dip four green peppers in very hot lard for a second, then remove the skin, cut off the top, and clean out the insides. Fill with a purée of fresh mushrooms, sprinkle with bread crumbs, put small bits of butter on top of each, and bake in oven for ten minutes. Serve as a garnish; or as a vegetable, with sauce Madére, or tomato sauce.

AUGUST 6

BREAKFAST
  Grapes
  Hominy in cream
  Rolls
  Coffee

LUNCHEON
  Canapé St. Francis
  Eggs Montebello
  Cold roast beef
  Cosmopolitan salad
  Buttermilk

DINNER
  Consommé paysanne
  Salted almonds
  Salmon steak, Calcutta
  Parisian potatoes, Hollandaise
  Broiled squab on toast
  Artichokes with melted butter
  Stewed corn
  Hearts of romaine, Roquefort
    dressing
  Assorted French pastry
  Coffee

Eggs Montebello. Poach four eggs, allow them to become cool, roll in flour, then in bread crumbs, and fry in swimming hot lard or butter. Serve on a napkin, and garnish with fried parsley. Serve sauce Montebello separate.

Sauce Montebello. Equal parts of Béarnaise and tomato sauce mixed.

Cosmopolitan salad. Put in a salad bowl in bouquets such vegetables as peas, string beans, carrots, cauliflower, asparagus, Brussels sprouts, etc. There should be at least four different kinds. In the center place a handful of shelled shrimps or lobster cut in slices, or crab meat. Serve with French dressing, well seasoned.

Consommé paysanne. Cut two leaves of white cabbage in one inch squares, and put in a casserole. Add one sliced carrot, one sliced turnip, one leek and two leaves of celery, also sliced. Also add two ounces of butter, cover, and simmer in oven until soft. Be careful that it does not burn. Drain off the butter, add one quart of consommé, and boil for ten minutes. Add a little chopped chervil.

Salmon steak, Calcutta. Put two slices of salmon, about one and one-half inches thick, in a flat buttered pan, season with salt and pepper, add one-half glass of white wine and one-half cup of fish stock, cover with buttered paper, and cook in oven for twenty minutes. Then put the fish on a platter and keep hot. Pour over the fish a sauce made as follows: Heat two ounces of butter in a casserole, add one spoonful of flour and one of curry powder, and heat through. Then add the broth the fish was cooked in, and one pint of fish stock, and boil for ten minutes. Bind with the yolks of two eggs and one-half cup of cream. Strain, put back in the casserole, and whip one ounce of fresh butter into it. When the butter is melted it is ready to pour over the fish. Garnish the fish with fleurons.

Parisian potatoes, Hollandaise. Cut a quart of potatoes with a round Parisian spoon, put in cold water, add a little salt, and boil very slowly. When done, drain off the water, and put the potatoes in the oven to dry. Then put the potatoes in one ounce of melted butter mixed with a little chopped parsley, roll carefully so they will not break, and serve.

AUGUST 7

BREAKFAST
Sliced nectarines in cream
Scrambled eggs with smoked beef
Rolls
Coffee

LUNCHEON
Omelet Levy
Lamb kidneys en brochette, bacon
Lyonnaise potatoes
Field salad
Camembert cheese with crackers
Demi tasse

DINNER
Potage Cameroni
Ripe olives
Sand dabs, sauté meunière
Sweetbreads, Figaro
Roast sirloin of beef, Mounet Sully
Broiled tomatoes
Escarole salad
Puff paste basket
Coffee

Omelet Levy. Make a plain omelet with eight eggs, and put on a quite-large china platter. Garnish with one bouquet of pimentos cut in small dices and heated in butter; one bouquet of green peppers cut in the same manner and sautéed in butter; one bouquet of asparagus tips, and one of chicken hash in cream.

Lamb kidneys en brochette with bacon. Remove the skin from two lamb kidneys, split them open, and put a skewer through them. Season with salt and pepper, roll in oil, and broil. When done place on a piece of dry toast, lay two strips of bacon on top. And put a spoonful of maître d'hôtel butter on top of all.

Potage Cameroni. Make one quart of consommé brunoise, add six chickens' livers cut in small squares and sautéed in butter; and one-half cup of boiled macaroni cut in half inch pieces. Serve grated cheese separate.

Sweetbreads, Figaro. Braised sweetbreads served with their own gravy, and garnished with one timbale of spinach for each person. Serve sauce Figaro separate.

Sauce Figaro. Reduce one pint of tomato sauce one half by boiling slowly. Allow to become cold, add one pint of mayonnaise sauce, mix well, and season with salt and Cayenne pepper.

Roast sirloin of beef, Mounet Sully. Roast a sirloin of beef, place on a platter, and garnish with fresh artichoke bottoms filled with peas au beurre, and potatoes Julienne. Serve Béarnaise sauce separate.

Puff paste basket. Roll out some puff paste about one-quarter inch thick. Cut out the paste with an oval cutter. Wash the tops, and then make a shallow incision in the tops with another oval cutter about one-half inch smaller. Bake. Remove the soft inside paste, and fill with sweetened whipped cream. Make a handle out of some candied angelica, and stick it on the whipped cream, making it look like a basket.

AUGUST 8

BREAKFAST
Orange juice
Kippered Alaska cod in cream
Baked potatoes
Rolls
Coffee

LUNCHEON
California gray shrimps in shell
Cold consommé in cups
Cold sirloin of beef, with meat jelly
Potato and beet salad
Schloss cheese with crackers
Coffee

DINNER
Consommé Monaco
Celery
Broiled striped bass, maître d'hôtel
Virginia ham glacé, champagne sauce
Timbale of spinach
Mashed potatoes
Watercress salad
Strawberry ice cream
Assorted cakes
Coffee

Kippered Alaska cod in cream. Kippered Alaska black cod is a delicate smoked fish. Remove the skin, place in a sauce pan and cover with thick cream. Bring slowly to a boil, and let stand for about ten minutes at boiling point. Another method of cooking is to put the fish in a sauté pan, cover with water, and bring to a boil. Then drain off the water, add some cream sauce and a small piece of butter, season with salt and pepper, and boil for five minutes.

Consommé Monaco. Cut one breast of a boiled chicken or fowl and two truffles in small dices. Add to one quart of hot well-seasoned consommé.

Virginia ham, glacé. Soak a Virginia ham in cold water over night. Then put the ham in a large kettle and cover with cold water, bring to a boil, and then set at side of stove and allow to simmer for three hours. The ham is done when the skin is easy to loosen. Then remove the skin, and put the ham in another pot with one quart of sherry wine, and set in oven to bake. Baste continually. After twenty minutes dust the top with powdered sugar, and bake until brown.

Champagne sauce, I. Put two ounces of sugar in a casserole and cook to a brown caramel color, but be careful not to burn. Then add one glass of vinegar and boil until nearly dry. Then add one pint of sauce Madère and boil for ten minutes. Strain, and season well.

II. Put one quart of champagne in a casserole and reduce until nearly dry, then add one pint of sauce Madère, season with salt and Cayenne pepper, boil for ten minutes, and strain.

Timbale of spinach. Pass one pint of freshly-chopped spinach through a fine sieve, season with salt and pepper, add one spoonful of cream sauce and a raw egg, mix well, and put in small buttered timbale moulds. Cook for twenty minutes in bain-marie. Serve as a garnish, or as a vegetable with cream, tomato, or Madeira sauce.

AUGUST 9

BREAKFAST
Fresh strawberries with cream
Flannel cakes, maple syrup
Coffee

LUNCHEON
Cantaloupe
Poached eggs, d'Orleans
Mutton chops, Argenteuil
Lettuce salad
Puff paste sandwich
Coffee

DINNER
Rice soup, Palermo
Radishes
Frogs' legs, sauté à sec
Tenderloin of beef, Gambetta
Romaine salad
Biscuit glacé, mapleine
Assorted cakes
Demi tasse

Poached eggs, d'Orleans. Make four round pieces of dry toast, lay a thin slice of smoked beef tongue on each, and a poached egg on top of the tongue. Cover with Béarnaise sauce.

Mutton chops, Argenteuil. Broil some mutton chops and put on a platter. Garnish with asparagus tips. Pour a little Hollandaise sauce over the tips; and a little brown gravy or sauce Madère over the chops.

Puff paste sandwich (pastry). Roll out some puff paste into a thin sheet, and spread with a thick layer of jam. Wash the edges of the sheet, and place another thin sheet of the same paste on top. Press together at the edges. Wash the top, and bake. When nearly done dust the top with powdered sugar, and bake in the oven until the sugar is melted. Serve cold.

Rice soup, Palermo. Heat two ounces of butter in a casserole, add two ounces of rice and one ounce of flour, and heat through. Then add three pints of chicken broth, and boil slowly. Keep stirring carefully so it will not burn on the bottom, but do not break the rice. When the rice is soft bind the soup with the yolks of three eggs mixed with one pint of cream. Keep stirring the soup until it nearly comes to a boil; taste to determine as to seasoning; add a tiny bit of grated nutmeg, a little Cayenne pepper, and the juice of two lemons, freshly squeezed.

Tenderloin of beef, Gambetta. Put a roast tenderloin of beef on a platter, garnish on one side with onions glacés, and on the other side with fresh mushrooms sauté in butter. Serve sauce Madère on top of the beef, and also separate in a bowl.

AUGUST 10

BREAKFAST
Sliced peaches with cream
Scrambled eggs with bacon
Rolls
Chocolate with whipped cream

LUNCHEON
Cold fonds d'artichauts, DuBarry
Cold Virginia ham and tenderloin of
  beef
Chilian salad
Lemon cake
Demi tasse

DINNER
Consommé Oriental
Ripe California olives
Fillet of halibut, Cubaine
Roast chicken
Asparagus, Hollandaise
New peas in butter
Duchess potatoes
Chiffonnade salad
Fancy ice cream
Assorted cakes
Coffee

Cold fonds d'artichauts, Du Barry. Boil four fresh artichoke bottoms in salt water, to which has been added the juice of a lemon. Also boil a head of cauliflower. When both are cold fill the bottoms with some of the cauliflower, and cover with a well-seasoned thick mayonnaise sauce. Place each artichoke on a leaf of lettuce, and serve.

Chilian salad. Place in a salad bowl equal parts of apple, celery and pimentos, all cut Julienne style. Serve with mayonnaise sauce.

Lemon cake. Bake a sponge cake, as described elsewhere. Cut in three layers, and fill between with lemon butter filling. Glacé the top with thin white icing flavored with lemon juice. Serve when the icing is dry.

Orange cake. Same as lemon cake, but fill the cake with orange butter filling, and glace the top with pink icing flavored with orange. Serve with a slice of orange on top of each portion of cake.

Lemon butter filling. One-half pound of sugar, four ounces of sweet butter, two lemons, the yolks of two eggs, and two whole eggs. Grate the lemon rinds into the sugar, squeeze in the juice of the lemons, add the eggs, yolks and butter, mix well, and stir over a slow fire until it thickens. Do not let it boil. Use cold.

Orange butter filling. Prepare in the same manner as lemon butter filling, but use oranges.

Consommé Oriental. Cut carrots and turnips in the shape of half moons. Boil in salted water until soft, and serve in hot consommé with an equal quantity of plain boiled rice.

Fillet of halibut, Cubaine. Cut four fillets of halibut, season with salt and pepper, and roll in flour. Heat two ounces of butter in a frying pan, then add the fish and sauté on both sides until done. Put the fish on a platter and pour Créole sauce over it. Serve boiled rice separate.

AUGUST 11

BREAKFAST
Grapenuts with cream
Boiled eggs
Dry toast
Ceylon tea

LUNCHEON
Shrimp patties in cream
Calf's liver sauté, Lyonnaise
German fried potatoes
Field salad
Camembert cheese with crackers
Coffee

DINNER
Potage Parmentier
Pim olas
Planked striped bass
Venison chops, port wine sauce
Hashed brown sweet potatoes
Artichokes au gratin
Endive salad
Strawberry meringue
Coffee

Shrimp patties in cream. Make four patty shells and keep them hot. Wash one pound of picked shrimps in warm water. Make a pint of cream sauce, add the shrimps, season with salt and Cayenne pepper, and fill the patties. Serve on napkins, with parsley in branches, and a lemon cut in four.

Calf's liver sauté, Lyonnaise. Cut four slices of calf's liver about one inch thick. Season with salt and pepper, and roll in flour. Put two ounces of butter in a frying pan, and heat, add the liver and fry on both sides. When nearly done remove from the pan and place on a platter. Slice two onions very thin, put in the pan and fry until yellow. Then add one spoonful of flour, heat through, add a cupful of stock, bouillon, or hot water, season with salt and pepper, and add some chopped parsley and the juice of a lemon. Boil for a few minutes, and pour over the liver.

Potage Parmentier. Cut four stalks of leek and one onion in thin slices. Put in a casserole with three ounces of butter, cover, and simmer until done. Then add two pounds of raw white potatoes cut in half inch squares, two quarts of bouillon or stock, and one quart of water, a handful of salt, and a bouquet garni. Boil slowly until the potatoes are done, remove the bouquet, taste to see if salt is needed, and add a little pepper and chopped parsley.

Venison steak, port wine sauce. Cut four venison chops about one and one-quarter inches thick, and season with salt and pepper. Put a spoonful of melted butter in a sauté pan, heat, then add the chops and sauté until done. Place on a platter and pour port wine sauce over them.

Port wine sauce. Make any kind of brown gravy after cooking venison chops, saddle, or any roast. Melt two spoonfuls of currant jelly in a casserole, in a wine glassful of port wine, and reduce one-half. Then add one cup of brown gravy, dish gravy, or sauce Madère, season with salt and pepper, and boil for five minutes. Serve with game or mutton.

AUGUST 12

BREAKFAST
Fresh raspberries with cream
Omelet with fine herbes
Crescents
Breakfast rolls
Cocoa

LUNCHEON
Cantaloupe
Eggs, Mollet, Bordelaise
Broiled lamb chops
String beans with parsley
Browned mashed potatoes
Dandelion salad
German apple cake
Coffee

DINNER
Consommé fermière
Radishes.   Salted almonds
Broiled lobster, maitre d'hôtel
Sweetbreads braisé, St. Albans
Roast squab, au jus
Summer squash, au beurre
Parisian potatoes
Escarole salad
Vanilla ice cream
Orange cake
Coffee

Eggs Mollet, Bordelaise. Put four Eggs Mollet (which see) in a deep dish, and cover with sauce Bordelaise.

Consommé fermiére. Put two ounces of butter in a casserole; add equal parts of carrots, turnips, and cabbage cut in thin round slices the size of a silver quarter. Simmer until done, then drain off the butter, add one and one-half quarts of consommé, and boil for fifteen minutes. Serve with chopped parsley on top, and with bread crusts fried in butter separate.

Sweetbreads braisé, St. Albans. Place some braised sweetbreads on a platter, and garnish with one head of fresh stuffed mushrooms and one small chicken patty for each person. Make a gravy as described elsewhere for sweetbreads braisé, to which should be added one spoonful of tomato sauce.

Grape jelly. To every eight pounds of fruit add one cup of water, bring to a boil, crush, and strain through a jelly bag. Measure the juice, and then measure and set aside an equal quantity of granulated cane sugar. Then boil the juice for half an hour. Melt the sugar, add to the juice and boil for ten minutes.

Gooseberry jam. To each eight pounds of half-ripe gooseberries add one teacupful of water. Boil until soft, add eight pounds of heated sugar, and continue boiling until clear.

Spiced vinegar, for pickles. One gallon of cider vinegar, one pound of brown sugar, two tablespoonfuls each of mustard seed, celery seed and salt; one tablespoonful each of turmeric powder, black pepper, and mace; two nutmegs grated; three onions; and one handful of grated horseradish.

Spiced cherries. Nine pounds of fruit, four pounds of sugar, one pint of malt or cider vinegar, one-half ounce of cinnamon bark, and one-half ounce of whole cloves. Make a syrup of the ingredients, and boil for a few minutes before adding the fruit. Cook the fruit in the syrup until the skins break; then take out, and boil the syrup down until thick. Pour over the fruit while hot.

Spiced sweet apples. Take equal parts of sugar and vinegar, add a dozen cloves and a stick of cinnamon bark, bring to a boil, add sweet apples, and cook until the apples are tender.

Spiced tomatoes. Take red and yellow pear-shaped tomatoes, prick with a needle to prevent bursting, sprinkle with salt, and let stand over night. Pack neatly in glass jars, and cover with a vinegar made as follows: One pint of cider or malt vinegar; one tablespoonful of sugar; and one teaspoonful each of cloves, allspice, and black pepper. The spices should be ground. Bring to the boiling point, and pour over the tomatoes. Seal when cold.

AUGUST 13

BREAKFAST
  Sliced fresh pineapple
  Oatmeal with cream
  Dry toast
  Oolong tea

LUNCHEON
  Lobster canapé
  Scrambled eggs, Mauresque
  Cold smoked beef tongue
  Romaine salad
  American cheese with crackers
  Assorted cakes
  Demi tasse

DINNER
  Potage Nassau
  Ripe California olives
  Pompano sauté, meunière
  Roast ribs of prime beef
  Stewed tomatoes
  Succotash
  New peas
  Mashed potatoes
  Lettuce and grapefruit salad
  Compote of peaches
  Coffee cream cakes
  Demi tasse

Lobster canapé. Cut the tail of a lobster in thin slices and lay on four pieces of toast. Cover with thick well-seasoned mayonnaise, and garnish the edges with chopped hard-boiled eggs and chopped parsley. Serve on a folded napkin, and garnish with parsley in branches and two lemons cut in half.

Scrambled eggs, Mauresque. Cut some Lyon sausage and boiled ham in small dices, put in a casserole with a piece of butter, and heat. Then add the beaten eggs, cream, and a little salt and pepper. Scramble in the usual manner, and serve in a deep china dish.

Potage Nassau. Peel eight white onions, and put in a casserole with one quart of water and a little salt. Boil for twenty minutes, and then drain off the water. Heat three ounces of butter in another casserole; then add three spoonfuls of flour, heat through; then add one pint of milk and one quart of bouillon and the onions, and boil for forty minutes. Strain through a fine sieve, put back in casserole, season with salt and Cayenne pepper, and stir-in three ounces of sweet butter. When the butter is melted, serve hot, with small crusts of bread cut in small squares, and fried in butter.

AUGUST 14

BREAKFAST
Fresh strawberries with cream
Broiled salted mackerel
Baked potatoes
Rolls
Coffee

LUNCHEON
Cold consommé in cups
Cold salmon, mayonnaise
Culemo salad
French pastry
Demi tasse

DINNER
Pea soup with vermicelli
Crisp celery
Codfish steak, à l'Anglaise
Fillet of beef, Dumas
Chicory salad
Fancy ice cream
Assorted cakes
Coffee

Pea soup with vermicelli. One quart of purée of pea soup mixed with one pint of consommé vermicelli.

Codfish steak à l'Anglaise. Heat two ounces of butter in a sauté pan; add two slices of fresh codfish cut about one and one-half inches thick, and one sliced onion. Season with salt and pepper, and simmer until the fish is done. Then remove the fish to a platter; sprinkle a spoonful of flour in the pan, heat through, add one-half glass of white wine, and boil for a few minutes. Then add one cup of hot milk and one-half cup of fish broth, and boil for ten minutes. Season with salt and pepper, add a little chopped parsley and a chopped hard-boiled egg and the juice of a lemon, and pour over the fish. Serve hot.

Fillet of beef, Dumas. Use a roast tenderloin of beef; or broiled fillet of beef steaks. Place on a platter, and cover with sauce Madère to which has been added a slice of boiled ham and a small can of French mushrooms cut in small dices. Garnish one side of the beef with potatoes Parisian, and the other side with artichokes cut in quarters and boiled in salted water.

AUGUST 15

BREAKFAST
Fresh grapes
Boiled eggs
Buttered toast
Coffee

LUNCHEON
Casawba melon
Fried fillet of sole, sauce Tartar
Cold tenderloin of beef
Salade Château de Madrid
Camembert cheese with crackers
Coffee

DINNER
Potage Dieppoise
Queen olives.   Radishes
Broiled fresh mackerel, anchovy
   butter
Potatoes Hollandaise
Sweetbreads, Lieb, with peas
Roast imperial squab
Asparagus with melted butter
Endive and beet salad
Corn starch blanc mange
Alsatian wafers
Coffee

Salade Château de Madrid. Peel a half dozen fresh mushrooms, and cut them, raw, in Julienne style. Place them in a salad bowl with equal parts of green peppers and pimentos, also cut Julienne. In the center put an equal part of plain boiled rice; and a dressing made with one spoonful of vinegar, the juice of a lemon, two spoonfuls of olive oil, a pinch of Cayenne pepper, a little paprika, salt and pepper, and some chopped parsley and chervil.

Potage Dieppoise. Put in a casserole four leaves of white cabbage, and two stalks of leeks and one of celery cut in thin slices. Add three ounces of butter, cover, and simmer until done. Then add one pound of raw potatoes cut in thin slices the size of a silver quarter, and three pints of bouillon. Season with salt and pepper, and boil until done.

Broiled fresh mackerel, anchovy butter. Broil the mackerel and place on a platter. Pour over it an anchovy butter made as described elsewhere. Garnish with parsley in branches and quartered lemons.

Sweetbreads, Lieb. Soak four sweetbreads in cold water for an hour. Then put on fire in three pints of cold water and a spoonful of salt. Bring to a boil, and then cool off in cold water. Then trim the sweetbreads, season with salt and pepper, roll in oil, and broil. The sweetbreads must be whole; not split. When done place on a slice of Virginia ham and cover with sauce Colbert, and garnish with fleurons. The preceding is for one person only.

Endives with beets. Cut endives salad lengthwise, place on a large china platter, season with salt and pepper, sprinkle with chopped beets and parsley, and a mixture of one-third of vinegar to two-thirds of olive oil.

AUGUST 16

BREAKFAST
Baked apples with cream
Small sirloin steak
Broiled bacon
Browned hashed potatoes
Rolls
Coffee

LUNCHEON
Grapefruit with cherries
Eggs Buckingham
Salade Russe
Vanilla Darioles
Demi tasse

DINNER
Potage Italienne
Salted pecans
Boiled turbot, nonpareil
Roast chicken
Purée of chicory
Summer squash in butter
Rissolées potatoes
Lemon water ice
Macaroons
Coffee

Eggs, Buckingham. Put in a buttered shirred egg dish a slice of toast, lay a slice of ham on top, and a soft poached egg on top of the ham. Cover with cream sauce, sprinkle with grated cheese, and bake in a hot oven until brown on top.

Vanilla Darioles. Mix one ounce of flour with three ounces of sugar, two eggs and five yolks of eggs. Then add one pint of milk and some vanilla flavoring, and strain. Line about one dozen dariole or small timbale moulds with very thin tartelette dough. Put a piece of butter the size of a marble in the bottom of each, and fill with the above preparation. Bake in a medium-hot oven, and when done unmould; and serve either hot or cold, with vanilla sauce.

Orange Darioles. Same as vanilla darioles, but flavor with the rind and juice of an orange. Serve with orange sauce.

Lemon Darioles. Prepare in the same manner as orange darioles, but use a lemon to flavor same. Serve with lemon sauce.

Potage Italienne. Soak half a pound of dry mushrooms in cold water for a few hours. Then put in a casserole with one quart of consommé, one pint of purée of tomatoes, and one-half pound of boiled spaghetti cut in pieces two inches long. Boil for ten minutes. Crush two pieces of garlic and fry in a spoonful of oil for a second, add to the soup, season with salt and pepper, and sprinkle with a little chopped parsley. Serve grated cheese separate.

Boiled turbot, nonpareil. Put the whole turbot in a fish kettle, cover with cold water, add a glass of white wine, a handful of salt, one sliced carrot, onion and lemon, and a bouquet garni. Boil slowly for about ten minutes, then allow to stand for about thirty minutes in the hot water. Then put the fish on a folded napkin on a platter, and garnish with parsley in branches and quartered lemons. Serve sauce non pareil separate.

Sauce nonpareil. Put in a casserole the yolks of five eggs and the juice of a lemon. Set the casserole in a bain-marie, and stir well. Then add, little by little, three-quarters of a pound of butter, and one-quarter of a pound of crayfish butter, or lobster butter. Then strain through a fine cheese cloth, season with salt and pepper, or Cayenne, add one dozen écrevisse tails cut in two; or the tail of a lobster cut in small squares.

Purée of chicory. See March 14th, Purée of salad.

AUGUST 17

BREAKFAST
  Stewed prunes
  Ham and eggs
  Rolls
  Coffee

LUNCHEON
  Cantaloupe
  Poached eggs, Balti
  Ham croquettes, cream sauce
  Peas à la Française
  Schloss cheese with crackers
  Coffee

DINNER
  Consommé Montesquieu
  Mortadella
  Pompano, sauté meunière
  Leg of mutton, Mexicaine
  String beans
  Potatoes sauté
  Hearts of lettuce,
  Thousand Island dressing
  French pastry
  Demi tasse

Poached eggs, Balti. Spread some fresh caviar on four pieces of toast, lay a poached egg on top of each, and cover with sauce Madère.

Ham croquettes. Cut about one pound of ham trimmings in very small squares. Cut a can of French mushrooms in small dices, and squeeze the water out of them. Heat an ounce of butter in a casserole, add a dozen shallots chopped fine, and simmer for five minutes. Then add a spoonful of flour and heat through; then add a cupful of bouillon or stock, and boil for a minute; then add the mushrooms and the ham, and cook for ten minutes. Bind with the yolks of two eggs, season with a little Cayenne pepper, and add some chopped parsley. Then take off the fire and work in two ounces of good butter. When the butter is dissolved put on a pan or platter, and allow to become cold. Form the croquettes in any shape desired, roll in flour, then in beaten eggs, and then in bread crumbs, and fry in hot swimming lard. Serve with cream or tomato sauce, or sauce Madère. The butter is added to prevent the croquettes from being hard, when cooked.

Virginia ham croquettes. Make from Virginia ham; otherwise same as above.

Consommé Montesquieu. Equal parts of boiled ham, breast of chicken, and French mushrooms, cut Julienne style. Also an equal part of the small flowers of boiled cauliflower. Serve all in hot, well-seasoned consommé.

Leg of mutton, Mexicaine. Put a leg of mutton in a roasting pan with a sliced onion and carrot, four leaves of celery, and one Chili pepper. Season the leg with salt and pepper, and rub with a little garlic; place a small piece of butter on top, and set in oven to roast. When done remove the leg to a platter, drain the grease from the pan, add one spoonful of meat extract, a cup of bouillon or stock, and a little salt, and boil for a few minutes. Pour a little of the gravy over the mutton and serve the rest in a bowl. Garnish the leg with one stuffed pimento à la Créole for each person.

Stuffed pimentos, Créole. Make a rice Créole. Fill pimentos with this rice, place on a buttered pan, put small pieces of butter on top of each, and bake in a medium-hot oven. Serve as a garnish, or as a vegetable with tomato sauce.

AUGUST 18

BREAKFAST
  Orange juice
  Broiled Spanish mackerel
  Baked potatoes
  Rolls
  English breakfast tea

LUNCHEON
  Eggs Mollet, Florentine
  Cold leg of mutton
  Lima bean salad
  Swiss cheese with crackers
  Assorted fruit
  Coffee

DINNER
  Chicken soup, Fougarmont
  California ripe olives
  Brook trout, Volper
  Louis potatoes
  Roast beef, Jules-Albert
  Stewed tomatoes
  Fried egg plant
  Endives salad, French dressing
  Vanilla ice cream
  Assorted cakes
  Coffee

Eggs Mollet, Florentine. Put some purée of spinach in a vegetable dish, place four eggs Mollet on top.

Chicken soup, Florentine. Cut a spring chicken, bones and all, in pieces one inch square. Heat three ounces of butter in a casserole, add the chicken, and cook until golden yellow; add two spoonfuls of flour and heat through; add three pints of chicken broth, a bouquet garni, and one-half cup of raw rice. Boil for one hour, then remove the bouquet garni, add one pint of boiling milk, and season with salt and pepper and a little chopped parsley.

Brook trout, Volper. Put in a casserole two quarts of cider, one sliced onion, one carrot, one piece of celery, one piece of leek, a little parsley, one bay leaf, one clove, and one spoonful of salt. Bring to a boil, and then add eight brook trout. Set the vessel on the side of the range, and let stand at boiling point for ten minutes; then remove the trout to a platter. Serve with the following sauce: Heat two ounces of butter in a casserole, add two spoonfuls of flour and one and one-half pints of the cider in which the fish was cooked. Boil for twenty minutes. Then add two more ounces of fresh butter, season well with salt and pepper, and strain over the fish. Garnish with bread cut in heart shapes, and fried in butter. Sprinkle with chopped parsley.

Louis potatoes. Cut some potatoes with a small round Parisian spoon, parboil in water, and finish cooking in just enough cream to cover the potatoes. Season with a little salt, and serve in a deep dish with the cream.

Roast beef, Jules-Albert. Season a five pound piece of sirloin of beef with salt and pepper, and rub with garlic. Put in an earthern pot and pour a glassful of olive oil over it. Let it stand in the ice box for two days. Then put on fire and roast for about forty minutes, basting often. Then remove the beef to a platter, and add to the roasting pan one spoonful of flour; heat; add one cup of bouillon and one-half glass of white wine, season with salt and pepper, boil for ten minutes, and strain. Pour a little over the beef, and serve the rest in a sauce boat.

AUGUST 19

BREAKFAST
    Fresh raspberries with **cream**
    Omelet with chives.
    Rolls
    Coffee

LUNCHEON
    Grapefruit, cardinal
    Fried eggs, Infante
    Imported Frankfort sausages
    Potato salad
    Limburger cheese with pumpernickel
    Rye bread
    Coffee

DINNER
    Consommé with celery and rice
    Antipasto
    Fillet of sole, au vin blanc
    Roast chicken
    Asparagus, Hollandaise
    Potato croquettes
    Romaine salad
    Lemon darioles
    Coffee

Fried eggs, Infante. Cook some chickens' livers sauté in butter, and add a little sauce Madère. Pour the livers around some fried eggs.

Imported Frankfurter sausages. These sausages can be obtained in cans. Remove from can immediately upon opening, otherwise they will turn bad. Put the sausages in water almost at the boiling point, and keep them at that temperature for twelve minutes, but do not let them boil. Serve on a platter, garnished with parsley in branches.

Consommé with celery and rice. Cut a stalk of celery in small squares, wash well, and boil in salted water until soft. Boil about one-quarter of a pound of rice in salted water until soft. Serve both in three pints of hot well-seasoned consommé.

Omelet with chives. Beat eight eggs, season with salt and pepper, add one spoonful of chives sliced very fine, and cook the omelet in the usual manner.

AUGUST 20

BREAKFAST
    Blackberries with cream
    Plain pancakes
    Breakfast sausages
    Rolls
    Coffee

LUNCHEON
    Cantaloupe
    Eggs, Meyerbeer
    Cold ham and tongue, meat jelly
    Chiffonnade salad
    German prune cake
    Demi tasse

DINNER
    Potage brunoise, with rice
    Carciofini
    Boiled codfish, Flamande
    Potatoes, natural
    Sweetbreads, sans gêne
    Roast turkey, cranberry sauce
    Broiled sweet potatoes
    Stewed corn
    Sliced tomatoes, vinaigrette
    Corn starch blanc mange with
        sabayon
    Coffee

Eggs Meyerbeer. Shirred eggs with a broiled split lamb's kidney and a slice of truffle on top of each one. Pour a little sauce Madère over the white of the eggs.

Potage brunoise, with rice. To three pints of consommé brunoise add one-quarter of a pound of boiled rice.

Boiled codfish, Flamande. Put three slices of fresh codfish, cut about one and one-half inches thick, in a kettle with water. Season with salt, add one-half glass of vinegar, bring to a boil, and let stand at the boiling point for half an hour. Then place on a folded napkin, with parsley in branches, and two lemons cut in two. Serve sauce Flamande separate.

Sauce Flamande. Heat two ounces of butter in a casserole, add two spoonfuls of flour, one spoonful of vinegar, one quart of the fish broth in which the codfish was cooked, one spoonful of French mustard, a little salt and pepper, one bay leaf, one clove, and a little grated nutmeg. Boil for twenty minutes, strain through a fine cheese cloth, and put back in casserole. Then add, little by little, three ounces of good butter. When the butter is melted add the juice of a lemon and some fresh-chopped parsley.

Sweetbreads, sans gêne. Put some braised sweetbreads on a platter, and garnish with one stuffed head of fresh mushroom to each person. Cover with sauce Colbert.

AUGUST 21

BREAKFAST
Baked pears with cream
Broiled salted mackerel
Boiled potatoes
Rolls
Coffee

LUNCHEON
Canapé thon mariné
Cold eggs, Riche
Broiled lamb chops
French fried potatoes
Cold artichokes, vinaigrette
Cottage cheese with crackers
Coffee

DINNER
Purée of lentils with tapioca
California ripe olives
Broiled pompano, fleurette
Duchess potatoes
Boiled fowl, celery sauce
Spinach, English style
Orange darioles
Demi tasse

Canapé thon mariné. Butter four pieces of toast, lay thin slices of thon mariné on top, spread a little mayonnaise over all with a knife, garnish the edges with chopped boiled eggs and chopped parsley. Serve on a napkin with parsley in branches, and quartered lemons.

Cold eggs, Riche. Make four eggs Mollet. When the eggs have become cold cut with the point of a knife, and let the yolks run out. Then fill with a few chopped anchovies, place on a china platter, and cover with sauce Figaro.

Purée of lentils with tapioca. Mix one quart of purée of lentils with one pint of consommé tapioca.

Boiled fowl. Put a soup hen on the fire in two quarts of water, add a little salt, bring to a boil, and skim. Then add one carrot, one onion, one leek, one piece of celery and a bouquet garni. Cook until the fowl is soft. Serve with cream, celery, oyster, or other sauce; as you may desire.

Celery sauce. Warm three ounces of butter in a casserole; add two stalks of celery, cut in small squares, well-washed and dried; and one and one-half spoonful of flour. Heat through, and then add two pints of chicken broth and a little salt. Boil until the celery is soft; then bind with the yolks of two eggs and a cup of cream.

AUGUST 22

BREAKFAST
  Sliced peaches with cream
  Oatmeal
  Rolls
  Coffee

LUNCHEON
  Casawba melon
  Eggs Lenox
  Tripe sauté, Lyonnaise
  Mashed potatoes
  Field salad
  Raspberry tartelette
  Demi tasse

DINNER
  Consommé Colbert
  Radishes.   Salted almonds
  Lobster en court bouillon
  Roast leg of lamb
  String beans
  Potatoes au gratin
  Fried egg plant
  Watercress salad
  Whipped cream in cups
  Lady fingers
  Coffee

Eggs Lenox. Boil hard one dozen eggs, remove the shells and cut in four. Put the eggs in one-half cup of cream sauce, and season with salt and pepper. Put in a deep buttered earthern dish, pour a cupful of tomato sauce on top, sprinkle with grated cheese, put small bits of butter on top, and bake in oven until brown.

Consommé Colbert. Add to consommé printanier one poached egg for each person. Sprinkle with chopped chervil.

Lobster en court bouillon. Heat in a sauté pan one spoonful of olive oil and one ounce of butter. Add two leeks and one onion sliced fine. Fry till crisp and yellow, add one glassful of white wine, one bay leaf, one clove, one bouquet of tied parsley, one pint of fish broth, one clove of garlic, some chopped parsley, and two tomatoes cut in four. Then add two live lobsters cut in pieces one inch thick, including the shell and claws. Season with salt and pepper and a pinch of Cayenne, and boil slowly for forty minutes. When done remove the bay leaf, clove and bouquet of parsley, and serve with the broth and all.

Whipped cream in cups. Whip some cream quite stiff, and add a little powdered sugar and vanilla. Fill some cups; decorate the tops with some of the same whipped cream, but put on in fancy shape with the aid of a pastry bag. Serve with lady fingers.

AUGUST 23

BREAKFAST
Blackberries with cream
Plain poached eggs on toast
Broiled bacon
Rolls
Uncolored Japan tea

LUNCHEON
Hors d'oeuvres variés
Cold consommé in cups
Omelet Impératrice
English mutton chop, tavern
Escarole and chicory salad
Roquefort cheese with crackers
Assorted fruit
Demi tasse

DINNER
Purée of white bean soup, Allemande
Plain celery
Sand dabs, meunière
Sugar-cured ham glacé, champagne
  sauce
Spinach in cream
Potatoes au gratin
Wine jelly with whipped cream
Assorted cakes
Coffee

Omelette Impératrice. Slice a breast of boiled chicken, and mix with half a cup of cream sauce. Season with salt and pepper. Make the omelet, and before turning over on platter lay the chicken stew in the center. Pour thin cream sauce around the omelet.

Purée of white bean soup, Allemande. Make a purée of white beans as described elsewhere. Add four Frankfort sausages, peeled and cut in thin slices.

Sugar-cured ham glacé. Put a ham in a kettle and cover with cold water. Bring to a boil, and allow to simmer on side of range, at boiling point, for about three hours. Then pull the skin from the ham, sprinkle heavily with powdered sugar, place in a roasting pan, put a pint of sherry wine in the bottom, set in oven, and roast until brown. Serve on a platter garnished with watercress. Serve champagne sauce separate.

Wine jelly with whipped cream. Make some wine jelly as described elsewhere. Pour into ·moulds and set in ice box until firm. Unmould on a cold dish, and decorate with sweetened whipped cream.

AUGUST 24

BREAKFAST
Sliced bananas with cream
Browned corned beef hash
Rolls
Coffee

LUNCHEON
Cantaloupe
Eggs, Opéra
Spring lamb Irish stew
French pastry
Coffee

DINNER
Consommé with Italian paste
Lyon sausage
Stewed striped bass, Américaine
Hollandaise potatoes
Roast chicken
Succotash
Cauliflower, Polonaise
Hearts of lettuce salad
Corn starch blanc mange with berries
Macaroons
Demi tasse

Eggs, Opéra. Garnish some shirred eggs on one side with asparagus tips in butter, and on the other side with chickens' livers sauté au Madère.

Consommé with Italian paste. Boil some Italian paste in salted water for eight minutes. Then drain off water, and cool the paste in cold water. Serve in hot consommé, with grated cheese separate.

Stewed striped bass, Américaine. Cut four pounds of striped bass in pieces two inches thick. Put them in a buttered sauté pan with an onion chopped fine; season with salt and pepper, add a glassful of white wine, and one quart of canned tomatoes just as they come from the can; and a bouquet garni. Cover, and simmer for half an hour. Then remove the fish to a platter, take out the bouquet garni, and reduce the broth one-half. Add, little by little, three ounces of sweet butter, stir until the butter is melted, add a little chopped parsley, and pour over the fish.

Corn starch blanc mange. Put a pint of milk on the fire. Moisten three spoonfuls of corn starch in a little cold milk, and then stir it into the boiling milk. Add two ounces of sugar and two well-beaten eggs. Cook for a few minutes, and pour into small moulds. When cold, unmould, and serve with cold cream.

Corn starch blanc mange with Sabayon. Prepare as above, and serve covered with thick Sabayon sauce.

Corn starch blanc mange with berries. Prepare a corn starch blanc mange, and serve with sweetened strawberries, raspberries, blackberries, or loganberries, around the edge of the dish.

Corn starch blanc mange with stewed fruit. Serve corn starch blanc mange with cold stewed apples, pears, peaches, plums, or apricots, around the bottom of the dish.

Corn starch food. (For infants or invalids.) Boil one pint of milk. Add three tablespoonfuls of corn starch diluted with a little cold water, and two ounces of sugar. Stir into the boiling milk, boil for a few minutes, and serve hot or cold.

AUGUST 25

BREAKFAST
Grapes
Scrambled eggs with tomatoes
Rolls
Coffee

LUNCHEON
Tomatoes, surprise
Eggs, de Lesseps
Rump steak, Dickinson
French fried potatoes
Jerusalem artichokes in cream
Camembert cheese with crackers
Assorted fruit   Demi tasse

DINNER
Purée of turnips, Caroline
Mortadella.   Salted almonds
Broiled fillet of sole, maitre d'hôtel
Leg of veal, au jus
Carrots, Vichy
Peas in butter
Château potatoes
Field and beet salad
Strawberry ice cream
Assorted cakes
Coffee

Scrambled eggs with tomatoes. Peel four tomatoes, cut in two, and squeeze out the water. Then cut in small squares, and put in a sauté pan with one ounce of butter, season with salt and pepper, and simmer until done. Then add eight beaten eggs, one-half cup of cream, one ounce of butter, a little more salt and pepper; and then scramble with the tomatoes.

Tomatoes, surprise. Peel four tomatoes, cut off the tops, and scoop out the centers with a small spoon. Season the inner side of the tomatoes with salt and pepper, and turn upside down so the water will run out. Cut some celery in small dices, wash well, and mix with mayonnaise sauce, season with salt and pepper; and then fill the tomatoes. Serve on lettuce leaves.

Eggs, de Lesseps. Butter shirred egg dishes, crack two eggs in each, and lay one-quarter of a calf's brains that has been previously heated, on each. Season with salt and pepper, and set in oven for a few minutes. Put a small piece of butter in a frying pan and cook until smoking, and nearly black; pour over the egg and brain. Put a spoonful of vinegar in the frying pan and heat, and also pour over the egg. Sprinkle with a little chopped parsley and a few capers.

Rump steak, Dickinson. Broil a rump steak, and place on a platter. Parboil four slices of beef marrow and lay on top with some green and red peppers cut in triangular shapes. Pour sauce Colbert around the steak.

Jerusalem artichokes in cream. Peel a quart of Jerusalem artichokes, and put in a casserole with water, salt and a piece of lemon. Boil until done, drain off the water, and cut the artichokes in any shape desired, or sliced. Make a pint of cream sauce, put the artichokes in it, and boil for a few minutes. Season well.

Purée of turnips, Caroline. Peel six turnips, cut in four, put in a casserole with two quarts of chicken or veal broth, half a pound of rice, and a bouquet garni. Boil until done, remove the bouquet, and strain through a fine sieve. Put back in the casserole, bring to a boil; and add slowly, bit by bit, four ounces of sweet butter; season with salt and pepper, and serve with small pieces of bread cut in dices and fried in butter.

Mortadella. Imported Italian sausages, which comes in cans, sliced. Very fine.

AUGUST 26

BREAKFAST
Stewed prunes
Buckwheat cakes, maple syrup
Crescents
English breakfast tea

LUNCHEON
Eggs, Don Juan
Broiled veal kidneys, with bacon
Lyonnaise potatoes
Celery Victor
Napoleon cake
Coffee

DINNER
Consommé Châtelaine
Queen olives
Fried soft clams, Tartar sauce
Tenderloin of beef, Cardinalice
Lima beans, au paprika
St. Francis potatoes
Endives salad
Mirlitons
Coffee

Eggs, Don Juan. Make four pieces of toast, lay six fillets of anchovies on each, and cover with scrambled eggs.

Consommé Châtelaine. Equal parts of small chicken dumplings, boiled rice and new peas, served in hot consommé.

Fried soft clams, sauce Tartar. Take the bellies of one dozen soft clams and roll in flour, then in beaten eggs, and finally in fresh bread crumbs. Fry in swimming hot lard or butter. Season with salt, place on a platter, on a napkin; and garnish with fried parsley and quartered lemons. Serve Tartar sauce separate.

Tenderloin of beef, Cardinalice. Roast a tenderloin of beef, and lay sliced truffles heated in Madeira wine, on top. For each person, garnish with one-half tomato seasoned with salt and pepper, a small bit of butter placed on top and baked in the oven, and one pimento heated in butter. Serve separate, sauce Béarnaise and tomato sauce mixed. This is also a good way to serve tenderloin or sirloin steaks.

Lima beans, au paprika. Boil one quart of Lima beans in salted water. When done drain off the water. Heat through in a casserole, two ounces of butter and six chopped shallots. Then add one teaspoonful of flour and one teaspoonful of paprika, and one-half cup of bouillon, stock, or water; and boil for ten minutes. Then add the Lima beans, and simmer for a few minutes. If necessary, add a little more salt.

Mirlitons (cake). Beat well together four eggs and three ounces of sugar. Add one gill of orange flower water and one pint of cream. Strain, and put into tartelette moulds lined with tartelette dough rolled very thin. Dust some powdered sugar over them, and bake in a moderate oven.

AUGUST 27

BREAKFAST
Cantaloupe
Ham and eggs
Rolls
Coffee

LUNCHEON
Cold celery broth
Cold salmon, mayonnaise
Sliced cucumbers
Roquefort cheese and crackers
Coffee

DINNER
Potage bourgeoisie
Pim olas
Skate fish au beurre noir
Potatoes, nature
Boiled beef, horseradish sauce
German cabbage
Roast squab
Chiffonnade salad
Biscuit glacé, vanilla
Assorted cakes
Coffee

Cold celery broth. Wash two stalks of celery, and cut in small pieces. Put in a vessel with three pounds of chopped raw shin of beef, the whites of six eggs, one onion, and a spoonful of salt. Mix well, and add slowly one gallon of stock or bouillon; or three quarts of water; and boil for two hours. Strain through a fine cloth, put in ice box, and serve when cold.

Potage bourgeoisie. In a kettle put a fresh brisket of beef, two marrow bones, and a handful of salt; and cover with cold water. Bring to a boil, skim well, add a small piece of Savoy cabbage, one carrot, one onion, one piece of celery, a dozen stalks of leek tied in a bunch, a bouquet garni, and a spoonful of whole black peppers. Boil slowly for about three hours and a half; then remove the beef; and take out the leeks and carrot and cut them in small round pieces. Take the fat off of the broth, and strain the broth over the leeks and carrot. Boil for a few minutes, and season with salt and pepper. Before serving add some chopped chervil, and some bread crusts cut in half inch squares, and fried in butter.

German cabbage. Heat three ounces of butter in a casserole, add three chopped onions, and simmer until done. Then add one spoonful of flour and one pint of bouillon from boiled beef, season with salt and pepper; and then add two heads of sliced Savoy cabbage, and cover the pot. Cook for one hour; then add one-half glass of white wine vinegar, and one spoonful of chopped parsley, and boil for thirty minutes.

AUGUST 28

BREAKFAST
  Sliced figs with cream
  Hominy
  Pulled bread
  Chocolate

LUNCHEON
  Olive and anchovy salad
  Eggs, Canada
  Broiled pigs' feet   Chow chow
  Potatoes, surprise
  Corn starch blanc mange with stewed
    fruits
  Demi tasse

DINNER
  Potage Colbert
  Salted hazelnuts
  Eels, marinière
  Roast leg of mutton
  String beans with shallots
  Mashed potatoes
  Endives salad
  Dariolets, Duchess
  Coffee

Olive and anchovy salad. Lay on a ravier, or flat celery dish, two dozen fillets of anchovies, crosswise. Cut the stones out of one dozen large queen olives, and slice the olives thin. Lay them over the anchovies, sprinkle with a very little salt, some fresh-ground black pepper, a spoonful of vinegar, and a spoonful of olive oil. Garnish with hard-boiled eggs cut in four, and chopped parsley.

Eggs, Canada. Cut the tops from four solid even-sized tomatoes, scoop out the insides, season with salt and pepper, break a raw egg in each, put a small piece of butter on top, season with salt and pepper, place on a buttered plate and bake in the oven for about eight or ten minutes. Serve on a china platter with a little tomato sauce around the tomatoes. Sprinkle with chopped parsley.

Potatoes, surprise. Bake four medium-sized potatoes, cut off the tops, and scoop out the insides. Mix the insides with two ounces of sweet butter, a little chopped chives, and salt and pepper. Mix lightly with a spoon, and refill the potatoes. Replace the top, and bake in oven again for three minutes. Serve on napkins.

Potage Colbert. Wash and dry two heads of chicory salad, slice fine, and fry in a casserole in three ounces of butter. Then add one and one-half ounces of flour, three pints of veal or beef broth, and one bouquet garni; and boil for an hour. Remove the bouquet, and strain the rest through a fine sieve. Put back in the vessel, season to taste with salt and Cayenne pepper, and when nearly boiling add the yolks of two eggs beaten with one cup of cream. Before serving add one lightly-poached egg to each person.

Eels, marinière. Remove the skin, and cut an eel in pieces three inches long. Put in a buttered pan, add one dozen finely chopped shallots, one glass of white wine, and one cup of fish broth. Cover, and boil until the eels are done. Then place on a platter. Heat one ounce of butter in a casserole, add a spoonful of flour and the broth in which the eels were cooked, and boil for five minutes. Bind with the yolks of two eggs and one-half cup of cream, add a little chopped parsley, and pour over the fish. Do not strain the sauce.

String beans with shallots. Boil two pounds of string beans in salted water. Simmer, without allowing to color, six chopped shallots in two ounces of butter. Then add the string beans, one ounce of butter, and some chopped parsley, season with salt and pepper, and simmer for a few minutes.

AUGUST 29

BREAKFAST
    Stewed dried fruit
    Boiled eggs
    Dry toast
    Coffee

LUNCHEON
    Grapefruit with cherries
    Eggs Benoit
    English mutton chops, Kentucky
        sauce
    Broiled sweet potatoes
    Romaine salad
    Brie cheese with crackers
    Coffee

DINNER
    Consommé tapioca, écrevisse butter
    California ripe olives
    Sand dabs, meunière
    Roast turkey, cranberry sauce
    Green corn
    Spinach with eggs
    Rissolée potatoes
    Cold artichoke, vinaigrette
    Roman punch
    Assorted cakes
    Coffee

Eggs Benoit. Spread some paté de foie gras on four pieces of toast, lay a poached egg on top of each; and a head of fresh mushrooms sauté in butter on top of each egg. Cover with Madeira sauce.

English mutton chop, Kentucky sauce. Broil the chop. Serve Kentucky sauce separate.

Kentucky sauce. Put in a casserole one pint of claret, half a pint of whiskey or cognac, one pint of chicken broth, half a pint of tomato ketchup, quarter of a pound of brown sugar, a little salt and one-half teaspoonful of tabasco sauce. Bring to a boil, and thicken with one-half cup of corn starch mixed with a little cold water. Boil for ten minutes, and then strain. Serve with mutton or game.

Stewed dried fruit (in general). Take pears, apricots, peaches, figs, or other fruit, and soak in cold water for about one hour. Then drain, add a little sugar, to taste, and boil until soft. Allow to become cold before serving.

Consommé tapioca, au beurre d'écrevisses (écrevisse butter). Make two quarts of consommé tapioca, and while boiling add, little by little, three ounces of écrevisse butter. When the butter is melted, and while the soup is boiling, add a little Cayenne pepper and a pony of cognac, and serve.

AUGUST 30

BREAKFAST
Apple sauce
Plain omelet
Pulled bread
Cocoa

LUNCHEON
Canapé of fresh caviar
Eggs Chambord
Breaded veal cutlets
Macaroni Caruso
Edam cheese with crackers
Coffee

DINNER
Potage Plessy
Celery
Boiled turbot, Hollandaise
Potatoes, nature
Sirloin steak, Bordelaise
Broiled fresh mushrooms
Soufflé potatoes
French asparagus, melted butter
Chicory salad
Raspberry water ice
Assorted cakes
Coffee

Eggs Chambord. Poached eggs on toast, covered with sauce Chambord.

Sauce Chambord. Put in a casserole the head of a salmon cut in small pieces. Add three ounces of butter, one sliced carrot, one onion, a little parsley in branches, one bay leaf, four cloves, one spoonful of whole black peppers, one clove of garlic, and a little salt. Simmer until the head is cooked, then add one pint of claret and reduce until nearly dry. Then add one quart of fish broth or stock and boil for ten minutes. Thicken with two ounces of butter and one ounce of flour kneaded together, mix well, add two tablespoonfuls of anchovy essence, and boil for five minutes. Strain through a fine sieve, put back in casserole, bring to a boil, add two ounces of fresh butter, whip well, and season with salt and Cayenne pepper. Strain through fine cheese cloth. Serve with fish or eggs.

Macaroni Caruso. Boil one pound of macaroni in salted water. When done drain off the water, add one-half pound of sliced fresh mushrooms sauté in butter, a very little garlic fried in oil, a cup of tomato sauce, and one-half cup of grated cheese. Also serve grated cheese separate.

Potage Plessy. Slice ten onions very fine, and put in a casserole with a quart of water, bring to a boil, and then drain. Heat three ounces of butter in a casserole, then add two ounces of flour and two quarts of bouillon, and stir well. Then add the onions, season with salt and pepper, boil for an hour, and strain through a fine sieve. Put back in the casserole and add two ounces of sweet butter. When the butter is melted add bread crumbs fried in butter.

AUGUST 31

BREAKFAST
Fresh raspberries with cream
Baked beans, Boston style
Boston brown bread
Coffee

LUNCHEON
Cantaloupe
Eggs Bernadotte
Calf's head, vinaigrette
Plain boiled potatoes
German prune cake
Demi tasse

DINNER
Potage Montglas
Dill pickles
Boiled striped bass, Indian soy sauce
Chicken sauté, Alsacienne
Peas à la Française
Chicory salad, Escoffier dressing
Floating island
Macaroons
Coffee

Eggs Bernadotte. Lay four poached eggs on four pieces of toast, put two fillets of anchovies crosswise on each egg. Mix one pint of cream sauce with one dozen sliced queen olives, and pour over the eggs.

Potage Montglas. Mix one pint of purée of tomatoes with one quart of Consommé sago. Add the breast of a boiled fowl cut Julienne style, the tip of a smoked beef tongue cut in small squares, and one-quarter of a pound of macaroni cut in pieces one inch long. Serve grated cheese separate.

Boiled striped bass, Indian soy sauce. Put a whole striped bass in a fish kettle, cover with cold water, add a handful of salt, two sliced lemons, one small piece of ginger root, one sliced onion, and a bouquet garni. Bring to a boil, and set on side of stove at boiling point for twenty minutes. When done place on a platter, on a napkin, and garnish with small round boiled potatoes, parsley in branches, and two lemons cut in half. Serve sauce separate.

Indian soy sauce. Put two ounces of butter in a casserole, add two chopped shallots, and heat. Then add one spoonful of flour, one pint of boiling milk, one-half pint of Indian soy sauce, and season with salt and Cayenne pepper. Boil for a few minutes; then add a cup of thick cream and the juice of a lemon. The Indian soy sauce may be obtained in bottles.

Chicken sauté, Alsacienne. Cut a chicken in four. Heat one ounce of butter in a sauté pan, add the chicken, season with salt and pepper and a chopped shallot, and cook until golden yellow. Then add one-half spoonful of flour, and toss. Then add one-half glass of white wine, one cup of bouillon, and a spoonful of meat extract; and simmer for fifteen minutes. Serve on a platter garnished on one side with noodles, and on the other side with flour dumplings. Sprinkle with chopped parsley.

Escoffier dressing. Mix well together one-fourth cup of imported Escoffier sauce, which may be obtained in bottles, three-fourths of a cup of Chili sauce, a cup of mayonnaise to which has been added the juice of half a lemon, a little chives cut fine, and salt, pepper and paprika to taste. Pour over the salad.

SEPTEMBER 1

BREAKFAST
Orange marmalade
Buckwheat cakes
Breakfast sausages
Rolls
Coffee

LUNCHEON
Canapé de sardine
Eggs Grazienna
Pork tenderloin, sauce piquante
Lorraine potatoes
Dandelion salad
Oregon cream cheese with crackers
Coffee

DINNER
Little Neck clams
Fish broth, with whipped cream
Chow chow
Broiled barracouda, sauce Rouge-
    mont
Potato brioche
Tournedos, Café Julien
String beans with tomatoes
Escarole salad
Strawberries à la mode
Assorted cakes
Demi tasse

Eggs Grazienna. Mix a cupful of boiled peas with a spoonful of cream sauce and a little salt and sugar. Heat well, and place on a platter. Put four fried eggs on top of the peas and pour a little tomato sauce around the bottom of the platter.

Fish broth with whipped cream. Make a fish broth, serve whipped cream and cheese straws on the side.

Potato brioche. Make a potato croquette preparation. Roll out, in flour, into the shape of a ball, place on a buttered pan, brush the tops with yolks of eggs, and bake in oven until nicely colored.

Sauce Rougemont (cold). Chop very fine some fresh mustard and tarragon, and mix with well-seasoned mayonnaise. If fresh mustard is not available use a little French mustard.

Broiled barracouda, sauce Rougemont. Split a barracouda, season well with salt and pepper, roll in oil, and broil. Place on a platter and garnish with parsley in branches and quartered lemons. Serve sauce Rougemont separate.

Tournedos, Café Julien. Take tournedos, or filet mignons, or small tenderloin steaks, or sirloin steaks; season well with salt and pepper, roll in oil, and broil. When done place on a platter, and garnish, for each person, with one fresh boiled artichoke bottom filled with French peas. Pour sauce Madère over the meat.

String beans with tomatoes. Peel and cut four tomatoes in four. Put in a casserole with one ounce of butter, season with salt and pepper, and simmer for ten minutes. Add two pounds of fresh boiled string beans, and two more ounces of fresh butter. Season with salt and pepper to taste, and simmer for five minutes. Sprinkle with parsley chopped fine.

SEPTEMBER 2

BREAKFAST
  Sliced pineapple
  Fried eggs with salt pork
  Rolls
  Coffee

LUNCHEON
  Little Neck clam cocktails
  Eggs à la tripe
  Cold roast beef
  String bean salad
  Duchess darioles
  Demi tasse

DINNER
  Potage Maintenon
  California ripe olives
  Pompano sauté, meunière
  Roast duckling, apple sauce
  Baked creamed squash
  Sweet potatoes sauté
  Green peas
  Waldorf salad
  Fancy ice cream
  Assorted cakes
  Coffee

Fried eggs with salt pork. Put four slices of salt pork in a frying pan and fry until done. Then break four eggs on top of the pork, season with a little pepper, and bake in oven for three minutes.

Dariole Duchess. Mix one ounce of flour and three ounces of sugar with two whole eggs and five yolks. Then add one pint of milk to which has been added six crushed macaroons. Line about a dozen dariole moulds, or small timbales, with tartelette dough, or puff paste parings. (Paste left over when making vol au vent or puff paste cakes). The paste should be rolled out very thin. Into the bottom of each lined mould place a little chopped candied fruit, then fill with the above preparation. Dust some powdered sugar on top, and bake in a rather hot oven. Unmould and serve with fruit sauce.

Potage Maintenon. Put a soup hen and two pounds of veal bones in a pot in one gallon of water, add a spoonful of salt, one onion, one carrot, one stalk of celery, one-half stalk of leek, and a bouquet garni. Bring to a boil, skim well, and then simmer until the fowl is done. Then take out the fowl and cut the white meat in small squares. Strain the broth. Heat in a casserole four ounces of butter, add one-half cup of rice and two and one-half ounces of flour. When heated through add the broth, stir well, and let it simmer slowly. When once boiling be careful that the rice does not stick to the bottom and burn. Also be careful when stirring that you do not break the rice. Taste, season with salt and a little Cayenne pepper; and when the rice is soft thicken the soup with the yolks of four eggs mixed with a cup of cream and a very little grated nutmeg. Do not let the soup boil after adding the thickening.

SEPTEMBER 3

BREAKFAST
  Fresh raspberries and
    strawberries with cream
  Calf's liver and bacon
  Rolls
  Coffee

LUNCHEON
  Cantaloupe and watermelon, surprise
  Shirred eggs, Caroli
  Veal kidneys sauté, au Madère
  Mashed potatoes
  Salade Brésilienne
  Camembert cheese with crackers
  Coffee

DINNER
  Consommé brunoise and vermicelli
  Pickles.   Radishes
  Planked black bass
  Cucumber salad
  Deviled chickens' legs with
    Virginia ham
  Spinach with cream
  Egg plant, Sicilienne
  French pastry
  Demi tasse

Cantaloupe and watermelon, surprise. Cut out with a round Parisian spoon equal parts of cantaloupe and watermelon. Mix, and serve in grapefruit suprême glasses. Serve salt, pepper and powdered sugar separate.

Eggs, Caroli. Place in a buttered shirred egg dish one slice of smoked beef tongue, break two eggs on top, season with salt and pepper, sprinkle with grated cheese, put small bits of butter on top, and bake in oven until brown.

Consommé brunoise and vermicelli. One quart of consommé brunoise mixed with one pint of consommé vermicelli. Serve grated cheese separate.

Planked black bass. Season a whole black bass with salt and pepper, and lay on a buttered plank. Put a little butter on top of the fish, and set in oven to bake. When the fish is done make a border around the edge of the plank with potato croquette preparation, using a pastry bag with a star tube to squeeze the potato through. Then set back in oven and cook until the border is brown. Pour two spoonfuls of maître d'hôtel butter over the fish, and garnish with parsley in branches and quartered lemons.

Deviled chickens' legs and Virginia ham. Use the legs from soup hens or roasted chickens. Spread with a mixture of half English and half French mustard, roll in bread crumbs, sprinkle with olive oil, broil, and place on a platter. Broil one slice of Virginia ham for each person, and lay on top of the chickens' legs. Pour tomato sauce around them.

Egg plant, Sicilienne. Peel an egg plant and cut in thin slices. Mix in a bowl two cups of grated cheese, one egg, half a cup of very thick cream, a little chopped chives, salt and a little Cayenne pepper. Spread on a slice of egg plant, and lay another slice on top, in the form of a sandwich. Roll in flour, then in beaten eggs, and finally in bread crumbs. Fry in very hot swimming butter, and serve on folded napkin.

SEPTEMBER 4

BREAKFAST
  Stewed prunes
  German pancakes
  Corn muffins
  Ceylon tea

LUNCHEON
  Hors d'oeuvres assortis
  Cold consommé in cups
  Baked oysters, Cruyère
  Russian salad
  Mirlitons au rhum
  Coffee

DINNER
  Potage Ruffo
  Queen olives
  Bouillabaisse Marseillaise
  Roast leg of lamb
  Corn à la Marie
  Potato croquettes
  Lima beans in butter
  Chicory and romaine salad
  Vanilla ice cream
  Lady cake
  Demi tasse

Baked oysters, Cruyère. Season one dozen oysters on the half shell with salt and pepper, lay on each a very thin slice of Swiss cheese, put a small bit of butter on top, and bake in a very hot oven for six minutes. Serve in the shells, on a platter, garnished with quartered lemons.

Mirlitons au rhum. Beat until very light, six eggs, six ounces of powdered sugar, and six ounces of almonds chopped very fine. Then add two tablespoonfuls of rum, one ounce of flour, and four ounces of melted butter. Pour into tartalette moulds, that have been lined with very thin dough. Dust the tops with powdered sugar, and bake in a rather hot oven. Glace the tops with thin icing flavored with rhum.

Potage Ruffo. Mix one quart of purée of tomato soup with one pint of consommé, add one-half pound of macaroni that has been boiled in salted water, and cut in pieces one-half inch long. Serve grated cheese separate.

Corn à la Marie. Put two ounces of butter and two peeled and quartered tomatoes in a casserole, and simmer for five minutes. Then add the corn cut from six boiled ears, season with salt, pepper, and a pinch of sugar, and simmer for five minutes.

Lady cake. One pound of sugar, three-quarters of a pound of sweet butter, one pound of flour, two ounces of corn starch, half a teaspoonful of baking powder, the whites of sixteen eggs, and rose flavoring. Mix the sugar with the butter and half of the whites of eggs. Mix the flour, corn starch and baking powder together, and add it to the first mixture. Beat the remainder of the whites of eggs until very hard, and add them to the preceding. Add the rose flavoring, mix lightly, put in mould and bake in the same manner as pound cake.

SEPTEMBER 5

BREAKFAST
Orange marmalade
Poached eggs with bacon
Rolls
Coffee

LUNCHEON
Grapefruit with chestnuts
Eggs Mollet, Auben
Lamb hash, Sam Ward
Escaloped tomatoes
Sierra cheese with crackers
Coffee

DINNER
Blue Point oysters on half shell
Consommé federal
Salted Brazil nuts
Boiled Lake Tahoe trout, Hollandaise
Potatoes, nature
Sweetbreads braisé, Georginette
Roast chicken
New beets, Californienne
Baked kohl rabi
Hearts of lettuce, egg dressing
Lemon water ice
Lady fingers
Demi tasse

Eggs Mollet, Auben. Make four croustades, lay an egg Mollet in each, and pour a little sauce Italienne over them.

Lamb hash, Sam Ward. Put two ounces of butter and one chopped onion in a casserole and simmer until yellow. Then add one pound of raw potatoes cut in small squares, and two pounds of left-over lamb cut in the same manner; season with salt and pepper, add one cup of bouillon, cover, and simmer for nearly an hour. Then dish up and sprinkle with chopped parsley.

Escaloped tomatoes. Drain into a bowl the juice from canned tomatoes. Butter a baking dish, cover the bottom with a layer of the tomatoes, add bits of butter, season with salt and pepper, and sprinkle with fresh bread crumbs. Then repeat with tomatoes, seasoning, and crumbs, in order, until the dish is full. Then add the tomato juice, sprinkle some crumbs on top, and bake in oven for twenty minutes. Serve in same dish.

Consommé federal. Make a consommé royal, season with a little Cayenne pepper, and add six thin slices of truffle for each person.

Sweetbreads braisé, Georginette. Make a purée of sorrel (see vegetable). Add to the purée some sliced canned mushrooms; or fresh mushrooms sauté in butter. Put the sorrel on a platter, lay sweetbreads braisé on top, and pour the gravy around the bottom of the platter.

New beets, Californienne. Put in a sauté pan two ounces of butter, three cloves, one teaspoonful of tarragon vinegar, one-half teaspoonful of sugar, and some fresh-cooked and peeled, small beets. Simmer for a few minutes.

Baked kohl rabi. Peel some kohl rabi, slice thin, and boil in salted water. Then arrange in a baking dish, cover with well-seasoned cream sauce, sprinkle with grated cheese and bread crumbs in equal parts, put small bits of butter on top, and bake in oven until brown.

SEPTEMBER 6

BREAKFAST
Baked pears with cream
Broiled salmon bellies with
  melted butter
Plain boiled potatoes
Rolls
Coffee

LUNCHEON
Cantaloupe
Eggs, Jockey Club
Cold chicken and tongue, meat jelly
String bean and tomato salad
American dairy cheese with crackers
Coffee

DINNER
Macaroni soup, with leeks
California ripe olives
Fillet of flounder, Chilienne
Roast loin of veal, au jus
Stuffed egg plant
Asparagus tips in cream
Cleo potatoes   Escarole salad
Chocolate éclairs   Demi tasse

Eggs, Jockey Club. Shirred eggs garnished with veal kidneys sauté au Madère.

String bean and tomato salad. Equal parts of fresh-boiled cold string beans and peeled and quartered tomatoes. Put the beans around the edge of a salad bowl and the tomatoes in the center. Serve with French dressing and fresh-chopped parsley.

Macaroni soup with leeks. Slice six stalks of leek very thin, and put in casserole with three ounces of butter. Simmer until the leeks are cooked; then add two quarts of bouillon, stock or chicken broth; and bring to a boil. Then add six ounces of macaroni that has been boiled in salted water for fifteen minutes and then cut in pieces one inch long. Boil again for fifteen minutes, and season with salt and pepper. It is ready to serve when the macaroni is soft. Serve grated cheese separate.

Fillet of flounder, Chilienne. Put four fillets of flounder in a flat buttered baking dish, season with salt and pepper, lay four parboiled oysters on top of each fillet, and cover all with sauce Créole. Sprinkle with grated cheese and bread crumbs, put small bits of butter on top, and bake in oven for thirty minutes. Serve in the same dish, sprinkled with chopped parsley.

Stuffed egg plant. Three tablespoonfuls of sweet butter, one-half cupful of fresh bread crumbs, one cup of bouillon, the breast or leg of a cooked chicken chopped very fine, one egg, one-half glass of white wine, one pony of sherry wine, one tablespoonful of flour; and for seasoning use salt and pepper, and a little grated nutmeg, if desired. Cut three egg plants in two lengthwise, and scoop out the centers, leaving the shell a half inch thick. Soak half a cup of bread crumbs in a little stock or bouillon for five minutes; then add the chicken, two spoonfuls of butter, the egg, well beaten, and the chopped centers of the egg plant. Season, fill the egg plant shells, sprinkle with fresh bread crumbs, put small bits of butter on top, set in pan with a spoonful of olive oil, pour in the rest of the bouillon and white wine, and bake in a moderate oven. Serve on hot dishes, with the following sauce. Heat one spoonful of flour with one spoonful of butter, add the sherry wine and a cupful of the broth from the pan in which the egg plant was baked, and cook for five minutes. Pour the sauce around the egg plant.

Asparagus tips in cream. Make half a pint of cream sauce, and season well. Heat a can of asparagus tips in its own water; drain, lay in a deep vegetable dish, and pour the cream sauce over them.

SEPTEMBER 7

BREAKFAST
  Fresh grapes and apricots
  Oatmeal with cream
  Crescents
  Chocolate with whipped cream

LUNCHEON
  Herring salad, Moscovite
  Eggs, Germaine
  Lamb chops sauté, aux fines herbes
  Peas and shallots in cream
  Mashed potatoes au gratin
  Lemon pie, special
  Coffee

DINNER
  German carrot soup
  Salami.   Green olives.   Celery
  Sand dabs, Gaillard
  Braised beef, comfortable
  Green corn
  Potato croquettes
  Romaine salad
  Fancy ice cream
  Assorted cakes
  Coffee

Herring salad, Moscovite. Soak half a dozen salted herrings in cold water for two hours. Then skin them, remove the bones, slice very thin, and place on a china platter. Chop two pickled beets, and place around the herring. Chop separately the whites and yolks of two hard-boiled eggs, and place on top of the herring. Pour the following dressing over all: Put in a bowl two spoonfuls of fresh-grated horseradish, a little salt and fresh-ground black pepper, one spoonful of tarragon vinegar, two spoonfuls of olive oil, and a little chopped cloves and parsley. Mix well.

Eggs, Germaine. Broil four large heads of fresh mushrooms and place them on four small round pieces of toast. Put a poached egg on top of each mushroom; and cover with sauce Colbert, to which has been added a little chopped tarragon.

Lamb chops sauté, aux fines herbes. Season eight lamb chops with salt and pepper, and fry in melted butter. Then place the chops on a platter. Put two ounces of butter in the frying pan, cook until the butter is brown, and pour over the chops. Sprinkle with chopped parsley, chervil, tarragon, and the juice of a lemon.

Peas and shallots in cream. Put in a sauté pan one dozen peeled shallots and simmer in two ounces of butter until golden yellow. Then add one quart of shelled peas, one cup of water, a little salt and a pinch of sugar. Then put on the cover and boil until soft. Drain off half of the broth and add one pint of rich cream sauce. Boil again for a few minutes.

German carrot soup. Grate the red parts of six carrots and put in a casserole with two ounces of butter and one chopped onion. Simmer for twenty minutes. Then add one pint of chicken broth, or veal broth, or any kind of stock; and one bouquet garni. Boil for twenty minutes, then remove the bouquet, and pass the rest through a fine sieve. Put back in casserole, add one pint of cream sauce, bring to a boil, and bind with the yolks of two eggs mixed with one cup of cream. Strain again; and before serving add a quarter of a pound of boiled noodles. Season with salt and a little Cayenne pepper.

Sand dabs, Gaillard. Season four sand dabs with salt and pepper, put in a buttered pan, lay four raw oysters on top of each fish, add one-half glass of white wine, cover with buttered paper, and cook in oven for ten minutes. Then remove the paper and pour one pint of cream sauce over the fish. Sprinkle with two chopped hard-boiled eggs, put a few bits of butter on top, and bake in oven until brown.

Braised beef, comfortable. Braise the beef, as described elsewhere. Add to the sauce one can of sliced mushrooms. Garnish the beef with a timbale of spinach for each person.

SEPTEMBER 8

BREAKFAST
  Sliced peaches with cream
  Picked-up codfish in cream
  Rolls
  Coffee

LUNCHEON
  Cold consommé, in cups
  Cold braised beef, meat jelly
  Cole slaw
  Omelette Célestine
  Demi tasse

DINNER
  Mutton broth, Kitchener
  Radishes
  Oysters, Newburg
  Fried chicken, Savoy
  Canned corn fritters
  Egg plant in casserole
  Lettuce salad
  French pastry
  Coffee

Omelette Célestine. Prepare an omelet, and before turning on platter fill with a little currant jelly. Sprinkle with powdered sugar, and burn with a hot iron. Cut some lady fingers in two, mix with a little sweetened whipped cream, and place at one end of the omelet. At the other end place some macaroons mixed with sweetened whipped cream.

Mutton soup, Kitchener. Put in a casserole three pounds of shin of beef, and a rack of lamb consisting of about six chops. Cover with about a gallon of water, add a little salt, bring to a boil, and skim. Then add two carrots, two turnips, one stalk of celery, two stalks of leeks, a bouquet garni, a spoonful of whole black peppers tied in cheese cloth, and one-half pound of large barley. Boil slowly. When the lamb is done remove, cut the chops apart and lay in soup tureen. When the vegetables are done remove the bouquet and the pepper bag; and cut the leeks, celery, carrots and turnips in small squares. Continue boiling the beef and barley until soft. Then remove the beef, which may be used the following day for an entrée dish if desired. Add to the soup two ounces of sweet butter, a glass of dry sherry wine, and the cut vegetables. Test for seasoning; and pour over the chops in the tureen. Sprinkle with chopped parsley.

Oysters, Newburg. Put two dozen oysters, with their juice, in a pan. Bring to a boil, drain off the broth, add one cup of cream sauce, boil once, then bind with the yolks of four eggs mixed with one-half cup of cream. Season with a little salt and Cayenne pepper, let come nearly to a boil, and add one-half glass of sherry wine. Serve in a chafing dish.

Fried chicken, Savoy. Joint two small frying chickens, season with salt and pepper, roll in flour, then in beaten eggs, and finally in bread crumbs. Fry in swimming hot melted butter. When done pour a cupful of tomato sauce on a platter, lay the chicken on it, and garnish with asparagus tips à la Hollandaise.

Canned corn fritters. One tablespoonful of melted butter, one can of crushed corn, one cupful of flour, one teaspoonful of baking powder, three tablespoonfuls of milk, and salt and white pepper to taste. Put all in a bowl and mix well. Drop on a hot buttered griddle in spoonfuls, and brown on both sides. Can be made with fresh corn if desired. Serve with roast or fried chicken.

Egg plant in casserole. Slice very thin, one large, or two small, egg plants, three small onions, one clove of garlic, three tomatoes, and one green pepper. Arrange alternately in a buttered casserole, season with salt and pepper, pour four tablespoonfuls of melted butter over all, cover, and cook with a slow fire. Serve hot or cold.

SEPTEMBER 9

BREAKFAST
Fresh strawberries with cream
Boiled eggs
Buttered toast
Oolong tea

LUNCHEON
Poached eggs, Florentine
Tripe étuvé, bonne femme
Bischwiller potatoes
Alligator pear salad
Roquefort cheese with crackers
Coffee

DINNER
Oysters on half shell
Consommé Portugaise
California ripe olives
Salmon steak, Colbert
Noisettes of lamb, Ducale
Asparagus Hollandaise
York potatoes
Dandelion salad, egg dressing
Wine jelly with apricots
Silver cake
Coffee

Poached eggs, Florentine. Cut a can of pimentos in strips their full length and about one-quarter inch wide. Heat in a sauté pan with a little butter, and seasoned with salt and pepper. Lay them on a platter, crosswise, and place six poached eggs on top. Pour Madeira sauce around them.

Tripe étuvé, bonne femme. Cut two pounds of cooked tripe in strips about one-half inch wide and three inches long. Put two ounces of butter and two chopped onions in a casserole, and simmer until done. Then add spoonful of flour, and heat through. Then one glass of white wine, one pint of stock, and the tripe. Season with salt and fresh-ground pepper, add a bouquet garni, cover the casserole, and cook in oven for one hour. When the tripe is done remove the bouquet, and add some fresh-chopped parsley.

Bischwiller potatoes. Cut two pounds of peeled potatoes lengthwise, in eight pieces each. Put in casserole and cover with cold water, add a little salt, and boil. When done drain off the water and put the potatoes on a long platter. Fry until crisp two sliced onions in two ounces of butter. Pour the butter and onions over the potatoes. Sprinkle with chopped parsley.

Consommé Portugaise. Peel four tomatoes, cut in two, squeeze out the water, and cut in small dices. Bring three pints of consommé to a boil, add the tomatoes and one cup of boiled rice. Canned tomatoes may be used if desired.

Salmon steak, Colbert. Cut two slices of salmon about one inch thick. Season with salt and pepper, roll in flour, then in beaten eggs, and then in fresh bread crumbs. Fry in frying pan with hot melted butter. When done place on a platter, on a napkin, and garnish with fried parsley and quartered lemons. Serve sauce Colbert separate.

Noisettes of lamb, Ducale. Season four noisettes of lamb with salt and pepper, and fry in sauté pan with one spoonful of butter. When done place on a platter and garnish with fresh-boiled artichoke bottoms filled with French peas in butter. Pour sauce Madère over the noisettes.

Silver cake. Ten ounces of sugar, six ounces of butter, the whites of six eggs, half a pint of milk, three-quarters of a pound of flour, and one-half ounce of baking powder. Mix well the sugar and the butter, and then stir in the whites of eggs and milk. Add the flour with the baking powder mixed in, and the rind of one lemon. Mix the whole lightly, and bake in the same manner as pound cake.

SEPTEMBER 10

BREAKFAST
  Sliced nectarines with cream
  Broiled salt mackerel
  Baked potatoes
  Rolls
  Coffee

LUNCHEON
  Casawba melon
  Eggs Chambery
  Ragout à la Deutsch
  German apple cake
  Iced tea

DINNER
  Cream of farina, lié
  Sweet pickles.   Salted almonds
  Fillet of sole, Pondichery
  Veal chops, Montgolfier
  English spinach
  Duchess potatoes
  Escarole and chicory salad
  Rice darioles
  Demi tasse

Eggs Chambery. Make a purée of chestnuts, spread on four pieces of buttered toast, lay a poached egg on each, and cover with brown sauce (sauce Madère).

Cream of farina, lié. Bring to a boil one pint of chicken broth, then let one-half pound of farina run into it; and cook for about thirty minutes. Then add one pint of boiling milk, season with salt and pepper; and boil again. Then pass through a sieve, put back in the casserole, and bind with the yolks of two eggs mixed with a large cup of cream. Strain again.

Fillet of sole, Pondichery. Cut four fillets of sole, season with salt and pepper, place in a buttered sauté pan, add one-half glass of white wine and one-half cup of fish broth. Cover with buttered paper, and cook in oven for ten minutes. Then place the fish on a platter. Make a sauce as follows: Heat two ounces of butter in a casserole, add one heaping spoonful of flour and heat through. Then add the broth from the fillet of sole, and an additional cup of broth; one spoonful of curry powder, and a cup of tomato sauce. Season with salt and pepper, boil for a few minutes, and strain over the fish.

Veal chops, Montgolfier. Season four veal chops with salt and pepper, and place in a sauté pan with two ounces of butter and an onion cut in four. Sauté until the onion and chops are golden yellow. Then place the chops on a platter. In the sauté pan put one-half spoonful of flour, and simmer; then add one cup of broth or stock, and boil for a few minutes. Cut a stalk of celery in small squares, and parboil in salted water for ten minutes. Then drain off the water, and add the celery to the sauce from the chops; and boil for ten minutes. Then add the chops, and simmer for ten minutes. Remove the chops to the platter, and season the sauce well with salt and pepper. Add one ounce of sweet butter and some chopped parsley, and pour over the chops.

Rice darioles. Cook one-quarter pound of rice in one quart of milk; with one-half split vanilla bean. When cooked add one-quarter pound of sugar, one gill of cream, and the yolks of four eggs. Mix well. Line one dozen dariole moulds with thin dough, cover the bottoms with a little apricot marmalade, and fill with the rice. Put a small piece of butter on top of each, and bake in oven. Serve with apricot sauce.

SEPTEMBER 11

BREAKFAST
  Baked apples with cream
  Scrambled eggs, with lobster
  Rolls
  Coffee

LUNCHEON
  Eggs Molière
  Frogs' legs, Greenway
  Cold squab
  Sliced grapefruit and lettuce salad
  Stilton cheese with crackers
  Demi tasse

DINNER
  Consommé with noodles
  California ripe olives
  Boiled salmon, sauce Maximilienne
  Potatoes, nature
  Filet mignon, Du Barry
  Chiffonnade salad
  Pancakes with raspberry syrup
  Coffee

Eggs Molière. Cut off the tops from four medium tomatoes, scoop out the insides, season with salt and pepper, lay an egg Mollet in each, and fill to the top with cream sauce to which has been added a few slices of mushrooms and truffles. Sprinkle with bread crumbs, and bake in hot oven until brown on top.

Frogs' legs, Greenway. Heat two ounces of butter in a sauté pan; then add two dozen hind legs of frogs, cut in two and seasoned with salt and pepper. Toss for two minutes in the pan over the fire; then sprinkle with a spoonful of flour, and toss again; then add a half glass of white wine and one large cup of chicken broth, and simmer for five minutes. Then bind with the yolks of two eggs mixed with one-half cup of cream, add a little chopped tarragon, chives and parsley. Serve in chafing dish.

Sauce Maximilienne. Add some chopped truffles to lobster sauce.

Filet mignon, Du Barry. Broiled filet mignons garnished with fresh bottoms of artichokes filled with cauliflower; and with a sauce Madère to which has been added some sliced canned French mushrooms.

Pancakes with raspberry syrup. Make a French pancake dough or batter. Cook small individual flat pancakes, place in a buttered chafing dish, and pour a little raspberry syrup over each in turn. Serve in the chafing dish.

Scrambled eggs, with lobster. Cut the tail of a boiled lobster in small squares, put in a sauté pan with two ounces of butter, season with salt and pepper, and simmer for a few minutes. Then add twelve beaten eggs, one-half cup of cream, and one ounce of sweet butter. Season with salt and pepper, and scramble in the usual manner.

SEPTEMBER 12

BREAKFAST
  Sliced oranges
  Broiled Alaska black cod
  Baked potatoes
  Rolls
  Chocolate with whipped cream

LUNCHEON
  Egg salad
  Broiled sweetbreads on toast
  Purée of Lima beans
  Fried egg plant
  Royal cake
  Iced tea

DINNER
  Blue Points, mignonette
  Purée of peas, with noodles
  Celery.   Pim olas
  Planked striped bass
  Roast chicken
  Young artichokes, en cocotte
  Baked sweet potatoes with sugar
  Cold asparagus, mayonaise
  Fancy ice cream
  Alsatian wafers
  Demi tasse

Egg salad. Boil one dozen eggs eight minutes, remove the shells, and cut the eggs in half. Place on a platter on lettuce leaves, season with salt and fresh-ground blackpepper, sprinkle with two spoonfuls of vinegar, three of olive oil, and some chopped chervil and parsley.

Royal cake. Bake a French sponge cake (which see), cut into four layers, and fill between with royal butter. Gláce the whole with orange icing, and form on top a crown, using a pastry bag and some royal butter. Decorate around the top of the cake with candied fruits.

Royal butter. The yolks of four hard-boiled eggs, six ounces of sweet butter, one-quarter pound of powdered sugar, and one teaspoonful of orange flower water. Crush and work the yolks smooth in a bowl, stir in the butter, sugar and flavoring, and mix well. Allow it to become very cold; pass it through a fine sieve and it will come out like vermicelli. Use it for cake filling and cake decorations.

Purée of peas with noodles. Make a purée of pea soup, and to each quart add three ounces of boiled noodles.

Young artichokes, en cocotte. Select very small California artichokes, trim them, and put in an earthen cocotte dish with one spoonful of hot olive oil, season with salt and pepper, cover, and cook slowly for about twenty-five minutes. Then add to each dozen artichokes one small can of American peas, and one head of lettuce salad sliced very thin. Cover again, and cook in oven for about twenty minutes more.

Baked sweet potatoes, with sugar. Boil half a dozen sweet potatoes until nearly done; cut in half, or in thick slices; lay in a buttered baking dish, spread with butter, sprinkle with a spoonful of brown sugar, season with salt and pepper, add one spoonful of hot water, set in oven and finish cooking, basting often until brown.

SEPTEMBER 13

BREAKRAST
  Baked bananas
  Boiled eggs
  Dry toast
  Coffee

LUNCHEON
  Grapefruit with cherries
  Scrambled eggs, Nantaise
  Deviled ham
  Purée of salad
  York potatoes
  Roquefort sandwiches
  Coffee

DINNER
  Consommé Napier
  Radishes, Antipasto
  Oysters Mornay
  Roast leg of lamb
  Stewed onions
  Scalloped pumpkin and rice
  Sybil potatoes
  Endives salad
  Roman punch
  Macaroons
  Demi tasse

Scrambled eggs, Nantaise. Split some sardines and lay on four pieces of buttered toast. Cook the scrambled eggs, and pour over the sardines.

Deviled ham. Slice some boiled or raw ham, spread with French and English mustard mixed, roll in fresh bread crumbs, and boil. Then place on platter, and serve with sauce diable, tomato sauce, or sauce Colbert. Garnish the platter with watercress and quartered lemons.

York potatoes. Add some boiled ham cut in small squares to Duchesse potatoes.

Consommé Napier. Add to boiling consommé a marrow bone cut as thin as your butcher can cut it with a saw. Serve at once.

Oysters Mornay. Parboil two dozen oysters in their own juice, then place them on a flat buttered baking dish, season with salt and pepper, cover with cream sauce, sprinkle with grated cheese, put small bits of butter on top, and bake in oven until brown.

Stewed onions. Peel some small white onions, and boil in salted water until tender. Then drain, and turn into a hot vegetable dish. Melt two tablespoonfuls of butter in a sauce pan, stir in one tablespoonful of flour, mix well, add one-half pint of boiling milk, season with salt and pepper, boil for five minutes, and pour over the onions.

Scalloped pumpkin and rice. Use a buttered fireproof dish. Put in a layer of stewed pumpkin, cover with a layer of boiled rice, then a spoonful of cream sauce, and continue in this order until the dish is nearly full. Sprinkle with oread crumbs, put small bits of butter on top, and bake in oven until brown.

Stewed pumpkin. Peel the pumpkin, cut in one-inch squares, place in a well-buttered casserole, season with salt and pepper, put small pieces of butter on top, add one spoonful of broth, cover, and bake in oven for thirty minutes. Serve in a vegetable dish, sprinkled with chopped parsley.

SEPTEMBER 14

BREAKFAST
Fresh strawberries with cream
Boiled salt mackerel, with
   melted butter
Boiled potatoes
Rolls
Coffee

LUNCHEON
Stuffed eggs, Epicure
Salisbury steak, Stanley
Spanish beans
Watercress salad
Wine jelly with peaches
Lady fingers
Demi tasse

DINNER
Toke Point oysters, mignonette
Cream of tomatoes
Ripe California olives
Sand dabs, meunière
Roast duckling, apple sauce
Corn oysters
Green peas
Baked sweet potatoes
Lettuce salad
French pastry
Demi tasse

Stuffed eggs, Epicure. Boil six eggs until hard, remove the shells, and cut in two lengthwise. Mix the yolks with one spoonful of purée de foie gras, and the chopped breast of a boiled chicken. Season with salt and pepper, pass through a fine sieve, put in bowl, add two ounces of sweet butter, mix well, and fill the eggs. Serve on lettuce leaves.

Salisbury steak, Stanley. Pass two pounds of raw beef through a fine meat grinder, season with salt and pepper and add a cup of thick cream. Make four, or six, oval steaks, roll in fresh bread crumbs, then in oil, and broil. Place on a platter. Split some bananas, roll in flour, fry in butter, and lay two pieces on top of each steak. Pour horseradish sauce around the steaks.

Spanish beans. One pint of red kidney beans, one pint of tomatoes, one onion chopped fine, one clove of garlic, one tablespoonful of oil, one-half pound of bacon or pork, one-half pound of beef cut in dices, one tablespoonful of powdered Spanish pepper, and a little salt and pepper. Soak the beans over night, parboil, and drain. Add the tomatoes, onion, garlic, meat, etc., season with salt and pepper, and pour in enough water to keep it from being too sticky, or thick. Cook slowly all day, or until the meat is tender, and the beans thoroughly cooked. About half an hour before serving add the Spanish pepper, and a tablespoonful of corn meal. The cooking may be finished in a fireproof dish, in the oven, if preferred.

Wine jelly with apricots. Fill some individual moulds, or glasses, half full of liquid jelly, place in the center of each one-half of a canned, or fully ripe, apricot; and place in ice box to set. When firm, fill to the tops with more jelly, and again set in ice box until ready to use.

Wine jelly with peaches. Prepare in the same manner as above.

Wine jelly with any kind of berries. Prepare in the same manner as above, using selected ripe berries of any kind.

Corn oysters. Mix well together two cupfuls of grated green corn, one beaten egg, one cup of flour, and a little salt and pepper. Drop from a spoon into very hot fat, in a frying pan. Serve on a napkin.

SEPTEMBER 15

BREAKFAST
Fresh raspberries with cream
Oatmeal
Pulled bread
Crescents
Chocolate

LUNCHEON
Hors d'oeuvres, assorted
Omelette Bayonnaise
Paprika schnitzel with spatzel
Swiss cheese with crackers
Pears
Coffee

DINNER
Consommé with stuffed cabbage
Sardines
Fillet of sole, Meissonier
English mutton chops
Broiled fresh mushrooms
Colache (vegetable)
Rissolée potatoes
Escarole salad
Fancy ice cream
Assorted cakes
Coffee

Omelette Bayonnaise. For four persons, take the bottoms of two boiled artichokes and cut in squares. Add one-half can of French mushrooms, sliced. Mix with a very little tomato sauce. Make the omelet, and before turning over on the platter fill with the above preparation. Make four fillets of anchovies on top of the omelet, and pour Béarnaise sauce around it.

Pulled bread. Take a large loaf of fresh bread and remove the inside, pulling it into large flakes. Put the flakes on a baking pan and bake in a moderate oven until crisp and brown.

Consommé with stuffed cabbage. Add to hot consommé one small stuffed cabbage to each person.

Stuffed cabbage. May be made any size, using the whole cabbage; or as small around as a silver half dollar, for garnishing. Parboil a whole cabbage; or some leaves only. Make a stuffing as follows: Soak two rolls in milk for ten minutes, then squeeze out, and chop fine. Add one onion, chopped and fried in butter; one pound of sausage meat; a whole raw egg, and some chopped parsley, chervil and chives. Season with salt and pepper, and mix well. Fill the whole head of cabbage if desired. Or, take two leaves and season with salt and pepper, put a spoonful of the stuffing in the center, and fold the leaves in the form of a ball. Place the stuffed cabbage in a buttered pan with a sliced carrot and onion, a bay leaf and a clove. Cover with bouillon, put a buttered paper over the top of the pan, and cook in the oven until the cabbage is soft. If served as a vegetable serve a brown meat gravy, or sauce Madère, or tomato sauce.

Fillet of sole, Meissonier. Trim four fillets of sole, fold them in half, season with salt and pepper, lay in buttered sauté pan, add one-half glass of white wine and one-half cup of fish broth, cover with buttered paper, and cook in oven for ten minutes. Put the fillets on a platter and cover with the following sauce: Cut a carrot and a turnip in very small dices, like brunoise, and put in a casserole with one ounce of butter. Cover the casserole, and simmer for twenty minutes or over, but be careful that it does not burn. Put two ounces of butter in another casserole, add a spoonful of flour and the broth from the cooked sole. If too thick add a little fish stock. Boil for five minutes, bind with the yolks of two eggs mixed with half a cup of cream, strain, and add the carrots and turnips, from which the butter has been drained. Season well.

Colache (vegetable). Pare three good-sized summer squash, and cut in small squares; three peeled and quartered tomatoes, and the corn cut from four ears. Put two ounces of butter in a casserole with one chopped onion, and simmer until the onion is yellow. Then add the squash, corn and tomatoes, and steam slowly for about three-quarters of an hour. Season with salt and pepper.

SEPTEMBER 16

BREAKFAST
  Sliced peaches with cream
  Ham and eggs
  Rolls
  Coffee

LUNCHEON
  Cantaloupe
  Broiled oysters with bacon
  Pig's knuckles and sauerkraut
  Boiled potatoes
  Assorted cheese with crackers
  Coffee

DINNER
  Ditalini soup, à la royal
  Pickles.   Ripe California olives
  Sand dabs, Carnot
  Larded tenderloin of beef, Sigurd
  Lettuce braisé
  Cold asparagus, mayonnaise
  Black cake
  Compote of apricots   Coffee

Broiled oysters with bacon. Drain the juice from two dozen large oysters, season with salt and pepper, roll in melted butter, then in fresh bread crumbs, place in a thin-wired special oyster broiler, sprinkle with olive oil, and broil. When done, place on four pieces of buttered toast, put a spoonful of maitre d'hôtel butter on top, and two strips of broiled bacon on top of all. Serve with lemons cut in half, and parsley in branches.

Pig's knuckles and sauerkraut. If fresh pig's knuckles are used salt must be added to the water; with salted knuckles it is unnecessary. Put the knuckles in a kettle filled with cold water, and bring to a boil. Skim, then add one onion, one carrot, one leek, one branch of celery, and a bouquet garni. Boil slowly until soft. Place on a platter and garnish with sauerkraut.

Ditalini soup à la royal. Ditalini is a species of macaroni, prepared in small pieces. Bring two quarts of chicken broth to a boil, add one-half pound of ditalini, and boil until the paste is soft. Then bind the soup with the yolks of three eggs mixed with half a pint of cream. Season well with salt and pepper, and serve at once. Serve grated cheese separate.

Sand dabs, Carnot. Place four cleaned and well seasoned sand dabs in a buttered pan, add one-half glass of white wine and one-half cup of fish stock; cover, and cook. When done place on a platter and pour a white wine sauce over the fish. Garnish with small patties filled with oyster crabs.

Oyster crab patties. Wash one-half pint of oyster crabs, and drain well. Put the crabs in a sauté pan with one ounce of butter, season with salt and pepper, and toss over the fire for five minutes. Then add a pony of sherry wine, and simmer for two minutes. Then add one-half cup of cream sauce, or white wine sauce, and fill the patties. Serve hot. For garnishing fish, make very small patties. If served as a fish course, serve on a platter garnished with parsley in branches.

Larded tenderloin of beef, Sigurd. Roast a larded tenderloin of beef, place on a platter, and garnish one side with stuffed tomatoes Créole; and the other side with potato croquettes. Serve sauce Périgueux separate.

Black cake (Christmas cake). One pound of butter, one pound of sugar, one pound of flour, ten eggs, one-half pint of brandy, three pounds of currants, one pound of citron, two pounds of seeded raisins, one-half pound of orange-peel, one-quarter pound of molasses, one-half ounce of powdered cloves, one-half ounce of ginger, one ounce of allspice, one-half ounce of cinnamon, and the rind and juice of two lemons. Mix thoroughly and bake.

SEPTEMBER 17

BREAKFAST
Stewed prunes
Boiled eggs
Buttered toast
English breakfast tea

LUNCHEON
Cold consommé in cups
Poached eggs, Dauphine
Broiled squab on toast
Sauté potatoes
Lorenzo salad
Camembert cheese with crackers
Kalte Schahle

DINNER
California oysters on half shell
Cream of corn and onions
Queen olives.   Radishes
Boiled salmon, Badu-Cah
Parisian potatoes with parsley
Roast turkey, cranberry sauce
Corn fritters, Susan Jones
Peas.   Endives salad
Vanilla ice cream
Seed biscuits
Demi tasse

Poached eggs, Dauphine. Lay some poached eggs on toast and garnish with asparagus tips. Pour over the eggs some sauce Madère, to which has been added some sliced French mushrooms.

Lorenzo salad. Cut some pears in squares, and add equal parts of water-cress and lettuce. Season with French dressing to which has been added two spoonfuls of chutney sauce.

Kalte Schahle. This is a German summer drink, and is made as follows: Put in a pitcher a large piece of ice, and then add three large glasses of beer, two large glasses of lemonade made with very little sugar, two spoonfuls of small raisins, and three spoonfuls of grated pumpernickel.

Cream of corn and onions. Heat two ounces of butter in a casserole; then add two spoonfuls of flour, one quart of chicken broth, six sliced onions, and six grated ears of corn. Season with salt and pepper, and boil for one hour. Then add one pint of milk, and boil again. Strain through a fine sieve, put back in casserole, add one-half pint of sweet cream, bring nearly to a boil, and add two ounces of butter. When the butter is melted, serve.

Boiled salmon, Badu-Cah. Cut two slices of salmon about one inch thick, and put in pot in cold water; add half of a sliced onion, half of a carrot, one bouquet garni, one-half spoonful of salt, and one wineglassful of vinegar. Boil slowly for twenty minutes. Serve on a platter, on a napkin, garnished with two lemons cut in half, and parsley in branches. Serve separate, lobster sauce to which has been added two spoonfuls of capers.

Lobster sauce. Make two pints of white wine sauce, and whip into it two large spoonfuls of lobster butter. Season with salt and Cayenne pepper. Strain, and add half a cupful of lobster cut in small dices. For Badu-Cah, omit the lobster.

Cranberry sauce. Boil one-half gallon of ripe cranberries with one-quart of water. Boil until soft, strain, add one and one-half pounds of sugar, and boil for five minutes. Pour in moulds, and serve cold.

This sauce may be made without straining if desired.

Corn fritters, Susan Jones. One pint of grated corn, half a teacupful of milk, half a teacupful of flour, a small teaspoonful of baking powder, a tablespoonful of melted butter, two eggs, one teaspoonful of salt, and a little pepper. Mix, and drop from a spoon into hot fat, and fry.

Seed biscuits. Four ounces each of sugar and butter, one pound of flour, three eggs, half ounce of caraway seeds, and lemon flavoring. Mix to a dough, roll out about one-quarter inch thick, cut in round shapes, wash the tops with beaten eggs, and bake in a medium oven.

SEPTEMBER 18

BREAKFAST
Baked bananas
Codfish in cream
Baked potatoes
Rolls
Coffee

LUNCHEON
Cantaloupe
Eggs, Isabella
Mixed grill, special
Escarole salad
Petaluma cream cheese with crackers
Coffee

DINNER
Consommé printanier royal
California ripe olives
Ecrevisses en buisson
Boiled leg of mutton, caper sauce
Mashed turnips
Steamboat fried potatoes
Lettuce and grapefruit salad
Orange soufflé glacé, St. Francis
Tango cake
Demi tasse

Baked bananas. Peel six bananas and cut them in half, lengthwise. Lay in a pan close together. Mix a little powdered cinnamon with some sugar, and spread over the bananas. Put some small bits of butter on top, and bake for twenty minutes. While baking, baste a couple of times with a little syrup. Serve with its own juice.

Orange soufflé glacé, St. Francis. Take six nice oranges and cut off the tops. Take out the insides. Put some sliced fruit, such as apples, oranges, pineapple, grapefruit, etc., in the bottom of the orange shell, and fill about one-third full. Add one-third of vanilla ice cream, and finally finish with a meringue made of the whites of three eggs, six ounces of sugar, and the grated rind of an orange. Dust some powdered sugar on top, and bake in a very hot oven until brown.

Eggs, Isabella. Put some thick Créole sauce on a platter, lay four poached eggs on top, and cover with a little cream sauce.

Petaluma cream cheese. This cheese is a specialty of Petaluma, California. Serve plain; or mixed with salt, pepper, chopped chives, and caraway seeds. Or serve with powdered sugar and cream, separate.

Tango cake. One-quarter pound of burnt almonds, powdered very fine, one-quarter pound of melted butter, three-quarters of a pound of sugar, two ounces of grated chocolate, one-quarter pound of biscuit crumbs, the grated rind of one lemon, the yolks of seven eggs, three whole eggs, the whites of seven eggs beaten very hard, and one pony of rum. Beat the eggs and yolks with the sugar until light; then add the almonds, chocolate, crumbs and lemon rind, and mix well. Add the rum and melted butter; and finally the whites of eggs, mixing lightly. Line a ring mould with very thin tartelette dough, cover the bottom with apricot jam, and then fill with the above preparation. Bake in a warm (not hot), oven. When done, glace with icing flavored with rum. While the icing is still soft sprinkle with assorted colored nonpareil seeds. These seeds may be obtained of grocers dealing in fancy groceries.

Steamboat fried potatoes. Peel three fresh-boiled potatoes, and cut crosswise in pieces one and one-half inches thick. Fry in a pan with half butter and half chicken fat. Season with salt and pepper, and cook until golden yellow.

SEPTEMBER 19

BREAKFASAT
  Stewed pears with claret
  Oatmeal and cream
  Dry toast
  Oolong tea

LUNCHEON
  Shrimp salad, Anastine
  Shirred eggs, Imperial
  Breast of squab, au jus
  Peas
  Chocolate cream pie
  Coffee

DINNER
  Oysters on half shell
  Potage Carpure
  Dill pickles.   Lyon sausage
  Sand dabs, sauté meunière
  Roast chicken
  Cauliflower Hollandaise
  Potatoes au gratin
  Endives salad
  Coffee ice cream
  Anise toast
  Demi tasse

Stewed pears with claret. Peel a dozen nice pears, put them in an earthen pot, add one pint of water, one-half pint of claret, one-half pound of sugar, and a piece of cinnamon stick. Cover the pot, and cook in oven for about two hours. Serve cold.

Shrimp salad, Anastine. Six shallots, one-half stalk of celery, one-half can of pimentos, and some parsley. Chop all very fine, and put in salad bowl with two pounds of picked shrimps. Mix, and add one-half teaspoonful of salt, some fresh-ground black pepper, two spoonfuls of tarragon vinegar, and four spoonfuls of olive oil. Serve in a salad bowl, with leaves of lettuce around the sides; and with hard-boiled eggs cut in four.

Shirred eggs, Imperial. Cut fresh goose liver in small pieces, and fry in pan seasoned with salt and pepper. Then place the liver in a buttered shirred egg dish, break eggs on top, season with salt and pepper, and cook until the eggs are done.

Breast of squab, au jus. Cut the breasts from four large squabs, season with salt and pepper, and roll in flour. Heat two ounces of butter in a sauté pan, add the breasts, and fry for ten minutes. Place the breasts on a platter, and put in the pan one spoonful of meat extract and one-half cup of stock. Season with salt and pepper, reduce one-half by boiling, and pour over the squab. Sprinkle with chopped parsley.

Chocolate cream pie. One quart of milk, the yolks of eight eggs, one-half pound of sugar, two ounces of corn starch, two ounces of powdered cocoa, and one ounce of butter. Dissolve the corn starch in a little milk, and stir into the yolks of eggs. Put the milk on the fire, add the sugar, cocoa, and butter, and bring to a boil. Then pour it into the yolks and corn starch, and set back on the stove until it thickens. Have a pie crust already baked, fill it with this cream, decorate the top with meringue, and set it in the oven to brown the top. Serve cold. The above will make about two pies.

Potage Carpure. Slice a head of lettuce very fine, wash, and drain well. Then put in a casserole with two ounces of butter, cover, and simmer for ten minutes. Then add chicken broth, or clear veal or beef broth (three pints), season with salt and pepper, and boil slowly for about fifteen minutes. Bind with the yolks of three eggs mixed with half a pint of cream. Serve with bread sliced thin, and dried in the oven, like toast.

Anise toast. One-half pound of sugar, four whole eggs, the yolks of two eggs, one-half ounce of anise seed, one-half pound of flour, and lemon flavoring. Beat the eggs, yolks and sugar over the fire until light; then remove and continue beating until cold. Add the flour, seeds, and flavor; dress on a buttered pan in long strips, and bake. When cold cut in slices, and toast in the same manner as zwieback.

SEPTEMBER 20

BREAKFAST
    Strawberries with cream
    Broiled salt mackerel
    Boiled potatoes
    Rolls   Coffee

LUNCHEON
    Eggs, Derby
    Cold chicken, Isabella
    Compote of peaches
    Devil cake   Demi tasse

DINNER
    Consommé Chartreuse. Queen olives
    Terrapin sauté au beurre
    Roast lamb, mint sauce
    Timbale of spinach
    Potatoes, Hollandaise
    Lettuce and grapefruit salad
    Vanilla ice cream
    Baisés (chocolate drops)   Coffee

Eggs, Derby. Cut a can of goose liver au natural in slices one-half inch thick, season with salt and pepper, roll in flour, and fry in butter. Place on a platter, put a poached egg on top of each slice, and pour sauce Madère, to which has been added sliced mushrooms, over the eggs.

Cold chicken, Isabella. Boil a fat chicken. When cold, slice the breast very thin. Make a pint of mayonnaise, and add a spoonful of paprika to it. Mix a cup of cold boiled rice with one spoonful of the mayonnaise, season with salt, and place in the center of a china platter. Lay the breast of chicken on top, and pour the rest of the sauce over all. Lay a few leaves of tarragon crosswise on top. At each end of the platter place two bouquets of asparagus tips. Sprinkle with finely chopped chervil.

Baisés (chocolate drops). One pound of sugar (half powdered and half icing), the whites of three eggs, two ounces of chocolate, and vanilla flavoring. Dissolve the chocolate, and stir into the sugar and whites of eggs, over the fire, until all is melted and smooth; but do not let it come to a boil. Dress on a buttered pan, like peppermint drops. Allow to dry out for a few hours, and bake in a moderate oven.

Devil cake. One-half pound of almond paste, one-half pound of sugar, one-half pound of butter, four ounces of grated chocolate, twelve yolks and twelve whites of eggs, and four ounces of flour. Cream the sugar with the butter, and work in the yolks. Rub the almond paste smooth with four of the whites of eggs, and add, with the grated chocolate, to the sugar, butter and yolks. Beat the rest of the whites of eggs very hard and stiff, and add them to the mixture, with the flour. Fill a butered cake mould, and bake. Allow to become cool; then cut into three layers, and fill between with chocolate filling. Glace the top with very dark chocolate frosting.

Consommé Chartreuse. Boil one cup of chestnuts in salted water until tender. Then drain off the water, and pass the chestnuts through a fine sieve. When the chestnuts are cold put in a bowl, add four whole eggs, and one pint of lukewarm consommé; season with salt and pepper; mix well; put in buttered timbale moulds, set them in bain-marie, and boil for twenty minutes, when they will set like custard when cold. Turn out of moulds, and cut in slices one-eighth inch thick. Serve in hot consommé.

Terrapin au beurre. Boil two terrapin (see index), cut up; season with salt, pepper and a little paprika and celery salt. Heat three ounces of butter in a pan, add the terrapin, and toss for about ten minutes. Put the terrapin in a chafing dish, add to the pan two ounces of butter, cook till brown, and pour over the terrapin. Sprinkle a pony of dry sherry wine over all, cover the dish, and allow to stand for a few minutes before serving.

SEPTEMBER 21

BREAKFAST
  Sliced pineapple
  Hominy with cream
  Crescents
  Russian caravan tea

LUNCHEON
  Canapé Riga
  Consommé in cups
  Chicken hash, with poached eggs
  Roquefort cheese with crackers
  Coffee

DINNER
  Oysters on half shell
  Bean and cabbage soup
  Celery
  Fillet of Tahoe trout, au vin blanc
  Roast loin of pork, apple sauce
  Sweet potatoes sauté
  Artichokes, Hollandaise
  Green corn
  Waldorf salad
  Cold chocolate pudding
  Coffee

Bean and cabbage soup. Soak two pounds of white beans in water over night. Put in a vessel two pounds of salt pork, three pounds of shin of beef, two gallons of cold water, and a tablespoonful of salt. Bring slowly to a boil, and skim well. Add the beans, and boil for an hour. Then add a small head of cabbage that has been cut in one-inch squares, one onion, one carrot, a bouquet garni, and one mashed clove of garlic. Boil slowly for two hours, then remove the pork, beef, carrot, onion and bouquet garni. Season to taste with salt and pepper, and add a little chopped parsley.

Cold chocolate pudding. One pint of cream, one-half pint of milk, the yolks of four eggs, six ounces of sugar, three ounces of chocolate, one-half ounce of gelatine, and a little vanilla flavoring. Soak the gelatine in a little cold water. Dissolve the chocolate and sugar on the fire; then add the yolks and milk, and stir until it thickens, but do not let it come to a boil. Remove from the fire, add the gelatine and vanilla flavoring, and stir until the gelatine is melted. Then strain, and cool. Whip the cream until stiff, mix with the foregoing, and immediately pour into pudding moulds. Set in the ice box to harden. Serve with cold chocolate sauce.

Cold chocolate sauce. Three-quarters of a pound of sugar, one-half pound of water, and four ounces of powdered chocolate. Bring the water to a boil, and dissolve the chocolate and sugar in it. Bring to a boil again; take off the fire, and allow to become cool. Serve with bavarois, puddings, blanc mange, ice creams, etc.

Italian wine sauce, for puddings. Two ounces of sago, one-half pint of water, one-half pint of claret, one-quarter pound of sugar, the juice of an orange, and a pony of rum. Soak the sago in the water for over an nour; then boil until clear. Then add the claret, sugar, and orange juice, and continue on fire until it thickens. Then add the rum. Serve with corn meal, sago, tapioca, or rice pudding.

SEPTEMBER 22

BREAKFAST
    Baked apples with cream
    Plain scrambled eggs
    Dry toast
    Coffee

LUNCHEON
    Cantaloupe
    Pompano en papillote
    Broiled sweetbreads on toast
    Succotash
    Soufflée potatoes
    French pastry
    Demi tasse

DINNER
    California oyster cocktail
    Consommé Trianon
    Ripe olives
    Fried eels, sauce rémoulade
    Breast of chicken with figs
    Artichokes, sauce Italienne
    Broiled fresh mushrooms
    Potatoes à la Reine
    Romaine salad, Roquefort dressing
    Biscuit glacé, St. Francis
    Alsatian wafers
    Coffee

Consommé Trianon. Cut some green, red, and natural royal in triangle shapes, and serve in hot consommé.

Consommé with green royal. Mix four eggs with one pint of warm consommé, add green coloring, strain, put in buttered timbale moulds, and cook in bain-marie. Cut in any shape, and serve in hot consommé.

Consommé with red royal. Obtain some red coloring from a fancy grocer. Mix the yolks of four eggs with one pint of warm consommé, add some coloring, strain, and cook in bain-marie. Cut in any shape desired, and serve in hot consommé.

Fried eels, sauce rémoulade. Cut the eels in pieces two inches long, and boil in water with a little salt and vinegar, one sliced onion, one carrot, and a bouquet garni. Allow to become cool in its own gravy. Then take out of the gravy, roll in flour, then in beaten eggs, then in bread crumbs, and fry in very hot swimming fat until golden yellow. Season with salt, and serve on a platter, on a napkin. Garnish with fried parsley and quartered lemons. Serve sauce rémoulade separate.

Breast of chicken with figs. Cut the breasts from two young raw roasting chickens, remove the skin, season with salt and pepper, roll in table cream, then in flour, and fry in very hot melted butter. When the breasts are done, pour three spoonfuls of cream on a platter and lay the breasts on top. Heat some preserved figs, and garnish with two for each person. Or dry figs may be warmed in consommé, and used instead, if desired.

SEPTEMBER 23

BREAKFAST
  Fresh raspberries with cream
  Griddle cakes with maple syrup
  Rolls
  Coffee

LUNCHEON
  Grapefruit en supreme
  Eggs Belley
  Roast loin of pork, apple sauce
  Fried sweet potatoes
  Cold artichokes, mayonnaise
  Camembert cheese with crackers
  Coffee

DINNER
  Chicken broth, San Remo
  Celery
  Oysters, Victor Hugo
  Small tenderloin steak,
    Cercle Militaire
  Peas in cream
  Pont Neuf potatoes
  Chiffonnade salad
  Philadelphia vanilla ice cream
  Assorted cakes
  Demi tasse

Eggs Belley. Slice some smoked beef very fine, parboil, and add to plain scrambled eggs, with a little chopped chives.

Chicken broth, San Remo. Make two quarts of plain chicken broth, add to it one-half cup of sliced soft-boiled carrots, and one cup of boiled rice. Serve grated cheese separate.

Oysters, Victor Hugo. Season two dozen oysters on the half shell with salt and pepper. Put in a bowl one cupful of fresh-grated horse radish, a little chopped parsley, one-half cup of fresh bread crumbs, one spoonful of grated cheese, and one spoonful of butter. Mix well, and spread over the oysters. Put in oven to bake, and when done serve in the same shells. Serve one-half lemon to each person.

Small tenderloin steak, Cercle Militaire. Season four small tenderloin steaks with salt and pepper, roll in oil, and broil. Broil in the same manner, and at the same time, four whole lamb kidneys. When done place the steaks on a platter with the kidneys on top. Boil four artichokes, remove the leaves, and toss the bottoms in a sauté pan with a little butter. Season with salt and pepper, and use to garnish the steaks. Heat two ounces of butter in a sauté pan, add six chopped shallots, when hot add a piece of lemon and a little chopped parsley, and pour over the kidneys and steaks.

SEPTEMBER 24

BREAKFAST
  Orange marmalade
  Boiled eggs
  Buttered toast
  Ceylon tea

LUNCHEON
  Cantaloupe
  Poached eggs, Mexicaine
  Broiled pig's feet
  Lyonnaise potatoes
  Lettuce salad
  Meringue Chantilly
  Demi tasse

DINNER
  Consommé Madrilène
  Ripe olives.   Celery
  Planked black bass
  Roast Muscovy duck, apple sauce
  Artichokes, Barigoule
  Laurette potatoes
  Fresh asparagus, Hollandaise
  Westphalian ham
  Frozen egg nogg
  Assorted cakes
  Coffee

Poached eggs, Mexicaine. Slice one green pepper, and simmer in butter. Slice one-half can of cèpes, and toss in olive oil over fire. Slice two pimentos; and mix all together with one cup of tomato sauce. Season well, pour on a platter, and lay six poached eggs on top.

Roast Muscovy duck. Clean a Muscovy duck, season with salt and pepper, and stuff with a piece of celery and two shallots chopped very fine. Put the duck in a roasting pan with a sliced onion and carrot, add a little water, and put in a hot oven. The water will evaporate quickly, and the fat from the duck will be sufficient to roast it. Baste often. When done place the duck on a platter, remove the fat from the pan, add one cup of stock and a spoonful of meat extract, boil for five minutes, and pour over the duck.

Artichokes, Barigoule. Parboil six artichokes in salted water for two minutes. Then remove the hairy part, between the leaves and the bottoms; and fill with a stuffing made as follows: Simmer twelve chopped shallots in a casserole in two ounces of butter; then add one-half pound of chopped fresh mushrooms, and simmer again for ten minutes. Then add one-half glass of white wine, and boil until nearly dry, but be careful that it does not burn. Then add one-half cup of brown gravy, season with salt and pepper and a little chopped garlic and parsley, and boil for five minutes. Then thicken with the yolks of three raw eggs, and if necessary add a very little fresh bread crumbs. When the artichokes are filled tie a thin slice of salt pork over the tops, lay in a sauté pan, with sliced onions, sliced carrots, a bouquet garni, and one-half pint of bouillon. Cover, set in the oven and cook for about forty-five minutes. If the leaves loosen easily they are done. Serve on a platter with sauce Madère.

Fresh asparagus and Westphalia ham. Boil some fresh asparagus, and serve with Hollandaise sauce. Serve at the same time raw sliced Westphalian ham.

SEPTEMBER 25

BREAKFAST
Sliced peaches with cream
Breakfast sausages
Flannel cakes, maple syrup
Rolls
Coffee

LUNCHEON
Oysters, Louis
Vogeleier omelet
Spring lamb Irish stew
   with dumplings
Camembert and Brie cheese
   with crackers
Coffee

DINNER
Homemade clam soup
Dill pickles.   Salted pecans
Fillet of sole, Paul Bert
Leg of veal, au jus
Spinach
Mashed potatoes
Lettuce salad
German apple cake
Demi tasse

Oysters, Louis. Season two dozen oysters on the half shell with salt and pepper, sprinkle with one dozen shallots chopped fine. Put one-half teaspoonful of bread crumbs, mixed with a little paprika, on each oyster. Put a small bit of butter on top of each, and bake in oven for about ten minutes. Serve in the shells, with one-half lemon to each person.

Spring lamb Irish stew with dumplings. Make an Irish stew (see index), and cook some dumplings in the broth, as given below.

Dumplings, for stews, pot pie, etc. One quart of flour, three heaping teaspoonfuls of baking powder, one-half teaspoonful of salt, and some sweet milk. Sift the baking powder, salt and flour, four times. Add enough milk to make rather a stiff dough or batter. Drop by spoonfuls into boiling broth. There should be broth enough to cook up around the dumplings, but not enough to cover them. Boil for half an hour, and do not lift the cover until done.

Homemade clam soup. Put three dozen Little Neck clams with their juice in a sauce pan. Add one pint of cold water, bring to a boil, and skim well. Then add one-half pint of boiling cream and two ounces of butter. When the butter is melted add one cup of broken saltine crackers, and season with salt, pepper, and a little chopped parsley.

Fillet of sole, Paul Bert. Put four fillets of sole in a buttered pan, season with salt and pepper, add one-half cup of fish stock, and one-half glass of white wine, cover with a buttered paper, and cook for ten minutes. Place fillets on a platter, reduce the stock nearly dry, add one cup of tomato sauce and one cup of Béarnaise sauce, mix well, and strain over the fish.

SEPTEMBER 26

BREAKFAST
  Fresh strawberries with cream
  Plain poached eggs on toast
  Rolls
  Coffee

LUNCHEON
  Pimentos Suédoise
  Sand dabs, meunière
  Fried loin of lamb chops,
     tomato sauce
  Lima beans with shallots
  Potato salad
  Chocolate éclairs
  Demi tasse

DINNER
  Toke Point oysters
  Sorrel soup with rice
  Chow chow
  Baked lobster, cardinal
  Ham glacé, champagne sauce
  Cooked lettuce salad
  Duchess potatoes
  Fruit salad
  Philadelphia lemon water ice
  Assorted cakes
  Coffee

Pimentos Suédoise. Spread the contents of a can of pimentos flat on the table, lay a fillet of anchovies in oil on each pimento, and roll up in the form of a sausage with the anchovy in the center. Lay them on a ravier dish, season with salt and pepper, one-third of vinegar and two-thirds olive oil, and sprinkle with chopped parsley.

Fried loin of lamb chops. Have your butcher cut six nice loin chops about one and one-quarter inch thick, and well trimmed. Season with salt and pepper, roll in flour, then in beaten egg, and finally in bread crumbs. Put some lard or melted butter in a sauté pan, and when hot add the chops and fry until nice and brown. Place on a platter, garnish with parsley in branches and lemons cut in half. Serve any sauce desired, separate.

Lima beans with shallots. Put one dozen chopped shallots in a casserole with two ounces of butter. When hot, add one teaspoonful of flour, one-half cup of bouillon, one quart of boiled Lima beans, and season with salt, pepper and a little chopped parsley. Boil for ten minutes.

Baked lobster, Cardinal. Boil four small lobsters. When done, split in two, remove the meat, and save the shells. Put two ounces of butter in a sauté pan, add the lobster meat cut in slices one-half inch thick, season with salt and pepper, and toss over the fire for a few minutes. Then add one-half glass of sherry wine, and reduce until nearly dry. Then add one cup of cream sauce and boil for few minutes. Then add one spoonful of lobster butter, mix well; and then fill the shells. Sprinkle with fresh bread crumbs, place small bits of butter on top, and bake in oven until golden brown. Serve on a platter, on a folded napkin, and garnish with parsley in branches and two lemons cut in half.

SEPTEMBER 27

BREAKFAST
Grapes
Ham and eggs
Rolls
Coffee

LUNCHEON
Cantaloupe
Eggs Bennett
Broiled quail on toast
Soufflée potatoes
Cold fresh asparagus, mustard sauce
Roquefort cheese with crackers
Coffee

DINNER
Consommé national
Plain celery.   Ripe olives
Fillet of sand dabs, meunière
Sweetbreads, royal
Roast leg of lamb, mint sauce
String beans
Stewed tomatoes
St. Francis potatoes
Sliced tomatoes
French pastry
Coffee

Eggs Bennett. Boil six eggs until hard, remove the shells, and cut in two lengthwise. Remove the yolks, chop fine, and mix with one ounce of butter, and twelve anchovies in oil cut in small squares. Fill the whites of the eggs with this mixture, place on a buttered baking dish, cover with a well-seasoned cream sauce, sprinkle with grated cheese, put small bits of butter on top, and bake in the oven until brown.

Broiled quail on toast. Split the quail, season with salt and pepper, roll in oil, and broil. When done place each quail on a piece of buttered toast, put a spoonful of maître d'hôtel butter on top of each, and garnish with watercress and lemons cut in half.

Consommé national. Cut some plain; green, and red royal in small stars, and serve in hot consommé.

Sweetbreads, royal. Parboil one pound of sweetbreads, pull off the skins, and cut in slices one-quarter inch thick. Peel twenty small heads of fresh mushrooms, wash well, and dry on a napkin. Put two ounces of butter in a sauté pan with the sweetbreads and mushrooms, season with salt and pepper, and simmer slowly for ten minutes. Then add half a pint of cleaned and well-washed oyster crabs, and simmer again for five minutes. Then add one-half pint of cream, and boil. Thicken with the yolks of three eggs well-mixed with a small cup of cream, but do not let it come to a boil after the cream has been added. Taste to see if seasoning is right, add half a glass of dry amontillado sherry wine, and serve in chafing dish.

SEPTEMBER 28

BREAKFAST
  Baked apples with cream
  German pancakes
  Rolls
  Coffee

LUNCHEON
  Grapefruit, cardinal
  Scrambled eggs, Norwegian
  Honeycomb tripe sauté, aux fines
    herbes
  Alsatian potatoes
  Watercress salad
  Pear tartelette.   Coffee

DINNER
  Potage Navarraise
  Salted pecans
  Oysters en brochette, à la diable
  Roast chicken
  Stewed tomatoes, family style
  Mashed potatoes
  Peas à la Française
  Lettuce, mayonnaise dressing
  Crust with peaches (Croute aux
    pêches)
  Demi tasse

Scrambled eggs, Norwegian. Make four pieces of anchovy toast, put some plain scrambled eggs on top, and lay some fillets of anchovies crosswise over the eggs.

Honeycomb tripe sauté, aux fines herbes. Cut three pounds of boiled tripe in strips, put in a sauté pan with four ounces of butter, season with salt and pepper, and cook over a quick fire. When nearly crisp add parsley, chives and chervil, all chopped fine; and serve in a deep dish. Serve quartered lemons on a platter, on a napkin, separate.

Potage Navarraise. Heat two ounces of butter in a casserole, add a spoonful of flour, and cook until golden yellow. Then add one quart of consommé and one pint of tomato sauce, or tomato purée; season with salt and pepper, boil for ten minutes, and strain. Boil one-half pound of vermicelli in salted water until soft, and add to the soup. Serve grated cheese separate.

Oysters en brochette. Cut the beard, or gills, from two dozen large oysters. Broil twelve slices of bacon, and cut them in three pieces each. Take a silver or steel skewer and put a slice of bacon on it, then an oyster, then bacon, then an oyster, and so continue until the skewer is full. Season with salt and pepper, roll in melted butter, then in fresh bread crumbs, and broil. When done, serve on a platter with maître d'hôtel sauce, and garnish with lemons cut in four, and parsley in branches.

Oysters en brochette, à la diable. .The word, brochette, means skewer. Make four skewers full of oysters and bacon as described above. Season with salt and pepper. Mix a tablespoonful of French mustard and a tablespoonful of English mustard together, and roll the skewered oysters in it, then in fresh bread crumbs, and then broil. Serve with maître d'hôtel sauce over the oysters, and devil sauce separate.

Crusts with peaches (croute aux pêches). Stew a dozen nice peaches (see index). Cut a dozen slices of bread about one-half inch thick, and in round shape, about three inches in diameter. Butter them, put on a pan, and roast in the oven; turning over so they will become brown on both sides. Place on a platter, set a peach on top of each crust, and pour its own syrup, to which has been added a little kirschwasser, over all.

Crusts with pears. Prepare in the same manner as above.

Crusts with apples. Prepare in the same manner as above. Canned fruit may be used if desired, for any of the above.

SEPTEMBER 29

BREAKFAST
Grapefruit juice
Oatmeal with cream
Rolls
English breakfast tea

LUNCHEON
Canapé of fresh Beluga caviar
Omelet with peas
Sirloin steak, Saxonne
Julienne potatoes
Lettuce salad
Meringue glacé à la vanille
Demi tasse

DINNER
Toke Point oysters, mignonette
Consommé Medina
Ripe California olives
Sand dabs, sauté meunière
Roast young turkey, cranberry sauce
Baked sweet potatoes
Fresh asparagus, Hollandaise
Fried egg plant
Watercress salad
Mince pie
Coffee

Omelet with peas. Mix a cup of boiled peas with two spoonfuls of cream sauce, and season with salt and a little sugar. Make an omelet with twelve eggs, and before turning over on platter fill with the peas. Pour a thin cream sauce around the omelet.

Sirloin steak, Saxonne. Season two sirloin steaks with salt and pepper, roll in oil, and broil. When done place on a platter, and garnish with four stuffed tomatoes with rice, and four stuffed cucumbers (see index). Pour a little sauce Madère over the steaks.

Consommé Medina. Boil six chicken livers in bouillon. When done, cut in Julienne style. Boil one-quarter pound of spaghetti until soft, cut in pieces one inch long, and add with the chickens' livers, to one and one-half quarts of very hot consommé. Serve grated cheese separate.

Pickled nasturtion seeds. Select the small and green seeds, and put them in salted water; changing the water twice in the course of a week. Then pour off the brine and cover with scalding vinegar with a little alum in it. Use in salads.

Pickled artichokes. Select small and tender artichokes, trim the bottoms, remove the hardest leaves, and allow to stand in alum water until ready to cook. Then bring to the boiling point, and allow to become cool slowly. Pack in glass jars, and cover with a liquor made as follows: To one gallon of vinegar add a teacup of sugar, one cup of salt, a teaspoonful of alum, and one-quarter ounce of cloves and black pepper. Bring to the boiling point. pour over the artichokes, and seal while hot.

Pickled onions. Select very small white onions, peel them, and boil in equal parts of sweet milk and water for ten minutes. Drain well, place in glass jars, and pour scalding spiced vinegar over them immediately. Use no sugar, and no allspice in the vinegar as it would tend to darken the onions.

Pickles. Take one hundred green cucumbers two inches long, or under; and peel as many small white onions as desired. Wash well, and put into a stone jar. Sprinkle plenty of table salt over them, and toss all about with the hands. Allow to stand for twenty-four hours, then drain off the liquor, place the cucumbers and onions in glass jars, and cover with spiced vinegar without sugar. Add a small red pepper to each jar. Seal hot.

Sweet pickled peaches. Select clingstone peaches, and peel; or rub the down off with a coarse crash towel. For eight pounds of fruit use four pounds of sugar, one quart of vinegar, one ounce of stick cinnamon, and one ounce of whole cloves. Boil the sugar and vinegar with the cinnamon for two minutes. Stick one or two cloves in each peach, and put in the boiling syrup. When the peaches are done place in jars, and put others in the syrup to cook until all are done. Then reduce the syrup to half the original quantity, and pour over the fruit. Seal hot. Plums and pears may be pickled in the same manner.

Green tomato pickle. Slice one peck of green tomatoes and one dozen large onions very thin. Put the tomatoes in a jar with salt sprinkled between layers, and allow to stand for a few hours. Put the onions in another jar, pour boiling water over them, and allow them to stand for a few hours also. Then squeeze the juice from both, and arrange them in a stone jar in alternate layers, sprinkling through them celery and mustard seed. Pour over all a quart of vinegar and a pint of sugar brought to a boil. It will be ready to use when cold.

Ripe cucumber sweet pickles. Pare twelve large ripe cucumbers, cut out the pulp, and cut them in strips. Boil together two pounds of sugar, one pint of vinegar, and one-half ounce of cinnamon and cloves. Skim well. Then put in the cucumbers, and cook until tender. Then remove the cucumbers, reduce the liquor, pour over the cucumbers, and cover tightly.

SEPTEMBER 30

BREAKFAST
Fresh raspberries with cream
Shirred eggs, Brunswick
Rolls
Coffee

LUNCHEON
Cantaloupe
Fried fillet of sole, Tartar sauce
Cucumber salad
Cold turkey and ham with chow chow
Baked potatoes
Brie cheese with crackers
Demi tasse

DINNER
Potage Schorestène
Dill pickles.   Radishes
Frogs' legs, sauté à sec
Small tenderloin steak, Nicholas II
Brussels sprouts, au beurre
Potatoes au gratin   Escarole salad
Baked brown bread pudding   Coffee

Shirred eggs, Brunswick. Butter a shirred egg dish, lay a slice of raw tomato about one-half inch thick in the bottom, heat through, turn it over, and break two eggs on top. Season with salt and pepper, and finish cooking.

Potage Schorestène. Chop fine, one pound of sirloin, or top sirloin, of beef. Put in a casserole with three quarts of consommé and boil slowly for one hour. Then strain through a coarse sieve. The meat must be all forced through the sieve, and served in the soup.

Small tenderloin steak, Nicholas II. Cut four small steaks, and season with salt and pepper. Put two ounces of butter in a frying pan and fry the steaks, and when nearly done remove them to a casserole. Heat eight whole truffles in sherry wine, and use them to garnish the steaks. Also lay on each steak a slice of goose liver sauté in butter. Pour a little sauce Madère over all.

Baked brown bread pudding. One quart of graham bread crumbs, one quart of milk, one gill of molasses, two ounces of butter, two ounces of sugar, three eggs, and one-half teaspoonful of cinnamon. Make the crumbs very fine. Then melt the butter in the milk, with the sugar, molasses, cinnamon, and eggs. Then stir in the crumbs, and bake in buttered moulds for about one-half hour. Serve hot, with cream sauce flavored with a little cinnamon.

Sweet grape juice. Crush twenty pounds of Concord grapes in three quarts of water, and put them in a porcelain kettle. Set the kettle on the fire, and stir well until it reaches the boiling point; then allow it to simmer for fifteen or twenty minutes. Strain through a cloth, and add three pounds of white sugar. When the sugar is dissolved strain again through a cloth, and heat to the boiling point. Pour into hot pint or quart bottles, and seal instantly with new corks, only. After the corks have been inserted dip the necks of the bottles into hot sealing wax.

Canned pumpkin or squash. Peel the squash or pumpkin, and cut in small squares. Boil, without seasoning, until soft. Mash through a fruit press. Fill hot quart glass jars, and seal tight. Keep in a cool dark place.

Preserved violets. Cut the stems from one pound of large full-blown violets. Boil one and one-half pounds of granulated sugar, until a little dropped in cold water makes a soft ball. Then throw the violets into the sugar, remove the pan from the fire for a moment, and stir gently. Then return the pan to the fire, boil up once, and then change the violets immediately to another vessel. Let them stand over night, and then drain off the syrup through a sieve. Put the syrup in a copper pan, add a cupful of sugar, and cook until it hardens in water. Then put in the violets, change to another vessel, and allow to stand again over night. Again drain off the syrup, and boil it for a few minutes. Then add the violets, and remove the pan at once from the fire, and stir lightly until it begins to crystalize. Then pour the whole on sheets of paper, shake, and separate the flowers carefully with the fingers. When dry pick them from the sugar, arrange on a wire grating, and allow them to become cool.

Canned minced meat. Three pounds of boiled beef, one pound of beef suet, three pounds of brown sugar, one-half peck of apples, two pounds of raisins, one pound of currants, one pound of citron, one grated nutmeg, one tablespoonful of powdered mace, and allspice and cinnamon to suit the taste. Chop the meat, suet and apples, slice the citron fine, and mix all together with the seasoning. Pour on enough boiled cider to make a thick batter. Heat it thoroughly and put into one quart glass jars. Seal while hot, and set away in a cool dark place.

OCTOBER 1

BREAKFAST
Orange and grapefruit juice, mixed
Broiled salt mackerel
Baked potatoes
Rolls
Coffee

LUNCHEON
Hors d'oeuvres assorted
Eggs Castro
Spring lamb steak, Bercy
French fried potatoes
Cold asparagus, mayonnaise
Strawberry whipped cream
Hazelnut macaroons   Demi tasse

DINNER
Consommé Georgia
Ripe California olives
Pompano sauté meunière
Virginia ham glacé, champagne sauce
Spinach in cream Laurette potatoes
Hearts of lettuce salad
Fancy ice cream
Assorted cakes   Coffee

Eggs Castro. Cook four artichokes, clean the bottoms, lay a poached egg on each, and cover with the following sauce: Mix half a cup of cream sauce with three-quarters of a cup of Hollandaise sauce, add a few sliced canned mushrooms, and season with salt and a little Spanish or Cayenne pepper.

Strawberry whipped cream. Crush one-half pint of strawberries with one-quarter of a pound of sugar. Whip one pint of cream until stiff, then add the crushed strawberries, mix well, and serve in saucers.

Raspberry, peach or banana whipped cream. Prepare in the same manner as strawberry whipped cream.

Hazelnut macaroons. Roast some shelled hazelnuts in the oven, and as soon as brown rub them well on a coarse sieve to remove the skins. Crush three-quarters of a pound of the hazelnuts and one-quarter pound of almonds with two pounds of sugar. Add eight or ten whites of eggs, and stir to a paste. Dress on paper, and bake in the same manner as ordinary macaroons.

Consommé Georgia. Peel two tomatoes, cut in two, squeeze out the juice, and cut in small squares. Cut two pimentos in small squares. Boil two peeled green peppers in bouillon, and cut in small squares. Slice twelve heads of canned mushrooms very fine. Add all of the above, together with a cup of plain boiled rice, to two quarts of very hot and well-seasoned consommé.

OCTOBER 2

BREAKFAST
   Sliced peaches with cream
   Omelet with bacon
   Corn muffins
   Coffee

LUNCHEON
   Cantaloupe
   Consommé in cups
   Lamb chops, Beau-sejour
   Château potatoes
   Romaine salad
   Compote of pears
   French sponge cake
   Coffee

DINNER
   Shrimp soup, family style
   Salted Brazil nuts.   Radishes
   Fillet of turbot, Bagration
   Roast leg of lamb, purée of chestnuts
   Boiled Parisian potatoes
   Fresh asparagus, Hollandaise
   Fancy ice cream
   American gugelhoff
   Coffee

Lamb chops, Beau-sejour. Make a risotto, and put in small buttered timbale moulds. Use one timbale to garnish each two broiled lamb chops. Pour some tomato sauce over the chops.

French sponge cake (Génoise legère). Put six eggs and four yolks into a basin with half a pound of sugar, and whip over a slow fire for about fifteen minutes, but do not let it become too hot. Then take off the fire, and continue beating until cold. Then mix in lightly half a pound of sifted flour, a quarter of a pound of melted butter, and some vanilla flavoring. Put in buttered moulds, and bake in a rather cool oven for over half an hour. When cold glacé with white frosting, and decorate the top with candied fruit.

Shrimp soup, family style. Add to one quart of fish broth one pound of picked shrimps, and bring to a boil. Then add one pint of boiling cream, season with salt and pepper and chopped parsley, add one-half cup of broken saltine crackers, and two ounces of sweet butter. It is ready to serve when the butter is melted.

Fillet of turbot, Bagration. Put four fillets of turbot in a buttered sauté pan, season with salt and pepper, add one-half glass of white wine and one-half cup of fish broth, cover with buttered paper, and put in oven. When done, remove the fish to a platter. With the trimmings of the turbot make a fish forcemeat. Mash the trimmings well in a mortar, pass through a sieve, add one egg, season with salt and pepper, make into small round balls, and boil in fish broth for three minutes. Put these fish balls into white wine sauce, pour over the fish, and serve hot.

American gugelhoff. One pound of flour, one-half pint of milk, one ounce of yeast, four eggs, three ounces of sugar, six ounces of butter, two ounces of Malaga raisins, and the rind of a lemon and a pinch of mace for flavoring. Have the milk luke-warm, dissolve the yeast in it, add all the other ingredients, and mix to a batter. Put into a basin, cover with a cloth, and allow to raise for about two hours. Butter the moulds well, sprinkle them with coarse-chopped almonds, fill the moulds half full with the raised dough, allow to raise until the moulds are about three-quarters full, and then bake in a medium oven.

OCTOBER 3

BREAKFAST
  Stewed prunes
  Boiled eggs
  Dry toast
  Coffee

LUNCHEON
  Canapé Eldorado
  Poached eggs, Taft
  Beef steak, Jusienne
  Potatoes au gratin
  Chicory salad
  Banana pie
  Demi tasse

DINNER
  Consommé Frascati
  Chow chow
  Boiled brook trout, sauce mousseline
  Potatoes, Nature
  Lamb chops, Beaugency
  Peas and carrots in cream
  Chiffonnade salad
  Pears à la Piedmont
  Alsatian wafers
  Coffee

Canapé Eldorado. Spread a leaf of lettuce with some mayonnaise sauce, lay a boiled artichoke bottom on top, and three small Mexican tomatoes stuffed with anchovies on top of the artichoke. Decorate with anchovy butter.

Poached eggs, Taft. Fry four slices of egg plant, lay a slice of boiled Virginia ham on top of each, a poached egg on top of each slice of ham, and cover with Hollandaise sauce. Cut a "T" out of a truffle and lay on top of the sauce.

Beef steak, Jusienne. Season four small steaks with salt and pepper, and fry in sauté pan with melted butter. When done place on a platter and garnish with lettuce braisé, peas in butter, and onions glacés. Pour sauce Madère over the steaks.

Consommé Frascati. Cut two potatoes in small dices, and parboil for five minutes in salted water. Drain off the water, add six heads of peeled fresh mushrooms sliced very thin, and two quarts of consommé. Cook slowly until the potatoes are soft.

Banana pie. Mash enough bananas to make two cupfuls of pulp. Force through a sieve with a potato masher, add one-half cup of sugar, two crushed and sifted soda crackers, one-half cup of milk, the juice and rind of a lemon, two spoonfuls of molasses, a pinch of powdered cinnamon, and two eggs. Mix well together, and bake in an open pie, in the same manner as a pumpkin pie.

Lamb chops, Beaugency. Broil the chops, place on a platter, and garnish with fresh artichoke bottoms filled with parboiled beef marrow cut in small dices. Serve sauce Choron separate.

Pears, Piedmont. Peel and remove the cores from a dozen nice pears, and stew them in syrup. Fill the centers with pear marmalade and chopped candied fruits. Cook some rice in the same manner as for rice croquettes. Dress a layer of the rice on a platter, place the pears on top, and serve with wine sauce. (See index for Italian wine sauce).

OCTOBER 4

BREAKFAST
  Baked apples with cream
  Griddle cakes, maple syrup
  Crescents
  English breakfast tea

LUNCHEON
  Cantaloupe
  Scrambled eggs, Bullit
  Broiled honeycomb tripe
  Sauté potatoes
  Field salad
  Roquefort cheese with crackers
  Coffee

WEDDING DINNER
  Fresh caviar with dry toast
  Toke Point oysters, mignonette
  Clear green turtle, amontillado
  Crisp celery.   Ripe olives
  Salted mixed nuts
  Frogs' legs, Jerusalem
  Sweetbreads braisé, Liencourt
  Peas à la Française
  Saddle of lamb, au jus
  Jets de houblons
  Cardon à la moelle
  Potatoes à la Reine
  Sorbet au champagne
  Stuffed capon, St. Antoine
  Lettuce salad with Roquefort dress-
    ing
  Assorted fancy cakes
  Wedding cake
  Assorted cheese
  Fruit and bonbons
  Demi tasse

Scrambled eggs, Bullit. Peel six heads of fresh mushrooms, slice very thin, and put in a sauce pan with one ounce of butter. Simmer until done, then add twelve beaten eggs, one cup of cream, two ounces of sweet butter, and a little salt and pepper. Scramble the eggs, and dish up on a platter on top of four slices of fried egg plant.

Sweetbreads, Liencourt. Braise some sweetbreads (see index), place on a platter with their own gravy, and garnish with fresh bottoms of artichokes filled with purée of fresh mushrooms.

Purée of fresh mushrooms. Wash thoroughly two pounds of fresh mushrooms, press in a cloth to extract the water, and chop very fine. Put two ounces of butter in a casserole, add the mushrooms, season with salt and pepper, cover and simmer for twenty minutes. Then add half a cup of fresh bread crumbs and a little chopped parsley, and bind with the yolks of two eggs.

Wedding cake (home made). One pound of sugar, one and one-half pounds of butter, ten eggs, one and one-half pounds of flour. Mix in the same manner as for pound cake, and then add one and one-half pounds of seedless raisins, one pound of currants, one pound of chopped citron, one-half pound of chopped orange peel, one tablespoonful of mixed spices (cinnamon, cloves, mace, ginger, etc.), the juice and rind of a lemon, and one-half pint of brandy. Put in a mould lined with buttered paper, and bake in a slow oven for about two hours. The cake will improve if allowed to set a few days after being baked.

As a table decoration.—Glacé the wedding cake with very thick white frosting, and then decorate it with royal icing (see glacé royal), using a fancy pastry tube.

Wedding cake in boxes.—When the cake has set for a few days after baking, cut in size to fit your boxes, and wrap each piece in wax paper. Tie the boxes with white ribbons.

OCTOBER 5

BREAKFAST
  Fresh raspberries with cream
  Broiled kippered herrings
  Baked potatoes
  Rolls
  Coffee

LUNCHEON
  Canapé of sardines
  Poached eggs, Velour
  Filet mignon, Monegasque
  Lettuce salad
  Camembert cheese with crackers
  Coffee

DINNER
  Hare soup, Uncle Sam
  Pim olas
  Sand dabs, meunière
  Roast leg of lamb, au jus
  Lima beans
  Mashed potatoes
  Romaine salad
  Crèpes Suzette
  Demi tasse

Poached eggs, Velour. Split two English muffins, toast and butter them, lay a slice of broiled ham on top of each, a poached egg on top of the ham, and cover with Béarnaise sauce.

Filet mignon, Monegasque. Broil some small tenderloin steaks, place on a platter, lay a slice of broiled tomato on top of each, and garnish with the bottoms of fresh artichokes filled with Parisian potatoes. Pour sauce Madère, to which has been added some sliced green olives, over the steaks.

Hare soup, Uncle Sam. Cut the saddle and hind legs from a large Belgian hare, and put the remainder in a roasting pan with two sliced onions, one carrot, one stalk of leek, one-half stalk of celery, a few pepper berries, two cloves, three bay leaves, two sprigs of thyme, and three ounces of butter. Season with salt and pepper, and put in oven and roast until done. Then sprinkle with three spoonfuls of flour, and roast again until the flour is brown. Then put in a casserole with two gallons of water and a little salt and one pound of lentils, and boil for four hours. Then force all that is possible through a fine sieve. Roast the legs and saddle of the hare, and cut the meat in half-inch squares. Put the strained soup back in the casserole, bring to a boil, add the cut-up hare meat and one glassful of sherry wine, and season if necessary with salt and Cayenne pepper.

Crèpes Suzette. Make some French pancakes, as thin as possible. Then make a cream with one-half pound of sweet butter, one-half pound of sugar, the grated peel of two oranges, and a dash of brandy or kirschwasser. Mix the sugar and butter to a light cream, then add the liquor and orange, and mix thoroughly. Spread some of the cream over each pancake, and then fold in the form of an English pancake. Place them in a chafing dish, pour two ponies of brandy or kirschwasser over them, and light just before serving.

OCTOBER 6

BREAKFAST
  Stewed prunes
  Shirred eggs
  Rolls
  Coffee

LUNCHEON
  Grapefruit en surprise
  Eggs, Sara Bernhardt
  Fried pig's feet, tomato sauce
  Château potatoes
  Applie pie
  Coffee

DINNER
  Blue Point oysters
  Consommé with noodles
  Celery.   Radishes
  Fillet of halibut, Pondicherry
  Roast chicken
  Chestnuts Boulettes
  Artichokes, Hollandaise
  Potato croquettes
  Endive salad
  Vanilla ice cream
  Alsatian wafers
  Demi tasse

Eggs, Sarah Bernhardt. Soak half a pound of salt codfish in water over night, then boil for ten minutes, and shred it. Put twelve beaten eggs in a casserole, season with a little salt and pepper, add two chopped truffles, the shredded codfish, and half a cup of thick cream; and then scramble. When done dish up in a deep china dish and lay sliced truffles heated in butter, on top.

Consommé with noodles. Boil one-half pound of noodles in salted water. When done add them to two quarts of hot consommé. Serve grated cheese separate.

Fillet of halibut, Pondicherry. Place four fillets of halibut in a sauté pan, season with salt and pepper, add one-half cup of fish broth and one-half glass of white wine, cover with buttered paper, and bake in oven for ten minutes. Heat two ounces of butter in a casserole, add one teaspoonful of flour and one of curry powder, heat through, then add the broth from the fish and a cup and a half of fish broth additional, and boil for ten minutes. Then bind the sauce with the yolks of two eggs mixed with half a cup of cream, season with salt and pepper, and strain. Then put the sauce back in the casserole, add two ounces of sweet butter, and when the butter is melted pour the sauce over the fish.

Chestnuts Boulettes. One cup of boiled and mashed chestnuts, one tablespoonful of whipped cream, one-half tablespoonful of butter, a pinch of salt, the yolks of two eggs, a little sugar, the whites of two eggs well beaten, and if desired, one teaspoonful of sherry wine Mix well together, form into small balls, dip in beaten eggs, roll in crumbs, and fry in hot swimming fat.

OCTOBER 7

BREAKFAST
Sliced bananas with cream
Sausage cakes
Buckwheat cakes
Rolls
Coffee

LUNCHEON
Fresh artichokes à la Russe
Eggs bonne femme
Broiled Alaska black cod
Paul Stock potatoes
Cucumber salad
Limberger cheese with crackers
Coffee

DINNER
Little Neck clam cocktail
Onion and tomato soup
Ripe California olives
Sand dabs, sauté meunière
Sirloin steak, Braconière
New peas in cream
Rissolée potatoes
Escarole salad
Roly-poly pudding
Coffee

Fresh artichokes à la Russe. Boil the bottoms of four artichokes in salted water, and allow them to become cold. Then fill them with fresh caviar, place on a platter on a folded napkin, and garnish with two lemons cut in half and parsley in branches.

Eggs bonne femme. Fry eight slices of bacon on both sides, in a frying pan, then add eight eggs, season with a little pepper, and cook in oven for three minutes. Serve on a platter, with mixed chopped parsley, chervil and chives sprinkled over the eggs.

Paul Stock potatoes. Bake four potatoes, remove the peels, and put the potatoes in a chafing dish. Add three ounces of sweet butter, season with salt and paprika and a spoonful of chives cut fine, and mix with a fork until the butter is melted. Serve in a chafing dish.

Onion and tomato soup. Slice four onions very fine, put in a casserole with two ounces of butter, and simmer until done. Then add four peeled and chopped tomatoes, and two quarts of bouillon, chicken broth, or consommé. Season with salt and pepper, and boil for half an hour. Serve grated cheese separate, and rolls cut in thin slices and toasted.

Sirloin steak, Braconière. Broil a sirloin steak, place on a platter, and garnish with onions glacés and broiled fresh mushrooms. Pour sauce Madère over the steak.

Roly-poly pudding. One pound of suet, one pound of flour, one cup of milk, and one pinch of salt. Chop the suet very fine, mix with the flour, salt and milk, making a rather hard dough. Roll out about one-quarter inch thick, and spread with a layer of any kind of jam. Roll up in the form of a sausage, put a wet cloth around it, and tie with a string at both ends. Steam or boil for an hour. Then unwrap, cut in individual pieces, and serve hot, with hard and brandy sauces.

OCTOBER 8

BREAKFAST
    Fresh strawberries with cream
    Ham and eggs
    Rolls
    Coffee

LUNCHEON
    Grapefruit à la rose
    Eggs, Boston style
    Lamb or mutton chops, Bignon
    String beans
    Mashed potatoes
    Tutti frutti pudding
    Demi tasse

DINNER
    Seapuit oysters
    Consommé Pemartin
    Celery.   Salted almonds
    Brook trout, Cambacérès
    Cucumber salad
    Breast of squab, Eveline
    Asparagus, Hollandaise
    Coupe Victor
    Ginger bread
    Demi tasse

Eggs, Boston style. Make four codfish cakes, put a poached egg on top of each, and cover with cream sauce.

Lamb or mutton chops, Bignon. Broil the chops, place on a platter, and garnish with one tomato stuffed with rice Créole to each person, one dozen green olives, and a small can of French mushrooms. Cut the mushrooms in small squares, put them in a sauté pan with one-half glass of sherry wine and cook until nearly dry. Then add two cups of brown sauce (sauce Madère), and pour over the chops.

Tutti frutti pudding. Sift one-quarter of a pound of flour into a sauce pan, add one pint of boiling milk and two ounces of butter, and stir over the fire with a wooden spoon, until it detaches from the pan. Then remove from the fire and add two ounces of butter, four ounces of sugar, the yolks of eight eggs, and four ounces of chopped candied fruits. Mix well. Beat the whites of six eggs very stiff and add them to the mixture, stirring them in lightly. Put in a buttered mould, and cook in bain-marie in the oven for about thirty minutes. When done unmould, and serve with apricot sauce flavored with a little kirschwasser.

Consommé Pemartin. Chop two truffles very fine, put in a casserole with one large glassful of Pemartin sherry wine and boil for two minutes. Then add two quarts of consommé, season well with salt and Cayenne pepper, and serve very hot.

Brook trout, Cambacérès. Season six brook trout with salt and pepper and place in a shallow buttered dish with one-half glass of white wine. Sprinkle with chopped tarragon, pour two pints of tomato sauce over all, lay a few bits of butter on top, and bake in the oven for twenty or thirty minutes, according to the size of the fish. Serve in the dish in which they were cooked.

Breast of squab, Eveline. Broil the breasts, and place on a platter with maître d'hôtel sauce on top. Garnish one side with spaghetti in cream and the other side with new peas in butter.

Ginger bread. One quart of flour, one ounce of butter, half a pint of molasses, two teaspoonfuls of allspice, a teaspoonful of ginger, two eggs, and a quarter of a teaspoonful of carbonate of soda. Sift the flour, the allspice and the ginger together. Pour a spoonful of hot water on the soda, and mix with the molasses, the eggs, and the melted butter. Then stir all together, mixing well, and bake in a thin layer; or divide into small rolls or cakes.

Coupe Victor. Take equal parts of raspberries and strawberries; and to each basket allow four spoonfuls of sugar and four spoonfuls of kirschwasser. Mix well, and set on ice to chill thoroughly. If there is not time to chill in this manner cover with cracked ice for a few minutes. Serve in punch glasses with a teaspoonful of lemon water ice on top. The water ice may be omitted if desired, but be sure to have the fruit well chilled.

OCTOBER 9

BREAKFAST
Fresh grapes
Broiled smoked Alaska black cod
Baked potatoes
Rolls
Coffee

LUNCHEON
Carciofini
Eggs Argenteuil
Chicken hash à l'Italienne
Cranberry water ice
Assorted cakes
Coffee

DINNER
Merry widow cocktail
Chicken soup à la Française
Celery
Scallops à la poulette
Roast leg of mutton
Stewed tomatoes
Peas in cream
Duchesse potatoes
Chicory salad
French pastry
Demi tasse

Broiled smoked Alaska black cod. Get a kippered Alaska black cod, roll in oil and broil. Serve with maître d'hôtel butter, and garnish with lemons cut in half, and parsley in branches. This fish is excellent prepared in the same manner as finnan haddie or smoked salmon, or served raw as a hors d'oeuvre.

Eggs Argenteuil. Scoop out the centers from four English muffins, toast them, and place a poached egg in each, cover with sauce Hollandaise, and lay two slices of truffle heated in butter on top of each.

Chicken hash, Italienne. Put two ounces of butter in a sauté pan with one chopped onion, or six chopped shallots. Fry, and then add one-half spoonful of flour and cook until brown. Then add one glass of sherry wine, and one cup of broth or stock, one whole boiled fowl cut in small dices, and one pound of dried mushrooms that have been previously soaked in cold water for one hour. Season with salt and pepper, and boil all together for thirty minutes. Serve toast Melba separate.

Chicken soup à la Française. Put a fat soup hen in a casserole with three quarts of water, a little salt, one onion, one carrot, and a bouquet garni. When coming to a boil skim well, cover, and simmer slowly until the hen is cooked.

Then remove the hen and cut the meat in half inch squares. Strain the broth, bring to a boil, and add two cupfuls of boiled rice and the chicken meat. Season well with salt and pepper, and add some chopped chervil.

Merry widow cocktail. Use wide glasses. Put in the bottom the tails of six écrevisses, or crawfish. Lay six asparagus tips on top, season with salt and pepper, and cover with plenty of mayonnaise. Set in the ice box as near the ice as possible, to chill thoroughly.

Scallops à la poulette. Parboil the scallops from two to three minutes in their own juice, but not longer, as they will become tough and rubbery. Drain, and keep the juice. Heat two spoonfuls of flour and two spoonfuls of butter, and add the juice and a little stock, making a thin sauce. Season with salt and pepper, add the yolk of one egg and two spoonfuls of cream, but do not boil. Mix in the scallops, and serve. Oysters and clams may be prepared in the same manner.

Cranberry water ice. Cook the berries in a very small quantity of water in a granite or porcelain lined kettle, as otherwise the berries will become discolored. Then strain the cooked berries through a hair-sieve, making a thin purée. To every quart of berries add the juice of two lemons. For each quart of berries dissolve a pint of sugar in a cup of water, and add to the purée. Taste to see if sweet enough. Freeze in the same manner as other water ices. Serve as an ice, for dessert, or between courses; although the latter manner of serving ices is going out of vogue.

OCTOBER 10

BREAKFAST
  Baked pears with cream
  Plain omelet
  Buttered toast
  Ceylon tea

LUNCHEON
  Cantaloupe
  Eggs Andalouse
  Broiled Imperial squab on toast
  Saratoga chip potatoes
  Cold artichokes, mayonnaise
  Montmorency pudding
  Coffee

DINNER
  Oysters on half shell
  Cream of summer squash
  Dill pickles.   Salted almonds
  Fillet of flounder, Norvegienne
  Roast tenderloin of beef, Boucicault
  Julienne potatoes
  Hearts of romaine salad
  Red currant water ice
  Assorted cakes
  Demi tasse

Eggs Andalouse. Make a risotto, place it on a platter, lay a poached egg on top, and cover with sauce Hollandaise. Pour tomato sauce around the rice to cover the bottom of the platter.

Cream of summer squash. Put three ounces of butter in a casserole, add two pounds of peeled summer squash cut in small pieces, and simmer for fifteen minutes. Then sprinkle with two small spoonfuls of flour, heat the flour through, and then add two quarts of chicken or other clear white broth. Boil for ten minutes, season with salt and pepper to taste, strain through a fine sieve, put back in the casserole, and before serving add one pint of boiling thick cream.

Fillet of flounder, Norvegienne. Place four fillets of flounder in a buttered pan, season with salt and pepper, add one-half glass of white wine and one-half cup of fish stock, cover, and cook for ten minutes. Place on a platter, some spinach in cream, lay the fish on top, and cover with sauce Hollandaise.

Roast tenderloin of beef, Boucicault. Put a roast tenderloin of beef on a platter, and garnish with stuffed cabbage. Pour sauce Madére over the meat.

Montmorency pudding. Butter a pudding mould very generously. Line it with stale cake, putting quartered fresh or glacé cherries on each piece. Make a custard with four eggs, a quarter of a pound of sugar and a pint of milk. Pour this over the cake, filling the mould. Bake for thirty minutes. Then remove from mould and serve hot, with brandy sauce to which has been added some fresh or glacé cherries chopped fine.

Red currant water ice. Strain one quart of ripe red currants. Canned ones may be used when the fresh are out of season. Add the juice of two lemons, and additional sugar, if necessary. Dissolve the sugar in hot water before adding. Freeze, using plenty of salt with the ice.

OCTOBER 11

BREAKFAST
Sliced peaches and cream
Boiled eggs
English breakfast tea
Butter toast

LUNCHEON
Hors d'oeuvres assorted
Eggs McKenzie
Meat croquettes
Cucumbers on toast
Camembert cheese. Crackers. Coffee

DINNER
Oysters on half shell
Hungarian soup   Ripe California olives
Halibut Metternich
Baked porterhouse steak
Potatoes rissolées
Plain spinach
Lettuce salad
Mince pie. American cheese. Coffee

Hungarian soup. Sauté half a pound of lean beef that has been cut into small cubes. Add six onions, thoroughly minced, and when slightly brown add four tablespoonfuls of flour. Mix well. Add three quarts of stock and a quart of tomatoes that have been strained through a sieve. Simmer slowly for one hour. Then add a teaspoonful of caraway seeds, half as much marjoram, and a large crushed garlic clove. Cook for another half hour or longer, very slowly. The stock should be made with a knuckle of veal and beef.

Baked porterhouse. Have a thick steak. Put into a Dutch oven, sprinkle with salt and pepper, and two ounces of butter. On top place three whole peeled tomatoes, one green pepper, two tablespoonfuls of Worcestershire sauce, two of mushroom or tomato catsup and a little chopped parsley. Baste frequently.

Meat croquettes. Chop a large onion and simmer in a pan with two ounces of butter. Mince the meat, and add one raw egg and mix well. Season with pepper, salt and some chopped parsley, and add a quarter cup of brown gravy. Allow to cool, roll out and form into croquettes. Dip in a mixture made of one egg and a spoonful of cream, and roll in sifted crumbs. Fry in swimming fat. Serve with tomato or Madeira sauce.

Eggs McKenzie. Peel four tomatoes, cut off the tops and scoop out the insides. Break an egg in each tomato, season with salt and pepper, cover with a little Bordelaise sauce, sprinkle with grated cheese, put small bits of butter on top, place on a buttered dish and bake in oven.

Cucumbers on toast. Peel and quarter two good sized cucumbers, and soak in salted water for about thirty minutes. Then boil in slightly salted water until tender, but not soft. Drain, and place each piece on a round of buttered toast. Make a sauce by rubbing together a tablespoonful of butter and a tablespoonful of flour, stir in a cup of the water in which the cucumbers were boiled, add a teaspoonful of lemon juice, salt and pepper to taste, and pour over the cucumbers and toast. Garnish with strips of pimentos.

Halibut Metternich. Cut two slices of halibut, one and one-half inches thick. Put in a vessel in cold water, season with salt, bring to a boil, and skim. Add a glass of milk, boil for about twenty-five minutes, until soft. Make a sauce in a casserole with two spoonfuls of butter, and two spoonfuls of flour. When hot add two cups of the fish broth, boil for ten minutes, and strain. Then add six chopped hard-boiled eggs and salt and pepper to taste. Put the fish on a buttered baking dish, pour the sauce over same, sprinkle with grated cheese, put small bits of butter on top, and bake in the oven until brown.

OCTOBER 12

BREAKFAST	LUNCHEON
Fresh strawberries and cream	Grapefruit cardinal
Baked beans, Boston style	Clam broth in cups
Boston brown bread	Eggs Conté
Coffee	Veal sauté, Catalane
	Romaine salad
	Assorted cheese and crackers
	Coffee

DINNER
Consommé Nelson
Radishes and celery
Sand dabs, meunière
Coquille of chicken, Mornay
Roast leg of mutton, Kentucky sauce
String beans in butter
Potatoes Anna
Field and beet salad
Charlotte Russe
Demi tasse

Eggs Conté. Butter a shirred egg dish. Place a spoonful of cooked lentils in center of dish, cover with two strips of fried bacon, break two eggs on top, season with salt and pepper, and bake in oven till eggs are done.

Veal Sauté, Catalane. Cut five pounds of breast and shoulder of veal in pieces two inches square. Put three spoonfuls of olive oil in a sauté pan and set on the stove until hot, then add the veal, season with salt and pepper, and toss over a quick fire until golden brown. Then sprinkle one spoonful of flour and cook until golden yellow. Add one pint of hot water or stock, six peeled and chopped tomatoes, one crushed garlic clove, and a bouquet garni. Bring to a boil, skim well, and cover. Boil until meat is soft. Before serving remove the bouquet garni, and add two dozen small onions glacés, and two dozen stoned queen olives.

Consommé Nelson. Put three pounds of fish bones and three quarts of water in a casserole, also one sliced onion, one carrot, one piece of leek, one leaf of celery, a little parsley in branches, one bay leaf, one clove, and season with salt and pepper. Boil for one-half hour, and clarify as follows: In a casserole put one pound of raw chopped beef and the whites of six eggs. Mix well. Add, little by little, the strained fish broth, set on the stove and bring to a boil. Then put to one side and allow to simmer for fifteen minutes. Strain through cheese cloth or napkin, add two cups of boiled rice, season well, and serve.

Coquille of chicken, Mornay. Boil a soup hen. When done cut the meat from the bones, and slice in thin pieces. Season with salt and pepper, add a cup of cream sauce, and mix. Then place in four buttered coquilles or shells, cover lightly with more cream sauce, sprinkle with grated cheese, put small bits of butter on top, and bake in oven until brown. Serve on platter with folded napkin, garnish with two lemons cut in two, and parsley in branches.

OCTOBER 13

BREAKFAST
Oatmeal in cream
Boiled eggs
Dry toast
Coffee

LUNCHEON
Cantaloupe
Scrambled eggs, Magda
Chicken sauté, Josephine
Asparagus tips, Hollandaise
Escarole salad
Danish apple cake.   Demi tasse

DINNER
Oysters on half shell
Potage Villageois
Lyon sausage.   Radishes.   Pickles
Fillet of sole, Judic
Tenderloin steak, Bernardi
Potatoes Sybil
Endive salad
Fancy ice cream and cakes.   Coffee

Scrambled eggs, Magda. In a casserole put two ounces of butter, twelve beaten eggs, one-half cup of cream, season with salt and pepper, and then scramble. When nearly done add one tablespoonful of grated Swiss cheese, one-half teaspoonful of mustard flour, and one tablespoonful of mixed, chopped parsley, chervil and chives.

Chicken sauté, Josephine. Cut two spring chickens in quarters, and season with salt and pepper. In a sauté pan put two ounces of butter and a spoonful of olive oil. Set on the stove until hot, add the chicken, and sauté. When nearly done add six chopped shallots, one tablespoonful of carrot cut in very small dices, one bay leaf cut very fine, one-half of a clove, a little parsley, and two heads of mushrooms, all chopped very fine. Also one spoonful of raw ham cut in very small squares. When the chicken is cooked remove to a platter, and to the sauté pan add one pony of brandy and reduce one-half. Then add two more ounces of sweet butter and the juice of a lemon, and pour over the chicken.

Danish apple cake. Pare and core six apples. Mix one and one-half cups of fine bread crumbs, one-half cup of sugar and one-half teaspoonful of cinnamon. Butter a deep cake mould and put a layer of the crumb mixture, with a bit of butter, at the bottom. Then a layer of the sliced apples, and continue alternately until the material is all used. Bake in a moderate oven for about two hours, and serve cold with whipped cream.

Potage Villageois. In a casserole put three ounces of butter and three stalks of leeks cut in Julienne shape. Simmer for fifteen minutes. Then add six leaves of Savoy cabbage, cut Julienne, and simmer again for ten minutes. Then add two quarts of stock, bouillon, chicken broth or consommé, season well with salt and pepper, and boil for forty minutes. Then add one-half pound of vermicelli and boil for fifteen minutes, or until the vermicelli is done.

Fillet of sole, Judic. Put four fillets of sole in a buttered pan, season with salt and pepper, put a little butter on top, squeeze the juice of a lemon over all, and bake in the oven until done. Then place four pieces of lettuce braisé on a platter, lay the fillets on top, cover with cream sauce, sprinkle with grated cheese, put small bits of butter on top, and bake again in the oven until brown.

Tenderloin steak, Bernardi. Broil a tenderloin steak. Place on a platter and garnish with croustades filled with spinach in cream, and artichoke bottoms filled with macédoine of vegetables. Pour some sauce Madére over the meat.

OCTOBER 14

BREAKFAST
  Stewed prunes
  Bacon and eggs
  Coffee
  Rolls

LUNCHEON
  Eggs Nantaise
  Pompano sauté, d'Orsay
  Broiled honeycomb tripe
  Maitre d'hôtel potatoes
  Lettuce salad
  Apple snow and cakes
  Coffee

DINNER
  Potage Champenoise
  Ripe olives
  Boiled brook trout, Romanoff
  Hollandaise potatoes
  Shoulder of mutton, Budapest
  Peas à la Française
  Laurette potatoes
  Celery mayonnaise
  Biscuit glacé, St. Francis
  Assorted fancy cakes
  Demi tasse

Eggs Nantaise. Split and toast two English muffins. Lay a few boiled asparagus tips on each half. Put a poached egg on top and cover with cream sauce.

Pompano sauté, d'Orsay. Season the pompano with salt and pepper, roll in flour and fry with melted butter. Then place the fried fish on a platter, and sprinkle with plenty of chopped parsley and lemon juice. In a hot pan put two ounces of butter, and when brown pour over the fish.

Apple snow. Peel, core and slice three large apples. Preferably sour ones. Cook in a little water and vinegar until soft. Then drain, and rub the apples through a sieve. When cold gradually add the whites of three eggs whipped very stiff, and half a cup of powdered sugar. Dress in dishes of fancy shape, and garnish with dots of currant jelly.

Potage Champenoise. Mix one quart of cream of potatoes with one quart of cream of celery. Add as garniture one-half cup of carrots and celery cut in very small dices, and boiled soft in consommé.

Boiled brook trout, Romanoff. Put six one-half pound trout in boiling water, to which has been added one-half glass of vinegar, and cook for about fifteen minutes. Serve on a platter on folded napkin. Garnish with parsley in branches and two lemons cut in half. Serve separate, sauce mousseline, to which has been added six chopped anchovies.

Shoulder of mutton, Budapest. Season the mutton well with salt and pepper and place in a roasting pan with a sliced carrot, an onion, a few branches of parsley, a leaf of celery and of leek, a few pepper berries, half of a bay leaf and a clove. Put an ounce of butter on top, and roast. Then remove the shoulder to a platter, drain off fat, and add to the pan one cup of bouillon and a spoonful of meat extract. Boil for a few minutes and strain over the meat. Garnish with risotto to which has been added a few pimentos cut in small squares.

OCTOBER 15

BREAKFAST
Fresh raspberries and cream
Waffles
Honey in comb
English breakfast tea

LUNCHEON
Herring Livonienne
Eggs en cocotte, Ribeaucourt
Beef tongue, Menschikoff
Potato salad
Roquefort cheese and crackers
Coffee

DINNER
Cream of peas, Suzon
Celery.   Radishes.   Pickles
Fillet of pompano, Pocharde
Roast tame duckling, apple sauce
Fried sweet potatoes
Succotash
Stewed tomatoes
Chocolate ice cream
Macaroons
Demi tasse

Herring, Livonienne. Soak two salted herrings in cold water for two hours. Then skin and bone them, and cut in half inch squares. Add one sliced boiled potato, and a peeled apple cut in small squares. Salt a little if necessary, season with pepper, one spoonful of olive oil and the juice of two lemons. Serve on a celery dish, sprinkled with chopped tarragon and parsley.

Eggs en cocotte, Ribeaucourt. Butter four cocotte dishes and break an egg in each. Cut in small squares, two slices of tongue, one slice of boiled ham, and four heads of canned mushrooms. Mix with two spoonfuls of brown gravy, season with salt and pepper, and put on top of the eggs. Sprinkle with a little grated cheese, and bake in the oven for eight minutes.

Beef tongue, Menschikoff. Place some sliced boiled beef tongue on a platter and garnish with small onions glacé, small vinegar pickles, and Madeira sauce with a few raisins in it.

Cream of peas, Suzon. Make a cream of peas soup. Add one spoonful of whipped cream for each person, and mix while hot. Put a poached egg on each plate and serve the soup over the eggs.

Cream of peas. To one quart of shelled new peas add one pint of chicken broth, and boil until the peas are soft. Strain and return to casserole and add one pint of hot table cream, and, little by little, one large spoonful of table butter. Season with salt and Cayenne pepper.

Cream of peas, St. Germain. Add a head of lettuce to the peas and prepare as above. When strained for the second time add one cup of fresh-boiled new peas to the soup.

Fillet of pompano, Pocharde. Cut four fillets of Florida pompano. Or Pacific pompano may be used. The latter are much smaller. Put the fish in a buttered pan, and season with salt and pepper. Add one-half glass of claret, one-half glass of white wine, and one-half cup of fish broth. Boil until done. In a sauce pan put one table spoonful of flour and place on stove. When hot add the broth in which the fish were cooked, and boil for five minutes. Then bind the sauce with the yolks of two eggs mixed with one-half cup of cream and one ounce of butter. Whip well and strain over the fish.

OCTOBER 16

BREAKFAST
Baked apples in cream
Boiled eggs
Dry toast
Coffee

LUNCHEON
Casawba melon
Eggs Mollet, à l'aurore
Sweetbreads, Saint Mondé
Lettuce salad
Mince pie
American cheese
Demi tasse

DINNER
Potage grenade
Salted almonds
Écrevisses Georgette
Roast leg of mutton, mint sauce
String beans
Mashed potatoes
Tomato salad
French pastry
Coffee

Eggs Mollet, à l'aurore. Place four eggs Mollet on four pieces of buttered toast. Cover with well seasoned tomato sauce.

Sweetbreads, Saint Mondé. Prepare braised sweetbreads as described elsewhere. Place on a platter and garnish with artichoke bottoms filled with asparagus tips with a little Hollandaise sauce on top; and others filled with French peas in butter with Madeira sauce.

Potage grenade. Cut in thin slices, the size of a silver quarter, two turnips, one stalk of leeks, one-half stalk of celery and a small head of Savoy cabbage. Put in a sauce pan with three ounces of butter, season with salt and a teaspoonful of sugar, and place in the oven to smother. Be careful that it does not burn. When soft add two quarts of consommé, and boil for one-half hour. Then add two tomatoes peeled and cut in small dices, boil for one minute, season with salt and pepper, and serve with a little chopped chervil.

Écrevisses Georgette. Bake four medium-sized potatoes. Then cut off the tops, remove the insides, and refill with Écrevisses Voltaire.

Écrevisses Voltaire. Boil two dozen écrevisses en buisson. Remove the tails from the shells and place them in a sauce pan with two ounces of butter and six sliced heads of fresh white mushrooms. Season with salt and a little Cayenne pepper, and simmer for ten minutes. Then add a pony of brandy, and simmer for a few minutes. Then add a large cup of cream, and boil for five minutes. Then add two sliced truffles. Bind with the yolks of two eggs mixed with one-half glass of dry sherry wine. Serve in chafing dish.

OCTOBER 17

BREAKFAST
Oatmeal and cream
Ham and eggs
Coffee
Rolls

LUNCHEON
Mortadelle
Poached eggs, Zurlo
Broiled honeycomb tripe
Lyonnaise potatoes
Field salad
Port de Salut cheese
Crackers
Coffee

DINNER
Consommé Leopold
Chow chow
Broiled smelts, à l'Américaine
Chicken Leon X
Peas à la Française
Duchesse potatoes
Lettuce and grapefruit salad
Fancy ice cream
Assorted cakes
Demi tasse
Mint wafers

Mortadelle. This is an Italian sausage, very highly seasoned, and comes in cans already sliced. Serve on a platter garnished with chopped meat, jelly and parsley in branches.

Poached eggs, Zurlo. Form some flat potato croquettes, and fry. Place a poached egg on top of each, and cover with cream sauce.

Consommé Leopold. Slice very fine one handful of sorrel and a head of lettuce. Wash well, and boil in two quarts of chicken broth for about thirty minutes. Serve with chervil.

Broiled Smelts, à l'Américaine. Split and remove the bones from twelve large smelts. Season with salt and pepper, roll in oil, and broil. When done place on a platter, garnish with six slices of broiled tomatoes, two lemons cut in half, and parsley in branches. Pour a little maître d'hôtel sauce over all.

Chicken Leon X. Put on fire, in cold water, one large fat roasting chicken or capon. Add salt, one carrot, and a bouquet garni. Boil until soft. Make a sauce with two ounces of butter mixed with two ounces of flour. When hot add one pint of the chicken broth. If too thick add a little more of the broth. Boil for half an hour. Then bind with the yolks of three eggs mixed with a cup of cream. Strain, and add two ounces of sweet butter. Stir the sauce well until the butter is melted. Place the chicken on a platter and garnish with macaroni cooked in cream. Pour a little of the sauce over the chicken. To the remainder of the sauce add in equal parts some sliced truffle, sliced canned French mushrooms and parboiled goose liver. Serve this sauce separate.

Mint wafers (after dinner mints). To half a gill of water add one pound of powdered sugar, and mix over fire until dissolved and hot. Add three or four drops of oil of peppermint. Then drop, about the size of a half silver dollar, on waxed paper or a greased pan, using the tip of a spoon or a paper bag. Allow to become cold and dry.

OCTOBER 18

BREAKFAST
  Grapefruit juice
  Poached eggs on toast
  Uncolored Japan tea
  Crescents

LUNCHEON
  Omelette Cherbourg
  Homemade beef stew
  Lorette salad
  Alhambra ice cream
  Assorted cakes
  Demi tasse

DINNER
  Cream of asparagus, Favori
  Salted mixed nuts.   Celery
  Sole Héloise
  Roast leg of veal, au jus
  Spinach in cream
  Potatoes au gratin
  Romaine salad
  Pancakes à la Lieb
  Demi tasse

Omelette Cherbourg. Mix a cup of picked shrimps with two spoonfuls of cream sauce. Heat well, and season with salt and pepper. Make the omelette in the usual manner, and before turning over on platter fill with the prepared shrimps. Pour a thick cream sauce around the omelette.

Lorette salad. One-third field salad, one-third boiled celery root, and one-third pickled beets. Season with French dressing.

Alhambra ice cream. Half vanilla and half strawberry ice cream served in any fancy form.

Cream of asparagus, Favori. Make a cream of asparagus soup and serve wtih plenty of boiled asparagus tips in it.

Sole Héloise. Remove the skin from both sides of a large sole. Place on a buttered pan, season with salt and pepper, add one-half glass of white wine, cover with a piece of buttered manila paper, and bake in the oven for about twenty minutes. Remove the sole to a platter, and put in the pan three ounces of butter, a little pepper, chopped parsley, chervil, tarragon, and chives. When hot add the juice of two lemons, season well, and pour over the sole.

OCTOBER 19

BREAKFAST
  Fresh strawberries and cream
  Broiled fresh mackerel
  Baked potatoes
  Rolls
  Coffee

LUNCHEON
  California oyster cocktail
  Consommé in cups
  Shirred eggs, Metternich
  Pears, mayonnaise
  Cheese toast
  Coffee

DINNER
  Potage Ferneuse
  Ripe olives
  Sand dabs, sauté meunière
  Roast ribs of beef
  String beans in butter
  Stewed tomatoes
  St. Francis potatoes
  Escarole salad
  Romaine ice cream
  Alsatian wafers
  Demi tasse

Shirred eggs, Metternich. Place two eggs in a buttered shirred egg dish with six canned mushrooms sliced very fine. Season with salt and pepper, sprinkle with grated cheese, place a small piece of butter on top, and bake.

Pears, mayonnaise. Use whole fresh pears cooked in syrup, or canned ones. Place the pears on lettuce leaves and cover with thick mayonnaise. On slices of toast place small pieces of American dairy cheese. Bake in the oven, and serve separate.

Cheese toast. Spread any such cheese as Parmesan, American, Sierra or Camembert, on slices of toast, and set in the oven until hot. Serve at once.

Potage Ferneuse. Slice six white turnips very fine, put in a casserole, with two ounces of butter. Cover, and simmer for fifteen minutes. Then add one cup of rice and three pints of bouillon, consommé, or chicken broth. Boil for one hour, strain through fine wire sieve, and put back in vessel. When hot stir in well three ounces of sweet butter, season with salt and a little Cayenne pepper.

Romaine ice cream. To coffee ice cream add a little rum before serving.

OCTOBER 20

BREAKFAST
  Baked apples
  Oatmeal and cream
  English breakfast **tea**
  Crescents

LUNCHEON
  Hard boiled eggs, vinaigrette
  Fried scallops, Tartar
  Broiled squab on **toast**
  Stewed corn
  Romaine salad
  Camembert **cheese**
  Crackers
  Coffee

DINNER
  Toke Point oysters
  Potage bouquetière
  Celery
  Fresh herring, à l'Egyptienne
  Small boiled potatoes
  Cucumber salad
  Chicken en cocotte, Bazar
  Cold asparagus, mustard **sauce**
  French pastry
  Assorted fruits
  Demi tasse

Hard boiled eggs, vinaigrette. Remove the shells from six hard boiled eggs, and cut in two. Place them on a china platter, sprinkle with salt, pepper, chopped parsley, a little chopped chervil, one spoonful of vinegar **and two** of olive oil.

Potage bouquetière. Consommé, tapioca and printanier mixed.

Fresh herring, à l'Egyptienne. Clean four fresh herring, season with salt and pepper, and fry in hot olive oil. Remove the fish to a platter, and add to the frying pan one sliced onion, and fry until done. Then add two peeled and quartered tomatoes, one bay leaf, one clove, and a sprig of thyme. Season with salt and pepper, and simmer for a few minutes. Then put the fish back in the pan, add the juice of two lemons and a little chopped parsley, and simmer together for five minutes. Serve both fish and sauce on a platter.

Chicken en cocotte, Bazar. Season a spring chicken with salt and pepper, and put in a cocotte (earthen casserole) with two ounces of butter and **six** small onions. Set in the oven, and baste well until golden yellow. Then add one spoonful of white wine and two peeled and quartered tomatoes. Cover the casserole and simmer for ten minutes. Add two dozen Parisienne potatoes and serve.

OCTOBER 21

BREAKFAST
  Stewed prunes
  Ham and eggs
  Rolls
  Coffee

LUNCHEON
  Grapefruit à la rose
  Eggs, ministerielle
  Beef goulash, Hungarian style
  Mince pie
  Coffee

DINNER
  Consommé Diane
  Chow chow.   Salted almonds
  Sole Déjazet
  Roast chicken
  Summer squash
  Château potatoes
  Lettuce salad
  Vanilla ice cream
  Assorted cakes
  Coffee

Consommé Diane. Take any game bird, such as grouse, partridge, quail, pheasant or guinea hen, and roast just enough to give a color. Then put in soup stock and boil until soft. Clarify the broth with chopped beef, and stain. Cut the breast out of the bird, cut in small squares, and serve in the consommé. Add some dry sherry wine and a little Cayenne pepper before serving.

Sole Déjazet. Remove the skin from a good sized sole, wash well, and dry in a napkin. Season with salt and pepper, dip in milk, roll in flour, then in beaten eggs, and finally in bread crumbs. Put in frying pan with melted butter and fry until done. Place on a platter, and pour some butter, which has been browned in a pan, over the fish. Lay a dozen tarragon leaves on top of the fish, garnish with quartered lemons and parsley in branches.

OCTOBER 22

BREAKFAST
  Baked apples with cream
  Omelette with chipped beef
  Rolls
  Coffee

LUNCHEON
  Hors d'oeuvres assorted
  Smoked black Alaska cod in cream
  Lamb kidneys en pilaff
  Mashed potatoes
  Camembert cheese
  Almond biscuits
  Coffee

DINNER
  California oysters on half shell
  Potage Livonien
  Olives.   Salted pecans
  Alsatian fish
  Roast ribs of beef
  Canned asparagus, Hollandaise
  Rissolées potatoes
  Escarole salad
  Lemon pie, special
  Coffee

Potage Livonien. In a casserole put one onion chopped fine, and three ounces of butter. Simmer until yellow. Then add one-quarter of a pound of sliced sorrel and one-half pound of sliced spinach. Simmer again for ten minutes. Then add one quart of chicken broth and one large cup of cream sauce. Boil one-half hour. Season well, and serve.

Smoked Alaska black cod in cream. Remove the skin from two pounds of smoked Alaska black cod. Cut in pieces two inches square, lay in a sauté pan, add one pint of thick table cream and boil for five minutes. Then thicken with the yolks of two eggs mixed with a little cream. Serve in a chafing dish.

Alsatian fish. Heat two tablespoonfuls of oil and thicken with one table, spoonful of flour. Remove from the fire and thin out with boiling water. Chop fine some parsley, onions and two cloves of garlic, and add to the pan. Season the fish with salt and pepper, place in the sauce, and cook for about twenty minutes.

Lamb kidneys en pilaff. Slice fine a half dozen lamb kidneys, and prepare in the same manner as chicken livers en pilaff. (See January 8th.)

Almond biscuit. To every ounce of almond flour add the whites of two eggs beaten to a stiff froth. Salt to taste and beat well together. Put in buttered patty tins and bake in a moderately quick oven from fifteen to twenty minutes. The whole must be done quickly, and baked as soon as the ingredients are mixed.

Lemon pie, special. Mix in saucepan the yolks of sixteen eggs, three-quarters of a pound of sugar, and the juice and rinds of six lemons, and cook over a slow fire until it thickens. Then remove from the fire and stir in the whites of eight eggs beaten very hard. Pour the mixture into two pie plates, lined with thin pie dough, and bake in a medium hot oven for about twenty-five minutes.

OCTOBER 23

BREAKFAST
Prunes Victor
Boiled eggs
Coffee and rolls
Snails (bread)

LUNCHEON
Avocado, French dressing
War griddle cakes
Tripe, Wm. H. Crane
Mashed potatoes
Coffee

DINNER
Orange and grapefruit, St. Francis
Stuffed chicken with California
     raisins
Rice Californienne
Lettuce and tomato salad
Olympic club cheese
Coffee

War griddle cakes. Soak stale bread in sour milk. Add enough flour or corn meal to make a batter. To a gallon add three eggs, baking powder, and salt. Cook in the same manner as wheat cakes.

Orange and grapefruit, St. Francis. Sliced oranges and grapefruit, in equal parts. Sprinkle with powdered sugar, and moisten with Dubonnet. Serve in double supreme glasses with a few fresh strawberries on top.

Prunes Victor. Put two pounds of dry prunes in an earthen pot, add two quarts of water, the rind of a lemon, one stick of cinnamon, one-half cup of sugar, and a vanilla bean. Put on hot stove and bring to a boil. Then move to one side of fire and simmer slowly for six hours. Or, set in a moderate oven for six hours. Allow to become cool, and add a pony of good cognac. Use the prune juice for a morning drink, and serve the prunes with cream.

Chicken stuffed with raisins. Soak a small loaf of bread in warm milk, squeeze out lightly, and add an equal volume of raisins. Season with salt and pepper, fill the chicken, and roast in the usual manner.

California raisins may be used in many dishes, such as soup, fish, entrees, roasts, bread, puddings, ice cream, etc.

Rice Californienne. Wash a pound of rice in cold water. Chop an onion, smother in butter, add the rice, one quart of broth, and season with salt and pepper. Bring to a boil, cover, and set in oven for thirty-five minutes. Before serving add one-half cup of grated cheese.

Tripe, Wm. H. Crane. Wash the tripe well, and cut in round pieces about five inches in diameter. Place them in a saucepan with a few carrots, two or three onions, some whole peppers, salt, white wine, and good white broth. Boil until thoroughly tender. Then place the tripe in a stone jar and strain the liquid over it. Keep in a cool place. When needed turn them in flour, and fry quickly in a frying pan in very hot butter. Serve with some parsley butter.

Avocado, French dressing. Split the avocado, remove the pit, and fill half full with a dressing made with salt, pepper, a little French mustard, and one-third vinegar and two-thirds olive oil.

French dressing. Two teaspoonfuls of salt, one teaspoonful of mustard, one-quarter teaspoonful of black pepper, one-half teaspoonful of paprika, the juice of one lemon, and the same amount of vinegar.   Put in a quart bottle, fill with olive oil, and shake thoroughly.

Salad dressing.   One-half cup of tomato catsup, one-half cup of cream, two teaspoonfuls of lemon juice, and black and red pepper and salt to taste.

Snails.   Dissolve one ounce of yeast in warm water. Make a dough with one pound of flour, four ounces of sugar, two eggs, two ounces of butter, two ounces of lard, one ounce of salt, one cup of water, and the dissolved yeast, Allow to raise for about an hour. Then roll the dough into a square sheet about one-quarter inch thick.   Brush over with butter and bestrew with sugar, cinnamon, and currants.   Roll the sheet into a roll and cut in slices one-quarter inch thick.   Lay the slices on a greased pan and allow to raise until double the size.   Bake in a moderate oven.

Olympic club cheese.   Scrape clean three best quality camembert cheeses. Put in a copper casserole with one-quarter pound of good Roquefort cheese, one-half pound of table butter, two tablespoonfuls of sifted flour and one pint of cream. Boil until the whole is melted together.   Then strain through cheese cloth, put in an earthen pot, and allow to become cool.

OCTOBER 24

BREAKFAST
   Stewed rhubarb
   Omelette with parsley
   Spoon or mush bread
   Coffee

LUNCHEON
   Oysters Bellevue
   Cold Virginia ham
   Corn pudding
   Loganberry ice cream
   Lady fingers
   Demi tasse

DINNER
   Canapé P. P. I. E.
   Onion soup au gratin
   Ripe olives
   Roast turkey, cranberry sauce
   Sweet potato pudding
   Coffee

Canapé P. P. I. E. (Panama-Pacific International Exposition). Make some pieces of buttered toast. Put fresh caviar in the center and anchovies around the edge. Serve on napkins with quartered lemons and parsley in branches.

Oysters Bellevue. In a lighted chafing dish put four pats of table butter, one-half teaspoonful of English mustard, a little salt, pepper and celery salt. Stir until the butter melts. Then add a teacupful of very finely chopped celery, and stir well until the celery is nearly cooked. Then pour in slowly, while stirring, one pint of rich cream, and allow to come to the boiling point. Then put in a dozen freshly opened oysters and cook for four or five minutes. Add a tablespoonful of good sherry or Madeira, and serve on very hot plates.

Spoon or mush bread. Scald two cups of corn meal in two cups of boiling water, allow to cool slightly, then add one cup of buttermilk, one teaspoonful of soda, two tablespoonfuls of lard or butter (butter preferred), one egg, and salt to taste. If you have no buttermilk use baking powder and sweet milk.

Corn pudding. One quart of corn cut from the ear and chopped fine, one egg, a tablespoonful of butter, and salt and pepper to taste. Thin with sweet milk, and bake in a hot oven.

Sweet potato pudding. Grate a large sweet potato and mix with one cup of sugar, one-half cup of butter, and two or three eggs, according to the size of the potato. Thin with sweet milk, flavor with ginger and spices, or vanilla can be used. Beat the eggs well before adding to the mixture. Bake in a moderate oven very slowly. The potatoes in the west are not as sweet as the southern variety, therefore more sugar may be required. A good rule is to bake a small portion first to see if the flavor is right. It is considered a luxury in certain parts of the South.

Loganberry ice cream. Put in a pan one quart of milk and one-half pound of sugar, and place on the fire. Mix the yolks of sixteen eggs with one-half pound of sugar. Stir the milk and sugar, after it has reached the boiling point, into it. Replace on the fire and stir until it becomes creamy, but do not let it boil. Then remove from the fire, add one quart of cream, strain and freeze. When nearly frozen add one quart of bottled loganberry juice, and finish freezing. A few drops of red coloring can be added if a bright color is desired.

OCTOBER 25

BREAKFAST
  Baked prunes
  Scrambled eggs
  Corn bread (2)
  Cocoa

LUNCHEON
  Anchovy salad
  Lamb hash, J. A. Britton
  Cheese cake
  Coffee

DINNER
  Cold artichokes, St. Francis dressing
  Brook trout, Café de Paris
  Breast of chicken, James Woods
  Salad Algerienne
  Frozen loganberry juice
  Macaroons

SUPPER
  Welsh rabbit, special
  Raisin bread
  Ale

Baked prunes. Select large prunes, place them in a baking pan side by side so they hardly touch, cover with water and cook in a moderate oven for an hour. Then pour off three-quarters of the juice, which may be kept for a beverage, and to the prunes add a little sugar, a stick of cinnamon, and the rind of a lemon. Cover the pan tightly, place back in a moderate oven and bake for at least one hour.

Corn bread (II). Put in a pan one egg beaten light, one cup of milk, one tablespoonful of sugar, one-half teaspoonful of salt, one cup of yellow corn meal, one cup of flour, and two and one-half teaspoonfuls of baking powder. If too thin add a little more white flour. Beat well together, and add four tablespoonfuls of melted butter or bacon drippings.

Graham bread. Same as for corn bread, but use no white flour.

Raisin bread. Warm one pint of milk and dissolve one-half ounce of yeast in it. Then add two ounces of butter, two eggs, two ounces of sugar. a pinch of salt and one-half pound of raisins. Mix well. Then stir in two pounds of flour, and make a smooth dough. Allow to raise for about three hours. Then fold the dough, put it in moulds, and let it again raise for about one hour. Bake in a moderate oven for about forty-five minutes.

Lamb hash, J. A. Britton. Take even quantities of left over roast lamb and mashed potatoes and pass through a fine meat chopper. Season well, add a piece of sweet butter, some chopped parsley and a little bouillon, and cook together. Serve hot, with a fried egg on top.

St. Francis dressing. One green pepper, an equal amount of raw celery and an equal amount of hard boiled eggs all chopped fine. Add one-half cup of Chili sauce, one-half cup of mayonnaise, one tablespoonful of white wine vinegar, two spoonfuls of olive oil, and salt, pepper and Cayenne. Mix well. Can be served with almost any kind of salad.

Brook trout, Café de Paris. Butter well an earthern dish, sprinkle with chopped shallots and parsley, lay the trout on top, season with salt and pepper, add a little white wine and fish broth, lay a few pieces of butter on top, and bake in oven until done. Serve in the dish in which they were cooked.

Breast of chicken, James Woods. Remove the skin from a nice young roasting chicken, lift off the breasts, season with salt and pepper, roll in cream, then in flour, and fry in butter. Place on a buttered shirred egg dish a piece of toast, then a thin slice of broiled Virginia ham, then the breasts of chicken, then a few heads of fresh mushrooms tossed in butter, then a little cream and a piece of butter, season all well, cover with a glass mushroom cover, and bake in oven for ten minutes.

Salad Algerienne. Sliced pineapple, oranges, grapefruit and bananas **in**

equal quantities. Serve in a bowl with lettuce leaves around the sides, and mayonnaise dressing made with plenty of lemon juice.

Frozen loganberry juice. Mix one quart of loganberry juice, one quart of water, one pound of sugar, and the juice of two lemons. Strain and freeze.

Welsh rabbit. Break an egg in a deep plate, add a teaspoonful of vinegar, and English mustard, paprika and salt to taste. Mix thoroughly. Then grate or crumble four ounces of good American cheese, place in a chafing dish, and add a small quantity of ale or beer. Just enough to keep the cheese from frying. Use a hot flame, and with two forks in one hand stir continually, in one direction. Do not permit the cheese to boil. When the cheese is melted add the egg and seasoning, and stir until blended. Then add a pinch of bicarbonate of soda, and serve on buttered toast which has been previously prepared. The rabbit can be prepared for any number of persons by allowing four ounces of cheese to each person, and one egg for each pound, or less, of cheese.

Cheese cake. Work thoroughly together one and one-half cup of butter and one and one-half cup of sugar until it is creamy. Then stir in eight eggs, one by one, then the juice and rind of one lemon, then one and one-half pound of cottage cheese, then one cup of cream and four spoonfuls of flour. Bake in spring form pans lined with thin pie dough.

OCTOBER 26

BREAKFAST
Oatmeal with cream
Bacon and eggs
Mixed bran biscuits
Coffee

LUNCHEON
Little Neck clams, mignonette
Consommé in cups
Cold Virginia ham
Lettuce salad
Pink pudding, Victor
Demi tasse

AFTERNOON TEA
Brioche
Coffee cake
Tea, chocolate or coffee

DINNER
Purée of pea soup
Ripe olives
Sand dabs, meunière
Saddle of lamb, jardinière
Hearts of palm, Victor
Figs Roma
Lady fingers
Demi tasse

Brioche. Dissolve one ounce of yeast in one gill of tepid water and add about one-third of a pound of flour, to make a medium firm sponge. Cover with a cloth and set in a warm place to raise. Then work into a smooth paste two-thirds of a pound of flour, three-quarters of a pound of butter, one ounce of sugar, a little salt, and six eggs. Beat the eggs in gradually. Then spread the sponge over the top and mix into the paste. Cover with a cloth and allow to raise until double in size. Then work together again, and place in a box for several hours to harden before using. Mould into small round balls, place in baking pans, and allow to raise until about one-third above their original size. Brush over with egg, make a cross-cut on top, and bake in a rather brisk oven.

Coffee cake. Put one pound of flour in a bowl. Dissolve an ounce of yeast in a gill of lukewarm milk, add it to the flour with two eggs, and work to a medium-stiff dough. Cover with a cloth and allow to raise till double in size. Then work in thoroughly three ounces of butter, two ounces of sugar, a pinch of salt, a pinch of nutmeg, and the juice and rind of one lemon. Allow to raise again for about an hour, when the dough will be ready to bake. This dough is the foundation for all kinds of coffee cake.

Pink pudding, Victor. Cook one-quarter pound of rice in one quart of milk with a vanilla bean and one-half pound of sugar. When done allow to cool, and then add one quart of whipped cream, some chopped fruits, and one drop of red coloring. Dissolve four sheets of gelatine in a little warm milk, stir into the above, put into moulds, and set in ice box until firm. Serve with fruit sauce.

Figs Roma. Line a bowl (timballe) with lady fingers. Put a layer of vanilla ice cream in the bottom, then a layer of about a dozen peeled and quartered figs, sprinkle this with good rum, cover thickly with sauce au marasquin, and sprinkle some macaroon crumbs on top. Serve in plates with ice around the bowl.

Four o'clock tea bran bread. Make a batter with two cups of bran, one cup of Educator entire wheat flour, one cup of white flour, one-half teaspoonful of salt, one teaspoonful of soda, one-half cup of molasses, one-half cup of water and two cups of milk, or one cup of milk and another one of water. Spread the batter about one inch thick in the pan, and cook in a slow oven.

Wheat bran gems. Make a batter with two cups of wheat bran, one cup of whole wheat flour, one teaspoonful of baking soda, one-half cup of molasses, three tablespoonfuls of hot milk, and three tablespoonfuls of boiling water. Put the dough in buttered gem pans, and cook for about twenty-five minutes.

Bran bread. Mix together two cups of wheat bran, one and one-half cups of flour, one-half teaspoonful of salt, one teaspoonful of soda, one-half cup of molasses, one-half cup of water, and two cups of milk, or one cup of milk and another cup of water. Put the dough in the pans about one inch thick, and bake in a slow oven.

Bran biscuits. Mix two cups of wheat bran, one cup of white flour, two teaspoonfuls of baking powder, one very small teaspoonful of salt, a piece of lard the size of an egg, and enough milk to make a stiff dough. Work well together, roll out about a half an inch thick, cut out with forms, and bake in a slow oven.

Hearts of palm, Victor. Hearts of palm can be obtained in cans similar to asparagus, and may be served in the same way, with Hollandaise, Polonaise, vinaigrette, or other sauces. Hearts of palm, Victor, is served cold, with Victor dressing (see April 21).

OCTOBER 27

BREAKFAST
Oatmeal
Strawberries with cream
Lamb chops with bacon
Boiled eggs
Rolls
Coffee

LUNCHEON
Grapefruit with maraschino
Consommé in cup
Salted almonds
Loin of pork, apple sauce
Lettuce salad
Meringué glacée à la vanille
Black coffee

DINNER
Purée of peas, Varsovienne
Olives
Celery
Sand dabs, sauté meunière
Roast chicken
Mashed potatoes
Canned asparagus, sauce Hollandaise
Escarole salad, French dressing
Omelet with strawberries
Coffee

Oatmeal. To one quart of water, boiling, add eight ounces of cracked wheat. Boil for one-half hour. Salt.

Consommé. Mix one-half pound of beef, chopped fine, with one white of an egg. Add slowly one quart of stock and let boil for half hour. Strain through napkin or fine cheese cloth.

Loin of pork. Place pork in roasting pan and pepper and salt well. Add one sliced onion, carrot, bay leaf, clove, a little celery and one teaspoonful of whole black peppers. Put in moderate oven and roast for about one and one-quarter hours. Baste often to keep juicy and of a fine color. When done remove from pan, skim part of the fat from the gravy and add one-half spoonful of flour, let simmer till brown, add one cup of stock and boil for a few minutes.

Purée of pea soup. Soak three-quarters of a pound of green split peas in cold water for three hours. Wash well and put on fire in cold water. Put in sauté pan one sliced onion, carrot, stalk of leek, a little celery and parsley, a bay leaf and clove, and a ham bone or skin of bacon or salt pork. Simmer in butter until soft. Add the peas and boil together until soft. Salt and pepper to taste and strain through sieve. If too thick add some stock of broth of any kind.

Varsovienne. Fried thin-sliced bacon.

Aux croutons. Bread cut in small dices and fried in butter.

Sand dabs, meunière. Remove the skin from the sand dabs, salt, pepper and roll in flour, and fry in fresh butter in shallow frying pan. When brown remove fish to platter, place piece of butter in pan, cook till brown, and pour over fish. Add the juice of one lemon and chopped parsley. Garnish the platter with parsley and quartered lemons.

Roast chicken, plain. Prepare sauce as for loin of pork. Omit flour for thickening. Serve with its own gravy.

Hollandaise sauce. Put the yolks of five eggs in saucepan. Place the saucepan in pot containing very hot water, on range. Stir the yolks well and add pieces of sweet butter the size of a hazelnut, until one pound is used. As the butter melts in the eggs be careful that the sauce does not get too hot. Add salt and Cayenne pepper to taste.

Salted almonds. Scald the almonds, allow to cool and remove the thin paper-shells. Put the almonds on a pan and roast in hot oven until brown. Wet with a solution of gum arabic and water, using about four teaspoonfuls to the pound of nuts. Dust over with table salt and stir until dry.

Meringue shells. To the whites of eight eggs use one pound of powdered sugar. Beat the whites very firm and stiff. Add a handful of sugar and beat thoroughly. Remove the whip and stir in the remainder of the sugar with a large spoon. Form in the size of an egg and dress on a buttered pan dusted with flour. Sprinkle with powdered sugar and bake in a moderate oven.

Vanilla ice cream. One pint of cream, one quart of milk, eight yolks of eggs, half pound of sugar and one vanilla bean. Place the milk, half of the sugar and the split vanilla bean on the fire to boil. Mix the remainder of sugar with the yolks of eggs, stir in the boiling milk and cook until creamy. Allow to cool, strain and freeze.

Plain omelet. Beat six eggs. Put in hot frying pan a piece of butter, add the eggs and roll quickly over hot fire to form. Salt. For a sweet omelet sprinkle with sugar.

Omelet with strawberries. Dust a plain omelet with plenty of powdered sugar. Burn bands across the top with a red-hot poker or special iron, and garnish with stewed strawberries.

Stewed strawberries. Wash a basket of strawberries thoroughly. Dry in napkin and roll in two ounces of granulated sugar. Put in saucepan and place on fire. Allow to remain until sugar is melted and berries are soft. Do not leave on fire too long.

French dressing for salad. To one-third of white wine vinegar use two-thirds of olive oil. Mix with salt, pepper, a little powdered mustard, dash of Worcestershire sauce and a little paprika.

Coffee. To seven ounces of ground coffee use two quarts of water. (Use eight ounces for after dinner coffee.) If you do not use a special coffee percolator pour the boiling water over the grounds, contained in a bag. Draw off and repeat twice.

Plain celery. Stalks of celery well washed and split in four.

Ripe olives. California olives allowed to ripen on the trees, and specially prepared in packing houses. Serve with cracked ice.

Oysters on half shell. Serve on cracked ice with half of lemon or lime.

OCTOBER 28

BREAKFAST
Cantaloupe
Hominy with cream
Scrambled eggs with smoked beef
Dry toast
Coffee

LUNCHEON
Canapé of caviar
Radishes
Hungarian goulash
Potato croquettes
Assorted fruits

DINNER
Purée of tomato soup
Celery
Boiled codfish, egg sauce
Roast leg of lamb
String beans in butter
Potatoes rissolées
Chicory salad
Vanilla ice cream
Lady fingers
Coffee

Hominy. To one quart of boiling water add eight ounces of hominy. Cook twenty minutes. Salt to taste. Serve cream separate.

Scrambled eggs plain. Beat six eggs, add two ounces of butter, spoonful of cream and a little salt and pepper. Stir on fire with a wooden spoon until cooked.

Scrambled eggs with smoked beef. Slice the beef very thin. Boil in water for a few minutes, add the eggs and serve on toast.

Canapé of caviar. Spread caviar, which has been kept on ice, on thin toast. Sprinkle thick with chopped hard-boiled eggs all around. Garnish with leaf of lettuce filled with chopped onion, parsley in branches, and one-fourth of a lemon. Serve on napkin.

Hungarian goulash. One pound of shoulder of veal, one pound loin of lean pork. Cut in pieces one inch square. Mix a little flour, salt, pepper and plenty of paprika. Put in sauce pan a piece of butter, two chopped onions and the fat from the loin of pork. Simmer till brown, then add the meats and flour; a little bouillon, stock or water; one-half cup of purée of tomatoes, a little thyme, one bay leaf, one clove and a little chopped parsley and celery. Cover tight and cook for three-quarters of an hour. Then add three potatoes cut the same as the meat, and cook till done.

Beef goulash. Same as the above except use beef, and the fat of pork, only.

Potato croquettes. Boil one pound of potatoes. Pour off water and let evaporate well. When quite dry mash fine, mix with the yolks of two eggs, salt and pepper. Roll on floured board into the form of a large cork. Dip in flour, then in beaten raw eggs, then in bread crumbs, and fry in swimming lard.

Purée of tomatoes. Put in sauce pan one sliced onion, a little celery and leek, one bay leaf, one clove, a spoonful of whole peppers, piece of butter, piece of hambone or pig skin, and allow to simmer. Then add one gallon of fresh or canned tomatoes, salt, and a teaspoonful of sugar. When cooked add a piece of butter. Strain well.

Purée of tomato soup. Add some chicken broth or bouillon to the purée of tomatoes. Serve bread crumbs fried in butter

Boiled codfish, or any white fish. Put fish in cold water. Add cup of milk to keep it white. Salt and boil. When done let stand for ten minutes. Serve on napkins with small boiled potatoes, parsley in branches, and quartered lemons.

Egg sauce. Add some chopped boiled eggs to cream sauce. Sprinkle with a little chopped parsley.

Cream or Béchamel sauce. Melt two ounces of butter in two ounces of flour. When warm, but not brown, add one pint of boiling milk. Stir well and cook for a few minutes. Strain.

String beans. Boil in salt water. Place in pan, add piece of butter and salt and pepper.

Escarole salad. Serve with French dressing. This salad goes well with piece of bread rubbed with garlic, and served in bowl.

Chicory salad. Serve with French dressing. Use crust of bread rubbed with garlic if desired.

OCTOBER 29

BREAKFAST
Stewed prunes
Pettijohns in cream
Ham and eggs
Rolls
Tea

LUNCHEON
Chicken broth in cups
Lamb hash
Cheese balls
Lettuce salad
Coffee

DINNER
Little Neck clams on shell
Giblet soup, English style
Frog legs, sauté à sec
Roast teal duck
Fried hominy and currant jelly
Boiled artichokes, Hollandaise sauce
Romaine salad
Philadelphia ice cream
Macaroons
Coffee

Pettijohns. To one quart of boiling water add eight ounces of Pettijohns. Cook ten minutes. Salt. Serve cream separate.

Fried ham. Thin slices of raw ham fried in butter. If fried too much ham will get hard.

Fried eggs. Use strictly fresh eggs and fry in hot butter. Salt and pepper.

Ham and eggs. Put ham in frying pan and fry one side. Turn, and crack eggs on top and fry.

Chicken broth. Put to boil in cold water two fat soup hens. Skim well, add one-half onion, a little celery, salt to taste, and cook for three hours, when fowls should be soft. Strain the bouillon and serve in cups. The cooked fowls may be used for sandwiches, chicken salad, chicken à la King, etc.

Boiled fowl. See chicken broth above.

Lamb hash. Cut cold boiled or roast lamb in small dices. Add one-half as much cold boiled potatoes. Put piece of butter in saucepan with one chopped onion and simmer until brown. Add lamb and potato, salt, pepper, cup of stock or bouillon and cook for ten minutes. Serve on toast with chopped parsley.

Cheese balls. Mix one and one-half cups of grated Parmesan or American cheese, one tablespoonful of flour, one-quarter teaspoonful of salt, a few grains of Cayenne pepper and the whites of three eggs beaten stiff. Shape in small balls or croquettes, roll in cracker dust, fry in deep fat and drain on brown paper. New lard is necessary for frying, and they must not stand, but serve immediately.

Lettuce salad. Wash, dry in napkin, and serve with French dressing.

Giblet soup à l'Anglaise. (English style). Cut turkey or chicken gizzards in small dices. Also a carrot, turnip, piece of celery and a piece of leek. Add one-third pound of barley, large spoonful of flour and four ounces of butter. Simmer all together, add two quarts of stock or bouillon, season with salt, pepper and teaspoonful of Worcestershire sauce and cook for one hour. Serve with a sprinkle of chopped parsley.

Frogs' legs sauté à sec. Season the frogs' legs with salt and pepper and dip in flour. Put a piece of butter in sauté pan and place on stove over a quick fire. When hot add the frogs' legs and fry for a few minutes. Remove to a chafing dish and put a fresh piece of butter in the sauté pan, brown, and pour over the legs, with chopped parsley, and garlic, if desired.

Roast teal duck. Season with pepper and salt and roast in very hot oven for ten minutes. Rare, seven and one-half minutes.

Fried hominy. Boil ten ounces of hominy in one quart of water for thirty minutes. Spread in pan to a depth of one inch or more, to cool. Cut in diamond shape one-quarter inch thick, roll in flour, beaten eggs and bread crumbs, and fry in swimming fat.

Boiled artichokes. Boil in salt water with a few slices of lemon. When soft serve on napkins with parsley in branches. Sauce separate.

Romaine salad. Romaine should not be washed, or the leaves broken Wipe with a napkin if it is dusty and serve with French dressing.

Philadelphia ice cream. Dissolve one-half pound of sugar in one quart of cream. Flavor to taste. Strain and freeze.

Little Neck clams on shell. Serve on cracked ice with half a lemon or lime.

OCTOBER 30

BREAKFAST
  Sliced oranges
  Force and cream
  Poached eggs on toast
  Coffee

LUNCHEON
  Canapé Hambourgeoise
  Broiled honeycomb tripe,
    maître d'hôtel
  Lyonnaise potatoes
  Field salad
  German apple cake
  Coffee

DINNER
  Purée of lentils
  Ripe olives
  Fillet of sole, au vin blanc
  Lamb chops with bacon
  Asparagus tip salad
  Tartelette with pears
  Coffee

Sliced oranges. Peel and slice the oranges and put on compote dish. Serve powdered sugar separate.

Force and cream. Serve raw with powdered sugar and cream separate.

Poached eggs. Break the eggs in boiling water, to which may be added a soupspoonful of vinegar if desired. Add plenty of salt to the water to take away the vinegar taste. Serve on toast and garnish with parsley in branches.

Canapé Hambourgeoise. Place on toast one sliced gherkin with a slice of smoked salmon on top, and a little anchovy sauce in center. Garnish around edge with chopped boiled egg, parsley and lemon.

Boiled honeycomb tripe. Cut honeycomb tripe in round pieces, five inches in diameter. Put in vessel with one onion, carrot, bay leaf, clove, a little celery and thyme and whole black peppers. Cover with water, salt and boil until done.

Broiled honeycomb tripe. Take boiled tripe, roll in olive oil, then in fresh bread crumbs, and broil. Serve with lemon and parsley garnishing, and maître d'hôtel sauce on top.

Maître d'hôtel sauce. One-quarter pound of fresh butter, juice of one lemon, and chopped parsley. Mix well. This sauce is not to be used hot.

Lyonnaise potatoes. Slice an onion, fry in butter, and mix with sauté potatoes.

Field salad. Wash and clean the salad well. Serve with French dressing and chopped parsley.

Purée of lentils (soup). Put in pot one pound of well-washed lentils and one quart of stock. Skim when it comes to a boil, and salt. Put in sauté pan an onion, carrot, bay leaf, clove, some parsley, celery, leek, whole black pepper, a ham bone or small piece of pigskin, and a piece of butter, and allow to simmer. Add to the lentils, and boil. When done strain through sieve and serve with small dices of bread fried in butter.

Fillet of sole, au vin blanc. Remove the skin from the fillets of sole. Put in buttered pan, add salt and a little Cayenne pepper, one-half glass of white wine, and one-half glass of stock. Cover with buttered manilla paper and put in oven to boil. When done put on platter and cover with sauce "au vin blanc." (See below.)

Sauce au vin blanc (white wine sauce). Cut up some large fish bones, put in pot and cover with water. Add salt, an onion, carrot, bay leaf, clove, a little thyme and whole black peppers. Boil for half an hour. Put in another saucepan three ounces of butter. When warm add two spoonfuls of flour, stir, add the strained fish stock; also add the stock left from the fillets, and boil for ten minutes. Beat well the yolks of two eggs and one-half cup of cream, and thicken the sauce with same. Strain.

Lamb chops with bacon. With each broiled lamb chop serve two slices of broiled bacon. Garnish with watercress.

Asparagus tip salad. Canned asparagus tips garnished with lettuce leaves. Serve with French dressing.

German apple cake. Make a dough with one pound of flour, one pound of butter, one cup of milk and a pinch of salt. Line a cake pan with the dough rolled thin, and cover with sliced apples. Dust some powdered sugar mixed with ground cinnamon over the apple, and bake. When nearly done pour over it a custard made of one pint of milk, one-quarter pound of sugar and three eggs, mixed well. Put again in the oven until the custard is set.

Tartelette of pears. One pound of flour, one-half pound of butter, two ounces of sugar, two eggs, one pinch of salt and one pony of water. Rub the butter into the flour, then add the sugar, salt, eggs and water. Work it lightly to a rather firm dough. Line some tartelette molds thinly with the dough. Peel and slice the pears and arrange them in the tartelette, put a pinch of sugar mixed with a very little cinnamon, on top. Place in a pan and bake. While they are baking mix one pint of apricot pulp with three-quarters of a pound of sugar, and boil for a few minutes. When the tartelettes are done remove from the moulds, and use a brush to coat the tops with the apricot marmalade. Allow to cool before serving.

OCTOBER 31

BREAKFAST
  Bananas in cream
  Buckwheat cakes
  Fried country sausages
  Cocoa

LUNCHEON
  Cold poached egg with mayonnaise
  Broiled finnan haddie
  Rump steak, Bércy
  Château potatoes
  Pickled beets
  Assorted fruits

DINNER
  Cream of cauliflower
  Butterfish, sauté meunière
  Shoulder of veal, au jus
  Carrots, Vichy
  Duchess potatoes
  Watercress salad
  Roquefort cheese
  Toasted crackers
  Coffee

Bananas and cream. Peel and slice the bananas. Serve cream and powdered sugar separate.

Buckwheat cakes. One-quarter pound of buckwheat flour, one-quarter pound of white flour, one tablespoonful of baking powder, one ounce of sugar, one ounce of molasses, one egg and just enough milk to make a thin dough. Mix well and cook on hot iron plate rubbed with a piece of raw lard. Serve with strained honey or syrup, separate.

Mayonnaise sauce. Put in bowl three yolks of eggs, a pinch of salt, a little Cayenne pepper, a pinch of English mustard flour and a dash of Worcestershire sauce. Stir well. Add, little by little, one pint of olive oil and an occasional few drops of vinegar or lemon juice. When finished, stir in one spoonful of boiling water, which will keep the sauce from curdling.

Cold poached eggs with mayonnaise. Serve on the top of toast. Pour mayonnaise over the egg, only. Garnish with lemon quarters and parsley.

Finnan haddie in cream. Remove the skin and bones and boil for one minute in plain water. Then separate the fish in small pieces, add one cup of cream and one-half cup of cream sauce, and boil for ten minutes. Serve in chafing dish.

Rump steak, Bércy. Broil steak. Sauce Bércy as follows: Simmer slightly in butter two chopped shallots. Add half cup of sauce maître d'hôtel, and one parboiled marrow, cut in small pieces. Pour over steak and put in oven for two minutes. Serve with chopped parsley.

Château potatoes. Cut raw potatoes in shape of a half-moon, and the size of an egg. Put in cold water, salt, and boil for five minutes. Then place in pan with butter and roast in oven for ten minutes. Salt again.

Boiled beets. Wash the beets well and boil with the skin on, in salt water. When soft remove the skin with the fingers while still hot.

Pickled beets. Use fresh-boiled and very hot beets. Put in a piece of cheese cloth, one onion, bay leaf, clove and one spoonful of whole black peppers, and tie tightly together. Place this in center of earthern pot with a layer of the hot sliced beets around the sides and over the top. To each dozen beets put four pieces of lump sugar on top. Salt and cover with white wine vinegar. Let stand, covered, at least two days before serving. If not all used at once, a wooden spoon must be used to remove the beets from the pot, otherwise they will spoil.

Cream of cauliflower soup. Put in saucepan one-half onion, a little leek, a piece of butter the size of two eggs, and let simmer slowly. Add one cup of flour, simmer a little more. Put in the stems of cauliflower and one quart of milk, boil till done, and strain through sieve. Put in pot, add one gill of cream and piece of sweet butter and stir well until butter is melted. Add salt and a little Cayenne pepper. Cut the heart of the cauliflower in small flowers, boil in salt water until soft, and add before serving.

Butter fish, meunière. See sand dabs, meunière.

Shoulder of veal, au jus. Roast either with or without bones. If boneless roll and tie firmly with a string. Season with salt and pepper and put in pan with an onion, carrot, bay leaf, clove and piece of butter. Put in oven and baste often. When done remove meat to platter, put a little water in the pan and let simmer for a few minutes, and add to the veal.

NOVEMBER 1

BREAKFAST
  Fresh figs in cream
  Boiled eggs
  Milk toast
  Coffee

LUNCHEON
  Smoked salmon
  Broiled sweetbreads
  New peas
  Moka cake
  Tea

DINNER
  Old fashioned pepper pot
  Celery
  Lake Tahoe trout, Sauce Génoise
  Hollandaise potatoes
  Roast mallard duck
  Fried hominy
  Currant jelly
  Summer squash in butter
  Vanilla ice cream
  Champagne wafers
  Coffee

Fresh figs in cream. Peel and slice the figs, and cool on ice before serving. Powdered sugar and cream separate.

Milk toast. Put in soup tureen the toast, in small pieces, and cover with boiling milk.

Smoked salmon. Slice the salmon very thin, serve on lettuce leaves, with quartered lemon and parsley in branches on the side.

Broiled veal sweetbreads. Soak the sweetbreads in cold water for two hours. Parboil and cool in cold water, and dry with a napkin. Split, salt and pepper, dip in oil and broil. Serve with maître d'hôtel sauce.

New peas, plain. Boil peas in salt water. When done allow to cool. Then put in saucepan with a piece of fresh butter, a little salt and a pinch of sugar, and allow to simmer for a few seconds.

Lake trout, boiled. In three quarts of water boil an onion, carrot, bay leaf, clove, some whole black pepper, salt, parsley and one glass of vinegar. Pour over fish and boil slowly for fifteen minutes. Serve on napkin garnished with lemon, parsley in branches and small round boiled potatoes.

Sauce Génoise. Take a raw salmon head, (a trout head will do), and cut in small pieces. Put in sauté pan with a piece of butter, a sliced onion, carrot, thyme, bay leaf, cloves, and some whole black pepper, and simmer for fifteen minutes. Then add one glass of claret, reduce; add one quart of brown gravy, cook for ten minutes and strain. Before serving stir in well the juice of one lemon and a piece of fresh butter. Sprinkle with chopped parsley.

Hollandaise potatoes. Shape potatoes in the form of a small egg. Boil in salt water, drain off and evaporate well. Serve on napkin.

Roast mallard duck. Roast about sixteen or eighteen minutes. See teal duck.

Summer squash in butter. Peel the squash and cut in quarters. Remove the seeds, and boil in salt water for five minutes. Put in sauté pan with a piece of butter and simmer slowly till soft. Salt and pepper, and sprinkle chopped parsley on top.

NOVEMBER 2

BREAKFAST
  Stewed rhubarb
  Boiled salt mackerel
  Plain boiled potatoes
  Dry toast
  Coffee

LUNCHEON
  Canapé of anchovies
  Omelette du Czar
  Spring lamb Irish stew
  Camembert cheese
  Crackers
  Coffee

DINNER
  Cream of celery soup
  Barracouda sauté, aux fines herbes
  Larded tenderloin of beef
  String beans
  Baked potatoes
  Sliced tomatoes, French dressing
  Vanilla custard pie
  Demi tasse

Boiled salt mackerel. Soak the mackerel in water over night. Boil in plenty of water and serve on napkin with lemon and parsley.

Canapé of anchovies. Lay split anchovies on thin buttered toast with chopped eggs around the edges. Serve on napkin, with lemon and parsley in branches.

Omelette du Czar. Pour horseradish sauce in cream, around the edge of a plain omelet.

Spring lamb Irish stew. Take four pounds of neck, shoulder and breast of lamb and cut in pieces two inches square. Put in vessel with cold water and salt, and bring to a boil. Drain off and cool the meat, put back in vessel in sufficient water to cover, with a boquet garni, one dozen small onions, one dozen small carrots, (large carrots may be cut to size of onions), two dozen raw potatoes cut in small oval shapes, and salt. Put on fire and cook till soft. remove bouquet garni, mix one cup of flour with cold water and strain into the boiling stew, stirring at the same time. Boil for five minutes. Before serving add chopped parsley and a spoonful of Worcestershire sauce, if desired.

Cream of Celery Soup. Use celery instead of cauliflower, and prepare the same as cream of cauliflower.

Baracouda sauté, aux fines herbes. Put seasoned fish, well rolled in flour, in pan in hot butter. When done lay fish on platter, and brown a fresh piece of butter in pan. Add the juice of one lemon, and pour over the fish. Serve with chopped parsley, chervil and chives.

Larded Tenderloin of Beef. Trim the tenderloin. Lard with fresh or salt pork cut in two inch strips, one-quarter of an inch square. Lay on in rows three-quarters of an inch apart, starting from the thick end of the tenderloin and continuing its entire length. Put in pan with a sliced onion, sliced carrot, bay leaf, clove, parsley in branches, and some butter on top of the meat. Put in oven and baste continuously for about thirty-five minutes. Remove the grease from the pan, add one cup of stock or water, reduce, salt, pepper and strain. Madeira sauce may be served with same if desired.

Sliced tomatoes, French dressing. Peeled tomatoes garnished with leaves of lettuce, and French dressing over same.

Vanilla custard pie. Six eggs, one quart of milk, one-half pound of sugar, and half of a vanilla bean. Mix the eggs with the sugar, add the milk. and strain. Line a large pie dish with thin pie dough. Fill with the custard and bake in moderate oven until set.

NOVEMBER 3

BREAKFAST
  Orange marmalade
  English breakfast tea
  Tea biscuits
  Ham and eggs

LUNCHEON
  Grapefruit
  Bouillon in cups
  Boiled beef, horseradish sauce
  Vegetable garnishing for beef
  Romaine salad
  Apple pie
  Coffee

DINNER
  Petite marmite
  Broiled lobster
  Potted squab chicken, plain
  Waffle potatoes
  Peach compote
  Boiled artichokes, Hollandaise sauce
  Coffee ice cream
  Pound cake
  Demi tasse

Tea biscuits. Three pounds of flour, one-half pound of butter, one quart of milk, three ounces of baking powder, three ounces of sugar, and a little salt. Sift the sugar, salt and baking powder with the flour; add the butter and milk, and make a dough on the table about one-half inch thick. Cut with a round cutter about the size of a dollar, place in a buttered pan, moisten the top with milk, and bake in a hot oven for about fifteen minutes.

Boiled beef with vegetables. The meat should be juicy, well-flavored and tender. The brisket, cross rib and rump are the best portions. The wide ribs at the end of a rib roast are also very good. Tie the beef with a string and put into boiling water; clear from scum, add salt, and garnish with carrots, onions, turnips, celery, leeks and Savoy cabbage. The cabbage may be tied with a string to prevent disintegration. A good way is to put all the vegetables into a net as they can thus be withdrawn at once. Allow the meat to simmer gently on the side of the range, but do not let it come to a boil. When done cut in slices, not too thin, and garnish with the vegetables neatly arranged around the beef. Serve separately, either cream horseradish sauce, piquante, tomato, or bouillon horseradish sauce. A little of its own broth should be poured over the meat before serving.

Horseradish sauce in cream. Cream sauce with fresh-grated horseradish and salt and pepper.

Horseradish sauce with bouillon. Put two fresh-grated horseradish roots in sauté pan with four ounces of butter. Cover and put in oven for five minutes. Add two grated rolls and return to oven for two minutes more. Then add bouillon enough to form the sauce. The bread will swell and give the necessary body. Add a pinch of sugar, salt and pepper.

Cold horseradish sauce, English style. To two fresh-grated horseradish roots add salt, a teaspoonful of English mustard, a teaspoonful of Worcestershire sauce, and a spoonful of vinegar, mixed well. Then add one pint of stiff-whipped cream.

Bouillon. Broth from boiled beef, strained.

NOVEMBER 4

BREAKFAST
Casaba melon
Boiled eggs
Cold Lyon sausage
Rolls
Coffee

LUNCHEON
Consommé in cup
Pompano sauté, Tempis
Broiled veal chops
St. Francis potatoes
Brazilian salad
Brie cheese Toasted crackers Coffee

DINNER
Cherrystone oysters on half shell
Cream of artichokes
Boiled rock cod, sauce fleurette
Sirloin steak, sauce Madére
Broiled fresh mushrooms
Delmonico potatoes
Celery Victor
Bavarois à la vanille
Macaroons
Coffee

Lyon sausage. An imported sausage. Slice thin and garnish with chopped meat jelly and parsley in branches.

Pompano sauté, meunière. Prepare the same as sand dabs, meunière. Sprinkle with chopped salted almonds over top.

Broiled veal chops. Salt and pepper the chops and dip in olive oil. Broil over slow charcoal broiler. Serve with maître d'hôtel sauce and watercress.

St. Francis potatoes. Peel three cold baked potatoes, chop veryfine, put in sauté pan with one-half pint of cream, three ounces of butter, salt and pepper. Simmer for five minutes.

Brazilian salad. Proportions should be one-half Lima beans, one-quarter raw celery, and one-quarter raw green peppers, cut in the form of matches. Pour French dressing over all and sprinkle with chopped parsley.

Oysters on half shell. Serve on cracked ice with one-half lemon or lime.

Boiled rock cod. See codfish.

Sauce fleurette. Cream sauce with chives, chervil and parsley, chopped fine and well seasoned.

Sirloin steak. Salt and pepper the steak, dip in olive oil and broil. Serve with maître d'hôtel sauce and chopped parsley.

Sauce Madére. Put in sauce pan one glass of sherry wine and reduce over fire one-half. Add one and one-half cups of brown gravy, boil for a few minutes, and add a little good Maderia before serving.

Broiled fresh mushrooms. Cut the stems from the mushrooms and wash the heads in three waters, to free them from sand, dry on napkin. Season with salt, pepper and a little olive oil, and broil over a slow fire for about ten minutes, according to their size. Serve on dry toast with maître d'hôtel sauce on top.

Celery Victor. (Salad). Wash six stalks of large celery. Make a stock with one soup hen or chicken bones, and five pounds of veal bones, in the usual manner, with carrots, onions, bay leaves, parsley, salt and whole pepper. Place celery in vessel and strain broth over same, and boil until soft. Allow to cool in the broth. When cold press the broth out of the celery gently with the hands, and place on plate. Season with salt, fresh-ground black pepper, chervil, and one-quarter white wine tarragon vinegar to three-quarters of olive oil.

Delmonico potatoes. Put hashed in cream potatoes in a buttered shirred egg dish, sprinkle with grated Parmesan cheese, and bake in oven until brown.

NOVEMBER 5

BREAKFAST
  Wine grapes
  Bacon and eggs
  Rolls
  Coffee

LUNCHEON
  Buttermilk
  Waffles and honey
  Coffee

DINNER
  Little neck clams on shell
  Potage Lamballe
  Ripe California olives
  Boiled river salmon, sauce mousseline
  Potatoes nature
  Roast sirloin of beef, sauce Madére
  Cauliflower au gratin
  Potatoes Laurette
  Cole slaw
  Chocolate ice cream
  Assorted cakes
  Coffee

Bacon and eggs. See ham and eggs.

Fried bacon. Thin slices of bacon fried slowly in pan in own fat. Should be crisp.

Waffles. One-half pound of flour, one-half teaspoonful of baking powder, two eggs, two ounces of sugar, two ounces of butter, a little mace and a little milk. Make a batter a little stiffer than for wheatcakes. Bake in waffle iron, but do not have the iron too hot.

Potage Lamballe. One-half purée of peas and one-half consommé with tapioca, mixed.

Boiled salmon, mousseline. Boil salmon in the same manner as trout.

Sauce mousseline. To one pint of Hollandaise add one cup of whipped cream and stir in gently.

Little neck clams. Same as oysters on shell.

Potatoes nature. Plain boiled potatoes cut in the shape of a small egg.

Roast sirloin of beef. See tenderloin of beef.

Cauliflower au gratin. Put some dry, boiled cauliflower on a buttered dish, cover with well-seasoned cream sauce, sprinkle with grated Parmesan cheese, put a little butter on top and bake in oven until brown.

Potatoes Laurette. To a cup of boiling water add one ounce of butter and stir in one-half cup of sifted flour, mixing it well. Allow to cool slightly and add the yolks of two eggs. Mix this dough with equal parts of fresh-boiled potato that has been passed through a sieve. Roll in flour in the form of a pencil and about two inches long, dip in egg and bread crumbs, and fry in swimming fat or lard. Serve on a napkin.

Cole slaw. Slice the leaves of a white cabbage very fine. Put in salad bowl and use dressing as desired. See salad dressings.

Chocolate ice cream. Prepare the same as vanilla ice cream, but in place of the vanilla bean use two ounces of cocoa, or two ounces of melted chocolate.

NOVEMBER 6

BREAKFAST
  Scrambled eggs with ham
  Stewed fruits
  Coffee

LUNCHEON
  Canapé of sardines
  Fried smelts, Tartar sauce
  Broiled lamb chops
  Stewed celery in cream
  French fried potatoes
  Vanilla custard pie

DINNER
  Tuna fish salad
  Chicken broth in cups
  Queen olives
  Roast capon, au cresson
  French peas
  Parisian potatoes
  Lettuce salad, egg dressing
  Fancy ice cream
  Lady fingers
  Coffee

Scrambled eggs with ham. Boiled ham cut in small dices and one small piece of butter. Put in vessel and add scrambled eggs. See plain scrambled eggs.

Canapé of sardines. Skin and split the sardines. Place on buttered toast, garnished with chopped eggs around the edges, and serve on napkin with quartered lemon and parsley in branches.

Fried smelts. Season the smelts, roll in flour, then in beaten eggs, and finally in bread crumbs. Fry in swimming fat and serve on napkin with fried parsley and lemons quartered. Sauce separate.

Fried parsley. Parsley in branches, well-washed and dried in towel. Fry in very hot swimming fat or lard for a second, as it fries very quickly. Salt and pepper. Can be used for garnishing fried fish and other dishes.

Tartar sauce. One chopped gherkin in vinegar, one tablespoonful of capers, a little chervil, parsley, chives and a tablespoonful of French mustard. Stir well into a cup of mayonnaise sauce.

Stewed celery in cream. Cut stalks or outside leaves of celery into one inch lengths. Wash well, parboil in salt water and allow to cool. Put back in salt water and boil until soft. Add one-half cup of cream sauce, a small piece of butter, one-half cup of cream, and season with salt and Cayenne pepper. Simmer for five minutes.

French fried potatoes. Cut raw potatoes in strips one-third inch thick and two inches long. Fry in swimming lard, but do not have it too hot. When potatoes are done remove from pan and let the fat become as hot as possible. Fry the potatoes again until they are a golden yellow. Remove, salt, and serve on a napkin. Do not cover, as this will cause them to become soft and spongy.

Tuna fish salad. (Thon mariné). This fish can be obtained in cans. Put in salad bowl some sliced lettuce with the tuna on top. Garnish with lettuce leaves and serve with French dressing. Do not mix until ready to serve.

Fancy ice cream. Fill fancy lead moulds with any kind of ice cream, using different colors in the same mould if desired. Cover with cracked ice and rock salt for thirty minutes. Remove and serve on doilies.

NOVEMBER 7

BREAKFAST
Strawberries in cream
Oatmeal
Shirred eggs
Rolls   Coffee

LUNCHEON
Potato and leek soup
Broiled halibut steak, maître d'hôtel
Homemade beef stew
Lemon water ice
Fruit cake
Demi tasse

DINNER
California oysters on shell
Consommé with sago
Écrevisses en buisson
Leg of veal, au jus
Browned mashed potatoes
Peas and carrots in cream
Hearts of lettuce, French dressing
Omelet with jelly
Coffee

SUPPER
Welsh rabbit

Shirred eggs, plain. Put eggs on buttered shirred egg dish and cook slowly. Salt and pepper.

Potato and leek soup. Simmer in butter one chopped onion and four stalks of leeks cut in small dices. When golden yellow add one tablespoonful of flour, mix, add one pound of potatoes cut in dices one-quarter inch square, one quart of stock or bouillon, and a boquet garni. Boil until potatoes are done. Season with salt, pepper, a little grated nutmeg and chopped parsley.

Bouquet garni. Tie in a bundle a small piece of celery, of leek, and of parsley in branches, with a bay leaf, two cloves, a sprig of thyme, and, if desired, a clove of garlic, in the center. This is used for flavoring stews, soups, fish, etc.

Broiled halibut, maître d'hôtel. Cut halibut in slices one inch thick. Salt and pepper, dip in olive oil and broil. Serve with maître d'hôtel sauce, quartered lemon and parsley.

Homemade beef stew. Three pounds of rump, hip, or flank beef, cut into squares two inches thick. Season the meat and simmer in sauce pot with two chopped onions and three ounces of butter. When brown add two tablespoonsful of flour and simmer again. Then add hot water enough to cover the meat, and a bouquet garni. Cook for one hour and then add one pound of potatoes cut in squares one inch thick, and leave on fire until potatoes are soft. Take out the bouquet, add one cup of purée of tomatoes and boil for five minutes. Serve with a sprinkle of chopped parsley.

Consommé with sago. Bring one quart of consommé to a boil and then let one-third of a pound of sago run slowly into it. Cook for ten minutes.

Écrevisses en buisson. To three quarts of boiling water add one sliced onion, one carrot, a bouquet garni, one glassful of vinegar, and salt. Boil for five minutes. Then put in three dozen écrevisses, or crayfish, and boil for ten minutes. Serve on napkin with parsley and lemon, or serve in its broth if desired. For most écrevisse dishes the sauce is made "en buisson" first and then prepared in fancy fashion following.

Leg of veal, au jus. Put leg of veal in pan and treat same as roast veal. Baste often.

Browned mashed potatoes. Put in buttered egg dish some mashed potatoes. Sprinkle with grated Parmesan cheese, place a little butter on top, and bake in oven.

Peas and carrots in cream. Put in pot one pint of boiled peas, one pint of boiled French carrots, one cup of thick cream, salt and a pinch of sugar. Boil for a few minutes and thicken with a half cup of cream sauce.

Omelet with jelly. See omelet with strawberries. Roll the omelet in pan, put any kind of jelly in center, turn over on platter, and burn with hot iron.

NOVEMBER 8

BREAKFAST
Bananas and cream
Force and cream
Crescent rolls   Cocoa

LUNCHEON
Cream of potato soup
Radishes
Broiled tenderloin steak, Bordelaise
    sauce
Gendarme potatoes
Asparagus tip salad
Vanilla éclairs   Demi tasse

AFTERNOON TEA
Preserved strawberries   Dry toast
Chicken sandwiches
Assorted cakes   Oolong tea

DINNER
Purée of tomatoes, with rice
Lobster Newburg
Roast chicken
Artichokes, Hollandaise
Waffle potatoes
Pistache ice cream
Alsatian wafers   Coffee

Force and cream. Serve raw force on a compote dish, with cream and powdered sugar separate.

Cream of potato soup. Simmer a little sliced onion, leeks, celery, one bay leaf, a clove and a piece of pig skin, or a raw ham bone, in butter. Then add one cup of flour and simmer again. Pour in two quarts of boiling milk and two pounds of sliced raw potatoes and boil until the potatoes are soft. Season with salt and a little Cayenne pepper, and strain through a fine sieve. Before serving add the yolk of one egg mixed with a cup of thick cream, and stir in gradually three ounces of sweet butter.

Radishes. Wash well. The red skin of the turnip-shaped species may be cut back, beginning at the bottom point and extending toward the top, in the form of open leaves, to make them look like open roses, if desired. Serve on cracked ice.

Broiled tenderloin steak. Salt and pepper the steak and dip in olive oil before broiling. Garnish with watercress and serve with maître d'hôtel sauce.

Bordelaise sauce. Simmer four shallots, chopped very fine, in two ounces of butter. When thoroughly warmed through add one-half glass of Bordeaux claret and reduce until nearly dry. Then add one pint of brown gravy and boil for five minutes. Then add one-quarter of a pound of sliced parboiled beef marrow, and a little chopped garlic, if that flavor is desired. Sprinkle with chopped parsley, and before serving stir in slowly two ounces of fresh butter. Serve poured over meats, or separate.

Gendarme potatoes. Peel some small potatoes and cut lengthwise in eight or more pieces. Put in roasting pan with salt, pepper and a piece of butter, and roast in oven for seven minutes. Add a sliced onion, mix well, and again roast, turning often.

Chicken sandwich. Slice boiled or left over roast chicken, very thin. Cut the bread thin and spread with sweet butter. Place the chicken between slices of the bread with a sprinkle of salt and pepper. Trim, and cut in shape desired.

Purée of tomato soup, with rice. Add one-half cup of boiled rice to each portion of purée of tomato soup.

Artichoke, Hollandaise. See boiled artichokes. Sauce Hollandaise served separate.

Lobster, Newburg. Cut the meat from the tails of California lobsters, in slices one-quarter inch thick. Put in sauté pan with butter, salt and pepper, and simmer for five minutes, or until the meat has a little color, over a quick fire. Then add for each lobster tail one cup of thick cream and one pony of brandy, and cook for two minutes. Thicken with yolks of two eggs mixed with a little cream, some very dry sherry wine, and a pinch of Cayenne pepper. Serve in chafing dish. Serve Maderia or sherry wine separate.

NOVEMBER 9

BREAKFAST
  Orange juice
  Cream toast
  Coffee

LUNCHEON
  Eggs au beurre noir
  Hamburg steak
  Lorraine potatoes
  Cole slaw, Thousand Island dressing
  Limburger cheese
  Rye bread and pumpernickle
  Coffee

DINNER
  Cream of chicken
  Salted English walnuts
  Fillet of sole, Joinville
  Roast tame duckling, apple sauce
  Sweet potatoes, Southern style
  Cold asparagus, mustard sauce
  Strawberry ice cream
  Cakes
  Coffee

SUPPER
  Chicken salad

Orange juice. Strain the juice of peeled oranges through a napkin, and serve in glass surrounded with fine ice.

Eggs au beurre noir. Use soft-fried or shirred eggs. Put a piece of butter in hot frying pan and when nearly black and smoking add a dash of vinegar, and pour over the eggs. Drop a few capers and chopped parsley on top, and salt and pepper.

Hamburg steak. To one and one-half pounds of trimmed beef, add four ounces of beef marrow, and pass through meat chopper, medium fine. Simmer some chopped onions in butter until nice and brown. Mix the meat and onions with salt, pepper, one raw egg, some chopped parsley, and a dinner roll soaked in water and chopped fine. Form the meat in round steaks one-half inch thick, roll in bread crumbs, and fry in pan in butter for about ten minutes. Remove the steaks carefully. Add a spoonful of flour to gravy in pan, simmer a little, and then add one-half cup of stock or water, pepper and salt, and strain before serving.

Lorraine potatoes. Simmer one chopped onion and one-quarter pound of salt pork cut in small dices, in one ounce of butter, for five minutes. Then add three pounds of potatoes cut in pieces one inch square, one pint of stock or bouillon, salt and pepper, and a bouquet garni. Cook until soft and sprinkle with chopped parsley before serving.

Thousand Island dressing, for salads. Two soupspoonfuls of mayonnaise, one soupspoonful of Chili sauce, one soupspoonful of French dressing, one teaspoonful of chopped pimentos, one-half teaspoonful of chopped olives, salt and pepper, all well mixed. Use a very cold salad bowl.

Cream of chicken. Place a soup hen in a soup kettle with three quarts of water, a leek, carrot, a little parsley and celery, six pepper berries, and two cups of rice. Boil until fowl is soft. Remove and cut away the white meat from the breast and set aside. Chop the remainder of the meat very fine, return to the kettle, and then strain the entire contents through a sieve. To the strained broth add one quart of milk, and strain again. Then add one-half pint of cream and the yolk of one egg, mixed; also a piece of sweet butter the size of an egg. Then add the breast of the fowl cut in small squares.

Roast tame duckling. See roast chicken. Also see stuffings.

NOVEMBER 10

BREAKFAST
   Shredded wheat biscuit
   Boiled eggs
   Rolls
   Coffee

LUNCHEON
   Holland herring
   Boiled potatoes
   Waffles and honey
   Coffee

DINNER
   Lynn Haven oysters on half shell
   Philadelphia pepper pot
   Roast canvas-back duck
   Hulled corn
   Currant jelly
   Cauliflower au gratin
   Celery mayonnaise
   Neapolitan ice cream
   Assorted cakes
   Demi tasse

Shredded wheat biscuits. Put the biscuit in a deep dish. A little boiling water poured over it will enable you to economize on cream.

Philadelphia pepper pot. Simmer in kettle four large onions chopped fine, one piece of celery, two leeks, one green pepper cut in very small squares, and one-quarter pound of butter. When done add two soupspoonsful of flour, and simmer again; add two quarts of stock, two pounds of tripe and one pound of potatoes cut in small squares, a bouquet garni and salt. Cook for two hours. Before serving remove the bouquet garni, add a tablespoonful of fresh-ground pepper, a little chopped parsley and some flour dumplings. Let the flour dumpling dough run through an ordinary sieve into boiling water and boil for just a minute.

Flour dumplings. One cup of flour, two eggs, three-fourths of a cup of milk, salt, and a little nutmeg. Mix well. Pass through colander with holes of about one-third inch in diameter, into boiling salt water. Boil for about three minutes, drain off water, put on platter and pour some brown butter over them.

Brown butter sauce. Put good-sized piece of sweet butter into frying pan and allow to brown. May be served poured over the dish, or in separate sauce bowl.

Hulled corn. May be obtained in cans. Follow directions on same. To hull corn is quite a complicated process, requiring the use of lye, etc.

Canvas-back duck. Same directions as for teal duck. Roast for about eighteen minutes.

Celery mayonnaise. Cut raw celery in strips like matches and wash well, then put in napkin on cracked ice, so it will become crisp. Serve with well-seasoned mayonnaise sauce, either on top or separate, as desired.

Pound cake. One-half pound of butter, one-half pound of sugar, one-half pound of flour, five eggs, a little rum and a teaspoonful of baking powder. Beat the butter with sugar until white, add the eggs one by one, while beating briskly. Mix the flour and the baking powder in together, and last of all add the rum. Put in mould and bake in oven for one hour.

Fruit cake. To the pound cake batter add one-half pound of chopped mixed glacé fruits, and one-half pound of raisins.

NOVEMBER 11

BREAKFAST
  Pearl grits and cream
  Fried eggs
  Rolls
  Chocolate

LUNCHEON
  Cold assorted meats
  Potato salad
  Iced tea

AFTERNOON TEA
  Chicken à la King
  Bread and butter sandwiches
  Raspberry water ice
  Champagne wafers
  Almond cake
  Tea
  Chocolate
  Whipped cream

DINNER
  Consommé with tapioca
  Boiled salmon, mousseline sauce
  Potatoes Hollandaise
  Roast goose, apple sauce
  St. Francis potatoes
  Celery Victor
  Baked Alaska
  Coffee

Pearl grits with cream. See hominy in cream.

Potato salad. Slice three boiled potatoes while hot. Add one small onion chopped fine, some chopped parsley, salt and pepper, two spoonsful of olive oil, and one each of boiling bouillon, or boiling water, and vinegar. Mix carefully so as not to break the potatoes, and serve in salad bowl with lettuce garnishing.

Chicken à la King. Take the breast of a boiled chicken or hen (fowl), and cut in very thin, diamond-shape pieces. Put in pan and add three-quarters of a pint of cream, salt and Cayenne pepper. Boil from three to five minutes. Add a glass of best sherry or Madeira wine. Boil for a minute and thicken with the yolks of two eggs, mixed with one-quarter pint of cream. Put some sliced truffles on top.

Raspberry water ice. One-half pound of sugar, one pint of water, and one pint of fresh raspberry pulp strained through a fine sieve. Squeeze in the juice of one lemon, add a little coloring if desired, strain and freeze.

Consommé with tapioca. To one quart of boiling consommé add slowly one cup of tapioca, and boil for eight minutes.

Bread and butter sandwiches. Spread sweet butter on thin slices of bread, and place face to face in pairs. Cut in any fancy shape, or roll and tie with soft baby ribbon.

NOVEMBER 12

BREAKFAST
  Honey in comb
  Boiled eggs
  Postum cereal
  Dry toast

LUNCHEON
  Cold goose and Virginia ham
  Port de Salut cheese
  Crackers
  Coffee

DINNER
  Oyster soup, family style
  Salted English walnuts
  Fried chicken, country style
  Au gratin potatoes
  Cauliflower, Polonaise
  Escarole and chicory salad
  Chocolate profiterole
  Coffee

SUPPER
  Canapé regalia

Postum cereal. A prepared breakfast food obtainable from all grocers. Follow directions on package.

Oyster soup, family style. Boil two dozen oysters with their juice. In a separate vessel boil one quart of milk and one pint of cream. Put both together and add two ounces of sweet butter, and salt and pepper. Before serving stir in some fine cut chives and one-half cup of broken crackers.

Au gratin potatoes. Fill a shallow buttered dish with hashed in cream potatoes. Sprinkle with grated Parmesan cheese, put a little butter on top, and bake in oven until brown.

Cauliflower, Polonaise. Put on a platter some fresh-boiled cauliflower and sprinkle with two finely chopped boiled eggs, salt and pepper and some chopped parsley. In a pan on range put three ounces of sweet butter. When warm add two tablespoonsful of fresh bread crumbs and allow to become well browned. Pour over cauliflower when very hot.

Fried chicken, country style. Put the dressed chicken in salt water and leave for about one hour. Then wash and dry between towels, season with pepper and a small amount of salt, and dredge well with flour. Place in frying pan about three tablespoonsful of lard and two or three slices of fat breakfast bacon. When bacon is brown remove, and strain the lard, being careful that it is not burned. Have the lard very hot and fry the chicken. When brown, and well done, remove the chicken and strain the lard again through a hair sieve, then return lard to range, and stir in thoroughly one tablespoonful of flour, being careful to have no lumps. Immediately before serving stir into the sauce one pint of cream, and let boil for one minute. Dress with the bacon and parsley in branches.

Canapé Regalia. Regalia is a special fish paste obtainable in cans. To one small can add two ounces of butter, mix well, and spread on fresh toast. Garnish with chopped eggs, serve on napkin with lemon in quarters and parsley in branches.

NOVEMBER 13

BREAKFAST
  Bananas and cream
  Scrambled eggs with chives
  Dry toast
  Coffee

LUNCHEON
  Pickled oysters
  Consommé in cups
  Broiled bluefish, maître d'hôtel
  Tripe, Lyonnaise
  Mashed potatoes
  Hearts of lettuce, egg dressing
  Chocolate éclairs
  Demi tasse

DINNER
  Potage Cambridge
  Boiled sheepshead, Hollandaise sauce
  Potatoes nature
  Chicken, Diva
  French peas
  Endive salad
  Strawberries with cream
  Assorted cakes
  Corn bread, Maryland
  Coffee

Pickled oysters. Parboil one carrot and one celery root cut in strips, and one onion sliced fine. Pour off water and finish cooking in one glassful each of white wine, and white wine vinegar, with a spoonful of pepper berries tied in cheese cloth. When done remove the peppers, add three dozen oysters and bring to a boil. Serve cold with parsley.

Broiled bluefish. Split the bluefish, remove the bones, season with salt and pepper, dip in oil and broil. Serve maître d'hôtel sauce on top, and quartered lemons and parsley.

Boiled sheepshead, Hollandaise sauce. Same as boiled salmon, Hollandaise.

Maryland corn bread. Beat two eggs until very light, and stir in one pint of sweet milk. Then sift one-half pint of coarse corn meal, add a teaspoonful of yeast powder, half a teaspoonful of salt, and a tablespoonful of melted lard or butter. Stir this into the milk and eggs. Mixture must be a thin batter. Bake in small bread pan or muffin rings.

Chicken, Diva. Prepare the chicken as for roast and stuff with rice stuffing. Put chicken in kettle and cover with stock or water. When done prepare a suprême sauce with the stock, pour over the chicken, and sprinkle with chopped Virginia ham. Carve at table.

Rice stuffing. Simmer a small chopped onion in butter, add one cup of washed rice, three cups of stock or bouillon, season, and cook in oven for twenty minutes. Then add two truffles cut in small squares. This stuffing is used for poultry, game, peppers, tomatoes, etc.

Suprême sauce. Melt three ounces of butter, add two ounces of flour, and simmer, but do not allow to brown. Add one and one-half pint of chicken stock, reduce for ten minutes, thicken with the yolk of one egg, a cup of cream and a small piece of sweet butter. Season with salt and a little Cayenne pepper. This sauce may be used with many entrée dishes.

Potage Cambridge (soup). Melt three ounces of butter in vessel, add two ounces of flour, and simmer for five minutes, or until golden yellow. Add one pint of veal broth or stock, one-half pint of purée of tomatoes and the trimmings of a few fresh mushrooms. Cook for twenty minutes, strain through sieve and add fine-cut strips of fresh mushrooms sauté in butter. A pony of dry sherry wine may be added if desired.

Strawberry ice cream. One pint of cream, one quart of milk, the yolks of eight eggs, one-half pound of sugar, one pint of strawberry pulp or strained strawberries, the juice of one lemon and a little coloring. Put the milk with half the sugar on the fire to boil. Mix the remainder of the sugar with the eggs, stir the boiling milk into it, and cook until it becomes creamy, but do not allow it to boil. Remove from the fire, add the cream, strawberry pulp and lemon juice, cool and freeze.

NOVEMBER 14

BREAKFAST
Grapefruit with vanilla sugar
Finnan haddie in cream
Puff paste crescents
Oolong tea

LUNCHEON
Green onions
Radishes
Eggs ministerielle
Vermicelli aux croutons
Cold asparagus, mustard sauce
Cup custard
Coffee

DINNER
Clam chowder, Manhattan style
Queen olives
Fillet of sole, Marguery
Omelet with spinach
Broiled fresh mushrooms
Coffee ice cream
Assorted cakes
Demi tasse

Puff paste crescents. Two pounds of flour, one pound of butter, one pint of milk, one ounce of salt, one and one-half ounces of sugar and two ounces of yeast dissolved in warm water. Mix one-half pound of the flour with one-half pint of water and the dissolved yeast. Stand in warm place for about twenty minutes. Put the remainder of flour on board and mix in the yeast paste; when sufficiently risen, add salt, sugar and milk, make a stiff dough and allow to stand for a few minutes. Roll out, put the butter into the dough as for ordinary puff paste, and roll in the same way, but giving it only half the number of turns.

Stock for soup. Two pounds of beef bones and a marrow bone, if you can obtain one, two gallons of water, a carrot, onion, leek, piece of parsley, a bouquet garni, salt and pepper. Boil for three hours. Strain.

Puff paste (feuilletage). Take one pound of flour and one cup of water and make a smooth paste, but not too soft. Form into a square loaf and let it set for about fifteen minutes. Roll out on floured board about one-half inch thick, and place in the center one pound of butter, well-worked and flexible. Fold the edges of the paste over the butter and roll out about one-quarter inch thick, taking care that the butter does not run out of the dough. Brush off the flour and fold in three. Roll out again to the same thickness as before and repeat the folding. Put in cool place or ice box for about one-half hour, then roll and fold as before. Again rest for one-half hour, and then roll and fold again. The paste will then have six turns in all, and after a little rest it can be used.

Brown gravy. One pound of veal bones, cut in pieces and browned in oven, with one carrot, one onion, a little thyme, one bay leaf, two cloves and three ounces of butter. Baste well, then add three ounces of flour, allow to brown a little, and then add two quarts of water and boil for two full hours. Season with salt, and strain. This gravy is used as a foundation for many fancy sauces, such as sauce Madère, etc.

NOVEMBER 15

BREAKFAST
Stewed rhubarb
Grape-nuts with cream
Yarmouth bloaters
Rolls
Coffee

LUNCHEON
Shrimp salad
Lamb chops
Julienne potatoes
French string beans
Chocolate macaroons
Coffee

DINNER
Seapuit oysters on half shell
Onion soup au gratin
Salted pistachio nuts
Whitefish, maître d'hôtel
Sweetbreads braisé, au jus
Purée St. Germain
Olivette potatoes
Roast leg of lamb, mint sauce
Romaine salad
Pineapple punch
Lady fingers
Coffee

Stewed rhubarb. Peel one pound of rhubarb, cut in two inch pieces, and place in shallow pan. Put on top one-quarter pound of sugar, a small piece of cinnamon, and one-half pint of water. Cover and put in oven for about twenty minutes. Remove, take out the cinnamon, and serve cold in its own juice. Cream and powdered sugar separate.

Grape-nuts with cream. Serve as prepared in package. Cream and powdered sugar separate.

Yarmouth bloater. Imported in cans. Put on broiler and heat through. Serve with maître d'hôtel sauce, quartered lemons and parsley.

Shrimp salad. Season fresh-boiled shrimps with salt, pepper and a little vinegar. Put some sliced lettuce in the bottom of a salad bowl, lay the shrimps on top, and cover with mayonnaise sauce. Garnish with quartered hard boiled eggs, fancy-cut beets, capers and queen olives. Serve very cold.

Julienne potatoes. Cut raw potatoes in thin strips like matches, and full length of potatoes. Fry in swimming fat, lard preferred, until crisp. Remove from fat, salt, and serve on napkin. Do not cover.

Onion soup, au gratin. Simmer three very finely sliced onions in butter until brown. Add one cup of bouillon or consommé, and boil for a few minutes. Put in earthern pot, or petite marmite, and place some slices of toasted French bread, previously prepared, on top. Put one-half cup of grated Parmesan cheese on the bread, set in very hot oven, and bake until the cheese is browned. Season to taste.

Whitefish, maître d'hôtel. Split the fish and remove the bones. Salt, pepper, dip in oil and broil. Serve with maître d'hôtel sauce, quartered lemons **and** parsley.

Purée St. Germain (vegetable). Strain cooked peas through a fine sieve. Put in pan with a piece of butter, salt and a pinch of sugar. Stir well, and when hot, add a very little thick cream. The purée should be firm, like mashed potatoes.

NOVEMBER 16

BREAKFAST
    Stewed prunes
    Malta Vita with cream
    Poached eggs on toast
    Rolls
    Coffee

LUNCHEON
    Hors d'oeuvres variés
    Fried fillet of sole, rémoulade sauce
    Broiled quail on toast
    Chiffonnade salad
    Soufflée potatoes
    Savarin au fine champagne
    Demi tasse

DINNER
    Cotuit oysters on half shell
    Petite marmite   Salted almonds
    Terrapin, Maryland style
    Roast ribs of beef
    Stewed tomatoes   Mashed potatoes
    Cold artichokes, mustard sauce
    English breakfast tea ice cream
    Assorted cakes   Coffee

Stewed prunes. Wash well one pound of prunes, and soak in cold water for two hours. Put on fire in same water, add a small piece of cinnamon stick, the peel of a quarter of a lemon, and two ounces of sugar, and cook on slow fire until soft. It will require about one hour. If an earthern pot with cover is used, put in bake oven for about two hours. The flavor will be better.

Malta Vita. Serve with powdered sugar, and cream, separate.

Hors d'oeuvres variés. (Appetisers assorted). Hors d'oeuvres are different delicacies, and, except in rare instances, are served cold. They consist of caviar, pickled oysters, Lyon sausages, any kind of fish salad, paté de foie gras, smoked salmon, smoked goose breast, and many others. From one dish to two dozen kinds may be served, allowing the guests to make a selection. Each kind should be served on a separate platter, or silver bowl.

Caviar. Leave the caviar three hours on ice. Serve in a glass dish. For each person have a round platter with napkin, a lettuce leaf filled with fine chopped onion and a quarter of a lemon. Thin dry toast and sweet butter separate.

Paté de goie gras. (Goose liver patty.) Obtainable in cans or terrines, of different sizes. Remove the fat, which is put on top as a preservative, and with a soup spoon, which has been dipped in hot water, cut the paste in thin slices, and serve on lettuce leaves on a napkin. Garnish with meat jelly and parsley in branches. Let the paté de foie gras stand in ice box a few hours before opening and serving.

Lyon sausage. A kind of imported beef sausage. Slice thin.

Stuffed eggs. Cut hard boiled eggs in two, either way. Mix the yolks with equal parts of sweet butter and pass through a sieve. Add salt, paprika, a little anchovy paste, and some chives. Mix well, and fill the halved eggs. Or the yolks may be mixed with butter, and some poppy or celery seeds, etc. Also with any kind of purée, such as purée of tomatoes, regalia, chicken, etc. If the filling is put in a pastry bag with a star mould in the bottom, to squeeze it through, the eggs can be filled in an attractive and novel manner. Serve very cold.

Sardines. Serve cold with quartered lemons, on lettuce leaves.

Sliced tomatoes. Have the tomatoes very cold. Peel and slice, and serve on lettuce leaves, with French dressing. To peel, put tomatoes in hot water for ten seconds, and peel immediately.

NOVEMBER 17

BREAKFAST
Baked apples
Boiled eggs
Toast
Coffee

LUNCHEON
Grapefruit with cherries
Steak and kidney pie
Cream cheese
Maryland beaten biscuits

DINNER
Consommé Madriléne
Ripe California olives
Sand dabs, meuniére
Butterball duck with currant jelly
Fried hominy
French endive salad
Asparagus, Hollandaise
Fancy ice cream
Assorted cakes
Coffee

Grapefruit with cherries. Cut the grapefruit in two pieces. Split some maraschino cherries and decorate. Pour a little maraschino on top.

Steak and kidney pie. Use individual pie dishes. A slice of raw sirloin steak one-half inch thick, cut in two. Two lamb kidneys cut in two. Salt, pepper, and roll in flour, put in pie dish and cover with a little cold water. Cover with piecrust dough and bake in oven for about eighteen minutes. Serve in the dishes in which they were baked, on napkins.

Butterball duck. Roast in hot oven for about twelve minutes.

Assorted cakes. Any kind of small cakes. Serve on a compotier, on doily. The more varied the assortment the better.

Maryland beaten biscuits. To one pint of sifted flour add one heaping teaspoonful of lard, or butter, and a little salt. Mix with one pint of sweet milk to stiff dough. Beat with a mallet for one hour. The succcess of same depends upon the beating. Shape as for tea biscuits and bake.

Macaroons. Mix one pound of almond paste with one pound of powdered sugar. Add the whites of six eggs and a spoonful of flour and mix well. Squeeze through a pastry bag onto paper, moisten the tops with water, using a brush, and bake in a very slow oven for about twenty minutes.

Lady fingers. Eight eggs, with the yolks and whites separate, one-half pound of sugar, one-half pound of flour, and some vanilla flavoring extract. Beat the sugar with the yolks until light; then beat the whites very stiff. Mix the flour with the yolks and sugar, then add the beaten whites and mix lightly. Dress on paper with a plain pastry bag, in the shape wanted. Dust powdered sugar on top and bake in a moderate oven.

NOVEMBER 18

BREAKFAST
  Guava jelly
  Oatmeal with cream
  Rolls
  Coffee

LUNCHEON
  Mariniert herring
  Plain boiled potatoes
  Calf's liver, sauce piquante
  Fried egg plant
  Oregon cream cheese and crackers
  Coffee

DINNER
  Purée of game, hunter style
  Salted English walnuts
  Roast capon
  Compote of pears
  Stewed celery, au Madère
  Paille potatoes
  Bavarois à la vanille
  Fancy macaroons
  Coffee

Mariniert herring. Soak six salt herrings in water for twelve hours. Then put in pot with one sliced onion, some whole parsley, a spoonful of whole black pepper berries, three bay leaves and six cloves. Mix one teaspoonful of English mustard with a cup of vinegar and pour over herring. Cover all with thick cream, shake well to thoroughly mix, and let stand for two days before serving. Serve with thin slices of one lemon on top, or, if desired, the lemon may be put with the herring for a day.

Calf's liver, sauté. Slice the liver one-quarter inch thick, salt, pepper, roll in flour and fry in butter. Do not fry too long as it will make the liver tough. Serve on a platter with its own gravy, chopped parsley, and quartered lemons.

Sauce piquante. Simmer one chopped onion with a piece of butter. Add two spoonsful of crushed pepper berries and half a glass of vinegar. Reduce almost dry. Then add one pint of brown gravy, boil for fifteen minutes, and strain. Chop fine one-half cup of gherkins, put into the sauce and boil for a few minutes. Add a sprinkle of chopped parsley.

Fried egg plant. Peel and cut the egg plant into slices one-quarer of an inch thick. Salt, pepper, roll in flour, then in beaten eggs, and finally in bread crumbs. Fry in swimming lard, fat, or butter. Place on napkin, sprinkle with a little more salt, and garnish with parsley.

Purée of game soup. Simmer the carcasses or meat of almost any kind of game, such as duck, rabbits, nares, venison, bear, etc. Cut in pieces and add one carrot, an onion, two bay leaves, two cloves, a piece of celery, a little thyme, some pepper berries and four ounces of butter. Roast all together until nice and brown. Add a cup of flour and simmer again until the flour is of a brownish color. Then add one and one-half quarts of bouillon, or stock, and boil for an hour. Strain, pressing all the soft parts of the game through the sieve, and season with salt and Cayenne pepper. Before serving add one-half glass of dry sherry wine or Madeira.

Purée of game, St. Hubert. Add to above soup some square cut pieces of roasted game, before serving.

Stewed celery, au Madère. Wash well and cut the celery stalks in pieces one inch long. Parboil in salt water, cool, and put back to boil in enough stock to cover. When nearly done drain off most of the stock, add a cup of brown gravy, and boil until soft. Salt and pepper, and add a little dry sherry or Madeira before serving.

Paille potatoes (straw). Cut in thin strips like straws the full length of the potato. Fry in very hot lard, serve in napkin, and salt when first removed from fat.

Fancy macaroons. Mix one pound of almond paste, three-quarters of a pound of powdered sugar, the whites of five eggs and one spoonful of flour. Put in pastry bag with a fancy tube and squeeze the paste through, about the size of a half dollar. Put half of a glacé cherry on top and let stand over night in a dry place. Bake in oven for ten minutes.

NOVEMBER 19

BREAKFAST
  Stewed apples
  Pettijohns with cream
  Ham and eggs
  Dry toast
  Oolong tea

LUNCHEON
  Canapé Riga
  Planked smelts, en bordure
  Sirloin steak, sauce Colbert
  Haricots panachés
  Lettuce and tomato salad
  Pistache éclairs
  Coffee

DINNER
  Potage santé
  Salted pecans
  Crab meat, au beurre noisette
  Roast tame duckling, apple sauce
  Corn fritters and potato croquettes
  Waldorf salad
  Fancy ice cream
  Assorted cakes
  Coffee

Canapé Riga. One-half tuna fish (thon mariné) and one-half caviar mixed. Spread on thin toast, buttered. Decorate around the edges with chopped eggs, quartered lemon and parsley in branches.

Planked smelts, en bordure. Split some large smelts down the back and remove the bones. Place on a buttered plank with salt, pepper and a little butter on top. Put some potato, prepared as for potato croquettes, into a pastry bag with a star tube, and press out a border around the fish about an inch high. Put in oven and bake for about fifteen minutes. Serve with a little maître d'hôtel butter on top, and garnish with quartered lemons and parsley.

Sauce Colbert. Chop three shallots very fine, and simmer in butter. Add one-half glass of claret, and reduce almost dry. Then add one pint of brown gravy and cook for ten minutes. Before serving add three ounces of sweet butter, the juice of one lemon, and some chopped parsley.

Potage santé (soup). Wash a good handful of sorrel and slice very thin. Put in pot with three ounces of butter and simmer slowly for ten minutes. Then add one quart of bouillon, or consommé, and boil for a few minutes. Thicken with the yolks of two eggs mixed with a cup of cream. Before serving put in some French bread, or rolls, that have been dried in the oven, and cut like chip potatoes.

Boiled crabs. Put two live crabs in a pot and cover with cold water. Add one glass of white wine vinegar, an onion, carrot, a bouquet garni and salt. Boil for thirty-five minutes and let become cool without removing from the water. Serve cracked, cold, with mayonnaise or any kind of cold sauce; or remove from shell and serve as a salad; or prepare hot in many ways.

Crab meat, au beurre noisette. Put some fresh-boiled crab meat on a platter and season with salt and pepper. In a frying pan put a quarter pound of sweet butter. Simmer until of a hazel color, and pour over crab meat. Sprinkle with chopped chervil, or parsley, on top, and garnish with lemon.

Waldorf salad. Half white celery and half apple, cut in small squares. Put both in salad bowl, but do not mix. Cover with mayonnaise and season to taste.

NOVEMBER 20

BREAKFAST
    Honey in comb
    Waffles
    Kippered herring
    Baked potatoes
    Rolls and coffee

LUNCHEON
    Eggs Marigny
    French pastry
    Iced tea

DINNER
    Consommé Cialdini
    Radishes
    Fillet of bass, 1905
    Larded sirloin of beef, Richelieu
    Salade Doucette
    Meringue glacé, Chantilly
    Coffee

Eggs Marigny. Put in a buttered cocotte dish a very thin, small, slice of ham, with two parboiled oysters on top. Break an egg over all, salt, pepper, cover with cream sauce and a little grated cheese, and bake in oven until done.

Consommé Cialdini. Cut some carrots, turnips and potatoes, with a fancy cutting spoon, to the size of a large pea. Cook each separate in salt water. When done put in consommé and add the boiled white meat of chicken cut in small squares, a few boiled or canned peas, and some chervil. Serve separate some very thin slices of French bread or rolls.

Larded sirloin of beef. Remove the skin and fat of the sirloin, half way near the thick part. Lard same and roast in the usual manner.

Richelieu. A garnish for beef and other meats. Is prepared in various styles. Here are four good ones.

Stuffed tomatoes with rice Créole, Stuffed fresh mushrooms à la D'Uxelles, braised lettuce and potatoes château.

Tomatoes, whole and baked, string beans, mushrooms and potatoes château.

Bouquet of all kinds of vegetables, fillets of anchovies, mushrooms and green olives.

Buttons of artichokes stuffed, stuffed tomato, mushrooms, lettuce braisé and potatoes château.

Fillet of bass, 1905. I originated this style in 1905, hence the name. Cut fillets of any kind of bass in pieces about three inches square, and free from skin and bones. Place on a piece of toast in a buttered shirred egg dish; salt, pepper, and place three nice heads of fresh mushrooms sauté in butter, on top of the fish. Put a soupspoonful of maître d'hôtel butter on top of the mushrooms, cover with a glass globe and bake in oven for twenty minutes. Just before serving uncover the fish, pour a little white wine sauce on top, re-cover, and serve.

Salade Doucette. Field salad.

Meringue glacé, Chantilly. Same as meringue glacé à la vanille. But decorate with whipped cream, passed through a pastry bag with a star tube.

NOVEMBER 21

BREAKFAST
  Bar le Duc jelly
  Horlick's malted milk
  Boiled eggs
  Maryland beaten biscuits

LUNCHEON
  Stuffed eggs
  Broiled salmon steak, anchovy butter
  Olivette potatoes
  Breaded lamb chops, Milanaise
  Pickled beets
  German apple cake   Coffee

DINNER
  Seapuit oysters on shell
  Consommé royal
  Skatefish au beurre noir   Potatoes nature
  Roast top sirloin of beef, forestière   Yorkshire pudding
  Chiffonnade salad
  Fancy ice cream   Assorted cakes   Coffee

Stuffed eggs with crab meat. Cut in two some hard-boiled eggs and remove the yolks. Fill the whites with fine-chopped crab meat mixed with a very thick mayonnaise. Chop the yolks and mix with a little chopped parsley, and sprinkle over the eggs. Serve very cold.

Broiled salmon steak. Cut a slice of salmon about one inch thick, salt, pepper, dip in oil and broil. Serve on platter with maitre d'hôtel sauce, and garnish with quartered lemons and parsley in branches. Or serve with anchovy butter or other sauce, either on top or separate.

Anchovy butter. Fresh butter mixed with anchovy paste and the juice of a lemon.

Breaded lamb chops. Salt and pepper the chops, roll in flour, then in beaten eggs, then in bread crumbs, and fry in butter.

Spaghetti Milanaise. Boiled spaghetti cut in two inch lengths, a slice of boiled ham, a slice of tongue, six mushrooms and one truffle cut in strips the same size as the spaghetti. Put all in one pot, add a little tomato sauce, salt and pepper, and let simmer for a few minutes. Serve grated Parmesan cheese separate. If served as a garnish with "lamb chops, Milanaise," mix the cheese before serving.

Consommé Royal. Beat four eggs and season well. Add one pint of warm (not hot), consommé, put in a buttered mould and set in a pan of hot water. Cook slowly in a moderate oven. When the custard is done allow to cool, and cut in any shape desired. Serve hot consommé, with royal custard as a garnish.

Skatefish au beurre noir. Place the skate in boiling water for a few minutes, when the skin may readily be scraped off. Put in cold water, add a little milk to make the fish white, salt, and bring to a boil. Take off the fire, but leave in the water for ten minutes. Then put fish on platter, salt, pepper, sprinkle with a little vinegar, a few capers and some chopped parsley. Put in frying pan a quarter pound of butter, allow to become almost black, and pour over fish.

Roast top sirloin of beef. Same as roast sirloin of beef.

Forestière, for sauce. Sliced fresh mushrooms, simmered in butter. Add brown gravy and boil for ten minutes. Before serving stir in a little sherry wine.

Yorkshire pudding. One cup of milk, one-half cup of flour, two eggs, and one teaspoonful of baking powder. Mix well, add salt, pepper and one-half cup of chopped beef suet. Bake in roasting pan with beef fat from your roast. When done cut in squares.

NOVEMBER 22

BREAKFAST
  Grapefruit
  Germea with cream
  Crescents
  Cocoa

LUNCHEON
  Scrambled eggs, Morocquaine
  Lamb trotters, poulette
  Potatoes St. Francis
  Moka éclairs
  Tea

DINNER
  Bisque of clams
  Frogs' legs, sauté à sec
  Tournedos Massenet
  Jets de houblons
  Endives au cerfeuil
  Mince pie
  American cheese
  Coffee

Germea and cream. Powdered sugar and cream separate.

Scrambled eggs, Morocquaine. Cut cèpes in small squares, fry in butter and place in middle of scrambled eggs. Tomato sauce around the edge.

Lamb trotters, poulette. Cook lambs' feet in stock or water with salt, and one carrot, an onion and a bouquet garni. When done pour poulette sauce over all.

Sauce poulette. Simmer three shallots in butter, but do not brown. Add one-half glass of white wine and reduce till almost dry. Then add chives sliced fine, sliced French mushrooms, and one pint of sauce Allemande. Boil for a few minutes, and bind with the yolk of an egg and a piece of fresh butter.

Bisque of clams. Simmer one onion, a little celery and leeks, one bay leaf and a few pepper berries in butter. Add the juice of one quart of clams, one pint of fish broth or water, and one cup of rice, and boil for an hour. Strain through a fine sieve, put back on fire and add one pint of cream. When hot add three ounces of butter, salt and a little Cayenne pepper. Parboil the clams, add the juice to the soup, cut the clams in small pieces and serve in the soup terrine. If desired both clams and broth can be used in making the bisque, and all strained before serving.

Tournedos Massenet. Small tenderloin steaks sauté in butter, and seasoned with salt and pepper. Garnish in bouquets with hearts of artichokes cut in four, sliced cèpes, small squares of tomatoes sauté in butter, French fried onions, and Olivette potatoes. Serve with sauce Madère.

Jets de houblons. (Hop sprouts). Can be obtained in cans. Warm in their own juice, drain, serve in vegetable dish, and cover with Hollandaise sauce.

Mince meat. One pound of beef suet chopped fine, one pound of boiled beef cut in very small dices, one pound of seedless raisins, one pound of cleaned currants, one-half pound of seeded Sultana raisins, one-half pound of citron cut in very small dices, one-pound of orange and lemon peel mixed and chopped fine, two pounds of chopped peeled apples, one ounce of ground cinnamon, one ounce of cloves, allspice, ginger and mace mixed, one pint of rum, and one pint of brandy. Mix well, put in jars and keep in cool place. Use as needed.

Mince pie. Line pie plate with dough as for apple pie. Put in mince meat, and finish as for apple pie. Serve warm with a piece of American cheese on the side.

NOVEMBER 23

BREAKFAST
  Baked apples
  Baked beans, Boston style
  Boston brown bread
  Coffee

LUNCHEON
  Écrevisse salad, gourmet
  Eggs, Henri IV
  Broiled squab chicken
  Soufflé potatoes
  Apricot compote
  French pastry   Coffee

DINNER
  Lynn Haven oysters on shell
  Chicken okra soup
  Salted Jordan almonds
  Fillet of halibut, Mornay
  Roast ribs of beef
  Stuffed tomatoes, Noyer
  Sweet potatoes, Southern style
  Wine jelly
  Caroline cakes
  Coffee

Stuffed tomatoes, Noyer. Cut the tops off two nice tomatoes, scoop them out and season with salt and pepper. Mix fresh bread crumbs and chopped English walnuts in equal parts and fill the tomatoes with same. Put a piece of butter on top and bake in moderate oven for ten minutes.

Baked apples. Wash and core the apples. With a sharp knife cut a circle through the skin, around the apple, above the center, to prevent the apples from bursting. Place on a pan and fill the hole in each with sugar mixed with a little ground cinnamon. Put a small piece of butter on top of each, and a little water in the bottom of the pan. Bake in a moderate oven. Serve with their own juice. Cream separate.

Baked beans, Boston style. Soak three pounds of white beans over night in cold water. Then put same in a one and one-half gallon earthern pot with one-half cup of molasses, one soupspoonful of English mustard mixed with a cup of water, a little salt, and one whole piece of fat, parboiled salt pork. Pour in just enough water to moisten, cover, and put in bake oven for four hours. Or in a not too hot range oven for two and one-half hours. If range is used, be careful that they do not burn. Serve from pot, or in small individual pots, with Boston brown bread separate.

Écrevisse salad, gourmet. Cover the bottoms of four dinner plates with chicory salad. In the center make a nest of celery cut in thin strips like matches. On top of that one well-washed fresh mushroom head, cut the same way, and to cap all, put the tails of six écrevisses. Sprinkle with salt and pepper, and a sauce of one-third tarragon vinegar and two-thirds olive oil. Cut two truffles like matches, and with some fine chervil, sprinkle all over the salad.

Eggs Henri IV. Breaded poached eggs fried in swimming lard. Place on a piece of toast spread with purée de foie gras, and cover with sauce Périgordine.

Sauce Périgordine. To one cup of brown gravy add one spoonful of chopped truffles reduced in sherry wine. Season with salt and Cayenne pepper.

Broiled squab chicken. Split a squab from the back, salt, pepper, moisten with a little olive oil and broil. Serve on toast, with maître d'hôtel sauce, quartered lemons and watercress.

NOVEMBER 24

BREAKFAST
Florida grapefruit
Eggs Bércy
Rolls
Coffee

LUNCHEON
Consommé in cups
Fried smelts, Tartar sauce
Broiled pig's feet, special
Fried apples
Romaine salad
French pastry   Coffee

DINNER
Seapuit oysters
Potage Lamballe
Boiled beef garnished with vegetables
Horseradish à l'Anglaise   Pickles
Asparagus, Hollandaise
Fancy ice cream
Assorted cakes   Coffee

Eggs Bércy. Fry some small breakfast sausages and cut in pieces one inch long. Make some shirred eggs. When half cooked add the sausages and a very little tomato sauce. Season with salt and pepper and finish cooking.

Broiled pig's feet, special. Take some boiled pig's feet, split, and remove the upper bones. Season with salt, pepper and olive oil, roll in fresh bread crumbs, and broil. See sauce below.

Sauce special. Two-thirds tomato ketchup, one-third tomato sauce, a little paprika, a little Worcestershire sauce. Bring to a boil and serve.

Boiled pig's feet. Roll two pig's feet very tightly together with cheesecloth, so they will lay straight when cooked. Put in vessel, cover with cold water, season with salt, whole black peppers, carrot, onion, and a bouquet garni. Boil until well done. If necessary to keep them after cooking, place in an earthern pot in their own broth.

Fried apples. Peel, core, and cut the apples in five or six pieces. Roll in flour and fry in swimming fat or lard. Serve on a napkin.

Icing or frosting, for glacé cakes, éclairs, etc. One and one-half pounds of icing sugar, a pony of water or fruit juice, and the whites of two eggs. Mix and heat over slow fire, stirring continually with a wooden spoon. Do not let it boil. Flavor according to desire. For chocolate frosting add a little melted cocoa.

Cream puffs. One-quarter pound of butter, one cup of water, one cup of milk, four eggs and one-quarter pound of flour. Put the butter, water and milk into a sauce pan and boil. Remove from the fire and add the flour, mixing with a wooden spoon. Then add the eggs one by one, beating well. Dress them on a buttered pan, and about two inches in diameter. Moisten the tops with eggs, and sprinkle with chopped almonds. Bake in a medium oven for about twenty minutes, then slit one edge and fill with sweet whipped cream. Dust some powdered sugar on top and serve.

Chocolate éclairs. Same dough as for cream puffs. Dress them on a buttered pan in the shape of lady fingers, and bake in hot oven. Split at one side and fill with sweet whipped cream. Coat with chocolate icing. Pastry cream may be used instead of whipped cream, if desired.

Pastry cream. Pint of milk, one-half of a vanilla bean, one-quarter pound of sugar, three eggs and one ounce of corn starch. Mix the eggs, sugar and corn starch. Boil the vanilla bean and add to the eggs. Mix well with a whip, put on fire and keep stirring until thick. When cold use it for filling small cakes, cream puffs, éclairs, etc.

NOVEMBER 25

BREAKFAST
Preserved figs
Wheat cakes
Rolls
Coffee

LUNCHEON
Anchovy salad
Poached eggs, sans gêne
Navarin of lamb, printanier
Baba au rhum
Demi tasse

DINNER
California oysters on half shell
Purée of lentils
Stuffed roasted chicken
String beans
Duchess potatoes
Cold French asparagus,
   French dressing
Almond cake
Coffee

SUPPER
Salade Olga

Wheat cakes. Sift together into a bowl one-half pound of flour and one teaspoonful of baking powder. Add one ounce of sugar, one ounce of melted butter, one egg and a little milk. Mix all into a medium thick batter. Bake on a hot griddle iron. Serve honey or maple syrup, and sweet butter separate.

Breakfast rolls. Three pounds of flour, one ounce of salt, one ounce of sugar and two ounces of yeast. Scald the milk and pour it over the sugar, salt and butter. Melt the yeast in luke-warm water, mix with the milk, etc., and add half of the flour. Beat well, cover, and let raise. Then add the remainder of the flour and let it raise again until it is twice its original volume. Put on table, roll in shape desired, place on pan, and let raise again. Brush the top with melted butter, and bake.

Anchovy salad. Put sliced lettuce on the bottom of a pickle dish. Place fillets of anchovies crosswise over the lettuce. Garnish all around with chopped eggs, beets and parsley. Season with French dressing.

Poached eggs, sans gêne. Place a hot poached egg on a heart of artichoke, cover with a slice of parboiled beef marrow. Serve with sauce Bordelaise.

Navarin of lamb, printanier. (Lamb stew). Take three pounds of shoulder, or breast of lamb, and cut in pieces two inches square. Salt, pepper, and put in sauté pan with a little fat or butter, and allow to roast until nice and brown. Then add a cup of flour and let same become brown. Add a cup of purée of tomatoes and enough hot water to cover the meat, and boil for ten minutes. Parboil three carrots and three turnips and cut in small pieces, and add together with twelve whole small onions fried brown in butter, twelve small round potatoes, and a bouquet garni. Cook until soft, remove the bouquet garni, and serve with chopped parsley and fresh cooked peas on top.

Duchess potatoes. Make dough as for potato croquettes. Roll on table with a little flour, and cut in the shape of a cork. Flatten and cut a cross on the top with a small knife, brush with yolks of eggs, put on buttered pan and bake in oven. By using a pastry bag with a star mould the tops can be decorated with the dough, in the form of a rose, in place of the cross.

Salade Olga. Cut into small dices two apples, one stalk of celery, two buttons of cooked artichokes, a few asparagus tips, and one truffle. Season with salt, pepper, and a very little vinegar and oil. Place in salad bowl with leaves of lettuce around the sides, and cover with mayonnaise. Garnish with fancy-cut pickled beets and artichokes. Sprinkle with hard-boiled yolks of eggs chopped fine, and parsley.

NOVEMBER 26

BREAKFAST
Oatmeal with cream
Boiled salt mackerel, melted butter
Baked potatoes
Rolls
Coffee

LUNCHEON
Stuffed eggs, Nantua
Mutton chop, grilled
Saratoga chip potatoes
Chiffonnade salad
Camembert cheese
Coffee

DINNER
Cream of asparagus
Whitebait on Graham bread
Rheinbraten
Romaine salad
Cup custard
Lady fingers
Coffee

Stuffed eggs, Nantua. Cut four hard-boiled eggs in two, lengthwise, and remove the yolks. Mix a piece of butter, the size of an egg, with a little anchovy paste, a very little salt, pepper, paprika, chopped parsley, and the yolks strained through a coarse sieve. Dress or fill the eggs through a pastry bag, put a slice of pimento on top of each, and serve very cold.

Mutton chops, grilled. Salt and pepper the chops, roll in oil and broil. Garnish with watercress.

Saratoga chip potatoes. Round the potatoes off lengthwise to about the size of a silver dollar. Slice very thin, fry in swimming fat until crisp, remove and salt. Serve on napkin. Do not cover or they will become soft.

Chiffonnade salad. Equal parts of romaine, lettuce, chicory, escarole, sliced cucumbers and quartered tomatoes. Put in salad bowl, pour French dressing over all, and garnish with chopped beets, eggs and parsley.

Cream of asparagus. Prepare same as cream of cauliflower. Use either canned or fresh asparagus.

Whitebait on Graham bread. Wash the whitebait and dry, then put in bowl, season with salt and pepper, and cover with milk. Remove and roll in flour, using a colander to allow the flour to sift through. Fry in swimming lard, which is ready in advance, and very hot. Serve on napkin, and garnish with Graham bread and butter sandwiches, fried parsley, quartered lemon, and sauce Tartar separate, or any kind of cold sauce.

Rheinbraten. Cut sirloin steaks one-half inch thick. Season with salt and paprika on both sides, and fry in hot butter. Dish up on platter with paprika sauce, and garnish with paprika potatoes.

Paprika sauce. Simmer one chopped onion and a chopped slice of raw ham, in a little butter. Add one cup of cream, two cups of cream sauce, a soupspoonful of paprika, and a little salt. Boil for ten minutes and strain.

Paprika potatoes. Slice fresh-boiled potatoes and put in sauce pan. Cover with paprika sauce, salt, and boil for a few minutes.

NOVEMBER 27

BREAKFAST
  Assorted fruits
  Boiled eggs
  Rolls
  Coffee

LUNCHEON
  Cold assorted meats
  Potato salad
  Coffee

DINNER
  Clear green turtle, au Xérès
  Toke Point oysters, mignonette
  Salted almonds.   Celery
  Radishes.   Ripe olives
  Planked striped bass
  Sweetbread patties, cream sauce
  Roast stuffed turkey, with chestnuts
  Cranberry sauce
  Sweet potatoes, Southern style
  Succotash
  Hearts of lettuce, egg dressing
  Plum pudding,
      hard and brandy sauces
  Mince pie
  Fancy ice cream
  Assorted cakes
  Roquefort cheese and crackers
  Assorted fruits
  Coffee

Mignonette sauce. Take one-half cup of whole white peppers and crush with a bottle on a hard table or marble slab, but not too fine. Mix with four finely chopped shallots, a little chives, one spoonful of salt and one-half pint of white wine or tarragon vinegar. Serve in a green pepper, or a small glass, in center of plate surrounded with oysters or clams.

Planked striped bass. Split the bass, remove the bones, place on buttered plank, season with salt, pepper and a little melted butter over all. Bake in oven until nearly done. Take out and decorate with a pastry bag and a star mould, with some potato prepared as for potato croquettes, forming a border around the fish. Put back in oven and bake until nice and brown. Pour maître d'hôtel sauce on top, garnish with quartered lemons and parsley in branches.

Turkey stuffed with chestnuts. Stuff the turkey with chestnut dressing. Put some thin-sliced pork fat over the breast and tie together. Place in pan with an onion, carrot, a little thyme, bay leaf and fresh piece of butter. Salt, put in oven and baste all the time. When turkey is done remove from pan, and let gravy set for a few minutes. Take off the fat, add a little stock or water, reduce one-half, add a little meat extract and strain.

Dressing for chicken, turkey, suckling pig, etc. Bake six onions, with the skins on, in oven for ten minutes. Remove the skins and chop very fine. Add turkey, chicken or suckling pig livers cut in very small squares. Then add fresh bread crumbs, a piece of fresh butter, salt and pepper. Mix well, add a little powdered thyme, chopped parsley, add garlic if desired. If for suckling pig add some sage.

Chestnut dressing. Split the shells of two pounds of chestnuts with a sharp pointed knife. Put in oven and when they burst open remove and peel. Put in pot with a small piece of celery, salt, cover with water, boil till done, allow to cool, and mix with dressing described above.

Apple dressing. Peel half a dozen apples, remove the cores, cut in six pieces, put in pan with three ounces of butter and simmer slowly for ten minutes. Mix with above dressing, omitting chestnuts.

NOVEMBER 28

BREAKFAST
Hothouse raspberries with cream
Oatmeal and cream
Stewed lamb kidneys
Rolls
Coffee

DINNER
Consommé aux quenelles
Ripe California olives
Cultivated brook trout, Hollandaise
Potatoes nature
Roast ribs of prime beef
Stewed tomatoes
Mashed potatoes
Lettuce salad
English breakfast tea ice cream
Assorted fancy cakes
Coffee

LUNCHEON
Grapefruit with cherries
Turkey hash on toast
Coffee éclairs
Oolong tea

SUPPER
Welsh rabbit

Stewed lamb kidneys. Split six kidneys, remove the skin, and cut in thin slices. Have a pan ready with hot butter and fry on a quick fire for a few seconds. Take kidneys from pan, and add one soupspoonful of flour to the sauce and let simmer until brown. Add one cup of stock or hot water, salt and pepper, and reduce one-half. Return the kidneys to the sauce, but do not let them boil or they will become hard. Before serving add a little sherry wine or chopped parsley.

Turkey hash on toast. Cut turkey in small dices, put in sauce pan, cover with two-thirds boiling cream and one-third cream sauce, season, boil for a few minutes, and serve on hot dry toast.

Welsh rabbit. Cut one pound of American cheese in very small dices. Put in pan with a small pinch of Cayenne pepper, one spoonful of ale or beer, one teaspoonful of Worcestershire sauce, and put on fire to melt. Do not stir until cheese is quite soft; then stir well with whip till it is melted and boiling. Pour over toast on a very hot china platter or shirred egg dish.

French bread. One gallon of warm water, two ounces of yeast, three ounces of salt, three ounces of sugar and three ounces of lard. Dissolve the yeast, salt, sugar and lard in the water, and mix in flour enough to form a medium-stiff dough. Work it until smooth, cover with a cloth and let it raise for one-half hour. Then form the dough into long loaves and about two inches thick. Lay them on a cloth dusted with flour and let them raise to nearly double in size. Moisten the tops with milk, make several diagonal cuts on each loaf half way through, and bake in a rather hot oven.

Homemade bread. One quart of warm water, one quart of warm milk, two ounces of yeast, one ounce of salt and one-quarter of a pound of melted lard or butter. Dissolve the yeast in the milk and butter, and add the salt and butter, or lard. Add enough flour to make a medium dough, mix, beat well and cover. Allow to raise for about four hours. Divide the dough in four parts, roll and place in moulds or pans and let raise another hour before baking.

NOVEMBER 29

BREAKFAST
  Orange juice
  Scrambled eggs with anchovies
  Rolls
  Coffee

LUNCHEON
  Écrevisses with mayonnaise
  Lamb chops sauté, aux cèpes
  Sybil potatoes
  Cup custard
  Coffee

DINNER
  Toke Point oysters on half shell
  Cream of summer squash
  Filet mignon, Chéron
  Georgette potatoes
  Ravachol salad
  Pistache ice cream
  Baked Alaska
  Coffee

Scrambled eggs with anchovies. Put some fillets of salted anchovies in oil and leave for a few days; or use anchovies in oil. Salt the scrambled eggs lightly and lay the anchovies crosswise over the top.

Écrevisses with mayonnaise. Prepare the écrevisses en buisson. When cold remove the tails from the shells and serve on platter with lemons and parsley. Mayonnaise separate.

Lamb chops sauté, aux cépes. Fry the chops in sauté pan, in oil. When done put on platter. Slice some cépes, (a specie of mushroom) season with salt and pepper and fry for a few seconds. Just before removing from the fire add a little garlic, and pour all over the chops. Sprinkle with chopped parsley.

Georgette potatoes. Use potato croquette dough. Roll on table to the thickness of a cork and about ten inches long. Make a hollow the entire length and fill with purée of spinach. Bring the edges of the hollow together and roll again so the spinach will be in the middle of the potato dough and not visible. Cut in pieces two inches long, roll in bread crumbs, and fry in the same manner as croquettes.

Ravachol salad. Use whole leaves of romaine. Place alternate slices of grape fruit and orange on top until the leaves are covered. Put some narrow strips of red pepper across the top, pour French dressing over all, and decorate with unsweetened whipped cream.

Filet mignon, Chéron. Small fillets of beef sauté in butter. Cover with Béarnaise sauce, and garnish with artichoke buttons, macédoine, (mixed vegetables) and fleurons.

Fleurons. Used for garnishing entrées, Newburg or chafing dish preparations, fish, etc. Take some puff paste, with six turns, roll it to about one-eighth inch in thickness, cut with a half moon cutter about two inches in diameter, and place on a pan moistened with water. Wash the tops with eggs and bake in a hot oven.

NOVEMBER 30

BREAKFAST
  Hominy and cream
  Calf's liver and bacon
  Baked potatoes
  Rolls
  Coffee

LUNCHEON
  Stuffed tomatoes, Nana
  Poached eggs, Persanne
  Broiled squab on toast
  Cold asparagus, mustard sauce
  Saratoga chip potatoes
  German apple cake
  Coffee

DINNER
  Onion soup, au gratin
  Celery
  Planked striped bass
  Roast leg of veal, au jus
  Cardon à la moelle
  Potatoes à la Reine
  Escarole and chicory salad
  Neapolitan ice cream
  Assorted cakes
  Coffee

Stuffed tomatoes, Nana. Put four nice medium sized tomatoes in boiling water for fifteen seconds. Then dip in cold water and peel. Cut off the tops, scoop out and fill with the following: One-half of the breast of a boiled chicken, chopped very fine, some chopped walnuts, a little mayonnaise sauce, a little whipped cream, and salt and pepper. Mix well. After filling place the tomatoes on lettuce leaves and cover with thin mayonnaise. Serve very cold.

Calf's liver and bacon. Slice the liver about two-thirds of an inch thick. Salt, pepper, pass through olive oil and broil, but not too well done or the liver will be hard. Serve broiled bacon on top, maître d'hôtel sauce, and garnish with lemon and parsley.

Mustard sauce, cold. For asparagus, artichokes, etc. To one cup of mayonnaise sauce add one soupspoonful of French mustard. Mix well.

Lunch rolls. Two pounds of flour, one ounce of yeast, one ounce of salt, one pint of water. Dissolve the yeast and salt in the water, add the flour and mix, making a rather hard dough. Put into a basin, cover with a cloth, and allow to stand for four hours. Then divide the dough in four parts, roll each one separately into the form of a stick about fourteen inches long and one inch thick. Put on a cloth on a special roll plank made for the purpose. Take care that the rolls are sufficiently far apart so they will not touch when they raise. Let them set for about one-half hour. Then cut each roll of dough in three parts with a sharp knife, make two incisions in the top of each, put into a pan and bake for about twenty minutes.

Cardons à la moelle. Cardon is a vegetable, a thistle-like plant related to the artichoke. It can be obtained in cans. Empty into a vessel and warm in its own juice. Parboil some sliced beef marrow, put into a brown gravy with the juice of one lemon and some chopped parsley. Remove cardon from its broth, put on a platter and pour the brown sauce and marrow over all.

DECEMBER 1

BREAKFAST
  Preserved figs with cream
  Force with cream
  Dry toast
  Coffee

LUNCHEON
  Cold fillet of sole, Raven
  Spring lamb Irish stew
  Cream puffs
  Coffee

DINNER
  Consommé Sévigné
  Salted Brazil nuts
  Sweetbreads braisé, Pompadour
  Château potatoes
  Terrine de foie gras à la gelée
  Hearts of romaine,
    Roquefort dressing
  Meringue à la crème, Chantilly
  Coffee

Cold fillet of sole, Raven. Cook four fillets of sole in white wine and place on a platter. Simmer two spoonsful of finely chopped shallots in butter, add a few chopped fresh mushrooms, one chopped tomato and the wine used for cooking the fish. Reduce until it becomes thick, cool off, add some chives and chervil chopped fine, and a little mayonnaise. Spread over the fillets, and cover with a mayonnaise rose. Decorate to taste with fancy-cut truffles, pickles, etc. Serve very cold.

Consommé Sévigné. White meat of chicken and smoked beef tongue cut Julienne. (in the shape of matches). Serve in consommé with a sprinkle of chopped chervil.

Sweetbreads braisé, Pompadour. Braise the sweetbreads until about two-thirds done. Cool a little and cover with a thin layer of chicken force meat. Decorate all around with chopped tongue, with chopped truffles in the center. Replace in pan, using the same stock used before, but strained. Cover with buttered manilla paper and return to oven to finish cooking. Serve with own gravy and a little Maderia sauce.

Terrine de foie gras à la gelée. Put the foie gras on ice for a few hours. Carve from the terrine with a table spoon and place on a platter covered with a napkin. Decorate with meat jelly cut in triangles and chopped, and parsley in branches.

Gelée. (Meat jelly). Take any kind of good stock. Put in the whites of six eggs to each gallon to clarify it. Add one pound of chopped raw beef to the gallon. Also one sliced onion, one carrot, one leek, a little celery and parsley, a few pepper berries, one bay leaf and a clove. Stir well and add slowly the hot stock. Soak twelve leaves of gelatine in cold water for ten minutes and add. Bring to a boil slowly, stirring from time to time. When it comes to a boil it must be clear. Strain through very fine cheese cloth, being careful not to stir up the meat so that it will cloud the broth. Season with salt and a very little Cayenne, add a glass of good sherry, and allow to cool.

Meringue à la crème, Chantilly. Whip some cream until stiff, add some powdered sugar, flavor with vanilla. Put one spoonful between each two meringue shells, dress on a plate, and decorate with some of the same cream passed through a pastry bag with a star mould.

DECEMBER 2

BREAKFAST
Baked apples
Oatmeal with cream
Butter toast
Coffee

LUNCHEON
Eggs, Tivoli
Miroton of beef, en bordure
Cabinet pudding
Coffee

DINNER
Blue Point oysters
Consommé Doria
Fillet of sole, St. Malo
Tournedos, Boulanger
Soufflé potatoes
Roquefort cheese
Crackers
Coffee

Eggs, Tivoli. Cut a piece of homemade bread into a cube and fry in butter. Open one side with a sharp knife and scoop out the center. Place in the cavity a poached egg, cover with cream sauce, sprinkle a little grated cheese on top, and bake until brown.

Miroton of beef, en bordure. Use left over boiled or braised beef, and cut in thin slices. Put into sauce pan one sliced onion with a piece of butter, and simmer until nice and brown. Then add one gill of vinegar, and a spoonful of French mustard and reduce until almost dry. Now add the sliced beef, cover with brown gravy, season with salt, pepper and a little chopped parsley, and boil for a few minutes. Dish into a deep platter, or individual shirred egg dishes, make a border of potato croquet dough, sprinkle grated cheese on top and bake till brown.

Consommé Doria. Consommé tapioca, with chopped truffles and sherry wine.

Fillet of sole, St. Malo. Fillet of sole au vin blanc with the addition of lobster sauce with scallops, and lobster and oysters cut in small squares.

Tournedos, Boulanger. Small fillets of beef sauté, with sauce Madére. Garnished with fried calf's brains and artichoke bottoms stuffed with spinach.

Soufflé potatoes. Peel the potatoes to oval shape. Do not wash but wipe with a napkin. Cut lengthwise in strips about an eighth of an inch in thickness. Place in swimming fat or lard that is merely warm and put on fire to get hot. When the potatoes are nearly done they will swim on top of the fat and swell up like little cushions. When all are on top take out and throw into very hot fat to color them. Remove, salt, and serve on napkin.

DECEMBER 3

BREAKFAST
Preserved figs
Boiled eggs
Corn muffins
Coffee

LUNCHEON
Grapefruit
Eggs en cocotte, Italienne
Chicken hash, Victor
Endive salad
Cup custard
Coffee

DINNER
Hors d'oeuvre variés
Cream of squash
Aiguillettes of bass, à la Russe
Squab sauté, Tyrollienne
Anna potatoes
Strawberry ice cream
Assorted cakes
Coffee

Corn Muffins. One-half pound of corn meal, one-half pound of flour, two ounces of melted butter, four eggs, one pint of sour milk, one-half cup of molasses, one teaspoonful of soda and one teaspoonful of salt. Sift together the corn meal, flour and salt. Dissolve the soda in the sour milk, add the eggs, well beaten, the molasses, the butter and the sifted ingredients. Beat well and bake in a well-greased muffin pan.

Eggs en Cocotte, Italienne. Put in buttered cocotte dish one raw egg, cover with sauce Italienne, put a little grated cheese and a small piece of butter on top and bake in oven.

Italienne sauce. Chop six shallots very fine and simmer in sauce pan with two ounces of butter. Do not let the shallots become brown or they will lose their flavor. Add some chopped fresh or canned mushrooms (about a can full), and one glass of white wine, and boil until reduced almost dry. Then add one and one-half pints of brown gravy, and boil again for a few minutes. Season with salt and pepper to taste, and sprinkle with chopped parsley. This sauce is used for many entrée dishes.

Endive salad. Endive is a species of chicory salad, originally imported from France. Cut in two lengthwise and lay on platter or individual plates. Serve with a sauce of salt, pepper, and one-fourth tarragon vinegar to three-fourths olive oil. Sprinkle with chopped chervil.

Chicken hash, Victor. Take the white meat of a boiled chicken or soup hen and cut in half inch squares, and half as much fresh-boiled potatoes cut the same way. Chop six shallots very fine and simmer in four ounces of sweet butter, but do not let them become colored. Add the chicken and potatoes, and cover with clear chicken broth. Season with salt, pepper and a little chives, and let simmer for five minutes. Serve in a chafing dish with a sprinkle of chopped chervil on top. Melba toast separate.

DECEMBER 4

BREAKFAST
Grapefruit juice
Shredded wheat biscuit with cream
English muffins
Coffee

LUNCHEON
Casaba melon
Eggs aromatic
English lamb chops,
    XX Century Club
Lettuce salad
Pistache éclairs
Coffee

DINNER
Blue Point oysters
Fillet of bass, shrimp sauce
Braised beef, Cumberland style
Baked Hubbard squash
Mashed potatoes
Endive salad
Vanilla ice cream
Assorted cakes
Coffee

Eggs aromatic. Fry the eggs in oil or poach. Place on toast, cover with tomato sauce, and put a few leaves of fresh mint on top before serving.

English lamb chops, XX Century Club. Broil the chops, garnish with pimentos stuffed with purée of sweet potatoes. Serve with sauce Madére.

Pistache Éclairs. Same as chocolate éclairs. Cover with pistache icing.

Pistache icing. To white icing add some pistache essence, or orange flower extract, and a little green coloring.

Fillet of bass, shrimp sauce. Place the fillets in a buttered pan, season with salt, add one-half glass of white wine, and a little stock or water. When cooked dish up on platter and cover with shrimp sauce.

Shrimp sauce. To some white wine sauce (sauce vin blanc) add some shrimps.

Braised beef with calf's feet. Take a piece of round or rump of beef, season with salt and pepper, put in pot with two onions cut in four, two carrots and a piece of butter. Roast until nice and brown. Then add one spoonful of flour and brown again. Add one glass of claret, one quart of stock, three tomatoes cut in four, or canned tomatoes, and a bouquet garni. Bring to a boil, cover tight and put in oven till very well done. This is braised beef, plain. When served Cumberland style (with calf's feet) add the feet at the same time as the claret and stock, and strain the sauce when done. If the feet are not served with the beef they may be used as an entrée.

Baked Hubbard squash. Cut the squash in four, remove the seeds, salt and pepper, put a piece of butter on top of each piece of squash and bake in oven.

DECEMBER 5

BREAKFAST
  Sliced oranges
  Boiled salt mackerel
  Baked potatoes
  Corn bread
  Coffee

LUNCHEON
  Clam broth in cups
  Ripe olives
  Fillet of turbot, Pelissier
  Potatoes Parisienne
  Spinach aux croutons
  Omelette au rhum
  Coffee

DINNER
  Lobster chowder
  Celery.   Salted English walnuts
  Aiguillettes of sole, Venitienne
  Planked striped bass
  Cucumber salad
  Brussels sprouts and chestnuts
  Apple Charlotte
  Coffee

Clam broth. Take hard or soft clams and wash well. Put in vessel with just water enough to cover, a little salt and a small piece of raw celery. Boil for fifteen minutes, and strain through cheese cloth.

Clam broth, Chantilly. Serve whipped cream separate, or on top of each cup.

Consommé en Bellevue. Half chicken broth and half clam broth mixed. Serve in cups with whipped cream on top.

Clam chowder. Chop two onions, one leek, a piece of celery and one green onion in small pieces, also cut one-half pound of salt pork in small squares. Put all together in a vessel with two ounces of butter and simmer till well done. Then add one gallon of stock or fish broth, four potatoes cut in half inch squares, salt, pepper, a little paprika, one teaspoonful of sugar, one teaspoonful of chopped thyme, a little chopped parsley, and four peeled tomatoes cut in small dices; or chopped canned tomatoes. Bring to a boil and let cook for about one hour. Put one hundred well-washed Little Neck clams in a separate vessel and put on fire with one-half glass of water and boil for ten minutes. Strain the broth and add to the chowder. Remove the clams from the shells, cut in four pieces and add to the chowder with one cup of cracker meal, and boil for four minutes. Serve with broken crackers.

Lobster chowder. Same as clam chowder with the exception of lobster cut in small dices instead of the clams.

DECEMBER 6

BREAKFAST
  Bananas with cream
  Boiled eggs
  Dry toast
  Chocolate
  Whipped cream

LUNCHEON
  Fish salad, ravigote
  Broiled lamb chops
  French fried potatoes
  Cauliflower Polonaise
  German coffee cake
  Lunch rolls
  Tea

DINNER
  Cream of endives
  Fillet of flounder, Chevreuse
  Chicken sauté, Ambassadrice
  Carrots, Vichy
  Fondante potatoes
  Escarole salad
  Peach ice cream
  Assorted cakes
  Coffee

SUPPER
  Oysters poulette
  St. Francis rolls
  Nesselrode pudding
  Lady fingers
  Demi tasse

Oysters poulette. Open three dozen oysters, put in vessel with their own juice and bring to a boil. Drain off the broth, cover oysters with a pint of poulette sauce, and serve in chafing dish.

Carrots, Vichy. Slice some tender carrots very fine, place in buttered sauce pan, season with salt and a little pepper, and simmer over a slow fire. Then add a little chicken broth or soup stock and cook until soft. Mix one teaspoonful of flour with three ounces of butter, add to the carrots and simmer for five minutes. Serve with chopped parsley.

Chocolate. For each person take one rib or bar of chocolate. Cut in very small pieces, put in pot and add one spoonful of water and let chocolate melt. Add one large cup of very hot milk for each person, and bring nearly to the boiling point.

Fish salad, ravigote. Any kind of boiled fish that may be left over. Remove the bones and skin, break the fish in small pieces and lay on lettuce leaves. Cover with Tartar sauce, garnish with sliced pickles, pickled beets and hard-boiled eggs.

Cream of endives. Prepare the same as cream of cauliflower, using endives instead.

Fillet of flounder, Chevreuse. Stuff the fillets with halibut force meat, put in buttered pan and cook in white wine. Cover with Béarnaise sauce mixed with a little purée of tomatoes.

Chicken sauté, Ambassadrice. Jointed chicken sauté in butter, sauce suprême, garnished with truffles, mushrooms and goose liver sauté

Goose liver sauté. Salt and pepper some fresh goose livers, roll in flour, put in pan with fresh butter and simmer until done. For garnishing entrée dishes the imported goose liver au natural can be obtained in cans. Remove the fat from the top of the can, cut the liver out in slices, season with salt and pepper, put in flour, and fry very quickly in sweet butter. Serve as a garnish or as an entrée.

Goose liver sauté aux truffes. Put goose liver sauté in chafing dish and cover with sauce Périgord.

Sauce Périgord. Slice six truffles very thin, put in vessel with a glass of dry sherry wine and reduce until it is nearly dry. Then add one-half pint of brown gravy, seasoned with salt and Cayenne pepper, and cook for ten minutes.

DECEMBER 7

BREAKFAST
  Oatmeal with cream
  Baked beans, Boston style
  Boston brown bread
  Coffee

LUNCHEON
  Mariniert herring
  Boiled potatoes
  Rolls
  Coffee

DINNER
  Chicken okra soup
  Salted pecans
  Fillet of sole, Normande
  Roast ribs of beef
  Asparagus, Hollandaise
  Brabant potatoes
  Bijou salad
  Hazelnut ice cream
  Alsatian wafers
  Coffee

Corn bread. One-half pound of yellow corn meal, one-half pound of flour, one teaspoonful of baking powder, three eggs, one ounce of melted butter, one teaspoonful of salt, one pint of milk and one-half cup of boiling water. Pour the boiling water over the corn meal and allow it to become cold. Beat the yolks of the eggs and add to the corn meal, then add the milk, flour and the baking powder, salt and melted butter. Mix and then add the whites of the eggs beaten very stiff. Pour into a shallow well-greased pan and bake in a hot oven for about twenty-five minutes.

Boston brown bread. One pound of rye flour, one pound of Graham flour, two pounds of corn meal, one pound of wheat flour, one quart of molasses, one and one-half quarts of milk, two ounces of salt and three ounces of baking powder. Put all the flour and the baking powder in one vessel, then add the molasses, milk and salt and make a soft dough. Fill brown bread moulds about three-fourths full, put in steam cooker for three and one-half hours, then remove from steam and bake in oven for twenty minutes.

Chicken okra soup. Remove the breast from a raw fowl, and with the remainder make a chicken broth. Cut the breast in small dices, put in vessel with a chopped onion and a chopped green pepper and a small piece of but or, simmer till onion is soft, then add the chicken broth, two peeled tomatoes cut in small dices, or some canned tomatoes, salt and pepper. Let boil slowly for one-half hour, then add one pound of okra cut in pieces three-quarters of an inch in length, and cook until okra is soft. Add one teaspoonful of Worcestershire sauce and a cup of boiled rice and serve with chopped parsley. If desired a slice of ham may be cut in small squares and added at the same time as the chicken breast.

DECEMBER 8

BREAKFAST
Stewed prunes
Scrambled eggs with asparagus tips
Buttered toast
Coffee

LUNCHEON
Hors d'oeuvres variés
Eggs Boremis
Hungarian beef goulash
Apple pie
Coffee

DINNER
Cream of spinach
Fillet of bass, Dieppoise
Chicken sauté, Marengo
Potatoes à la Reine
Dandelion salad
Apricot ice cream
Macaroons
Coffee

Scrambled eggs with asparagus tips. Put some asparagus tips in butter, season with salt and pepper, simmer till hot, and add to the eggs.

Eggs Boremis. Put an egg in a well-buttered cocotte dish, season with salt and pepper, put plenty of grated cheese and a piece of butter on top of all, and bake in oven.

Cocoa. Put two tablespoonsful of cocoa in a pot with one-half cup of water and boil for a minute. Add two cups of milk, bring to a boil, and strain. Serve powdered sugar separate. May also be made with water only, omitting the milk.

Fillet of bass, Dieppoise. Cook the fillets "au vin blanc." Dish up on platter with lobster sauce and oysters, mushrooms, truffles, shrimps and mussels cut in small squares.

Chicken sauté, Marengo. Joint of chicken, season with salt and pepper and put in pan in very hot olive oil. When nice and brown on both sides add four chopped shallots and a little garlic and allow them to get hot, but not brown. Then add one-half glass of white wine and reduce. Add one cup of brown gravy, one cup of chopped tomatoes and one can of French mushrooms. Cook for fifteen minutes. Dish up and garnish with eggs and croûtons fried in oil, chopped parsley, and a few slices of truffle on top.

Pie paste. One and one-half pounds of flour, one-half pound of lard, one-half pound of butter and a pinch of salt. Mix all together and add enough water, (about one cup), to make a rather stiff dough. Keep in cool place or ice box.

Apple pie. For two pies line the plates with pie paste rolled very thin. Slice six good sized apples, add one-quarter of a pound of sugar and a teaspoonful of powdered cinnamon, mix and fill the plates. Wet the edges of the dough and cover with paste also rolled thin. Wash over with egg, make a few cuts in the center so the steam may escape while baking, and put in a moderate oven. When done dust with powdered sugar, and serve hot or cold as desired. If the apples are coarse it will be well to boil them a little in water with a piece of cinnamon and a very little sugar.

DECEMBER 9

BREAKFAST
Baked apples with cream
Hominy with cream
Rolls
Coffee

LUNCHEON
Grapefruit en suprême
Eggs Benedict
Lamb hash
Chocolate layer cake
Coffee

DINNER
Potage Coulis
Salted pecans
Fillet of turbot, Royaldi
Chicken, Edward VII
Potato croquettes
Chiffonnade salad
Parfait au chocolate
Assorted cakes
Coffee

Grapefruit en suprême. Serve in a long-stemed double grapefruit glass. put shaved ice in large glass around the smaller one. In small glass put sliced grapefruit mixed with powdered sugar. Tie a ribbon, with neat bow, around the glass.

Eggs Benedict. Split an English muffin, toast on the inside, place on each half a small slice of broiled ham, on the ham a poached egg, cover with Hollandaise sauce, and place a piece of truffle on top.

Layer cake. Eight eggs, one-half pound of sugar, one-half pound of flour, one-quarter pound of melted butter, and some flavoring extract. Beat the eggs with the sugar, on slow fire until warm, remove and continue beating until cold. Mix the flour in lightly and then add the melted butter, little by little, and the flavoring. Do not mix too much. Pour into a well-buttered mould and bake in a moderate oven for about three-quarters of an hour. Allow to cool, cut in three or four slices, and fill with cream, or jelly, or marmalade, as desired. Glacé the top with icing and decorate. The American style layer cake is mixed in the same manner, but baked in shallow moulds, requiring only about ten minutes in the oven. The filling is then placed between the cakes. instead of slicing.

Chocolate layer cake. Bake some layers as for moka cake, and put three or four, one on top of another, with chocolate butter cream filling between. The filling is made in the same manner as moka filling, but use one ounce of melted chocolate or cocoa instead of the coffee flavor. Glacé the top of the cake with chocolate frosting and decorate with some of the chocolate cream filling, using pastry bag with fancy tube.

Chicken, Edward VII. Boil the chicken in stock and stuff with rice as for Chicken Diva. Add small squares of truffles and goose liver natural. Serve with curry sauce.

DECEMBER 10

BREAKFAST
Stewed rhubarb
Boiled eggs
Dry toast
Coffee

LUNCHEON
Canapé Riga
Eggs Coquelicot
Tripe and oysters in cream
Camembert cheese
Crackers
Coffee

DINNER
Potage Hollandaise
Stuffed fillet of sole, Diplomate
Tournedos de Goncourt
String beans, aux fines herbes
Julienne potatoes
Salade Brésilienne
Floating island
Pound cake
Coffee

Eggs Coquelicot. Line a timbale mould with a whole red pepper, (canned pimento) and break an egg into it, season with salt and pepper, and put timbale in a pan in boiling water, and place in oven until egg is cooked. Put some chicken hash in cream on a platter and turn egg and pepper on top to look like a little red cap. Serve with cream sauce around the hash.

Tripe and oysters in cream. Simmer six chopped shallots in butter, but do not allow them to color. Add two pounds of tripe cut in strips, one cup of stock, one bouquet garni, and boil for one hour. Remove the bouquet garni, drain off the broth. Add two cups of cream sauce and three dozen parboiled oysters. Simmer for a minute, and season with salt and a little Cayenne pepper.

Potage Hollandaise. (Soup). Bind a velouté of chicken with cream and yolks of eggs. Serve with brunoise garnishing.

Velouté. Used for the foundation of many soups. Put in vessel five ounces of butter and four ounces of flour and simmer for a few minutes. Add two quarts of chicken broth, stock or bouillon, cook for half an hour and bind with one cup of cream and the yolks of two eggs.

Consommé brunoise. Cut in very small dice, (nearly fine chopped), one carrot, one turnip, one leek, a stalk of celery and a little white cabbage, and parboil in salt water. Then drain off the water, put in well-buttered casserole, add a pinch of sugar, cover with buttered manilla paper and with the casserole cover on top of that, and put in the oven to braise. If too dry a half cup of stock may be added. Cook until vegetables are soft. Use for potage garnishing, Consommé brunoise, and other dishes. For soups use one heaping spoonful of brunoise to each plate.

Fillet of sole, Diplomate. Slice fine six fresh mushrooms, season with salt and pepper, and simmer in butter. When done add one spoonful of meat extract. Split four fillets of sole and fill with the above dressing and cook "au vin blanc." Then place on a platter, cover with cream sauce well seasoned, put grated cheese on top and bake in oven.

Tournedos de Goncourt. Broiled fillet of beef served with Béarnaise sauce mixed with a little purée of tomatoes, and garnished with tomatoes glacées.

Tomatoes glacées. Put six whole peeled tomatoes on a buttered pan, season with salt and pepper, put a small piece of butter on top of each, and bake in moderate oven for ten minutes.

DECEMBER 11

BREAKFAST
  Grapefruit juice
  Omelet with ham
  Puff paste crescents
  Oolong tea

LUNCHEON
  Canapé Martha
  Cold assorted meats
  Potato salad
  Cherry tartelettes
  Coffee

DINNER
  Blue Points
  Consommé brunoise
  Braised salmon, Parisienne
  Boiled leg of mutton, caper sauce
  Mashed turnips
  Roast chicken
  Hearts of lettuce salad
  Biscuit glacé
  Assorted cakes
  Coffee

Omelet with ham. Cut a slice of cooked ham in small squares, put in omelet pan with a small piece of butter. When hot add three beaten eggs and follow directions for plain omelet, but use a little less salt.

Canapé Martha. Cut a round piece of toast and put some lobster croquette farcé on top in the shape of a pyramid. Put a thin slice of Swiss cheese on top and bake in oven. Garnish with lemon and parsley.

Cherry tartelette. Line tartelette moulds and follow directions as for pear tartelettes, but fill with canned cherries.

Braised salmon, Parisienne. Put a slice of salmon in buttered pan, season with salt and pepper, sprinkle with chopped shallots and parsley, add one one-half glass of white wine, cover and simmer until cooked. Remove fish to platter, and in the pan pour some white wine sauce, (sauce au vin blanc). Let boil for five minutes and pour over fish. Don't strain.

Boiled leg of mutton, caper sauce. Put the leg of mutton in pot and cover with boiling water. Add one carrot, a leak, onion, a little celery and a bouquet garni. Season with salt, and boil for about forty-five minutes.

Caper sauce. Melt three ounces of butter in sauce pan, add three ounces of flour and allow to become hot. Add three pints of stock, bouillon, or the stock from the leg of mutton. Boil for ten minutes, season to taste, bind with the yolk of one egg and a piece of butter, strain, and add one-half cup of capers.

Mashed turnips. Boil or steam a half dozen white or Russian (yellow) turnips. Strain through a fine sieve or colander, add salt and pepper and three ounces of butter. A potato boiled with the turnips will reduce the strong turnip odor.

DECEMBER 12

BREAKFAST
Stewed prunes
Codfish balls
Rolls
Coffee

LUNCHEON
Oyster broth
Chow chow
Bouillabaisse Marseillaise
Asparagus Hollandaise
Omelette au confiture
Coffee

DINNER
Clam chowder
Celery
Oysters à la Hyde
Striped bass, meunière
Potatoes nature
Combination salad
Fancy ice cream
Alsatian wafers
Coffee

Codfish balls. Soak one pound of salt codfish in cold water over night. Then boil in fresh water for ten minutes. Boil two potatoes in salt water and strain through colander or sieve. Shred the codfish very fine and mix with the potato and the yolks of three eggs working well together. Allow to become cool, form into balls, roll in flour and fry in melted butter until nice and golden yellow. Serve on napkins with quartered lemons and parsley in branches.

Bouillabaisse Marseillaise. (Fish stew). Simmer in shallow sauté pan six chopped shallots, one-half onion sliced very fine and one stalk of white leek also finely sliced, in two spoonsful of olive oil, for about one minute. Then add a clove of chopped garlic, one glass of white wine, one pint of fish stock or hot water, salt, pepper, a little Cayenne, a bouquet garni and the tail of a live lobster cut in six slices, and one dozen of well washed Little Neck clams shell and all, boil for ten minutes. Add some solid meat of white fish such as rock cod, bass, tomcods, etc., and a pinch of whole saffron tied in a cloth. Boil again for twenty-five minutes. Do not skim. Remove the saffron and serve in deep dish with the broth. Sprinkle some chopped parsley over the top. Serve separate, slices of bread fried in oil and then rubbed with garlic.

Omelette au confiture. (Jelly omelet). Same as strawberry omelet. Put currant jelly or any kind of marmalade in center of omelet before turning over on platter.

Oysters à la Hyde. Parboil one-half cup of white celery chopped fine, for ten minutes, and allow to cool. Put in sauce pan two dozen large raw oysters with their own juice, add two tablespoonsful of cracker meal, two ounces of butter, one cup of cream and the parboiled celery. Season with salt, pepper, a little Cayenne, and boil for two minutes. If the sauce is not sufficiently thick add a little more cracker meal. Serve in chafing dish.

DECEMBER 13

BREAKFAST
  Griddle cakes
  Honey
  Breakfast sausage
  Rolls
  Coffee

DINNER
  Little Neck clams
  Potage Mongol
  Fillet of sole, Joinville
  Chicken sauté, Bordelaise
  Artichokes Hollandaise
  Potatoes Laurette
  Biscuit Tortoni
  Macaroons
  Coffee

LUNCHEON
  Casaba melon
  Consommé Ditalini
  Eggs Créole
  Stuffed lamb chops, Soubise
  Champs Elysées potatoes
  Romaine salad
  Napoleon cake
  Coffee

SUPPER
  Oysters mignonette
  Salted almonds
  Sweetbreads à la King
  Parfait Napolitain
  Cakes
  Demi tasse

Breakfast sausages. Small pork sausages fried in pan with a small piece of butter. Serve on platter with their own fat.

Consommé Ditalini. Boil some Ditalini (a species of Italian paste), in salt water, drain off and serve in consommé. Grated cheese separate.

Eggs Créole. Put in buttered shirred egg dish one spoonful of Créole sauce, break two eggs in center, and bake in oven.

Créole sauce. Put in sauce pan three ounces of butter, one sliced onion, and three sliced green peppers. Simmer for ten minutes, or until soft, then add one quart of canned tomatoes with their juice, one can of sliced French mushrooms, one-half can of sliced pimentos, a very little finely chopped garlic, and salt and pepper. Cook slowly for one hour. Fresh tomatoes may be substituted for canned, if desired; and if the sauce is too thick some brown gravy or bouillon may be added.

Fillet of sole, Joinville. Cook the fillets "au vin blanc." Serve crayfish sauce or écrevisse, or shrimp sauce with sliced French mushrooms, truffles and lobster.

Potage Mongol. One-third purée of peas, one-third consommé Julienne, one-third purée of tomatoes. Well mixed.

Chicken sauté, Bordelaise. Jointed chicken sauté in butter with a shallot. Serve brown gravy with mushrooms and cèpes sauté, and garnish with fried onions.

Cèpes sauté. Cèpes are a species of mushrooms and may be obtained in cans. Slice and fry in butter and olive oil in equal parts, season with salt and pepper, and when nearly golden yellow add a very finely chopped shallot and some chopped parsley, and simmer for a minute longer. Often used for garnishing entrées, etc.

Fried onions. Cut large onions in thin slices and separate into rings. Put in milk, then in flour, and fry in hot swimming lard. When brown remove, salt, and serve on napkin, or use for garnishing.

DECEMBER 14

BREAKFAST
  Preserved figs
  Oatmeal with cream
  Chickens' livers sauté, au Madère
  Rolls
  Coffee

LUNCHEON
  Cold assorted meats
  Alligator pear, French dressing
  Roquefort cheese
  Crackers
  Coffee

DINNER
  Lynnhaven oysters
  Purée of Lima beans, aux croûtons
  Ripe olives
  Sand dabs, meunière
  Louisiana gumbo filé
  Boiled rice
  Russian salad
  Peach Melba
  Assorted cakes
  Coffee

Chickens' livers sauté, au Madère. Cut the livers in three, salt and pepper and fry in sauté pan in butter. Drain off and add a cup of sauce Madère. Do not let them boil in the sauce.

Purée of Lima beans. Take a can of Lima beans, or a quart of fresh beans, put in vessel, cover with chicken broth or bouillon and boil till done. Then strain through fine sieve, put back in vessel, add two ounces of sweet butter, and season to taste. Serve with small squares of bread fried in butter.

Louisiana gumbo filé. Two chickens, one quart of large oysters, one quart of cooked shrimps, six bell peppers, four large onions, one quart of tomatoes, one-half pound of butter, two bunches of celery, one small bunch of parsley, one-quarter teaspoonful of tobasco sauce, and black pepper and salt to suit.

First.—Cut the chicken the same way as for fricassée, and wipe dry.

Second.—Cut onions and brown in butter, and strain.

Third.—Fry chicken brown in strained butter, then set to one side.

Fourth.—Add two tablespoonsful of flour to strained butter and brown gradually. When a rich brown add two quarts of boiling water, then add the tomatoes. Now bring to boiling point and strain through a fine strainer.

Fifth.—Place strained liquor in a large stew pan and add one teaspoonful of salt and a half teaspoonful of black pepper, then add the chicken. Should the liquor not sufficiently cover the chicken add more hot water to about two inches above. Then add the bell peppers and celery without cutting up. Boil over slow fire until chicken can be picked off the bones with fork. Then remove chicken and strip meat from bones and cut in small pieces, remove the celery and bell peppers, and replace chicken. Add the shrimps, oysters and tobasco sauce. Boil for ten minutes. Then gradually add sufficient "filé powder" to bring to a rich creamy consistency. Add to each plate two large tablespoonsful of boiled rice. Serve immediately.

Boiled rice. Wash one-half pound of rice and soak in cold water for an hour. Cook over hot fire in four quarts of boiling water for fifteen minutes, or until the grains can be mashed between the fingers. Strain through a colander.

DECEMBER 15

BREAKFAST
  Hothouse raspberries with cream
  Boiled eggs
  Dry toast
  Coffee

LUNCHEON
  Livermore salad
  Fillet of halibut, Mornay
  French pastry
  Rolls
  Tea

DINNER
  Potato and leek soup
  Queen olives
  Black bass, Cambacère
  Vol au vent Toulouse
  Roast lamb, mint sauce
  Rissolées potatoes
  Field salad
  Vanilla ice cream
  Lady fingers
  Coffee

Livermore salad. Broil three country sausages, allow to cool and slice thin. Mix with one peeled tomato cut in small squares, one-half cup of string beans, chives, chervil, salt and pepper, and one-third of white wine vinegar to two-thirds of olive oil.

Fillet of halibut, Mornay. Place the halibut fillets in buttered pan, season with salt and pepper, cover with fish stock or water, and boil. When nearly done remove from pan and put on buttered platter, cover with Mornay sauce, sprinkle with grated cheese and place small pieces of butter on top. Bake in oven till nice and brown. See sauce below.

Sauce Mornay. For four persons use one pint of thick cream, season with salt and Cayenne pepper, bind with the yolks of two eggs and one tablespoonful of grated cheese.

Mint sauce. Use one-quarter pound of brown sugar to one quart of vinegar. Bring to the boiling point, cool off and add some fresh mint leaves chopped fine.

Rissolées potatoes. Cut potatoes in the form of a small egg or a ball. Boil for seven minutes, then put in pan with butter and brown. Sprinkle with salt.

Vol au vent, Toulouse. Boiled breast of chicken cut in small squares; chicken dumplings, dessertspoon size; one can of French mushrooms, whole; one sliced truffle, and two sweetbreads sliced and boiled in chicken broth. Put all in casserole, add one-half wine glass of dry sherry wine, allow to become hot, and add sauce Allemande to cover. It will now be like a stew. Season to taste and fill the heated "vol au vents," or patties.

Black bass, Cambacère. Simmer six finely chopped shallots in butter. While hot add three sliced fresh mushrooms, one peeled tomato cut in squares, and one-half glass of white wine. Reduce almost dry. Then add one pint of white wine sauce. Cook the fish "au vin blanc" style and pour the sauce over same.

DECEMBER 16

BREAKFAST
Sliced pineapple
Rolled oats with cream
Rolls
Coffee

LUNCHEON
Omelette Lorraine
Cold lamb with jelly
Salade Américaine
French pancake
Coffee

DINNER
Potage Flamande
Boiled codfish, sauce Horose
Potatoes nature
Tenderloin of beef, Bristol
Lettuce salad
Ice cream
Assorted cakes
Demi tasse

Omelette Lorraine. Serve the omelette with small sausages, broiled bacon and Madeira sauce.

Salade Américaine. Parboil one-half cup of okra cut in pieces one inch long. Peel a tomato and a boiled potato and cut in strips. Put in bowl with the okra, which has been allowed to cool, and garnish the top with very finely chopped Virginia ham over one half, and with chopped green peppers over the other half. Serve with French dressing.

Pancakes. For two persons take three-fourths of a cup of flour, the same of milk, one egg and a pinch of salt. Mix together into a thin batter. Bake on a pancake pan, well buttered.

English pancakes. Mix and cook the cakes as above. Stack one on another in a chafing dish, sprinkling each with a little lime juice and powdered sugar.

Pancakes Lieb. Same as above, but instead of the lime juice, spread each cake with sweet butter and powdered sugar. Keep hot with chafing dish.

French pancakes. Same ingredients as above, but cover each cake with currant jelly and roll into a roll. Sprinkle with powdered sugar and burn with a redhot iron in stripes.

Potage Flamande. Potato soup garnished with brunoise.

Boiled codfish, sauce Horose. Boil the codfish, place on napkin, garnish with small boiled potatoes, quartered lemons and parsley. See sauce below.

Sauce Horose. Two-thirds Hollandaise sauce and one-third tomato sauce mixed.

Tenderloin of beef, Bristol. Roast tenderloin of beef, sauce Madère, garnished with rice croquettes in pear form, purée of green peas and Laurette potatoes.

Rice croquettes. Put two ounces of butter and a finely chopped onion in vessel and simmer until yellow. Then add one cup of washed rice, one-half cup of bouillon and a pinch of salt, and cook in oven for ten minutes. Then add one cup of sauce Allemande and again put in oven for twenty minutes. When rice is well done bind with the yolks of two eggs and one spoonful of grated Parmesan cheese. Allow to cool and roll in the shape of a pear or ball or other desired shape. Bread and fry in swimming lard.

DECEMBER 17

BREAKFAST
Sliced oranges
Boiled eggs
Corn muffins
English breakfast tea

LUNCHEON
Consommé Rivoli
Olives
Kingfish, meunière
Loin of mutton, charcutière
Corn fritters
Mashed potatoes
Coffee éclairs
Demi tasse

DINNER
Cream of chicken, à la Reine
Celery.   Salted pecans
Fillet of sole, Maximilian
Roast chicken, Rosabelle
Escarole salad
Frozen raisin punch
Lady fingers
Coffee

Consommé Rivoli. Consommé garnished with carrots cut in half moon shape and boiled in consommé, small chicken dumplings and royal custard also cut in half moon shape.

Kingfish, meunière. Wash and dry the fish and season with salt and pepper. Roll in flour and sauté in pan with butter. When done put on platter and cover with sauce meunière. Garnish with quartered lemons and parsley. See sauce below.

Sauce meunière. This is a butter sauce and is principally used for fish. Place the fish or meat on a platter and sprinkle with a little salt and pepper, chopped parsley and the juice of a lemon. Heat in frying pan four ounces of butter to a hazelnut color and pour over the dish.

Loin of mutton, charcutière. Salt and pepper the loin well on the inside, and roll up. Put in roasting pan and roast in the usual manner. To make charcutière use the mutton pan gravy, or take Madeira sauce, and add two sliced pickles and one dozen sliced green olives.

Corn fritters. One-half cup of flour, one egg, one-half cup of milk, one teaspoonful of baking powder and salt and pepper. Mix well and then add one and one-half cups of grated fresh corn, or a can of drained corn. Fry in pan with hot butter. Serve on napkin.

Cream of chicken, à la Reine. Cream of chicken served with small chicken dumplings.

Fillet of sole, Maximilian. Cook fish as for "au vin blanc." Cover with Hollandaise sauce mixed with one tablespoonful of hot meat extract.

Roast chicken, Rosabelle. Garnish the chicken with hearts of artichokes and whole tomatoes, Macédoine. Sauce Madère. This garnish is fine with most any kind of meat.

Frozen raisin punch. Strain the juice of three lemons, add one pint of water, one-half pound of granulated sugar and freeze in the usual manner. Have ready one-half pound of boiled in sugar, and chopped, seeded or seedless raisins. Let the raisins cool, and add with the whites of two eggs, well beaten, to the contents of the freezer, and finish. Serve in glasses with kirschwasser or maraschino poured over the top.

DECEMBER 18

BREAKFAST
Wheat cakes
Honey
Rolls
Coffee

LUNCHEON
Omelette du Czar
Pickled ham with red cabbage
Rolled oats pudding
Coffee

DINNER
Purée of white beans
Pickles
Striped bass, Portugaise
Braised beef
Macaroni in cream
Chiffonnade salad
Oriental cup
Cakes
Coffee

Omelette du Czar. Grate a horseradish root and place in pan with piece of butter. When hot add one-half cup of cream sauce and mix well. Make the omelet, and before turning on the platter put the horseradish in the center. Serve with cream sauce around the edge.

Pickled ham. Take a fresh leg of pork, rub with salt and pepper and put in earthern jar. Cover with red or white wine, or water mixed with wine, as you prefer; one onion, one carrot, a piece of celery, parsley in branches, a few pepper berries and a bouquet garni. After two or three days take out the leg of pork and roast in the ordinary manner. Half of the pork pickle may be used to make a flour gravy if desired.

Red cabbage. Slice a head of red cabbage very fine. Put in vessel with salt, pepper, one glassful of red wine and two cups of fat bouillon. Cover and cook in oven for two hours.

Red cabbage, German style. One sliced red cabbage, one-half glass of vinegar, three sliced apples, two cups of bouillon, and a small piece of salt pork or bacon. Put in oven and cook as above.

Purée of white beans. Soak two pounds of white beans over night. Put in pot and cover with stock or bouillon. Cook until soft, strain through fine sieve, put back in pot and add enough bouillon to make a soup. Season to taste, add two ounces of sweet butter, and serve with small squares of bread fried in butter, separate.

Striped bass, Portugaise. Take a whole bass and cut in slices two inches thick. Put in a buttered pan one-half of an onion chopped, three chopped shallots, a little chopped garlic and parsley, two tomatoes cut in small squares and a bouquet garni. Place the fish on top, season with salt and pepper, add one glass of white wine, one cup of stock or fish broth, cover and cook slowly. When done remove the bouquet, place the fish on platter and reduce the broth one-half. Add four ounces of butter, mix well and pour over the fish. Sprinkle with a little fresh-chopped parsley mixed with a little finely chopped garlic.

Macaroni in cream. Boil the macaroni in salt water. When done drain, add cream sauce, a little sweet butter, salt and Cayenne pepper. Serve grated cheese separate.

DECEMBER 19

BREAKFAST
Picked up codfish in cream
Rolls
Coffee

LUNCHEON
Grapefruit with maraschino
Poached eggs, à l'Indienne
Nivernaise salad
German huckleberry pie
Coffee

DINNER
Oysters on half shell
Clam broth in cups
Salted almonds
Boiled whitefish, Golfin
Hollandaise potatoes
Salade Rejane
Pistache ice cream
Assorted cakes
Coffee

Picked-up codfish in cream. Soak one pound of codfish in cold water over night. Cut two fresh-boiled potatoes in small squares. Put the codfish in cold water and boil for ten minutes, drain, and shred the fish in small pieces. Put in pot with the potatoes, add two cups of cream sauce, salt and a little Cayenne pepper, and simmer for ten minutes.

Poached eggs, à l'Indienne. Lay hot poached eggs on plain boiled rice and cover with curry sauce.

Curry sauce. Simmer one onion, one leek, a small piece of celery, one bay leaf, a branch of thyme and a little garlic in three ounces of butter. Then add two spoonsful of curry powder and two of flour. When hot add one quart of stock, one sliced apple, one sliced banana sauté in butter, and one-half cup of Indian chutney. Boil for twenty minutes, strain through a fine sieve and salt to taste. This sauce is used for chicken, fish, oysters, lamb, veal, etc., and should be made respectively with chicken broth, fish broth, juice of oysters, and so forth.

Salade Nivernaise. Cut in dices cooked carrots, beets and turnips. Place in salad bowl in separate piles with a bouquet of watercress in center. Season with French dressing.

Boiled whitefish, Golfin. Boil in the same manner as codfish. Serve on napkin, garnished with parsley, lemon and small boiled potatoes. Serve sauce separate. See below.

Sauce Golfin. White wine sauce mixed with small strips of boiled smoked tongue and gherkins.

Salade Rejane. Boiled celery root and artichoke buttons, and two tomatoes cut in squares. Place in salad bowl in separate piles. Slice two pimentos and place in center. Season with French dressing.

Pistache ice cream. Prepare a vanilla ice cream mixture. Crush one-quarter pound of pistachio nuts to a very fine paste, mix with a little orange flower water and two ounces of sugar. Infuse in the vanilla ice cream mixture, and strain when hot. Allow to become cold, color a very light green, and freeze.

DECEMBER 20

BREAKFAST
  Sliced bananas
  Shredded wheat biscuit with cream
  Dry toast
  Tea

LUNCHEON
  Consommé Orleans
  Poached eggs, Diane
  Tripe à la Créole
  Boiled rice
  Demi tasse
  Coffee éclairs

DINNER
  Potage Alexandra
  Fish patties, Bagration
  Veal kidney roast
  Turnips glacés
  Gendarmes potatoes
  Celery root, field and beet salad
  Bavarois au chocolat
  Macaroons
  Coffee

Consommé Orleans. Boiled barley well-washed so it will not discolor the soup, small chicken dumplings, peas, one peeled tomato cut in very small squares, and some chopped chervil. Put in consommé just before dishing up.

Poached eggs, Diane. Line a tartelette mould with paste and fill with raw white beans to support the walls, and bake in oven. Then throw out the beans and fill with tomatoes sauté in butter, place a poached egg on top, cover with Hollandaise sauce, and put in hot oven for a second.

Tripe à la Créole. Cut two pounds of boiled tripe in strips, put in casserole one pint of Créole sauce and boil for thirty minutes. Serve with boiled rice.

Potage Alexandra. Half velouté of chicken and half cream of potatoes.

Veal kidney roast. Secure a loin of veal with the kidneys left in, roll, season well and roast in the same manner as shoulder of veal.

Fish patties, Bagration. Small pieces of sole, twelve oysters, and twelve Little Neck clams boiled in white wine. Drain and add six heads of French mushrooms sliced, one sliced truffle, and enough white wine sauce to make the consistency of a stew. Have the patty shells very hot, and fill.

Turnips glacés. Cut the turnips in pieces four times the size of an almond, and put to boil in salt water. When nearly done drain, add a small piece of butter and put in oven until yellow. Then add one spoonful of meat extract and glacé them.

Gendarme potatoes. Cut the potatoes in the same shape as for French fried. Put in pan with piece of butter and roast in oven. When half done add one sliced onion and finish roasting. Sprinkle with salt and chopped parsley before serving.

Celery root, field and beet salad. Boil two peeled celery roots. When cold slice and put in salad bowl with field salad on top, and decorate with sliced boiled beets. Season with French dressing.

DECEMBER 21

BREAKFAST
Stewed rhubarb
Boiled eggs
Dipped toast
Rolls
Coffee

LUNCHEON
Sweet-and-sour bananas
Consommé Massenet
Blood pudding
Mashed turnips
Camembert cheese
Crackers
Coffee

DINNER
Potage Reine Margot
Celery
Boiled salmon, sauce Riche
Olivette potatoes
Breast of chicken, Alexandra.
Hearts of lettuce
Philadelphia ice cream
Assorted cakes
Coffee

Sweet-and-sour bananas. Put six ounces of brown sugar and some pepper berries tied in cheese cloth, in one quart of vinegar and bring to the boiling point. Then add three sliced green peppers and boil for two minutes, add six sliced pimentos and remove the pepper berries. Peel one dozen bananas and put them in an earthern jar and pour the boiling vinegar and peppers over them. Let stand for twelve hours and serve cold.

Consommé Massenet. Garnish the consommé with boiled carrots cut in half-moon shape, and boiled macaroni cut in pieces one-half inch long. Sprinkle with chopped chervil.

Blood pudding. Made of pork blood, etc., and may be obtained from your butcher. Broil or fry in butter.

Potage Reine Margot. To cream of chicken add some almonds mashed fine, mixed with a little cream, and strained. This is called almond milk.

Sauce Riche. Mix a tablespoonful of anchovy paste with a pint of Hollandaise sauce, add one truffle, three heads of French mushrooms, and one dozen shrimps cut in small squares.

Breast of chicken, Alexandra. Take the breasts of a raw roasting chicken, season with salt and pepper, put in sauté pan with butter. Cook until nice and yellow, add one-half cup of cream and finish cooking. Place the breasts on two oval croustades filled with string beans sauté. Add the cream gravy to a cup of Mornay sauce, with a little paprika, cover the breasts with this sauce and bake in oven till golden yellow. Serve on napkin with parsley in branches.

Vanilla Bavarois. Boil one quart of milk with one-half of a split vanilla bean. Stir in gradually, until it gets creamy, six ounces of sugar mixed with the yolks of four eggs. Add five leaves of gelatine that have been washed in cold water, stirring until melted. Strain, when cold add one pint of rich, very stiff, whipped cream. Pour into moulds of fancy shape and place in ice box for about two hours. Serve with vanilla sauce or sweetened whipped cream flavored with vanilla.

DECEMBER 22

BREAKFAST
  Baked apples with cream
  Scrambled eggs with fine herbes
  Crescents
  Coffee

LUNCHEON
  Croustade Cancalaise
  Consommé Fleury
  Ragout à la Deutsch
  Roquefort cheese
  Crackers
  Coffee

DINNER
  Potage Faubonne
  Médaillon of sole, St. Victor
  Roast squab
  Asparagus Hollandaise
  Duchess potatoes
  Romaine salad
  Pineapple water ice
  Assorted cakes
  Coffee

Scrambled eggs with fine herbs. Add to the eggs some fine cut chives, parsley and chervil.

Croustade Cancalaise. Drain off the juice from pickled oysters and fill the croustades with them. Cover with sauce Tyrolienne and garnish with chopped hard-boiled eggs.

Consommé Fleury. Sliced sorrel boiled in water for a second, boiled rice, small asparagus tips and peas, in equal parts. Serve in consommé.

Ragout à la Deutsch. One-half pound of sliced raw tenderloin of beef, and three lamb kidneys, season with salt and pepper and fry in frying pan with very hot butter. When done remove the meat and place in a deep dish. Put three chopped shallots and a green pepper cut in small dices, in the butter in frying pan and simmer for a minute. Drain, add two cups of brown gravy and one cup of sauté potatoes. Mix with the meat, but do not allow to boil. Serve from the deep dish or casserole.

Potage Faubonne. Make a purée of white beans and bind with the yolk of one egg mixed with a little cream. Serve small squares of bread fried in butter, separate.

Médaillon of sole, St. Victor. Cook the fish in white wine and allow to become cold. Mix the stock with white wine sauce, bring to a boil and reduce until it becomes very thick. Strain and mix with equal parts of mayonnaise, whipping well so it will not turn. Let the sauce become cold and pour over the fish, and place in the ice box. Boil three eggs for seven minutes, cool, split in two crosswise, remove the yolk and fill with fresh caviar. Turn the eggs upside down and cover with some of the fish sauce, colored a delicate rose. Cut some peeled tomatoes in the form of strawberries, and make a vegetable salad mixed with a little thick mayonnaise. Make a pyramid of the salad in the middle of the dish, place the fillet of sole around it, and garnish with the eggs and tomatoes. Sprinkle with chopped parsley.

DECEMBER 23

BREAKFAST
  Honey in comb
  Waffles
  Yarmouth bloater
  Rolls
  Coffee

LUNCHEON
  German pancakes
  Chocolate
  Whipped cream

DINNER
  Potage Mathilda
  Lobster croquettes, cream sauce
  Plain potted squab chicken
  Stewed tomatoes
  Lettuce braisé
  Château potatoes
  Cold artichokes, mustard sauce
  Charlotte aux pommes
  Coffee

German pancakes. Two eggs, one-half cup of milk, one-half cup of flour, a pinch of salt, a little nutmeg and one teaspoonful of sugar. Mix well. Have a large frying pan ready with hot butter. Be sure and have the butter run all over the inside of the pan so the pancake will not stick to the sides when it rises. Pour in the batter and place in oven. When nearly done, powder with sugar and put back in oven to brown. Serve with lemon and powdered sugar.

Potage Mathilda. Cream of cucumbers with small squares of bread fried in butter.

Rice Créole. Put in sauce pan three ounces of butter, one chopped onion, a slice of raw ham cut in small squares, and one green pepper cut in small dices. Simmer until the onions are soft, then add one cup of washed rice, one peeled and chopped tomato, two red peppers (pimentos), cut in small dices, two cups of stock or bouillon, and a little salt. Cover and put in oven until the rice is soft. Before serving add two spoonsful of grated Parmesan or Swiss cheese. This rice may be used for stuffing green peppers, tomatoes, onions, etc.

Chicken croquettes. Three cups of chicken hash made from white and dark meat, one cup of chopped fresh or canned mushrooms, and one-half onion chopped very fine. Simmer in butter. Then add two cups of Allemande or cream sauce, season with salt and Cayenne pepper. Put on fire and reduce until thick. Bind with the yolks of two eggs. Allow to become cold, and form in pyramid shape or in the shape of a large cork, bread, and fry in swimming fat until well colored. Serve on napkin with sauce separate, or around the croquettes. A chopped truffle may be added before simmering, if desired.

Sweetbread croquettes. Three cups of sweetbreads parboiled and cut in small dices, and if desired, one chopped truffle. Simmer with chopped onions, and then follow recipe for chicken croquettes.

Lobster croquettes. Three cups of lobster cut in small dices, one cup of canned or fresh mushrooms, and one truffle chopped fine. Simmer all in butter, then add one-half glass of sherry wine and cook for two minutes, then add two cups of cream sauce and reduce. Bind with the yolks of three eggs. Follow directions for chicken croquettes for cooking and serving.

DECEMBER 24

BREAKFAST
Preserved figs with cream
Shirred eggs
Dry toast
Cocoa

LUNCHEON
Petite marmite
Broiled lobster
Roast beef
Cléo potatoes
String bean salad
Lemon pie
Coffee

DINNER
Potage Duchesse
Fillet of sole, Marguery
Roast lamb, mint sauce
Succotash
Broiled fresh mushrooms on toast
Alligator pear salad
Peach Tetrazzini
Assorted cakes
Coffee

Petite marmite. Put in a vessel with cold water to cover, five pounds of short ribs of beef and a soup hen. Season with a spoonful of salt, and bring to a boil, and skim carefully so the broth will be clear. Then add two large carrots, three turnips, a piece of cabbage, one stalk of celery and four leeks, all tied in a cheese cloth; one bouquet garni, and a large marrow bone. When beef and fowl are well done remove, take off the skin and fat and cut the meat in pieces one inch square. Remove the bouquet garni, and cut the cabbage, carrots, turnips, celery and leeks in round pieces one-half inch in diameter. Put the beef, chicken and vegetables in another pot and strain the broth over them. Boil slowly for five minutes. Have your butcher saw some raw marrow bones in wafers as thin as paper, and add them to the soup at the last moment. Serve very hot in soup tureen, with a sprinkle of chopped chervil. Cut some crust of bread or rolls in diamond shape, bake in oven till brown, and serve separate. Special earthern petite marmite pots are carried at the large stores, and are preferable to tureens for serving.

Broiled lobster. Cut a live lobster in two lengthwise, season with salt and pepper, sprinkle with olive oil, and broil on hot iron. Serve with maître d'hôtel sauce, garnished with lemons and parsley.

Cléo potatoes. Cut raw potatoes in pear shapes the size of an egg, parboil in salt water, then put in a well-buttered pan pointed end up, sprinkle with melted butter and roast in oven, basting all the time till brown. When done, salt and serve on napkin, garnished with parsley.

String bean salad. Put in salad bowl some cold boiled string beans, sprinkle with very finely-sliced chives, chopped parsley, salt and fresh-ground black pepper, and one-third vinegar and two-thirds olive oil.

Potage Duchesse. Cream of rice with royal in strips.

Fillet of sole, Marguery. Prepare the sole as for "au vin blanc." Place on top of each fillet two parboiled mussels, and two heads of French mushrooms, cover with sauce "au vin blanc," sprinkle with bread crumbs made from stale rolls, and a little butter, and bake in hot oven until a light yellow color.

DECEMBER 25

BREAKFAST
Hothouse raspberries with cream
Oatmeal
Rolls
Coffee

LUNCHEON
Eggs ministerielle
Cold assorted meats
Chiffonnade salad
Pont Neuf cake
Demi tasse

DINNER
Blue Points, mignonette
Bisque d'écrevisses
Salted almonds.   Celery
Ripe California olives
Fillet of trout, Café de Paris
Sweetbreads braisé, au jus
Purée de marrons
Roast goose, apple sauce
Sweet potatoes, Southern style
Pâté de foie gras de Strasbourg
Lettuce salad, aux fines herbes
Frozen diplomate pudding
Assorted cakes
Pont l'évêque cheese   Crackers
Nuts and raisins   Coffee

Eggs ministerielle. Cut sandwich bread in slices about two inches thick. With a round cutter about three inches in diameter cut out the white of the bread. With another cutter about an inch and a half in diameter cut out the center of the round slices, leaving a ring of bread. Soak these rings in thick cream for a second, put on buttered dish, break an egg in the center of each, salt and pepper, cover with a light cream sauce, sprinkle with grated cheese, and bake in oven for about eight minutes.

Pont Neuf potatoes. Three times the size of regular "French" fried potatoes.

Sweetbreads braisé au jus. (Glacé). Place in buttered sauté pan one sliced onion, one carrot, a little parsley, a bay leaf and a clove, and a few pepper berries. Put three parboiled sweetbreads, which may be larded with fresh or salted pork if desired, on top, add one-half cup of bouillon, salt, and put over fire to boil. When reduced place in oven, add a small quantity of meat extract, and glacé by basting continually with its own broth, until well browned. When done lay on platter and strain the broth over them.

Bisque d'écrevisses. Remove the tails of three dozen écrivisses. Use two-thirds of the shells, broken up, to make the soup, and one-third for écrevisse butter. Simmer in butter one onion, one carrot, a leek and a little celery, all cut up; with one bay leaf, some thyme and one spoonful of black pepper berries. Then add the broken shells, two spoonsful of flour, one glass of white wine, one-half glass of brandy, one gallon of bouillon and one cup of raw rice. Season with salt and Cayenne pepper, cook till rice is very soft, and strain through fine sieve. Bisque should be a little thicker than other cream soups. Before serving add two spoonsful of écrevisse butter and stir well, then add the écrevisse tails and one-half glass of Cognac.

Écrevisse butter. Break fine in mortar some écrevisse (crayfish) shells. Put in sauce pan with one-half pound of butter, one-half onion, one-half carrot, a small piece of celery, one-half of a leek stalk, a little thyme, one bay leaf and a few pepper berries, and simmer in oven till butter is clarified, or clear, and all the other liquids evaporated. Squeeze through cheese cloth into a bowl standing in ice. The butter will rise to the top, and may be easily removed when cold. This butter is used with many sauces, soups, etc.

Lobster butter. Use lobster shells and prepare in the same manner as ecrevisse butter. This butter is used for lobster sauce, Newburg dishes, soups, etc.

DECEMBER 26

BREAKFAST
- Stewed prunes
- Boiled eggs
- Toast
- Tea

LUNCHEON
- Grapefruit en suprême
- Cold goose and ham, apple sauce
- Romaine salad
- Brie cheese
- Crackers
- Coffee

DINNER
- Potage bonne femme
- Roast ruddy duck
- Fried hominy and currant jelly
- Cold asparagus, mustard sauce
- Baba au rhum
- Coffee

Potage bonne femme. Purée of white beans with Julienne of vegetables.

Fillet of sole, Florentine. Put the fillet of one sole in a buttered pan, salt, add one-half glass of water mixed with white wine, and boil until done. In the center of a buttered platter put a cup of purée of spinach and place the boiled fillet on top, cover with Mornay sauce, with grated cheese and small bits of butter on top of the sauce. Bake in oven until brown.

Roast ruddy duck. Roast for twelve minutes, in the same manner as teal duck.

Baba au rhum. One-half pound of flour, one ounce of yeast, three ounces of butter, two ounces of sugar, two ounces of currants and the rind and juice of one lemon. Dissolve the yeast in one cup of warm milk and make a soft sponge with half of the flour, cover and let rise in a warm place. Work the sugar and the butter together until creamy, add the eggs and lemon and the rest of the flour. When the sponge has risen to twice its original size mix with the batter; at the same time adding the currants. Fill baba moulds half full and let raise until nearly to the edge of the moulds. Bake in a rather hot oven. When done soak well in a syrup made with one pint of water, one pound of sugar, one gill of rum and the juice of a lemon. Pour some of the sauce over the babas when serving.

Savarin au kirsch. Make a dough the same as for baba au rhum, but omit the currants. Fill a round crown-shaped savarin mould half full, allow to raise, and bake. Soak in a syrup made of one pint of water, one pound of sugar, and one gill of kirschwasser. Serve warm.

Savarin Chantilly. Same as savarin au kirsch, but decorated with whipped cream, and served cold.

Savarin Montmorency. Like savarin au kirsch, but serve hot with stewed stoned cherries as sauce.

Savarin mirabelle. Same as savarin au kirsch, but serve hot with stewed stoned mirabelles.

DECEMBER 27

BREAKFAST
Preserved figs
Ham and eggs
Toasted corn muffins
Coffee

LUNCHEON
Consommé in cups
Ripe olives
Panfish sauté, meunière
Stewed tripe, Blanchard
Savarin au kirsch   Coffee

DINNER
Potage Flamande
Frogs' legs, sauté à sec
Roast sirloin of beef, Porte Maillot
Lettuce braisé
Château potatoes
Endive salad
Biscuit glacé
Assorted cakes
Coffee

Stewed tripe, Blanchard. Simmer a chopped onion in three ounces of butter, add one pint of bouillon, or stock, or chicken broth, one spoonful of flour, one pound of tripe cut in strips, one cupful of raw round potatoes cut out with a small-size "Parisian" spoon, one bouquet garni and one gill of white wine. Cover and cook for one hour, or until potatoes are very soft. Before serving remove bouquet garni and sprinkle with fresh-chopped parsley.

Potage Flamande. Potato soup mixed with brunoise.

Frogs' legs, sauté à sec. To have the best flavor frogs should be killed just before cooking. Remove the skins and cut off the hind legs, salt and pepper them and roll in flour. Sauté one dozen frogs' legs in three ounces of hot butter in a frying pan, for a few minutes over a good fire. Then add a chopped shallot and let simmer for a few minutes. The legs should then be crisp. Serve on a platter with chopped parsley and lemon.

Roast sirloin of beef, Porte Maillot. Roast the sirloin, serve with sauce Madére, garnish with small French carrots, celery braisé, lettuce braisé and château potatoes.

Lettuce braisé. Wash four heads of large romaine lettuce in cold water, parboil in salt water, cool, and squeeze dry with the hands. Cut each head in four lengthwise, remove the stem, season with salt and pepper, and fold so both ends come together. Place a piece of pigskin in the bottom of a buttered pan, put the lettuce on top, and add a sliced onion, one carrot and a bay leaf. Cover with buttered manilla paper and allow to simmer for a while. Then add one cup of stock, put in oven and cook until soft. Used for garnishing entrées, etc.

Biscuit glacé. Put in double boiler eight yolks of eggs, one-half pound of sugar, and one-half of a split vanilla bean. Cook until it thickens, stirring continually. Then remove from the fire and beat with an egg whip until cold and very light. Remove the vanilla bean, add one quart of whipped cream and mix lightly. Put in fancy paper cases or fancy moulds, and freeze. Before serving decorate the tops with whipped cream, or any kind of ice cream or water ice.

Biscuit glacé, St. Francis. Fill some oblong paper cases with biscuit glacé foundation, put in ice box to freeze, decorate the tops with pistachio and strawberry ice cream before serving.

Biscuit glacé of strawberry, raspberry, coffee, pistachio, chocolate, apple, mapleine, pineapple, kirsch, peppermint, etc. Same as Biscuit Glacé, but decorate with the desired ice cream or water ice before serving.

DECEMBER 28

BREAKFAST
  Broiled Finnan haddie
  Baked potatoes
  Rolls
  Coffee

LUNCHEON
  Canapé of sardines
  Boston baked beans
  Brown bread
  Coffee

DINNER
  Seapuit oysters
  Cream of rice
  Salted pecans
  Fillet of flounder, Café Riche
  Spring lamb tenderloin, Thomas
  Roast chicken, au jus
  Hearts of romaine, egg dressing
  Strawberry parfait
  Macaroons
  Coffee

Broiled Finnan haddie. (Smoked haddock). Remove the bones, roll in oil and put on iron to broil. When done on both sides place on platter, cover with maître d'hôtel sauce or plain melted butter, garnish with parsley in branches and quartered lemons.

Cream of rice. Melt in sauce pan two ounces of butter, add one-quarter pound of rice flour, and when hot, one and one-half pints of chicken broth. Boil for ten minutes and strain. Season with salt and Cayenne pepper, and add one-half pint of hot cream and a small piece of butter before serving.

Salted Pecans. Roast one-half pound of shelled pecans to a light brown color, wet with a solution of water and a little gum Arabic, or the white of an egg, while they are still hot, and then dust over with one spoonful of fine table salt and stir until dry.

Salted English walnuts. Follow directions for pecans.

Fillet of flounder, Café Riche. Put the fillets in a buttered pan, cover with white wine, and boil. When done place on platter, pour Génoise sauce with the addition of a spoonful of beef extract, over the fish.

Spring lamb tenderloin, Thomas. Broil the tenderloin and dish up on buttered toast, and cover with sauce Colbert. Garnish on one side with small boiled potatoes covered with cream sauce, and flageolet beans on the other.

Flageolet beans. These are French beans and can be obtained in cans. Put on the fire in salt water, bring to the boiling point, and drain. Add sweet butter, salt and pepper, mix well and serve immediately.

Egg dressing, for salads. Chop two hard-boiled eggs, and put in salad bowl with one-half teaspoonful of French mustard, one pinch of salt, some fresh-ground pepper, a little chopped parsley, a little chervil, two spoonsful of vinegar and four of olive oil. Mix well.

Strawberry parfait. With one quart of strawberry ice cream mix one pint of sweet whipped cream. Put in moulds or glasses and serve with whipped cream on top.

Parfaits. Pistachio, vanilla, chocolate, peach and café, all prepared the same as strawberry.

Neapolitan parfait. Put in mould or glass, three kinds of parfaits, as strawberry, vanilla and pistachio. Allow to become very hard in ice box, and serve whipped cream on top.

Wilson parfait. Peach parfait with the addition of some chopped peeled peaches. Serve with whipped cream and a crystallized violet on top.

DECEMBER 29

LUNCHEON
  Canapé Monte Carlo
  Poached eggs, Persanne
  Tosca salad
  French pastry
  Coffee

BREAKFAST
  Baked apples
  Oatmeal with cream
  Rolls
  Coffee

DINNER
  Consommé Madrilène
  Ripe California olives
  Boiled salmon, sauce Anglaise
  Ragout fin
  Stanislaus salad
  Cream cheese with Bar le Duc
  Crackers
  Coffee

Canapé Monte Carlo. Purée of foie gras lightly mixed with a little stiff mayonnaise and spread on thin toast. Garnish around the edge with chopped yolks of hard-boiled eggs, and serve on napkins with parsley in branches.

Eggs Persanne. Place hot poached eggs on a round toast, cover with tomato sauce and sprinkle with fine chopped ham and parsley.

Tosca salad. Cut in fine strips about one inch long some boiled ham, tongue, cooked potatoes and buttons of artichokes. Arrange in salad bowl with some asparagus tips in the center, garnish with the chopped yolks and whites of hard-boiled eggs, separate; and serve with French dressing.

Consommé Madrilène. Slice a handful of sorrel and cook for five minutes in consommé. Add vermicelli and one tomato cut in small dices. Serve grated cheese separate.

Boiled salmon, sauce Anglaise. Cook the salmon in the same manner as for Hollandaise. For sauce Anglaise use one pint of Hollandaise sauce, mixed with two chopped hard-boiled eggs, sliced chives, chopped parsley and chervil. Serve separate.

Stanislaus salad. Remove the inside leaves of a whole head of lettuce, leaving a green bowl. Put in bottom, celery cut in long strips, with slices of grapefruit and seedless grapes cut in half, on top. Sprinkle with chopped walnuts. Serve with French dressing.

Ragout fin. Slice some parboiled tender sweetbreads, chickens' livers, chickens' combs, chickens' kidneys and truffles, and sauté in butter, cooking each separately. Then put all in one pan, add a half glass of good sherry, boil for one minute, add a half pint of brown gravy, simmer for a few minutes, and serve with chopped chervil on top. Chickens' combs and kidneys come in bottles from France. If you wish you may cut the tips from raw rooster combs, put in boiling water for a minute, when they can be rubbed with salt to remove the skin. Then soak in cold water to cause the blood to run out, and boil in salt water till soft.

Cream cheese with Bar le Duc. Mix some cream cheese with a little whipped cream and spread on plate in the shape of a ring. Put some red Bar le Duc jelly in center. Serve toasted crackers separate.

DECEMBER 30

LUNCHEON   BREAKFAST
    Plain consommé in cups   Grapefruit
    Fried fillet of sole, rémoulade   Pork sausages   Apple sauce
    Brie cheese and crackers   Coffee   Wheat cakes   Coffee

DINNER
    Potage Jackson   Crab meat Monza
    Chicken dumplings, sauce Allemande
    Braised beef à la mode   Peas à la Français
    Duchess potatoes
    Pineapple biscuit glacé
    Assorted cakes   Coffee

Fried fillet of sole. Clean and trim the fillets, season with salt and pepper, roll in flour, then in beaten eggs, then in bread crumbs, and fry in swimming hot lard for five minutes. Remove and serve on napkin with quartered lemons and fried parsley. Sauce separate.

Rémoulade sauce. Take a handful of spinach, one of watercress and one of parsley and mash fine in a mortar. Put in a cloth and press out the juice. Mix the juice with a pint and a half of mayonnaise, add four chopped gherkins and some sliced chives.

Crab meat, Monza. Wash carefully one pound of fresh mushrooms, and cut each one in four. Put in sauté pan with two ounces of butter and simmer for thirty minutes. When the mushrooms are soft add the meat of one crab cooked in cream. Before serving add one gill of dry sherry wine.

Crab meat in cream. Remove the meat from the shell of a boiled crab. In a sauce pan put a piece of butter the size of an egg, and place on stove. When warm add two spoonsful of flour and allow to become hot, then add one pint of boiling milk and one-fourth of a pint of hot cream. Stir well and boil for ten minutes. Season with salt and Cayenne pepper, then add the crab meat and serve in deep dish. Serve dry toast separate.

Chicken dumplings. (Quenelles de volaille). Take the breast of a raw fowl and trim carefully away the fat, using the white meat only. Chop very fine and pass through a fine sieve, place in a bowl on ice, season with salt and Cayenne pepper, and with a wooden spoon stir in little by little some very thick cream (not whipped), which has been kept on ice. Add the cream until you have nearly double the amount of force meat. Have two teaspoons in cold water. Take one and fill with the force meat, make a little hole in the middle and fill with goose liver puree and close up. Remove the dumpling from the first spoon with the other one and place on a buttered pan, and continue. When enough are formed cover with stock and bring to the boiling point, then set off the fire and let stand for ten minutes on the back of the range. The force meat may be used for small dumplings without the purée of goose liver; or some other filling may be used. Make them small for garnishing consommé, vol au vent, patties, financiére, tortu, etc. The force meat is also used to make timbales of chicken.

Sauce Allemande. Cut up three pounds of veal bones, put in vessel with two gallons of water, bring to a boil and skim. Add one onion, a carrot, a little celery and leek, some pepper berries, two cloves, a sprig of thyme and some salt. Boil for two hours and strain. Put in sauce pan three ounces of butter, when hot add two ounces of flour and heat again. Then add a pint and a half of the broth, boil for ten minutes, season and strain. This is the foundation of many fancy sauces.

Potage Jackson. Potato soup with small pieces of macaroni added.

DECEMBER 31

LUNCHEON
    Poached eggs, Zingara
    Calf's head, vinaigrette
    Boiled potatoes
    Lemon pie
    Coffee

BREAKFAST
    Raw apples
    Rolled oats with cream
    Buttered toast
    Cocoa with whipped cream

DINNER
    Toke Point oysters
    Potage Américaine
    Fillet of sole, Valeska
    Saddle of lamb, international
    Chiffonnade salad
    Coffee ice cream
    Alsatian wafers
    Demi tasse

Poached eggs, Zingara. Poached eggs on toast. Cover with tomato sauce and small strips of tongue.

Potage Américaine. Put in a pot one onion, one leek, and a little celery, and simmer in three ounces of butter until soft. Then add two spoonsful of flour and simmer again. Now add one peeled and cut up squash, a bouquet garni and two quarts of stock, and boil till well done. Remove the bouquet garni and strain the remainder through a fine sieve. Season with salt and pepper. Before serving add one cup of cream and two cups of plain boiled rice.

Fillet of sole, Valeska. This is stuffed fillet of sole with a slice of lobster and a slice of truffle on top, and cooked in white wine. Reduce broth and add Hollandaise sauce, and stir in a spoonful of écrevisse butter to give a pink color.

Saddle of lamb, international. Put saddle of lamb in a roasting pan with one carrot, an onion, a piece of celery, a few pepper berries and some parsley in branches. Season the saddle with salt and pepper, rubbing in well. Spread some butter over the top and roast in oven, basting continually so it will not become dry. Cook for forty minutes, then take saddle from the pan, remove the fat and add to the gravy a spoonful of flour and a cup of stock or hot water, salt, cook for five minutes and strain. Before serving add one-half gill of sherry wine. For international garnishing use a bouquet each of purée of peas, mashed potatoes and purée of chestnuts.

Coffee ice cream. Add to vanilla ice cream before freezing one pint of strong coffee and one-quarter pound of sugar.

Calf's head, plain. Cut the flesh, tongue and brains from the skull and put in cold water for six hours. Put the brains aside. (See index for calf's brains.) Put the rest of the meat on the fire in water with a handful of salt, bring to a boil and allow to cool. Then cut in square pieces, leaving the tongue whole. Put the cut-up pieces in a pot, cover with water, add one handful of salt, a carrot, an onion, a spoonful of black pepper berries, one bouquet garni and a lemon cut in two. Boil till well done. If not to be used right away put in earthen jar and strain the broth over it.

Vinaigrette sauce. Chop fine one small sour pickle and add salt, some fresh-ground black pepper, one spoonful of vinegar, two spoonsful of olive oil, some sliced chives, chopped parsley and chervil. If desired, add one chopped shallot and a spoonful of chopped capers.

Selections from The Hotel St. Francis Menu Files

Hotel St. Francis, Oriental Dinner, May 15, 1917:

Fruit Salad, Oriental
Cream of Chicken, Sam Yong
Mixed Chinese Nuts
Halibut, Veronica
Chop Suey
Roast Duckling, Apple Sauce
Noodles
Cold Artichoke
Mikados Glacee
Mignardises
Demi Tasse

Hotel St. Francis, Californian Dinner, March 31, 1917:

California Oysters
Clear Green Turtle, Sherry
Salted Almonds
Sand Dabs, Meuniere
Sweetbreads Braise, with Peas
Broiled San Francisco Jumbo Squab
Chateau Potatoes
Cold Fresh Asparagus, Mustard Sauce
Cafe Parfait
Assorted Cakes
Demi Tasse

French Dinner, March 15, 1917:

Coeur de Palmier, Victor
Creme de Volaille, a la Reine
Amandes Salees
Truite de Rivière, Meuniere
Pommes Parisienne
Pigeonneau au Cresson
Petits Pois Etuvés
Salade de Saison
Pudding Diplomate Glacé
Petits Fours
Demi Tasse

To meet Mr. Masaya Suzuki, director of The Sumitomo Bank, Limited, and director-in-chief of The Sumitomo General Head Office. Mr. Seiichi Koh, host, April 10, 1919:

Canape Favorite
Toke Point Oysters
Green Turtle Soup
Almonds   Celery   Olives
Seafood, Mariniere
Noisette of Spring Lamb, Colbert
Sherbet Fleur de Palma
Sweetbreads Conte de Nassau
Breast of Chicken, St. Francis
Potatoes Clarence
Heart of Lettuce, Fines Herbes
Biscuit Emaline
Friandises
Coffee
Amontillado Sherry
Pommery Greno
Liqueurs

Hotel St. Francis, Mexican Dinner, May 23 1917:

Ecrevisses, Gourmet (Cold)
Abalone Chowder
Salted Jordan Almonds
Boiled Striped Bass, Hollandaise
Potatoes Nature
Pilaff Mexicaine
Roast Imperial Squab
Asparagus Tips
Salade de Saison
Fancy Ice Cream
Wafers
Demi Tasse

Hotel St. Francis, Italian Dinner, April 27, 1917:

Hors d'Oeuvres, Italienne
Bisque d'Ecrivesses
Salted Almonds
Shad au Gratin, Piedmontaise
Macaroni, Caruso
Stuffed Imperial Squab
Potatoes, Tetrazzini
Cold Artichoke
Tutti Frutti
Friandises
Bonbon Italien
Demi Tasse

Hotel St. Francis, Southern Dinner, May 28, 1917:

Pickled Oysters, New Orleans
Giblet Soup, with Barley
Salted Nuts
Boiled Salmon, Genoise
Vol au Vent, Toulouse
Roast Squab
Potatoes Sybil
Cold Asparagus
Coupe Carolina
Assorted Cakes
Demi Tasse

Patek-Newman wedding, August 24, 1915

Fresh caviar
Toke Points
Essence of Chicken
Celery   Olives   Salted Nuts
Frogs' Legs, Newman
Noisettes of Lamb, Colbert
Peas Etuvé
Champagne Punch
Breast of Duckling
Pommes a la Reine
Salad Veronica
Fancy Ice Cream
Cakes
Coffee

Mr. Raphael Weill, May 23, 1915:
California Oysters on Half Shell
Salmon Belly, Béchamel
White Corn Bread, sliced
Saddle of Lamb
Chicory Salad
Asparagus, Sauce Mousseline
Hot Waffles
Cafe au Lait

Chi Psi Fraternity, August 28, 1915:
Toke Points
Clear Bortsch
Salted Almonds   Celery   Olives
Lobster Newburgh
Vol au Vent, Financiere
Chateaubriand, Colbert
Peas a la Fraincaise
Pommes Chateau
Champagne Punch
Breast of Squab
Salad de Saison
Fancy Ice Cream
Cakes

Hayashi Banquet, March 24, 1916:
California Oysters on Half Shell
Potage Lemardelais
Salted Walnuts   Olives   Celery
Mountain Trout, Meunière
Pommes Maitre d'Hotel
Noisette of Baby Lamb, Perigord
Croustade St. Germain
Sorbet Doi
Roast Guinea Hen
Lettuce and Tomato Salad
Glacé Madeleine
Mignardises
Coffee

Mr. A. Johnston, dinner to Charles Schwab,
May 9, 1915:
Crab Cocktail, Moscovite
Chicken Gumbo, Princess
Almonds   Olives
Sweetbreads, Eugenie
Roast Guinea Hen
Grilled Sweet Potato
Artichokes, French Dressing
Fancy Ice Cream
Assorted Cakes
Coffee

Mr. James Woods, dinner to Mr. Boomer
of New York, May 13, 1915:
Hors d'Oeuvres
Beef Tea en Tasse Diable
Olives   Almonds
Frog
Vol au Vent of Chicken
Saddle of Lamb
Potatoes Reine
Chicory
Asparagus, Hollandaise Sauce
Bavarois
Cakes
Coffee

Knights of the Royal Arch, May 20, 1915
Toke Points
Cream of Celery
Olives   Almonds
Striped Bass, Joinville
Tournedos Forestiere
Pommes Rissolé
Peas Etuvé
Champagne Punch
Roast Squab Chicken
Salad de Saison
Fancy Ice Cream
Cakes
Coffee

Mrs. Neustadter, February 14, 1916:
California and Toke Points
Consomme de Volaille, Royal
Almonds   Olives
Frogs a la Michels
Asparagus, Hollandaise
Chicken Poëlé
Brandied Peaches
Pommes Fondantes
Goose Liver Sauté
Lettuce, French Dressing
Fancy Ice Cream
Assorted Cakes
Coffee

Real Estate Banquet, February 5, 1916:
Toke Points
Mongol
English Walnuts   Olives   Celery
Fillet of Bass, Joinville
Sweetbread Cutlets, Virginia
Peas
Roast Squab
Potatoes Chateau
Salad de Saison
Fancy Ice Cream
Assorted Cakes
Coffee

Mr. L. J. Scroffy, February 4, 1916:
Fresh Caviar
Celery   Olives   Almonds
Terrapin Maryland
Wild Rice
Virginia Ham Glacé, Ferrari
Faison Truffles
Salad de Saison
Pudding Glacé, Diplomate
Mignardises
Coffee

Mrs. J. C. Cowdin, January 27, 1916:
Canape de Caviar Frais
Huitres de Californie
Bortsch Clair en Tasse
Celeri   Olives Mures   Amandes Salees
Poitrine de Faisan aux Figues
Pommes a la Reine
Petits Pois a la Francaise
Foie d'Oie a la Gelee
Salad de Laitue
Coupe St. Jacques
Mignardises
Demi Tasse

Mrs. Samuel Rissinger, January 5, 1916:
Hors d'Oeuvres Russe
Potage Lord Mayor
Almonds   Olives   Celery
Frogs, Michels
Breast of Pheasant, Rossini
Figs au Madère
Fresh Asparagus, Hollandaise
Salad Veronica
Apple Charlotte
Ice Cream Pralinee
Cakes
Coffee

Bagmen of Bagdad, December 30, 1915:
Toke Points
Green Turtle Soup
Celery   Olives   Almonds
Terrapin Maryland
Noisette of Lamb, Colbert
Haricot Panachée
Potatoes Rissolée
Champagne Punch
Breast of Duck, Currant Jelly
Fried Hominy
Cold Asparagus, Mustard Sauce
Pudding Glacé
Assorted Cakes
Coffee

Mr. Horace Hill, December 22, 1915:
California Oysters on Half Shell, Mignonette
Chicken Gumbo, Princess
Celery   Olives   Almonds
Vol au Vent of Crab Meat, Monza
Saddle of Spring Lamb
Puree of Chestnut
Peas a la Francaise
Aspic de Foie Gras, Romaine
Orange Soufflé Glacé
Assorted Cakes
Demi Tasse

Mrs. Jules Levy, January 10, 1917:
Toke Points
Petite Marmite with Marrow Dumplings
Cheese Straws
Frogs, Neptune
Breast of Duckling a l'Orange
Potatoes Fondantes
Sweet and Sour String Beans
Fresh Asparagus, Hollandaise
Foie d'Oie aux Truffes
Lettuce Salad
Omelette Soufflé aux fraises
Demi Tasse

Mr. Otto Irving Wise, December 27, 1916:
Queux d'Ecrevisse, Moscovite
Broth in Cups
Celery   Olives   Almonds
Frogs Marinière
Boneless Squab Guinea Hen
Pommes a la Reine
Artichoke Bottom, Hollandaise
Mousse de Foie Gras, Virginie
Lettuce Salad, French Dressing
Pudding Diplomate
Fancy Cakes
Coffee

Mr. L. A. Schwabacher, December 2, 1916:
Canape de Caviar
Queux d'Ecrevisse, Moscovite
Broth in Cups au Cerfeuil
Celery   Olives   Almonds
Frogs' Legs a la Schwabacher
Ris de Veau Braise
Truffes de Perigord en Serviette
Boneless Squab Guinea Hen, Farcis
Pommes a la Reine
Asperges Nouvelles, Hollandaise
Mousse de Foie Gras, Virginie
Salad de Laitue
Pudding Diplomate
Mignardises
Demi Tasse

Mr. Colum, June 28, 1919:
Canape Caviar with Cocktail
Toke Points
Green Turtle Soup
Almonds   Olives
Lobster Newburg
Ham Glacé, Champagne Sauce
Timbale of Spinach
Iowa Corn Bread
Vol au Vent Toulouse
Kirsch Punch
Guinea Hen
Potatoes Chateau
Salad
Ice Cream   Cakes
Coffee

Mrs. J. Ehrman, Supper, October 27, 1915:
Oysters on Half Shell
Frogs in Rings
Broiled Squab on Toast
Shoestring Potatoes
Lettuce Salad
Chocolate Parfait
Strawberry Water Ice
Assorted Cakes
Coffee

Mr. Charles Schwab, May 15, 1915:
Supreme Frascate
Potage Lemardelais, Passe
Almonds   Olives
Fillet of Trout, Cafe de Paris
Breast of Chicken, Colbert
Peas a la Francaise
Artichokes, Hollandaise Sauce
Terrine de Foie Gras
Lettuce aux Cerfeuil
Bavarois aux Fraise and Framboise
Assorted Cakes
Coffee

Pacific Musical Club, Supper, February 23 1916:
Toke Points
Salted Almonds
Broiled Squab
Sybil Potatoes
Salad de Saison
Ice Cream, Mozart
Fancy Cakes
Coffee

St. Ignatius University, November 9, 1916:
Blue Points
Clear Turtle
Almonds   Celery   Olives
Sole Normande
Filet Mignon, Sauce Madère
Haricots Panaches
Potatoes Noisette
Champagne Punch
Roast Squab Chicken
Salad de Saison
Glacé Madeleine
Fancy Cakes
Coffee

Mr. T. F. Baxter, Supper, November 20, 1916:
California Oysters on Half Shell, Mignonette
Crab Meat, Monza
Breast of Squab, Colbert
Lettuce Salad
Fancy Ice Cream
Assorted Cakes
Coffee

First Subscription Ball, Mrs. S. S. Martin, Supper, December 22, 1915:
Scrambled Eggs
Bacon
Sausages
Toast Melba
Coffee

Mr. Ercole Canessa, Luncheon, May 29, 1915:
Hors d'Oeuvres
Salted Almonds
Fillet of Sand Dabs, Victor, Tartar Sauce
Breast of Chicken, Colbert
Peas   Soufflé Potato
Soufflé Chocolat
Sauce Vanilla
Demi Tasse

Prudential Insurance Company of America, Luncheon, February 15, 1916:
Canape of Anchovies
Potage Lambale
Olives
Lobster Newburgh
Loin of Lamb, Zahler
Salad de Saison
Hot Mince Pie
Black Coffee

Mrs. A. Welch, Luncheon, February 16, 1916:
Fruit Cocktail in Coupe
Chicken Broth in Cups
Almonds
Fillet of Sole, Tartare
Broiled Squab
Pommes Chateau
Cold Asparagus, Mustard Sauce
Fancy Ice Cream
Cakes Caroline
Coffee

Dr. Hugo Lieber, May 18, 1915:
California Oysters
Strained Gumbo
Olives   Almonds
Fillet of Sole, Florentine
Breast of Chicken, Colbert
Pomme Foudaietes
Lettuce
Asparagus, Hollandaise Sauce
Ice Cream   Cakes
Coffee

Mrs. Hiram Johnson, July 22, 1915:
Cantaloupe Moscovite
Beef Tea in Cups
Salted Almonds
Fillet of Trout, Cafe de Paris
Breast of Chicken with Truffles
Potatoes Noisettes
Hearts of Lettuce
Biscuit Glacé, St. Francis
Friandises
Demi Tasse

National Association of Professional Base-ball, November 10, 1915:
Toke Points
Cream a la Reine
Celery   Olives   Almonds
Fillet of Sole, Joinville
Chicken Croquettes with Peas
Roman Punch
Imperial Squab
Salad de Saison
Fancy Ice Cream
Fancy Cakes
Coffee

Inland Iron Company, May 27, 1915:
Crab Cocktail, Moscovite
Clear Bartsch in Cups
Salted Almonds   Ripe Olives
Sand Dabs, Meuniere
Sweetbread Cutlets, St. Germain
Chateaubriand, Sauce Madère
Artichokes
Pommes Fondantes
Sorbet au Champagne
Roast Imperial Squab
Salad de Saison
Ice Cream
Mignardises
Coffee

Prudential Insurance Company, May 24, 1919:
Cherry Stone
Clear Green Turtle
Salted Almonds   Ripe Olives
Aiguillette of Sole, Marjory
Filet Mignon with Fresh Mushrooms
Flageolet aux Fines Herbes
Potato Chateau
Orange Sherbet
Roast Imperial Squab
Chiffonade Salad
Fancy Ice Cream
Assorted Cakes
Coffee

Mr. Henry T. Scott, May 19, 1915:
Bouchees Fui with Cocktail
Fresh Caviar
California Oyster Soup
Almonds   Olives
Sand Dabs, Sauté, Meuniere
Pommes Parisienne, Persillade
Breast of Duck
New String Beans
Chicory and Escarole Salad
Mousse of Fresh Strawberries
Assorted Cakes
Coffee

*Dinner in honor of Baron S. Goto, given by
Consul General T. Ohta:*
Grapefruit and Orange au Marasquin
Potage Lemardelais
Salted Pecans   Ripe Olives
Bass Under Glass with Fresh Mushrooms
Noisette of Baby Lamb, Colbert
String Beans
Sorbet Mikado
Breast of Chicken, Lucullus
Potatoes Julienne
Cold Fresh Asparagus, Mustard Sauce
Fancy Ice Cream
Friandises
Demi Tasse
*White Wine   Red Wine
Champagne
White Creme de Menthe
Cognac
Cigarettes
Cigars*

Mr. Raphael Weill, May 13, 1915:
California Oysters on Half Shell
Brandade
Saddle of Lamb
Petits Pois a la Francaise
Chicory
Blanc Mange
Petits Fours
Coffee

Mrs. George Marye, July 20, 1915:
Grapefruit Supreme
Salted Almonds and Pecans
Fillet of Sand Dabs, Mornay
Noisettes of Lamb, Sauce Diable
Corn
Boneless Squab, Stuffed
Hearts of Lettuce, Russian Dressing
Fresh Peach Ice Cream
Assorted Cakes
Coffee

Mrs. H. Sinsheimer, October 27, 1915:
Toke and California Oysters
Einlauf Suppe
Almonds
Frogs Raphael, Weill
Eingedampfte Chicken
French Fried Potatoes
String Beans au Beurre
Bottoms of Artichokes, Lettuce Victor
Orange Soufflé Glacé St. Francis
Fancy Cakes
Coffee

Retail Dry Goods Association, October 10,
1916:
Blue Points
Potage Lord Mayor
Celery   Olives   Almonds
Fillet of Sole, Bagration
Tournedos Forestière
Potatoes Noisette
Peas Etuvé
Champagne Punch
Roast Squab Chicken
Salade de Saison
Frozen Diplomate Pudding
Fancy Cakes
Coffee

*Golden Gate Thoroughbred Breeders' As-
sociation,* September 19, 1915:
Toke Points
Clear Turtle
Celery   Olives   Almonds
Aiguillette of Sole, Marguery
Vol au Vent Vaupaliere
Filet Mignon Madère
Peas a la Francaise
Champagne Punch
Breast of Squab
Potatoes Noisettes
Salade de Saison
Fancy Ice Cream
Assorted Cakes
Coffee

Fire Chief's Banquet of San Francisco,
September 30, 1915:
Toke Points
Potage Lord Mayor
Celery   Olives   Almonds
Fillet of Bass, Marinière
Tournedos with Fresh Mushrooms
Peas a la Francaise
Potato Risolée
Roman Punch
Roast Squab
Salade de Saison
Fancy Ice Cream
Assorted Cakes
Coffee

Telephone Pioneers of America, September
21, 1915:
Caviar d'Astrakan
Toke Points
Potage Windsor
Celery   Almonds   Olives
Ecrevessis Voltaire
Mousse de Ris de Veau Royal
Chateaubriand Bayard
Petits Pois a la Francaise
Sorbet Ambassadrice
Poitrine de Guinea aux Fines Herbes
Pommes Noisettes
Salade Veronica
Glaces Fantaisies
Mignardises
Cafe Noir

West Virginia Banquet (West Virginia Building, Exposition Grounds), November 5, 1915:

Toke Points
Strained Gumbo, Princesse
Celery   Olives   Almonds
Fillet of Bass, Joinville
Sweetbread Braise with Peas
Champagne Punch
Roast Imperial Squab
Pommes Chateau
Salad de Saison
Fancy Ice Cream
Assorted Cakes
Coffee

Mrs. Henry T. Scott, August 30, 1915:

Canape Caviar with Cocktail
Clear Bortsch in Cups
Cheese Straws
Salted Pecans
Sand Dabs, Meunière
Mousse of Virginia Ham
Timbale of Spinach
Breast of Pheasant, Lucullus
Salad Veronica
Coupes Curasco
Fancy Cakes
Coffee

Carlos Sanjinis (Bolivian Consul), August 23, 1915:

Toke Points
Green Turtle Soup, Xerxes
Almonds   Olives   Celery
Lobster Newburgh
Noisette of Lamb, Perigordine
Peas a la Francaise
Pommes a la Reine
Champagne Punch
Breast of Chicken, Virginia Ham
Celery Victor
Fancy Ice Cream
Assorted Cakes
Coffee

Papyrus Club, May 15, 1918.

Coupe Printaniere au Kirsch
Consomme Tomato Chantilly
Olives
Sand Dabs, Meuniere
Pommes Hollandaise
Chateau Briand Forestiere
Cold Asparagus, Mustard Sauce
Meringue Glacee
Demi Tasse

Dinner to Mr. Thomas Coleman, Manager Hotel St. Francis, September 26, 1918.

Toke Points
Clear Turtle
Olives   Almonds
Ecrevisses Voltaire
Breast of Chicken, Colbert
Peas Etuvé   Potatoes Fondante
Hearts of Lettuce St. Francis
Fancy Ice Cream
Cakes Caroline
Coffee

Mrs. Anita Baldwin, August 14, 1915:

Fruit Salad Supreme
Consomme
Almonds   Olives
Frogs, Neptune
Mousse of Virginia Ham
Puree of Fresh Artichokes
Breast of Chicken
Pommes Souffleé
Alligator Pears
Pudding Nesselrode
Fancy Cakes
Coffee

Mrs. E. H. Stotesbury, July 25, 1915:

Astrakan Caviar
Chicken Broth
Cheese Straws
Salted Pecans and Almonds
Sand Dabs, Tempis
Pommes Parisienne
Virginia Ham
English Spinach
Corn Lieb
Breast of Squab Chicken
Salad Ravajole
Coupes Fraise
Fancy Cakes
Coffee
Candy

Monsieur Gregoire, French Building, P. P. I. E., November 15, 1919:

Bouchees Fines
Huitres Mignonettes
Bisque d'Ecrevisses
Almonds   Celery   Olives
Truite de Rivière
Tournedos Cheron
Pommes Soufflée
Poitrine de Volaille, Virginie
Coeur de Laitue
Glacé Madeleine
Friandises
Coffee

Students Army Training Corps, December 7, 1918.

Oyster Cocktail
Potage Mongol
Olives   Celery   Almonds
Filet of Sole, Joinville
Roast Imperial Squab
Peas Etuvé   Potatoes Parisienne
Salad de Saison
Fancy Ice Cream
Assorted Cakes
Coffee

Mr. Jesse Lillienthal (Luncheon) November 7, 1918.

California Oyster Cocktail
Olives   Celery
Filet Mignon Grilled
Pommes Chateau
New String Beans
Individual Alaska
Demi Tasse

Mr. Mulcahy, February 26, 1918:
Toke Points Mignonette
Clear Bortsch in Cups
Celery   Olives   Almonds
Ecrevisses Voltaire
Noisette of Lamb with Fresh Mushrooms
Peas Etuvé—Pommes Lorette
Breast of Duck
Fried Hominy
Endive, Victor Dressing
Asparagus Glaceé
Assorted Cakes
Cafe Marcel

———————

Colonel Tessier, November 4, 1918:
Potage St. Germain
Almonds
Fillet Sand Dabs, Sauce Ecrevisses
Poulet Poele
Pommes Champs Elysées
Petits Pois Parisienne
Lettuce Salad, Fines Herbes
Soufflee, Vanilla Sauce
Fruit
Coffee

———————

Mr. T. Ohta:
Blue Points Mignonette
Clear Green Turtle Soup
Salted Nuts   Celery   Olives
Ecrevisses Voltaire
Mackerel Mikado
Jumbo Squab, Parisienne
Asparagus, Hollandaise
Salad Fruitiere
Fresh Figs, Sake
Friandises
Demi Tasse

*Luncheon to Major Harley, Mr. French and
Friends,* November 5, 1918:
Ecrevisses Gourmets Cold
Broiled Chicken
Peas Etuvé—Potatoes Champs Elysees
Cream Cheese and Bar le Duc
Demi Tasse

———————

Mr. M. J. Cohen, April 16, 1917:
Toke Points
Potage Lord Mayor
Celery   Olives   Almonds
Terrapin Maryland
Whole Squab Chicken
Potatoes Chateau
Cold Asparagus, Figaro
Fancy Ice Cream
Cakes
Demi Tasse

———————

Mr. Mogi, January 16, 1918:
Fresh Caviar on Ice Socle
Clear Green Turtle, Amontillado
Almonds   Celery   Olives
Frogs Legs, Michels
Sweetbread aux Truffes
Petits Pois
Goose Liver with Apples
Punch Mikado
Pheasant, Bread Sauce
Potatoes Champs Elysees
Melon Richelieu
Cakes
Coffee

INDEX

☆

The Classified Index follows on pages 398 to 412, inclusive. The general Alphabetical Index is on pages 413 to 430 inclusive.

CEREALS

Boiled farina in milk, July 6
Fried hominy, Oct. 29
Force and cream, Oct. 30; Nov. 8
Germea, Nov. 22
Grapenuts, Nov. 15
Hominy, Oct. 28
Malta vita, Nov. 16
Pearl grits, March 5
Pearl grits with cream, Nov. 11
Pettijohns, Oct. 29
Shredded wheat biscuits, Nov. 10

CHEESE

Cheese balls, Oct. 29
Cottage cheese, May 24
Cream cheese with Bar-le-Duc, Dec. 29
Olympic Club cheese, Oct. 23
Petaluma cream cheese, Sept. 18
Souffle au fromage (cheese souffle), April 4
St. Francis cheese, July 1

CHICKEN

A la King, Nov. 11
Austrian fritters, April 22
A l'Estragon, March 8
Boiled fowl, Oct. 29
Breast of chicken, Alexandra, Dec. 21
Breast of chicken with Virginia ham, Feb. 22
Breast of chicken with figs, Sept. 22
Breast of chicken, James Woods, Oct. 25
Baked chicken with rice, March 19
Broiled chicken, Tyrolienne, May 28
Breast of chicken en aspic, July 26
Boiled fowl, celery sauce, Aug. 21
Chicken croquettes, Dec. 23
Cold chicken, ısabella, Sept. 20
Coquille of chicken, Mornay, Oct. 12
Diva, Nov. 13
Deviled chicken's legs, April 30
Deviled chicken's legs with Virginia ham, Sept. 3
Edward VII, Dec. 9
Essence of chicken in cup, Feb. 6
En cocotte, Bazaar, Oct. 20
Fried, Maryland, Jan. 20
Fried, Villeroi, June 26
Fried, Savoy, Sept. 8
Fried, country style, Nov. 12
Fricassee, à l'ancienne, June 26
Hash, Victor, Dec. 3
Hash, on toast, Feb. 15
Hash, à l'Italienne, Oct. 9
Leon X, Oct. 17
Livers, sauté, forestière, Feb. 8
Livers sauté, au Madère, Dec. 14
Plain, roasted, Oct. 27
Patties, Toulouse, May 12
Potpie, home style, Feb. 18
Sauté, Ambassadrice, Dec. 6
Sauté, Marengo, Dec. 8
Sauté, Parisienne, Feb. 12
Sauté, Montmorency, Feb. 23
Sauté, Salonika, March 3
Sauté, Hongroise, March 17
Sauté, Portugaise, March 18
Sauté, Chasseur, April 3
Sauté, D'Austin, April 16
Sauté, Madeleine, April 29
Sauté, Demidoff, May 3
Sauté, au Madère, May 13
Sauté, Amphitian, May 16
Sauté, demi-deuil, May 31
Sauté, Archiduc, June 14
Sauté, Viennoise, July 3
Sauté, Lafitte, July 7
Sauté, Alsacienne, Aug. 31
Sauté, Josephine, Oct. 13
Stuffed chicken with California raisins, Oct. 23
Tyrolienne, March 26
Valencienne, Jan. 7

SQUAB CHICKEN

Broiled, Nov. 23
Michels, July 22
Plain potted, Jan. 10
Sauté, Sutro, Feb. 26

CAPON

Galantine, July 19
Stuffed, Bruxelloise, Feb. 27
Stuffed, St. Antoine, Jan. 4

BEEF

Braised beef, with calf's feet, Dec. 4
Beefsteak, Provencale, Jan. 13
Beefsteak, Bismarck, Jan. 18
Beef tongue, boiled, Jan. 29
Beef à la mode, May 21
Braised beef, June 12
Beef marrow, Princess, July 8
Braised beef, comfortable, Sept. 7
Beef-steak, Jussien, Oct. 3
Baked porterhouse, Oct. 11
Beef tongue, Menschikoff, Oct. 15
Beef tongue, Parisienne, March 11
Broiled tenderloin steak, Nov. 8
Broiled sirloin steak, Cliff House, June 9
Corned beef and cabbage, Jan. 27
Corned beef hash, March 31
Corned beef hash, browned, March 31
Corned beef hash, au gratin, March 31
Chipped beef on toast, June 8
Filet mignon, April 14
Filet mignon, Athenienne, June 16
Filet mignon, Bayard, March 4
Filet mignon, Cheron, May 25; Nov. 29
Filet mignon, DuBarry, Sept. 11
Filet mignon, Marchale, May 20
Filet mignon, Trianon, April 14
Fillet of beef, Charcutière, April 15
Fillet of beef, Cendrillon, May 5
Fillet of beef, Lombard, May 12
Fillet of beef, Balzag, June 26
Fillet of beef, Dumas, Aug. 14
Hamburg steak, Nov. 9
Hashed fillet of beef, Sam Ward, April 29
Larded sirloin of beef, Nov. 20
Larded tenderloin of beef, April 28
Larded tenderloin of beef, Montbasson, April 28
Larded tenderloin of beef, St. Martin, June 1
Larded tenderloin of beef, Vigo, June 22
Larded tenderloin of beef, Lili, July 2
Larded tenderloin of beef, Sigurd, Sept. 16
Larded rump of beef, June 12
Miroton of beef, en bordure, Dec. 2
Minced tenderloin, à l'estragon, Feb. 21
Meat croquettes, Oct. 11
Ox tail braisé, May 4
Planked sirloin steak, Jan. 22
Porterhouse steak, Bercy, May 20
Porterhouse steak, Jolly, June 20
Planked sirloin steak, St. Francis, July 17
Rump steak, Bercy, Oct. 31
Roast top sirloin of beef, Nov. 21
Rheinbraten, Nov. 26
Rump steak, Dickinson, Aug. 25
Roast beef, Jules Albert, Aug. 18
Roast sirloin, fermière, June 14
Roast sirloin, Monet-Sully, Aug. 7
Roast tenderloin, Berthieu, July 13
Roast tenderloin, Boucicault, Oct. 10
Roast tenderloin, vert pré, July 24
Sirloin steak, sauce Madère, Nov. 4
Sirloin of beef, roasted, Nov. 5
Sirloin steak, marchand de vin, Feb. 11
Sweet-sour beef tongue, March 1
Sirloin steak, Dickinson, April 7
Small tenderloin steak, Demidoff, April 17
Sour schmorrbraten, May 16
Smoked beef tongue, with spinach, May 22
Small tenderloin steak, Fedora, May 27
Steak, Tartar, July 21
Small sirloin steak à la Russe, July 29

FISH—Continued
Turbot, fillet of, Tempis, July 31
Turbot, fillet of, Windsor, April 27
Victoria, Feb. 28
Vol au vent of salmon, Genoise, May 1
Whitefish, baked, St. Menehould, Aug. 2
Whitefish, boiled, Netherland style, Jan. 1
Whitefish, broiled, maitre d'hotel, Nov. 15
Whitefish, fried, March 15
Whitebait on graham bread, Nov. 26
Yarmouth bloater, Nov. 15

FRUIT
Bananas sliced, with whipped cream, June
Berries with whipped cream, June 3
Cactus fruit with lemon, Feb. 7
California raisins, Oct. 23
Cantaloupe and watermelon, surprise, Sept. 3
Fruit salad, au kirsch, Feb. 3
Fruit salad, au marasquin, Feb. 3
Fruit salad, Chantilly, Feb. 3
Fruit salad glacé, April 18
Figs sliced, with cream, June 4
Fruits sliced, with whipped cream, June 3
Grapefruit a l'anisette, April 8
Grapefruit a la Rose, April 25
Grapefruit and orange en supreme, Feb. 18
Grapefruit, Cardinal, July 10
Grapefruit cocktail, April 18
Grapefruit en supreme, Dec. 9
Grapefruit en supreme with kirsch, April 15
Grapefruit with cherries, Nov. 17
Grapefruit with chestnuts, Jan. 30
Orange and Grapefruit, St. Francis, Oct. 23
Orange en supreme, March 18
Orange en supreme au curacao, May 5
Peaches, sliced, with whipped cream, June 3
Peach, Morelli, April 27
Pears, mayonnaise, Oct. 19
Strawberries, Parisienne, May 22
Strawberries Romanoff, April 18

FRUIT, COOKED
Apple, baked, Nov. 23
Apple compote, June 23
Apricot compote, June 23
Apples fried, Nov. 24
Apple sauce, April 12
Bananas, baked, Sept. 18
Compote of pineapple, June 13
Gooseberry compote, June 29
Grapefruit marmalade, April 10
Nectarine compote, June 23
Orange compote, July 4
Peaches, baked, June 22
Peach compote, June 23
Peaches with brandy sauce, May 19
Pears, baked, June 22
Pears in syrup, April 1
Pears, stewed, with claret, Sept. 19
Plum compote, June 23
Prunes, Nov. 16
Prunes, baked, Oct. 25
Prune compote, June 23
Prunes, Victor, Oct. 23
Rhubarb, Nov. 15
Strawberries, Oct. 27

GAME
Butterball duck, roasted, Nov. 17
Canvas-back duck, roasted, Nov. 10
Hare, saddle of, sour cream sauce, March 30
Mallard duck, roasted, Nov. 1
Partridge, roasted, Feb. 15
Pheasant pie, cold, July 10
Pheasant, roasted, Jan. 9
Puree of game, for garnishing, Feb. 20
Quail, broiled, on toast, Sept. 27
Reindeer chops, March 4
Reindeer, roast leg of, April 17
Ruddy duck, roasted, Dec. 26
Teal duck, roasted, Oct. 29
Venison, roast saddle of, July 9
Venison chop (steak), port wine sauce, Aug. 11

GOOSE
Goose liver sauté, Dec. 6
Goose liver sauté, aux truffes, Dec. 6
Goose, stuffed, with chestnuts, Jan. 18

GARNITURES FOR ENTREES, ETC.
Bercy, Feb. 7
Boulanger, Dec. 2
Bristol, Dec. 16
Cheron, Nov. 29
Clermont, Jan. 3
De Goncourt, Dec. 10
Ducale, Feb. 22
Financiere, March 2
International, Dec. 31
Malvina, Feb. 7
Porte Maillot, Dec. 27
Richelieu, Nov. 20
Rosabelle, Dec. 17
Rossini, Feb. 5
Toulouse, Jan. 25

HORS D'OEUVRES
Antipasto, Feb. 6
Artichokes, fresh, a la Russe, Oct. 7
Barquette a l'Aurore, Jan. 14
Canape Eldorado, Oct. 3
Canape Hambourgeoise, Oct. 30
Canape Julia, Feb. 22
Canape Martha, Dec. 11
Canape Monte Carlo, Dec. 29
Canape Norway, May 31
Canape, P. P. I. E., Oct. 24
Canape Riga, Nov. 19
Canape Romanoff, April 1
Canape St. Francis, June 11
Canape Regalia, Nov. 12
Canape Thon Marine, Aug. 21
Canape of anchovies, Nov. 2
Canape of caviar, Oct. 28
Canape of chicken, March 3
Canape of lobster, Aug. 13
Canape of raw meat, Feb. 19
Canape of raw beef, May 22
Canape of sardines, Nov. 6
Caviar, Nov. 16
Cold fonds d'artichauts, Du Barry, Aug. 10
Crab legs, Stock, June 3
Croquettes Livannienne, Jan. 6
Croustades Cancalaise, Dec. 22
Egg salad, Sept. 12
Fillet of herring, marine, Feb. 21
Fish salad, ravigote, Dec. 6
Hard boiled eggs, vinaigrette, Oct. 20
Herring Livonienne, Oct. 15
Herring salad, July 29
Herring salad, Moscovite, Sept. 7
Hors d'oeuvres varies, Nov. 16
Indian canape, March 28
Kieler sprotten, April 10
Lyon sausage, Nov. 4
Lyon sausage, Nov. 16
Marinite herring, Nov. 18
Matjes herring, March 28
Matjes herring, Krasnapolsky, July 25
Merry Widow cocktail, July 9
Mortadella, Aug. 25; Oct. 17
Olive and anchovy salad, Aug. 28
Oysters marine, April 23
Pain mane, Jan. 17
Pancake Molosol, Jan. 11
Pate de foie gras, Nov. 16
Pickled oysters, Nov. 13
Pickled salmon, St. Francis, April 29
Pimientos, a l'huile, Jan. 24
Pimentos Suedoise, Sept. 26
Pimentos, vinaigrette, Aug. 3
Pim olas, June 6
Plain celery, Oct. 27
Radishes, Nov. 8
Ripe olives, Oct. 27
Ripe olives with garlic and oil, April 22

OYSTERS—Continued

En brochette, Sept. 28
En brochette, a la Diable, Sept. 28
Kirkpatrick, Jan. 31
Louis, Sept. 25
Mignonette, April 17
Mornay, Sept. 13
Newburg, Sept. 8
On half shell, Oct. 27; Nov. 4
Oysters or crab, Poulette, March 29
Pickled, cold, Nov. 13
Stewed, Jan. 13
Supreme, St. Francis, May 3
Victor, March 10
Victor Hugo, Sept. 23
Yaquina, Jan. 10

PASTRY

Alexandria pudding, July 25
Almond cake, April 5
Almond cream cake, April 5
Almond rocks, July 21
Allumettes, June 7
American gugelhoff, Oct. 2
Angel cake, or Angel food, June 18
Anise seed cake, Feb. 20
Anise toast, Sept. 19
Anisette cake, July 29
Apple cobbler, July 16
Apple cottage pudding, July 11
Apple Moscovite, Feb. 22
Apple snow, Oct. 14
Apple strudel, April 13
Apple turnover, May 30
Apricot cobbler, July 16
Apricot layer cake, Feb. 27
Apricot meringue, July 18
Baba au rhum, Dec. 26
Baises (chocolate drops), Sept. 20
Baked apple roll, June 15
Baked apricot roll, June 15
Baked blackberry roll, June 15
Baked huckleberry roll, June 15
Baked loganberry roll, June 15
Banana whipped cream, Oct. 1
Bavarois a la vanille, Dec. 21
Bavarois a la vanille with Bar le Duc, Feb. 2
Bavarois Noisette, March 28
Bavarois, raspberry, Jan. 29
Beignets soufflés, June 14
Berliner pfannenkuchen, June 30
Bird's nests, July 30
Blackberry meringue, July 18
Black cake, Sept. 16
Blanc mange aux fruits, June 16
Blanc mange aux liqueurs, June 16
Blanc mange, chocolate, June 16
Blanc mange, coffee, June 16
Blanc mange, vanilla, June 16
Boiled custard, July 15
Boston brown pudding, July 11
Bouchette, June 15
Bouchette Palmyra, July 15
Brandy sauce, Feb. 17
Bread custard pudding, July 8
Brioche, Oct. 26
Brown Betty, April 9
Cabinet pudding, Jan. 31
Cakes, assorted, Nov. 17
Cannelons a la creme, May 28
Carmel custard, Jan. 28
Caroline cake, March 16
Charlotte Russe, April 16
Cheese cake, Oct. 25; Jan. 14
Cherry tartelette, Dec. 11
Chocolate bouchette, June 15
Chocolate eclairs, Nov. 24
Chocolate layer cake, Feb. 27; Dec. 9
Chocolate macaroons, April 6
Chocolate profiterole, Jan. 20
Chocolate pudding, cold, Sept. 21
Cinnamon cake, July 3

PASTRY—Continued

Cocoa cake, April 9
Cocoanut pudding, July 8
Coffee bouchette, June 15
Coffee cake, Oct. 26
Coffee cake dough, June 30
Coffee cream cake, July 3
Coffee custard, April 10
Coffee fruit cake, July 3
Cold chocolate sauce, Sept. 21
Compote with rice, July 31
Cornet a la creme, May 28
Corn starch blanc mange, Aug. 24
Corn starch blanc mange with berries, Aug. 24
Corn starch blanc mange with Sabayon, Aug. 24
Corn starch blanc mange, stewed fruits, Aug. 24
Corn starch food (for invalids), Aug. 24
Corn starch pudding, July 1
Cottage pudding, July 11
Cream fritters, June 5
Cream puffs, Nov. 24
Cream sauce, Jan. 24
Crepes suzette, Oct. 5
Croute a l'Ananas (pineapple crust), July 23
Croute aux fruits (fruit crust), July 23
Crullers, June 30
Crusts with apples, Sept. 28
Crusts with peaches, Sept. 28
Crusts with pears, Sept. 28
Cup custard, Jan. 26
Danish apple cake, Oct. 13
Dariole Duchesse, Sept. 2
Dartois Chantilly, April 23
Devil cake, Sept. 20
Diplomate pudding, March 18
Doughnuts, June 30
English rice pudding, April 24
Frankfort pudding, April 21
French layer cake, Feb. 27
French pastry, Feb. 13
French sponge cake (Genoise legere), Oct. 2
Fried cream, March 11
Fritters, surprise, July 20
Fruit cake, Nov. 10
Fruit cake (white), Feb. 25
German almond strips, June 23
German apple cake, Oct. 30
German coffee cake, July 3
German huckleberry cake, June 24
Gingerbread, Oct. 8
Ginger snaps, May 15
Hard sauce, Feb. 17
Hazelnut macaroons, Oct. 1
Homemade apple pudding, March 20
Homemade cookies, Feb. 2
Honey cake, June 23
How to cook sugar to a blow, June 21
Icing or frosting, Nov. 24
Imperial pancake, April 26
Italian meringue, June 21
Italian wine sauce, Sept. 21
Jam roll pudding, April 27
Jelly roll, May 29
Kisses, June 7
Lady cake, Sept. 4
Lady fingers, Nov. 17
Langues de chat, June 23
Layer cake, Feb. 27; Dec. 9
Lemon butter filling, Aug. 10
Lemon cake, Aug. 10
Lemon dariole, Aug. 16
Lemon sauce, March 27
Macaronade Celestine, July 15
Macaroons, Nov. 17
Macaroons, fancy, Nov. 18
Meringue a la creme, Chantilly, Dec. 1
Meringue peaches, March 10
Meringue shells, Oct. 27
Mint wafers, Oct. 17
Mirlitons, Aug. 26
Mirlitons au rhum, Sept. 4
Moka cake (Mocha cake), Feb. 18

SHELL FISH—Continued
Terrapin au beurre, Sept. 20
Terrapin, Baltimore, March 21
Terrapin, Jockey Club, March 21
Terrapin, Maryland, March 21

SHELL FISH—CLAMS
Batelière, March 6
Créole, Feb. 1
En cocotte, Californienne, July 3
Fried soft clams, Tartare, Aug. 26
Little necks on half shell, Nov. 5
Scalloped, Aug. 3
Soft clams, Newburg, Feb. 5
Stuffed, July 7
With wine sauce, April 5

SOUPS
Consomme
Ab-del-Cader, June 14
Allemande, June 22
Alexandria, Aug. 1
Andalouse, June 16
Aux éclairs, May 18
Aux pluches, May 26
Aux quenelles, April 14
Aux quenelles, Doria, May 22
Bellevue, Dec. 5
Bohemienne, June 28
Bouillon, Nov. 3
Brétonne, Jan. 22
Brunoise, Dec. 10
Brunoise and vermicelli, Sept. 3
Cameroni, July 11
Camino, March 17
Caroline, June 2
Celery and rice, Aug. 19
Célestine, April 28
Charles Quint, July 8
Chartreuse, Sept. 20
Châtelaine, Aug. 26
Chevalière, July 23
Chicken broth, Oct. 29
Chiffonnade, May 3
Cialdini, Nov. 20
Clam broth, Dec. 5
Clam broth, Chantilly, Dec. 5
Colbert, Feb. 25; Aug. 22
Crème de volaille, Jan. 14
Créole, June 24
Croute au pot, May 5
D'Artagnan, Jan. 12
Daumont, April 16
De la Mariée, Jan. 16
Diable, May 14
Diane, Oct. 21
Ditalini, Dec. 13
Doria, Dec. 2
Du Barry, March 11
Favorite, Jan. 7
Federal, Sept. 5
Fermière, Aug. 12
Fleury, Dec. 22
Florentine Feb. 21; July 4
Frascati, Oct. 3
Garibaldi, July 15
Georgia, Oct. 1
Gumbo, strained, in cups, Feb. 27
Imperatrice, Jan. 18
Inauguration, July 28
Irma, June 18
Italian paste, Aug. 24
Japonnaise, June 4
Julienne, Jan. 4
Léopold, Oct. 17
Madriliene, Dec. 29
Magadore, June 26
Marchand, June 6
Marie, Louise, July 2
Massenet, Dec. 21
Medina, Sept. 29
Monaco, Aug. 8

SOUPS, CONSOMME—Continued
Monte Cristo, July 26
Montesquieu, Aug. 17
Napier, Sept. 13
National, Sept. 27
Nelson, Oct. 12
Nicoise, July 6
Noodles, Oct. 6
Oriental, Aug. 10
Orleans, Dec. 20
Oyster broth, April 8
Palestine, July 13
Parfait, April 6; Jan. 24
Paysanne, Aug. 6
Pemartin, Oct. 8
Perles de Nizam, May 24
Plain, Oct. 27
Portugaise, Sept. 9
Printanière, April 30
Profiteroles, May 28
Rachel, Feb. 17
Rivoli, Dec. 17
Ravioli, May 12
Rothschild, Aug. 4
Royal, Nov. 21
Royal, with carrots, May 8
Royal, green, Sept. 22
Royal, red, Sept. 22
Russe, April 26
Sago, Nov. 7
Sarah Bernhardt, May 20
Scotch, Jan. 11
Sévigné, I, Dec. 1
Sévigné, II, April 18
Sicilienne, July 21
Soubise, April 22
Stuffed cabbage, Sept. 15
Tapioca with écrevisse butter, Aug. 29
Talleyrand, July 17
Tapioca, Nov. 11
Théodora, April 20
Tosca, May 16
Turbigo, June 10
Trianon, July 19; Sept. 22
Vanderbilt, July 30
Viveurs, May 7
Valencienne, May 10; June 20
Venitienne, May 30
Vermicelli, Feb. 10
Xavier, June 22

CREAM SOUPS
Algerienne, May 25
Artichokes, June 11
Asparagus, Nov. 26
Asparagus, Favori, Oct. 18
Crème Bagration, May 17
Bananas, March 5
Bisque d'ecrevisses, Dec. 25
Bisque of California oysters, Jan. 5
Bisque of clams, Nov. 22
Bisque of crabs, Jan. 23
Cardinal, May 27
Cauliflower, Oct. 31
Celery, Nov. 2
Celery, Kalamazoo, Feb. 8
Chicken, Nov. 9
Chicken a la Reine, Dec. 17
Chicken, Hortense, April 1
Congolaise, May 31
Corn and onions, Sept. 17
Countess, June 25
Endives, Dec. 6
Farina, March 7
Farina lie, Sept. 10
Flageolets, July 24
Frogs' legs, Feb. 24
Green corn, I, March 9
Green corn, II, June 3
Lettuce, March 2
Lima beans, Feb. 19
Maintenon, Jan. 18
Parisienne, April 13

www.ingramcontent.com/pod-product-compliance
Lightning Source LLC
Chambersburg PA
CBHW080509090426
42734CB00015B/3005